USE THIS MAMMOTH, AUTHORITATIVE REFERENCE TO SETTLE ANY ARGUMENT ABOUT THE WONDERS OF OUR WORLD

THE ULTIMATE HEIST: The largest bank robbery took place in Lebanon in 1976, when bandits made off with somewhere between $20 and $50 million—no one is quite sure. [pp. 440–441]

HISTORY'S HARDEST-WORKING EASTER BUNNY: The greatest egg hunt in the United States happened at Coquina Beach in Manatee, Florida, on March 23, 1991, with more than 40,000 children searching for 120,000 plastic and candy eggs. [p. 462]

VALENTINE'S DAY HAUL: The biggest win at a slot machine was $6,814,823.48 by Cammie Brewer at the Club Cal-Neva, Reno, on February 14, 1988. [p. 226]

A COMMUNICATIONS BREAKDOWN: Ida and Simon Stern decided to get divorced. He was 97. She was 91. [p. 484]

PLUS!!!

THE 12,471-FOOT-HIGH-KITE! [pp. 468, 470]
THE $56,000 PIG [p. 113]
THE 500,000-LINE POEM [p. 334]
THE 4-ACRE NIGHTCLUB [p. 228]

AND

THE WORLD'S L THE BRIGHTEST COM OR-CYCLE [p. 266], A VIE EVER MADE [p. 37

Bantam Books in the Guinness Series

GUINNESS BOOK OF OLYMPIC RECORDS
THE GUINNESS BOOK OF RECORDS 1995

THE GUINNESS BOOK OF RECORDS 1995

Editor
Peter Matthews

Executive Editor, U.S. Edition
Michelle Dunkley McCarthy

Editor, U.S. Edition (New York)
Mark Young

Founding Editor
Norris McWhirter

BANTAM BOOKS
NEW YORK • TORONTO • LONDON • SYDNEY • AUCKLAND

This edition contains the complete text of the original hardcover edition.
NOT ONE WORD HAS BEEN OMITTED.

THE GUINNESS BOOK OF RECORDS 1995
A Bantam Book / Published by arrangement with
Guinness Publishing, Ltd.

Bantam edition / April 1995

ISBN 0-553-56942-2

Published simultaneously in the United States and Canada

Bantam Books are published by Bantam Books, a division of Bantam Doubleday Dell Publishing Group, Inc. Its trademark, consisting of the words "Bantam Books" and the portrayal of a rooster, is Registered in U.S. Patent and Trademark Office and in other countries. Marca Registrada. Bantam Books, 1540 Broadway, New York, New York 10036

PRINTED IN THE UNITED STATES OF AMERICA

OPM 0 9 8 7 6 5 4 3 2 1

CONTENTS

FEATURES

INTRODUCTION

WELCOME TO THE 34th edition of *The Guinness Book of Records.* As with the previous 33 editions, the book has been completely revised and updated. A comparison of this edition with that of a decade ago will show the tremendous changes in the standards of records, the categories included (for example, this edition includes a feature on the Internet, the largest computer network), and indeed, in our whole way of life. Mothers are older, cars are faster, more of space appears before our lenses every year. (Maybe there is even something in the air that allows for taller and taller card houses.) A comparison with last year's edition will also show this. A more striking contrast, however, between this edition and last year's is in presentation. This year the book sports a brand-new design that we hope will fascinate and involve readers as much as the records themselves.

NEW IN THE book this year, in response to popular demand, is a series of interviews with some of the record-holders. What makes them tick? What makes them choose a record to break and stay with it until it topples? These features will provide a greater insight into the levels of determination, effort and talent required to earn a spot in our pages.

OF COURSE, PEOPLE'S interest in the Guinness brand of superlatives is nothing new. Since the publication of the first edition in Great Britain in 1955, "our" record-holders have found themselves in the spotlight of public attention.

THE FIRST BOOK was the brainchild of Sir Hugh Beaver, a Guinness executive. After a day of game shooting in Ireland, Beaver and his shooting party got bogged down in an argument over which bird was the fastest game bird in Europe. The extensive library at Castlebridge House, the site of the shoot, could not provide the answer.

BEAVER THOUGHT THERE must be numerous one-upmanship battles going on nightly in pubs and inns throughout the British Isles, while the patrons partook of his employer's brew. He decided to produce a book to settle these arguments.

BEAVER CHALLENGED NORRIS and Ross McWhirter, statisticians in London, to compile a book of records. The first copy was bound by the printers in 1955. The book shot to the top of the British best-seller list, and each successive annual edition has done the same.

OVER THE LAST forty years the book has become a worldwide success. The first United States edition was published in 1956. Editions in France (1962) and Germany (1963) followed. The 1995 edition will be published throughout the world, in more than 30 languages.

THE PURPOSE OF *The Guinness Book of Records* has always been to provide accurate, easy-to-find information on the achievements of humans (and nonhumans) in every field of endeavor. The book has also become a unique outlet for individuals to demonstrate their talents.

GUINNESS WANTS TO help people achieve their record-breaking ambitions. The criteria used to establish a record are as follows: the record must be measurable, must be independently corroborated, must be completely objective, and should preferably be the subject of worldwide interest and participation. Unique skills, unusual happenings and one-of-a-kind occurrences do not qualify for entry into the book.

IF YOU WISH to attempt a published record, write to the following address requesting the specific guidelines for that event:

Facts On File, Inc.
460 Park Avenue South
New York, NY 10016
Attn: The Guinness Book of Records

IF YOU WOULD like to attempt a potential new record category, you should submit a brief proposal outlining your idea to the same address.

WE ARE A very small editorial team, and we receive hundreds of letters every week. Please submit your requests at least two months in advance of your attempt so that we can give your inquiry the attention it deserves. We can only respond to requests that include a stamped, self-addressed envelope.

ACKNOWLEDGMENTS

I WOULD LIKE to thank the many people who have provided us with the information needed to produce an accurate account of the world and its records.

REGRETTABLY, SPACE PREVENTS me from mentioning everyone. However, I would like to give special thanks to the editor and staff of the *Facts On File News Digest*, whose resources, talents and consideration have greatly added to the success of this edition.

I AM GRATEFUL for the contributions of three individuals: Christine Heilman, Jill Lazer, Dawn Ryddner and Tobey Grumet. Their talents, dedication and good humor have helped enormously in the production of this book. Finally, I must acknowledge the contribution of my colleague, Michelle Dunkley McCarthy. After five editions, the 1995 book marks her departure from the Guinness family.

Mark C. Young
Editor, U.S. Edition

HUMAN BEING

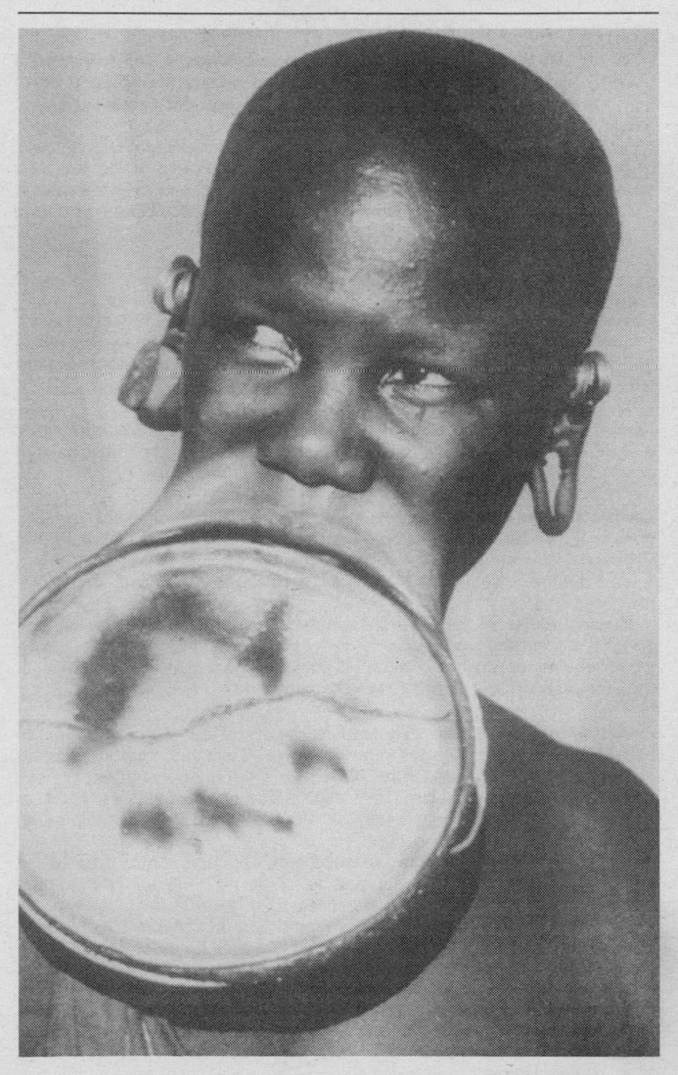

ORIGINS

EARLIEST HUMANS

If the age of the Earth–Moon system (latest estimate 4,540 ± 40 million years) is likened to a single year, hominids appeared on the scene at about 3:35 P.M. on 31 Dec, and the life span of a 120-year-old person would be about 84/100ths of a second.

Human beings (*Homo sapiens*) are a species in the subfamily Homininae of the family Hominidae of the superfamily Hominoidea of the suborder Simiae (or Anthropoidea) of the order Primates of the infraclass Eutheria of the subclass Theria of the class Mammalia of the subphylum Vertebrata (Craniata) of the phylum Chordata of the subkingdom Metazoa of the animal kingdom.

Earliest primates Primates appeared in the Paleocene epoch about 65 million years ago. The earliest members of the suborder Anthropoidea are known from both Africa and South America in the early Oligocene, 30–34 million years ago. Finds from the Fayum, Egypt, may represent primates from the Eocene period, 37 million years ago.

Earliest hominoid The earliest hominoid fossil is a jawbone with three molars, discovered in the Otavi Hills, Namibia on 4 Jun 1991. It was dated at 12–13 million years and named *Otavi pithecus namibiensis*.

Earliest hominid The earliest hominid relic is an Australopithecine jawbone with two molars, each 2 in long, found near Lake Baringo, Kenya in February 1984 and dated to 4 million years ago by associated fossils and to 5.4–5.6 million years ago through rock correlation by potassium–argon dating.

Parallel tracks of hominid footprints extending over 80 ft were discovered at Laetoli, Tanzania in 1978, by Paul Abell and Dr Mary Leakey, in volcanic ash dating to 3.6 million years ago. The height of the smallest of the seemingly three individuals was estimated to be 3 ft 11 in.

Earliest of the genus Homo The earliest species of this genus is *Homo habilis*, or "Handy Man," from Olduvai Gorge, Tanzania, named by Louis Leakey, Philip Tobias and John Napier in 1964 after a suggestion from Prof. Raymond Arthur Dart (1893–1988). The greatest age attributed to fossils of this genus is about 2.4 million years for a piece of cranium found in western Kenya in 1965.

The earliest stone tools are abraded core-choppers dating from *c.* 2.7 million years ago. They were found at Hadar, Ethiopia in November–December 1976 by Hélène Roche (France). Finger-held (as opposed to fist-held) quartz slicers found by Roche and Dr John Wall (New Zealand) close to the Hadar site by the Gona River can also be dated to *c.* 2.7 million years ago.

Earliest Homo erectus The oldest example of this species (upright man), the direct ancestor of *Homo sapiens*, was discovered by Eugène Dubois

The earliest hominid fossil, a jawbone with three molars, was found in the Otavi Hills, Namibia in 1991. It is dated at 12–13 million years old. (Muséum National d'Histoire Naturelle)

A 3.6-million-year-old hominid footprint (left) discovered at Laetoli, Tanzania in 1978. (Science Photo Library/John Reader)

(Netherlands; 1858–1940) at Trinil, Java in 1891. Javan *H. erectus* was redated to 1.8 million years in 1994.

Earliest Homo sapiens Through the Pleistocene epoch (1.6 million to 10,000 years ago) the trend towards large brains continued. *Homo sapiens* ("wise man") appeared about 300,000 years ago as the successor to *Homo erectus*.

United States Over 500 artifacts 11,000 to 16,000 years old were found in Washington Co., PA in April 1973 after being brought to the attention of the University of Pittsburgh by Albert Miller, whose family owned the land. The dig, led by Dr James Adovasio, started in June 1973 and lasted until June 1983.

The site dates to the Pre-Clovis Paleo-Indian culture and it is believed that the *Homo sapiens* Paleo-Indians were the initial inhabitants of the site.

In 1968 a burial site containing bones of two individuals believed to be an infant and an adolescent were uncovered by construction workers in Wilsall, MT.

The bones were dated by the MAS technique to not less than 10,600 years ago. The remains are believed to be of members of the Paleo-Indian culture, with the artifacts in the style of the Clovis Age.

Oldest human body The body of a Late Stone Age man, who is thought to have died *c.* 3300 B.C., was found almost perfectly preserved in an Austrian glacier in September 1991.

Oldest mummy Mummification dates from 2600 B.C. The oldest complete mummy is of Wati, a court musician of *c.* 2400 B.C., from the tomb of Nefer in Saqqâra, Egypt, found in 1944.

DIMENSIONS

GIANTS

Growth of the body is determined by growth hormone. This is produced by the pituitary gland, set deep in the brain. Overproduction in childhood produces abnormal growth, and true gigantism is the result. The true height of human giants is frequently obscured by exaggeration and commercial dishonesty. The only admissible evidence on the actual height of giants is that collected since 1870 under impartial medical supervision.

Tallest men The tallest man in medical history of whom there is irrefutable evidence was Robert Pershing Wadlow, born on 22 Feb 1918 in Alton, IL. Weighing 8½ lb at birth, he began his abnormal growth at the age of two following a double hernia operation. At age 10 he was 6 ft 5 in tall.

On 27 Jun 1940 Dr C.M. Charles of Washington University's School of Medicine in St Louis, MO, and Dr Cyril MacBryde measured Robert Wadlow at 8 ft 11.1 in (arm span 9 ft 5¾ in) in St Louis. Wadlow died 18 days later on 15 Jul 1940, weighing 439 lb, in a hotel in Manistee, MI as a result of a septic blister on his right ankle caused by a poorly fitting brace. He was buried in Oakwood Cemetery, Alton, IL in a coffin measuring 10 ft 9 in.

His greatest recorded weight was 491 lb on his 21st birthday. His shoes were size 37AA (18½ in) and his hands measured 12¾ in from the wrist to the tip of the middle finger.

Living There are two claimants to the title of tallest person in the world: Haji Mohammad Alam Channa (b. 1956) of Bachal Channa, Sehulan Sharif, Pakistan, and the world's tallest living woman, Sandy Allen (see Tallest women), both of whom are around 7 ft 7¼ in tall.

Tallest women The tallest woman in medical history was the giantess Zeng Jinlian (b. 26 Jun 1964) of Yujiang village in the Bright Moon Commune, Hunan Province, central China, who measured 8 ft 1¾ in when she died on 13 Feb 1982. This figure represented her height with assumed normal spinal curvature, because she suffered from severe scoliosis (curvature of the spine) and could not stand up straight. She began to grow abnormally

Sandy Allen, the world's tallest living woman, seen here with champion bedmaker Nurse Michelle Benkel. (K. Herschell for Guinness Publishing)

from the age of four months and stood 5 ft 1½ in before her fourth birthday. Her hands measured 10 in and her feet 14 in in length. Both her parents and her brother were of normal size.

Living The world's tallest woman is Sandy Allen, born 18 Jun 1955 in Chicago, IL. A 6½ lb baby, she began growing abnormally soon after birth. At 10 years of age she stood 6 ft 3 in, and she measured 7 ft 1 in when she was 16. On 14 Jul 1977 this giantess underwent a pituitary gland operation, which inhibited further growth at 7 ft 7¼ in. She now weighs 462 lb and takes a size 16 EEE shoe.

Most variable stature Adam Rainer, born in Graz (Austria; 1899–1950), measured 3 ft 10½ in at the age of 21. He then suddenly started growing at a rapid rate, and by 1931 he had reached 7 ft $1\frac{3}{4}$ in. He became so weak as a result that he was bedridden for the rest of his life. At the time of his death on 4 Mar 1950, age 51, he measured 7 ft 8 in and was the only person in medical history to have been both a dwarf and a giant.

Tallest married couple Anna Hanen Swan (1846–88) of Nova Scotia, Canada was said to be 8 ft 1 in but actually measured 7 ft $5\frac{1}{2}$ in. At the church of St Martin-in-the-Fields, London, Great Britain on 17 Jun 1871 she married Martin van Buren Bates (1845–1919) of Whitesburg, KY, who stood 7 ft $2\frac{1}{2}$ in, making them the tallest married couple on record.

Tallest twins The world's tallest identical twins are Michael and James Lanier (b. 27 Nov 1969) of Troy, MI. They measured 7 ft 1 in at the age of 14 years and both now stand 7 ft 4 in. Their sister Jennifer is 5 ft 2 in tall.

The world's tallest female identical twins are Heather and Heidi Burge (b. 11 Nov 1971) of Palos Verdes, CA. They are both 6 ft $4\frac{3}{4}$ in tall.

DWARFS

The strictures that apply to giants apply equally to dwarfs, except that exaggeration gives way to understatement. In the same way as 9 ft is the limit towards which the tallest giants tend, so 22 in is the limit towards which the shortest adult dwarfs tend (compare with the average length of newborn babies, which is 18–20 in).

DISSIMILAR!

Fabien Pretou (b. 15 Jun 1968; 6 ft 2 in) married Natalie Lucius (b. 19 Jan 1966; 3 ft 1 in) in Seyssinet-Pariset, France on 14 Apr 1990.

Shortest person The shortest mature human of whom there is independent evidence is Gul Mohammad (b. 15 Feb 1957) of Delhi, India. On 19 Jul 1990 he was examined at Ram Manohar Hospital, New Delhi, and found to measure $22\frac{1}{2}$ in in height and to weigh $37\frac{1}{2}$ lb. The other members of his immediate family are of normal height.

The shortest-ever female was Pauline Musters, a Dutch dwarf. She was born at Ossendrecht, Netherlands, on 26 Feb 1876 and measured 12 in at birth. At nine years of age she was 21.65 in tall and weighed only 3 lb 5 oz. She died on 1 Mar 1895 in New York City at the age of 19. Although she was billed at 19 in, a postmortem examination showed her to be exactly 24 in (there was some elongation after death). Her mature weight varied from $7\frac{1}{2}$–9 lb.

Living The shortest living female is Madge Bester (b. 26 Apr 1963) of Johannesburg, South Africa, at $25\frac{1}{2}$ in. She suffers from *Osteogenesis imperfecta* and is confined to a wheelchair. The disease is characterized by brittle bones and other deformities of the skeleton. Her mother, Winnie, is not much taller, measuring $27\frac{1}{2}$ in, and she too is confined to a wheelchair.

Twins The shortest twins ever recorded were the dwarfs Matjus and Bela Matina (b. 1903–d. *c.* 1935) of Budapest, Hungary, who later became United States citizens. They both measured 30 in.

Living The world's shortest living twins are John and Greg Rice (b. 3 Dec 1951) of West Palm Beach, FL, who both measure 34 in.

The shortest identical twin sisters are Dorene Williams of Oakdale and Darlene McGregor of Alameda, CA (b. 1949), who each stand 4 ft 1 in.

Oldest Hungarian-born Susanna Bokoyni ("Princess Susanna") of Newton, NJ died at the age of 105 years on 24 Aug 1984. She was 3 ft 4 in tall.

WEIGHT

Heaviest male The heaviest human in medical history was Jon Brower Minnoch (b. 29 Sep 1941) of Bainbridge Island, WA, who had suffered from obesity since childhood. The 6-ft-1-in-tall former taxi driver weighed 392 lb in 1963, 700 lb in 1966, and 975 lb in September 1976.

In March 1978, Minnoch was rushed to University Hospital, Seattle, saturated with fluid and suffering from heart and respiratory failure. It took a dozen firemen and an improvised stretcher to move him from his home to a ferryboat. When he arrived at the hospital he was put in two beds lashed together. It took 13 people just to roll him over. Consultant endocrinologist Dr Robert Schwartz calculated that Minnoch must have weighed more than 1,400 lb when he was admitted. A great deal of this was water accumulation due to his congestive heart failure. After nearly 16 months on a 1,200-calorie-a-day diet, he was discharged at 476 lb. In October 1981 he had to be readmitted, after having put on 197 lb. When he died on 10 Sep 1983 he weighed more than 798 lb.

Heaviest living male The heaviest living man is T.J. Albert Jackson (b. 1941 Kent Nicholson), also known as "Fat Albert," of Canton, MS. He has weighed 891 lb and has a 120-in chest, a 116-in waist, 70-in thighs and a 29½-in neck.

Heaviest female The heaviest woman ever recorded is Rosalie Bradford (USA; b. 1944), who registered a peak weight of 1,200 lb in January 1987. In August of that year she developed congestive heart failure and was rushed to a hospital. She was put on a carefully controlled diet and by February 1994 weighed 283 lb. Her target weight is 150 lb. See On the Record Feature (p. 8).

Heaviest twins Billy Leon (1946–79) and Benny Loyd (b. 7 Dec 1946) McCrary, alias McGuire, of Hendersonville, NC were normal in size until the age of six, when they both contracted German measles. In November 1978 they weighed 743 lb (Billy) and 723 lb (Benny) and had 84-in waists. As professional tag-team wrestling performers they were billed at weights up to 770 lb. Billy died at Niagara Falls, Ontario, Canada on 13 Jul 1979.

Weight loss *Dieting* The greatest recorded slimming feat by a male was that of Jon Brower Minnoch (see Heaviest male), who had reduced to 476 lb by July 1979, a weight loss of at least 920 lb in 16 months.

Rosalie Bradford (see Heaviest female) went from a weight of 1,200 lb in January 1987 to 283 lb in February 1994, a loss of a record 917 lb.

WEIGHT LOSS

After losing 917 pounds, what do you do for an encore? "I've got over 100 pounds to go," says Rosalie Bradford.

Always chubby as a child, Bradford reached obesity around the time of her marriage. Her weight escalated after the birth of her first child. She weighed about 600 pounds at the time of her hospitalization, and just kept on gaining as a combination of health and weight-related complaints forced her to stay in bed. Then a neighbor wrote a letter to TV diet guru Richard Simmons.

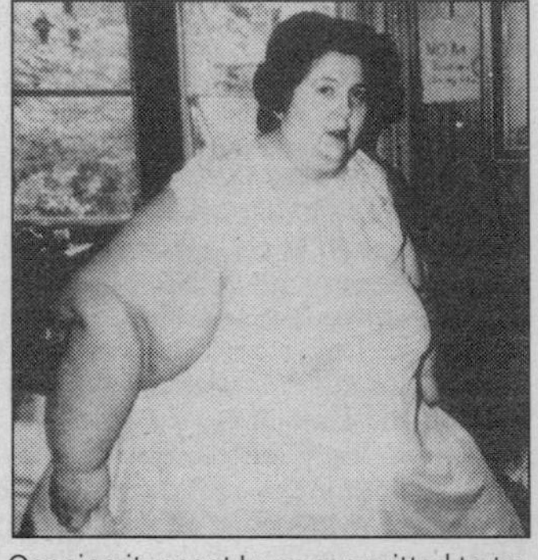

"He called me up and said two things: 'God doesn't make junk' and 'You're worth the effort.' Well, I took what he said to heart. He sent me a diet package, and I couldn't open it for months. Opening it meant I was committed to try, and then I might fail again. At first I couldn't plan my meals for the day.

I had to lose 500 pounds before I could even stand up." Bradford had been in bed for eight years, and returning to her feet meant physical therapy as well as more dieting.

"It's amazing," she agrees. "I used to ask God to come down one night when He wasn't feeling too lousy, wave His magic wand and dump all that fat on the floor. It didn't work that way, and now I've learned what it means to take slow little steps towards doing the right thing. It's going to be a lifelong effort. And now? Now I'm just waiting for the movie!"

At 850 lb in 1989, upper right; at 300 lb in 1993, above.

Sweating Ron Allen (b. 1947) sweated off 21½ lb of his weight of 239 lb in Nashville, TN in 24 hours in August 1984.

Weight gain The reported record for weight gain is held by Jon Brower Minnoch (see Heaviest male) at 196 lb in 7 days in October 1981 after readmittance to University Hospital, Seattle, WA. Arthur Knorr (USA; 1916–60) gained 294 lb in the last six months of his life.

Greatest differential The greatest weight difference recorded for a married couple is *c.* 1,300 lb in the case of Jon Brower Minnoch (See Heaviest male) and his 110-lb wife Jeannette in March 1978.

Lightest The lightest adult was Lucia Zarate (Mexico, 1863–89), an emaciated dwarf of 26½ in, who weighed 4.7 lb at the age of 17. She "fattened up" to 13 lb by her 20th birthday. At birth she had weighed 2½ lb.

BIRTH & FAMILIES

Birthrate *Highest and lowest* The crude birthrate—the number of births per 1,000 population—for the whole world was estimated to be 27 per 1,000 in the period 1985–90. The highest rate estimated by the United Nations for the period 1985–90 was 55.6 per 1,000 for Malawi. Excluding Vatican City, where the rate is negligible, the lowest recorded rate was 9.5 per 1,000 for San Marino.

United States The National Center for Health Statistics (NCHS) estimates that 4,039,000 babies were born in 1992. The estimated United States crude birthrate (the number of babies for every 1,000 people) is 15.7. Official statistics for 1993 show that California led with 510,077 births, while Wyoming had the fewest, with 6,703. The most live births registered in the United States in any year were 4,300,000 in 1957. The highest birthrate recorded after 1909, the first year official records were recognized, was 30.1 in 1910.

Natural increase The rate of natural increase (crude birthrate minus crude death rate) for the whole world was estimated to be 17.3 (27.0 minus 9.7) per 1,000 in the period 1985–90, compared with a peak of 20.6 per 1,000 in 1965. The highest of the latest available recorded rates was 37.4 (43.0 less 5.6) for Oman in 1985–90. The lowest rate of natural increase in any major independent country in recent times was in Hungary, which experienced a decline in the same period, with a figure of –1.7 per 1,000 (11.9 births and 13.6 deaths).

MOTHERHOOD

Most children The greatest officially recorded number of children born to one mother is 69, by the wife of Feodor Vassilyev (b. 1707–*fl.* 1782), a peasant from Shuya, 150 miles east of Moscow, Russia. In 27 confinements she gave birth to 16 pairs of twins, seven sets of triplets and four sets of quadruplets. The case was reported to Moscow by the Monastery of Nikolskiy on 27 Feb 1782. Only two of those who were born in the period *c.* 1725–65 failed to survive their infancy.

The world's most prolific mother is currently Leontina Albina (nee Espinosa; b. 1925) of San Antonio, Chile, who in 1981 produced her 55th and last child. Her husband Gerardo Secunda Albina (variously Alvina; b. 1921) states that they were married in Argentina in 1943 and had five sets of triplets (all boys) before coming to Chile. Only 40 (24 boys and 16 girls) survive.

Oldest mother The oldest reported age for a pregnancy is 63. Menopause is the end of a woman's reproductive life and occurs in the majority of women between the ages of 45 and 55 years. Recent hormone treatment techniques, however, have led to postmenopausal women becoming pregnant. It is therefore now feasible for a woman of *any* age to give birth.

BABIES

Heaviest single birth Big babies (i.e., those over 10 lb) are usually born to mothers who are large, overweight or have some medical problem such as diabetes. The heaviest baby born to a healthy mother was a boy weighing 22 lb 8 oz who was born to Signora Carmelina Fedele of Aversa, Italy in September 1955.

Mrs Anna Bates (nee Swan; 1846–88), the 7-ft-5½-in Canadian giantess, gave birth to a boy weighing 23 lb 12 oz (length 30 in) at her home in Seville, OH on 19 Jan 1879, but the baby died 11 hours later.

Twins The world's heaviest twins, collectively weighing 27 lb 12 oz, were born to Mrs J.P. Haskin of Fort Smith, AR on 20 Feb 1924.

LONGEST!

Interval between twins

Mrs Danny Petrungaro (nee Berg; b. 1953) of Rome, Italy, who had been on hormone treatment after suffering four miscarriages, gave birth normally to a girl, Diana, on 22 Dec 1987, but the other twin, Monica, was delivered by cesarean on 27 Jan 1988, 36 days later.

Quadruplets The world's heaviest quadruplets (two girls, two boys) weighed 22 lb 15¾ oz collectively and were born to Mrs Tina Saunders at St Peter's Hospital, Chertsey, Great Britain on 7 Feb 1989.

Quintuplets Two cases have been recorded for heaviest quintuplets, both recording a total weight of 25 lb. The first set was born on 7 Jun 1953 to Mrs Lui Saulian of Zhejiang, China, and the second set to Mrs Kamalammal of Pondicherry, India on 30 Dec 1956.

Lightest single birth A premature baby girl weighing 9.9 oz was reported to have been born on 27 Jun 1989 at the Loyola University Medical Center, IL.

Lightest twins Mary, 16 oz, and Margaret, 19 oz, were born on 16 Aug 1931 to Mrs Florence Stimson of Old Fletton, Great Britain.

Fastest triplet birth Bradley, Christopher and Carmon were born naturally to Mrs James E. Duck of Memphis, TN in two minutes on 21 Mar 1977.

Test-tube babies There are various methods by which babies can be conceived outside of the mother's body. These children are usually known as "test-tube" babies and the technique as IVF (in-vitro fertilization).

First The world's first test-tube baby was born to Lesley Brown, age 31, who gave birth by cesarean section to Louise (5 lb 12 oz) in Oldham General Hospital, Great Britain at 11:47 P.M. on 25 Jul 1978. Louise was externally conceived on 10 Nov 1977.

The first test-tube baby in the United States was Elizabeth Jordan Carr (5 lb 12 oz), who was delivered by cesarean section to Judy Carr, age 28, in Norfolk General Hospital, VA on 28 Dec 1981. Elizabeth was externally conceived on 15 Apr 1981. Dr Howard Jones of Eastern Virginia Medical School performed the in-vitro procedure.

Twins The world's first test-tube twins, Stephen and Amanda, were delivered by cesarean section to Mrs Radmila Mays, age 31, at the Queen Victoria Medical Centre, Melbourne, Australia on 5 Jun 1981. Amanda weighed in at 5 lb 6 oz and Stephen at 5 lb 3 oz.

Triplets The world's first test-tube triplets (two girls and one boy) were born at Flinders Medical Centre, Adelaide, Australia on 8 Jun 1983. At the request of the parents, no names were released.

Quintuplets Alan, Brett, Connor, Douglas and Edward were born to Linda and Bruce Jacobssen at University College Hospital, London, Great Britain on 26 Mar 1985.

First birth from frozen embryo Zoe (last name withheld) was delivered by cesarean section weighing 5 lb 13 oz on 28 Mar 1984 in Melbourne, Australia. Scientists from Monash University announced the birth.

United States A boy (9 lb 8 oz) was delivered by cesarean section on 4 Jun 1986 to Monique (last name withheld), age 36, in Cottage Hospital, Santa Barbara, CA. A second child (name withheld) was born on 23 Oct 1989 by the same procedure, and it is believed that this is the only case of siblings from frozen embryos. Dr Richard Marrs was in charge of the procedure.

Most-premature babies James Elgin Gill was born to Brenda and James Gill on 20 May 1987 in Ottawa, Ontario, Canada 128 days premature and weighing 1 lb 6 oz.

In the United States the most premature baby is Ernestine Hudgins, who was born on 8 Feb 1983 in San Diego, CA about 18 weeks premature and weighing 17 oz.

Twins Joshua and Evan Ernsteen were born on 18 Aug 1992 at Evanston Hospital, IL, 112 days premature.

Triplets The lightest and most premature triplets in the United States were Brandi Nichole, Christian Kipling and Kelli Amanda Karasiewicz, who were born to Rick and Gwen Karasiewicz on 9 Dec 1980 in Columbia, SC, 88 days premature and weighing 1 lb 11 oz, 1 lb 15 oz and 1 lb 10 oz respectively.

Quadruplets Tina Piper of St Leonards-on-Sea, Great Britain, had quadruplets on 10 Apr 1988, after exactly 26 weeks of pregnancy. Oliver, 2 lb 9 oz (d. Feb 1989), Francesca, 2 lb 2 oz, Charlotte, 2 lb 4½ oz, and Georgina, 2 lb 5 oz, were all born at The Royal Sussex County Hospital, Brighton, Great Britain.

MULTIPLE BIRTHS

Conjoined twins Conjoined twins were formerly called "Siamese," from the celebrated Chang and Eng Bunker ("Left" and "Right" in Thai), born at Meklong, Thailand on 11 May 1811 of Chinese parents. They were joined by a cartilaginous band at the chest. They married (in 1843) the Misses Sarah and Adalaide Yates of Wilkes County, NC, and fathered 10 and 12 children respectively. They died within three hours of each other on 17 Jan 1874, age 62.

Rarest The most extreme form of conjoined twins is dicephales tetrabrachius dipus (two heads, four arms and two legs). The only fully reported example is Masha and Dasha Krivoshlyapovy, born in Russia on 4 Jan 1950.

Earliest successful separation The earliest successful separation of conjoined twins was performed on xiphopagus (joined at the sternum) girls at Mount Sinai Hospital, Cleveland, OH by Dr Jac S. Geller on 14 Dec 1952.

Longest-parted twins Through the help of New Zealand's television program *Missing* on 27 Apr 1989, Iris (nee Haughie) Johns and Aro (nee Haughie) Campbell (b. 13 Jan 1914) were reunited after 75 years' separation.

United States Fraternal twins Lloyd Earl and Floyd Ellsworth Clark were born on 15 Feb 1917 in Nebraska. They were parted when only four months old and lived under their adopted names, Dewayne William Gramly (Lloyd) and Paul Edward Forbes (Floyd). Both men knew that they had been born twins but it wasn't until 16 Jun 1986 that they were reunited, after having been separated for over 69 years.

Quindecaplets It was announced by Dr Gennaro Montanino of Rome that he had removed by hysterotomy after four months of pregnancy the fetuses of ten girls and five boys from the womb of a 35-year-old housewife on 22 Jul 1971. A fertility drug was responsible for this unique instance of quindecaplets.

Highest number at a single birth The highest number reported at a single birth were two males and eight females at Bacacay, Brazil on 22 Apr 1946. Reports of ten at a single birth were also received from Spain in 1924 and from China on 12 May 1936.

The highest number medically recorded is nine (nonuplets) born to Mrs Geraldine Broderick at Royal Hospital for Women, Sydney, Australia on 13 Jun 1971. None of the five boys (two stillborn) and four girls lived for more than six days. The birth of nine children has also been reported on at least two other occasions: Philadelphia, PA on 29 May 1971; and Bagerhat, Bangladesh *c.* 11 May 1977; in both cases none survived.

Most sets of multiple births in a family *Quintuplets* There is no recorded case of more than a single set.

Quadruplets Four sets to Mde Feodor Vassilyev, Shuya, Russia (b. 1707) (see Motherhood).

Triplets 15 sets to Maddalena Granata, Italy (b. 1839–*fl.* 1886).

Twins 16 sets to Mde Vassilyev (see above). Mrs Barbara Zulu of Barbeton, South Africa bore three sets of girls and three mixed sets in seven years (1967–73). Mrs Anna Steynvaait of Johannesburg, South Africa produced two sets within 10 months in 1960.

DESCENDANTS

In polygamous countries (countries that allow a man to have more than one wife at a time), the number of a person's descendants can become incalculable. The last Sharifian emperor of Morocco, Moulay Ismail (1672–1727), known as "The Bloodthirsty," was reputed to have fathered a total of 525 sons and 342 daughters by 1703 and to have achieved a 700th son in 1721.

At his death on 15 Oct 1992, Samuel S. Must, age 96, of Fryburg, PA, had 824 living descendants. The roll call comprised 11 children, 97 grandchildren, 634 great-grandchildren and 82 great-great-grandchildren.

Mrs Peter L. Schwartz (1902–88) of Missouri had 14 children, 13 of whom are still living; 175 grandchildren; 477 great-grandchildren; and 20 great-great-grandchildren.

Seven-generation family Augusta Bunge (nee Pagel; b. 13 Oct 1879) of Wisconsin learned that she was a great-great-great-great-grandmother when she received news of the arrival of her great-great-great-great-grandson, Christopher John Bollig (b. 21 Jan 1989).

Great-great-great-grandmother Harriet Holmes of Newfoundland, Canada (b. 17 Jan 1899) became the youngest living great-great-great-grandmother on 8 Mar 1987 at the age of 88 years 50 days.

Family tree The lineage of K'ung Ch'iu or Confucius (551–479 B.C.) can be traced back further than that of any other family. His great-great-great-great-grandfather K'ung Chia is known from the eighth century B.C. This man's 85th lineal descendants, Wei-yi (b. 1939) and Wei-ning (b. 1947), live today in Taiwan.

LONGEVITY

No single subject is more obscured by vanity, deceit, falsehood and deliberate fraud than human longevity.

Centenarians surviving beyond their 113th year are extremely rare, and the present absolute proven limit of human longevity does not yet admit of anyone living to celebrate his or her 121st birthday.

Data on documented centenarians has shown that only one 115-year life can be expected in 2.1 billion lives.

In 1990 the United States population of people 65 and over was 31.7 million, representing 12.6 percent of the population. Since 1900 the American population 65 and over has increased tenfold, from 3.1 million. As of 1 Jul 1990 there were 35,808 centenarians.

Life expectancy World life expectancy is rising from 47.5 years (1950–55) towards 63.9 years (1995–2000). In the decade 1890–1900, life expectancy among the population of India was 23.7 years.

The highest average life expectancy at birth is in Japan, with 82.1 years for women and 76.1 years for men in 1991. The lowest life expectancy at birth for the period 1985–90 is 39.4 years for males in Ethiopia and Sierra Leone, and 42.0 years for females in Afghanistan.

Oldest authentic centenarian The greatest *authenticated* age to which any human has ever lived is 120 years 237 days in the case of Shigechiyo Izumi of Asan on Tokunoshima, an island 820 miles southwest of Tokyo, Japan. He was born at Asan on 29 Jun 1865 and was recorded as a 6-year-old in Japan's first census of 1871. He died in his ranch house on 21 Feb 1986 after developing pneumonia. He worked until the age of 105. His wife died when only 90 years of age. He drank *Sho-chu* ("firewater" distilled from sugar) and took up smoking when 70 years old. He attributed his long life to "God, Buddha and the Sun."

Oldest living The oldest living person whose date of birth can be authenticated is Jeanne Louise Calment. She was born in France on 21 Feb 1875, when Ulysses S. Grant was still the president of the United States, and she met Vincent van Gogh in her father's hardware store when she was 14. Now 119 years old, she lives in a nursing home in Arles, southern France.

United States The oldest living person in the United States is Mrs Wilhelmina "Minnie" Kott (nee Geringer), who was born in Chicago, IL on 7 Mar 1879.

Oldest twins Eli Shadrack and John Meshak Phipps were born on 14 Feb 1803 at Affinghton, VA. Eli died at Hennessey, OK on 23 Feb 1911 at the age of 108 years 9 days, on which day John was still living in Shenandoah, VA.

Female On 17 Jun 1984, identical twin sisters Mildred Widman Philippi and Mary Widman Franzini of St Louis, MO celebrated their 104th birthday. Mildred died on 4 May 1985, 44 days short of the twins' 105th birthday.

Oldest living twins John Henry Laur and Thomas Docherty Laur are the oldest living male identical twins in the United States. They were born in Warren Township, Midland County, MI on 2 Dec 1901.

Oldest living triplets Faith, Hope and Charity Cardwell were born in Sweetwater, TX on 18 May 1899, and live together in a Sweetwater retirement home.

Oldest quadruplets The Ottman quads of Munich, Germany—Adolf, Anne-Marie, Emma and Elisabeth—were born on 5 May 1912. Adolf was the first to die, on 17 Mar 1992, at the age of 79 years 316 days.

United States The Morlok quads of Lansing, MI—Edna, Wilma, Sarah and Helen—celebrated their 63rd birthday on 18 May 1993.

The world's longest-lived human was Shigechiyo Izumi. Here he is seated before a statue of himself honoring his longevity.

AUTHENTIC LONGEVITY RECORDS

Country	Age	Name	Born	Died
Japan	120 yr 237 days	Shigechiyo Izumi	29 Jun 1865	21 Feb 1986
France	119 yr 46 days	Jeanne Louise Calment	21 Feb 1875	*fl.** April 1994
United States[1]	116 yr 88 days	Carrie White (Mrs; nee Joyner)	18 Nov 1874	14 Feb 1991
Great Britain	115 yr 229 days	Charlotte Hughes (Mrs; nee Milburn)	1 Aug 1877	17 Mar 1993
Canada	113 yr 124 days	Pierre Joubert	15 Jul 1701	16 Nov 1814
Australia	112 yr 330 days	Caroline Maud Mockridge	11 Dec 1874	6 Nov 1987
Wales	112 yr 292 days	John Evans	19 Aug 1877	10 Jun 1990
Spain[2]	112 yr 228 days	Josefa Salas Mateo	14 Jul 1860	27 Feb 1973
Norway	112 yr 61 days	Maren Bolette Torp	21 Dec 1876	20 Feb 1989
Morocco	112 yr +	El Hadj Mohammed el Mokri (Grand Vizier)	1844	16 Sep 1957
Poland	112 yr +	Roswlia Mielczarak (Mrs)	1868	7 Jan 1981
Netherlands	111 yr 354 days	Thomas Peters	6 Apr 1745	26 Mar 1857
Ireland	111 yr 327 days	The Hon. Katherine Plunket	22 Nov 1820	14 Oct 1932
Scotland	111 yr 238 days	Kate Begbie (Mrs)	9 Jan 1877	5 Sep 1988
South Africa[3]	111 yr 151 days	Johanna Booyson	17 Jan 1857	16 Jun 1968
Sweden[4]	111 yr 90 days	Wilhelmine Sande (Mrs)	24 Oct 1874	21 Jan 1986
Italy	111 yr 12 days	Domenico Minervino	10 May 1880	21 May 1991
Czechoslovakia	111 yr +	Marie Bernatková	22 Oct 1857	*fl.* October 1968
Germany[5]	111 yr	Maria Corba	15 Aug 1878	*fl.* March 1990
Finland	111 yr +	Fanny Matilda Nystrom	30 Sep 1878	1989
Channel Islands	110 yr 321 days	Margaret Ann Neve (nee Harvey)	18 May 1792	4 Apr 1903
Northern Ireland	110 yr 234 days	Elizabeth Watkins (Mrs)	10 Mar 1863	31 Oct 1973
Yugoslavia	110 yr +	Demitrius Philipovitch	9 Mar 1818	*fl.* August 1928
Greece	110 yr +	Lambrini Tsiatoura (Mrs)	1870	19 Feb 1981
USSR	110 yr +	Khasako Dzugayev	7 Aug 1860	*fl.* August 1970

[1] *Rena Glover Brailsford died in Summerton, SC on 6 Dec 1977 reputedly aged 118 years. The 1900 U.S. Federal Census for Crawfish Springs Militia District of Walker County, GA, records an age of 77 for a Mark Thrash. If the Mark Thrash (reputedly born in Georgia in December 1822) who died near Chattanooga, TN on 17 Dec 1943 was he, and the age attributed was accurate, then he would have survived for 121 years. According to Jackson Pollard's Social Security payments, he was born on 15 Dec 1869 in Georgia, but no birth certificate or family bible are available.*
[2] *Benita Medrana of Avila died on 28 Jan 1979, allegedly aged 114 years 335 days.*
[3] *Susan Johanna Deporter of Port Elizabeth, South Africa was reputedly 114 years old when she died on 4 Aug 1954.*
[4] *Mrs Sande was born in present-day Norway.*
[5] *An unnamed female died in Germany in 1979 aged 112 years, and an unnamed male, aged also 112 years, died in 1969.*
* Note: *fl.* is the abbreviation for the Latin *floruit,* meaning he or she was living at the relevant date.

TOP • 5 • FIVE

65+ POPULATION

State	Total (1,000's)
California	3,136
Florida	2,369
New York	2,364
Pennsylvania	1,829
Texas	1,717

Data: AARP/AOA

Most living ascendants Megan Sue Austin of Bar Harbor, ME had a full set of grandparents and great-grandparents and five great-great-grandparents, making 19 direct ascendants, when she was born on 16 May 1982.

ANATOMY & PHYSIOLOGY

HANDS, FEET AND HAIR

Touch The extreme sensitivity of the fingers is such that a vibration with a movement of 0.02 microns can be detected.

Longest fingernails Fingernails grow at a rate of about 0.02 in a week—four times faster than toenails. The aggregate measurement of those of Shridhar Chillal (b. 1937) of Pune, Maharashtra, India, on 3 Mar 1993 was 205 in for the five nails on his left hand (thumb 48 in, index finger 36 in, second finger 39 in, third finger 42 in, and pinkie 40 in). He last cut his nails in 1952.

Fewest toes The two-toed syndrome exhibited by some members of the Wadomo tribe of the Zambezi Valley, Zimbabwe and the Kalanga tribe of the eastern Kalahari Desert, Botswana is hereditary via a single mutated gene. They are not handicapped by their deformity, and can walk great distances without discomfort.

Largest feet If cases of elephantiasis are excluded, then the biggest feet currently known are those of Matthew McGrory (b. 17 May 1973) of Pennsylvania, who wears size 23 shoes.

> **GUESS WHAT?**
>
> **Q.** WHAT IS THE FASTEST TAP DANCING RATE?
>
> **A.** LOOK IN "DANCING" (ARTS & ENTERTAINMENT)

Balancing on one foot The longest recorded duration for balancing on one foot is 55 hr 35 min, by Girish Sharma at Deori, India from 2–4 Oct 1992. The disengaged foot may not be rested on the standing foot, nor may any object be used for support or balance.

Motionlessness António Gomes dos Santos of Zare, Portugal stood motionless for 15 hr 2 min 55 sec on 30 Jul 1988 at the Amoreiras Shopping Center, Lisbon.

Longest hair Human hair grows at a rate of about 0.5 in a month. If left uncut it will usually grow to a maximum of 2–3 ft.

The longest documented length of hair belongs to Mata Jagdamba of Ujjain, India (b. 1917); it measured 13 ft 10½ in on 21 Feb 1994.

United States The hair of Diane Witt of Worcester, MA measured over 12 ft 8 in in March 1993.

Most valuable hair On 18 Feb 1988 a bookseller from Cirencester, Great Britain paid £5,575 ($10,035) for a lock of hair that had belonged to British naval hero Lord Nelson (1758–1805) at an auction held at Crewkerne, Great Britain.

Hair splitting The greatest reported achievement in hair splitting by a human was that of Alfred West (Great Britain; 1901–85), who succeeded in splitting a human hair 17 times into 18 parts on eight occasions.

The longest strand of hair belongs to yogini Mata Jagdamba of Ujjain, India. It measures 13 ft 10½ in. (Guinness Rishi)

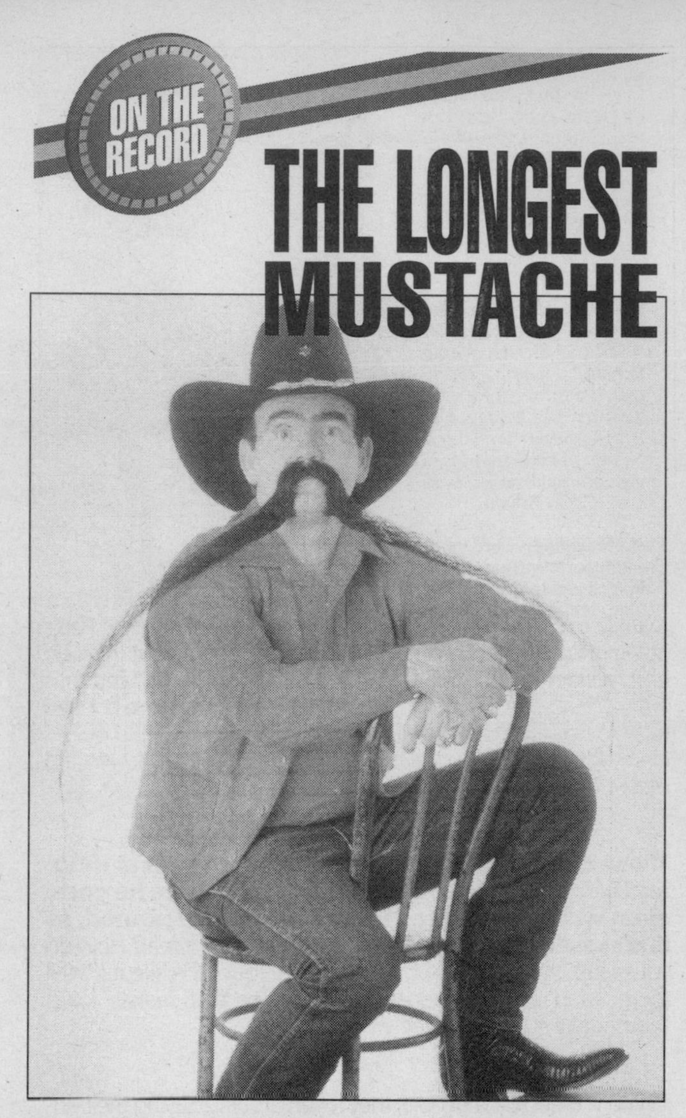

THE LONGEST MUSTACHE

Paul Miller was out driving around Hollywood with his wife one day when the sheriff pulled over their pickup truck. "Pardon me, ma'am," said the sheriff to Mrs.

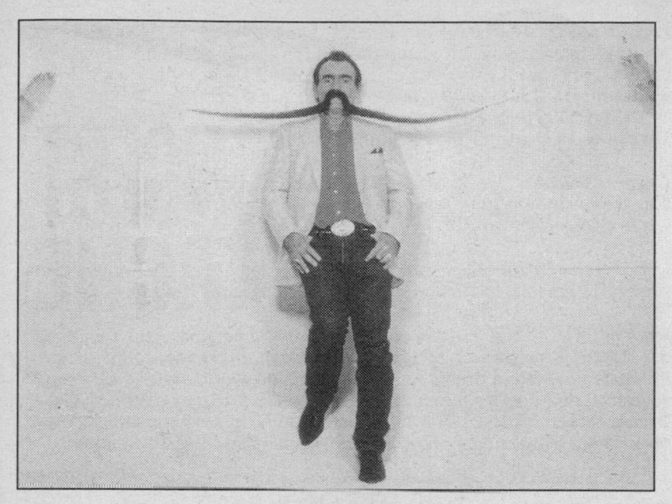

Miller displays America's longest mustache. (Dennis Slagle)

Miller, "you're carrying too wide a load for this road." He had a twinkle in his eye though, because the "wide load" was Paul, riding in the back seat with his mustache extending out through both windows. "That's a true story," Miller guffaws, "and that was back when my mustache was only five feet long!" He hopped out of the pickup, "looking like any old burglar they'd pulled over." Instead of being frisked, he had his picture taken with the men in blue. "We got along great!"

These days Miller's mustache is over eight feet long, and he's still grabbing attention everywhere he goes, even when his mustache is rolled up and pinned, as it is most days. "Everyone wants to know, 'Is it real? How do you sleep? Why did you grow it? Does your wife like it?' I tell them, 'I don't know—she hasn't talked to me in 18 years!'" jokes the happily married Miller.

"When I meet some people, they'll start arguing, saying their uncle had one longer. So I'll start unrolling it, asking 'Was it this long?' And I'll keep unrolling it until it's beyond my reach. Then they'll say at last, 'No, not that long.'"

Longest beard The beard of Hans N. Langseth (b. 1846 near Eidsvoll, Norway) measured 17½ ft at the time of his burial in Kensett, IA in 1927 after 15 years' residence in the United States. It was presented to the Smithsonian Institution, Washington, D.C., in 1967.

The beard of Janice Deveree, "the bearded lady" (b. Bracken Co., KY, 1842), was measured in 1884 at 14 in.

Longest mustache The mustache of Kalyan Ramji Sain of Sundargarth, India, grown since 1976, reached a span of 133½ in (right side 67¾ in and left side 65¾ in) in July 1993.

United States Paul Miller of Alta Loma, CA had grown a mustache measuring 8 ft 2 in long in March 1994. See On the Record Feature (p. 20–21).

Shaving The fastest barbers on record are Denny Rowe and Tom Rodden. Denny Rowe shaved 1,994 men in 60 min with a retractor safety razor in Herne Bay, Great Britain on 19 Jun 1988, taking on average 1.8 sec per volunteer, and drawing blood four times. Tom Rodden of Chatham, Great Britain shaved 278 even braver volunteers in 60 min with a straight razor on 10 Nov 1993, averaging 12.9 sec per face. He drew blood only once.

TEETH

Earliest Tooth enamel is the only part of the human body that remains basically unchanged throughout life. It is also the hardest substance in the body.

The first deciduous or milk teeth normally appear in infants at 5–8 months, these being the upper and lower jaw first incisors. Molars usually appear at 24 months, but in a case published in Denmark in 1970, a six-week-premature baby was documented with eight teeth at birth, of which four were in the molar region.

Most dentists The country with the most dentists is the United States, where there were 190,842, with 139,404 registered members of the American Dental Association, at the end of 1993.

Most dedicated dentist Brother Giovanni Battista Orsenigo of the Ospedale Fatebenefratelli, Rome, Italy, a dentist, conserved all the teeth he extracted during the time he practiced his profession from 1868 to 1904. In 1903 the number was found to be 2,000,744 teeth, indicating an average of 185 teeth, or nearly six total extractions, a day.

Most valuable tooth In 1816 a tooth belonging to British scientist Sir Isaac Newton (1643–1727) was sold in London, Great Britain for £730 ($3,650). It was purchased by a nobleman who had it set in a ring, which he wore constantly.

Earliest false teeth From discoveries made in Etruscan tombs, partial dentures of bridgework type were being worn in what is now the Tuscany region of Italy as early as 700 B.C. Some were permanently attached to existing teeth and others were removable.

Lifting and pulling with teeth Walter Arfeuille of Ieper-Vlamertinge, Bel-

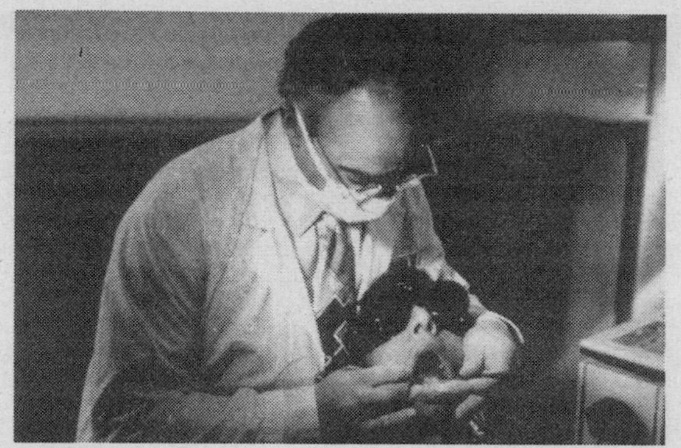

There are more dentists in the United States than in any other country. (Gamma/Hensey)

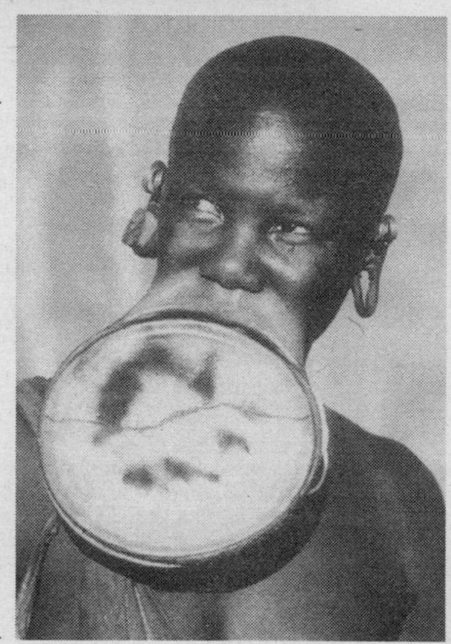

The ceremonial lip plate worn by the women of the Surma tribe of Ethiopia. (Robert Estall Photographs/A. Fisher & C. Beckwith)

PULLING!

Robert Galstyan of Masis, Armenia pulled two railroad cars coupled together, weighing a total of 483,197 lb, a distance of 23 ft along a railroad track with his teeth at Shcherbinka, Greater Moscow, Russia on 21 Jul 1992.

gium lifted weights totaling 621 lb a distance of 6¾ in off the ground with his teeth in Paris, France, on 31 Mar 1990.

OPTICS

Highest acuity The human eye is capable of judging relative position with remarkable accuracy, reaching limits of between 3 and 5 seconds of arc.

In April 1984 Dr Dennis M. Levi of the College of Optometry, University of Houston, TX, repeatedly identified the relative position of a thin bright green line within 0.85 sec of arc. This is equivalent to a displacement of some ¼ in at a distance of one mile.

Light sensitivity Working in Chicago, IL in 1942, Maurice H. Pirenne detected a flash of blue light of 500 nm in total darkness, when as few as five quanta or photons of light were available to be absorbed by the rod photoreceptors of the retina.

BONES

Longest Excluding a variable number of sesamoids (small rounded bones), there are 206 bones in the adult human body, compared with 300 in children (as they grow, some bones fuse together). The thigh bone or femur is the longest. It constitutes usually 27.5 percent of a person's stature, and may be expected to be 19¾ in long in a 6-ft-tall man. The longest recorded bone was the 29.9-in femur of the German giant Constantine, who died in Mons, Belgium, on 30 Mar 1902, age 30. The femur of Robert Wadlow, the tallest man ever recorded, measured an estimated 29½ in.

Smallest The stapes or stirrup bone, one of the three auditory ossicles in the middle ear, measures 0.10–0.13 in in length and weighs from 0 .03–0.066 grains.

MUSCLES

Largest Muscles normally account for 40 percent of human body weight. The bulkiest of the 639 named muscles in the human body is usually the gluteus maximus or buttock muscle, which extends the thigh. During pregnancy a woman's uterus can increase its weight from about 1 oz to over 2.2 lb.

Smallest The stapedius, which controls the stapes (see above), is less than 0.05 in long.

Longest The longest muscle in the human body is the sartorius, which is a narrow, ribbonlike muscle running from the pelvis across the front of the thigh to the top of the tibia below the knee.

Strongest The strongest muscle in the human body is the masseter, of which there are two, one on each side of the mouth, which is responsible for the action of biting. In August 1986, Richard Hofmann (b. 1949) of Lake City, FL achieved a bite strength of 975 lb for approximately two seconds in a research test using a gnathodynamometer at the College of Dentistry, University of Florida. This figure is more than six times the normal biting strength.

Most active It has been estimated that the eye muscles move 100,000 times a day or more. Many of these eye movements take place during the dreaming phase of sleep.

Longest muscle name The muscle with the longest name is the *levator labii superioris alaeque nasi*, which runs inwards and downwards on the face, with one branch running to the upper lip and the other to the nostril. It is the musclc that everts or curls the upper lip, and its action was particularly well demonstrated in the performances of Elvis Presley (1935–77).

Largest chest measurements In the extreme case of Robert Earl Hughes (USA; 1926–58) the chest measurement was 124 in, and T.J. Albert Jackson, currently the heaviest living man, has a chest measurement of 120 in.

The largest muscular chest measurement is that of Isaac Nesser of Greensburg, PA, at 74 1/16 in.

Largest biceps Isaac Nesser has biceps 29 in in circumference when cold (not pumped).

WAISTS

Largest The largest waist ever recorded was that of Walter Hudson (1944–91) of New York, which measured 119 in at his peak weight of 1,197 lb.

Smallest The smallest waist in someone of normal stature was that of Mrs Ethel Granger (1905–82) of Peterborough, Great Britain, reduced from a natural 22 in to 13 in over the period 1929–39. A measurement of 13 in was also claimed for the French actress Mlle Polaire (real name Emile Marie Bouchand; 1881–1939).

NECKS

Longest The maximum measured extension of the neck by the successive fitting of copper coils, as practiced by the women of the Padaung or Kareni tribe of Myanmar, is 15 3/4 in. When the rings are removed, the muscles supporting the head and neck shrink to their normal length.

BRAINS

Heaviest The heaviest brain ever recorded was that of a 30-year-old male, which weighed 5 lb 1.1 oz and was reported by Dr T. Mandybur and Karen Carney of the Department of Pathology and Laboratory Medicine at the University of Cincinnati, OH in December 1992.

Lightest The lightest "normal" or non-atrophied brain on record was one weighing 2 lb 6.7 oz reported by Dr P. Davis and Prof. E. Wright of King's College Hospital, London, Great Britain in 1977. It belonged to a 31-year-old woman.

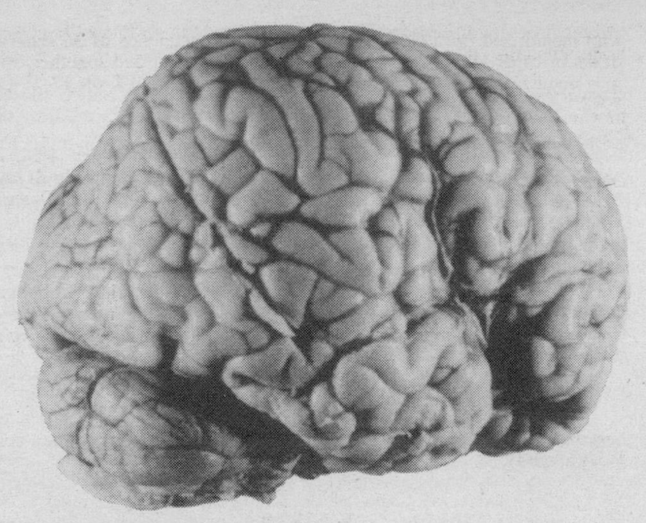

The heaviest brain ever recorded was that of a 30-year-old male. It weighed 5 lb 1.1 oz. The average brain weighs 3 lbs. (Jay Card/University of Cincinnati)

Most expensive skull The skull of Emanuel Swedenborg (1688–1772), the Swedish natural philosopher and theologian, was bought in London, Great Britain by the Royal Swedish Academy of Sciences for £5,500 ($10,505) on 6 Mar 1978.

Computation Mrs Shakuntala Devi of India multiplied two 13-digit numbers (7,686,369,774,870 × 2,465,099,745,779) randomly selected by the Computer Department of Imperial College, London on 18 Jun 1980, in 28 sec. Her answer, which was correct, was 18,947,668,177,995,426,462,773,730. Some experts on calculating prodigies refuse to give credence to Mrs Devi on the grounds that her achievements are so vastly superior to the calculating feats of any other judged prodigy that the judgment must have been defective.

Memory Bhandanta Vicittabi Vumsa (1911–93) recited 16,000 pages of Buddhist canonical texts in Yangon, Myanmar in May 1974. Gon Yangling, 26, has memorized more than 15,000 telephone numbers in Harbin, China, according to the Xinhua News Agency.

Card memorizing Dominic O'Brien (Great Britain) memorized on a single sighting a random sequence of 40 separate decks of cards (2,080 cards in all) that had been shuffled together, with only one mistake, at the BBC studios, Elstree, Great Britain on 26 Nov 1993. He also memorized a single deck of shuffled cards in 43.59 seconds at the Guinness World of Records exhibition, London, Great Britain on 25 Mar 1994.

The United States record is held by Frost McKee of Georgetown, TX, who memorized on a single sighting a random sequence of 36 separate decks of cards (1,872 cards in all) that had been shuffled together, with only eight mistakes, at the Ramada Inn, Georgetown, TX on 17–18 Oct 1992.

Greatest number of places of pi Hideaki Tomoyori (b. 30 Sep 1932) of Yokohama, Japan recited pi from memory to 40,000 places in 17 hr 21 min, including breaks totaling 4 hr 15 min, on 9–10 Mar 1987 at the Tsukuba University Club House.

Mental health The country with the most psychologists and psychiatrists is the United States. The registered membership of the American Psychological Association (instituted in 1892) was 124,000, and the membership of the American Psychiatric Association (instituted in 1844) was 38,156 as of 1 Jan 1994.

VOICE

Greatest range The normal intelligible outdoor range of the male human voice in still air is 600 ft. The *silbo*, the whistled language of the Canary Island of La Gomera, is intelligible across the valleys at five miles under ideal conditions. There is a recorded case of the human voice being detectable at a distance of 10½ miles across still water at night.

Fastest talker Few people are able to speak *articulately* at a sustained speed above 300 words per minute.

Steve Woodmore of Orpington, Great Britain spoke 595 words in a time of 56.01 sec, or 637.4 words per minute, on the British TV program *Motor Mouth* on 22 Sep 1990.

United States John Moschitta (USA) recited 545 words in 55.8 sec, or 586 words per minute, on 24 May 1988 in Los Angeles, CA.

GUESS WHAT?

Q. WHICH PRESIDENT GAVE THE SHORTEST INAUGURATION SPEECH?

A. LOOK IN "LEGISLATURES" (BUSINESS & PUBLIC AFFAIRS)

Backwards talking Steve Briers of Kilgetty, Great Britain recited the entire lyrics of Queen's album *A Night at the Opera* backwards on 6 Feb 1990 in a time of 9 min 58.44 sec.

United States The American record is held by David Fuhrer of California, who recited the entire lyrics of Queen's album *A Night at the Opera* backwards at Trax Recording Studio, CA on 28 Jul 1989 in a time of 10 min 19 sec.

Hamlet's soliloquy Sean Shannon, a Canadian residing in Oxford, Great Britain, recited Hamlet's soliloquy "To be or not to be" (260 words) in a time of 24 sec (equivalent to 650 words per min) on British Broadcasting Corporation's *Radio Oxford* on 26 Oct 1990.

Screaming The loudest scream was one of 128 decibels at 8 ft 2 in produced by Simon Robinson of McLaren Vale, South Australia at The Guinness Challenge at Adelaide, Australia on 11 Nov 1988.

Shouting Annalisa Wray (b. 21 Apr 1974) of Comber, Northern Ireland, achieved 119.4 decibels in a shouting contest at the Seventh International Rally Arura held in Coleraine Academical Institution, Coleraine, Northern Ireland on 11 Aug 1992.

Donald H. Burns of St George's, Bermuda achieved a shout of 119 decibels when he appeared on the Fuji TV film *Narvhodo the World* at Liberty State Park, NJ on 18 Jan 1989.

Whistling Roy Lomas achieved 122.5 decibels at 8 ft 2 in in the Deadroom at the British Broadcasting Corporation studios in Manchester, Great Britain on 19 Dec 1983.

Yodeling The most rapid recorded yodel is 22 tones (15 falsetto) in 1 sec, by Peter Hinnen of Zürich, Switzerland on 9 Feb 1992.

BLOOD

Groups On a world basis Group O is the most common (46 percent), but in some areas, for example Norway, Group A predominates.

The rarest type in the world is a type of Bombay blood (subtype h-h) found so far only in a Czechoslovak nurse in 1961, and in a brother (Rh positive) and sister (Rh negative) surnamed Jalbert in Massachusetts, reported in February 1968.

The most common subgroup in the United States is O+, which is found in 38.4 percent of the population. The rarest generic blood group is AB–, which occurs in only 0.7 percent of persons in the United States.

Recipient A 50-year-old hemophiliac, Warren C. Jyrich, required 2,400 donor units of blood, equivalent to 1,900 pints of blood, when undergoing open heart surgery at the Michael Reese Hospital, Chicago, IL in December 1970.

Largest vein The largest is the inferior vena cava, which returns the blood from the lower half of the body to the heart.

Largest artery The largest artery is the aorta, which is 1.18 in in diameter where it leaves the heart. By the time it ends at the level of the fourth lumbar vertebra it is about 0.68 in in diameter.

Most alcoholic The University of California Medical School, Los Angeles reported in December 1982 the case of a confused but conscious 24-year-old female, who was shown to have a blood alcohol level of 1.8 grains per 0.18 pt. After two days she discharged herself.

CELLS

Biggest The largest is the megakaryocyte, a blood cell, measuring 200 microns. It spends its life in the bone marrow, rarely venturing out in the main stream of the blood itself. In the marrow it produces the "stickiest" particles in the body—the platelets, which play an important role in stopping bleeding.

Smallest Some of the smallest cells are brain cells in the cerebellum that measure about 0.005 mm.

Longest The longest cells are neurons of the nervous system. Motor neurons 4.26 ft long have cell bodies (gray matter) in the lower spinal cord with axons (white matter) that carry nerve impulses from the spinal cord down to the big toe.

Fastest turnover of body cells The body cells with the shortest life are in the lining of the alimentary tract (gut), where the cells are shed every three days.

Longest life Those with the longest life are brain cells, which last for life. They may be three times as old as bone cells, which may live 25–30 years.

Longest memory The lymphocyte has the longest memory of any cell in the body. These white blood cells are part of the body's immune defense system. As successive generations of lymphocytes are produced during life, the cells never forget an enemy. So, for example, once a measles virus has introduced itself to the lymphocytes in the first years of life, these stalwarts of the immune system will still be ready to recognize and destroy the measles virus 70 years later. This is why you cannot get measles twice.

BODY TEMPERATURE

Highest Willie Jones, 52, was admitted to Grady Memorial Hospital, Atlanta, GA on 10 Jul 1980 with heatstroke on a day when the temperature reached 90°F with 44 percent humidity. His temperature was found to be 115.7° F. After 24 days he was discharged "at prior baseline status."

Lowest People may die of hypothermia with body temperatures of 95°F. The lowest authenticated body temperature is 57.5°F, for Karlee Kosolofski, age 2, of Regina, Saskatchewan, Canada on 23 Feb 1994. She had accidentally been locked outside her home for six hours in a temperature of –8°F. Despite severe frostbite, which required the amputation of her left leg above the knee, she has made a full recovery.

MEDICAL EXTREMES

Cardiac arrest The longest period of cardiac arrest in which the victim survived is four hours in the case of a Norwegian fisherman, Jan Egil Refsdahl (b. 1936), who fell overboard in the icy waters off Bergen on 7 Dec 1987. He was rushed to nearby Haukeland Hospital after his body temperature fell to 77°F and his heart stopped beating, but he made a full recovery after he was connected to a heart–lung machine normally used for heart surgery.

United States On 9 Oct 1986, Allen Smith, age 2, fell into the Stanislaus River in Oakdale, CA. He was spotted 90 minutes later and rushed to Modesto Memorial Hospital, where two hours later his heart began beating again spontaneously.

Cardiopulmonary resuscitation Brent Shelton and John Ash completed a CPR marathon (cardiopulmonary resuscitation—15 compressions alternating with two breaths) of 130 hr from 28 Oct–2 Nov 1991 at Regina, Saskatchewan, Canada.

United States Three teams of two, consisting of David Bailey and Les Williams, Angie Drinkard and Rich Martel, and Michelle Tyler and Sherri Johnson, all completed CPR marathons of 120 hr 6 min from 1–6 Sep 1988 at Melbourne, FL.

Longest coma Elaine Esposito (1934–78) of Tarpon Springs, FL, never stirred after an appendectomy on 6 Aug 1941, when she was 6 years old. She died on 25 Nov 1978 at the age of 43 years 357 days, having been in a coma for 37 years 111 days.

Longest and shortest dreams Dreaming sleep is characterized by rapid eye movements known as REM. The longest recorded period of REM is one of 2 hr 23 min on 15 Feb 1967 at the Department of Psychology, University of Illinois, Chicago by Bill Carskadon. In July 1984 the Sleep Research Center, Haifa, Israel recorded no REM in a 33-year-old male with a shrapnel brain injury.

Eating Michel Lotito (b. 15 Jun 1950) of Grenoble, France, known as Monsieur Mangetout ("Mr Eat-Everything"), has been eating metal and glass since 1959. Gastroenterologists have X-rayed his stomach and described his ability to consume 2 lb of metal per day as unique. His diet since 1966 has included 10 bicycles, a supermarket cart (in 4½ days), seven TV sets, six chandeliers, a low-calorie Cessna light aircraft and a computer. He is said to have provided the only example in history of a coffin (handles and all) ending up inside a man.

Longest without food and water The longest recorded case of survival without food *and* water is 18 days by Andreas Mihavecz, then 18, of Bregenz, Austria, who was put in a holding cell on 1 Apr 1979 in a local government building in Höscht, and then totally forgotten by the police. On 18 Apr 1979 he was discovered close to death. He had been a passenger in a car that crashed.

g forces Race car driver David Purley (1945–85) survived a deceleration from 108 mph to zero in a crash at Silverstone, Great Britain on 13 Jul 1977 that involved a force of 179.8 *g*. He suffered 29 fractures, three dislocations and six heart stoppages.

The highest *g* value endured voluntarily is 82.6 *g* for 0.04 sec by Eli L. Beeding, Jr. on a water-braked rocket sled at Holloman Air Force Base, NM on 16 May 1958. He was subsequently hospitalized for three days.

Heat endurance The highest dry-air temperature endured by naked men in US Air Force experiments in 1960 was 400° F, and by heavily clothed men 500° F. (Steaks require only 325° F to cook.)

In 1977, race car driver David Purley survived a crash that subjected him to a force of 179.8 g. (Allsport)

Hospital stay The longest stay in a hospital was by Miss Martha Nelson, who was admitted to the Columbus State Institute for the Feeble-Minded in Ohio in 1875. She died in January 1975 at the age of 103 years 6 months in the Orient State Institution, OH after spending more than 99 years in hospitals.

Most injections Samuel L. Davidson (b. 30 Jul 1912) of Glasgow, Scotland, has had at a conservative estimate 77,200 insulin injections since 1923.

Lung power The inflation of a standardized 3,503 meteorological balloon to a diameter of 8 ft against time was achieved by Nicholas Berkeley Mason in 45 min 7 sec for the *Tarm Pai Du* television program in Thailand on 6 Nov 1992.

Longest in "iron lung" John Prestwich (b. 24 Nov 1938) of Kings Langley, Great Britain has been dependent on a negative pressure respirator since his 17th birthday (24 Nov 1955) when he contracted polio.

United States Mrs. Laurel Nisbet (1912–85) of La Crescenta, CA was in an "iron lung" for 37 years 58 days continuously until her death.

Heaviest organ The heaviest internal organ is the liver at 3.3 lb. This is four times heavier than the heart.

Pill-taking The highest recorded total of pills swallowed by a patient is 565,939 between 9 Jun 1967 and 19 Jun 1988 by C.H.A. Kilner (1926–88) of Bindura, Zimbabwe.

Postmortem birth The longest gestation interval in a postmortem birth was one of 84 days in the case of a girl born on 5 Jul 1983 to a brain-dead woman in Roanoke, VA who had been kept on a life support machine since April.

Sneezing The longest sneezing fit ever recorded is that of Donna Griffiths (b. 1969) of Pershore, Great Britain. She started sneezing on 13 Jan 1981 and sneezed an estimated one million times in the first 365 days. She achieved her first sneeze-free day on 16 Sep 1983—the 978th day.

The fastest speed at which particles expelled by sneezing have ever been measured to travel is 103.6 mph.

DID YOU KNOW?

Charles Osborne (1894–1991) of Anthon, IA hiccupped every 1½ seconds for 69 years 5 months, until February 1990. He began hiccupping in 1922 when he was slaughtering a hog, and was unable to find a cure, but led a reasonably normal life in which he had two wives and fathered eight children. He died on 1 May 1991.

Snoring Melvyn Switzer of Dibden, Great Britain recorded peak levels of 91–92 decibels while sleeping at the South View Hotel, Lyndhurst, Great Britain on the evening of 29 Oct 1992.

Stretcher bearing The record for carrying a stretcher case with a 140-lb "body" is 167.86 miles in 49 hr 2 min from 29 Apr–1 May 1993. This was achieved by two four-man teams from the 85th CFB (Canadian Forces Base) Trenton in and around Trenton, Ontario, Canada.

United States A stretcher was carried 158.2 miles in 46 hr 35 min, from 27–29 May 1992, by two four-man teams from the 85th Medical Battalion, Ft Meade, MD.

Swallowing The worst reported case of compulsive swallowing of objects involved an insane female, Mrs H., who at the age of 42 complained of a "slight abdominal pain." She proved to have 2,533 objects, including 947 bent pins, in her stomach. These were removed by Drs Chalk and Foucar in June 1927 at the Ontario Hospital, Canada.

The heaviest object extracted from a human stomach has been a 5 lb 3 oz ball of hair from a 20-year-old female compulsive swallower at the South Devon and East Cornwall Hospital, Great Britain, on 30 Mar 1895.

Most tattoos The ultimate in being tattooed is represented by Tom Leppard of the Isle of Skye, Scotland. He has chosen a leopard-skin design, with all the skin between the spots tattooed saffron yellow. The area of his body covered is approximately 99.2 percent.

Bernard Moeller of Pennsylvania has the most separate designs, with 14,000 individual tattoos up to January 1993.

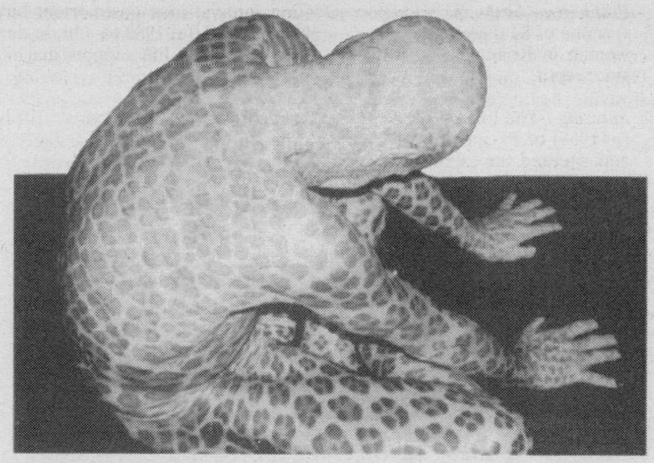

The appropriately named Tom Leppard sports a fetching all-over leopard-skin design that leaves less than one percent of his skin untattooed.

The world's most decorated woman is strip artiste "Krystyne Kolorful" (b. 5 Dec 1952, Alberta, Canada). Her 95 percent bodysuit took 10 years to complete.

Underwater submergence In 1986 2-year-old Michelle Funk of Salt Lake City, UT, made a full recovery after spending 66 minutes under water.

ILLNESS AND DISEASE

Commonest *Noncontagious* The commonest noncontagious diseases are periodontal diseases such as gingivitis (inflammation of the gums). In their lifetime few people completely escape the effects of tooth decay.

Contagious The commonest contagious disease in the world is coryza (acute nasopharyngitis), or the common cold.

Highest mortality There are a number of diseases that are generally considered to be universally fatal. AIDS (Acquired Immune Deficiency Syndrome) and rabies encephalitis, a virus infection of the central nervous system, are well-known examples. The *disease* rabies, however, should not be confused with being bitten by a rabid animal. With immediate treatment, the virus can be prevented from entering the nervous system, and chances of survival are high.

Historically, the pneumonic form of plague (bacterial infection), which caused the Black Death of 1347–51, killed everyone who caught it—some 75 million people worldwide.

Leading cause of death In industrialized countries, diseases of the heart and blood vessels account for more than 50 percent of deaths. The most common of these are heart attacks, strokes and gangrene of the lower limbs, usually due to atheroma (degeneration of the arterial walls) obstructing the flow of blood.

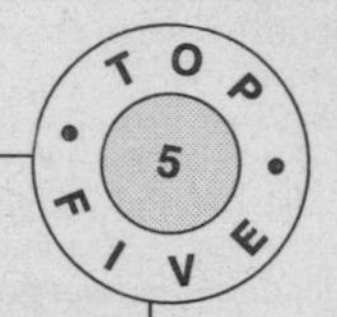

LEADING CAUSES OF DEATH IN THE US

Disease	Deaths
Heart disease	720,862
Cancer	514,657
Cerebral vascular disease	143,481
Chronic obstructive pulmonary diseases and allied conditions	90,650
Accidents and adverse effects	89,347

Centers for Disease Control, 31 Dec 1993

US AIDS CASES

State	Cases
New York	68,533
California	65,772
Florida	35,414
Texas	24,920
New Jersey	20,185

Metropoitan Area	Cases
New York	58,807
Los Angeles	22,803
San Francisco	18,135
Miami	10,920
Washington, D.C	10,177
Chicago	9,797
Houston	9,538

Centers for Disease Control, 31 Dec 1993

PHYSICIANS

Most and fewest physicians The country with the greatest number of physicians is China, which had 1,763,000 physicians in 1990, including those practicing dentistry and those practicing traditional Chinese medicine. The United States had 653,062 physicians on 1 Jan 1992.

Chad has the highest number of people per physician, with 47,640, while at the other extreme, in Italy there is one physician for every 225 people.

Medical families The four sons and five daughters of Dr Antonio B. Vicencio of Los Angeles, CA all qualified as doctors during the period 1964–82. The Barcia family of Valencia, Spain has had the same medical practice for seven generations, since 1792. Eight sons of John Robertson of Strathclyde, Great Britain graduated as medical doctors between 1892 and 1914.

OPERATIONS

Longest The most protracted reported operation was one of 96 hr performed from 4–8 Feb 1951 in Chicago, IL on Mrs Gertrude Levandowski for the removal of an ovarian cyst. During the operation her weight fell from 616 lb to 308 lb.

Most performed Dr M.C. Modi, a pioneer of mass eye surgery in India, since 1943 has performed as many as 833 cataract operations in one day, visited 46,120 villages and 12,118,630 patients, performing a total of 610,564 operations to February 1993.

Dr Robert B. McClure (b. 1901) of Toronto, Ontario, Canada performed a career total of 20,423 major operations from 1924 to 1978.

Most endured Since 22 Jul 1954 Charles Jensen of Chester, SD has had 934 operations (to the end of February 1993) to remove the tumors associated with basal cell nevus syndrome.

Oldest patient The greatest recorded age at which anyone has undergone an operation is 111 years 105 days in the case of James Henry Brett, Jr. (1849– 1961) of Houston, TX. He had a hip operation on 7 Nov 1960.

Fastest amputation The shortest time recorded for a leg amputation in the pre-anesthetic era was 13–15 seconds by Napoleon's chief surgeon, Dominique Larrey. There could have been no ligation of blood vessels.

Earliest general anesthesia The earliest recorded operation under general anesthesia was for the removal of a cyst from the neck of James Venable by Dr Crawford Williamson Long (1815–78), using diethyl ether $(C_2H_5)_20$, in Jefferson, GA on 30 Mar 1842.

Hemodialysis patient Raymond Jones (1929–91) of Slough, Great Britain suffered from kidney failure from the age of 34, and received continuous hemodialysis for 28 years. He averaged three visits per week to the Royal Free Hospital, London, Great Britain.

Munchausen's syndrome The most extreme recorded case of the rare and incurable condition known as Munchausen's syndrome (a continual desire

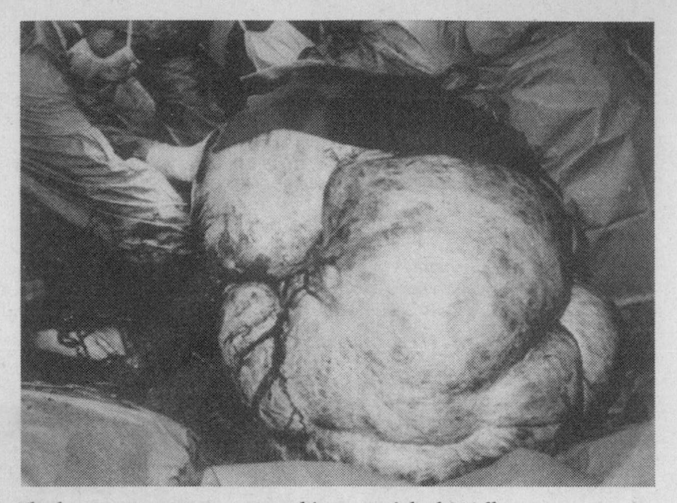

The largest tumor ever removed intact weighed 303 lb. The patient, who weighed 210 lb after the operation, made a full recovery. She left surgery on one gurney and the cyst on another. (Stanford University Medical Center)

to have medical treatment) was William McIloy (b. 1906), who cost Britain's National Health Service an estimated £2.5 million ($4 million) during his 50-year career as a hospital patient. During that time he had 400 major and minor operations, and stayed at 100 different hospitals using 22 aliases. The longest period he was ever out of the hospital was six months. In 1979 he hung up his bedpan for the last time, saying he was sick of hospitals, and retired to an old people's home in Birmingham, Great Britain, where he died in 1983.

Largest tumor The largest tumor ever reported was an ovarian cyst weighing an estimated 328 lb that was drained during the week prior to removal of the cyst shell by Dr Arthur Spohn in Texas in 1905. The patient made a full recovery.

The largest tumor ever removed *intact* was a multicystic mass of the ovary weighing 303 lb. The 3-ft-diameter growth was removed in its entirety in October 1991 from the abdomen of an unnamed 35-year-old woman by Prof. Katherine O'Hanlan of Stanford University Medical Center, California. The operation took over six hours; the patient left the operating theater on one gurney and the cyst on another. The patient weighed 210 lb after the operation and has made a full recovery.

Largest gallbladder On 15 Mar 1989 at the National Naval Medical Center in Bethesda, MD, Prof. Bimal C. Ghosh removed a gallbladder that weighed 23 lb from a 69-year-old woman. The patient had been complaining of increasing swelling around the abdomen, and after removal of this enlarged gallbladder, which weighed more than three times as much as the average newborn baby, the patient felt perfectly well and left the hospital 10 days after the operation.

Gallstones The largest gallstone reported in medical literature was one of 13 lb 14 oz removed from an 80-year-old woman by Dr Humphrey Arthure at Charing Cross Hospital, London, Great Britain on 29 Dec 1952.

In August 1987 it was reported that 23,530 gallstones had been removed from an 85-year-old woman by Mr K. Whittle Martin at Worthing Hospital, Sussex, Great Britain, after she complained of severe abdominal pain.

Most and fewest hospitals The country with the greatest number of hospitals is China, with 61,929 in 1989. Nauru has the most hospital beds per person (250 for every 10,000 people) and Bangladesh and Ethiopia the fewest (3 per 10,000).

Largest ambulances The world's largest are the 59-ft-long articulated Alligator Jumbulances Marks VI, VII, VIII and IX, operated by the ACROSS Trust to convey the sick and handicapped on vacations and pilgrimages across Europe. They are built by Van Hool of Belgium with Fiat engines, cost $350,000 and carry 44 patients and staff.

TRANSPLANTS

Heart The first heart transplant operation was performed on Louis Washkansky, age 55, at the Groote Schuur Hospital, Cape Town, South Africa between 1 A.M. and 6 A.M., on 3 Dec 1967, by a team of 30 headed by Prof. Christiaan Neethling Barnard. The donor was Miss Denise Ann Darvall, age 25. Washkansky lived for 18 days.

United States The first heart transplant was performed on a 2½-week-old baby boy at Maimonides Hospital, Brooklyn, NY on 6 Dec 1967 by a team of 22 headed by Dr Adrian Kantrowitz. The donor was a newborn infant. The baby boy lived 6½ hours. The first adult transplant was performed at the Stanford Medical Center in Palo Alto, CA on 6 Jan 1968 by Dr Norman E. Shumway on 54-year-old Mike Kasperak. Mr Kasperak, a retired steelworker, lived 14 days. From December 1967 until 31 Dec 1993 there have been 16,378 heart transplants. The greatest number performed in one year is 2,293, in 1993.

Double heart The first double heart transplant operation in the United States was performed on Darrell Hammarley, age 56, at the Stanford Medical Center in Palo Alto, CA on 20 Nov 1968. The first heart implanted failed to beat steadily and was replaced by a second transplant two hours later.

Longest surviving William George van Buuren of California (1929–91) received an unnamed person's heart at the Stanford Medical Center, Palo Alto, CA on 3 Jan 1970, and survived for 21 years 10 months 24 days. The surgeon who performed the operation was Dr Edward Stinson.

Youngest Paul Holt of Vancouver, British Columbia, Canada underwent a heart transplant at Loma Linda Hospital in California on 16 Oct 1987 at the age of 2 hr 34 min. He was born six weeks premature weighing 6 lb 6 oz.

Davina Thompson was the first person to undergo triple transplant surgery. She received heart, lung and liver transplants on 17 Dec 1986. (Rex Features/Brooker)

Animal-to-human The first operation in the United States was carried out on 23 Jan 1964 at the University of Mississippi Medical Center in Jackson, MS by a team of 12 headed by Dr James D. Hardy. The patient, age 64, received the heart of a chimpanzee, which beat for 90 minutes.

Heart–lung–liver The first triple transplant took place on 17 Dec 1986 at Papworth Hospital, Cambridge, Great Britain when Mrs Davina Thompson (b. 28 Feb 1951) of Rawmarsh, Great Britain underwent surgery for seven hours by a team of 15 headed by chest surgeon Dr John Wallwork and Prof. Sir Roy Calne.

Five-organ Tabatha Foster (1984–88) of Madisonville, KY, at 3 years 143 days of age received a transplanted liver, pancreas, small intestine, portions of stomach and large intestine in a 15-hour operation at the Children's Hospital, Pittsburgh, PA on 31 Oct 1987. Before the operation, she had never eaten solid food.

Artificial heart On 1–2 Dec 1982 at the Utah Medical Center, Salt Lake City, UT, Dr Barney B. Clark, 61, of Des Moines, WA was the first recipient of an artificial heart. The surgeon was Dr William C. DeVries. The heart was a Jarvik-7 designed by Dr Robert K. Jarvik. Dr Clark died on 23 Mar 1983, 112 days later. William J. Schroeder survived 620 days with an artificial heart in Louisville, KY from 25 Nov 1984 to 7 Aug 1986.

First synthetic heart implant Haskell Karp, age 47, of Skokie, IL, received the first synthetic heart implant on 4 Apr 1969, at St Luke's Episcopal Hospital, Houston, TX. Dr Denton A. Cooley led the team of doctors, which included the developer of the heart, Dr Domingo Liotta. The artificial heart was replaced by a human transplant on 7 April.

Kidney Dr Richard H. Lawler (USA; 1895–1982) performed the first transplant of a kidney in a human at Little Company of Mary Hospital, Chicago, IL, on 17 Jun 1950. The first successful kidney transplant operation was performed at Peter Bent Brigham Hospital (now Brigham and Women's Hospital) in Boston, MA on 23 Dec 1954 by a team of surgeons headed by Dr John P. Merrill. The patient, Richard Herrick, age 23, received a kidney from his identical twin, Ronald.

Longest surviving From 1977, when figures were first gathered, until 1993, there have been a total of 136,986 kidney transplants in the United States. The greatest number performed in one year is 10,894, in 1993.

The longest surviving kidney transplant patient is Johanna Leanora Rempel (nee Nightingale; b 24 Mar 1948) of Red Deer, Alberta, Canada who was given a kidney from her identical twin sister Lana Blatz on 28 Dec 1960. The operation was performed at the Peter Bent Brigham Hospital, Boston, MA. Both Johanna and her sister have continued to enjoy excellent health, and both have borne healthy children.

Lung The first lung transplant operation in the United States took place on 11 Jun 1963 at the University of Mississippi Medical Center in Jackson, MS. The surgery, which was headed by Dr James D. Hardy, lasted three hours and involved the replacement of the patient's left lung. The patient, John Richard Russell, survived 18 days.

LIVING WORLD

ANIMAL KINGDOM

GENERAL RECORDS

Oldest land animals Animals moved from the sea to the land 414 million years ago, according to discoveries made in 1990 near Ludlow, Great Britain. The first land animals include two kinds of centipede and a tiny spider found among plant debris, suggesting that life moved onto land much earlier than previously thought.

Loudest animal sound The low-frequency pulses made by blue whales when communicating with each other have been measured up to 188 decibels, making them the loudest sounds emitted by any living source. They have been detected 530 miles away.

Noisiest The noisiest land animal in the world is the howler monkey (*Alouatta*) of Central and South America. The males have an enlarged bony structure at the top of the windpipe that enables the sound to reverberate, and their fearsome screams have been described as a cross between the bark of a dog and the bray of a donkey increased a thousandfold. When they are in full voice they can be clearly heard for distances up to 10 miles.

The appropriately named howler monkey is the world's noisiest animal. (Jacana/J-P Varin)

Most fertile A single cabbage aphid (*Brevicoryne brassicae*) could theoretically (with unlimited food) give rise in a year to a mass of descendants weighing 906 million tons, more than three times the total weight of the world's human population.

Strongest In proportion to their size, the strongest animals are the larger beetles of the family Scarabaeidae, which are found mainly in the tropics. In one test, a rhinoceros beetle (*Dynastinae*) supported 850 times its own weight on its back (compared with 25 percent of its body weight for an adult elephant). As a comparison, in a trestle lift humans can support 17 times their own body weight.

Suspended animation In 1846 two specimens of the desert snail *Eremina desertorum* were presented to the British Museum (Natural History) in London as dead exhibits. They were placed on display, but four years later, in March 1850, one of the snails was found to be still alive. This hardy little creature lived for another two years before it fell into a torpor and then died.

STRONGEST BITE!

Experiments carried out with "Snodgrass gnathodynamometer" (shark-bite meter) at the Lerner Marine Laboratory in Bimini, Bahamas revealed that a 6-ft-6¾-in-long dusky shark (*Carcharhinus obscurus*) could exert a force of 132 lb between its jaws. This is equivalent to a pressure of 22 tons/in^2 at the tips of the teeth.

Regeneration The sponges (Porifera) have the most remarkable powers of regeneration of lost parts of any animal; they can regrow from tiny fragments of themselves. If a sponge is pushed through a fine-meshed silk gauze, each piece of separated tissue will live as an individual.

Slowest growth The slowest growth in the animal kingdom is that of the deep-sea clam *Tindaria callistisormis* of the North Atlantic, which takes *c*. 100 years to reach a length of 0.31 in.

Greatest weight loss During a 7-month lactation period, a 132-ton female blue whale (*Balaenoptera musculus*) can lose up to 25 percent of her body weight nursing her calf.

Most dangerous The malarial parasites of the genus *Plasmodium* carried by mosquitoes of the genus *Anopheles*, if we exclude wars and accidents, have probably been responsible for half of all human deaths since the Stone Age.

Largest animal-made structure The largest structure ever built by living creatures is the 1,260-mile-long Great Barrier Reef, off Queensland, Australia, covering an area of 80,000 miles^2. It consists of countless millions of

The world's largest structure made by animals, the Great Barrier Reef, consists of over 350 species of coral. (Planet Earth Pictures/K Amsler)

dead and living stony corals (order Madreporaria or Scleractinia). Over 350 species of coral are currently found there, and its accretion is estimated to have taken 600 million years.

Largest colonies The black-tailed prairie dog (*Cynomys ludovicianus*), a rodent of the family Sciuridae found in the western United States and northern Mexico, builds large colonies. One single "town" discovered in 1901 contained about 400 million individuals and was estimated to cover 24,000 $miles^2$.

Most acute sense of smell The most acute sense of smell exhibited in nature is that of the male emperor moth *Eudia pavonia*, which can detect the sex attractant of the virgin female at the almost unbelievable range of 6.8 miles upwind. This scent has been identified as one of the higher alcohols ($C_{16}H_{29}OH$), of which the female carries less than 0.0001 mg.

Greatest concentration The greatest concentration of animals ever recorded was a huge swarm of Rocky Mountain locusts (*Melanoplus spretus*) in Nebraska on 15–25 Aug 1875. They covered an area estimated at 198,600 $miles^2$ as they flew over the state. The swarm contained at least 12.5 trillion insects, with an aggregate weight of 27.5 million tons.

Most prodigious eater The larva of the Polyphemus moth (*Antheraea polyphemus*) of North America consumes an amount equal to 86,000 times its own birth weight in the first 56 days of its life. In human terms, this would be equivalent to a 7-lb baby taking in 300 tons of nourishment!

Largest eye The Atlantic giant squid has the largest eye of any animal, living or extinct. It has been estimated that one found at Thimble Tickle Bay,

Newfoundland, Canada had eyes 15¾ in wide—almost twice the width of this open book!

Largest flying creature The largest-ever flying creature was the pterosaur *Quetzalcoatlus northropi* ("feathered serpent"). About 70 million years ago it soared over what is now Texas, Wyoming and New Jersey; Alberta, Canada; and Senegal and Jordan. Partial remains discovered in Big Bend National Park, TX in 1971 indicate that this reptile must have had a wingspan of 36–39 ft and weighed about 190–250 lb.

DID YOU KNOW?

Because of their ultrasonic echolocation abilities, bats have the most acute hearing of any terrestrial animal. Vampire bats (family Desmodontidae) and fruit bats (Pteropodidae) can hear frequencies as high as 120–210 kHz, compared with 20 kHz for adult humans and 280 kHz for the common dolphin (*Delphinus delphis*).

MAMMALS

Largest The largest animal ever recorded is the blue or sulfur-bottom whale (*Balaenoptera musculus*), also called Sibbald's rorqual. Newborn calves measure 21 ft 3½ in–28½ ft in length and weigh up to 6,614 lbs.

Heaviest A female blue whale weighing 109 tons and measuring 90 ft 6 in was caught in the Southern Ocean on 20 Mar 1947.

Longest The longest specimen ever recorded was a female blue whale landed in 1909 at Grytviken, South Georgia, Falkland Islands in the South Atlantic; it measured 110 ft 2½ in in length.

Deepest dive On 25 Aug 1969 a bull sperm whale (*Physeter catodon*) was killed 100 miles south of Durban, South Africa after it surfaced from a dive lasting 1 hr 52 min. Inside its stomach were found two small sharks that had been swallowed about an hour earlier. These were *Scymnodon*, a type found only on the sea floor. At this distance from land the water is over 9,876 ft deep, which suggests that the sperm whale sometimes descends over 9,840 ft when seeking food and is limited by pressure of time rather than by water pressure.

Largest on land The largest land mammal ever recorded was *Indricotherium* (=*Baluchitherium*), a long-necked, hornless rhinocerotid that roamed across western Asia and Europe about 35 million years ago and

The mighty African bush elephant (above) is the world's largest land mammal. The smallest is Savi's white-toothed pygmy shrew (left). (Planet Earth Pictures/J Downer; Jacana/Mammi-france)

was first known from bones discovered in the Bugti Hills of Baluchistan, Pakistan in 1907–08. A restoration in the American Museum of Natural History, New York City measures 17 ft 9 in to the top of the shoulder hump and 37 ft in total length, and this gigantic browser weighed about 16–22 tons.

Living The largest specimen of the African bush elephant (*Loxodonta africana*) was a bull shot in Mucusso, Angola on 7 Nov 1974. Lying on its side this elephant measured 13 ft 8 in in a projected line from the highest point of the shoulder to the base of the forefoot, indicating that its standing height must have been about 13 ft. It weighed over 13.5 tons.

Largest marine The largest toothed mammal is the sperm whale (*Physeter catodon*), also called the cachalot. The 16-ft-5-in-long lower jaw of a sperm whale exhibited in the British Museum (Natural History) in London belonged to a bull measuring nearly 84 ft.

Tallest The giraffe (*Giraffa camelopardalis*), found in the dry savanna and semidesert areas of Africa south of the Sahara, is the tallest living animal. The tallest ever recorded was a Masai bull (*G. c. tippelskirchi*) named George, received at Chester Zoo, Great Britain on 8 Jan 1959 from Kenya. His "horns" *almost* grazed the roof of the 20-ft-high Giraffe House when he was nine years old. George died on 22 Jul 1969.

Smallest The smallest mammal in terms of length is Savi's white-toothed pygmy shrew, also called the Etruscan shrew (*Suncus etruscus*), which has a head and body length of 1.32–2.04 in, a tail length of 0.94–1.14 in and weighs 0.05–0.09 oz. It is found along the Mediterranean coast and southwards to Cape Province, South Africa.

Fastest on land Over a short distance (i.e., up to 1,800 ft) the cheetah or hunting leopard (*Acinonyx jubatus*) of the open plains of East Africa, Iran, Turkmenistan and Afghanistan has a probable maximum speed of about 60 mph on level ground.

The pronghorn antelope (*Antilocapra americana*) of the western United States has been observed to travel at 35 mph for 4 miles, at 42 mph for 1 mile, and at 55 mph for ½ mile.

Fastest marine On 12 Oct 1958 a bull killer whale (*Orcinus orca*), measuring an estimated 20–25 ft in length, was timed at 34.5 mph in the eastern Pacific. Similar speeds have also been reported for Dall's porpoise (*Phocoenoides dalli*) in short bursts.

Slowest The ai or three-toed sloth of tropical South America (*Bradypus tridactylus*) has an average ground speed of 6–8 ft per minute (0.07–0.1 mph), but in the trees it can accelerate to 15 ft per minute (0.17 mph).

Sleepiest and most wakeful Some armadillos (Dasypodidae), opossums (Didelphidae) and sloths (Bradypodidae) spend up to 80 percent of their lives sleeping or dozing, while it is claimed that Dall's porpoise (*Phocoenoides dalli*) never sleeps at all.

Oldest No other mammal can match the age of 120 years attained by humans (*Homo sapiens*; see Human Beings). It is probable that the closest approach is made by the Asiatic elephant (*Elephas maximus*). Sri Lanka's famous bull elephant Rajah, which had led the annual Perahera procession through Kandi carrying the Sacred Tooth of the Buddha since 1931, died on 16 Jul 1988, reportedly at the age of 81 years. The greatest age that has been verified with certainty is 78 years in the case of a cow named Modoc, which died at Santa Clara, CA on 17 Jul 1975.

Highest-living The yak (*Bos grunniens*), of Tibet and the Sichuanese Alps, China, climbs to an altitude of 20,000 ft when foraging.

Largest herds The largest herds on record were those of the springbok (*Antidorcas marsupialis*) during migration across the plains of the western parts of southern Africa in the 19th century. One herd estimated to be 24 km *15 miles* wide and more than 160 km *100 miles* long was reported from Karree Kloof, Orange River, South Africa in July 1896.

Largest litter The greatest number of young born to a *wild* mammal at a single birth is 31 (30 of which survived) in the case of the tailless tenrec (*Tenrec ecaudatus*) found in Madagascar and the Comoro Islands. The normal litter size is 12–15, although females can suckle up to 24.

GUESS WHAT?

Q. WHAT IS THE RECORD FOR MOST HUMAN BABIES?

A. LOOK IN "BIRTH & FAMILIES" (HUMAN BEING)

Longest gestation period The Asiatic elephant (*Elephas maximus*) has an average gestation period of 609 days (over 20 months) and a maximum of 760 days.

Shortest gestation period The gestation periods of the American opossum (*Didelphis marsupialis*), also called the Virginian opossum, and the rare water opossum or yapok (*Chironectes minimus*) of central and northern South America are normally 12–13 days but can be as short as eight days.

Youngest breeder The female true lemming (*Lemmus lemmus*) of Scandinavia can become pregnant at the age of 14 days. The gestation period is 16 to 23 days, and litter size varies from 1 to 13. Lemmings are also prolific animals; one pair was reported to have produced eight litters in 167 days, after which the male died.

CARNIVORES

Largest on land In 1894 a weight of 1,656 lb was recorded for a male Kodiak bear (*Ursus arctos middendorffi*) shot at English Bay, Kodiak Island, AK whose *stretched* skin measured 13½ ft from nose to tail. It is worth noting that these bears grow so large because they have a limitless supply of

The Kodiak bear is the world's largest carnivore. Below the bear enjoys a little fishing; above, it is adopting a more intimidating pose. (Images Colour Library)

food on Kodiak Island, not because they are an extraordinarily enormous species.

Smallest The Siberian least weasel (*Mustela rixosa pygmaea*) has an overall length of 6.96–8.14 in and weighs 1¼–2½ oz.

Largest feline The male long-furred Siberian tiger (*Panthera tigris altaica*) averages 10 ft 4 in in length from the nose to the tip of the extended tail, stands 39–42 in at the shoulder and weighs about 585 lb.

An Indian tiger (*Panthera tigris tigris*) shot in northern Uttar Pradesh in November 1967 measured 10 ft 7 in between pegs (11 ft 1 in over the curves) and weighed 857 lb (compared with 9 ft 3 in and 420 lb for an average adult male).

Captive The largest tiger in captivity, and the heaviest on record, is a nine-year-old Siberian male named Jaipur, owned by animal trainer Joan Byron-Marasek of Clarksburg, NJ. This specimen measured 10 ft 11 in in total length and weighed 932 lb in October 1986.

Smallest feline The rusty-spotted cat (*Felis rubiginosa*) of southern India and Sri Lanka has an overall length of 25–28 in (the tail measures 9–10 in) and weighs about 3 lb.

PRIMATES

Largest The male eastern lowland gorilla (*Gorilla g. graueri*) of the lowland forests of eastern Zaïre and southwestern Uganda stands 5 ft 9 in tall and weighs 360 lb.

Tallest The greatest height (top of crest to heel) recorded for a gorilla in the wild is 6 ft 2 in for a male of the mountain race shot in the eastern Congo (Zaïre) *c.* 1920.

Gamma, the oldest chimpanzee, who died of natural causes at the advanced age of 59. (Yerkes Regional Primate Research Center)

Heaviest The heaviest gorilla ever kept in captivity was a male of the mountain race named N'gagi, who died in San Diego Zoo in California on 12 Jan 1944 at the age of 18. He weighed 683 lb at his heaviest in 1943 and was 5 ft 7³/₄ in tall.

Smallest Adult specimens of the rare pen-tailed shrew (*Ptilocercus lowii*) of Malaysia have a total length of 9–13 in (head and body 4–5¹/₂ in; tail 5–7¹/₂ in) and weigh 1.23–1.76 oz.

Oldest The greatest age recorded for a nonhuman primate is 59 years 5 months for a chimpanzee (*Pan troglodytes*) named Gamma, who died at the Yerkes Primate Research Center in Atlanta, GA on 19 Feb 1992. Gamma was born at the Florida branch of the Yerkes Center in September 1932.

Monkey The world's oldest monkey, a male white-throated capuchin (*Cebus capucinus*) called Bobo, died on 10 Jul 1988 aged 53.

SEALS, SEA LIONS, WALRUSES

Largest The largest accurately measured specimen of the southern elephant seal (*Mirounga leonina*) was a bull that weighed at least 4.4 tons and measured 21 ft 4 in after flensing (stripping of the blubber or skin). Its original length was about 22¹/₂ ft. It was killed in the South Atlantic at Possession Bay, South Georgia on 28 Feb 1913.

Smallest The smallest pinnipeds are the ringed seal (*Phoca hispida*) of the Arctic and the closely related Baikal seal (*P. sibirica*) of Lake Baikal and

The world's largest seal—the southern elephant seal of the sub-Antarctic islands—in tuneful repose. (Jacana/Parer-Parer, Cook/Aus)

Caspian seal (*P. caspica*) of the Caspian Sea, Asia. Adult males measure up to 5½ ft in length and can weigh up to 280 lb.

Oldest A female gray seal (*Halichoerus grypus*) shot at Shunni Wick, Shetland, Great Britain on 23 Apr 1969 was believed to be "at least 46 years old" based on a count of dentine rings.

Fastest The maximum swimming speed recorded for a pinniped is a short spurt of 25 mph by a California sea lion (*Zalophus californianus*).

Deepest dive In May 1988 a team of scientists from the University of California at Santa Cruz tested the diving abilities of the northern elephant seal (*Mirounga angustirostris*) off Ano Nuevo Point, CA. One female reached a record depth of 4,135 ft, and another remained submerged for 48 minutes.

BATS

Largest The only flying mammals are bats (order Chiroptera), of which there are about 950 species. The largest in terms of wingspan is the Bismarck flying fox (*Pteropus neohibernicus*) of the Bismarck Archipelago and New Guinea. One specimen preserved in the American Museum of Natural History in New York City has a wingspan of 5 ft 5 in.

United States Mature specimens of the large mastiff bat (*Eumops perotis*), found in southern Texas, California, Arizona and New Mexico, have a wingspan of 22 in.

Smallest The smallest bat in the world is Kitti's hog-nosed bat at 6.3 in and 0.06–0.071 oz.

United States The smallest native bat is the Western pipistrelle (*Pipistrellus hesperus*), found in the western United States. Mature specimens have a wingspan of 7.9 in.

Oldest The greatest age reliably reported for a bat is 32 years for a banded female little brown bat (*Myotis lucifugus*) in the United States in 1987.

Largest colonies The largest concentration of bats found living anywhere in the world today is that of the Mexican free-tailed bat (*Tadarida brasiliensis*) in Bracken Cave, San Antonio, TX, where up to 20 million animals assemble after migration.

DEEPEST!

The little brown bat (*Myotis lucifugus*) has been recorded at a depth of 3,805 ft in a zinc mine in New York State. The mine serves as winter quarters for 1,000 members of this species.

RODENTS

Largest The capybara (*Hydrochaeris hydrochaeris*), also called the carpincho or water hog, of tropical South America has a head and body length of 3¼–4½ ft and can weigh up to 250 lb.

Smallest The northern pygmy mouse (*Baiomys taylori*) of central Mexico and southern Arizona and Texas measures up to 4.3 in in total length and weighs 0.24–0.28 oz.

Oldest The greatest reliable age reported for a rodent is 27 years 3 months for a Sumatran crested porcupine (*Hystrix brachyura*) that died in the National Zoological Park, Washington, D.C. on 12 Jan 1965.

Fastest breeder The female meadow vole (*Microtus agrestis*), found in Great Britain, can reproduce from the age of 25 days and can have up to 17 litters of 6–8 young in a year.

Longest hibernation The barrow ground squirrel (*Spermophilus parryi barrowensis*) of Point Barrow, AK hibernates for nine months of the year.

DEER

Largest The largest deer is the Alaskan moose (*Alces alces gigas*). A bull standing 7 ft 8 in between pegs and weighing an estimated 1,800 lb was shot on the Yukon River in the Yukon Territory, Canada in September 1897.

Smallest The smallest true deer (family Cervidae) is the northern pudu (*Pudu mephistopheles*) of Ecuador and Colombia. Mature specimens measure 13–14 in at the shoulder and weigh 16–18 lb.

Oldest The world's oldest recorded deer is a red deer (*Cervus elaphus scoticus*) named Bambi (b. 8 Jun 1963). Bambi is owned by the Fraser family of Kiltarlity, Great Britain.

United States The greatest reliable age recorded for a deer is 26 years 8 months for a red deer (*Cervus elaphus scoticus*) that died in the Milwaukee Zoo, WI on 28 Jun 1954.

KANGAROOS

Largest The male red kangaroo (*Megaleia rufa* or *Macropus rufus*) of central, southern and eastern Australia stands up to 7 ft tall, measures up to 8 ft ½ in in total length and weighs up to 187 lb.

Fastest The fastest speed recorded for a marsupial is 40 mph for a mature female eastern gray kangaroo (*Macropus giganteus* or *M. canguru*).

TUSKS

Longest The longest elephant tusks (excluding prehistoric examples) are a pair from Zaïre preserved in the National Collection of Heads and Horns

DID YOU KNOW?

Highest jump A captive eastern gray kangaroo once cleared an 8-ft fence when an automobile backfired, and there is also a record of a hunted red kangaroo clearing a stack of timber 10 ft high.

Longest jump During a chase in New South Wales, Australia in January 1951, a female red kangaroo made a series of bounds that included one of 42 ft. There is also an unconfirmed report of an eastern gray kangaroo jumping nearly 44½ ft on level ground.

kept by the New York Zoological Society (Bronx Zoo), New York City. The right tusk measures 11 ft 5½ in along the outside curve and the left tusk measures 11 ft. Their combined weight is 293 lb.

Heaviest A pair of tusks in the British Museum (Natural History), London collected from an aged bull shot in Kenya in 1897 weighed 240 lb (length 10 ft 2½ in) and 225 lb (length 10 ft 5½ in) respectively, giving a total weight of 465 lb.

HORNS

Longest The longest horns of any living animal are those of the water buffalo (*Bubalus arnee = B. bubalis*) of India. One bull shot in 1955 had horns measuring 13 ft 11 in from tip to tip along the outside curve across the forehead.

Domestic animal The largest spread on record is 10 ft 6 in for a Texas longhorn steer. The horns are currently on exhibition at the Heritage Museum, Big Springs, TX.

ANTLERS

Largest The record antler spread or "rack" is 6 ft 6½ in from a moose killed near the headwaters of the Stewart River in the Yukon Territory, Canada in October 1897. The antlers are now on display in the Field Museum, Chicago, IL.

HORSES

Earliest domestication Evidence from the Ukraine indicates that horses may have been ridden earlier than 4000 B.C.

Largest The tallest and heaviest documented horse was the shire gelding Sampson, bred by Thomas Cleaver of Toddington Mills, Great Britain. This horse (foaled 1846) measured 21.2½ hands (7 ft 2½ in) in 1850 and was later said to have weighed 3,360 lb.

Smallest The stallion Little Pumpkin (foaled 15 Apr 1973), owned by J.C. Williams Jr. of Della Terra Mini Horse Farm, Inman, SC, stood 14 in and weighed 20 lb on 30 Nov 1975.

The smallest species is the Falabela of Argentina, which was developed by Julio Falabela of Recco de Roca, Argentina. The smallest example was a mare that stood 15 in and weighed 26¼ lb.

Oldest The greatest age reliably recorded for a horse is 62 years in the case of Old Billy (foaled 1760), bred by Edward Robinson of Woolston, Great Britain. Old Billy died on 27 Nov 1822.

Oldest pony The greatest age reliably recorded for a pony is 54 years for a stallion (foaled 1919) owned by a farmer in central France.

United States The oldest pony in the United States was Trigger, who lived for 47 years (1945–92). He was owned by Dorothy B. Crouse of Whiteside, MO.

Mules Apollo (foaled 1977) and Anak (foaled 1976), owned by Herbert L. Mueller of Columbia, IL, are the largest mules on record. Apollo measures 19.1 hands (6 ft 5 in) and weighs 2,200 lb, with Anak at 18.3 hands (6 ft 3 in) and 2,100 lb. Both are the hybrid offspring of Belgian mares and mammoth jacks.

DOGS

The canine population of the United States for 1993 was estimated by the Pet Food Institute to be 53 million. There was at least one dog kept as a pet in 37.7 percent of the households in the United States.

Largest The heaviest (and longest) dog ever recorded is Aicama Zorba of La-Susa (whelped 26 Sep 1981), an Old English mastiff owned by Chris Eraclides of London, Great Britain. Zorba stands 37 in at the shoulder and weighed 343 lb in November 1989.

TOP 10 TEN

US DOGS

Breed	Registrations
Labrador Retrievers	124,899
Rottweilers	104,160
German Shepherds	79,936
Cocker Spaniels	75,882
Golden Retrievers	68,125
Poodles	67,850
Beagles	61,051
Dachshunds	48,573
Dalmatians	42,816
Shetland Sheepdogs	41,113

American Kennel Club; 1993

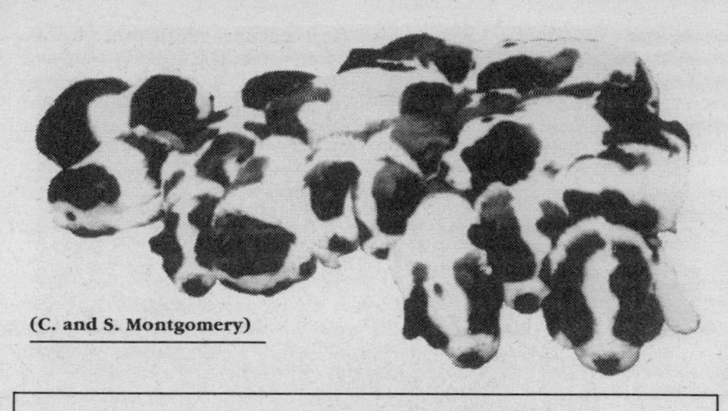
(C. and S. Montgomery)

LARGEST PET LITTERS

Animal/Breed	No.	Owner	Date
Cat *Burmese/Siamese*	19[1]	V. Gane, Church Westcote, Great Britain	7 Aug 1970
Dog *American foxhound*	23	W. N. Ely, Ambler, PA	19 Jun 1944
St Bernard	23[2]	R. and A. Rodden, Lebanon, MO	6–7 Feb 1975
Great Dane	23[3]	M. Harris, Little Hall, Great Britain	June 1987
Ferret *Domestic*	15	J. Cliff, Denstone, Great Britain	1981
Gerbil *Mongolian*	14[4]	S. Kirkman, Bulwell, Great Britain	May 1983
Guinea pig	12	Laboratory specimen	1972
Hamster *Golden*	26[5]	L. and S. Miller, Baton Rouge, LA	28 Feb 1974
Mouse *House*	34[6]	M. Ogilvie, Blackpool, Great Britain	12 Feb 1982
Rabbit *New Zealand white*	24	J. Filek, Cape Breton, Nova Scotia, Canada	1978

[1]*Four stillborn.*
[2]*Fourteen survived.*
[3]*Sixteen survived.*
[4]*Litter of fifteen recorded in the 1960s by George Meares, geneticist-owner of gerbil-breeding farm in St Petersburg, FL, using special food formula.*
[5]*Eighteen killed by mother.*
[6]*Thirty-three survived.*

The beautiful St Bernard, which, along with the Old English Mastiff, is the heaviest breed of domestic dog. (Spectrum Colour Library)

Tallest The tallest dog ever recorded was Shamgret Danzas (whelped 1975), owned by Wendy and Keith Comley of Milton Keynes, Great Britain. He stood $41^{1}/_{2}$ in, or 42 in when his hackles were raised, and weighed up to 238 lb. He died on 16 Oct 1984.

Smallest The smallest dog on record was a matchbox-sized Yorkshire terrier owned by Arthur Marples of Blackburn, Great Britain. This tiny creature, which died in 1945 at the age of nearly two years, stood $2^{1}/_{2}$ in at the shoulder and measured $3^{3}/_{4}$ in from the tip of its nose to the root of its tail. Its weight was just 4 oz.

The smallest living dog is a Yorkshire terrier named Summerann Thumberlina, 8 in long and weighing 20 oz. Born on 5 Jan 1992, she is owned by Maureen Howes of Stourport-on-Severn, Great Britain.

Oldest The greatest age recorded for a dog is 29 years 5 months for an Australian cattle-dog named Bluey, owned by Les Hall of Rochester, Victoria, Australia. The dog was obtained as a puppy in 1910 and worked among cattle and sheep for nearly 20 years. He was put to sleep on 14 Nov 1939.

Longest-serving guide dog The longest period of *active service* reported for a guide dog is 14 years 8 months (August 1972–March 1987) in the case of a Labrador retriever bitch named Cindy-Cleo (whelped 20 Jan 1971), owned by Aaron Barr of Tel Aviv, Israel. The dog died on 10 Apr 1987.

Highest Jump!

The canine "high jump" record for a leap and a scramble over a smooth wooden wall (without ribs or other aids) is 12 ft 2½ in, achieved by an 18-month-old lurcher dog named Stag at the annual Cotswold Country Fair in Cirencester, Great Britain on 27 Sep 1993. The dog is owned by Mr and Mrs P.R. Matthews of Redruth, Great Britain.

Duke, a three-year-old German shepherd, handled by Cpl Graham Urry of the Royal Air Force base at Newton, Great Britain, scaled a ribbed wall with regulation shallow slats to a height of 11 ft 9 in on the British Broadcasting Corporation *Record Breakers* TV program on 11 Nov 1986.

Most guide dogs placed In the United States, the record for the most guide dogs placed with users is held by the Seeing Eye of Morristown, NJ, with a total of 230 placements in 1991.

Most prolific The greatest sire ever was the champion greyhound Low Pressure, nicknamed Timmy (whelped Sep 1957), owned by Bruna Amhurst of London, Great Britain. From Dec 1961 until his death on 27 Nov 1969 he fathered over 3,000 puppies.

Longest jump A greyhound named Bang jumped 30 ft while chasing a hare at Brecon Lodge, Gloucestershire, Great Britain in 1849. He cleared a 4-ft-6-in gate and landed on a hard road, damaging his pastern bone.

Tracking In 1925 a Doberman pinscher named Sauer, trained by Detective-Sergeant Herbert Kruger, tracked a stock thief 100 miles across the Great Karroo, South Africa by scent alone.

Top show dog The greatest number of Best-in-Show awards won by any dog in all-breed shows is 203, compiled by the Scottish terrier bitch Ch. Braeburn's Close Encounter (whelped 22 Oct 1978) by 10 Mar 1985. She is owned by Sonnie Novick of Plantation Acres, FL.

Largest dog show The centennial of the annual Crufts show, held at the National Exhibition Center, Birmingham, Great Britain on 9–12 Jan 1991, attracted a record 22,993 entries.

Drug sniffing Snag, a US Customs Labrador retriever trained and partnered by Jeff Weitzmann, has made 118 drug seizures worth a canine record $810 million.

The greatest number of seizures by dogs is 969 (worth $182 million) in 1988 alone by Rocky and Barco, a pair of malinoises patrolling the Rio Grande Valley ("Cocaine Valley") along the Texas border, where the pair were so proficient that Mexican drug smugglers put a $30,000 price on their heads. The dogs hold the rank of honorary Sergeant Major and always wear their stripes on duty.

CATS

The feline population of the United States for 1993 was estimated by the Pet Food Institute to be 64 million. There was at least one cat in 32.9 percent of the households in the United States.

Largest The heaviest domestic cat was a neutered male tabby named Himmy, owned by Thomas Vyse of Redlynch, Queensland, Australia. At the time of his death (from respiratory failure) on 12 Mar 1986 at the age of 10 years 4 months he weighed 46 lb 15 1/4 oz (neck 15 in, waist 33 in, length 38 in).

Smallest A male blue point Himalayan-Persian cat named Tinker Toy, owned by Katrina and Scott Forbes of Taylorville, IL, is just 2 3/4 in tall and 7 1/2 in long.

Oldest The oldest reliably recorded cat was the female tabby Ma, owned by Alice St George Moore of Drewsteignton, Great Britain. This cat was put to sleep on 5 Nov 1957 at the age of 34.

Largest cat show The largest cat show in the United States was the Purina Cat Chow/CFA Invitational held at the Cervantes Convention Center, St. Louis, MO from 19–20 Nov 1988; it attracted a record 814 entries.

Best climber On 6 Sep 1950 a four-month-old kitten belonging to Josephine Aufdenblatten of Geneva, Switzerland followed a group of climbers to the top of the 14,691 ft Matterhorn in the Alps.

Most prolific A tabby named Dusty (b. 1935) of Bonham, TX produced 420 kittens during her breeding life. She gave birth to her last litter (a single kitten) on 12 Jun 1952.

TOP 10

US CATS

Breed	Registrations
Persian	48,010
Maine Coon	3,549
Siamese	2,979
Abyssinian	2,360
Exotic	1,288
Scottish Fold	1,282
Oriental Shorthair	1,219
American Shorthair	1,140
Burmese	980
Birman	932

Cat Fanciers' Association, Inc.; 1993

Oldest feline mother In May 1987 Kitty, owned by George Johnstone of Croxton, Great Britain, produced two kittens at the age of 30 years, making her the oldest feline mother on record. She died in June 1989, just short of her 32nd birthday, having given birth to a known total of 218 kittens.

RABBITS

Largest In April 1980 a five-month-old French lop doe weighing 26.45 lb was exhibited at the Reus Fair in northeast Spain.

Smallest The Netherland dwarf and the Polish dwarf both have a weight range of 2–2½ lb when fully grown. In 1975 Jacques Bouloc of Coulommière, France announced a new cross of the above breeds that weighed 14 oz.

Most prolific The most prolific domestic breeds are the New Zealand white and the Californian. Does produce 5–6 litters a year, each containing 8–12 kittens during their breeding life (compare with five litters and 3–7 young for the wild rabbit).

Longest ears "Sweet Majestic Star," a champion black English lop rabbit owned by Therese and Cheryl Seward of Exeter, Great Britain, had ears measuring 28½ in long and 7¼ in wide. He died on 6 Oct 1992. The ears of his grandson "Sweet Regal Magic" are the same length.

BIRDS

Earliest The earliest fossil bird is known from two partial skeletons found in Texas in rocks dating from 220 million years ago. Named *Protoavis texensis* in 1991, this pheasant-sized creature has caused much controversy by pushing the age of birds back 45 million years from the previous record, that of the more familiar *Archeopteryx lithographica* from Germany.

Largest The largest living bird is the North African ostrich (*Struthio c. camelus*). Males of this flightless (ratite) subspecies have been recorded up to 9 ft in height and 345 lb in weight.

Largest flying The world's heaviest flying (carinate) birds are the Kori bustard or paauw (*Ardeotis kori*) of northeast and southern Africa and the great bustard (*Otis tarda*) of Europe and Asia. Weights of 42 lb have been reported for the former, and there is an unconfirmed record of 46 lb 4 oz for a male great bustard shot in Manchuria that was too heavy to fly. The heaviest reliably recorded great bustard weighed 39 lb 11 oz.

Bird of prey The heaviest bird of prey is the Andean condor (*Vultur gryphus*), adult males averaging 20–25 lb. A weight of 31 lb has been claimed for an outsized male California condor (*Gymnogyps californianus*) now preserved in the California Academy of Sciences at San Francisco. This

The fastest-flying birds in level flight are found among the duck and goose families. Pictured here is the green-winged teal. (Planet Earth Pictures/J Downer)

OLDEST CAGED PETS

Species	Name, Owner, etc.	Age
Bird *Parrot*	*Prudle*, captured 1958, I. Frost, Seaford, Great Britain	35 yr
Budgerigar	*Charlie*, April 1948–20 Jun 1977, J. Dinsey, London, Great Britain	29 yr 2 mos
Rabbit *Wild*	*Flopsy*, caught 6 Aug 1964, d. 29 Jun 1983, L.B. Walker, Longford, Tasmania, Australia	18 yr 10¾ mos
Guinea pig	*Snowball*, d. 14 Feb 1979, M. A. Wall, Bingham, Great Britain	14 yr 10¼ mos
Gerbil *Mongolian*	*Sahara*, May 1973–4 Oct 1981, A. Milstone, Lathrup Village, MI	8 yr 4¼ mos
Mouse *House*	*Fritzy*, 11 Sep 1977–24 Apr 1985, B. Beard, West House School, Birmingham, Great Britain	7 yr 7 mos
Rat *Common*	*Rodney*, January 1983–25 May 1990, R. Mitchell, Tulsa, OK	7 yr 4 mos

species is appreciably smaller than the Andean condor and rarely exceeds 23 lb.

Largest wingspan The wandering albatross (*Diomedea exulans*) of the southern oceans has the largest wingspan of any living bird. The largest was a very old male with a wingspan of 11 ft 11 in, caught by members of the Antarctic research ship USGS *Eltanin* in the Tasman Sea on 18 Sep 1965.

Tallest The tallest of the flying birds are cranes, tall waders of the family Gruidae, some of which can stand almost 6 ft 6 in high.

Smallest The smallest bird is the bee hummingbird (*Mellisuga helenae*) of Cuba and the Isle of Pines. Adult males (females are slightly larger) measure 2.24 in in total length, half of which is taken up by the bill and tail, and weigh 0.056 oz (females are slightly heavier).

Bird of prey The smallest bird of prey is the 1.23 oz, 5½–6 in long, white-fronted falconet (*Microhierax latifrons*) of northwestern Borneo, which is sparrow-sized.

Most abundant The red-billed quelea (*Quelea quelea*), a seed-eating weaver of the drier parts of Africa south of the Sahara, has an estimated adult breeding population of 1.5 billion, and at least 1 billion are slaughtered annually without having any impact on this number.

United States The red-winged blackbird (*Agelaius phoeniceus*) has an estimated population of at least 30 million. The blackbird is found throughout the country, except for desert and mountainous regions.

Most talkative A number of birds are renowned for their talking ability (i.e., the reproduction of words) but the African gray parrot (*Psittacus erythacus*) excels in this ability. A female named Prudle, formerly owned by Lyn Logue (died January 1988) and now in the care of Iris Frost of Seaford, Great Britain, won the "Best talking parrot-like bird" title at the National Cage and Aviary Bird Show in London each December for 12 consecutive years (1965–76). Prudle, who has a vocabulary of nearly 800 words, was taken from a nest at Jinja, Uganda in 1958. She retired undefeated.

Largest vocabulary Puck, a budgerigar owned by Camille Jordan of Petaluma, CA, had a vocabulary estimated at 1,728 words on 31 Jan 1994.

Fastest-flying The fastest creature on the wing is the peregrine falcon (*Falco peregrinus*) when swooping from great heights during territorial displays. In one series of German experiments, a velocity of 168 mph was recorded at a 30° angle of descent, rising to a maximum of 217 mph at an angle of 45°.

United States America's fastest bird is the white-throated swift (*Aeronautes saxatilis*), which has been estimated to fly at speeds of 200 mph. The peregrine falcon (*Falco peregrinus*) has been credited with a speed of 175 mph while in a dive. The dunlin (*Calidris alpina*) has been clocked from a plane at 110 mph.

Fastest wing-beat The wing-beat of the horned sungem (*Heliactin cornuta*) of tropical South America is 90 beats/sec.

Slowest-flying The slowest-flying birds are the American woodcock (*Scolopax minor*) and the Eurasian woodcock (*S. rusticola*), which, during courtship flights, have been timed at 5 mph without stalling.

Oldest The greatest irrefutable age reported for any bird is over 80 years for a male sulfur-crested cockatoo (*Cacatua galerita*) named Cocky, who died at London Zoo, Great Britain in 1982.

Domestic The longest-lived domesticated bird (excluding the ostrich, which has been known to live up to 68 years) is the domestic goose (*Anser-anser domesticus*), which may live about 25 years. On 16 Dec 1976 a gander named George, owned by Florence Hull of Thornton, Great Britain, died at the age of 49 years 8 months. He was hatched in April 1927.

Longest flights The greatest distance covered by a ringed bird is 14,000 miles, by an arctic tern (*Sterna paradisea*), which was banded as a nestling on 5 Jul 1955 in the Kandalaksha Sanctuary on the White Sea coast, Russia, and was captured alive by a fisherman 8 miles south of Fremantle, Western Australia on 16 May 1956. The bird had flown south via the Atlantic Ocean and then circled Africa before crossing the Indian Ocean. It did not survive to make the return journey.

Highest-flying Most migrating birds fly at relatively low altitudes (i.e., below 300 ft) and only a few dozen species fly higher than 3,000 ft.

The highest irrefutable altitude recorded for a bird is 37,000 ft for a Ruppell's vulture (*Gyps rueppellii*) that collided with a commercial aircraft over Abidjan, Ivory Coast on 29 Nov 1973. The impact damaged one of the aircraft's engines, causing it to shut down, but the plane landed safely without further incident. Sufficient feather remains of the bird were recovered to allow the Museum of Natural History in Washington, D.C. to make a positive identification of this high-flier, which is rarely seen above 20,000 ft.

United States The highest verified altitude record for a bird in the United States is 21,000 ft for a mallard (*Anas platyrhynchos*) that collided with a commercial jet on 9 Jul 1963 over Nevada. The jet crashed, killing all aboard.

Fastest bird The fastest bird on land is the ostrich, which despite its bulk can run at a speed of up to 40 mph when necessary.

Most airborne The most aerial of all birds is the sooty tern (*Sterna fuscata*), which, after leaving the nesting grounds, remains continuously aloft from 3–10 years as a sub-adult before returning to land to breed.

Longest feathers The longest feathers grown by any bird are those of the phoenix fowl or onagadori (a strain of red jungle fowl *Gallus gallus*), which has been bred in southwestern Japan since the mid-17th century. In 1972 a tail covert measuring 34 ft $9^1/_2$ in was reported for a rooster owned by Masasha Kubota of Kochi, Shikoku, Japan.

Fastest swimmer The gentoo penguin (*Pygoscelis papua*) has a maximum burst of speed of *c*. 17 mph.

Deepest dive In 1969 a depth of 870 ft was recorded for a small group of emperor penguins (*Aptenodytes forsteri*) at Cape Crozier, Antarctica by a team of US scientists. One bird remained submerged for 18 minutes.

Keenest vision It has been calculated that a large eagle can detect a target object at a distance 3–8 times greater than that achieved by humans. A peregrine falcon (*Falco peregrinus*) can spot a pigeon at a range of over 5 miles under ideal conditions.

Greatest field of vision The woodcock (family Scolopacidae) has eyes set so far back on its head that it has a 360° field of vision, enabling it to see all around and even over the top of its head.

Highest g force Experiments have revealed that the beak of the red-headed woodpecker (*Melanerpes erythrocephalus*) hits the bark of a tree with an impact velocity of 13 mph. This means that when the head snaps back the brain is subject to a deceleration of about 10 *g*.

Longest bills The bill of thc Australian pelican (*Pelicanus conspicillatus*) is 13–18½ in long.

The longest bill in relation to overall body length is that of the sword-billed hummingbird (*Ensifera ensifera*) of the Andes from Venezuela to Bolivia. The bill measures 4 in in length and is longer than the bird's body.

Shortest bills The shortest bill is that of the glossy swiftlet (*Collocalia esculenta*), whose bill is almost nonexistent.

Largest egg On 28 Jun 1988 a 2-year-old cross between a northern and a southern ostrich (*Struthio c. camelus* and *Struthio c. australis*) laid an egg weighing a record 5.1 lb at the Kibbutz Ha'on collective farm, Israel.

United States The largest egg on the list of American birds is that of the trumpeter swan; it measures 4.3 in in length, 2.8 in in diameter. The average California condor egg measures 4.3 in in length and 2.6 in in diameter and weighs 9.5 oz.

Smallest egg The smallest egg laid by any bird is that of the vervain hummingbird (*Mellisuga minima*) of Jamaica. Two specimens measuring less than 0.39 in in length weighed 0.0128 oz and 0.0132 oz. (See Smallest nest.)

United States The smallest egg laid by a bird on the American list is that of the Costa hummingbird (*Calypte coastae*); it measures 0.48 in in length and 0.33 in in diameter with a weight of 0.017 oz.

Longest incubation The longest normal incubation period is that of the wandering albatross (*Diomedea exulans*), with a range of 75–82 days. There is an isolated case of an egg of the mallee fowl (*Leipoa ocellata*) of Australia taking 90 days to hatch, against its normal incubation of 62 days.

Shortest incubation The shortest incubation period is 10 days in the case of the great spotted woodpecker (*Dendrocopus major*) and the black-billed cuckoo (*Coccyzus erythropthalmus*).

Largest nest The incubation mounds built by the mallee fowl (*Leipoa ocellata*) of Australia measure up to 15 ft in height and 35 ft across, and it has been calculated that the nest site may involve the mounding of 8,100 ft^3 of material weighing 330 tons.

Smallest nest The smallest nests are built by hummingbirds (Trochilidae). That of the vervain hummingbird (*Mellisuga minima*) is about half the size of a walnut, while the deeper one of the bee hummingbird (*M. helenea*) is thimble-sized.

Bird-watchers The world's leading bird-watcher or "twitcher" is Phoebe Snetsinger of Webster Groves, MO, who has logged 7,530 of the 9,700 known species since 1965, representing over 74 percent of the available total.

24 hours The greatest number of species spotted in a 24-hour period is 342, by Kenyans Terry Stevenson, John Fanshawe and Andy Roberts on day two of the Birdwatch Kenya '86 event held on 29–30 November.

REPTILES

Earliest reptile fossil The oldest reptile fossil, nicknamed "Lizzie the Lizard," was found on a site in Scotland by palaeontologist Stan Wood in March 1988. The 8-in-long reptile is estimated to be 340 million years old, 40 million years older than previously discovered reptiles. "Lizzie" was officially named *Westlothiana lizziae* in 1991.

CROCODILIANS

Largest There are four protected estuarine crocodiles at the Bhitarkanika Wildlife Sanctuary, Orissa State, eastern India that measure more than 19 ft 8 in in length. The largest individual is over 23 ft long.

Smallest Osborn's dwarf crocodile (*Osteolaemus osborni*), found in the

OLDEST!

The greatest age authenticated for a crocodilian is 66 years for a female American alligator (*Alligator mississippiensis*) that arrived at Adelaide Zoo, South Australia on 5 Jun 1914 as a two-year-old and died there on 26 Sep 1978.

upper region of the Congo River, West Africa, rarely exceeds 3 ft 11 in in length.

LIZARDS

Largest The largest of all lizards is the komodo monitor or ora (*Varanus komodoensis*), found on the Indonesian islands of Komodo, Rintja, Padar and Flores. Adult males average 7 ft 5 in in length and weigh about 130 lb. The largest specimen to be accurately measured was a male presented to an American zoologist in 1928 by the Sultan of Bima that was taped at 10 ft 1 in. In 1937 this animal was put on display in St Louis Zoological Gardens, MO for a short period. It then measured 10 ft 2 in in length and weighed 365 lb.

Longest The slender Salvadori monitor (*Varanus salvadori*) of Papua New Guinea has been measured up to 15 ft 7 in, but nearly 70 percent of the total length is taken up by the tail.

Smallest *Sphaerodactylus parthenopion*, a tiny gecko indigenous to the island of Virgin Gorda, one of the British Virgin Islands, is the world's smallest lizard. It is known from only 15 specimens, including some pregnant females found between 10–16 Aug 1964. The three largest females measured 0.70 in from snout to vent, with a tail of approximately the same length.

Oldest The greatest age recorded for a lizard is over 54 years for a male slow worm (*Anguis fragilis*) kept in the Zoological Museum in Copenhagen, Denmark from 1892 until 1946.

TURTLES

Largest The largest turtle ever recorded is a male leatherback found dead on the beach at Harlech, Great Britain on 23 Sep 1988. It measured 9 ft 5½ in in total length over the carapace (nose to tail), 9 ft across the front flippers and weighed an astonishing 2,120 lb.

The greatest weight reliably recorded in the United States is 1,908 lb for a male leatherback captured off Monterey, CA on 29 Aug 1961, which measured 8 ft 4 in.

Smallest The smallest marine turtle in the world is the Atlantic ridley (*Lepidochelys kempii*), which has a shell length of 19.7–27.6 in and a maximum weight of 80 lb.

Oldest The greatest age recorded for a chelonian is over 152 years for a male Marion's tortoise (*Testudo sumeirii*), brought from the Seychelles to Mauritius in 1766 by the Chevalier de Fresne, who presented it to the Port Louis army garrison. This specimen, which went blind in 1908, was accidentally killed in 1918.

Fastest The fastest speed claimed for any reptile in water is 22 mph by a frightened Pacific leatherback turtle.

Deepest dive In May 1987 it was reported by Dr Scott Eckert that a leatherback turtle (*Dermochelys coriacea*) fitted with a pressure-sensitive

A leatherback turtle can dive to greater depths than any other chelonian. (Planet Earth Pictures/D. Perrine)

recording device had dived to a depth of 3,973 ft off the Virgin Islands in the West Indies.

SNAKES, GENERAL

Longest A reticulated python (*Python reticulatus*) measuring 32 ft 9½ in was shot in Celebes, Indonesia in 1912 . This species is also found in southeast Asia and the Philippines.

United States There are three species of snake in the United States with average measurements of 8 ft 6 in. These include the indigo snake (*Drymarchon corais*), the eastern coachwhip (*Masticophis flagellum*) and the black ratsnake (*Elaphe obsoleta*)—all found in the southeastern United States.

Shortest The shortest snake in the world is the rare thread snake (Leptotyphlops bilineata), which is known only from the islands of Martinique, Barbados and St Lucia in the West Indies. The longest examples measured 4¼ in.

Heaviest The anaconda (*Eunectes murinus*) of tropical South America and Trinidad is nearly twice as heavy as a reticulated python (*Python reticulatus*) of the same length. A female shot in Brazil *c.* 1960 was not weighed, but as it measured 27 ft 9 in in length with a girth of 44 in, it must have weighed about 500 lb. The average adult length is 18–20 ft.

Oldest The greatest reliable age recorded for a snake is 40 years 3 months 14 days for a male common boa (*Boa constrictor constrictor*) named Popeye, who died at the Philadelphia Zoo, PA on 15 Apr 1977.

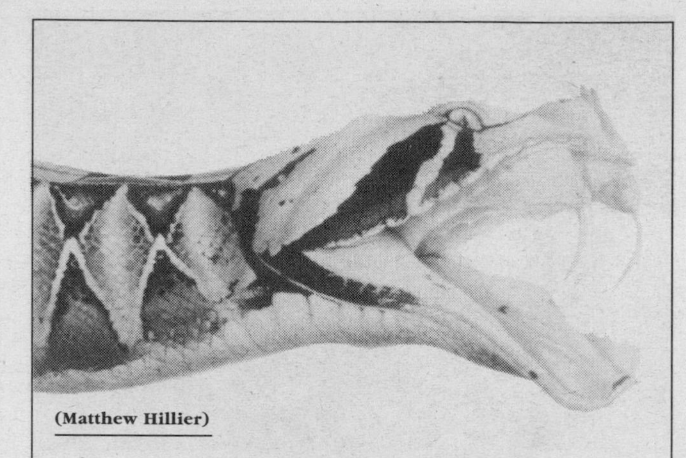

(Matthew Hillier)

A 6-ft gabon viper can sport fangs of around 2 in, and looks considerably sweeter with its mouth shut (below). (Jacana/M Liquet)

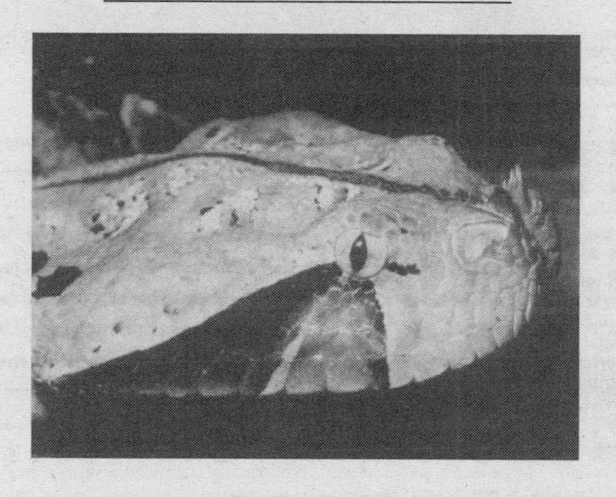

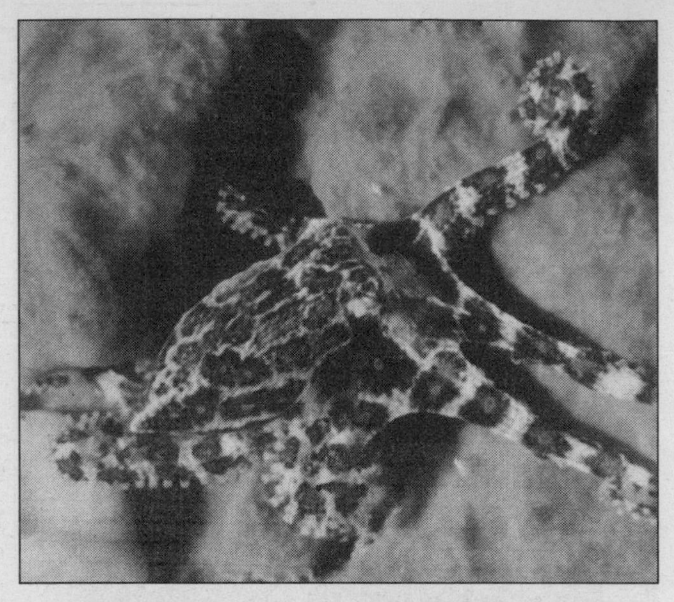

Southern blue-ringed octopus *Hapalochlaena masculosa*

LOOKS COULD KILL

Most animals—even the poisonous species—do not pose any real threat to human well-being. Animal weaponry is largely designed for debilitating prey, or is used by the possessor in reflexive acts of defense. Nevertheless, the exceptional few, on the rare occasions that they make human contact, are lethal. The world's most venomous creatures are pictured here—all of them exotic, strikingly beautiful, and VERY DANGEROUS.

BLUE-RINGED AND TERROR-TINGED

The deadly bite of this deceptively pretty octopus can kill in a matter of minutes. With a radial spread of just 4–6 in, the two main closely related species, *Hapalochlaena masculosa* and *H. lunulata,* contain a neurotoxic venom so potent that only rarely can an antivenin be used in time to save the victim.

Habitat: the coasts of Australia

Sea snake
Hydrophis belcheri

Australian box jellyfish
Cubomedusae
Chironex fleckeri

SEA SNAKE

All sea snakes are poisonous, though they cause few accidents due to their habitat. *Hydrophis belcheri* has a myotoxic venom a hundred times as toxic as that of the Australian taipan (*Oxyuranus scutellatus*), whose bite can kill a human being in minutes.

Habitat: Ashmore Reef in the Timor Sea, off northwest Australia

A STING IN THE TAIL

When approached by potential prey, the Australian box jellyfish suddenly releases a collagenous, stinging thread, which uncoils and turns inside out in the process, sometimes exposing lateral barbs. Some of the threads are hollow, and contain a cardiotoxic venom which can enter the body of the prey. The cubomedusan sea wasps—particularly the genera *Chironex* and *Chiopsalmus*—are especially dangerous. A sting can cause paralysis and death in a human within 3 minutes of contact.

Habitat: the coasts of Australia, especially Queensland, as far north as Malaya

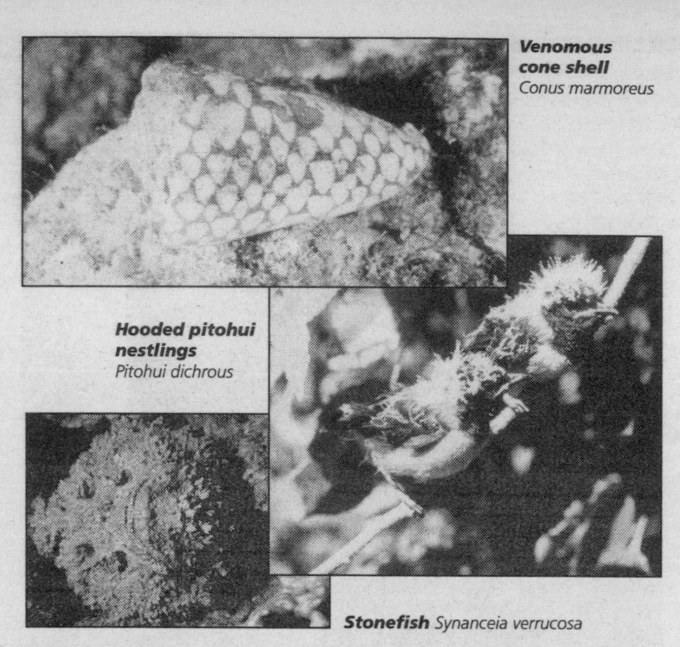

Venomous cone shell *Conus marmoreus*

Hooded pitohui nestlings *Pitohui dichrous*

Stonefish *Synanceia verrucosa*

MARINE MOLLUSK

There are some 400–500 species of cone shell, all of which can deliver a poisonous neurotoxin. The geographer cone (*Conus geographus*) and the court cone (*C. aulicus*) are considered to be the most deadly. The venom is injected by a unique fleshy, harpoon-like proboscis, and symptoms include impaired vision, dizziness, nausea and paralysis, sometimes followed by death.

Habitat: Polynesia to East Africa

A BIRD IN THE HAND

No birds were believed to be poisonous until just three years ago, when a graduate student at the University of Chicago felt numbness and burning in his mouth when he licked his hands after handling a hooded pitohui bird. The poison turned out to be identical to that of the poison-dart frog, though in a far less potent form.

Habitat: New Guinea

THE KILLER CATCH

The most poisonous fish in the world are the stonefish (Synanceidae), and in particular *Synanceja horrida,* which has the largest venom glands of any known fish. Direct contact with the spines of its fins, which contain a strong neurotoxic poison, often proves fatal.

Habitat: the tropical waters of the Indo-Pacific

KILLING 50 MEN WITH ONE FROG

These small, brightly colored creatures secrete some of the most deadly biological toxins known to humans. They come in varying colors—red, bright green, pink, orange and gold—and may be adorned with darker spots or stripes. In the Kokoi poison-arrow of Colombia, one ten-thousandth of a gram of its poison is enough to kill a man of average build. The native Indians of the rain forests can poison as many as 50 arrows with the fluids of one tiny specimen.

Habitat: the floor of the rain forest in South and Central America

Poison-arrow frog
Dendrobates tinctorius

Poison-arrow frog
Dendrobates auratus

Poison-arrow frog
Dendrobates pumilio

(Planet Earth Pictures; NHPA/B. Beehler)

VENOMOUS SNAKES

Longest The longest venomous snake in the world is the king cobra (*Ophiophagus hannah*), also called the hamadryad, which averages 12–15 ft in length and is found in southeast Asia and the Philippines. An 18-ft-2-in specimen, captured alive near Fort Dickson in the state of Negri Sembilan, Malaya in April 1937, later grew to 18 ft 9 in in London Zoo, Great Britain. It was destroyed at the outbreak of war in 1939.

Shortest The namaqua dwarf adder (*Bitis schneider*) of Namibia has an average adult length of 8 in.

Heaviest The heaviest venomous snake is probably the eastern diamond-back rattlesnake (*Crotalus adamanteus*) of the southeastern United States. One specimen, measuring 7 ft 9 in in length, weighed 34 lb.

Most venomous The most venomous land snake is the 6-ft-6¾-in-long smooth-scaled snake (*Parademansia microlepidotus*) of the Diamantina River and Cooper's Creek drainage basins in Channel County, Queensland and western New South Wales, Australia, which has a venom nine times as toxic as that of the tiger snake (*Notechis scutatus*) of South Australia and Tasmania. One specimen yielded 0.00385 oz of venom after milking, enough to kill 125,000 mice, but so far no human fatalities have been reported.

Snake bites More people die of snakebites in Sri Lanka than in any comparable area in the world. An average of 800 people are killed annually on the island by snakes, and more than 95 percent of the fatalities are caused by the common krait (*Bungarus caeruleus*), the Sri Lankan cobra (*Naja n. naja*), and Russell's viper (*Vipera russelli pulchella*).

The saw-scaled or carpet viper (*Echis carinatus*) bites and kills more people in the world than any other species. Its geographical range extends from West Africa to India.

United States The most venomous snake in the United States is the coral snake (*Micrurus fulvius*). In a standard LD99–100 test, which kills 99–100 percent of all mice injected with the venom, it takes 0.55 grain of venom per 2.2 lbs of mouse weight injected intravenously. In this test, the smaller the dosage, the more toxic the venom. However, the teeth of the coral snake point back into its mouth, and therefore it cannot inject the venom until it has a firm hold on the victim.

Longest fangs The longest fangs of any snake are those of the highly venomous gabon viper (*Bitis gabonica*) of tropical Africa. In a specimen of 6 ft length they measured 1.96 in.

Fastest The fastest-moving land snake is probably the slender black mamba (*Dendroaspis polylepis*) of the eastern part of tropical Africa. It is possible that this snake can achieve speeds of 10–12 mph in short bursts over level ground, and it is said to chase people aggressively.

FROGS

Largest The largest frog is the rare African giant frog or goliath frog (*Conraua goliath*) of Cameroon and Equatorial Guinea. A specimen captured in April 1989 on the Sanaga River, Cameroon by Andy Koffman of Seattle, WA had a snout-to-vent length of 14½ in (34½ in overall with legs extended) and weighed 8 lb 1 oz on 30 Oct 1989.

Smallest The smallest frog in the world is *Sminthillus limbatus* of Cuba, which is less than ½ in long.

Longest jump (*Competition frog jumps are the aggregate of three consecutive leaps.*)

The greatest distance covered by a frog in a triple jump is 33 ft 5½ in by a South African sharp-nosed frog (*Ptychadena oxyrhynchus*) named Santjie at a frog derby held at Lurula Natal Spa, Paulpietersburg, Natal, South Africa on 21 May 1977.

United States At the annual Calaveras Jumping Jubilee held at Angels Camp, CA on 18 May 1986, an American bullfrog (*Rana catesbeiana*) called Rosie the Ribeter, owned and trained by Lee Guidici of Santa Clara, CA, leapt 21 ft 5¾ in.

FISH

GENERAL RECORDS

Largest The largest fish in the world is the rare plankton-feeding whale shark (*Rhincodon typus*), which is found in the warmer areas of the Atlantic, Pacific, and Indian Oceans. The longest scientifically measured one on record was a 41½-ft specimen captured off Baba Island near Karachi, Pakistan on 11 Nov 1949. It measured 23 ft around the thickest part of the body and weighed an estimated 16½ tons.

Carnivorous The largest carnivorous fish is the great white shark (*Carcharodon carcharias*). The largest example accurately measured was 20 ft 4 in long and weighed 5,000 lb. It was harpooned and landed in the harbor of San Miguel, Azores in June 1978.

Smallest The shortest recorded marine fish—and the shortest known vertebrate—is the dwarf goby (*Trimmatom nanus*) of the Chagos Archipelago, central Indian Ocean. In one series of 92 specimens collected by the 1978–79 Joint Services Chagos Research Expedition of the British Armed Forces, the adult males averaged 0.34 in in length and the adult females 0.35 in.

FROG JUMPING

Lee Guidici, an elementary school teacher in Santa Clara, CA, makes an annual event of preparing for the great Calaveras County Frog-Jumping Contest made famous in the Mark Twain story.

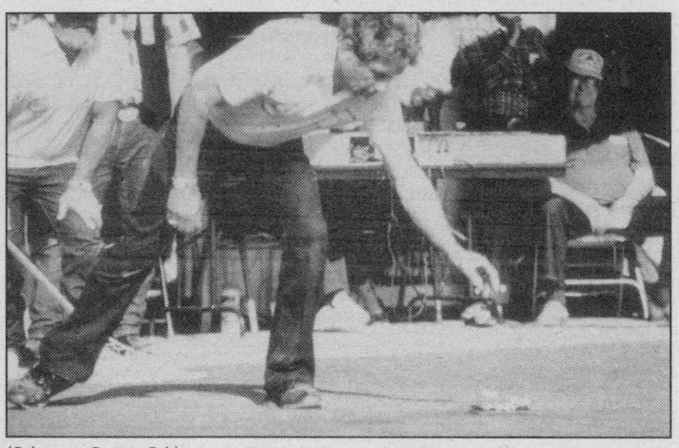

(Calaveras County Fair)

First he goes huntin' frog, equipped with a miner's hat ("to free both hands") and a boat. "I shine the lights into the water, and the frogs' eyes radiate back like stars." Then he barehands 'em. "Sometimes I bring my son and his friends out to help. They try and try, and they get embarrassed. That's when they say, 'I'll row the boat. You catch the frogs.'"

Guidici takes his catch to schools all over town, teaching the kids all about frogs and what it takes to jump them. There's a jumping contest, and the winning child earns a trip with Guidici to the big hop in Calaveras. Guidici's record-breaking frog, Rosie the Ribeter, was named by students at Santa Clara Middle School. Nowadays she's back home in an irrigation ditch in the San Joaquin Valley. Says Guidici fondly, "We put her out and said 'Thanks, you've done your job, now go ahead and have your little ones.' If they make the cut, that's great!" But, he allows, "Any frog that breaks this record now will only break it by a quarter-inch or so." Back home, he tells the schoolkids to hold their own human jumps. "I ask them to see if they can beat Rosie's jump in three jumps of their own. It gives them a real respect for amphibians."

Fastest The sailfish (*Istiophorus platypterus*) is considered to be the fastest species of fish over short distances, although the practical difficulties of measuring make data extremely difficult to secure. In a series of speed trials carried out at the Long Key Fishing Camp, FL, one sailfish took out 300 ft of line in 3 sec, which is equivalent to a velocity of 68 mph (compare with 60 mph for the cheetah).

Deepest Brotulids of the genus *Bassogigas* are generally regarded as the deepest-living vertebrates. The greatest depth from which a fish has been recovered is 27,230 ft in the Puerto Rico Trench (27,488 ft) in the Atlantic by Dr Gilbert L. Voss of the US research vessel *John Elliott*, who took a 6½-in-long *Bassogigas profundissimus* in April 1970. It was only the fifth such brotulid ever caught.

OLDEST!

In 1948 the death was reported of an 88-year-old female European eel (*Anguilla anguilla*) named Putte in the aquarium at Hälsingborg Museum, Sweden. She was allegedly born in the Sargasso Sea, in the North Atlantic, in 1860, and was caught in a river as a 3-year-old elver.

Oldest goldfish Goldfish (*Carassius auratus*) have been reported to live for over 50 years in China.

A goldfish named Fred, owned by A.R. Wilson of Worthing, Great Britain, died on 1 Aug 1980 at 41 years of age.

Shortest-lived The shortest-lived fish are probably certain species of the suborder Cyprinodontei (killifish), found in Africa and South America, which normally live about eight months.

Most eggs The ocean sunfish (*Mola mola*) produces up to 30 million eggs, each of them measuring about 0.05 in in diameter, at a single spawning.

Fewest eggs The mouth-brooding cichlid *Tropheus moorii* of Lake Tanganyika, East Africa, produces seven eggs or less during normal reproduction.

Most valuable The world's most valuable fish is the Russian sturgeon (*Huso huso*). One 2,706-lb female caught in the Tikhaya Sosna River in 1924 yielded 541 lb of best-quality caviar, which would be worth $300,000 on today's market.

The 30-in-long Ginrin Showa koi, which won the supreme championship in nationwide Japanese koi shows in 1976, 1977, 1979 and 1980, was sold two years later for 17 million yen (about $165,000). In March 1986 this ornamental carp was acquired by Derry Evans, owner of the Kent Koi Centre near Sevenoaks, Great Britain, for an undisclosed sum, but the 15-year-old fish died five months later. It has since been stuffed and mounted to preserve its beauty.

Most ferocious The razor-toothed piranhas of the genera *Serrasalmus, Pygocentrus* and *Pygopristis* are the most ferocious freshwater fish in the world. They live in the sluggish waters of the large rivers of South America, and will attack any creature, regardless of size, if it is injured or making a commotion in the water. On 19 Sep 1981 more than 300 people were reportedly killed and eaten when an overloaded passenger-cargo boat capsized and sank as it was docking at the Brazilian port of Obidos.

Most electric The most powerful electric fish is the electric eel (*Electrophorus electricus*), which is found in the rivers of Brazil, Colombia, Venezuela and Peru. An average-sized specimen can discharge 1 amp at 400 volts, but measurements up to 650 volts have been recorded.

FRESHWATER

Largest The largest fish that spends its whole life in fresh or brackish water is the rare pla beuk (*Pangasianodon gigas*). It is confined to the Mekong River and its major tributaries in China, Laos, Cambodia and Thailand. The largest specimen, captured in the River Ban Mee Noi, Thailand, was reportedly 9 ft 10¼ in long and weighed 533½ lb.

Smallest The shortest and lightest freshwater fish is the dwarf pygmy goby (Pandaka pygmaea), a colorless and nearly transparent species found in the streams and lakes of Luzon in the Philippines. Adult males measure only 0.28–0.38 in in length and weigh 0.00014–0.00018 oz.

STARFISH

Largest A specimen of the very fragile brisingid *Midgardia xandaros* collected by the Texas A & M University research vessel *Alaminos* in the southern part of the Gulf of Mexico in the late summer of 1968 measured 4½ ft tip to tip, but the diameter of its disc was only 1.02 in.

Smallest The smallest starfish is the asterinid sea star *Patiriella parvivipara*, discovered by Wolfgang Zeidler on the west coast of the Eyre peninsula, South Australia in 1975. It has a maximum radius of only 0.18 in and a diameter of less than 0.35 in.

Most destructive The crown of thorns (*Acanthaster planci*) of the Indo-Pacific region and the Red Sea has 12–19 arms and can measure up to 24 in in diameter. It feeds on coral polyps and can destroy 46½–62 in^2 of coral in one day. It has been responsible for the destruction of large parts of the Great Barrier Reef off Australia.

Deepest The greatest depth from which a starfish has been recovered is 24,881 ft for a specimen of *Porcellanaster ivanovi* collected by the Soviet research ship *Vityaz* in the Mariana Trench, in the western Pacific, *c*. 1962.

CRUSTACEANS

Largest marine The largest of all crustaceans (although not the heaviest) is the takashigani or giant spider crab (*Macrocheira kaempferi*), which is found in deep waters off the southeastern coast of Japan. One specimen with a claw-span of 12 ft 1¼ in weighed 41 lb.

Heaviest The heaviest of all crustaceans, and the largest species of lobster, is the American or North Atlantic lobster (*Homarus americanus*). On 11 Feb 1977 a specimen weighing 44 lb 6 oz and measuring 3 ft 6 in from the end of the tail fan to the tip of the largest claw was caught off Nova Scotia, Canada and later sold to a New York restaurant owner.

Largest freshwater The largest freshwater crustacean is a species of crayfish, or crawfish (*Astacopsis gouldi*) found in the streams of Tasmania, Australia. It has been measured up to 2 ft in length and may weigh as much as 9 lb. In 1934 an unconfirmed weight of 14 lb (total length 29 in) was reported for an outsized specimen caught at Bridport, Tasmania, Australia.

Largest concentration The largest single concentration of crustaceans ever recorded was an enormous swarm of krill (*Euphausia superba*) estimated to weigh 11 million tons and tracked by US scientists off Antarctica in March 1981.

Crabs, lobsters, shrimps, prawns, crawfish and other crustaceans. The heaviest crustacean, and the largest species of lobster, is the American or North Atlantic lobster. (Planet Earth Pictures/G van Ryckevorsel)

SPIDERS

Largest The world's largest spider is the goliath bird-eating spider (*Theraphosa leblondi*) of the coastal rain forests of northeastern South America. A male example collected by members of the Pablo San Martin Expedition at Rio Cavro, Venezuela in April 1965 had a leg span of 11.02 in.

Heaviest Female bird-eating spiders are more heavily built than males, and in February 1985 Charles J. Seiderman of New York City captured a female example near Paramaribo, Surinam that weighed a record peak 4.3 oz before its death from molting problems in January 1986. Other measurements included a maximum leg span of 10½ in, a total body length of 4 in, and 1-in-long fangs.

Smallest The smallest spider is *Patu marplesi* (family Symphytognathidae) of Western Samoa in the Pacific. The type specimen (male), found in moss at *c.* 2,000 ft in Madolelei, Western Samoa in January 1965, measured 0.017 in overall, which means that it was about the size of a period on this page.

Oldest The longest-lived of all spiders are the primitive Mygalomorphae (tarantulas and allied species). One female therasophid collected in Mexico in 1935 lived for an estimated 26–28 years.

United States The longest-lived species of American spider is the *Rhecosticta californica* of the family Theraphosidae, which has an average life span of 25 years.

Most venomous The world's most venomous spiders are the Brazilian wandering spiders of the genus *Phoneutria*, and particularly *P. fera*, which has the most active neurotoxic venom of any living spider. These large and highly aggressive creatures frequently enter human dwellings and hide in clothing or shoes. When disturbed they bite furiously several times, and hundreds of accidents involving these species are reported annually. When deaths do occur, they are usually in children under the age of seven. Fortunately, an effective antivenin is available.

Fastest The fastest-moving arachnids are the long-legged sun spiders of the order Solifugae, which live in the arid semidesert regions of Africa and the Middle East. They feed on geckos and other lizards and can reach speeds of over 10 mph.

SCORPIONS

Smallest The smallest scorpion in the world is *Microbothus pusillus* from the Red Sea coast, which measures about 1/2 in in total length.

Most venomous The most venomous scorpion in the world is the Palestine yellow scorpion (*Leiurus quinquestriatus*), which ranges from the eastern part of North Africa through the Middle East to the shores of the Red Sea. Fortunately, the amount of venom it delivers is very small (0.000009 oz) and adult lives are seldom endangered; however, it has been responsible for a number of fatalities among children under the age of five.

LARGEST!

The largest of the 800 or so species of scorpion is the tropical "emperor" (*Pandinus imperator*) of Guinea, adult males of which can attain a body length of 7 in or more.

WORMS

Longest The longest known species of earthworm is *Microchaetus rappi* (=*M. microchaetus*) of South Africa. In *c.* 1937 a giant earthworm measuring 22 ft in length when naturally extended and 0.8 in in diameter was collected in the Transvaal.

Shortest *Chaetogaster annandalei* measures less than 0.02 in in length.

INSECTS

It is estimated that there may be as many as 30 million species of insect—more species than all other animals put together—but thousands are known only from a single type or specimen.

Oldest A shrimplike creature found in 1991 in rocks dated as 420 million years old may be the world's oldest insect. Found in Western Australia, this euthycarcinoid was a large (5 in long) freshwater predator.

CHARMING THE WORMS FROM THE GROUND

Worms, which depend on moisture to survive,

CHARMING

normally burrow down into the top few feet of the

THE

earth. Continuous vibrations, from their underground

WORMS

perspective, can be caused only by the sound of rain,

FROM

and their penchant for soaking up the maximum

THE

amount of moisture draws them to

GROUND

the surface.

(Liverpool Daily Post and Echo)

Above, contestants at Willaston County Primary School encouraging the worms' advances. (Mr & Mrs G. D. Farr)

Visit the most charming of school festivals each summer at the Willaston County Primary School in Nantwich, Great Britain, and you will stumble across a vast expanse of three-yard-square plots, each peopled with focused, intent individuals staring or poking gently at the ground. They might be brandishing a garden fork, a watering can, or a radio. They are the contestants of the World Worm Charming Championship, inaugurated in 1980, and they have 30 minutes to entice the worms from the comfort of their earthly dwellings.

Anyone can enter; the championship, which is a burgeoning fund-raiser, attracts interest from all over the world. In 1993 there were 150 teams competing for the coveted Golden Rampant Worm trophy; local competition is fierce, however, and the trophy has never left the village of Willaston. There are two basic rules: no refreshment, stimulation, or drugs, and no digging. The idea is to lure out the worms by vibration.

The world record was set in 1980, when Tom Shufflebotham raised an astonishing 511 worms from a 3-yard plot in the allowed time. His method was "twanging"—a traditional technique in which a four-pronged pitchfork is placed in the ground and wiggled by the handle forwards and backwards, causing the vibrations that persuade the worms to emerge.

Heaviest The heaviest living insects are the Goliath beetles (family Scarabaeidae) of Equatorial Africa. The largest members of the group are *Goliathus regius*, *G. goliathus* (=*G. giganteus*) and *G. druryi*, and in one series of fully-grown males (females are smaller) the lengths from the tips of the small frontal horns to the end of the abdomen measured up to 4.33 in and the weights ranged from 2½–3½ oz.

Longest The longest insect in the world is *Pharnacia kirbyi*, a stick insect from the rainforests of Borneo. A specimen in the Natural History Museum, London, Great Britain has a body length of 12.9 in and a total length, including the legs, of 20 in.

Smallest The smallest insects recorded so far are the "feather-winged" beetles of the family Ptiliidae (trichopterygidae) and the "battledore-wing fairy flies" (parasitic wasps) of the family Mymaridae; they are smaller than some species of protozoa (single-celled animals).

Lightest The male bloodsucking banded louse (*Enderleinellus zonatus*) and the parasitic wasp (*Caraphractus cinctus*) may each weigh as little as 5,670,000 to an oz. Eggs of the latter each weigh 141,750,000 to an oz.

Loudest The loudest of all insects is the male cicada (family Cicadidae). At 7,400 pulses/min its tymbal organs produce a noise (officially described by the US Department of Agriculture as "tsh-ee-EEEE-e-ou") detectable more than a quarter of a mile distant.

Fastest-flying A maximum speed of 36 mph for the Australian dragonfly *Austrophlebia costalis* has been recorded for short bursts.

Fastest wing-beat The fastest wing-beat of any insect under natural conditions is 62,760 per min by a tiny midge of the genus *Forcipomyia*. The muscular contraction–expansion cycle of 0.00045 sec represents the fastest muscle movement ever measured.

Slowest wing-beat The slowest wing-beat of any insect is 300 per min by the swallowtail butterfly (*Papilio machaon*). The average is 460–636 per min.

Fastest-moving The fastest-moving insects are certain large tropical cockroaches, and the record is 3.36 mph, or 50 body lengths per second, registered by *Periplaneta americana* at the University of California at Berkeley in 1991.

Highest g force The click beetle (*Athous haemorrhoidalis*) averages 400 *g* when "jack-knifing" into the air to escape predators. One example measuring ½ in in length and weighing 0.00014 oz that jumped to a height of 11¾ in was calculated to have "endured" a peak brain deceleration of 2,300 *g* by the end of the movement.

Oldest The longest-lived insects are the splendor beetles (Buprestidae). On 27 May 1983 a *Buprestis aurulenta* appeared from the staircase timber in the the home of Mr W. Euston of Prittlewell, Great Britain, after 47 years as a larva.

Largest cockroach The world's largest cockroach is *Megaloblatta longipennis* of Colombia. A preserved female in the collection of Akira Yokokura of Yamagata, Japan measures 3.81 in in length and 1.77 in across.

Largest termite mound In 1968 W. Page photographed a specimen south of Horgesia, Somalia estimated to be 28½ ft tall.

Largest grasshopper The largest grasshopper in the world is an unidentified species from the border of Malaysia and Thailand measuring 10 in in length and capable of leaping 15 ft.

DRAGONFLIES

Largest *Megaloprepus caeruleata* of Central and South America has been measured up to 4.72 in across the wings and 7.52 in in body length.

United States The giant green darner (*Anax walsinghami*), found in the West, has a body length of up to 4½ in.

Smallest The world's smallest dragonfly is *Agriocnemis naia* of Myanmar. A specimen in the British Museum (Natural History), London, Great Britain had a wing spread of 0.69 in and a body length of 0.71 in.

United States The smallest dragonfly in the United States is the elfin skimmer (*Nannothaemis Bella*), which has a body length of ⅘ in.

FLEAS

Largest Siphonapterologists recognize 1,830 varieties, of which the largest-known is *Hystrichopsylla schefferi*, which was described from a single specimen taken from the nest of a mountain beaver (*Aplodontia rufa*) at Puyallup, WA in 1913. Females are up to 0.3 in long.

Longest jump The champion jumper among fleas is the common flea (*Pulex irritans*). In one American experiment carried out in 1910 a specimen allowed to leap at will performed a long jump of 13 in and a high jump of 7¾ in. In jumping 130 times its own height a flea subjects itself to a force of 200 *g*.

BUTTERFLIES

Largest The largest butterfly is the Queen Alexandra's birdwing (*Ornithoptera alexandrae*) of Papua New Guinea. Females may have a wingspan exceeding 11 in and weigh over 0.9 oz.

United States The largest *native* butterfly in the United States is the giant swallowtail (*Papilio cresphontes*), found in the eastern states, with a wingspan of up to 6 in.

Smallest The smallest of the 140,000 known species of Lepidoptera is *Stigmella ridiculosa*, which has a wingspan of 0.079 in with a similar body length and is found in the Canary Islands.

MIGRATION!

A tagged female monarch butterfly (*Danaus plexippus*) released by Donald Davis at Presqu'ile Provincial Park near Brighton, Ontario, Canada on 6 Sep 1986 was recaptured 2,133 miles away, on a mountain near Angangueo, Mexico on 15 Jan 1987. This distance was obtained by measuring a line from the release site to the recapture site, but the actual distance traveled could be double this figure.

United States The smallest butterfly in the United States is the pygmy blue (*Brephidium exilis*), found in the Southeast, with a wingspan of 3/8–3/4 in.

Largest butterfly farm The Stratford-upon-Avon Butterfly Farm, Warwickshire, Great Britain can accommodate 2,000 exotic butterflies in authentic rain forest conditions. The total capacity of all flight areas at the farm, which opened on 15 Jul 1985, is over 141,259 ft^3. The complex also comprises insect and plant houses and educational facilities.

United States Butterfly World, in Coconut Creek, FL, accommodates 2,000 butterflies in authentic rain forest or North American conditions. About 80 species of butterfly can be seen at any one time, and in the course of a year up to 300 species are shown in the three large screened aviaries for display and 36 separate screen enclosures for breeding.

MOLLUSKS

Largest The giant squid, *Architeuthis dux*, is the world's largest invertebrate. The heaviest ever recorded was a 2.2-ton monster that ran aground in Thimble Tickle Bay, Newfoundland, Canada on 2 Nov 1878. Its body was 20 ft long, and one tentacle measured 35 ft.

Longest The longest mollusk ever recorded was a 57-ft giant *Architeuthis longimanus* that was washed up on Lyall Bay, Cook Strait, New Zealand in October 1887. Its two long, slender tentacles each measured 49 ft 3 in.

Oyster opening The record for opening oysters is 100 in 2 min 20.07 sec, by Mike Racz in Invercargill, New Zealand on 16 Jul 1990.

Snail racing On 20 Feb 1990 a garden snail named Vern, owned by Sally De Roo of Canton, MI, completed a 12 1/5 in (3 cm) course at West Middle School in Plymouth, MI in a record 2 min 13 sec at 0.092 in/sec.

The Atlantic giant squid is a triple record breaker: largest mollusk, largest known invertebrate, and largest eye. (Ann Ronan Picture Library)

JELLYFISH

Largest An Arctic giant jellyfish (*Cyanea capillata arctica*) that washed up in Massachusetts Bay had a bell diameter of 7 ft 6 in and tentacles stretching 120 ft.

Most venomous The Australian sea wasp (*Chironex fleckeri*) is the most venomous jellyfish in the world. Its cardiotoxic venom has caused the deaths of 66 people off the coast of Queensland since 1880, with victims dying within 1–3 minutes if medical aid is not available. One effective defense is women's pantyhose, outsize versions of which are now worn by Queensland lifeguards at surfing tournaments.

SPONGES

Largest The largest sponge is the barrel-shaped loggerhead sponge (*Spheciospongia vesparium*) of the West Indies and the waters off Florida. Individuals measure up to 3 ft 6 in in height and 3 ft in diameter.

Heaviest In 1909 a wool sponge (*Hippospongia canaliculatta*) measuring 6 ft in circumference was collected off the Bahamas. When taken from the water it weighed between 80–90 lb but after it had been dried and relieved of all excrescences it weighed 12 lb. (This sponge is now preserved in the National Museum of Natural History, Washington, D.C.)

Smallest The widely distributed *Leucosolenia blanca* measures 0.11 in in height when fully grown.

Deepest Sponges have been recovered from depths of up to 18,500 ft.

DINOSAURS

Heaviest The main contender for the heaviest dinosaur is probably the titanosaurid *Antarctosaurus giganteus* ("Antarctic lizard") from Argentina and India, at 45–88 tons.

Largest The largest-ever land animals were sauropod dinosaurs, a group of long-necked, long-tailed, four-legged plant-eaters that lumbered around most of the world during the Jurassic and Cretaceous periods 208–65 million years ago.

Tallest The tallest and largest dinosaur is the *Brachiosaurus brancai* ("arm lizard") from the Tendaguru site in Tanzania, dated as Late Jurassic (150 million years ago). The site was excavated by German expeditions during the period 1909–11 and the bones prepared and assembled at the Humboldt Museum in Berlin. A complete skeleton was constructed from the remains of several individuals and put on display in 1937. It is also the world's largest and tallest mounted dinosaur skeleton, measuring 72 ft 9½ in in overall length (height at shoulder 19 ft 8 in), and has a raised head height of 46 ft. A weight of 30–40 tons is likely.

GUESS WHAT?

Q. WHAT IS THE HIGHEST GROSSING MOVIE OF ALL TIME?

A. SEE "MOVIES" (ARTS & ENTERTAINMENT)

Longest A diplodocid from New Mexico named *Seismosaurus halli* was estimated in 1991 to be 128–170 ft long based on comparisons of individual bones.

Smallest The chicken-sized *Compsognathus* ("pretty jaw") of southern Germany and southeast France, and an undescribed plant-eating fabrosaurid from Colorado, both measured 29½ in from the snout to the tip of the tail and weighed about 15 lb.

Largest predatory dinosaur The largest flesh-eating dinosaur recorded so far is *Tyrannosaurus rex* ("king tyrant lizard"), which 70 million years ago reigned over what are now the states of Montana, Wyoming and Texas and the provinces of Alberta and Saskatchewan, Canada. The largest and heaviest example, as suggested by a discovery in South Dakota in 1991, was 19½ ft tall, had a total length of 36½ ft and weighed an estimated 6–8 tons.

Longest neck The sauropod *Mamenchisaurus* ("mamenchi lizard") of the Late Jurassic of Sichuan, China had the longest neck of any animal that has ever lived. The neck measured 36 ft—half the total length of the dinosaur.

Most brainless *Stegosaurus* ("plated lizard"), which roamed across Colorado, Oklahoma, Utah and Wyoming about 150 million years ago, measured up to 30 ft in total length but had a walnut-sized brain weighing only 2½ oz. This represented 0.004 of 1 percent of its computed body weight of 1.9 tons (compare with 0.074 of 1 percent for an elephant and 1.88 percent for a human).

Largest footprints In 1932 the gigantic footprints of a large bipedal hadrosaurid ("duckbill") measuring 53½ in in length and 32 in wide were discovered in Salt Lake City, UT, and other reports from Colorado and Utah refer to footprints 37–40 in wide. Footprints attributed to the largest brachiosaurids also range up to 40 in wide for the hind feet.

Largest eggs The largest known dinosaur eggs are those of *Hypselosaurus priscus* ("high ridge lizard"), a 40-ft-long titanosaurid that lived about 80 million years ago. Examples found in the Durance valley near Aix-en-Provence, France in October 1961 would have had, uncrushed, a length of 12 in and a diameter of 10 in (capacity 5.8 pt).

PLANT KINGDOM

GENERAL RECORDS

Oldest "King Clone," the oldest known clone of the creosote plant (*Larrea tridentata*), found in southwest California, was estimated in February 1980 by Prof. Frank C. Vasek to be 11,700 years old.

Northernmost The yellow poppy (*Papaver radicatum*) and the Arctic willow (*Salix arctica*) survive, the latter in an extremely stunted form, on the northernmost land at Lat. 83° N.

Southernmost Lichens resembling *Rhinodina frigida* have been found in Moraine Canyon at Lat. 86°09′S, Long. 157°30′W in 1971 and in the Horlick Mountain area, Antarctica at Lat. 86°09′S, Long. 131°14′W in 1965.

The southernmost recorded flowering plant is the Antarctic hair grass (*Deschampsia antarctica*), which was found at Lat. 68°21′S on Refuge Island, Antarctica on 11 Mar 1981.

FLOWERS, FRUITS AND VEGETABLES

In the interest of fairness and to minimize the risk of mistakes being made, all plants should, where possible, be entered in official international, national or local garden contests. Only produce grown primarily for human consumption will be considered for publication. The assistance of *Garden News* and the World Pumpkin Confederation is gratefully acknowledged.

Type	Size	Grower/Location	Year
Apple	3 lb 2 oz	Miklovic family, Caro, MI	1992
Cabbage	124 lb	B. Lavery, Llanharry, Great Britain	1989
Cantaloupe	62 lb	G. Draughtridge, Rocky Mount, NC	1991
Carrot[1]	15 lb 7 oz	I. Scott, Nelson, New Zealand	1978
Celery	46 lb 1 oz	B. Lavery, Llanharry, Great Britain	1990
Cucumber[2]	20 lb 1 oz	B. Lavery, Llanharry, Great Britain	1991
Chrysanthemum	8 ft 10 in	M. Comer, Desford, Great Britain	1992
Dahlia	25 ft 7 in	R. Blythe, Nannup, Western Australia	1990
Garlic	2 lb 10 oz	R. Kirkpatrick, Eureka, CA	1985
Grapefruit	6 lb 8½ oz	J. and A. Sosnow, Tucson, AZ	1984
Grapes	20 lb 11½ oz	Bozzolo y Perut Ltda, Santiago, Chile	1984
Leek (pot)	12 lb 2 oz	P. Harrigan, Linton, Great Britain	1987
Lemon	8 lb 8 oz	C. and D. Knutzen, Whittier, CA	1983
Marrow	108 lb 2 oz	B. Lavery, Llanharry, Great Britain	1990
Onion	11 lb 2 oz	R. Holland, Cumnock, Great Britain	1992
Parsnip	171¾ in	B. Lavery, Llanharry, Great Britain	1990
Petunia	13 ft 8in	B. Lawrence, Windham, NY	1985
Philodendron	1,114 ft	F. Francis, University of Massachusetts	1984
Pineapple[3]	17 lb 8 oz	Dole Philippines Inc, South Cotabato, Philippines	1984
Potato[4]	7 lb 1 oz	J. East, Spalding, Great Britain	1963
	7 lb 1 oz	J. Busby, Atherstone, Great Britain	1982

Pumpkin	836 lb	N. Craven, Stouffville, Ontario, Canada	1993
Radish	37 lb 15 oz	Litterini family, Tanunda, South Australia	1992
Rhubarb	5 lb 14 oz	E. Stone, East Woodyates, Great Britain	1985
Runner bean	39 1/2 in	J. Taylor, Shifnal, Great Britain	1986
Rutabaga	53 lb 8 oz	P. Lillie, Uxbridge, Ontario, Canada	1993
Squash	821 lb	L. Stellpflug, Rush, NY	1990
Strawberry	8.17 oz	G. Anderson, Folkestone, Great Britain	1983
Sunflower[5]	25 ft 5 1/2 in	M. Heijms, Oirschot, Netherlands	1986
Tomato	7 lb 12 oz	G. Graham, Edmond, OK	1986
Tomato plant[6]	53 ft 6in	G. Graham, Edmond, OK	1985
Watermelon	262 lb	B. Carson, Arrington, TN	1990
Zucchini	64 lb 8 oz	B. Lavery, Llanharry, Great Britain	1990

[1]*A 6 ft 10 1/2 in long carrot was grown by Bernard Lavery of Llanharry, Great Britian in 1991.*

[2]*A Vietnamese variety 6 ft long was reported by L. Szabo of Debrecen, Hungary in September 1976. A.C. Rayment of Chelmsford, Great Britain grew one measuring 43 1/2 in in 1984–86.*

[3]*Pineapples weighing up to 28 lb 11 oz were reported from Tarauaca, Brazil in 1978.*

[4]*One weighing 18 lb 4 oz was reported dug up by Thomas Siddal in his garden in Chester on 17 Feb 1795. A yield of 515 lb was achieved from a 2 1/2 lb parent seed by Bowcock planted in April 1977.*

[5]*A sunflower with a head measuring 32 1/4 in in diameter was grown by Emily Martin of Maple Ridge, British Columbia, Canada in September 1983. A fully mature sunflower measuring just 2 1/5 in was grown by Michael Lenke of Lake Oswego, OR in 1985 using a patented bonsai technique.*

[6]*It was reported at the Tsukuba Science Expo Center, Japan on 28 Feb 1988 that a single plant produced 16,897 tomatoes.*

(continued)

US NATIONAL RECORDS

Entry	Record	Grower	Year
Beet	45½ lb	R. Meyer, Brawley, CA	1984
Collard[7]	35 ft tall	B. Rackley, Rocky Mount, NC	1980
Corn	31 ft high	D. Radda, Washington, IA	1946
Dahlia	16 ft 5in	S. & P Barnes, Chattahoochee, FL	1982
Eggplant	5 lb 5¼ oz	J. & J. Charles, Summerville, SC	1984
Gourd	93½ in long	B.W. Saylor, Licking, MO	1986
Gourd (weight)	78 lb	L. Childers, Stinesville, IN	1986
Kohlrabi	36 lb	E. Krejci, Mt Clemens, MI	1979
Lima bean	14in	N. McCoy, Hubert, NC	1979
Okra stalk	17 ft 6¼ in	C. H. Wilber, Crane Hill, AL	1983
	17 ft 6¼ in	B. & E. Crosby, Brooksville, FL	1986
Onion	7½ lb	N. W. Hope, Tempe, AZ	1984
Peanut	4in	E. Adkins, Enfield, NC	1990
Pepper	13½ in	J. Rutherford, Hatch, NM	1975
Pepper plant	12 ft 3in	F. Melton, Jacksonville, FL	1992
Rutabaga[8]	42.4 lb	J. & M. Evans, Palmer, AK	1993
Sweet potato	40¾ lb	O. Harrison, Kite, GA	1982
Tomato (cherry)	28 ft 7in	C. H. Wilber, Crane Hill, AL	1985
Zucchini	35.6 lb	D. Schroer, Homer, AK	1992

[7]This same collard holds the record for greatest width, measuring 62 in from leaf tip to leaf tip at its greatest point of width.
[8]A rutabaga weighing 51 lb was reported from Alaska in 1981, but this has not been substantiated.

Highest The greatest certain altitude at which any flowering plants have been found is 21,000 ft on Mt Kamet (25,447 ft) in the Himalayas by N.D. Jayal in 1955. They were *Ermania himalayensis* and *Ranunculus lobatus*.

Deepest The greatest depth at which plant life has been found is 884 ft, by Mark and Diane Littler off San Salvadore Island, Bahamas in October 1984. These maroon-colored algae survived although 99.9995 percent of sunlight was filtered out.

Deepest roots The greatest reported depth to which roots have penetrated is an estimated 400 ft for a wild fig tree at Echo Caves, near Ohrigstad, Transvaal, South Africa. A single winter rye plant (*Secale cereale*) has been shown to produce 387 miles of roots in 1.83 ft^3 of earth.

Fastest-growing Some species of the 45 genera of bamboo have been found to grow up to 3 ft per day (0.00002 mph).

BLOOMS AND FLOWERS

Earliest flower A flower believed to be 120 million years old was identified in 1989 by Dr Leo Hickey and Dr David Taylor of Yale University from a fossil discovered near Melbourne, Victoria, Australia. The flowering angiosperm, which resembles a modern black pepper plant, had two leaves and one flower and is known as the Koonwarra plant.

United States The fossil of a flowering plant with palmlike imprints was found in Colorado in 1953 and dated about 65 million years old.

Largest The largest of all blooms are those of the parasitic stinking corpse lily (*Rafflesia arnoldii*), which measure up to 3 ft across and 3/4 in thick, and attain a weight of 15 lb. The plants attach themselves to the cissus vines in the jungles of southeast Asia. True to its name, the plant has an extremely offensive scent.

Inflorescence The largest-known inflorescence (as distinct from the largest of all blooms) is that of *Puya raimondii*, a rare Bolivian monocarpic member of the Bromeliaceae family. Its erect panicle (diameter 8 ft) emerges to a height of 35 ft and each of these bears up to 8,000 white blooms. (See Slowest-flowering plant.)

Smallest flowering and fruiting The floating, flowering aquatic duckweed (*Wolffia angusta*) of Australia, described in 1980, is only 0.024 in long and 0.013 in wide. It weighs about 1/100,000 oz and its fruit, which resembles a minuscule fig, weighs 1/400,000 oz.

United States The smallest plant regularly flowering in the United States is *Wolffia globosa*, which is found in the San Joaquin Valley, central California, and rivers draining the Sierra Nevada Mountains. The plant weighs about 150 micrograms, and is listed as 0.015 in to 0.027 in length and 0.011 in in width.

Fastest-growing It was reported from Tresco Abbey, Isles of Scilly, Great Britain in July 1978 that a *Hesperoyucca whipplei* of the family Liliaceae grew 12 ft in 14 days, a rate of about 10 in per day.

ON THE RECORD

JACK-O-LANTERN

T.M. McCarthy

"Our goal this year was three thousand jack-o-lanterns," Nancy Sporborg announced from the top of the scissor-lift, hoisted alongside the giant pyramid of pumpkins. "And the count is four thousand"—the roar of applause from the crowd below drowned out her voice—"eight hundred"—the shouting grew even louder—"seventeen!" From below, the voices of children and their parents clamored to be heard. "Mrs. Sporborg! Here's one more!"

One at a time, please. That's how a "little old New Hampshire town" made its way into *The Guinness Book of Records*. It started because Nancy Sporborg, a corporate communications manager and mother of two, wanted to do something special for the town in which she grew up: Keene, New Hampshire. "I love Keene," she says, "and I was worried. It's an amazingly beautiful town, and it was beginning to die. It's about as New England as you can get, right down to a big white church on the town green, and we have tremendous pride in it— but there were more and more empty storefronts. I knew that if I wanted to keep some life in our downtown I would have to do something about it."

Tom Newcombe

It's been three years since Sporborg first thought of the Harvest Festival and the pumpkin carving extravaganza to go with it. "People here are conservative. They said 'No way' to the idea, and they thought I was crazy when I called Guinness. But I said, 'Just wait.' " The result was an outpouring of enthusiasm—and pumpkins. "Each person got the opportunity to bring a piece of themselves downtown. They carved faces, names, company logos. And they carved themselves a place in the record book."

Slowest-flowering The slowest-flowering of all plants is the rare *Puya raimondii*, the largest of all herbs, discovered at 13,000 ft in Bolivia in 1870. The panicle emerges after about 80–150 years of the plant's life. It then dies. One planted near sea level at the University of California's Botanical Garden, Berkeley in 1958 grew to 25 ft and bloomed as early as August 1986 after only 28 years. (See Largest blooms.)

Longest daisy chain The longest daisy chain measured 6,980 ft 7 in and was made in 7 hr by villagers of Good Easter, Great Britain on 27 May 1985. The team is limited to 16.

Longest lei A 14,550-ft paper flower lei was made by local citizens at the Hyatt Regency Waikiki, Honolulu, HI on 19 Dec 1992.

Orchids *Tallest* The tallest of all orchids is *Grammatophyllum speciosum*, a native of Malaysia. Specimens have been recorded up to 25 ft in height.

The tallest of all American orchids is the *Eulophia ecristata*, with a recorded height of 5.6 ft. There are five species of vanilla orchids that are vines and can spread to almost any length depending on the environment. These orchids root in the ground and will grow in any direction over their surroundings.

Largest flower The largest orchid flower is that of *Pathiopedilum sanderianum*, whose petals are reported to grow up to 3 ft long in the wild. It was discovered in 1886 in the Malay Archipelago. A plant of this variety grown in Somerset, Great Britain in 1991 had three flowers averaging 2 ft from the top of the dorsal sepal to the bottom of the ribbon petals, giving a record stretched length of 4 ft.

The largest flowering orchid in the United States is the yellow ladyslipper (*Cypripedium calceolus*) of the Pubescens variety. Its petals grow up to 7 in long.

Largest cactus The largest of all cacti is the saguaro (*Cereus giganteus* or *Carnegiea gigantea*), found in Arizona, southeastern California and Sonora, Mexico. The green fluted column is surmounted by candelabra-like branches rising to a height of 57 ft 11¾ in in the case of a specimen discovered in the Maricopa Mountains, near Gila Bend, AZ on 17 Jan 1988.

An armless cactus 78 ft in height was measured in April 1978 by Hube Yates in Cave Creek, AZ. It was toppled in a windstorm in July 1986 at an estimated age of 150 years.

Largest rhododendron Examples of the scarlet *Rhododendron arboreum* reach a height of 65 ft on Mt Japfu, Nagaland, India. The cross-section of the trunk of a *Rhododendron giganteum*, reputedly 90 ft high, from Yunnan, China, is preserved at Inverewe Gardens, Highland, Great Britain.

Largest rose tree A Lady Banks rose tree at Tombstone, AZ has a trunk 12 ft in circumference, stands 9 ft high and covers an area of 8,660 ft^2. It is supported by 68 posts and several thousand feet of piping, which enables 150 people to be seated under the arbor. The cutting came from Scotland in 1884.

Hanging basket A giant hanging basket measuring 20 ft in diameter and containing about 600 plants was created by Rogers of Exeter Garden Cen-

VEGETABLE GROWING

Champion vegetable grower Bernard Lavery scorns the notion of a green thumb. He offers this plan for giant growing success: "Use seed which has the genetic capabilities to grow giant vegetables. Then all you need to be a world champion is some fertile ground, a little love and care, and Lady Luck sitting on your shoulder throughout the growing season. It's great fun, it's easy, and anyone can do it."

If it were as simple as that for every farmer, supermarket bins would be filled with cabbage, celery, cucumbers and zucchini monsters like the ones that sprout—seemingly magically—from Lavery's patch. A seed and plant breeder, he has been growing record-breaking vegetables at his farm in Llanharry, Wales, for 20 years. "I derive an enormous amount of pleasure from stretching nature to its limits," Lavery enthuses.

But the proof is in the eating. "When they are freshly harvested and before they become overmature, giant vegetables taste truly magnificent," Lavery claims. His favorite part is growing, though, and his favorite veggies are pumpkins and squash. "They will increase with size by two or three inches a day. They seem to grow even as you are looking at them." Hmmm. Maybe it's not the thumb at all that holds the green magic: maybe it's all in the eyes.

Bernard Lavery and his prize produce (B Lavery)

tre, Great Britain in 1987. Its volume was approximately 4,167 ft^3 and it weighed an estimated 4.4 tons.

FRUITS AND VEGETABLES

Least nutritive The fruit with the lowest caloric value is the cucumber (*Cucumis sativus*), with 73 kilocal/lb.

Apple peeling The longest single unbroken apple peel on record is one of 172 ft 4 in, peeled by Kathy Wafler of Wolcott, NY in 11 hr 30 min at Long Ridge Mall, Rochester, NY on 16 Oct 1976. The apple weighed 20 oz.

Apple picking The greatest recorded performance is 15,830 lb picked in 8 hr by George Adrian of Indianapolis, IN on 23 Sep 1980.

Cucumber slicing Norman Johnson of Blackpool College, Great Britain set a record of 13.4 sec for slicing a 12-in cucumber, 1½ in in diameter, at 22 slices to the inch (total 264 slices) at West Deutscher Rundfunk in Cologne, Germany on 3 Apr 1983.

Most jack-o'-lanterns The record for most jack-o'-lanterns in one place at one time is 4,817, on 29 Oct 1993. The pumpkins were carved for the Harvest Festival in Keene, NH, a Center Stage Cheshire County event sponsored by Paragon Cable. See On the Record feature (p. 92–93).

Largest jack-o'-lantern The largest jack-o'-lantern in the world was carved from a 827 lb pumpkin by Michael Green, Regina Johnson and Daniel Salcedo at Nut Tree, CA on 30 October 1992.

Potato peeling The greatest quantity of potatoes peeled by five people to an institutional cookery standard with standard kitchen knives in 45 min is 1,064 lb 6 oz (net) by Marj Killian, Terry Anderson, Barbara Pearson, Marilyn Small and Janene Utkin at the 64th Annual Idaho Spud Day celebration, held in Shelley, ID on 19 Sep 1992. See On the Record feature (p. 97).

VINEYARDS

Largest The world's largest vineyard extends over the Mediterranean slopes between the Pyrenees and the Rhône in the *départements* Gard, Hérault, Aude and Pyrénées-Orientales, France. It covers an area of 2,075,685 acres.

United States The largest continuous vineyard in the United States is Minor Thornton Ranch in Fresno, CA. Owned by the Golden State Vintners Corp., the vineyard covers 5,200 acres and produces 6,500 tons of grapes each year.

Largest vine A grapevine planted in 1842 at Carpinteria, CA yielded more than 9.9 tons of grapes in some years, and averaged 7.7 tons per year until it died in 1920.

ON THE RECORD

POTATO PEELING

They grew up in potato country, with potato fields as far as the eye could see. They spend their days cooking for the Shelly, Idaho Public Schools. Why shouldn't they spend one day a year—Spud Day, of course—cutting up?

They're the Shelly Spuddettes—Janene Utkin, Terry Anderson, Barbara Pearson, Marilyn Small, and their chairwoman, Marj Killian. "I've never met a potato I didn't like," claims Killian. "We don't practice peeling; we don't need to." It was Spud Day itself that gave the team the idea. "Pillsbury donated 5,000 pounds of potatoes. They'd deliver 'em, and we'd get 'em washed and cleaned by noon. We figured, if we could do that, we could peel fast, too."

They were right, but it took a couple of years to hit the record. "The first year, we ran out of potatoes before the 45 minutes were up. We had to sit and watch everyone else peel away." This year the Spuddettes had their spuds ready. "My husband and I gathered all we could from the ones left on the ground after harvest. We added those to the donations." Once the title was won, the Spuddettes had to worry about something else—what to do with the taters. Killian kept a supply in her bathtub for weeks ("in water, with salt. They'll keep"). One cook made doughnuts—"They call them spudnuts"—and someone else made ice cream. Potato ice cream? It got the thumbs-up from Killian. "It's made from potatoes, isn't it? You can bet it's good!"

The team wears T-shirts that boast "Addicted to Spuds." Seems like a local affliction. "We honor the potato in Shelly," says Killian. "It's our livelihood. Why shouldn't the potato-peeling record be here?"

LEAVES

Largest The largest leaves of any plant belong to the raffia palm (*Raphia farinifera = R. raffia*) of the Mascarene Islands in the Indian Ocean, and the Amazonian bamboo palm (*R. taedigera*) of South America, whose leaf blades may measure up to 65½ ft in length, with petioles up to 13 ft.

The largest leaves to be found in outdoor plants in the United States are those of the climbing fern (*Lygodium japonicum*) of the Gulf coast, with leaves of 23 ft.

Undivided The largest undivided leaf is that of *Alocasia macrorrhiza*, found in Sabah, Malaysia. A specimen found in 1966 was 9 ft 11 in long and 6 ft 3½ in wide, with a surface area of 34.12 ft^2.

Clovers A fourteen-leafed white clover (*Trifolium repens*) was found by Randy Farland near Sioux Falls, SD on 16 Jun 1975. A fourteen-leafed red clover (*T. pratense*) was reported by Paul Haizlip at Bellevue, WA on 22 Jun 1987.

SEEDS

Largest The largest seed in the world is that of the giant fan palm *Lodoicea maldivica (= L. callipyge, L. seychellarum)*, commonly known as the double coconut or coco de mer, found wild only in the Seychelles in the Indian Ocean. The single-seeded fruit of this plant may weigh 44 lb.

Smallest The smallest are those of epiphytic (nonparasitic plants growing on others) orchids, at 35 million seeds/oz (compare with grass pollens at up to 6 billion grains/oz).

Most durable The most plausible, though inconclusive claim for the longevity of seeds is that made for the Arctic lupine (*Lupinus arcticus*) found in frozen silt at Miller Creek, Yukon, Canada in July 1954 by Harold Schmidt. The seeds were germinated in 1966 and were radiocarbon dated to at least 8000 B.C. and more probably to 13,000 B.C.

GRASSES

Commonest The world's commonest grass is Bermuda grass (*Cynodon dactylon*), which is native to tropical Africa and the Indo-Malaysian region, but which extends from Lat. 45°N to 45°S. It is possibly the most troublesome weed of the grass family, affecting 40 crops in over 80 countries. The Callie hybrid, selected in 1966, grows as much as 6 in a day, and stolons reach 18 ft in length.

Tallest A thorny bamboo culm (*Bambusa arundiancea*) felled at Pattazhi, Travancore, India in November 1904 was 121½ tall.

Widest lawn mower The widest gang mower in the world is the 5-ton 60-ft-wide 27-unit "Big Green Machine" used by the turf farmer Jay Edgar Frick of Monroe, OH. It mows an acre in 60 sec.

Longest distance The longest drive on a power lawn mower was 3,034 miles, when Ian Ireland of Harlow, Great Britain drove an Iseki

SG15 between Harlow and Southend Pier, Great Britain from 13 Aug to 7 Sep 1989. He was assisted by members of 158 Round Table, Luton, Great Britain and raised over £15,000 ($26,250) to aid the Leukemia Research Fund.

WEEDS

Largest The largest weed is the giant hogweed (*Heracleum mantegazzianum*), originally from the Caucasus. It reaches 12 ft tall and has leaves 3 ft long.

Most damaging The most damaging and widespread weed is the purple nutsedge, nutgrass or nutsedge (*Cyperus rotundus*), a land weed native to India. It attacks 52 crops in 92 countries, including the United States, where it is primarily found in the southern states.

Tallest The tallest weed in the United States is the Melaleuca tree (*Melaleuca quinquenervia*), introduced to the Florida and Gulf coasts from Australia in 1900. Growing to an average of 39 ft, the weed has infested 3.7 million of the 4.7 million acres of Florida wetlands. Very dense and resistant to fire, it is a fire hazard in that it contains "essential" petroleums that spread fire quickly.

Most spreading The greatest area covered by a single clonal growth is that of the wild box huckleberry (*Gaylussacia brachycera*), a mat-forming evergreen shrub first reported in 1796. A colony covering about 100 acres was found on 18 Jul 1920 near the Juniata River, PA. It has been estimated that this colony began 13,000 years ago.

Aquatic weeds The worst aquatic weed of the tropics and subtropics is the water hyacinth (*Eichhornia crassipes*), which is a native of the Amazon basin but extends from Lat. 40°N to 45°S.

TREES

Earliest The earliest species of tree still surviving is the maiden-hair tree (*Ginkgo biloba*), of Zhesiang, China, which first appeared about 160 million years ago, during the Jurassic era. It has been grown since *c.* 1100 in Japan, where it was known as *ginkyō* ("silver apricot") and is now known as *icho*.

Oldest The *potential* life span of a bristlecone pine is estimated at nearly 5,500 years, and that of a giant sequoia (*Sequoiadendron giganteum*) at perhaps 6,000 years. No single cell lives more than 30 years. The oldest recorded tree was a bristlecone pine (*Pinus longaeva*) designated WPN-114, which grew at 10,750 ft above sea level on the northeast face of Mt Wheeler, NV. It was found to be 5,100 years old.

Most massive The most massive tree on earth is the biggest known giant sequoia (*Sequoiadendron giganteum*), a tree named General Sherman, standing 275 ft tall, in Sequoia National Park, CA. In 1991 it had a girth of 102.6 ft, measured 4½ ft above the ground. General Sherman has been estimated to contain the equivalent of 5 billion matches. The red-brown bark may be up to 24 in thick in parts.

OLDEST TREE!

The oldest known *living* tree is the bristlecone pine named Methuselah, growing at 10,000 ft on the California side of the White Mountains, confirmed as 4,700 years old. In 1974 this tree produced 48 live seedlings.

Greatest spread The tree canopy covering the greatest area is that of the great banyan (*Ficus benghalensis*) in the Indian Botanical Garden, Calcutta, with 1,775 prop or supporting roots and a circumference of 1,350 ft. It covers some 3 acres and dates from before 1787.

Greatest girth A circumference of 190 ft was recorded for the European chestnut (*Castanea sativa*) known as the "Tree of the Hundred Horses" (*Castagno di Cento Cavalli*) on Mt Etna, Sicily, Italy in 1770 and 1780. It is now in three parts, widely separated.

United States The giant sequoia named General Sherman in Sequoia National Park, CA has a girth of 83 ft 2 in.

Wood cutting The first recorded lumberjack sports competition was held in 1572 in the Basque region of Spain.

The following records were set at the Lumberjack World Championships at Hayward, WI (founded 1960):

Power saw (three slices of a 20-in-diameter white-pine log with a single-engine saw from a dead start)—8.03 sec by Rick Halvorson (USA) in 1993.

Bucking (one slice from a 20-in diameter white-pine log with a crosscut saw)—one-man, 17.14 sec by David Hocquard (New Zealand) in 1992; two-man, 6.77 sec by Gilles Levesques and Gaston Duperre (both Canada) in 1992.

Standing block chop (chopping through a vertical 14-in diameter white-pine log 30 in in length)—22.05 sec by Melvin Lentz (USA) in 1988.

Underhand block chop (chopping through a horizontal 14-in diameter white-pine log 30 in in length)—17.84 sec by Laurence O'Toole (Australia) in 1985.

Springboard chopping (scaling a 9 ft spar pole on springboards and chopping a 14-in diameter white-pine log)—1 min 18.45 sec by Bill Youd (Australia) in 1985.

Tree topping Guy German climbed a 100-ft spar and sawed off the top (circumference 40 in) in a record time of 53.35 sec at Albany, OR on 3 Jul 1989.

Tallest According to the researches of Dr A.C. Carder, the tallest tree ever measured was an Australian eucalyptus (*Eucalyptus regnans*) at Watts River, Victoria, Australia, reported in 1872 by forester William Ferguson. It was 435 ft tall and almost certainly measured over 500 ft originally.

Living The tallest tree currently standing is the "National Geographic Society" coast redwood (*Sequoia sempervirens*) in Humboldt Redwoods State Park, CA. Its revised height, following earlier miscalculations, was 365 ft in October 1991, according to Ron Hildebrant of California.

Christmas tree The world's tallest cut Christmas tree was a 221 ft Douglas fir (*Pseudotsuga menziesii*) erected at Northgate Shopping Center, Seattle, WA in December 1950.

Tree climbing The fastest time up a 100-ft tree trunk and back down to the ground is 24.82 sec, by Guy German of Sitka, AK on 3 Jul 1988 at the World Championship Timber Carnival in Albany, OR.

The fastest time up a 29-ft-6-in coconut tree barefoot is 4.88 sec, by Fuatai Solo, 17, in Sukuna Park, Fiji on 22 Aug 1980.

Fastest-growing Discounting bamboo, which is not classified as a tree but as a woody grass, the fastest rate of growth recorded is 35 ft 3 in in 13 months by an *Albizzia falcata* planted on 17 Jun 1974 in Sabah, Malaysia.

Slowest-growing Excluding *bonsai*, the 14th century Oriental art of cultivating miniature trees, the extreme in slow growth is represented by the *Dioon edule* (Cycadaceae), measured in Mexico between 1981 and 1986 by Dr Charles M. Peters, who found the average annual growth rate to be 0.03 in; a specimen 120 years old measured 4 in in height.

Remotest The tree believed to be the remotest from any other is a sole Norwegian spruce on Campbell Island, Antarctica. Its nearest companion would be over 120 nautical miles away on the Auckland Islands.

Tree sitting The duration record for staying in a tree is more than 23 years, by Bungkas, who went up a palm tree in the Indonesian village of Bengkes in 1970 and has been there ever since. He lives in a nest which he made from branches and leaves. Repeated efforts have been made to persuade him to come down, but without success.

Tree planting Three hundred schoolchildren and adults from Walsall, Great Britain, planted 1,774 trees in 17 hr 20 min (over six days) between 25 Nov and 5 Dec 1993.

Largest forest The largest forested areas in the world are the vast coniferous forests of northern Russia, lying between Lat. 55°N and the Arctic Circle. The total wooded area amounts to 2.7 billion acres (25 percent of the world's forests), of which 38 percent is Siberian larch. The former USSR is 34 percent forested. In comparison, the largest area of forest in the tropics remains the Amazon basin, amounting to some 815 million acres.

United States The largest forest in the United States is the Tongass National Forest (16.7 million acres), in Alaska. The United States is 32.25 percent forested.

Longest avenue The world's longest avenue of trees is the Nikko Cryptomeria Avenue, comprising three parts converging on Imaichi City in the Tochigi Prefecture of Japan and measuring a total of 22 miles. It was planted in the period 1628–48, and over 13,500 of its original 200,000 Japanese cedar (*Cryptomeria japonica*) trees survive, at an average height of 88½ ft.

MICROBES

Largest The largest protozoans in terms of volume that are known to have existed were calcareous foraminifera (Foraminiferida) belonging to the genus *Nummulites*, a species of which, in the Middle Eocene rocks of Turkey, attained 8½ in in diameter.

The largest existing protozoan, a species of the fan-shaped *Stannophyllum* (Xenophyophorida), can exceed this in length (9¾ in has been recorded) but not in volume.

Smallest protophytes The marine microflagellate alga *Micromonas pusilla* has a diameter of less than 0.00008 in.

Fastest The protozoan *Monas stigmatica* has been found to move a distance equivalent to 40 times its own length in a second. No human can cover even seven times his own length in a second.

Fastest reproduction The protozoan *Glaucoma*, which reproduces by binary fission, divides as frequently as every three hours. Thus in the course of a day it could become a great-great-great-great-great-grandparent and the progenitor of 256 descendants!

FUNGI

Largest The world's largest fungus is a single living clonal growth of the underground fungus *Armillaria ostoyae*, reported in May 1992 as covering some 1,500 acres in the forests of Washington State. Estimates based on its size suggest that the fungus is 500–1,000 years old, but no attempts have been made to estimate its weight. Also known as the honey or shoestring fungus, it fruits above ground as edible gilled mushrooms.

Largest edible A giant puffball (*Calvatia gigantea*) measuring 8 ft 8 in in circumference and weighing 48½ lb was found by Jean-Guy Richard of Montreal, Canada in 1987.

Largest tree fungus The largest recorded tree fungus is the bracket fungus *Rigidoporus ulmarius* growing from dead elm wood on the grounds of the

International Mycological Institute at Kew, Great Britain. It measured 59 × 56¾ in with a circumference of 14 ft 10¾ in.

United States In April 1992 Freda Kaplan of San Ramon, CA found a puffball (*Langermannia gigantea*) measuring 7 ft 3 in in circumference on the Wiedemann ranch in San Ramon.

Heaviest Another similar clonal growth, but of the fungus *Armillaria bulbosa*, reported on 2 Apr 1992 to be covering about 37 acres of forest in Michigan, was calculated to weigh over 110 tons, which is comparable with blue whales. The organism is thought to have originated from a single fertilized spore at least 1,500 years ago.

Heaviest edible An example of the edible chicken of the woods mushroom (*Laetiporus sulphureus*) weighing 100 lb was found in the New Forest, Great Britain by Giovanni Paba of Broadstone, Great Britain on 15 Oct 1990.

Most poisonous The yellowish-olive death cap (*Amanita phalloides*) is the world's most poisonous fungus and is responsible for 90 percent of fatal poisonings caused by fungi. The estimated lethal amount for humans, depending on body weight, is about 1¾ oz of a fresh fungus. From 6–15 hours after eating, the victim experiences vomiting and delirium, followed by collapse and death. Among its victims was Cardinal Giulio de' Medici, Pope Clement VII (b. 1478), on 25 Sep 1534.

Aeroflora The highest total fungal spore count was 5,686,861/ft³ near Cardiff, Great Britain on 21 Jul 1971. The lowest counts of airborne allergens are zero.

BACTERIA

Oldest Viable bacteria were reported in 1991 to have been recovered from sediments 3–4 million years old from the Sea of Japan.

Living In 1991 it was reported that live bacteria were found in the flesh of a mastodon (an ancestor of the elephant) from Ohio, which died 12,000 years earlier and which, on the evidence of spear marks found in the ribs, represented the first proof of humans killing a prehistoric animal. The bacteria gave the flesh "a bad smell" even after such a long time.

Largest The largest bacterium is *Epulopiscium fishelsoni*, which inhabits the intestinal tract of the brown surgeonfish (*Acanthurus nigrofuscus*) from the Red Sea and the Great Barrier Reef. Measuring 80 × 600 μm or more and therefore visible to the naked eye, this mega-microorganism, first discovered by Israeli researchers in 1985, is 1 million times larger than the human food poisoner *Escherichia coli*.

Smallest free-living entity The smallest of all free-living organisms are the pleuro-pneumonia-like organisms of the *Mycoplasma*. One of these, *Mycoplasma laidlawii*, first discovered in sewage in 1936, has a diameter during its early existence of only 0.0000001 m. Examples of the strain known as H.39 have a maximum diameter of 3 × 0.0000001 m and weigh an estimated 0.0000000000000001 g.

Highest In April 1967 the National Aeronautics and Space Administration (NASA) reported that bacteria had been discovered at an altitude of 25½ miles.

Fastest The rod-shaped bacillus *Bdellovibrio bacteriovorus*, using a polar flagellum rotating 100 times/sec, can move 50 times its own length of 2 micrometers per sec. This would be the equivalent of a human sprinter reaching 200 mph.

Toughest The bacterium *Micrococcus radiodurans* can withstand atomic radiation of 6.5 million röntgens, or 10,000 times the dose that would be fatal to the average person. In March 1983 John Barras (University of Oregon) reported bacteria from sulfurous seabed vents thriving at 583°F in the East Pacific Rise at Lat. 21°N.

ZOOS, AQUARIA & PARKS

ZOOS

It has been estimated that throughout the world there are some 757 zoos, with an estimated annual attendance of 350 million.

Oldest The earliest known collection of animals was the one set up by Shulgi, a third-dynasty ruler of Ur from 2097–2094 B.C., at Puzurish in southeast Iraq. The oldest known zoo is the one at Schönbrunn, Vienna, Austria, built in 1752 by the Holy Roman Emperor Franz I for his wife Maria Theresa.

The oldest existing public zoological collection in the world is the Zoological Society of London, Great Britain, founded in 1826. In January 1993 the collection comprised 18,128 specimens, housed in Regent's Park, London, Great Britain (36 acres) and at Whipsnade Park, Bedfordshire, Great Britain (541 acres; opened 23 May 1931).

United States The Philadelphia Zoo received its charter from the state of Pennsylvania in 1859, but did not open to the public until 1874. Lincoln Park Zoo, a 60-acre public park owned by the city of Chicago, received a gift of two swans from Central Park, New York City in 1868 to start its collection. By 1870 a "small barn and paddocks" had been built to house additional animals that had been donated by the public. The current facility covers 35 acres.

According to the American Association of Zoological Parks and Aquariums, the top zoo for attendance is Lincoln Park Zoo, with 4 million visitors each year.

AQUARIA

Largest In terms of the volume of water held, the Living Seas Aquarium, opened in 1986 at the EPCOT Center, FL is the world's largest, with a total capacity of 6.25 million gal. It contains over 3,000 fish representing 65 species.

The largest in terms of marine life is the Monterey Bay Aquarium in California. The aquarium was opened on 20 Oct 1984 at a cost of $55 million. It contains over 6,500 specimens (525 species) of fauna and flora in its 95 tanks. The volume of water held is 750,000 gal. The average annual attendance is 1.7 million visitors; however, in 1985 there were 2.3 million visitors, the highest for any aquarium in the United States.

PARKS

Largest The world's largest national park is the National Park of North-Eastern Greenland, covering 375,289 miles^2 and stretching from Liverpool Land in the south to the northernmost island, Odaaq Ø, off Pearyland. Established in 1974 and enlarged in 1988, much of the park is covered by ice and is home to a variety of protected flora and fauna, including polar bears, musk-ox and birds of prey.

United States The largest public park in the United States is Wrangell–St Elias National Park and Preserve in Alaska. Of the 13.2 million acres, the National Park section is 8.33 million acres and the Preserve comprises 4.88 million acres.

Largest game reserve The world's largest zoological reserve is the Etosha National Park, Namibia. Established in 1907, it now covers an area of 38,427 miles^2.

AGRICULTURE

FARMS

Largest The largest farms in the world were *kolkhozy*—collective farms in the former USSR. These were reduced in number from 235,500 in 1940 to 26,900 in 1988 and represented a total cultivated area of 417.6 million acres. Units of over 60,000 acres were not uncommon.

The pioneer farm owned by Laucidio Coelho near Campo Grande, Mato Grosso, Brazil *c.* 1901 covered 3,358 miles^2 and supported 250,000 head of cattle at the time of the owner's death in 1975.

Cattle ranch The world's largest cattle ranch is currently the 11,600 miles^2 Anna Creek ranch in South Australia, owned by the Kidman family. The biggest component is Strangway, at 5,500 miles^2.

Chicken farm The Agrigeneral Company L.P. in Ohio has 4.8 million hens laying some 3.7 million eggs daily.

NATIONAL PARKS

ELOISE AND CHARLES SHIELDS

Charles, age 76, and Eloise, age 75, have had a love affair with America's national parks for over 45 years. When the National Park Service introduced a parks passport in 1985, the Shieldses had the book stamped at every park they visited. In 1991 a new passport book was issued, and the Shieldses decided to visit as many national parks as possible. Why?

"We thought it would be fun to see all the parks, and this got us into new areas we never would have gone to, learning about heroes of our country, our heritage, wonderful scenery and exciting experiences we had never dreamed of before."

By 1992, when they had been using the new passport book for almost a year, park rangers and personnel began telling Charles and Eloise that they had never seen so many stamps on a passport. That's when they decided to see all the national parks, and they've been working on that goal for the last two years.

Eloise at San Juan Island National Historical Park, Washington.

Niagara Falls, New York (Images)

By the spring of 1994, the Shieldses had visited 351 parks or national monuments out of a possible 368. What keeps them going?

"Our main goal in doing this was to inspire others to visit parks and discover a whole new world of fun, entertainment and see the broad scope of our country's past and present. We hope that others will imitate us and discover for themselves the beauty and excitement of America's national parks."

Monument Valley, Utah/Arizona border (S. Llewellyn-Jones)

Ochopee Post Office, Florida-
smallest post office in the U.S.
Big Cypress National Reserve.

Grand Canyon, Arizona (Images)

Community garden The largest such project is the one operated by the City Beautiful Council and the Benjamin Wegerzyn Garden Center in Dayton, OH. It comprises 1,173 plots, each measuring 812 ft^2.

Hop farm The world's leading hop growers are John I. Haas Inc., with farms in Idaho, Oregon and Washington; Tasmania, Australia; and Kent, Great Britain, covering a total net area of 6,146 acres. The largest field covers 1,715 acres near Toppenish, WA.

Mushroom farm The world's largest mushroom farm is owned by Moonlight Mushrooms Inc. and was founded in 1937 in a disused limestone mine near Worthington, PA. The farm employs over 1,106 people who work in a maze of underground galleries 156 miles long, producing over 54,000,000 lbs of mushrooms per year.

Rice farm The largest wild rice (*Zizania aquatica*) farm in the world is that of Clearwater Rice Inc. in Clearbrook, MN, covering 2,000 acres. In 1986 it yielded 577,000 lb, the largest amount to date.

Sheep ranch The largest sheep ranch in the world is Commonwealth Hill, in the northwest of South Australia. It grazes between 50,000 and 70,000 sheep, along with 24,000 uninvited kangaroos, in an area of 4,080 $miles^2$ enclosed by 138 miles of dog-proof fencing. The head count on Sir William Stevenson's 40,970-acre Lochinver station in New Zealand was 127,406 on 1 Jan 1993.

The largest sheep move on record occurred when 27 horsemen moved a flock of 43,000 sheep 40 miles from Barcaldine to Beaconsfield station, Queensland, Australia in 1886.

Turkey farm The farms of Bernard Matthews plc in Norfolk, Great Britain, produce 10 million turkeys per year and employ a staff of 2,500. The largest farm, at North Pickenham, Great Britain, produces 1 million turkeys.

Combine harvesting Philip Baker of West End Farm, Merton, Great Britain harvested 182.5 tons of wheat in eight hours using a Massey Ferguson MF 38 combine on 8 Aug 1989. On 9 Aug 1990 an international team from CWS Agriculture, led by estate manager Ian Hanglin, harvested 394.73 tons of wheat in eight hours from 108.72 acres at Cockayne Hatley Estate, Sandy, Great Britain. The equipment consisted of a Claas Commandor 228 combine fitted with a Shelbourne Reynolds SR 6000 stripper head.

Bale rolling Michael Priestley and Marcus Stanley of Heckington Young Farmers Club rolled a 3-ft-11-in-wide cylindrical bale over a 164-ft course in 18.06 sec at the Lincolnshire Federation of Young Farmers' Clubs annual sports day at Sleaford, Great Britain on 25 Jun 1989.

Baling A rick of 40,400 bales of straw was built between 22 Jul and 3 Sep 1982 by Nick and Tom Parsons with a gang of eight at Cuckoo Pen Barn Farm, Birdlip, Great Britain. It measured 150 × 30 × 60 ft high and weighed some 784 tons. The team baled, hauled and ricked 24,200 bales in seven consecutive days from 22–29 July.

Svend Erik Klemmensen of Trustrup, Djursland, Denmark baled 220

The largest wild rice farm in the world, covering 2,000 acres, is in Clearwater, MN.

US CROP PRODUCERS

Crop	Leading State	Annual Production
Barley	North Dakota	117,600,000 bushels
Corn	Illinois	1,300,000,000 bushels
Cotton	Texas	5,148,00 bales
Oats	North Dakota	37,100,000 bushels
Peanuts	Georgia	1,360,000,000 lbs
Potatoes	Idaho	121,460,000 cwt
Rice	Arkansas	62,094,000 cwt
Sugar beets	Minnesota	5,344,000 tons
Tobacco	North Carolina	596,285,000 lbs
Wheat	Kansas	388,500,000 bushels

USDA/NASS Crop Production 1993 Summary

tons of straw in 9 hr 54 min using a Hesston 4800 baling machine on 30 Aug 1989.

Plowing The fastest recorded time for plowing an acre by the Society of Ploughmen (Great Britain) rules is 9 min 49.88 sec, by Joe Langcake at Hornby Hall Farm, Brougham, Great Britain on 21 Oct 1989. He used a case IH 7140 Magnum tractor and a Kverneland four-furrow plow.

The greatest area plowed with a six-furrow plow to a depth of 9 in in 24 hours is 173 acres. This was achieved by Richard Gaisford and Peter Gooding of Wiltshire Young Farmers, using a Case IH tractor and a Lemken plow, at Manor Farm, Pewsey, Great Britain on 25–26 Sep 1990.

Field to loaf The fastest time for producing 13 loaves of bread (a baker's dozen) from growing wheat is 12 min 11 sec, by representatives from the villages of Clapham and Patching in Great Britain on 23 Aug 1992. They used 13 microwaves to bake the loaves. Using a traditional baker's oven to bake the bread, the record time is 19 min 45 sec, by a team organized by John Haynes of millers Read Woodrow at Alpheton, Great Britain on 19 Sep 1992.

United States The fastest time for producing 13 loaves in the United States is 21 min 22 sec, by Wheat Montana at Three Forks, MT on 29 Aug 1991.

CATTLE

India was the world's leading cattle farming nation in 1993, with an estimated 271.3 million head from a worldwide total of 1.05 billion head. However, the leading producer of milk in 1993 was the United States, with 68.7 million metric tons. As of 1 Jan 1994 there were 101.7 million head of cattle farmed in the United States. The leading cattle producer was Texas, with 14.8 million head.

Largest The heaviest breed of cattle is the Chianini, which was brought to the Chiana Valley in Italy from the Middle East in pre-Roman times. Four types of the breed exist, the largest of which is the Val di Chianini, found on the plains and low hills of Arezzo and Sienna. Bulls average 5 ft 8 in at the forequarters and weigh 2,865 lb (compare with 1,873 lb for cows), but Chianini oxen have been known to attain heights of 6 ft 2¾ in. The sheer expense of feeding such huge cattle has put the breed under threat of extinction in Italy, but farmers in North America, Mexico and Brazil are still enthusiastic buyers of the breed.

The heaviest bovine on record was a Holstein–Durham cross named Mount Katahdin, exhibited by A.S. Rand of Maine from 1906–10, which frequently weighed in at an even 5,000 lb. He was 6 ft 2 in at the shoulder with a 13 ft girth, and died in a barn fire *c.* 1923.

Smallest The smallest breed of domestic cattle is the Ovambo of Namibia. Bulls and cows average 496 lb and 353 lb respectively.

Oldest Big Bertha, a Dremon owned by Jerome O'Leary of Blackwatersbridge, County Kerry, Republic of Ireland, died less than three months short of her 49th birthday, on 31 Dec 1993.

MOST EXPENSIVE LIVESTOCK

Species	Animal, Seller, Buyer, etc.	Price
Cattle	Joe's Pride (beefalo); D.C. Basalo, Burlingame, CA to Beefalo Cattle Co., Calgary, Canada, 9 Sep 1974	$2,500,000
Sheep	Collinsville stud JC&S 43; bought by Willogoleche Pty Ltd, 1989 Adelaide Ram Sales, South Australia	$358,750
Goat	Angora buck; Waitangi Angoras, New Zealand, to Elliott Brown Ltd, Waipu, New Zealand, 25 Jan 1985	$79,000
Pig	Bud (cross-bred barrow); Jeffrey Roemisch, Hermleigh, TX to E.A. Bud Olson and Phil Bonzio, 5 Mar 1983	$56,000
Horse	Farceur (Belgian stallion); bought by C.G. Good, Ogden, IA, 16 Oct 1917	$47,000

Reproductivity On 25 Apr 1964 it was reported that a cow named Lyubik had given birth to seven calves in Mogilev. A case of five live calves at one birth was reported in 1928 by T.G. Yarwood of Manchester, Great Britain. The lifetime breeding record is 39 in the case of Big Bertha. (See Oldest.)

Birth weights The heaviest recorded live birth weight for a calf is 225 lb for a British Friesian cow at Rockhouse Farm, Bishopston, Great Britain in 1961.

Lightest The lowest live birth weight accurately recorded for a calf is 12 lb for a healthy female born on 5 Mar 1992 on the farm of Pat and Eileen Dugan of Towner, ND. She was a crossbreed of a charlois heifer and a black angus bull.

Milk yields As of 1993, the world's leading producer of cow's milk was the United States, with 68.7 million metric tons. Wisconsin led the country, producing 10.9 million tons. The highest recorded world lifetime yield of milk for a single cow is 465,224 lb, by the unglamorously named cow No. 289 owned by M.G. Maciel & Son of Hanford, CA, to 1 May 1984.

The greatest recorded yield for one lactation (maximum 365 days) is 55,661 lb in 1975 by the Holstein Beecher Arlinda Ellen, owned by Mr and Mrs Harold L. Beecher of Rochester, IN. The highest reported milk yield in a day is 241 lb, by a cow named Urbe Blanca in Cuba on or about 23 Jun 1982.

Hand-milking of cows Joseph Love of Kilifi Plantations Ltd., Kenya milked 117 gal from 30 cows on 25 Aug 1992.

The United States record for hand-milking is 88.2 gal, by Andy Faust at Collinsville, OK in 1937 in 12 hours.

Butterfat yields The world record lifetime yield is 16,370 lb, by the Holstein Breezewood Patsy Bar Pontiac in 3,979 days.

The world record for 365 days is 3,126 lb, by Roybrook High Ellen, a Holstein owned by Yashuhiro Tanaka of Tottori, Japan.

Cheese The world's biggest producer of cheese is the United States, with an estimated total for 1993 of 6.5 billion lbs. Cheese consumption for 1993 in the United States was 6.7 billion lbs, an annual per-person cheese consumption of 26 lbs, or a half-pound of cheese per week.

Oldest The oldest cheeses are the Arabian *kishk*, made of the dried curd of goats' milk. Today there are 450 named cheeses in 18 major varieties, but many are merely named after different towns and differ only in shape or the method of packing. France has 240 varieties. The most avid cheese-eaters are the people of France, with an annual average of 43.6 lb per person.

GOATS

Largest The largest goat ever recorded was a British Saanen named Mostyn Moorcock, owned by Pat Robinson of Ewyas Harold, Great Britain, which reached a weight of 400 lb (shoulder height 44 in and overall length 66 in). He died in 1977 at the age of four.

Oldest The oldest goat on record was a Golden Guernsey-Anglo Nubian cross named Naturemade Aphrodite (1975–93), belonging to Katherine Whitwell of Moulton, Great Britain, which died on 23 Aug 1993 aged 18 years and 1 month. Aphrodite bred for ten consecutive years, during which time she reared 26 kids, including five sets of triplets and one set of quads.

Reproductivity According to the British Goat Society, at least one or two cases of quintuplets are recorded annually out of the 10,000 goats registered, but some breeders only record the females born.

On 14 Jan 1980 a nanny goat named Julie, owned by Galen Cowper of Nampah, ID, gave birth to septuplets, but they all died, including the mother.

Milk yields The highest recorded milk yield for any goat is 7,714 lb in 365 days by Osory Snow-Goose, owned by Mr and Mrs G. Jameson of Leppington, New South Wales, Australia, in 1977.

Cynthia-Jean (Baba), owned by Carolyn Freund-Nelson of Northport, NY, has lactated continuously since June 1980.

PIGS

The world's leading producer of hogs in 1993 was China, with 384.2 million head from a world total of 754.1 million. As of 1 Dec 1993 there were 56.7 million heads of hogs farmed in the United States. The leading state was Iowa with 14.6 million head.

Largest The heaviest pig ever recorded was a Poland–China hog named Big Bill, who was so obese that his belly dragged along the ground. Bill weighed an astonishing 2,552 lb just before he was put away after suffering a broken leg in an accident en route to the Chicago World's Fair for exhibition in 1933. Other statistics included a shoulder height of 5 ft and a length of 9 ft. At the request of his owner, W.J. Chappall, this prized possession was mounted and put on display in Weekly County, TN until 1946, when the exhibit was acquired by a traveling carnival. On the death of the carnival's proprietor his family reportedly donated Big Bill to a museum, but no trace has been found of him since.

Smallest The smallest breed of pig is the Mini Maialino, developed by Stefano Morini of St Golo d'Enza, Italy, after 10 years of experimentation with Vietnamese pot-bellied pigs. The piglets weigh 14 oz at birth and 20 lb at maturity.

Reproductivity The highest recorded number of piglets in one litter is 34, farrowed on 25–26 Jun 1961 by a sow owned by Aksel Egedee of Denmark. In February 1955 a Wessex sow belonging to E.C. Goodwin of Paul's Farm, Leigh, Great Britain also had a litter of 34, of which 30 were stillborn.

Birth weights The average birth weight for a piglet is 3 lb. A Hampshire–Yorkshire sow belonging to Rev. John Schroeder of Mountain Grove, MO farrowed a litter of 18 on 26 Aug 1979. Five were stillborn, including one male that weighed 5 lb 4 oz.

The highest recorded weight for a piglet at weaning (eight weeks) is 81 lb for a boar, one of a litter of nine farrowed on 6 Jul 1962 by the Landrace gilt Manorport Ballerina 53rd, alias "Mary," and sired by a Large White named Johnny at Kettle Lane Farm, West Ashton, Great Britain.

In November 1957 a total weight of 1,134 lb was reported at weaning for a litter of 18 piglets farrowed by an Essex sow owned by Mrs B. Ravel of Seaton House, Thorugumbald, Great Britain.

POULTRY

Figures for 1993 showed the United States to be the largest producer of chicken meat, or broiler, with a total of 15.02 million tons. The most produced by a state was 2.3 million tons, by Arkansas. The leading egg producer, however, is China, where an estimated 215 billion were laid in 1993. United States egg production in 1993 was 71.39 billion. The greatest state production was in California, with 6.5 billion eggs.

Chicken Largest The heaviest breed of chicken is the White Sully, developed by Grant Sullens of West Point, CA by crossing and recrossing large Rhode Island Reds with other varieties. The largest recorded chicken is Big Snow, a rooster weighing 23 lb 3 oz on 12 Jun 1992, with a chest girth of 2 ft 9 in and standing 1 ft 5 in at the shoulder. Owned and bred by Ronald Alldridge of Deuchar, Queensland, Australia, Big Snow died of natural causes on 6 Sep 1992.

Reproductivity The highest authenticated rate of egg-laying is by a White Leghorn, No. 2988, which laid 371 eggs in 364 days in an official test conducted by Prof. Harold V. Biellier ending on 29 Aug 1979 at the College of Agriculture, University of Missouri.

The highest recorded annual average per bird for a flock is 315 eggs in 52 weeks (August 1991–August 1992) from 5,997 free-range ISA Brown layers, owned by Vernon Weicle of Park Farm, Heol-y-Cyw, Penwed, Wales.

Largest egg The heaviest egg reported was one of 16 oz, with double yolk and double shell, laid by a White Leghorn at Vineland, NJ on 25 Feb 1956. The largest egg recorded was one of nearly 12 oz for a five-yolked egg measuring 12¼ in around the long axis and 9 in around the short, laid by a Black Minorca at Mr Stafford's Damsteads Farm, Mellor, Great Britain in 1896.

Most yolks The highest claim for the number of yolks in a hen's egg is nine, reported by Diane Hainsworth of Hainsworth Poultry Farms, Mount Morris, NY in July 1971, and also from a hen in Kyrgyzstan in August 1977.

Flying Sheena, a barnyard bantam owned by Bill and Bob Knox, flew 630 ft 2 in at Parkesburg, PA on 31 May 1985.

Chicken and turkey plucking Ernest Hausen (1877–1955) of Fort Atkinson, WI died undefeated after 33 years as champion chicken plucker. On 19 Jan 1939 he was timed at 4.4 sec.

Vincent Pilkington of Cootehill, County Cavan, Republic of Ireland killed and plucked 100 turkeys in 7 hr 32 min on 15 Dec 1978. His record for a single turkey is 1 min 30 sec in Dublin on 17 Nov 1980.

Egg shelling Two kitchen hands, Harold Witcomb and Gerald Harding, shelled 1,050 dozen eggs in a 7¼-hr shift at Bowyers, Great Britain on 23 Apr 1971. Both men were blind.

Egg dropping The greatest height from which fresh eggs have been dropped (to the ground) and remained intact is 650 ft, by David S. Donoghue from a helicopter on 2 Oct 1979 on a golf course in Tokyo, Japan.

Duck Reproductivity An Aylesbury duck belonging to Annette and Angela Butler of Princes Risborough, Great Britain laid 457 eggs in 463 days, including an unbroken run of 375 in as many days. The duck died on 7 Feb 1986. Another duck of the same breed, owned by Edmond Walsh of Gormanstown, Republic of Ireland, laid eggs every year right up to her 25th birthday. She died on 3 Dec 1978 at the age of 28 yr 6 months.

Goose egg The heaviest goose egg on record was one of 24 oz that measured 13½ in around the long axis and had a maximum circumference of 9½ in around the short axis. It was laid on 3 May 1977 by a white goose named Speckle, owned by Donny Brandenberg of Goshen, OH. The average weight is 10–12 oz.

Turkey The greatest dressed weight recorded for a turkey is 86 lb for a stag named Tyson reared by Philip Cook of Leacroft Turkeys Ltd, Peterborough, Great Britain. It won the annual "heaviest turkey" competition held in London, Great Britain on 12 Dec 1989 and was auctioned for charity for a record £4,400 ($7,480).

SHEEP

The world's leading producer of sheep is Australia, with a total of 147.1 million head in 1993. As of 1 Jan 1994 there were 9.8 million head of sheep farmed in the United States. The leading state was Texas, with 1.7 million head.

Largest The largest sheep ever recorded was a Suffolk ram named Stratford Whisper 23H, which weighed 545 lb and stood 43 in tall in March 1991. It is owned by Joseph and Susan Schallberger of Boring, OR.

Smallest The smallest breed of sheep is the Ouessant, from the Ile d'Ouessant, Brittany, France, at 29–35 lb in weight and standing 18–20 in at the withers. The species was saved from extinction by breeding programs.

Oldest A crossbred sheep owned by Griffiths & Davies of Dolclettwr Hall, Taliesin, Great Britain gave birth to a healthy lamb in the spring of 1988 at the grand old age of 28, after lambing successfully more than 40 times. She died on 24 Jan 1989 just one week before her 29th birthday.

Reproductivity The record for lambs at a single birth is eight (five rams and three ewes) on 4 Sep 1991 from a Finnish Landrace ewe owned by the D.M.C. Partnership of Feilding, Manawatu, New Zealand. On 2 Dec 1992 a Charolais ewe owned by Graham and Jo Partt of Wem, Great Britain also gave birth to eight lambs, seven of which survived.

Birth weights *Heaviest* The highest recorded birth weight for a lamb is 38 lb at Clearwater, Sedgwick County, KS in 1975, but neither lamb nor ewe survived. Another lamb of the same weight was born on 7 Apr 1975 on the Gerald Neises Farm, Howard, SD but died soon afterwards.

Lowest The lowest live birthweight recorded for a lamb is 1 lb 15¾ oz for a female Texel (one of twins) born on 28 Mar 1991 at the farm owned by Verner and Esther Jensen in Rødekro, Denmark. This record was equaled on 8 Jun 1991 by a badger-faced Welsh mountain lamb named Lyle (also a twin) at Thorpe Park, Great Britain.

The eight lambs of the world's largest litter at 12 weeks. (Ken Mihaere)

Sheep's survival On 24 Mar 1978 Alex Maclennan found one ewe still alive after he dug out 16 sheep buried in a snowdrift for 50 days near the River Skinsdale on Mrs Tyser's Gordonbush Estate in Sutherland, Great Britain. The sheep's hot breath creates airholes in the snow, and the animals gnaw their own wool for protein, enabling them to survive in a snowdrift for a considerable length of time.

Sheep to shoulder At the International Wool Secretariat Development Center, Ilkley, Great Britain, a team of eight using commercial machinery produced a sweater—from shearing sheep to the finished article—in 2 hr 28 min 32 sec on 3 Sep 1986.

Fine spinning The longest thread of wool, hand-spun and plied to weigh 0.35 oz, was one with a length of 1,815 ft 3 in, achieved by Julitha Barber of Bull Creek, Western Australia, at the International Highland Spin-In, Bothwell, Tasmania, Australia on 1 Mar 1989.

GUESS WHAT?

Q. WHAT WEIGHS FOUR TONS AND "BLANKETS" 20 FOOTBALL FIELDS?

A. CHECK "BIG DEALS" (HUMAN ACHIEVEMENTS).

Shearing The fastest speed for sheep shearing in a working day was that recorded by Alan McDonald, who machine-sheared 805 lambs in nine hours (an average of 40.2 seconds per lamb) at Waitnaguru, New Zealand on 20 Dec 1990. The hand-shearing record is 353 lambs in nine hours, by Peter Casserly of Christchurch, New Zealand on 13 Feb 1976.

Longest fleece A Merino wether found on K.P. & B.A. Reynolds Company's Willow Springs Station, South Australia in November 1990 produced 65 lb of wool from a fleece 25 in long, representing a 7-year growth.

FISHERIES

United Nations Food and Agricultural Organization figures for 1990 (the last year for which comparable data is available) showed the world's leading fishing nation to be China, with a total catch of 13.44 million tons, followed by the former USSR (11.63 million tons) and Japan (11.59 million tons). The United States was in fifth place with 6.57 million tons out of a worldwide total of 108.86 million tons, down from a worldwide 112 million tons in 1989.

The record value for a catch by a single trawler is $473,957, from a 41,776-ton catch by the Icelandic vessel *Videy* at Hull, Great Britain on 11 Aug 1987. The greatest catch ever recorded from a single throw is 2,724 tons, by the purse seine-net boat M/S *Flømann* from Hareide, Norway in the Barents Sea on 28 Aug 1986. It was estimated that more than 120 million fish were caught in this shoal.

EARTH & SPACE

THE UNIVERSE

A light-year is the distance traveled by light (at a speed of 186,282.397 miles/sec) in one tropical year (365.24219878 mean solar days at January 0.12 hours Ephemeris time in A.D. 1900). This is equivalent to 5,878,499,814,000 miles.

Largest structure in the Universe In November 1989 Margaret Geller and John Huchra (both USA) announced the discovery of a "Great Wall" in space, a concentration of galaxies in the form of a "crumpled membrane" with a minimum extent of 280 × 800 million light-years and a depth of up to 23 million light-years.

Galaxies Largest In July 1990 Juan M. Uson, Stephen P. Boughn and Jeffrey R. Kuhn (all USA) announced the discovery of the largest galaxy—the central galaxy of Abell 2029, 1,070 million light-years distant in the Virgo Cluster. The galaxy has a major diameter of 5.6 million light-years, which is 80 times the diameter of our own Milky Way galaxy, and has a light output equivalent to 2 trillion times that of the Sun.

Brightest The brightest galaxy (or galaxy in the process of forming) is IRAS F10214 + 4724, which was detected as a faint source by Infra Red Astronomy Satellite (IRAS) in 1983 but was shown in February 1991 to have a far-infrared luminosity 3×10^{14} times greater than that of the Sun. It has a red shift of 2.286, equivalent to a distance of 11.6 billion light-years, but the remotest galaxy is the radio source 4C 41.17, determined by K. Chambers, G. Miley and W. Van Bruegel in January 1990 to have a red shift of 3.800, equivalent to a distance of 12.8 billion light-years.

Age of the Universe It is impossible to be definite about the origin of the Universe. The most widely accepted theory in the scientific community is that the initial formation of the galaxies within the Universe took place only a million years after the Big Bang (14 ± 3 billion years ago).

Farthest visible object The remotest heavenly body visible to the naked eye is the Great Galaxy in Andromeda (mag. 3.47), known as Messier 31. It was first noted from Germany by Simon Marius (1570–1624). It is a rotating nebula in spiral form at a distance from the Earth of about 2,309,000 light-years, and our galaxy is moving towards it. It is just possible that under ideal conditions for observations, Messier 33, the Spiral in Triangulum (mag. 5.79), can be glimpsed by the naked eye at a distance of 2,509,000 light-years.

Remotest object The interpretation of the red shifts of quasars in terms of distance is limited by a lack of knowledge of the Universal constants. The record red shift is 4.897 for the quasar PC 1247 + 3406, announced in May 1991. If it is assumed that there is an "observable horizon," where the speed of recession is equal to the speed of light, then a simple interpretation would place this quasar at 13,200 million light-years distant.

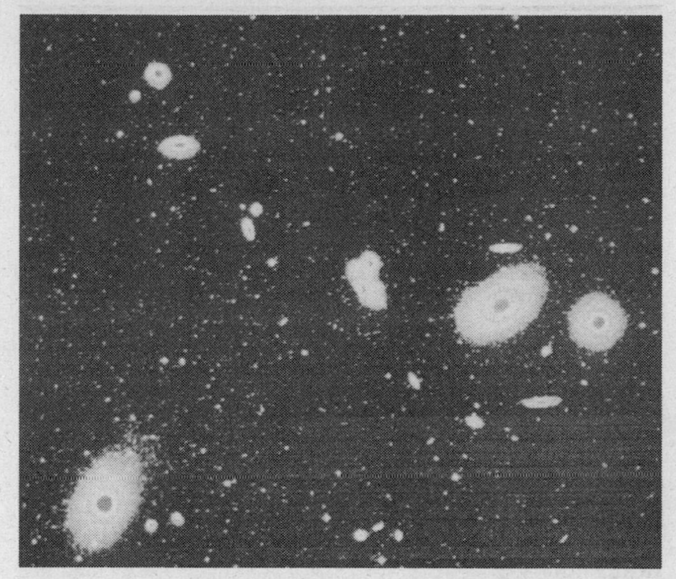

The Virgo Cluster is the nearest major cluster of galaxies to our own galaxy system and contains the universe's largest galaxy—Abell 2029. (Science Photo Library/Royal Observatory)

Quasars The discovery of the most luminous object in the sky, the quasar HS 1946 + 7658, which is at least 1.5×10^{15} times more luminous than the Sun, was announced in July 1991 following the Hamburg Survey of northern quasars. This quasar has a red shift of 3.02 and is therefore at a distance of 12,400 million light-years (7.3×10^{22} miles).

The most violent outburst observed in a quasar was recorded on 13 Nov 1989 by a joint US–Japanese team which noted that the energy output of the quasar PKS 0558-504 (which is about 2 billion light-years distant) increased by two-thirds in three minutes, equivalent to the total energy released by the Sun in 340,000 years.

STARS

Nearest The nearest star other than our own Sun is the very faint Proxima Centauri, discovered in 1915, which is 4.225 light-years (25 trillion miles) away.

The nearest star visible to the naked eye is the southern hemisphere binary Alpha Centauri, or Rigel Kentaurus (4.35 light-years distant), with an apparent magnitude of –0.29.

Largest The largest star is the M-class supergiant Betelgeuse (Alpha Orionis—the top left star of Orion), which is 310 light-years distant. It has a diameter of 400 million miles, which is about 500 times greater than that of the Sun. It is surrounded by a dust "shell" and also by an outer tenuous gas halo up to 530 billion miles in diameter.

Heaviest The heaviest star is the variable Eta Carinae, 9,100 light-years distant in the Carina Nebula, with a mass 200 times greater than that of our own Sun.

Most luminous If all the stars could be viewed at the same distance, Eta Carinae would also be the most luminous star, with a total luminosity 6,500,000 times that of the Sun. However, the *visually* brightest star viewed through a telescope is the hypergiant Cygnus OB2 No. 12, which is 5,900 light-years distant. It has an absolute visual magnitude of –9.9 and is therefore visually 810,000 times brighter than the Sun.

Smallest Neutron stars, which may weigh up to three times the mass of the Sun, have diameters of only 6–19 miles. Although black holes are pointlike sources, their distortion of local space–time means that they appear as black stars, with a diameter of 37 miles for one weighing 10 times the mass of the Sun.

GUESS WHAT?

Q. WHERE IS THE BEST VIEW OF THE STARS?

A. LOOK IN "TELESCOPES" (SCIENCE & TECHNOLOGY)

Lightest The white dwarf companion to the millisecond pulsar PSR 1957 + 20, the discovery of which was announced by A.S. Fruchter, D.R. Stinebring and J.H. Taylor in April 1988, has a mass only 0.02 that of the Sun and is being evaporated away by the fast-spinning neutron star.

Faintest GD 165B, the brown dwarf candidate companion to the white dwarf GD 165A, which is 117 light-years distant, is the faintest star. It has a luminosity ten thousand times less than that of the Sun and a visual brightness eight million times less. Its discovery was announced by E.E. Becklin and B. Zuckerman in September 1988.

Brightest (as seen from Earth) Sirius A (Alpha Canis Majoris), 8.64 light-years distant, is the brightest star in the sky, with an apparent magnitude of –1.46. It has a diameter of 1.45 million miles, a mass 2.14 times greater than that of the Sun, and is visually 24 times brighter.

Youngest The youngest stars appear to be two protostars known collectively as IRAS – 4 buried deep in dust clouds in the nebula NGC 1333, which is 1,100 light-years distant. Announced in May 1991 by a combined British, German and American team, these protostars will not blaze forth as full-fledged stars for at least another 100,000 years.

Oldest The oldest stars in the galaxy are located in the halo, high above the disc of the Milky Way. A group led by Timothy Beers (USA) discovered 70 of these stars by January 1991 but eventually expect to detect 500.

Longest name Torcularis Septentrionalis is the name applied to the star Omicron Piscium in the constellation Pisces.

Pulsars Slowest The pulsar that has the slowest spin-down rate, and is therefore the most accurate stellar clock, is PSR 1855 + 09 (discovered in December 1985) at only .0000000000000000021 revolutions per sec.

Fastest For pulsars whose spin rates have been accurately measured, the fastest-spinning is PSR 1937 + 214, which was discovered by a group led by Donald C. Backer in November 1982. It is in the minor constellation Vulpecula (the Little Fox), 16,000 light-years (9.4×10^{16} miles) distant, and has a pulse period of 1.5578064883 millisec, which is equivalent to a spin rate of 641.9282546 revolutions per sec.

Brightest supernova The brightest supernova ever seen is believed to be SN 1006, noted in April 1006 near Beta Lupi. It flared for two years and attained a magnitude of –9 to –10. The remnant is believed to be the radio source G.327.6 + 14.5, nearly 3,000 light-years distant. Others have oc-

An artist's impression of a binary star system consisting of a black hole and a normal orange-red star. The immense gravitational field of the black hole is sucking in the gas from the atmosphere of the normal star. (Science Photo Library/Dr Seth Shostak)

curred in 1054, 1604, 1885, and most recently on 23 Feb 1987. This last supernova was visible to the naked eye when at its brightest in May 1987.

Black holes The concept of superdense bodies was first proposed by the Marquis de Laplace (1749–1827). This term for a star that has undergone complete gravitational collapse was first used in 1967, and the first tentative identification of a black hole was announced in December 1972 in the binary-star X-ray source Cygnus X–1.

The best black hole candidate is the central star of the binary (or triple) star system V404, which is 5,000 light-years distant in the constellation Cygnus and which first showed a possible black hole signature, discovered by the Ginga satellite, in May 1989. In September 1991 its mass was firmly established as being greater than six times that of the Sun (and more likely eight to fifteen times).

Constellations The largest of the 88 constellations is Hydra (the Sea Serpent), which covers 1302.844 deg^2 or 3.16 percent of the whole sky and contains at least 68 stars visible to the naked eye (to 5.5 mag). The constellation Centaurus (Centaur), ranking ninth in area, however, embraces at least 94 such stars.

The smallest constellation is Crux Australis (Southern Cross), with an area of only 0.16 percent of the sky, or 68.477 deg^2 compared with the 41,252.96 deg^2 of the whole sky.

Zodiacal constellations The largest is Virgo with an area of 1,294.428 deg^2, and the smallest is Capricornus (Capricorn) with an area of 413.947 deg^2. Taurus is the zodiacal constellation with the most bright stars, with 125 down to magnitude 6.

THE SOLAR SYSTEM

Largest scale model The largest scale model of the solar system was developed by the Lakeview Museum of Arts and Sciences in Peoria, IL and inagurated in April 1992. See On the Record Feature (p. 126–127).

THE SUN

Distance extremes The true distance of the Earth from the Sun is 1.00000102 astronomical units or 92,955,902 miles. Our orbit being elliptical, the distance of the Sun varies between a minimum (perihelion) of 91,402,500 miles and a maximum (aphelion) of 94,509,300 miles. Based on an orbital circumference of 584,018,400 miles and an orbital period (sidereal year) of 365.256366 days, the average orbital velocity is 66,620 mph.

Temperature and dimensions The Sun is classified as a yellow dwarf type G2, although its mass at 2 octillion tons is 332,946.04 times that of the Earth and represents over 99 percent of the total mass of the solar system. The Sun's diameter is 865,040 miles and its density is 1.408 times that of water or a quarter that of the Earth.

The Sun has a central temperature of about 15,400,000 K (Kelvins) and a core pressure of 1.65 million tons/in^2. It uses up about 4.4 million tons of hydrogen per sec, although it will have taken 10 billion years to exhaust its energy supply (about 5 billion years from the present). The luminous intensity of the Sun is 2.7 octillion candela.

Sunspots To be visible to the *protected* naked eye, a sunspot must cover about 1/2,000th part of the Sun's disc and thus have an area of about 0.5 billion miles^2. The largest sunspot ever noted was in the Sun's southern hemisphere on 8 Apr 1947. Its area was about 7 billion miles^2 with an extreme longitude of 187,000 miles and an extreme latitude of 90,000 miles. Sunspots appear darker because they are more than 2,700°F cooler than the rest of the Sun's surface temperature of 9,945°F.

In October 1957 a smoothed sunspot count showed 263, the highest recorded index since records started in 1755. In 1943 one sunspot lasted for 200 days, from June to December.

PLANETS

Largest Jupiter, with an equatorial diameter of 88,846 miles and a polar diameter of 83,082 miles, is the largest of the nine major planets, with a mass 317.828 times, and a volume 1,323.3 times, that of the Earth. It also has the shortest period of rotation, resulting in a Jovian day of only 9 hr 50 min 30.003 sec in the equatorial zone.

Smallest and coldest The discovery of Pluto by Clyde William Tombaugh (USA) at the Lowell Observatory, Flagstaff, AZ was announced on 13 Mar 1930. The planet has a diameter of 1,417 miles. Although the surface temperature of Pluto is only approximately known, its surface composition suggests that it must be similar to the value of –391°F measured for Neptune's moon Triton, the lowest observed surface temperature of any natural body in the solar system.

Hottest For Venus a surface temperature of 864°F has been estimated from measurements made from the Russian *Venera* and US *Pioneer* surface probes.

Outermost The Pluto–Charon system orbits at a mean distance from the Sun of 3,674 million miles. However, this is less than the mean distance of the Kuiper Belt object 1992 QB_1—the discovery of which was announced by David Jewitt (Great Britain) and Jane Luu (USA) on 14 Sep 1992—which orbits at 4,074 million miles, although tentative evidence suggests that a second object, 1993 FW, discovered by Luu and Jewitt on 28 Mar 1993, may be even further out.

Nearest The fellow planet closest to the Earth is Venus, which is, at times, only 26 million miles inside the Earth's orbit, compared with Mars' closest approach of 35 million miles outside the Earth's orbit.

Fastest Mercury, which orbits the Sun at an average distance of 35,983,100 miles, has a period of revolution of 87.9686 days, thus giving the highest average speed in orbit of 107,030 mph.

Mars, located 1.2 miles from the museum. (Lakeview Museum, Peoria, IL)

THE SOLAR SYSTEM SCALE MODEL

Sheldon Schafer began his career in southern India, teaching science for the Peace Corps. He followed that up by working at a planetarium in Yonkers, New York, setting up scale models of the solar system in the hallways of elementary schools in the South Bronx. "We'd make the Sun the thumbnail on a kid standing at one end of the hall. Other kids would hold signs for the planets. It was 10 giant steps to Saturn, 40 to Pluto."

It was a great education for the kids, but it was frustrating for Schafer. "You can't represent both time and distance to scale without really making it a large scale." So he moved to Peoria, Illinois, a land with the space for a solar system spread over 60 miles of countryside—and into the universe beyond.

At the center of Schafer's universe is the Sun, painted on the 10-meter planetarium dome of the Lakeview Museum, where Schafer acts as deputy director. The planets are made of Plexiglas and were painted by Walter Kinsman, who used Voyager 2 photos as his guide. "He spent over a month with Jupiter in his living room," muses Schafer. Jupiter, the largest planet, is four feet in diameter in Schafer's solar system. Pluto is 40 miles from the Planetarium.

"I didn't set out to get into *The Guinness Book of Records*," says Schafer. "It's just icing on the cake." The Guinness cachet has helped Schafer convince scientists, students and other world travelers to transport models to new destinations. Comets from the Kuiper Belt and the Oort Cloud out beyond Pluto have been carried as far off as Japan and Antarctica. Beside each model stands a Plexiglas sign explaining that it's part of the world's largest scale model of the solar system. It would require out-of-this-world capabilities to beat this record!

Sheldon Schafer standing in Jupiter's orbit, 3.9 miles from the museum. (Lakeview Museum, Peoria, IL)

Highest surface feature By far the highest and most spectacular surface feature of any planet is Olympus Mons (formerly Nix Olympica) in the Tharsis region of Mars. It has a diameter of 310–370 miles and a height of 75,450–95,150 ft, making it more than 2½ times as tall as Mt Everest.

Brightest and faintest Viewed from the Earth, by far the brightest of the five planets visible to the naked eye is Venus, with a maximum magnitude of –4.4.

The faintest planet is Pluto, with a magnitude of 15.0.

Densest and least dense Earth is the densest planet, with an average density 5.515 times that of water, while Saturn has an average density only about one-eighth of this value or 0.685 times that of water.

Conjunctions The most dramatic recorded conjunction of the seven principal members of the solar system besides the Earth (Sun, Moon, Mercury, Venus, Mars, Jupiter and Saturn) occurred on 5 Feb 1962, when 16° covered all seven during an eclipse in the Pacific area. The next notable conjunction will take place on 5 May 2000.

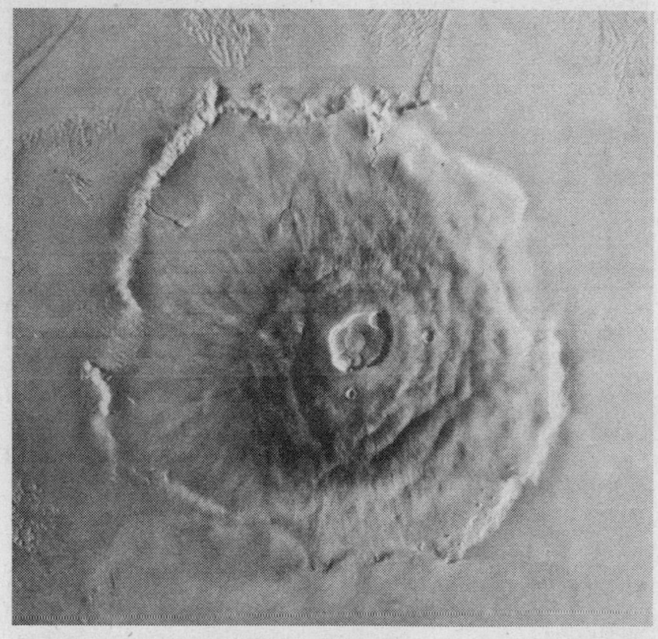

A computer-processed image of Olympus Mons, on Mars. The highest surface feature in the solar system, Mons' summit stands more than twice as high as Mount Everest. (Science Photo Library/US Geological Survey)

SATELLITES

Distance extremes The distance of satellites from their parent planets varies from the 5,827 miles of Phobos from the center of Mars to the 14,700,000 miles of Jupiter's outer satellite Sinope.

Largest The largest and heaviest satellite is Ganymede (Jupiter III), which is 2.017 times heavier than the Earth's Moon and has a diameter of 3,273 miles.

Smallest Of satellites whose diameters have been measured, the smallest is Deimos, the outermost moon of Mars. Although irregularly shaped, it has an average diameter of 7.8 miles.

Most and least The solar system has a total of 61 satellites, with Saturn having the most, 18, while Earth and Pluto only have one satellite each and Mercury and Venus have none.

The most recently discovered satellite, announced on 16 Jul 1990 by Mark R. Showalter (USA), is the Saturnian satellite Pan, which was found on *Voyager 2* photographs taken during the close approach in August 1981. It has a diameter of only about 12 miles and orbits within the 200-mile Encke gap in the A ring.

ASTEROIDS

Number and distance extremes There are estimated to be about 45,000 asteroids, but the orbits of only about 6,100 have been accurately computed. While most orbit between Mars and Jupiter, distances from the Sun vary between 12,980,000 miles for the Apollo asteroid 3200 Phaethon (discovered 11 Oct 1993) at perihelion and 4,431 million miles for the Kuiper Belt object 1992 QB_2 at aphelion. The closest known approach to the Earth by an asteroid was to within 93,000 miles on 20 May 1993 by $1993KA_2$, just a few hours before its discovery.

Largest and smallest The largest and first discovered (by G. Piazzi in Palermo, Sicily on 1 Jan 1801) is 1 Ceres, with an equatorial diameter of 596 miles. The smallest asteroid is $1993KA_2$, with a diameter of 16 ft.

Brightest The brightest asteroid is 4 Vesta (discovered on 29 Mar 1807) with an absolute magnitude of 3.16.

Faintest The faintest asteroid is 1993 KB_2, whose absolute magnitude of 29 makes it the faintest object ever detected.

THE MOON

The Earth's closest neighbor in space and its only natural satellite is the Moon, which has an average diameter of 2,159.3 miles and a mass of 8.1 $\times 10^{19}$ tons, or 0.0123 that of the Earth, so its density is 3.344 times that of water.

The Moon orbits at a mean distance from the Earth of 238,854.5 miles center-to-center. In the present century the closest approach (smallest perigee) was 221,441 miles center-to-center on 4 Jan 1912 and the farthest distance (largest apogee) was 252,718 miles on 2 Mar 1984. The orbital pe-

THE ASTEROID THAT CAME TOO CLOSE TO THE EARTH

An asteroid estimated to have been 16 ft in diameter passed within 93,000 miles of the Earth on 20 May 1993. We were not in any great danger as a result, but it was the closest observed natural object outside the atmosphere.

The asteroid, designated 1993 KA2, was discovered on 21 May 1993 by Tom Gehrels of the University of Arizona using the Spacewatch telescope. He followed it for more than five hours that night and observed it again the following night. From the data that he obtained, Brian Marsden of the Harvard–Smithsonian Center for Astrophysics calculated the orbit of 1993 KA2 and the circumstances of the close approach to the Earth the previous day. The object had come from the direction of the Sun, and at its closest to the Earth was above the southern North Atlantic Ocean. When it was discovered, 1993 KA2 was more than 430,000 miles away, receding and fading rapidly.

Many thousands of asteroids have well-determined orbits. Most orbit the Sun in the so-called asteroid belt between the orbits of Mars and Jupiter. However, many orbit outside this region, and some, like 1993 KA2, are known to come into the neighborhood of the Earth. The current location of 1993 KA2 is very uncertain and it must be considered lost.

What would it be like if a huge asteroid were to strike the Earth? This artist's impression shows what might happen if an asteroid c. 500 miles in diameter were to do so. Fortunately, however, such an event is very unlikely, and so it remains in the imagination of artists and science fiction writers. (Science Photo Library/NASA)

riod (sidereal month) is 27.321661 days, giving an average orbital velocity of 2,289 mph.

Craters Only 59 percent of the Moon's surface is directly visible from the Earth because it is in "captured rotation," i.e., the period of rotation is equal to the period of orbit. The largest wholly visible crater is the walled plain Baily, towards the Moon's South Pole, which is 183 miles across, with walls rising to 14,000 ft. The Orientale Basin, partly on the averted side, measures more than 600 miles in diameter.

The deepest crater is the Newton Crater, with a floor estimated to be between 23,000 and 29,000 ft below its rim and 14,000 ft below the level of the plain outside.

Highest mountains In the absence of a sea level, lunar altitudes are measured relative to an adopted reference sphere with a radius of 1,080 miles. The greatest elevation attained on this basis by any of the 12 US astronauts who have landed on the moon has been 25,688 ft on the Descartes Highlands by Capt. John Watts Young (USN) and Major Charles M. Duke, Jr. (USAF) on 27 Apr 1972.

Temperature extremes When the Sun is overhead the temperature on the lunar equator reaches 243°F (31°F above the boiling point of water). By sunset the temperature is 58°F, but after nightfall it sinks to –261°F.

ECLIPSES

Earliest recorded There appears to be no real evidence for ancient descriptions of eclipses prior to the partial eclipse observed in Nineveh in Assyria on 15 Jun 763 B.C. The first definite evidence for a total eclipse comes from Chu-fu, China, observed on 17 Jul 709 B.C.

Longest duration The maximum duration of an eclipse of the Sun is 7 min 31 sec. The longest of recent date was on 20 Jun 1955 (7 min 8 sec), west of the Philippines, although it was clouded out along most of its track.

Eclipse durations can be artificially "extended" when observers are airborne. The totality of the Sun was "extended" to 74 min for observers aboard a Concorde that took off from Toulouse, France and stayed in the Moon's shadow from 10:51 to 12:05 GMT on 30 Jun 1973 over the Atlantic before landing in Chad.

Most and least frequent The highest number of eclipses possible in a year is seven, as in 1935, when there were five solar and two lunar eclipses. In 1982 there were four solar and three lunar eclipses.

The lowest possible number in a year is two, both of which must be solar, as in 1944 and 1969.

The only recent example of three total solar eclipses occurring at a single location was at a point 44°N, 67°E in Kazakhstan, east of the Aral Sea. These took place on 21 Sep 1941, 9 Jul 1945 and 25 Feb 1952.

COMETS

Brightest The brightest comets are held to be either the Curls Comet of 1862 or the Ikeya-Seki Comet of 1965.

Periodical The brightest periodical comet is Halley's Comet, with a period of 76 years, its successive appearances having been traced back to 467 B.C. It was first depicted in the Nuremburg Chronicle of A.D. 684 and attracts great interest with each appearance.

Largest The tail of the brilliant Great Comet of 1843 trailed for 205 million miles. The bow shock wave of Holmes Comet of 1892 once measured 1.5 million miles in diameter.

Shortest period The periodic comet that returns most frequently is the increasingly faint Encke's Comet, first identified in 1786. It has an orbital period of 1,206 days (3.3 years) and has the closest approach to the Sun, at 32 million miles at perihelion, when its speed is 155,000 mph.

The most frequently observed comets are Schwassmann-Wachmann I, Kopff and Oterma, which can all be observed every year between Mars and Jupiter.

Longest period The longest period determined for a comet is 958 years, in the case of Comet 1894 Gale, equivalent to a mean distance of 9 billion miles.

Closest approach to Earth On 1 Jul 1770, Lexell's Comet, traveling at a speed of 86,100 mph (relative to the Sun), came within 745,000 miles of the Earth. The Earth is believed to have passed through the tail of Halley's Comet on 19 May 1910.

METEORITES

When a *meteoroid* (consisting of broken fragments of cometary or asteroidal origin and ranging in size from fine dust to bodies several miles in diameter) falls to the Earth's surface, the remnant, which may be either aerolite (stony) or siderite (metallic), is described as a *meteorite*. Such events occur about 150 times per year over the whole land surface of the Earth.

Oldest A revision in 1981 of the age estimates of meteorites suggests that the oldest accurately dated is the Krähenberg meteorite at 4,600 ± 20 million years, which is just within the initial period of solar system formation.

INJURED!

The only person injured by a meteorite in the United States was Mrs Ann Hodges of Sylacauga, AL. On 30 Nov 1954 a 9-lb stone, some 7 in in length, crashed through the roof of her home, hitting Mrs Hodges on the arm and bruising her hip. The physician who examined her, Dr Moody D. Jacobs, declared her fit but she was subsequently hospitalized as a result of the publicity.

The *Cape York* meteorite, which is the largest meteorite exhibited by any museum. (American Museum of Natural History)

Largest The largest known meteorite was found in 1920 at Hoba West, near Grootfontein in Namibia, and is a block 9 ft long by 8 ft wide, estimated to weigh 65 tons. The largest meteorite exhibited by any museum is the "Cape York" meteorite, weighing 68,085 lb, found in 1897 near Cape York, on the west coast of Greenland, by the expedition of Commander Robert Edwin Peary (USA; 1856–1920). It was known to the Inuits as the Abnighito and is now exhibited in the Hayden Planetarium in New York City. The largest piece of stony meteorite recovered is a piece weighing 3,902 lb, part of a 4.4-ton shower that struck Jilin, China on 8 Mar 1976.

Greatest explosion There was a mysterious explosion of 10–15 megatons in the basin of the Podkamennaya Tunguska River, 40 miles north of Vanavar, in Siberia, Russia, on 30 Jun 1908. The explosion devastated an area of 1,500 miles^2 and the shock was felt as far away as 625 miles. The cause has most recently been attributed to the energy released following a total disintegration at an altitude of 33,000 ft of a 98-ft-diameter common type stony asteroid traveling at hypersonic velocity at an incoming angle of 45 degrees.

Lunar Twelve known meteorites are believed to be of lunar origin, as distinguished by characteristic element and isotopic ratios. The first 11 were found in Antarctica but the most recently discovered, which has only a 1 in diameter and weighs 0.67 oz, was found at Calcalong Creek on the Nullarbor Plain to the north of the Great Australian Bight in January 1991. The name "Calcalong" is a corruption of the Aboriginal word meaning "seven sisters went up to the sky, chased by the Moon."

Craters It has been estimated that some 2,000 asteroid–Earth collisions have occurred in the last 600 million years. One hundred and two collision sites or astroblemes have been identified.

In 1962, a crater 150 miles in diameter and 1/2 mile deep in Wilkes Land, Antarctica was attributed to a meteorite. Such a crater could have been caused by a meteorite weighing 14,329,900,000 tons striking at 44,000 mph.

There is a craterlike formation or astrobleme 275 miles in diameter on the eastern shore of Hudson Bay, Canada.

The largest and best-preserved crater that was definitely formed by an asteroid is the Coon Butte or Barringer Crater, discovered in 1891 near Canyon Diablo, Winslow, AZ. It is 4,150 ft in diameter and now about 575 ft deep, with a parapet rising 130–155 ft above the surrounding plain. It has been estimated that an iron–nickel mass of some 2.2 million tons and a diameter of 200–260 ft gouged this crater in *c.* 25,000 B.C.

Tektites The largest tektite of which details have been published weighed 7 lb and was found in 1932 at Muong Nong, Saravane Province, Laos. It is now in the Louvre Museum, Paris, France.

Fireball The brightest fireball ever photographically recorded was by Dr Zdenek Ceplecha over Sumava, Czechoslovakia (now Czech Republic) on 4 Dec 1974; it had a momentary magnitude of –22 or 10,000 times brighter than a full Moon.

Meteor shower The greatest shower on record occurred on the night of 16–17 Nov 1966, when the Leonid meteors (which recur every 33 1/4 years) were visible between western North America and eastern Russia. It was calculated that meteors passed over Arizona at a rate of 2,300 per min for a period of 20 min from 5 A.M. on 17 Nov 1966.

THE EARTH

The Earth is approximately 4,540 million years old. It is not a true sphere, but is flattened at the poles and hence an oblate spheroid. The area of the surface is estimated to be 196,937,400 miles^2 and the volume about 259,875,300,000 miles^3.

The mass of the Earth is 6.6 sextillion tons and the density is 5.515 times that of water. The Earth picks up cosmic dust, but estimates of the amount vary widely, with 33,000 tons a year being the upper limit. The period of axial rotation, i.e., the true sidereal day, is 23 hr 56 min 4.0989 sec, mean time.

Largest diameter The equatorial diameter (7,926.3803 miles) is 26.5757 miles larger than the polar diameter of 7,899.8046 miles. The Earth has a pear-shaped asymmetry, with the north polar radius being 148 ft longer than the south polar radius. There is also a slight ellipticity of the equator, since its major diameter at longitude 14.96°W is 456 ft longer than its minor axis. The greatest departures from the reference ellipsoid are a protuberance of 240 ft in the area of Papua New Guinea and a depression of 344 ft south of Sri Lanka, in the Indian Ocean.

Greatest circumference The greatest circumference of the Earth, at the equator, is 24,901.458 miles, compared with 24,859.731 miles at the meridian.

FEATURES & THEIR DIMENSIONS

OCEANS

The area of the Earth covered by oceans and seas (the hydrosphere) is estimated to be 139,782,000 miles^2 or 70.98 percent of the total surface. The mean depth of the hydrosphere is 12,234 ft and the volume 323,870,000 miles^3, compared to 8.4 million miles^3 of fresh water. The total weight of the water is estimated to be 1.41 quintillion tons, or 0.024 percent of the Earth's total weight.

Largest The largest ocean in the world is the Pacific. Excluding adjacent seas, it represents 45.9 percent of the world's oceans and covers 64,186,300 miles^2 in area. The average depth is 12,925 ft.

Shortest distance The shortest navigable transpacific distance, from Guayaquil, Ecuador to Bangkok, Thailand, is 10,905 miles.

Deepest The deepest part of the ocean was first pinpointed in 1951 by the British Survey Ship *Challenger* in the Mariana Trench in the Pacific Ocean. On 23 Jan 1960 the US Navy bathyscaphe *Trieste* descended to the bottom at 35,813 ft. A more recent visit produced a figure of 35,839 ft ± 33 ft, from data obtained by the survey vessel *Takuyo* of the Hydrographic Department, Japan Maritime Safety Agency in 1984, using a narrow multibeam echo sounder.

A one-kilogram (2.2 lb) ball of steel dropped into water above the Mariana Trench would take nearly 64 min to fall to the seabed, where hydrostatic pressure is over 18,000 lb/in^2.

United States Defining US waters as within 200 nautical miles of any US territory (Economic Exclusive Zone [EEZ]), the deepest point in American waters is Challenger D in the Mariana Trench in the Pacific Ocean. Challenger D is 5,973 fathoms (35,838 ft) deep, 170 nautical miles SW of Guam at 11°22.4′N, 142°35.5′E.

Smallest The smallest ocean in the world is the Arctic Ocean, which measures 5,105,700 miles^2. Its average depth is 3,407 ft.

Largest sea The largest of the world's seas is the South China Sea, with an area of 1,148,500 miles^2.

Remotest spot from land The world's most distant point from land is a spot in the South Pacific, approximately 48°30′S, 125°30′W, which is about 1,660 miles from the nearest points of land, namely Pitcairn Island, Ducie Island

and Cape Dart, Antarctica. Centered on this spot is a circle of water with an area of about 8,657,000 miles^2—about 2 million miles^2 larger than Russia, the world's largest country.

Largest bay The largest bay in the world measured by shoreline length is Hudson Bay, Canada, with a shoreline of 7,623 miles and an area of 476,000 miles^2. Measured by area, the Bay of Bengal, in the Indian Ocean, is larger, at 839,000 miles^2.

Largest gulf The largest gulf in the world is the Gulf of Mexico, with an area of 596,000 miles^2 and a shoreline of 3,100 miles from Cape Sable, FL, to Cabo Catoche, Mexico.

Longest fjord The world's longest fjord is the Nordvest Fjord arm of the Scoresby Sound in eastern Greenland, which extends inland 195 miles from the sea.

Highest seamount The highest known submarine mountain, or seamount, is one discovered in 1953 near the Tonga Trench, between Samoa and New Zealand in the South Pacific. It rises 28,500 ft from the seabed, with its summit 1,200 ft below the surface.

Most southerly The most southerly part of the oceans is located at 85°34′S, 154°W, at the snout of the Robert Scott Glacier, 305 miles from the South Pole.

Sea temperature The temperature of water at the surface of the Earth's seas varies greatly. It is as low as 28°F in the White Sea and as high as 96°F in the shallow areas of the Persian Gulf in summer.

The highest temperature recorded in the ocean is 759°F, for a hot spring measured by an American research submarine some 300 miles off the west coast of the United States in 1985.

Clearest The Weddell Sea, 71°S, 15°W off Antarctica, has the clearest water of any sea. A Secchi Disk 1 ft in diameter was visible to a depth of 262 ft on 13 Oct 1986, as measured by Dutch researchers at the German Alfred Wegener Institute. Such clarity corresponds to what is attainable in distilled water.

STRAITS

Longest The longest straits in the world are the Tatarskiy Proliv or Tartar Straits between Sakhalin Island and the Russian mainland, running from the Sea of Japan to Sakhalinsky Zaliv—500 miles, thus marginally longer than the Malacca Straits, between Malaysia and Sumatra.

Broadest The broadest *named* straits in the world are the Davis Straits between Greenland and Baffin Island, Canada, with a minimum width of 210 miles. The Drake Passage, a deep waterway between the Diego Ramirez Islands, Chile and the South Shetland Islands, is 710 miles across.

Narrowest The narrowest navigable straits are those between the Aegean island of Euboea and the mainland of Greece. The gap is only 135 ft wide at Khalkis.

WAVES

Highest The highest officially recorded sea wave was calculated at 112 ft from trough to crest; it was measured by Lt Frederic Margraff (USN) from the USS *Ramapo* proceeding from Manila, Philippines to San Diego, CA on the night of 6–7 Feb 1933, during a 68-knot hurricane. The highest instrumentally measured wave was one 86 ft high, recorded by the British ship *Weather Reporter*, in the North Atlantic on 30 Dec 1972 at Lat. 59°N, Long. 19°W.

On 9 Jul 1958 a landslip caused a 100 mph wave to wash 1,720 ft high along the fjord-like Lituya Bay in Alaska.

CURRENTS

Greatest The greatest current in the oceans is the Antarctic Circumpolar Current or West Wind Drift Current. On the basis of four measurements taken in 1982 in the Drake Passage, between Chile and Antarctica, it was found to be flowing at a rate of 4.3 billion ft^3 per sec. Results from computer modeling in 1990 estimate a higher figure of 6.9 billion ft^3 per sec.

Strongest The world's strongest currents are the Nakwakto Rapids, Slings-by Channel, British Columbia, Canada (Lat. 51°05′N, Long. 127°30′W), where the flow rate may reach 16 knots.

United States The strongest current in the United States occurs on the coast of Alaska in Chatham Strait, Pt. Kootzhahoo at Pt. Bridge. The current ebbs at 7 knots. The strongest current on the east coast of the United States is at St Johns River in Pablo Creek, FL. The current ebbs at 5.2 knots.

TIDES

Greatest The greatest tides occur in the Bay of Fundy, which divides the peninsula of Nova Scotia, Canada from Maine and the Canadian province of New Brunswick.

Burncoat Head in the Minas Basin, Nova Scotia, has the greatest mean spring range, with 47 ft 6 in. A range of 54 ft 6 in was recorded at springs in Leaf Basin, in Ungava Bay, Quebec, Canada in 1953.

Least Tahiti, in the mid-Pacific Ocean, experiences virtually no tide.

Highest and lowest The highest and lowest tide in the United States is at Sunrise, AK on Turnagain Arm islet. Its range is 33.3 ft.

ICEBERGS

Largest The largest iceberg on record was an antarctic tabular iceberg of over 12,000 $miles^2$, 208 miles long and 60 miles wide, sighted 150 miles west of Scott Island, in the South Pacific Ocean, by the USS *Glacier* on 12 Nov 1956. The 200 ft thick arctic ice island T.1 (140 $miles^2$), discovered in 1946, was tracked for 17 years until it broke up in 1963.

Tallest The tallest iceberg measured was one of 550 ft reported off western Greenland by the US icebreaker *East Wind* in 1958.

DID YOU KNOW?

The highest tsunami was triggered by an underwater landslide that struck the island of Lanai in Hawaii *c.* 105,000 years ago and deposited sediment up to an altitude of approximately 1,230 ft. The highest known in modern times appeared off Ishigaki Island, Ryukyu Chain on 24 Apr 1771. It tossed an 830-ton block of coral more than 1.3 miles.

The worst tsunami in the United States occurred on 8 Sep 1900 in Galveston, TX, killing over 5,000 people.

Most southerly arctic The most southerly arctic iceberg was sighted in the Atlantic by a USN weather patrol at Lat. 28°44′N (approximately the same latitude as Miami, FL), Long. 48°42′W, in April 1935.

Most northerly antarctic The most northerly antarctic iceberg was a remnant sighted in the Atlantic by the ship *Dochra* at Lat. 26°30′S (approximately the same latitude as Rio de Janeiro, Brazil), Long. 25°40′W, on 30 Apr 1894.

LAND

There is strong evidence that about 300 million years ago the Earth's land surface comprised a single primeval continent of 60 million miles², now termed Pangaea, and even before its existence it is possible that there had been other supercontinents. Pangaea is believed to have split about 190 million years ago, during the Jurassic period, into two supercontinents, which are called Laurasia (Eurasia, Greenland and North America) and Gondwana (Africa, Arabia, India, South America, Oceania and Antarctica).

On 1 Feb 1994 the National Oceanic and Atmospheric Administration (NOAA) reported that the total land area of the United States is 3,018,698 miles².

Largest state The largest state in land area is Alaska, with 591,004 miles². The largest in the 48 coterminous states is Texas, with 267,017 miles² of land.

Smallest state The smallest state is Rhode Island, with 1,212 miles².

Longest coastline The state with the longest coastline is Alaska; it measures 33,904 miles.

Land furthest from the sea The point of land furthest from the sea is at Lat. 46°16.8′N, Long. 86°40.2′E in the Dzungarian Basin, which is in the Xinjiang Uighur Autonomous Region (Xinjiang Uygur Zu zhi ju), China's most northwesterly province. It is at a straight-line distance of 1,645 miles from the nearest open sea—Baydaratskaya Guba to the north (Arctic

Ocean), Feni Point to the south (Indian Ocean) and Bo Haiwan to the east (Yellow Sea).

CONTINENTS

Largest Of the Earth's surface, 41.25 percent, or 81.2 million miles^2, is covered by continental masses, of which only about 57,151,000 miles^2 (about two-thirds, or 29.02 percent of the Earth's surface) is land above water, with a mean height of 2,480 ft above sea level. The Eurasian landmass is the largest, with an area (including islands) of 20.7 million miles^2. The Afro-Eurasian landmass, separated artificially only by the Suez Canal, covers an area of 32.7 million miles^2 or 57.2 percent of the Earth's landmass.

Smallest The smallest continent is the Australian mainland, with an area of 2,941,526 miles^2, which, together with Tasmania, New Zealand, Papua New Guinea and the Pacific Islands, is described as Oceania.

PENINSULAS

Largest The world's largest peninsula is Arabia, with an area of about 1.25 million miles^2.

United States The Alaskan peninsula is the longest in the United States, with a length of 471 miles. The longest in the coterminous 48 states is the Florida peninsula, at 383 miles.

ISLANDS

Largest Discounting Australia, which is usually regarded as a continental landmass, the largest island in the world is Greenland, with an area of about 840,000 miles^2.

The largest sand island in the world is Fraser Island, Queensland, Australia with a sand dune 75 miles long.

Freshwater The largest island surrounded mostly by fresh water (18,500 miles^2) is the Ilha de Marajó in the mouth of the River Amazon, Brazil.

The world's largest inland island (i.e., land surrounded by rivers) is Ilha do Bananal, Brazil (7,700 miles^2). The largest island in a lake is Manitoulin Island (1,068 miles^2) in the Canadian section of Lake Huron.

Remotest The remotest island in the world is Bouvet Island (Bouvetøya), discovered in the South Atlantic by J. B. C. Bouvet de Lozier on 1 Jan 1739. Its position is 54°26′S, 3°24′E. This uninhabited Norwegian dependency is about 1,050 miles from the nearest land—the uninhabited Queen Maud Land in Antarctica.

The remotest inhabited island in the world is Tristan da Cunha, discovered in the South Atlantic by Tristão da Cunha, a Portuguese admiral, in March 1506. It has an area of 38 miles^2. After evacuation in 1961 (due to volcanic activity), 198 islanders returned in November 1963. The nearest inhabited land to the group is the island of St Helena, 1,315 nautical miles to the northeast.

Southernmost land The South Pole, unlike the North Pole, is on land. The Amundsen–Scott South Polar station was built there at an altitude of 9,370 ft in 1957. The station is drifting bodily with the ice cap 27–30 ft per year in the direction 43°W and was replaced by a new structure in 1975.

Northernmost land On 26 Jul 1978 Uffe Petersen of the Danish Geodetic Institute observed the islet of Odaaq Ø, 100 ft across, 0.8 miles north of Kaffeklubben Ø off Pearyland, Greenland at Lat. 83°40′32.5″N, Long. 30°40′10.1″W. It is 438.9 miles from the North Pole.

Greatest archipelago The world's greatest archipelago is the crescent of more than 17,000 islands, 3,500 miles long, that forms Indonesia.

Highest rock pinnacle The world's highest rock pinnacle is Ball's Pyramid near Lord Howe Island in the Pacific, which is 1,843 ft high, but has a base axis of only 660 ft.

Largest atoll The largest atoll in the world is Kwajalein in the Marshall Islands, in the central Pacific Ocean. Its slender coral reef 176 miles long encloses a lagoon of 1,100 miles^2.

The atoll with the largest land area is Christmas Atoll, in the Line Islands in the central Pacific Ocean. It has an area of 251 miles^2, of which 124 miles^2 is land.

Longest reef The Great Barrier Reef off Queensland, northeastern Australia is 1,260 miles in length. It is not actually a single reef, but consists of thousands of separate reefs. Large areas of the central section of the reef—approximately between Cooktown and Proserpine—have been devastated by the crown-of-thorns starfish (*Acanthaster planci*).

NEWEST!

The world's newest island is Pulau Batu Hairan ("Surprise Rock Island") in the South China Seas, some 40 miles to the northeast of Kudat, in Sabah, Malaysia. It was first sighted by three local fishermen on 14 Apr 1988. A week later it had doubled in height and now has an area of 1.9 acres and a maximum height of 10 ft.

The night before, they had heard some low rumbling sounds, probably the noise of the land mass as it was rising. Some superstitious residents expressed fears that a huge octopus might be lurking in the deep, and that the island might have been stirred up by its furious power.

ROCKS

The age of the Earth is generally considered to be 4,540 ± 40 million years. However, no rocks of this great age have yet been found on the Earth, since geological processes have presumably destroyed them.

Oldest The greatest reported age for any scientifically dated rock is 3,962 million years in the case of the Acasta Gneisses, found in May 1984. The rocks were discovered approximately 200 miles north of Yellowknife, Northwest Territories, Canada by Dr Samuel Bowring as part of an ongoing Canadian geology survey mapping project.

Older minerals that are not rocks have also been identified. Some zircon crystals discovered by Bob Pidgeon and Simon Wilde in the Jack Hills, 430 miles north of Perth, Western Australia in August 1984 were found to be 4,276 million years old. These are the oldest fragments of the Earth's crust discovered so far.

United States The oldest rocks in the United States are the Morton Gneisses, found in 1935 by G.A. Phiel and C.E. Dutton scattered over an area of 50 miles from New Ulm, Brown Co. to Renville Co. in Minnesota. In 1980 these rocks were dated at 3.6 billion years by Sam Goldrich of the US Geological Survey in Denver, CO, using the uranium-lead dating method.

Largest The largest exposed monolith in the world is Ayers Rock, known to Aborigines as Uluru, which rises 1,143 ft above the surrounding desert plain in Northern Territory, Australia. It is 1.5 miles long and 1 mile wide.

It was estimated in 1940 that La Gran Piedra, a volcanic plug located in the Sierra Maestra, Cuba, weighs 67,632 tons.

DEPRESSIONS

Deepest The deepest depression so far discovered is the bedrock of the Bentley subglacial trench, Antarctica at 8,326 ft below sea level. The greatest submarine depression is an area of the northwest Pacific floor that has an average depth of 15,000 ft.

The deepest exposed depression on land is the shore surrounding the Dead Sea, now 1,310 ft below sea level. The deepest point on the bed of this saltiest of all lakes is 2,388 ft below sea level.

The rate of fall in the lake surface since 1948 has been 13³/₄ in per year.

The deepest part of the bed of Lake Baikal in Russia is 3,875 ft below sea level.

United States The lowest-lying area in the United States is in Death Valley, CA at 282 ft below sea level.

Largest The largest exposed depression in the world is the Caspian Sea basin in Azerbaijan, Russia, Kazakhstan, Turkmenistan and Iran. It is more than 200,000 miles^2, of which 143,550 miles^2 is lake area.

The chief land area of the depression is the Prikaspiyskaya Nizmennost, lying around the northern third of the lake and stretching inland for a distance of up to 280 miles.

Gems, Jewels & Precious Metals

Amber

Largest The largest amber, *Burma Amber*, is 33 lb 10 oz and is located in the Natural History Museum, London, Great Britain.

Diamond

Largest The largest diamond is 3,106 carats and was found on 26 Jan 1905 in the Premier Mine, Pretoria, South Africa. Named *The Cullinan*, it was cut into 106 polished diamonds and produced the largest cut fine quality colorless diamond, weighing 530.2 carats.

The largest known single piece of rough diamond still in existence weighs 1,462 carats and is retained by De Beers Central Selling Organization in London, Great Britain.

Largest cut The largest cut diamond is the 545.67-carat gem known as the *Unnamed Brown*, which was fashioned from a 775.50-carat rough into a fire rose cushion cut. The stone was found at the Premier Diamond Mine and designed by master cutter Gabi Tolkowsky.

Smallest brilliant cut The smallest diamond is 0.000102 carat, with a diameter of 0.009 in. The diamond was polished with all 57 facets by D. Drukker & Zn NV of Amsterdam, Netherlands.

Highest-priced A superb 11-sided pear-shaped mixed-cut diamond of 101.84 carats was bought at Sotheby's, Geneva, Switzerland on 14 Nov 1990 for $12,760,000.

The highest price paid for a rough diamond was $10 million for a 255.10-carat stone from Guinea, by the William Goldberg Diamond Corporation in partnership with the Chow Tai Fook Jewelery Co. Ltd. of Hong Kong, in March 1989. *Many polished diamond sales are considered private transactions, and the prices paid are not disclosed.*

The record per carat is $926,315 for a 0.95-carat fancy purplish-red stone sold at Christie's, New York on 28 Apr 1987.

Emerald

Largest cut An 86,136-carat natural beryl was found in Carnaiba, Brazil in August 1974. It was carved by Richard Chan in Hong Kong and valued at £718,000 ($1,120,080) in 1982.

Largest single crystal The largest single emerald crystal of gem quality was 7,025 carats. It was found in 1969 at the Cruces Mine, near Gachala, Colombia, and is owned by a private mining concern.

Highest-priced The highest price paid for a single lot of emeralds was $3,080,000, for an emerald and diamond necklace made by Cartier, London, Great Britain in 1937 (a total of 12 stones weighing 108.74 carats), which was sold at Sotheby's, New York on 26 Oct 1989. The highest price for a single emerald is $2,126,646, for a 19.77-carat emerald and diamond ring made by Cartier in 1958, which was sold at Sotheby's, Geneva, Switzerland on 2 Apr 1987. This also represented the record price per carat for an emerald, at $107,569.

Gold

Largest mass of gold The 7,560-oz *Holtermann Nugget,* found on 19 Oct 1872 in the Beyers & Holtermann Star of Hope mine, Hill End, New South Wales, Australia, contained some 220 lb of gold in a 630-lb slab of slate.

Largest pure nugget The *Welcome Stranger,* found at Moliagul, Victoria, Australia in 1869, yielded 2,248 troy oz of pure gold from 2,280¼ oz.

Jade

Largest A single lens of nephrite jade was found in the Yukon Territory of Canada in July 1992. It weighed 636 tons and is owned by Yukon Jade Ltd.

Opal

Largest The largest single piece of gem-quality white opal was 26,350 carats, found in July 1989 at the Jupiter Field at Coober Pedy in South Australia. It has been named *Jupiter-Five* and is in private ownership.

Largest black A stone found on 4 Feb 1972 at Lightning Ridge, New South Wales, Australia produced a finished gem of 1,520 carats, called the *Empress of Glengarry.* It measures 4¾ x 3⅛ x ⅝ in, and is owned by Peter Gray.

Largest rough black The largest gem-quality uncut black opal was also found at Lightning Ridge, on 3 Nov 1986. After cleaning, it weighs 2,020 carats and measures 4 x 2⅝ x 2½ in. It has been named *Halley's Comet* and is owned by a team of opal miners known as The Lunatic Hill Syndicate.

Pearl

Largest The 14 lb 1 oz *Pearl of Lao-tze* was found at Palawan, Philippines on 7 May 1934 in the shell of a giant clam. This 9½-in-long by 5½-in-diameter molluscan concretion was bought at auction on 15 May 1980 in San Francisco, CA by Peter

(continued)

Hoffman and Victor Barbish for $200,000.

Largest abalone A baroque abalone pearl measuring 2¾ x 2 x 1⅛ in and weighing 469.13 carats was found at Salt Point State Park, CA in May 1990. It is owned by Wesley Rankin and is called the *Big Pink*.

Largest cultured A 1½-in round, 138.25-carat cultured pearl weighing 1 oz was found near Samui Island, off Thailand, in January 1988. The stone is owned by the Mikimoto Pearl Island Company, Japan.

Highest-priced *La Régente*, an egg-shaped pearl weighing 302.68 grains and formerly part of the French crown jewels, was sold at Christie's, Geneva, Switzerland on 12 May 1988 for $864,280.

Platinum

Largest The largest platinum nugget ever found weighs 340 oz and was discovered in the Ural Mountains in Russia in 1843. It was melted down shortly after its discovery.

Largest existing The largest surviving platinum nugget, the *Ural Giant*, weighs 277 oz and is currently in the custody of the Diamond Foundation in the Kremlin, Moscow, Russia.

Ruby

Largest star The *Eminent Star* ruby, believed to be of Indian origin, is the largest ruby, at 6,465 carats. It is an oval cabochon with a six-ray star, and measures 4¼ x 3⅝ x 2¼ in. It is owned by Kailash Rawat of Eminent Gems Inc. of New York.

Highest-priced A ruby and diamond ring made by Chaumet, in Paris, France, weighs 32.08 carats and was sold at Sotheby's, New York on 26 Oct 1989 for $4,620,000. The record per carat is $227,300 for a ruby ring with a stone weighing 15.97 carats, which was sold at Sotheby's, New York on 18 Oct 1988.

Sapphire

Largest star The largest star sapphire is the 9,719.50-carat gem *The Lone Star*. It was cut in London, Great Britain in November 1989 and is owned by Harold Roper.

Highest-priced A step-cut stone of 62.02 carats was sold as a sapphire and diamond ring at Sotheby's, St Moritz, Switzerland on 20 Feb 1988 for $2,791,723.

Topaz

Largest The rectangular, cushion-cut 22,892.5-carat *American Golden Topaz*, with 172 facets and 5⅞ in in overall width, has been on display at the Smithsonian Institution, Washington, D.C. since 4 May 1988.

The Old Pool in Boundary Waters (above), Far East Branch of Lechuguilla Cave, the deepest cave in the United States. (David Harris/Speleography)

The "Frozen Niagara" is just one of the spectacular sights that attract visitors to Mammoth Cave (right), the most extensive cave system in the world. (National Park Service)

CAVES

Longest The most extensive cave system in the world is that beneath the Mammoth Cave National Park, KY. Explorations by many groups of cavers have revealed that interconnected cave passages beneath the Flint, Mammoth Cave and Toohey Ridges make up a system with a total mapped length that is now 348 miles.

Largest The world's largest cave chamber is the Sarawak Chamber, Lubang Nasib Bagus, in the Gunung Mulu National Park, Sarawak, Malaysia, discovered and surveyed by the 1980 British–Malaysian Mulu Expedition. Its length is 2,300 ft; its average width is 980 ft; and it is nowhere less than 230 ft high. It would be large enough to hold 7,500 buses.

Underwater The longest explored underwater cave is the Nohoch Na Chich cave system in Quintana Roo, Mexico, with 77,900 ft of mapped passages. Exploration of the system, which began in November 1987, has been carried out by the CEDAM Cave Diving Team under the leadership of Mike Madden (USA).

The longest dive into a single flooded cave passage is 13,300 ft into the Doux de Coly, Dordogne, France by Olivier Issler (Switzerland) on 4 Apr 1991.

Greatest descent The world depth record was set by the Groupe Vulcain in the Gouffre Jean Bernard, France at 5,256 ft in 1989. However, this cave, explored via multiple entrances, has never been entirely descended, so the "sporting" record for the greatest descent into a cave is recognized as 4,947 ft in the Shakta Pantjukhina in the Caucasus Mountains of Georgia by a team of Ukrainian cavers in 1988.

Longest stalactite The longest stalactite in the world is a wall-supported column extending 195 ft from roof to floor in the Cueva de Nerja, near Málaga, Spain.

The longest freehanging stalactite in the world is one 33 ft long in the Gruta do Janelão, in Minas Gerais, Brazil.

Tallest stalagmite The tallest stalagmite in the world is one in the Krásnohorská cave, near Rožňava in Slovakia, which is generally accepted as being about 105 ft tall.

The tallest cave column is considered to be the Flying Dragon Pillar, 128 ft high, in Daji Dong, Guizhou, China.

Deepest The deepest cave in the United States is Lechuguilla Cave in Carlsbad Caverns, Carlsbad, NM, which currently measures 1,571 ft deep and over 68 miles long.

MOUNTAINS

Highest Mt Everest, a peak in the eastern Himalayas on the Tibet–Nepal border, was discovered to be the world's highest mountain in March 1856 by the Survey Department of the Government of India, from theodolite readings taken in 1849 and 1850. Its height was computed to be 29,002 ft, although recent satellite measurements now put it at 29,029 feet.

The mountain whose summit is farthest from the Earth's center is the Andean peak of Chimborazo (20,561 ft), 98 miles south of the equator in Ecuador, South America. Its summit is 7,057 ft further from the Earth's center than the summit of Mt Everest.

The highest island mountain in the world is Puncak Jaya in Irian Jaya, Indonesia. A survey by the Australian Universities' Expedition in 1973 yielded a height of 16,023 ft.

United States The highest mountain in the United States is Mt McKinley in Alaska, with a highest point of 20,320 ft. McKinley, so named in 1896, was called Denali (Great One) in the Athabascan language of Native North Americans. The highest mountain in the 48 contiguous states is Mt Whitney in California, with a highest point of 14,494 ft.

Tallest The world's tallest mountain measured from its submarine base (3,280 fathoms) in the Hawaiian Trough to its peak is Mauna Kea (White Mountain) on the island of Hawaii, with a combined height of 33,480 ft, of which 13,796 ft are above sea level.

Greatest ranges The greatest of all mountain ranges is the submarine Mid-Ocean Ridge, extending 40,000 miles from the Arctic Ocean to the Atlantic Ocean, around Africa, Asia and Australia, and under the Pacific Ocean to the west coast of North America. It has a greatest height of 13,800 ft above the base ocean depth.

The world's greatest land mountain range is the Himalaya-Karakoram, which contains 96 of the world's 109 peaks of over 24,000 ft. The longest range is the Andes of South America, which is approximately 4,700 miles in length.

HIGHEST HALITES!

Along the northern shores of the Gulf of Mexico for 725 miles there exist 330 subterranean "mountains" of salt, some of which rise more than 60,000 ft from bedrock and appear as the low salt domes first discovered in 1862.

Longest lines of sight Vatnajökull (6,952 ft), Iceland has been seen by refracted light from the Faeroe Islands 340 miles away.

United States In Alaska, Mt McKinley (20,320 ft) has been sighted from Mt Sanford (16,237 ft), a distance of 230 miles.

Greatest plateau The most extensive high plateau in the world is the Tibetan Plateau in Central Asia. The average altitude is 16,000 ft and the area is 715,000 miles^2.

Sheerest wall Mt Rakaposhi (25,550 ft) rises 3.72 vertical miles from the Hunza Valley, Pakistan in 6.2 horizontal miles with an overall gradient of 31°.

HIGHEST ALTITUDES IN THE US BY STATE

State *	Highest point	Elevation (ft)
Alaska	Mt McKinley	20,320
California	Mt Whitney	14,494
Colorado	Mt Elbert	14,433
Washington	Mt Rainier	14,410
Wyoming	Gannett Peak	13,804
Hawaii	Mauna Kea	13,796
Utah	Kings Peak	13,528
New Mexico	Wheeler Peak	13,161
Nevada	Boundary Peak	13,140
Montana	Granite Peak	12,799
Idaho	Borah Peak	12,662
Arizona	Humphreys Peak	12,633
Oregon	Mt Hood	11,239
Texas	Guadalupe Peak	8,749
South Dakota	Harney Peak	7,242
North Carolina	Mt Mitchell	6,684
Tennessee	Clingmans Dome	6,643
New Hampshire	Mt Washington	6,288
Virginia	Mt Rogers	5,729
Nebraska	Johnson Township	5,426
New York	Mt Marcy	5,344
Maine	Mt Katahdin	5,267
Oklahoma	Black Mesa	4,973
West Virginia	Spruce Knob	4,861
Georgia	Brasstown Bald	4,784
Vermont	Mt Mansfield	4,393
Kentucky	Black Mountain	4,139
Kansas	Mt Sunflower	4,039
South Carolina	Sassafras Mountain	3,560
North Dakota	White Butte	3,506
Massachusetts	Mt Greylock	3,487
Maryland	Blackbone Mountain	3,360
Pennsylvania	Mt Davis	3,213
Arkansas	Magazine Mountain	2,753
Alabama	Cheaha Mountain	2,405
Connecticut	Mt Frissell	2,380
Minnesota	Eagle Mountain	2,301
Michigan	Mt Arvon	1,979
Wisconsin	Timms Hill	1,951
New Jersey	High Point	1,803
Missouri	Taum Sauk Mount	1,772
Iowa	Sec. 29, T 100N, R 41W	1,670
Ohio	Campbell Hill	1,549
Indiana	Franklin Township	1,257
Illinois	Charles Mound	1,235
Rhode Island	Jerimoth Hill	812
Mississippi	Woodall Mountain	806
Louisiana	Driskill Mountain	535
Delaware	Ebright Road	442
Florida	Sec. 30, T 6N, R 20W	345

** Pete Allard, Jim Grace, Shuan Lacher, David Sandway and Dennis Stewart reached each high point of the 48 contiguous states in a record time of 30 days 10 hours 51 minutes and 55 seconds, 1–31 Jul 1991. They hiked a total of 253 miles and drove 17,284 miles during the entire trip.*

The 3,200-ft-wide northwest face of Half Dome, Yosemite, CA is 2,200 ft high but nowhere departs more than 7° from the vertical.

WATERFALLS

Highest The highest waterfall (as opposed to vaporized "bridal-veil fall") in the world is the Salto Angel (Angel Falls) in Venezuela, on a branch of the Carrao River, an upper tributary of the Caroni, with a total drop of 3,212 ft—the longest single drop is 2,648 ft. The Angel Falls were named after the US pilot Jimmie Angel (d. 8 Dec 1956), who recorded them in his log book on 16 Nov 1933.

United States The tallest continuous waterfall in the United States is Ribbon Falls in Yosemite National Park, California, with a drop of 1,612 ft. This is a seasonal waterfall and is generally dry from late July to early September.

Yosemite Falls, also in Yosemite National Park, has the greatest *total* drop at 2,425 ft, but actually consists of three distinct waterfalls. These are the Upper (1,430 ft), Middle (675 ft) and Lower falls (320 ft).

Greatest On the basis of the average annual flow, the greatest waterfall in the world is the Boyomoa Falls in Zaïre with 600,000 cusec.

The dramatic Khône Falls on the Mekong River in Laos is the widest waterfall in the world. (Explorer/P. Gontier)

The greatest peak flow ever was the Guaíra (Salto das Sete Quedas) on the Alto Paraná River between Braxil and Paraguay, which on occasions in the past attained a peak rate of 1.75 million cusec. However, the completion of the Itaipú Dam gates in 1982 ended this claim to fame.

Widest The widest waterfall in the world is the Khône Falls (50–70 ft high) in Laos, with a width of 6.7 miles and a flood flow of 1.5 million cusec.

RIVERS

Longest The two longest rivers in the world are the Nile, flowing into the Mediterranean, and the Amazon, flowing into the South Atlantic. Which is the longer is more a matter of definition than of simple measurement.

Not until 1971 was the true source of the Amazon discovered, by Loren McIntyre (USA) in the snow-covered Andes of southern Peru. The Amazon begins with snowbound lakes and brooks—the actual source has been named Laguna McIntyre—which converge to form the Apurimac. This joins other streams to become the Ene, the Tambo and then the Ucayali. From the confluence of the Ucayali and the Marañón the river is called the Amazon for the final 2,300 miles as it flows through Brazil into the Atlantic Ocean.

The Amazon has several mouths that widen toward the sea, so that the exact point where the river ends is uncertain. If the Pará estuary (the most distant mouth) is counted, its length is approximately 4,195 miles.

The length of the Nile watercourse, as surveyed by M. Devroey (Belgium) before the loss of a few miles of meanders due to the formation of Lake Nasser, behind the Aswan High Dam, was 4,145 miles. This course is unitary from a hydrological standpoint and runs from the source in Burundi of the Luvironza branch of the Kagera feeder of the Victoria Nyanza via the White Nile (*Bahr el-Jebel*) to the delta in the Mediterranean.

United States The longest river in the United States is the Mississippi, with a length of 2,348 miles. It flows from its source at Lake Itasca, MN through 10 states before reaching the Gulf of Mexico. The entire Mississippi River system, including the eastern and western tributaries, flows through 25 states in all.

Shortest As with the longest river, two rivers could also be considered to be the shortest river with a name. The Roe River, near Great Falls, MT, has two forks fed by a large freshwater spring. These relatively constant forks measure 201 ft (East Fork Roe River) and 58 ft (North Fork Roe River) respectively. The Roe River flows into the larger Missouri River. The D River, located at Lincoln City, OR, connects Devil's Lake to the Pacific Ocean. Its length is officially quoted as 120 ± 5 ft.

Largest basin The largest river basin in the world is that drained by the Amazon, which covers about 2,720,000 miles^2. It has countless tributaries and sub-tributaries, including the Madeira, which at 2,100 miles is the longest tributary in the world.

Longest estuary The world's longest estuary is that of the often-frozen Ob, in the north of Russia, at 550 miles. It is up to 50 miles wide, and is also the widest river that freezes solid.

Largest delta The world's largest delta is that created by the Ganges and Brahmaputra in Bangladesh and West Bengal, India. It covers an area of 30,000 miles^2.

United States The Mississippi River delta is the largest in the United States, with an area of about 10,100 miles^2.

Greatest flow The greatest flow of any river in the world is that of the Amazon, which discharges an average of 4.2 million cusec into the Atlantic Ocean, increasing to more than 7 million cusec in full flood. The lower 900 miles of the Amazon average 55 ft in depth, but the river reaches a maximum depth of 407 ft. The flow of the Amazon is 60 times greater than that of the Nile.

Submarine river In 1952 a submarine river 190 miles wide, known as the Cromwell Current, was discovered flowing eastward below the surface of the Pacific for 4,000 miles along the equator. In places it flows at depths of up to 1,300 ft. Its volume is 1,000 times that of the Mississippi.

Subterranean river In August 1958 a crypto-river (or concealed river), tracked by radioisotopes, was discovered flowing under the Nile with six times its mean annual flow, or 20 trillion ft^3.

Longest waterway The longest transcontinental waterway is 6,637 miles long and links the Beaufort Sea in northern Canada with the Gulf of Mexico in the United States. It starts at Tuktoyaktuk on the Mackenzie River and ends at Port Eads on the Mississippi delta. The final link was formed in 1976 with the completion of the South Bay Diversion Channel in Manitoba, Canada, joining the Churchill River system and the Nelson River system.

Largest swamp The world's largest tract of swamp is the Gran Pantanal of Mato Grosso state in Brazil. It is about 42,000 miles^2 in area.

Largest marsh The Everglades is a vast plateau of subtropical saw-grass marsh in southern Florida, covering 2,185 miles^2. Fed by water from Lake Okeechobee, the third largest freshwater lake in the United States, the Everglades is the largest subtropical wilderness in the continental United States.

RIVER BORES

The bore (an abrupt rise of tidal water) on the Qiantong Jiang in eastern China is the most remarkable of the 60 in the world. At spring tides the wave attains a height of up to 25 ft and a speed of 13–15 knots. It is heard advancing at a range of 14 miles.

The annual downstream flood wave on the Mekong, in southeast Asia, sometimes reaches a height of 46 ft.

The greatest volume of any tidal bore is that of the Furo do Guajarú, a shallow channel that splits Ilha Caviana in the mouth of the Amazon.

LAKES AND INLAND SEAS

Largest The largest inland sea or lake in the world is the Caspian Sea (in Azerbaijan, Russia, Kazakhstan, Turkmenistan and Iran). It is 760 miles long and its total area is 143,550 miles^2. Its maximum depth is 3,360 ft and the surface is 93 ft below sea level. (See also Depressions, largest.)

United States The largest lake in the United States is Lake Michigan, with a water surface area of 22,300 miles^2, a length of 307 miles, a breadth of 118 miles and a maximum depth of 923 ft. Both Lake Superior and Lake Huron have larger areas, but these straddle the border between Canada and the United States.

Deepest The deepest lake in the world is Lake Baikal in southern part of eastern Siberia, Russia. It is 385 miles long and between 20–46 miles wide. In 1974 the lake's Olkhon Crevice was measured by the Hydrographic Service of the Soviet Pacific Navy and found to be 5,371 ft deep, of which 3,875 ft is below sea level.

United States The deepest lake in the United States is 6-mile-long Crater Lake, in Crater Lake National Park in the Cascade Mountains of Oregon. Its surface is 6,176 ft above sea level and its extreme depth is 1,932 ft, with an average depth of 1,500 ft. The lake has neither inlets nor outlets; instead it is filled and maintained solely by precipitation.

Highest The highest navigable lake in the world is Lake Titicaca (maximum depth 1,214 ft, with an area of about 3,200 miles^2) in South America (1,850 miles^2 in Peru and 1,350 miles^2 in Bolivia). It is 100 miles long and is 12,506 ft above sea level. There are higher lakes in the Himalayas, but most are glacial and of a temporary nature only. A survey of the area carried out in 1984 showed a lake at a highest-ever height of 17,762 ft, named Panch Pokhri, which was 1 mile long.

Freshwater The freshwater lake with the greatest surface area is Lake Superior. The total area is 31,800 miles^2, of which 20,700 miles^2 are in Minnesota, Wisconsin and Michigan and 11,100 miles^2 in Ontario, Canada. It is 600 ft above sea level. The freshwater lake with the greatest volume is Lake Baikal in Siberia, Russia, with an estimated volume of 5,500 miles^3.

Largest lagoon Lagoa dos Patos, located near the seashore in Rio Grande do Sul, southernmost Brazil, is 174 miles long and extends over 3,803 miles^2, separated from the Atlantic Ocean by long sand strips. It has a maximum width of 44 miles.

Underground The world's largest underground lake is the Drachenhauchloch cave near Grootfontein, Namibia, discovered in 1986. The surface of the lake is some 217 ft underground, and its depth is 276 ft.

The United States' largest underground lake is the Lost Sea, 300 ft subterranean in the Craighead Caverns, Sweetwater, TN, measuring 4½ acres and discovered in 1905.

Lake in a lake The largest lake inside another lake is Manitou Lake

Lying in a deep structural hollow and flanked to the east by the Baikal Mountains, Russia's Lake Baikal is the world's deepest lake. (Science Photo Library/Novosti Press Agency)

Crater Lake in the Cascade Mountains of Oregon is the deepest in the United States. (US National Park Service)

(41.09 miles^2) on the world's largest lake island, Manitoulin Island (1,068 miles^2), in the Canadian part of Lake Huron. The lake itself contains a number of islands.

OTHER FEATURES

Largest gorge The largest land gorge in the world is the Grand Canyon on the Colorado River in north-central Arizona. It extends from Marble Gorge to the Grand Wash Cliffs, over a distance of 277 miles. It averages 10 miles in width and 1 mile in depth. The submarine Labrador Basin canyon, between Greenland and Labrador, Canada, is *c.* 2,150 miles long.

Deepest canyon A canyon or gorge is generally defined as a valley with steep rock walls and a considerable depth in relation to its width. The Grand Canyon (see above) has the characteristic vertical sections of wall, but is much wider than its depth. The Vicos Gorge in the Pindus mountains of northwest Greece is 2,950 ft deep and only 3,600 ft between its rims.

The deepest submarine canyon yet discovered is one 25 miles south of Esperance, Western Australia; it is 6,000 ft deep and 20 miles wide.

United States The deepest canyon in the United States is Kings Canyon, East Fresno, CA, which runs through Sierra and Sequoia National Forests. The deepest point, which measures 8,200 ft, is in the Sierra National Park Forest section of the canyon.

GUESS WHAT?

Q. WHAT DESERT INHABITANT IS 50 FEET TALL?

A. LOOK IN "PLANTS" (LIVING WORLD)

Deepest valley The Yarlung Zangbo valley is 16,650 ft deep where it turns through the Himalayas in eastern Tibet, before the river changes its name to the Brahmaputra. The peaks of Namche Barwa (25,436 ft) and Jala Peri (23,891 ft) are just 13 miles apart with the Yarlung Zangbo River in between, at an elevation of 8,000 ft.

Cliffs The highest sea cliffs in the world are those on the north coast of east Moloka'i, HI near Umilehi Point, which descend 3,300 ft to the sea at an average gradient of more than 55°.

Natural arches The longest natural arch in the world is the Landscape Arch in the Arches National Park, 25 miles north of Moab in Utah. This natural sandstone arch spans 291 ft and is set about 100 ft above the canyon floor. In one place erosion has narrowed its section to 6 ft. The Rainbow Bridge, UT, discovered on 14 Aug 1909, although only 270 ft long, is more than 22 ft wide and rises 290 ft in elevation.

Longest glaciers It is estimated that 5,250,000 miles², or 9.7 percent of the Earth's land surface, is permanently glaciated. The Antarctic ice sheet accounts for 86 percent of this and the Greenland ice sheet for 11 percent. The world's longest glacier is the Lambert Glacier, discovered by an Australian aircraft crew in Australian Antarctic Territory in 1956–57. Draining about a fifth of the East Antarctic ice sheet, it is up to 40 miles wide and, with its seaward extension, the Amery Ice Shelf, it measures at least 440 miles in length.

The fastest-moving major glacier is the Jacobshavn Isbrae in Greenland, flowing an average of 62 ft per day.

Thickest ice The greatest recorded thickness of ice is 2.97 miles, measured by radio echo soundings from a US Antarctic research aircraft at 69°9′38″S, 135°20′25″E, 250 miles from the coast of Wilkes Land, Antarctica on 4 Jan 1975.

Deepest permafrost The deepest recorded permafrost is more than 4,500 ft, reported from the upper reaches of the Viluy River, Siberia, Russia in February 1982.

Desert Nearly an eighth of the world's land surface is arid, with a rainfall of less than 10 in per year. The Sahara in North Africa is the largest desert in the world. At its greatest length it is 3,200 miles from east to west. From north to south it is between 800 and 1,400 miles. The area covered by the desert is about 3,579,000 miles².

United States The Mojave Desert is the largest in the United States. It covers approximately 15,000 miles².

Sand dunes The world's highest measured sand dunes are those in the Saharan sand sea of Isaouane-N-Tifernine of east-central Algeria at Lat. 26°42′N, Long. 6°43′E. They have a wavelength of 3 miles and attain a height of 1,525 ft.

NATURAL PHENOMENA

EARTHQUAKES

Greatest It is estimated that each year there are some 500,000 detectable seismic or microseismic disturbances, of which 100,000 can be felt and 1,000 cause damage. The deepest recorded hypocenters are of 447 miles in Indonesia in 1933, 1934 and 1943.

United States The strongest earthquake in American history, measuring 8.4 on the Richter scale, was near Prince William Sound, AK (80 miles east of Anchorage) on 27 Mar 1964. It killed 131 people and caused an estimated $750 million in damage; it also caused a tsunami 50 feet high that traveled 8,445 miles at 450 mph. The town of Kodiak was destroyed, and tremors were felt in California, Hawaii and Japan.

DEADLIEST NATURAL DISASTERS

Type of Disaster	Number killed	Location	Date
Circular Storm [1]	1,000,000	Ganges Delta Islands, Bangladesh	12–13 Nov 1970
Flood	900,000	Hwang-ho River, China	Oct 1887
Earthquake [2]	830,000	Shaanxi, Shanxi and Henan Provinces, China	2 Feb 1556
Landslides (triggered by a single earthquake)	180,000	Kansu Province, China	16 Dec 1920
Volcanic Eruption	92,000	Tambora, Sumbawa, Indonesia	5–10 Apr 1815
Avalanches [3]	*c.* 18,000	Yungay, Huascarán, Peru	31 May 1970
Tornado	*c.* 1,300	Shaturia, Bangladesh	26 Apr 1989
Hail	246	Moradabad, Uttar Pradesh, India	20 Apr 1888
Lightning	81	Boeing 707 jet airliner, struck by lightning near Elkton, MD	8 Dec 1963

[1] *This figure published in 1972 for the Bangladeshi disaster was from Dr Afzal, Principal Scientific Officer of the Atomic Energy Authority Centre, Dacca.*

[2] *The figure of 1,100,000 sometimes attributed to the Eastern Mediterrranean earthquake of 20 May 1202 is a gross exaggeration, since it includes those who died in a famine the following year.*

[3] *A total of 18,000 Austrian and Italian troops were reported to have been lost in the Dolomite valleys of northern Italy on 13 Dec 1916 in more than 100 snow avalanches. Some of the avalanches were triggered by gunfire.*

The most commonly used measure of the size of an earthquake is its surface magnitude (M_s), based on amplitudes of surface waves, usually at a period of 20 sec. The largest reported magnitudes on this scale are about 8.9, but the scale does not properly represent the size of the very largest earthquakes, above M_s about 8, for which it is better to use the concept of seismic moment, M_o, devised by K. Aki in 1966.

Moment can be used to derive a "moment magnitude," M_w, first used by Hiroo Kanamori in 1977. The largest recorded earthquake on the M_w scale is the Chilean shock of 22 May 1960, which had $M_w = 9.5$, but measured only 8.3 on the M_s scale.

Material damage The greatest physical devastation was in the earthquake on the Kanto plain, Japan, of Sep 1 1923 (Mag. $M_s = 8.2$, epicenter in Lat. 35°15′N, Long. 139°30′E). In Tokyo and Yokohama 575,000 dwellings were destroyed. The official total of people killed and missing in this *Shinsai* (great quake) and the resultant fires was 142,807.

United States The insured property loss of the Los Angeles earthquake of 17 Jan 1994 amounts to $2.5 billion. It is estimated that the overall loss could reach $20 billion, making it the third most expensive disaster ever for insurers. The earthquake measured 7.5 on the Richter scale.

VOLCANOES

The total number of known active volcanoes in the world is 1,343, of which many are submarine. The word *volcano* derives from the now-dormant Vulcano Island (from the Roman god of fire *Vulcanus*) in the Mediterranean.

Greatest explosion The greatest explosion in historic times (possibly since Santoriní in the Aegean Sea, 60 miles north of Crete, in 1628 B.C.) occurred at *c.* 10 A.M. (local time), or 3:00 GMT, on 27 Aug 1883, with an eruption of Krakatoa, an island (then 18 $miles^2$) in the Sunda Strait, between Sumatra and Java, in Indonesia. One hundred and sixty-three villages were wiped out and 36,380 people killed by the wave it caused. Pumice was thrown 34 miles high and dust fell 3,313 miles away 10 days later. The explosion was recorded four hours later on the island of Rodrigues, 2,968 miles away, as "the roar of heavy guns," and was heard over one-thirteenth of the surface of the globe.

This explosion, estimated to have had about 26 times the power of the greatest H-bomb test (by the USSR; for details of thermonuclear explosions, see Business & Public Affairs, Bombs), was still only a third of the Santoriní cataclysm.

United States The most deaths from a volcanic eruption in the United States was 60 people, on 18 May 1980 from the eruption of Mt St. Helens, WA.

Greatest volume of discharge The total volume of matter discharged in the eruption of Tambora, a volcano on the Indonesian island of Sumbawa, 5–10 Apr 1815, was 36–43 $miles^3$. A crater 5 miles in diameter was formed and the height of the island was lowered from 13,450 ft to 9,350 ft. More than 92,000 people were killed, or died as a result of the subsequent famine.

Most violent eruption The ejecta in the Taupo eruption in New Zealand *c.* A.D. 130 has been estimated at 33 billion tons of pumice moving at one time at 400 mph. It flattened 6,200 $miles^2$. Less than 20 percent of the 15.4 billion tons of pumice carried up into the air in this most violent of all documented volcanic events fell within 125 miles of the vent.

Longest lava flow The longest lava flow in historic times is a mixture of ropey lava (twisted cordlike solidifications) and blocky lava resulting from the eruption of Laki in 1783 in southeast Iceland, which flowed 40½–43½ miles. The largest prehistoric flow is the Roza basalt flow in North America *c.* 15 million years ago, which had an unsurpassed length (190 miles), area (15,400 $miles^2$) and volume (300 $miles^3$).

Largest active Mauna Loa in Hawaii has the shape of a broad gentle dome 75 miles long and 31 miles wide (above sea level), with lava flows

A view of the giant ash cloud formed by an eruption of Mt St. Helens. On 18 May 1980 an avalanche measuring a record 96 billion ft^3 was triggered by the volcano's eruption. (Science Photo Library/David Weintraub)

THE TALLEST GEYSER

WAIMANGU

Imagine a fountain of boiling water higher than the Empire State Building, and you can picture the tallest geyser on record.

A geyser is a spouting hot spring that discharges water and steam. The greatest height to which a geyser has ever erupted is 1,500 ft, in the case of Waimangu, near Rotorua in New Zealand. Waimangu was discovered on 30 Jan 1901 by Dr Humphrey Haines, who was investigating reports of huge steam clouds in the area.

Waimangu soon became a popular attraction, but its fame increased dramatically when four people were killed there in August 1903. They had been standing some 90 ft away from the geyser when it displayed, but because of the force of the eruption their bodies were found up to 1/2 mile away.

In late 1904 Waimangu ceased activity, and although the surrounding area erupted in 1917, the geyser itself did not. The ground in the area is still hot, but the dramatic sight of Waimangu erupting is now history.

that occupy more than 1,980 miles^2 of the island. It has a total volume of 10,200 miles^3, of which 84.2 percent is below sea level. Its caldera or volcano crater, Mokuaweoweo, measures 4 miles^2 and is 500–600 ft deep. Mauna Loa rises 13,680 ft and has averaged one eruption every 4$^1/_2$ years since 1843, although none have occurred since 1984.

United States The only active volcano in the contiguous 48 states is Mt St. Helens, located near Seattle, WA. There have been 25 registered eruptions over the past decade, the last on 14 Feb 1991. Mt St. Helens was 9,677 ft high before its 1980 eruption; it now stands at 8,364 ft.

Highest active The highest volcano regarded as active is Ojos del Salado at a height of 22,595 ft, on the frontier between Chile and Argentina.

Northernmost and southernmost The northernmost volcano is Beeren Berg (7,470 ft) on the island of Jan Mayen (71°05′N) in the Greenland Sea. It erupted on 20 Sep 1970, and the island's 39 inhabitants (all male) had to be evacuated. The most southerly known active volcano is Mt Erebus (12,447 ft), on Ross Island (77°35′S) in Antarctica.

Largest crater The world's largest caldera or volcano crater is that of Toba, north-central Sumatra, Indonesia, covering 685 miles^2.

AVALANCHES

Greatest The greatest natural avalanches, though rarely observed, occur in the Himalayas, but no estimates of their volume have been published. It was estimated that 120 million ft^3 of snow fell in an avalanche in the Italian Alps in 1885.

The 250-mph avalanche triggered by the Mt St. Helens eruption in Washington State on 18 May 1980 was estimated to measure 96 billion ft^3.

GEYSERS

Tallest Currently the tallest active geyser in the world is the National Park Service's Steamboat Geyser, in Yellowstone National Park, WY. During the 1980s this geyser erupted at intervals ranging from 19 days to more than four years, although there were occasions in the 1960s when it erupted as frequently as every 4–10 days. The maximum height ranges from 195–380 ft.

WEATHER

The meteorological records given here necessarily relate largely to the last 150–170 years, since data before that time are both sparse and often unreliable.

The longest continuous observations have been maintained at the Radcliffe Observatory, Oxford, Great Britain since 1814, and on a daily basis since 1874, though discontinuous records have enabled the Chinese to assert that 903 B.C. was a very bad winter.

Lowest ozone levels Ozone levels reached a record low at the South Pole, Antarctica on 12 Oct 1993, when a figure of 91 Dobson units (DU) was recorded. The minimum level needed to shield the Earth from solar ultraviolet radiation is 300 DU.

Most equable temperature *Short period* The location with the most equable recorded temperature over a short period is Garapan, on Saipan in the Mariana Islands, Pacific Ocean. During the nine years from 1927–35 inclusive, the lowest temperature recorded was 67.3°F on 30 Jan 1934 and the highest was 88.5°F on 9 Sep 1931, giving an extreme range of 21.2°F.

Long period Between 1911 and 1990 the Brazilian offshore island of Fernando de Noronha had a minimum temperature of 63.9°F on 27 Feb 1980 and a maximum of 90.0°F on 3 Mar 1968, 25 Dec 1972 and 17 Apr 1973, giving an extreme range of 26.1°F.

Annual mean temperature readings The highest annual mean temperature in the United States is 78.2°F at Key West, FL.

The lowest mean temperature reading is 36.5°F at International Falls, MN.

Greatest temperature ranges The greatest recorded temperature ranges in the world are around the Siberian "cold pole" in the east of Russia. Temperatures in Verkhoyansk (67°33′N, 133°23′E) have ranged 188 deg F, from –90°F to 98°F.

The greatest temperature variation recorded in a day is 100 deg F (a fall from 44°F to –56°F) at Browning, MT on 23–24 Jan 1916.

The most freakish rise was 49 deg F in 2 min at Spearfish, SD, from –4°F at 7:30 A.M. to 45°F at 7:32 A.M. on 22 Jan 1943.

Highest shade temperature The highest shade temperature ever recorded is 136°F at Al'Azīzīyah, Libya (alt. 367 ft) on 13 Sep 1922.

Hottest place On an annual mean basis, with readings taken over a six-year period from 1960 to 1966, the temperature at Dallol, in Ethiopia, was 94°F.

At Marble Bar, Western Australia (maximum 121°F), 162 consecutive days with maximum temperatures of over 100°F were recorded between 30 Oct 1923 and 8 Apr 1924.

United States The highest temperature ever recorded in the United States was 134°F at Greenland Ranch, Death Valley, CA on 10 Jul 1913. In Death Valley, maximum temperatures of over 120°F were recorded on 43 consecutive days, between 6 Jul and 17 Aug 1917.

Driest place The annual mean rainfall on the Pacific coast of Chile between Arica and Antofagasta is less than 0.004 in.

United States In 1929 no precipitation was recorded for Death Valley, CA. Currently the driest state is Nevada, with an annual rainfall of only 9 inches.

IT'S RAINING AGAIN!

Mawsynram in India is the wettest place in the world, with ten times more rain every year than New York and twenty times more than London.

A survey carried out by researchers from the Indian Meteorological Department between 1941 and 1979 showed that Mawsynram had on average 467½ in of rain per annum. Most of it falls in the monsoon season from June to September, and on average only 147 days each year have any rain. The weather station is located on the crest of the southern range of the Khasi Hills in Meghalaya, some 125 miles to the northeast of Dhaka, the capital of Bangladesh. Cherrapunji, which holds records for the greatest recorded rainfall in a month and also in a year, is only 10 miles away.

To appreciate just how much rain Mawsynram has, it is interesting to compare the figures with those for major cities around the world.

Beijing has 72 in

Tokyo has 61½ in

Sydney has 46½ in

New York has 43¼ in

Rio de Janeiro has 42½ in

Toronto has 30½ in

Mexico City has 28 in

Paris has 24½ in

Berlin has 23¾ in

London has 23¼ in

= 20 in of rain

Although Mawsynram has the most rain, Sydney, Paris, Berlin and London actually have rain on more days — 152, 162, 167 and 153 respectively. At the other extreme, it only rains in Beijing on 64 days each year.

Longest drought Desierto de Atacama, in Chile, experiences virtually no rain, although several times a century a squall may strike a small area of it.

United States The most intense drought in the United States lasted 57 months, from May 1952 to March 1957, in western Kansas. The Drought Severity Index reached a lowest point ever of –6.2, in September 1956.

Below –4.0 on this index indicates extreme drought conditions.

Most sunshine The annual average at Yuma, AZ is 90 percent (over 4,000 hours of sunshine).

St Petersburg, FL recorded 768 consecutive sunny days from 9 Feb 1967 to 17 Mar 1969.

Least sunshine At the South Pole there is zero sunshine for 182 days every year, and at the North Pole the same applies for 176 days.

Lowest screen temperature A record low of –128.6°F was registered at Vostok, Antarctica (alt. 11,220 ft) on 21 Jul 1983.

The coldest permanently inhabited place is the Siberian village of Oymyakon (pop. 4,000), 63°16′N, 143°15′E (2,300 ft), in Russia, where the temperature reached –90°F in 1933, and an unofficial –98°F has been published more recently.

United States The lowest temperature ever recorded in the United States was –79.8°F on 23 Jan 1971 in Prospect Creek, AK.

The lowest temperature in the continental United States was –69.7°F in Rogers Pass, MT on 20 Jan 1954.

Coldest place Polyus Nedostupnosti (Pole of Inaccessibility), Antarctica at 78°S, 96°E, is the coldest place in the world, with an extrapolated annual mean of –72°F.

The coldest measured mean is –70°F, at Plateau Station, Antarctica.

United States Langdon, ND had 41 days below 0°F, from 11 Nov 1935–20 Feb 1936. Langdon also holds the record for most days below 32°F, with 92 days from 30 Nov 1935–29 Feb 1936.

Wettest place By average annual rainfall, the wettest place in the world is Mawsynram, in Meghalaya State, India, with 467½ in per annum.

United States The wettest state is Louisiana, with an annual rainfall of 56 inches.

Most rainy days Mt Wai-‘ale-‘ale (5,148 ft), Kauai, HI has up to 350 rainy days per year.

Greatest rainfall A record 73.62 in of rain fell in 24 hours in Cilaos (alt. 3,940 ft), La Réunion, Indian Ocean on 15 and 16 Mar 1952. This is equal to 8,327 tons of rain per acre.

For a calendar month, the record is 366 in, at Cherrapunji, Meghalaya, India in July 1861.

The 12-month record was also set at Cherrapunji, with 1,041.8 in between 1 Aug 1860 and 31 Jul 1861.

United States In the United States, the 24-hr record is 19 in at Alvin, TX, on 25–26 Jul 1979. Over a 12-month period, 739 in fell at Kukui, Maui, HI from December 1981–December 1982. The greatest rainfall in the coterminous states is 184.56 in, at Wynoochee Oxbow, WA in 1931.

Longest-lasting rainbow A rainbow lasting over three hours was reported from the coastal border of Gwynedd and Clwyd, North Wales, Great Britain on 14 Aug 1979.

Worst flood damage As of 10 Aug 1993 it was reported that an estimated $12 billion in property and agricultural damage had been caused by the great Midwest flood of 1993. The flood affected parts of nine states and covered an area estimated at twice the size of New Jersey.

Deadliest flood The most deaths from a flood in the United States was more than 2,000 people, at Johnstown, PA on 31 May 1889. The water formed a wall 20–30 ft high, rushing through the valley on the way to Johnstown at a rate of 15 mph.

Greatest flood Scientists reported the discovery of the largest freshwater flood in history in January 1993. It occurred *c.* 18,000 years ago when an ancient ice dam lake in the Altay Mountains in Siberia, Russia, broke, allowing the water to pour out.

The lake was estimated to be 75 miles long and 2,500 ft deep. The main flow of water was reported to be 1,600 ft deep and traveling at 100 mph.

Windiest place Commonwealth Bay, George V Coast, Antarctica, where gales reach 200 mph, is the world's windiest place.

Highest surface wind speed A surface wind speed of 231 mph was recorded at Mt Washington (6,288 ft), NH on 12 Apr 1934. The fastest speed at a

MOST COSTLY HURRICANES IN US HISTORY

Year	Hurricane	Area	Losses (in millions)
1992	Andrew	Florida, Louisiana	$46,500
1989	Hugo	Georgia to Virginia	$4,195
1992	Iniki	Hawaii	$1,600
1979	Frederic	Florida to New York	$752
1983	Alicia	Texas	$675
1991	Bob	New Jersey to Maine	$620
1985	Elena	Gulf region	$543
1965	Betsy	Gulf region	$515
1985	Gloria	North Carolina to Maine	$418
1970	Celia	Texas	$309

Solurce: Insurance Information Institute

low altitude was registered on 8 Mar 1972 at the USAF base at Thule, Greenland (145 ft), when a peak speed of 207 mph was recorded. The fastest speed measured to date in a tornado is 280 mph at Wichita Falls, TX on 2 Apr 1958.

Hurricanes The greatest number of fatalities from an American hurricane is an estimated 6,000 deaths on 8 Sep 1900 in Galveston Island, TX.

Material damage The most costly hurricane in the United States was Hurricane Andrew, which hit southern Florida on 24 Aug 1992, crossed the Gulf of Mexico and caused further destruction in Louisiana. The hurricane killed 76 people, left approximately 258,000 people homeless and caused an estimated $46.5 billion in damages.

As of 1 Feb 1994 the Insurance Information Institute reported that $16.5 billion had actually been paid by insurers to claimants.

Fastest winds The fastest sustained winds in a hurricane in the United States measured 200 mph, with 210 mph gusts, on 17–18 Aug 1969, when Hurricane Camille hit the Mississippi/Alabama coast at Pass Christian, MS. Hurricane Camille also had the greatest storm surge in the United States.

Greatest speed The greatest forward speed by a hurricane in the United States was in excess of 60 mph, with an average speed of 58 mph, for the Great New England Hurricane on 21 Sep 1938, when it struck central Long Island at Babylon, NY. The hurricane continued on to landfall at Milford, CT.

Tornadoes The most deaths from one tornado in the United States is 695, on 18 Mar 1925 in Missouri, Illinois and Indiana. This tornado also ranks first as the tornado with the longest continuous track on the ground, 219 miles; first with a 3.5-hour continuous duration on the ground; first in total area of destruction, covering 164 miles^2; first in dimensions, with the funnel sometimes exceeding one mile wide; and third in forward speed, reaching a maximum of 73 mph, while averaging 62 mph over its duration. The state with the most tornadoes recorded in a year is Texas, with 232 in 1967.

Highest waterspout The highest waterspout was one observed on 16 May 1898 off Eden, New South Wales, Australia. A theodolite reading from the shore gave its height as 5,014 ft. It was about 10 ft in diameter.

Heaviest hailstones The heaviest hailstones on record, weighing up to 2¼ lb, are reported to have killed 92 people in the Gopalganj district of Bangladesh on 14 Apr 1986.

United States The heaviest hailstone in the United States weighed 1.671 lb, had a circumference of 17.5 in and a diameter of 5.62 in in Coffeyville, KS on 3 Sep 1970.

Greatest snowfall A total of 1,224½ in of snow fell over a 12-month period from 19 Feb 1971 to 18 Feb 1972 at Paradise, Mt Rainier, in Washington State.

The record for a single snowstorm is 189 in at Mt Shasta Ski Bowl, CA

Members of the US Air Weather Service measured the lowest sea-level barometric pressure while flying over Typhoon Tip as it raged across the Pacific. (USAF)

from 13–19 Feb 1959, and for a 24-hr period the record snowfall is 78 in, at Mile 47 Camp, Cooper River Division, AK on 7 Feb 1963. The greatest depth of snow on the ground was 37 ft 7 in at Tamarac, CA in March 1911.

Cloud extremes The highest standard cloud form is cirrus, averaging 27,000 ft and higher, but the rare nacreous or mother-of-pearl formation may reach nearly 80,000 ft. The lowest is stratus, below 1,500 ft. The cloud form with the greatest vertical range is cumulonimbus, which has been observed to reach a height of nearly 68,000 ft in the tropics.

Upper atmosphere The lowest temperature ever recorded in the atmosphere is –279° F at an altitude of 56 miles. This is in the region of noctilucent cloud formation in the mesosphere.

Thunder-days In Tororo, Uganda an average of 251 days of thunder per year was recorded for the 10-year period 1967–76.

Lightning Most times struck The only man in the world to be struck by lightning seven times is ex-park ranger Roy C. Sullivan (USA), the human lightning conductor of Virginia. His attraction for lightning began in 1942 (lost big toenail), and was resumed in July 1969 (lost eyebrows), in July 1970 (left shoulder seared), on 16 Apr 1972 (hair set on fire), on 7 Aug 1973 (hair set afire again and legs seared), on 5 Jun 1976 (ankle injured), and he was sent to Waynesboro Hospital with chest and stomach burns on 25 Jun 1977 after being struck while fishing. In September 1983 he died by his own hand, reportedly rejected in love.

Fog Longest Sea-level fogs—with visibility less than 0.56 miles—persist for weeks on the Grand Banks, Newfoundland, Canada, with the average being more than 120 days per year.

Cape Disappointment, WA has the most fog days in the United States, with an average of 2,552 hours (or 106 complete days) of heavy fog per year.

Least Key West, FL averages less than one day a year of heavy fog.

Largest mirage The largest mirage on record was that sighted in the Arctic at 83°N 103°W by Donald B. MacMillan in 1913. This type of mirage, known as the Fata Morgana, appeared as the same "hills, valleys, snow-capped peaks extending through at least 120 degrees of the horizon" that Peary had misidentified as Crocker Land six years earlier. On 17 Jul 1939 a mirage of the mountain Snaefellsjökull (4,744 ft) on Iceland was seen from the sea at a distance of 335–350 miles.

Barometric pressure The highest barometric pressure ever recorded was 32 in at Agata, Siberia, Russia (alt. 862 ft) on 31 Dec 1968. The lowest sea-level pressure was 25.69 in in Typhoon Tip, 300 miles west of Guam, Pacific Ocean, at Lat. 16°44′N, Long. 137°46′E, on 12 Oct 1979.

The highest barometric pressure recorded in the United States was 31.43 in at Barrow, AK on 3 Jan 1970. The highest in the coterminous states was 31.40 in, at Helena, MT on 9 Jan 1962. The lowest barometric pressure recorded in the United States was 26.35 for the 1935 Labor Day Hurricane, which crossed the US coastline at Matecumbe Key, FL at 10 P.M. on 2 Sep 1935.

SCIENCE & TECHNOLOGY

ELEMENTS

SUBATOMIC PARTICLES

Heaviest The heaviest particle whose existence is accepted is the neutral weak gauge boson, the Z°, of mass 91.17 GeV and lifetime 2.65×10^{-25} sec, the shortest lifetime of any particle.

Lightest The photon (and the theoretically predicted graviton) are both expected to have as close to zero mass as is possible within current cosmological models.

Most stable Experiments indicate that the lifetime of the most likely decay mode of a proton (to a positron and a neutral pion) has a lower limit of 3.1×10^{32} years.

Least stable The shortest-lived subatomic particle is the boson Z° particle, with a lifetime of 2.65×10^{-25} sec.

THE 109 ELEMENTS

Of the 109 known elements, the first 94 exist naturally. At room temperature the elements comprise 2 liquids, 11 gases and 85 known solids. Elements 85, 87 and 101 to 109 would also be solid at room temperature if they could be obtained in a coherent form.

Most common Hydrogen (H) is the most common element, accounting for over 90 percent of all known matter in the Universe and 70.68 percent by mass in the Solar System. The commonest element in the Earth's atmosphere is nitrogen (N), which is present at 78.08 percent by volume (75.52 percent by mass), and iron (Fe) is the most common element in the Earth itself, accounting for 36 percent of the planet's mass.

Newest Element 108, provisionally named unniloctium (Uno), but with the name hassium (Hs) proposed, was announced in April 1984 based on the observation of only three atoms at the Gesellschaft für Schwerionenforschung (GSI), Darmstadt, Germany.

Density *Solid* The densest solid at room temperature is osmium (Os) at 0.8161 lb/in³. The least dense element at room temperature is the metal lithium (Li) at 0.01927 lb/in³, although the density of solid hydrogen at its melting point of –434.546°F is only 0.00315 lb/in³.

Gas The densest gas at NTP (Normal Temperature and Pressure, 0°C and one atmosphere) is radon (Rn) at 0.6274 lb/ft³. The lightest gas is hydrogen (H) at 0.005612 lb/ft³.

Melting and boiling points *Highest* Metallic tungsten or wolfram (W) melts at 6,188°F. The graphite form of carbon (C) sublimes directly to vapor at

6,999°F and can only be obtained as a liquid above a temperature of 8,546°F and a pressure of 100 atmospheres.

Lowest Helium (He) cannot be obtained as a solid at atmospheric pressure. The minimum pressure necessary is 24.985 atmospheres at –458.275°F. Helium also has the lowest boiling point, at –458.275°F. For metallic elements, mercury (Hg) has the lowest melting and boiling points, at –37.892°F and 673.92°F respectively.

Purest In April 1978 P.V.E. McClintock of the University of Lancaster,

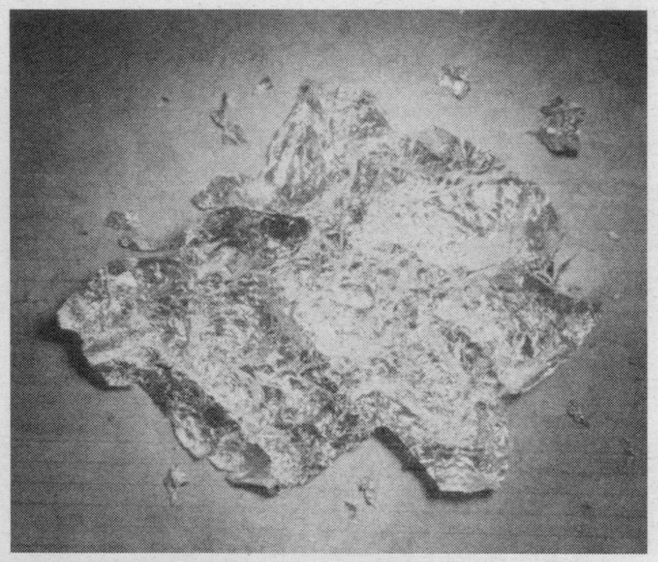

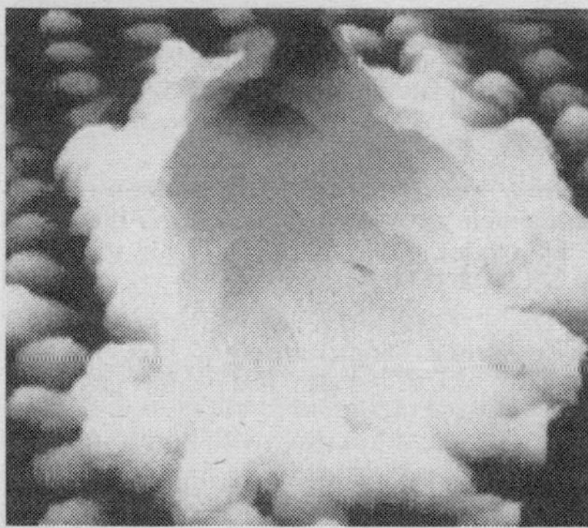

Gold is the easiest element to manipulate (above). An ounce of gold can be drawn out into a strand 43 miles long. (Science Photo Library/Erich Schrempp)

In this microscopic image (left), gold atoms are shown on a substrate of graphite (carbon). (Science Photo Library/Philippe Plailly)

Great Britain reported success in obtaining the isotope helium 4 (He-4) with impurity levels at less than two parts in 10^{15}.

Hardest The carbon (C) allotrope diamond has a Knoop value of 8,400.

Thermal expansion The metal with the highest expansion is cesium (Cs), at 94×10^{-5} per deg C, while the diamond allotrope of carbon (C) has the lowest expansion at 1.0×10^{-6} per deg C.

Most ductile 1 oz of gold (Au) can be drawn to a length of 43 miles.

Highest tensile strength Boron (B)has the highest tensile strength, at 5.7 GPa 8.3×10^5 lb/in^2.

Liquid range Based on the differences between melting and boiling points, the element with the shortest liquid range (on the Celsius scale) is the inert gas neon (Ne), at only 2.542 degrees (from –248.594 to –246.052°C [–415.469°F to –410.894°F]). The radioactive element neptunium (Np) has the longest liquid range, at 3,453 degrees (from 637 to 4,090°C [1,179°F to 7,394°F]).

Toxicity The severest restriction placed on any element in the form of a radioactive isotope is 2.4×10^{-16} grams/m^3 in air for thorium 228 (Th–228) or radiothorium, while the most severely restricted nonradioactive element is beryllium, with a threshold limit value in air of only 2 mg/m^3.

ISOTOPES

Most and fewest There are at least 2,550 isotopes, and cesium (Cs) has the most, with 37. The greatest number of stable isotopes is 10, for the metallic element tin (Sn). Hydrogen (H) has the fewest accepted isotopes, with just three.

Lightest and heaviest The lightest nuclide is hydrogen 1 (H 1) or protium, and the heaviest is meitnerium 266 (Mt-266)—meitnerium being the proposed name for element 109.

Most and least stable The most stable radioactive isotope is the double-beta decaying tellurium 128 (Te-128), with a half-life of 1.5×10^{24} years. Lithium 5 (Li-5) is the least stable, with a lifetime of 4.4×10^{-22} sec.

RAREST!

Only 0.0056 oz of the natural element astatine (At) is present in the Earth's crust; the isotope astatine 215 (At 215) accounts for only 1.6×10^{-10} oz. The least abundant element in the atmosphere is the radioactive gas radon (Rn), with a volume of 6×10^{-18} parts by volume.

CHEMICAL EXTREMES

Most powerful nerve gas Ethyl S-2-diisopropylaminoethylmethylphosphonothiolate or VX, developed at the Chemical Defense Experimental Establishment, Porton Down, Great Britain in 1952, is 300 times more powerful than the phosgene ($COCl_2$) used in World War I. The lethal dosage is 10 mg-minute/m^3 airborne or 0.3 mg orally.

Most lethal man-made chemical TCDD (2, 3, 7, 8-tetrachlorodibenzo-p-dioxin), the most dangerous of the 75 known dioxins, is admitted to be 150,000 times more deadly than cyanide.

Strongest acid The strongest super acid is an 80 percent solution of antimony pentafluoride in hydrofluoric acid (fluoroantimonic acid HF: SbF_5). This solution has not been measured directly, but even a 50 percent solution is 10^{18} times stronger than concentrated sulfuric acid.

Bitterest substance The bitterest-tasting substances are based on the denatonium cation and have been produced commercially as benzoate and saccharide. Taste detection levels are as low as one part in 500 million, and a dilution of one part in 100 million will leave a lingering taste.

Sweetest substance Talin from arils (appendages found on certain seeds) of katemfe (*Thaumatococcus daniellii*), discovered in West Africa, is 6,150 times as sweet as a 1 percent sucrose solution.

Most absorbent substance "H-span" or Super Slurper, composed of one-half starch derivative and one-fourth each of acrylamide and acrylic acid, can, when treated with iron, retain water 1,300 times its own weight.

Most refractory substance The most refractory substance is tantalum carbide ($TaC_{0.88}$), which melts at 7,214°F.

Most heat-resistant substance The existence of a complex material known as NFAARr or Ultra Hightech Starlite was announced in April 1993. Invented by Maurice Ward (Great Britain; b. 1932), it can temporarily resist plasma temperature (18,032°F).

Least dense solids These are the silica aerogels in which tiny spheres of bonded silicon and oxygen atoms are joined into long strands separated by pockets of air. In February 1990 the lightest of these aerogels, with a density of only 5 oz/ft^3, was produced at Lawrence Livermore Laboratory, CA. The main use will be in space to collect micrometeoroids and the debris present in comets' tails.

Highest superconducting temperature In May 1991, bulk superconductivity with a transition to zero resistance at –221.3°F was achieved at the Laboratorium für Festkörperphysik, Zurich, Switzerland, in a mixture of oxides of mercury, barium, calcium and copper, $HgBa_2Ca_2Cu_3O_1$+x and

$HgBa_2CaCu_2O_6$+x. Claims to have obtained higher temperatures have not been substantiated.

Most magnetic substance The most magnetic substance is neodymium iron boride ($Nd_2Fe_{14}B$) with a maximum energy product (the highest energy a magnet can supply when operating at a particular operating point) of up to 280 kJ/m^3.

Longest index The 12th collective index of *Chemical Abstracts*, completed in December 1992, contains 35,137,626 entries in 215,880 pages and 115 volumes and weighs 544 lb. It provides references to 3,052,700 published documents in the field of chemistry.

SMELLIEST!

The most evil of the 17,000 smells so far classified may be a matter of opinion, but ethyl mercaptan (C_2H_5SH) and butyl seleno-mercaptan (C_4H_9SeH) are pungent claimants, each with a smell reminiscent of a combination of rotting cabbage, garlic, onions, burned toast and sewer gas.

PHYSICAL EXTREMES

Highest temperature Temperatures produced in the center of a thermonuclear fusion bomb are of the order of 400,000,000°C. This temperature was attained in 1990 under controlled experimental conditions in the Tokamak Fusion Test Reactor at the Princeton Plasma Physics Laboratory, Princeton, NJ, by deuterium injection into a deuterium plasma.

Lowest temperature Absolute zero, 0 K on the Kelvin scale, corresponds to –459.67°F. The lowest temperature ever reached is 28×10^{-13} K in a nuclear demagnetization device at the Low Temperature Laboratory, Helsinki University of Technology, Finland in April 1993.

Highest pressures A sustained laboratory pressure of 170 GPa (11,000 tons force/in^2) was achieved in the giant hydraulic diamond-faced press at the Carnegie Institution's Geophysical Laboratory, Washington, D.C. and reported in June 1978.

Using dynamic methods and impact speeds of up to 18,000 mph, momentary pressures of 7,000 GPa (540,000 tons/in^2) were reported from the United States in 1958.

Lowest friction The lowest coefficient of static and dynamic friction of any solid is 0.03, for Hi-T-Lube with an MOS2 burnished (B) exterior. The 0.03

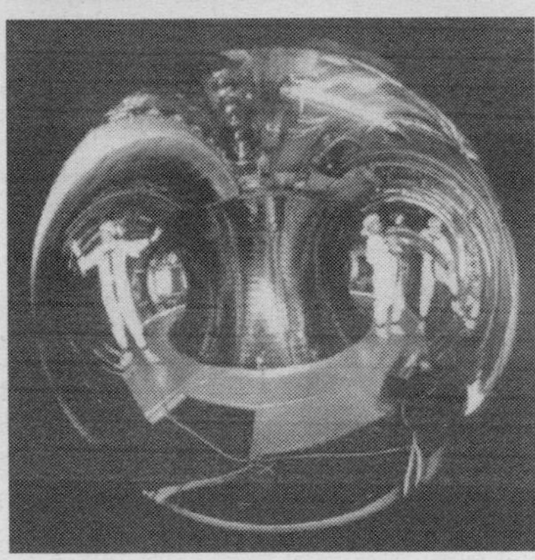

Princeton's Tokamak Fusion Test Reactor (TFTR) has generated the world's highest temperature. At left, scientists check the interior before a test run. (US Department of Energy/Science Photo Library; Roger Ressmeyer, Starlight/Science Photo Library)

result was achieved by sliding Hi-T-Lube (B) against Hi-T-Lube (B). This material was developed for NASA in 1965 by General Magnaplate Corp. in Linden, NJ and has been used on many space projects.

Highest velocity The highest velocity at which any solid visible object has been projected is 93 miles/sec (334,800 mph) in the case of a plastic disc at the Naval Research Laboratory, Washington, D.C., in August 1980.

Most powerful electric current If fired simultaneously, the 4,032 capacitors comprising the Zeus capacitor at the Los Alamos Scientific Laboratory, NM would produce, for a few microseconds, twice as much current as that generated anywhere else on Earth.

Hottest flame The hottest-burning substance is carbon subnitride (C_4N_2), which, at one atmosphere pressure, can produce a flame calculated to reach 9,010°F.

Highest measured frequency The highest *directly* measured frequency is a visible yellow-green light at 520.2068085 terahertz (a terahertz being a million million hertz) for the o-component of the 17–1 P (62) transition line of iodine-127.

The highest measured frequency determined by precision metrology is a green light at 582.491703 terahertz for the b_{21} component of the R (15) 43–0 transition line of iodine-127.

Smallest hole Holes 3.16 Å (3.16×10^{-10}m) in diameter were produced on the surface of molybdenum disulphide by Dr Wolfgang Henkl of the University of Munich, Germany, and Dr John Maddocks of the University of Sheffield, Great Britain, using a chemical method involving a mercury drill. The holes were drilled on 17 Jul 1992 at the University of Munich.

Brightest light The brightest artificial sources are laser pulses generated at the Los Alamos National Laboratory, NM, announced in March 1987. An ultraviolet flash lasting one picosecond (1×10^{-12} sec) is intensified to 5×10^{15} watts.

The most powerful searchlight ever developed was one produced during World War II by the General Electric Company Ltd at the Hirst Research Center in London, Great Britain. It had a consumption of 600 kW and a maximum beam intensity of 2.7 billion candles from its parabolic mirror (diameter 10 ft).

GUESS WHAT?

Q. Where is the hottest place in the world?

A. Look in "Weather" (Earth & Space)

Magnetic fields The strongest continuous field strength achieved was a total of 35.3 ± 0.3 teslas at the Francis Bitter National Magnet Laboratory, Massachusetts Institute of Technology in Cambridge, MA, on 26 May 1988, employing a hybrid magnet with holmium pole pieces.

The weakest measured magnetic field was one of 8×10^{-15} teslas in the heavily shielded room at the same laboratory. It is used for research into the very weak magnetic field generated in the heart and brain.

Highest vacuum A vacuum of the order of 10^{-14} torr was obtained at the IBM Thomas J. Watson Research Center, Yorktown Heights, NY in October 1976 in a cryogenic system with temperatures down to –452°F.

Highest voltage The highest-ever potential difference obtained in a laboratory was 32 ± 1.5 million volts by the National Electrostatistics Corporation at Oak Ridge, TN on 17 May 1979.

SCIENTIFIC INSTRUMENTS

Largest The largest scientific instrument is the electron–positron storage ring "LEP" at CERN, Geneva, Switzerland, which is 12½ ft in diameter and 17 miles in circumference.

Finest balance The Sartorius Model 4108 manufactured in Göttingen, Germany can weigh objects of up to 0.018 oz to an accuracy of 3.5×10^{-10} oz, equivalent to little more than 1/60 of the weight of the ink on this period.

Largest bubble chamber The $7 million installation completed in Oct 1973 at Fermilab, near Batavia, IL, is 15 ft in diameter. It contains 8,718 gallons of liquid hydrogen at a temperature of –413°F and has a superconducting magnet of 3 teslas.

Fastest centrifuge The highest man-made rotary speed ever achieved is 4,500 mph by a tapered 6-in carbon fiber rod in a vacuum at Birmingham University, Great Britain, reported on 24 Jan 1975.

Most powerful laser The most powerful laser is the "Nova" at the Lawrence Livermore National Laboratory, CA. Its 10 arms produce laser pulses capable of generating 100×10^{12} W of power, much of which is delivered to a target the size of a grain of sand in 1×10^{-9} sec. For this brief instant, that power is 200 times greater than the combined output of all the electrical generating plants in the United States. Fitted with two target chambers, the laser itself is 300 ft long and about three stories high.

Heaviest magnet The heaviest magnet is in the Joint Institute for Nuclear Research at Dubna, near Moscow, Russia, for the 10 GeV synchrophasotron measuring 196 ft in diameter and weighing 42,000 tons.

Largest electromagnet The world's largest electromagnet is part of the L3 detector, an experiment on LEP (large electron–positron collider). The octagonal-shaped magnet consists of 7,055 tons of low carbon steel yoke and 1,213 tons of aluminum coil. Thirty thousand amperes of current flow through the aluminum coil to create a uniform magnetic field of 5 kilogauss. The total weight of the magnet, including the frame, coil and inner support tube, is 7,810 tons, and it is composed of more metal than the Eiffel Tower.

Smallest microphone Prof. Ibrahim Kavrak of Bogazici University, Istanbul, Turkey developed a microphone for a new technique of pressure measurement in fluid flow in 1967. It has a frequency response of 10 Hz–10 kHz and measures 0.06×0.03 in.

Most powerful microscope The scanning tunneling microscope (STM) invented at the IBM Zürich research laboratory, Switzerland, in 1981 has a magnifying ability of 100 million and is capable of resolving down to 1/100 the diameter of an atom (3×10^{-10} m), making it the world's most powerful microscope.

Most powerful particle accelerator The world's highest energy "atom-smasher" is the 1.25-mile diameter proton synchroton "Tevatron" at the

Fermi National Accelerator Laboratory (Fermilab) near Batavia, IL. On 3 Jan 1987 a center of mass energy of 1.8 TeV (1.8×10^{12} eV) was achieved by colliding beams of protons and antiprotons.

Smallest optical prism A glass prism with sides 0.001 in—barely visible to the naked eye—was created at the National Institute of Standards and Technology laboratories in Boulder, CO in 1989.

Sharpest objects and smallest tubes The sharpest manufactured objects are glass micropipette tubes whose beveled tips have an outer diameter of 0.02 mm and an 0.01 mm inner diameter. The latter is 6,500 times thinner than a human hair. They are used in intracellular work on living cells.

Largest barometer An oil-filled barometer, of overall height 42 ft, was constructed by Allan Mills and John Pritchard of the Department of Physics and Astronomy, University of Leicester, Great Britain in 1991. It attained a standard height of 40 ft (at which pressure mercury would stand at $2^1/_2$ ft).

Smallest thermometer Dr Frederich Sachs, a biophysicist at the State University of New York at Buffalo, has developed an ultra-microthermometer for measuring the temperature of single living cells. The tip is one micron in diameter, about $^1/_{50}$ the diameter of a human hair.

Finest cut The $13 million large optics diamond turning machine at the Lawrence Livermore National Laboratory, CA was reported in June 1983 to be able to sever a human hair 3,000 times lengthwise.

Thinnest glass The thinnest glass, type D263, has a minimum thickness of 0.00098 in and a maximum thickness of 0.00137 in. It is made by Deutsche Spezialglas AG, Grünenplan, Germany for use in electronic and medical equipment.

Largest blown glass vessel A bottle standing 7 ft 8 in tall with a capacity of about 188 gal was blown at Wheaton Village, Millville, NJ on 26–27 Sep 1992 by a team led by glass artist Steve Tobin. The attempt was made during the "South Jersey Glass Blast," part of a celebration of the local glass-making heritage.

ECHO! ECHO!

The longest echo in any building is one of 15 sec following the closing of the door of the Chapel of the Mausoleum, Hamilton, Scotland, built 1840–55.

MATHEMATICS

In dealing with large numbers, scientists use the notation of 10 raised to various powers to eliminate a profusion of zeros. For example, 19,160,000,000,000 miles would be written 1.916×10^{13} miles. Similarly, a very small number, for example 0.0000154324 of a gram, would be written 1.54324×10^{-5}.

Largest numbers The largest lexicographically accepted named number in the system of successive powers of ten is the centillion, first recorded in 1852. It is the hundredth power of a million, or 1 followed by 600 zeros.

Prime numbers A prime number is any positive integer (excluding unity 1) having no integral factors other than itself and unity, e.g., 2, 3, 5, 7 or 11. The lowest prime number is thus 2.

The highest *known* prime number was discovered by computer scientists David Slowinski and Paul Gage at Cray Research Inc. in Minnesota in January 1994, while they were conducting tests on a CRAY C90 Series supercomputer. The new prime number has 258,716 digits, enough to fill over 21 pages of *The Guinness Book of Records*. In mathematical notation it is expressed as $2^{859,433}-1$, which denotes two multiplied by itself 859,433 times, minus one. Numbers expressed in this form are known as Mersenne prime numbers, named after Father Marin Mersenne, a 17th-century French monk who spent years searching for prime numbers of this type.

The largest known twin primes are $1,706,595 \times 2^{11,235} - 1$ and $1,706,595 \times 2^{11,235} + 1$, found on 6 Aug 1989 by a team in Santa Clara, CA.

Composite numbers The lowest nonprime or composite number (excluding 1) is 4.

Perfect numbers A number is said to be perfect if it is equal to the sum of its divisors other than itself, e.g., 1 + 2 + 4 + 7 + 14 = 28. The lowest perfect number is 6 (=1 + 2 + 3).

All perfect numbers have a direct relationship to Mersenne primes. The highest known perfect number, therefore, and the 33rd so far discovered, is $(2^{859,433}-1) \times 2^{859,433}$. It has a total of 517,430 digits (enough to fill over 41 pages of *The Guinness Book of Records*), and it is derived from the largest known Mersenne prime (see Prime numbers).

Newest mathematical constant The study of turbulent water, the weather and other chaotic phenomena has revealed the existence of a new universal constant, the Feigenbaum number. Named after its discoverer, Mitchell Feigenbaum (USA), this constant equals approximately 4.669201609102990.

Most difficult math problem Fermat's last theorem has precipitated more incorrect proofs than have been published for any other theorem. Pierre de Fermat inspired centuries of hopeless searching when he wrote the theorem in a notebook, adding, "I have found an admirable proof of this theorem, but the margin is too narrow to contain it." In June 1993 Andrew J. Wiles of Princeton University announced his discovery of the proof of the theorem. Subsequent study has revealed flaws that Prof. Wiles is working to correct.

Most-proved theorem A book published in 1940 entitled *The Pythagorean Proposition* contained 370 different proofs of Pythagoras' theorem.

Longest proof The proof of the classification of all finite simple groups is spread over more than 14,000 pages in nearly 500 papers in mathematical journals, contributed by more than 100 mathematicians over a period of more than 35 years.

Most prolific mathematician Leonard Euler (Switzerland; 1707–83) was so prolific that his papers were still being published for the first time more than 50 years after his death. His collected works have been printed bit by bit since 1910 and will eventually occupy more than 75 large volumes.

Most accurate version of pi The most decimal places to which *pi* (π) has been calculated is 2,260,321,336, by brothers Gregory Volfovich and David Volfovich Chudnovsky, on their homemade supercomputer m zero, in New York City in the summer of 1991.

Most inaccurate version of pi In 1897 the General Assembly of Indiana enacted Bill No. 246, stating that *pi* was *de jure* 4.

Most innumerate The Nambiquara of the northwest Mato Grosso of Brazil lack any system of numbers. They do, however, have a verb that means "they are alike."

Earliest measures The earliest known measure of weight is the *beqa* of the Amratian period of Egyptian civilization *c.* 3800 B.C., found at Naqada, Egypt. The weights are cylindrical, with rounded ends, and weigh 6.65–7.45 oz.

The unit of length used by the megalithic tomb-builders in northwestern Europe *c.* 3500 B.C. appears to have been 2.72 ± 0.003 ft. This was deduced by Prof. Alexander Thom (1894–1985) in 1966.

DID YOU KNOW?

"As I was going to St Ives, I met a man with seven wives. Every wife had seven sacks, every sack had seven cats, every cat had seven kits. Kits, cats, sacks and wives, how many were going to St Ives?"

Apart from slight differences in wording, this is identical to a puzzle found in the Rhind papyrus, an Egyptian scroll bearing mathematical tables and problems, copied by the scribe Ahmes *c.* 1650 B.C.

BOTTLE BATTLE

The Whitall Tatum Glass Factory Team proudly displaying their 108-gallon bottle. (Wheaton Village)

In the early 1900s a rivalry developed between glassblowers at the Whitall Tatum Company in Millville, New Jersey and the Illinois Glass Company of Alton, Illinois to see which firm could make the largest bottle. The culmination of this competition took place in late 1903 at Whitall Tatum, when a four-man crew set the record for the largest bottle ever blown—one of capacity 108 gal. It stood 5 ft 4 in tall and was 31 in wide.

Producing a container of this size was a monumental undertaking. Sadly, the bottle was broken on its return from St. Louis, where it was being exhibited, to Millville. The only surviving proof was a photograph showing the bottle towering over the team of brawny men who created it.

The intense heat of the gather will actually distort the workers' face shields. (Whcaton Village)

On 26 and 27 Sep 1992 a team of glassblowers led by glass artist Steve Tobin—the team consisting of Dale Leader, Daisuke Shintani, Chuck Smart, Don Friel and David Lewin—decided to attempt to beat the record at the Wheaton Glass Factory in Wheaton Village, Millville. They practiced for months to perfect the process they used to create the Big Bottle. Here's how they did it.

1 The end of a hollow pipe—which was about 4½ ft long altogether—was turned in a 2,200°F oven. The oven contained the molten glass, which was by that stage melted to the consistency of honey. As much of the glass as possible was gathered onto the edge of the pipe.

2 One of the glassblowers blew down the pipe, creating a small bubble of air in the gather of glass.

3 The pipe was returned to the furnace to gather more glass over and over again, until it had been in the furnace six times. "We built up one layer on top of the previous gather—like layers of skin on an onion," Friel said. "We shaped it, let it cool and went back. Each time, the size of the gather was twice what it was before." By the time the adequate amount of glass had been accumulated, the gather weighed around 90 pounds. It took four men to lift the pipe, and a crossbar was attached to the blowpipe to support it.

4 The pipe and glass were transported to a steel drum, 4 feet tall, lined with wooden slats, specially made for the purpose. Shintani sat on a set of steps so that he could reach over the glass, and he attached a hose to the neck of the blowpipe and inflated the glass with compressed air. As it grew it sagged and stretched, and the steps were raised by means of a forklift truck, suspending the glassblower high above the factory floor.

The new record-holders display their bottle. Standing: left, Steve Tobin; right, Daisuke Shintani. Sitting: left, Dale Leader; right, Donald Friel. (Wheaton Village)

5 Meanwhile, Tobin and Lewin kept reheating the glass with torches to prevent it from shattering as the air was blown in.

6 The bottle reached its full height of 7 feet 8 inches, and the bottle, still attached to the blowpipe, had to be removed from the mold.

7 The bottle had to be moved onto its side so that it could enter the specially constructed annealing oven, measuring 8 feet by 4 feet by 4 feet. Another special construction, a fire-resistant sling made of fabric, was used to carry the bottle.

8 It took four members of the team to transfer the bottle to the oven and two more members to open the doors of the oven. The procedure was accomplished in a matter of seconds.

9 Once the bottle was in the oven, the blowpipe had to be removed: the neck of the bottle was scored with a file and then hit repeatedly with a baseball bat.

10 The bottle was left in the oven for 20 hours to anneal.

11 The bottle was removed and put on permanent exhibition at the Museum of American Glass at Wheaton Village in Millville, New Jersey.

The bottle rises out of the mold and the neck is formed. (Wheaton Village)

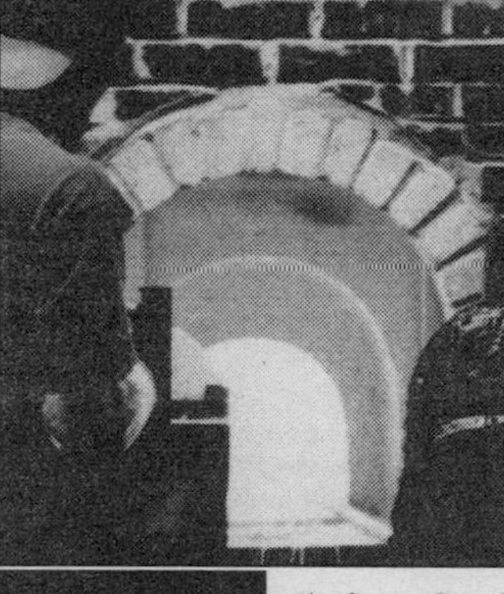

The first gather of glass launches the attempt to create the world's largest bottle. (Wheaton Village)

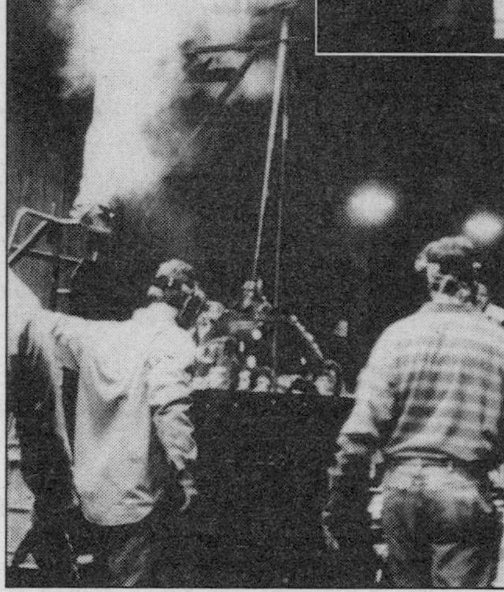

The glassblower is raised by a forklift as the compressed air is blown. The hot glass burns the sides of the wooden mold, creating steam.(Wheaton Village)

COMPUTING

Fastest The fastest general-purpose vector-parallel computer is the Cray Y-MP C90 supercomputer, with 2 gigabytes (gigabyte = one billion bytes) of central memory and with 16 CPUs (central processing units), giving a combined peak performance of 16 gigaflops (gigaflop = one billion flops [floating point operations] per second).

Several suppliers now market "massively parallel" computers which, with enough processors, have a theoretical aggregate performance exceeding that of a C90, though the performance on real-life applications can often be less. This is because it may be harder to harness effectively the power of a large number of small processors than a small number of large ones.

Fastest chip In March 1992 it was reported that DEC of Maynard, MA had developed an all-purpose computer chip, a 64-bit processor known as Alpha, which could run at speeds of up to 150 MHz (compared with 66 MHz for many modern personal computers). One Alpha chip is claimed to have about the same processing power as a CRAY-1, which went on sale in 1976 as the Cray company's first supercomputer.

Fastest transistor A transistor capable of switching 230 billion times per second was announced by the University of Illinois at Urbana–Champaign in October 1986. The devices were made of indium, gallium, arsenide and aluminum gallium arsenide and were developed in collaboration with General Electric Company.

Smallest modem The smallest modem is the SRM-3A, which is 2.4 in long, 1.2 in wide, and 0.8 in high, and weighs 1.1 oz. It is currently manufactured by RAD Data Communications Ltd of Tel Aviv, Israel.

Smallest robot The world's smallest robot is the "Monsieur" microbot, developed by the Seiko Epson Corporation of Japan in 1992. The light-sensitive robot measures less than 0.06 in^3, weighs 0.05 oz and is made of 97 separate watch parts (equivalent to two ordinary watches). Capable of speeds of 0.4 in/sec for about 5 min when charged, the "Monsieur" has earned a design award at the International Contest for Hill-Climbing Micromechanisms.

POWER

Steam engines Oldest The oldest steam engine in working order is the Smethwick Engine, dating from 1779. Designed by James Watt (1736–1819) and built by the Birmingham Canal Company, the pump—originally a 24-in bore with a stroke of 8 ft—worked on the canal locks at Smethwick,

INTERNET
THE INFORMATION HIGHWAY

(James Bartholomew)

Linking more than 27,000 computer networks and 20 million users worldwide, Internet is the world's largest computer network. Dr Vinton Cerf (left), co-creator of the system, describes the network and its potential.

How big is a billion? "It's a one with nine zeroes," says Vinton Cerf. He ought to know. A billion is how many networks he predicts Internet—the international web of computers he helped pioneer—will soon link. The Internet has gotten where it is today because Cerf and his collaborator, Robert E. Kahn, dreamed large. The two were commissioned by the U.S. government at the height of the Cold War, in 1973. Their mission: to create a way "to maintain Command Central in a post-nuclear attack environment." Unlike any other communications system, the Internet has no central control point. It can't be paralyzed if one part of the network shuts down; users just switch to other routes and continue communication.

Cerf and Kahn saw Internet's potential as a research tool. By the late 1980s, access was given to computer science, research and education. And then came e-mail. Cerf, who had worked to create a commercial electronic mail service, sought a link with Internet. Computers across the nation began blinking "YOU HAVE MAIL."

"In the long run," forecasts Cerf, "we'll see a global and ubiquitous communication ability." In some disciplines, it's already happening. In early 1994, a 129-digit number expected to take 40 quadrillion years to factor was beat by mathematicians who used the Internet to connect their computers. The decoded message, "The magic words are squeamish ossifrage," might not mean much to many, but to Cerf—and the message's decoders—it was proof of Internet's power. "In the blink of an eye the information is sewn together electronically in a seamless web."

"The thing that pleases me most is when I talk to parents whose college kids don't write home—but they send e-mail." Cerf spends his own time—where else?—on the Internet. "I'm part of a lively discussion group of Shakespeare managed by the University of Toronto."

Great Britain until 1891. The engine was presented to the Birmingham Museum of Science and Industry in 1960 and is regularly steamed for the public.

Largest The largest ever single-cylinder steam engine was designed by Matthew Loam of Cornwall and built by the Hayle Foundry Co. in 1849 for land draining at Haarlem, Netherlands. The cylinder was 12 ft in diameter and each stroke lifted 16,140 gal of water.

Most efficient The most efficient steam engine recorded was Taylor's engine built by Michael Loam for United Mines of Gwennap, Great Britain in 1840. It registered only 1.7 lb of coal per horsepower per hour.

Largest power plant The most powerful power station is currently the Itaipu power station on the Paraná River near the Brazil–Paraguay border. Opened in 1984, the station has now attained its ultimate rated capacity of 13,320 MW.

Largest battery The 10 MW lead-acid battery at Chino, CA has a design capacity of 40 MW/h. It will be used at an electrical substation for leveling peak demand loads. This $13 million project is a cooperative effort by Southern California Edison Company Electric Power Research Institute and International Lead Zinc Research Organization Inc.

Biggest blackout The greatest power failure in history struck seven northeastern US states and Ontario, Canada on 9–10 Nov 1965. About 30 million people in 80,000 miles^2 were plunged into darkness. Two people died as a result of the blackout. In New York City the power failed at 5:27 P.M. and was not fully restored for 13½ hr.

The Palo Verde complex is the largest nuclear power facility in the United States. (Palo Verde Nuclear Generating Station)

Largest boilers The largest boilers ever designed were those ordered in the United States from Babcock & Wilcox, with a capacity of 1,330 MW, involving the evaporation of 9.33 million lb of steam per hour.

Largest generators The largest operational is a turbo generator of 1,450 MW (net) being installed at the Ignalina atomic power station in southern Lithuania.

Largest nuclear power stations The world's largest nuclear power station, with 10 reactors and net output of 8,814 MW, is the station in Fukushima, Japan.

The largest nuclear power complex in the United States is at Wintersburg, AZ. The three Palo Verde units have a net summer capability of 3,663 MW.

The largest unit in the country is found in Bay City, TX. The South Texas 1 unit has a capability of 1,251 MW; the South Texas 2 unit's capability is 1,250 MW.

Largest nuclear reactor The largest single nuclear reactor in the world is the Ignalina station, Lithuania, which came fully on line in January 1984 and has a net capacity of 1,380 MW.

Solar power In terms of nominal capacity, the largest solar electric power facility in the world is the Harper Lake Site (LSP 8 and 9) in the Mojave Desert, run by UC Operating Services. These two solar electric generating stations (SEGS) have a nominal capacity of 160 MW (80 MW each). The station site covers 1,280 acres.

At year-end 1993, the total capacity of wind and solar (photovoltaic and thermal) electricity generating systems in the United States was approaching 2,000 MW. In 1993 wind turbines produced 2.9 billion kWh of electricity, the equivalent of burning 5.4 million barrels of oil—enough to meet the needs of a city the size of San Francisco for a year. Over 90 percent of the wind systems are located in California.

Transformers The world's largest single-phase transformers are rated at 1,500,000 kVA. Eight of these are in service with the American Electric Power Service Corporation. Of these, five step down from 765 to 345 kV.

DID YOU KNOW?

The duration record for spinning a clock-balance wheel by unaided hand is 5 min 26.8 sec, by Philip Ashley, 16, of Leigh, Great Britain on 20 May 1968. The record using 36 in of string with a 7¼-oz top is 58 min 20 sec, by Peter Hodgson at Southend-on-Sea, Great Britain on 4 Feb 1985. A team of 25 from the Mizushima Plant of Kawasaki Steel Works in Okayama, Japan spun a giant top 6 ft 6¾ in tall and 8 ft 6¼ in in diameter, weighing 793.6 lb, for 1 hr 21 min 35 sec on 3 Nov 1986.

An aerial view of the world's largest solar electric power facility, which is located in the Mojave Desert. Below bottom is one of the generating stations; below top, a close-up of one of the complexes. (Hank Morgan/Science Photo Library)

Transmission lines The longest span of any power line between pylons is 17,638 ft, across the Ameralik Fjord near Nuuk, Greenland. Built and erected by A.S. Betonmast of Oslo, Norway in 1991–92 as part of the 132kV line serving the 45MW Buksefjorden Hydro Power Station, the line weighs 42 tons.

Highest The world's highest transmission lines are those across the Straits of Messina, Italy, with towers of 675 ft (Sicily side) and 735 ft (Calabria side) 11,900 ft apart.

Highest voltages The highest voltages now carried are 1,330 kV for 1,224 miles on the D.C. Pacific Inter-tie in the United States.

Turbines *Largest* The largest hydraulic turbines are those rated at 815 MW (equivalent to 1.1 million hp), 32 ft in diameter with a 449 ton runner and a 350 ton shaft, installed by Allis-Chalmers at the Grand Coulee Dam Third Powerplant, WA.

Smallest A self-sustaining gas turbine with compressor and turbine wheels measuring just 2 in and an operating speed of 50,000 rev/min was built by Geoff Knights of London, Great Britain.

Wind generators The $14.2 million GEC MOD-5A installation on the north shore of Oahu, HI produces 7,300 kW when the wind reaches 32 mph with 400 ft rotors.

Oldest water mill The water mill with the oldest continuous commercial use is at Priston Mill near Bath, Great Britain, first mentioned in A.D. 931 in a charter to King Athelstan (924/5–939). It is driven by the Conygre Brook.

ENGINEERING

Oldest machinery The earliest mechanism still in use is the *dâlu*—a water-raising instrument known to have been in use in the Sumerian civilization, which originated *c.* 3500 B.C. in what is now lower Iraq.

Blast furnace The world's largest blast furnace, with a volume of 5,500 m^3, is the no. 5 furnace at the Cherepovets works in Russia.

Catalytic cracker The world's largest catalytic cracker is Exxon's Bayway Refinery plant at Linden, NJ, with a fresh feed rate of 5 million gals per day.

Conveyor belts The world's longest single-flight conveyor belt is one of 18 miles in Western Australia installed by Cable Belt Ltd of Camberley, Great Britain.

Gantry crane The 92.3 ft wide Rahco gantry crane at the Grand Coulee

Dam Third Powerplant, WA was tested to lift a load of 2,460 tons in 1975. It lowered a 1,972 ton generator rotor with an accuracy of 1.32 in.

Tallest mobile crane The 890-ton Rosenkranz K10001, with a lifting capacity of 1,100 tons, and a combined boom and jib height of 663 ft, is carried on 10 trucks, each limited to a length of 75 ft 8 in and an axle weight of 130 tons. It can lift 33 tons to a height of 525 ft.

Greatest load raised The heaviest lifting operation in engineering history was the raising of the entire 1-mile-long offshore Ekofisk complex in the North Sea, Great Britain, after subsidence of the seabed. The complex consists of eight platforms weighing some 44,090 tons. During 17–18 Aug 1987 it was raised 21 ft 4 in by 122 hydraulic jacks requiring a computer-controlled hydraulic system.

Most powerful diesel engines Five 12RTA84 type diesel engines have been constructed by Sulzer Brothers of Winterthur, Switzerland, for container-ships built for the American President Lines. Each 12-cylinder power unit gives a maximum continuous output of 57,000 bhp at 95 rev/min.

Largest dragline The world's largest walking dragline is "Big Muskie," the Bucyrus-Erie 4250W with an all-up weight of 13,200 tons and a bucket capacity of 5,933 ft^3 on a 310 ft boom. This is the largest mobile land machine and is now operating on the Central Ohio Coal Co. Muskingum site in Ohio.

Earthmover The giant wheeled loader developed for open-air coal mining in Australia by SMEC, a consortium of 11 manufacturers in Tokyo, Japan, is 55 ft in length, weighs 198 tons, and has rubber tires 11½ ft in diameter. The bucket has a capacity of 671 ft^3.

Escalators The world's longest is the four-section outdoor escalator at Ocean Park, Hong Kong, which has an overall length of 745 ft and a total vertical rise of 377 ft.

Shortest The ultimate in pampering for weary shoppers is the escalator at Okadaya More's shopping mall at Kawasaki-shi, Japan. It has a vertical height of 32.83 in and was installed by Hitachi Ltd.

Moving sidewalks The longest "moving sidewalks" are those installed in 1970 in the Neue Messe Center, Düsseldorf, Germany, which measure 738 ft between comb plates.

Escalator riding The record distance traveled on a pair of "up" and "down" escalators is 133.18 miles, by David Beattie and Adrian Simons at Top Shop in London, Great Britain, from 17 to 21 Jul 1989. They each completed 7,032 circuits.

Forging The largest forging on record is one of a 225-ton, 55-ft-long generator shaft for Japan, forged by the Bethlehem Steel Corporation of Pennsylvania in October 1973.

Forklift trucks Kalmar LMV of Sweden in 1991 manufactured three counterbalanced forklift trucks capable of lifting loads up to 99 tons at a

Escalator riding champs David Beattie and Adrian Simons (above) moving along during their record-setting ride.

The 70-floor Yokohama Landmark Tower (right) houses the world's fastest passenger elevators. Passengers travel from the second floor to the 69th in 40 seconds at an average 28 mph. (Mitsubishi Electric Corporation)

load center of 90.5 in. They were built to handle the Libyan Great Man-made River Project, comprising two separate pipelines, one 620 miles long running from Sawir to the Gulf of Sirte and the other 557 miles from Tazirbu to Benghazi, Libya.

• ***Lathe*** The largest is the 126-ft-long 460-ton giant lathe built by Waldrich Siegen of Germany in 1973 for the South African Electricity Supply Commission at Rosherville.

Largest nuts The largest nuts ever made weigh 5 tons each with an outside diameter of 52 in and a 25 in thread. Known as "Pilgrim Nuts," they are manufactured by Pilgim Moorside Ltd of Oldham, Great Britain for use on the columns of a large forging press.

Passenger elevators The fastest domestic passenger elevators in the world are in the 70-story, 971-ft-tall Yokohama Landmark Tower in Yokohama, Japan, opened to the public on 16 Jul 1993. Designed and built by Mitsubishi Electric Corporation of Tokyo, the lifts operate at 28 mph, taking passengers from the second floor to the 69th floor observatory in 40 sec.

Much higher speeds are achieved in the winding cages of mine shafts. A hoisting shaft 6,800 ft deep, owned by Western Deep Levels Ltd in South Africa, winds at speeds of up to 41 mph. Otitis media (popping of the ears) presents problems above even 10 mph.

Longest incarceration in an elevator Graham Coates of Brighton, Great Britain established an involuntary record when he was trapped in an elevator for 62 hr in Brighton on 24–28 May 1986.

Pipelines *Natural gas* The longest natural gas pipeline in the world is the Trans-Canada pipeline, which by 1974 had 5,654 miles of pipe up to 42 in in diameter.

Oil The longest crude oil pipeline in the world is the Interprovincial Pipe Line Company installation from Edmonton, Alberta, Canada to Buffalo, NY, a distance of 1,775 miles. Along the length of the pipe, 13 pumping stations maintain a flow of 8.3 million gals of oil per day.

Most expensive The world's most expensive pipeline is the Alaska oil pipeline running 800 miles from Prudhoe Bay to Valdez. On completion of the first phase in 1977, it had cost $8 billion. The pipe is 48 in in diameter and its capacity is now 2.1 million barrels per day.

Presses The world's two most powerful production machines are forging presses in the United States. The Loewy closed-die forging press, in a plant leased from the US Air Force by the Wyman-Gordon Company at North Grafton, MA, weighs 10,438 tons and stands 114 ft 2 in high. It has a rated capacity of 49,160 tons and became operational in October 1955. A similar press is in operation at the plant of the Aluminum Company of America in Cleveland, OH.

The greatest press force of any sheet metal forming press is 116,840 tons for a QUINTUS fluid cell press delivered by ASEA to BMG AG in Munich, Germany in January 1986.

Radar installations The largest of the three installations in the US Ballistic Missile Early Warning System (BMEWS) is that near Thule, in Greenland, 931 miles from the North Pole. It was completed in 1960 at a cost of $500 million.

Ropes The largest rope ever made was a coir fiber launching rope with a diameter of 47 in made in 1858 for the British liner *Great Eastern* by John and Edwin Wright of Birmingham, Great Britain. It consisted of four strands, each of 3,780 yarns.

Wire ropes The longest wire ropes in the world are the four made at British Ropes Ltd, Wallsend, Great Britain, each measuring 15 miles. The ropes are 1.3 in in diameter, weigh 120 tons each, and were ordered by the CEGB for use in the construction of the 2,000 MW cross-Channel power cable.

Shovel The Marion 6360 has a reach of 236 ft 9 in, a dumping height of 153 ft and a bucket capacity of 4,860 ft^3. Manufactured in 1964, it is operated for open-cast coal mining near Percy, IL by the Arch Mineral Corporation.

Steel production The world's largest producer of steel is the Nippon Steel Corporation of Japan, which produced 30.52 million tons of crude steel in the year ending March 1992, compared with 31.959 million tons in 1991. It now has 37,388 employees, compared with 51,441 in 1988.

The largest producer of steel in the United States in 1993 was USX Corporation, of Pittsburgh, PA, which produced 11.334 million tons of raw steel. The 1993 sales figure for the US Steel Group of USX was $5.6 billion and the number of employees for the year was 21,500.

Wind tunnel The world's largest wind tunnel is that of the NASA Ames Research Center in Mountain View, Palo Alto, CA. The largest test section measures 118 × 79 m and is powered by six 17,000 kW motors, giving a top speed of 124 mph.

MINES & DRILLING

Deepest The deepest penetration into the Earth's crust is a geological exploratory drilling near Zapolarny in the Kola Peninsula of Arctic Russia, begun on 24 May 1970 and reported in April 1992 to have surpassed a depth of 40,230 ft. The eventual target of 49,212 ft is expected in 1995.

Shaft sinking The one-month (31 days) world record is 1,251 ft for a standard shaft 26 ft in diameter, at Buffelsfontein Mine, Transvaal, South Africa, in March 1962.

Ocean drilling The deepest recorded drilling into the seabed is 6,563 ft, by the Ocean Drilling Program's vessel *JOIDES Resolution*, in the eastern equatorial Pacific in 1991. The deepest site at which drilling has been conducted is 23,077 ft below the surface on the western wall of the Mariana

MINING RECORDS

Earliest

World 100,000 B.C.—CHERT (silica) Nazlet Sabaha Garb, Egypt.

Deepest

World[1] 11,749 ft—GOLD Western Deep Levels, Carletonville, South Africa.

Coal

Largest (US) 27.9 million short tons per annum, ARCO Coal Co.'s Black Thunder Mine in Wright, WY.

Oldest (US)[2] *c.* 1750 at James River coalfield near Richmond, VA. This site is now abandoned.

Deepest (exploratory shaft) 6,700 ft, Donbas field, Ukraine.

(open cast, lignite) 1,066 ft, near Bergheim, Germany.

Copper

Deepest (open pit) 2,625 ft, Bingham Canyon, near Salt Lake City, UT.

Longest (underground) 994 miles, Division El Teniente, Codelco, Chile.

United States 356 miles of tunnels, San Manuel Mine, Magma Copper Co. in Arizona.

Gold

Richest 49.4 million fine oz (all-time yield), Crown Mines, Transvaal, South Africa.

Largest (world)[3] 12,107 acres, East Rand Proprietary Mines Ltd, Boksburg, Transvaal, South Africa.

Iron

Largest 22.4 billion tons (45–65% ore), Lebedinsky, Kursk region, Russia.

United States[4] 13.708 million metric tons at Mountain Iron, MN.

Lead

Largest >10 percent of world output, Viburnum Trend, MI.

Platinum

Largest 30.8 tons per year, Rustenburg Platinum Mines Group, Transvaal, South Africa.

Quarry

Largest (world) 2.81 miles^2, 3.698 billion tons (extracted), Bingham Canyon, UT.

Spoil Dump

Largest (world) 7.4 billion ft^3, New Cornelia Tailings, Ten Mile Wash, AZ.

Tungsten

Largest 2,205 tons per day, Union Carbide Mount Morgan mine, near Bishop, CA.

Uranium

Productivity 5,930 tons uranium per year, Cameco's Lake mine in Saskatchewan, Canada, 15.5 percent of world production.

[1] Sinking began in June 1957 and 14,000 ft is regarded as the limit. Its No. 3 vertical ventilation shaft is the world's deepest shaft, at 9,675 ft. This mine requires 141,150 tons of air per day, and uses enough refrigeration energy to make 41,440 short tons of ice. An underground shift comprises 11,150 men.

[2] The first recorded discovery of coal in the United States was in 1679 by French explorers, who reported a coal mine on the Illinois River.

[3] The world's most productive gold mine may be Muruntau, Kyzyl Kum, Uzbekistan, with an estimated 88 tons of gold per year. It has been estimated that South Africa has produced in 96 years (1886–1982) more than 31 percent of all gold mined since 3900 B.C. Over 51 percent of the world's output is produced at the 38 mines of the Witwatersrand fields, South Africa, first discovered in 1886. The largest gold mine currently in the United States is the Newmount Gold Company's Mine Complex in Eureka County and Elko County, NV.

[4] Minnesota produced the most iron in the United States in 1990, at 45.160 metric tons. The greatest year for the entire country was 1953, with 119.888 million metric tons.

Trench, Pacific Ocean, by the Deep Sea Drilling Project's vessel *Glomar Challenger*.

Ice-core drilling The deepest borehole in ice was reported in July 1993 to have reached the bottom of the Greenland ice sheet at a depth of 10,018 ft after five years' drilling by American researchers.

Fastest drilling The most footage drilled in one month is 34,574 ft, in June 1988 by Harkins & Company Rig Number 13 during the drilling of four wells in McMullen County, TX.

Coal shoveling The record for filling a 1,120 lb hopper with coal is 26.83 sec, by Brian McArdle at the Fingal Valley Festival in Fingal, Tasmania, Australia on 5 Mar 1994. The record by a team of two, also set at the Fingal Valley Festival on 5 Mar 1994, is 15.01 sec, by Brian McArdle and Rodney Spark, both of Middlemount, Queensland, Australia.

OIL

Production The world's largest oil producer in 1993 was Saudi Arabia, with 8,198,000 barrels per day (b/d). The United States was third, with 6,838,000 b/d.

Crude oil imports In 1993 the United States imported 7,523,000 b/d of crude oil and its by-products. Saudi Arabia was the leading supplier, providing 1,408,000 b/d, which represented 18.72 percent of US imports.

OPEC countries supplied the US with 4,251,000 b/d, or 56.51 percent of the total, while Persian Gulf countries supplied 1,994,000 b/d, or 26.51 percent.

Refineries The world's largest refinery is the Petroleos de Venezuela S.A. refinery in Judibana, Falcón, Venezuela. It is operated by the Lagoven subsidiary of Petroleos and in 1991 produced 530,000 barrels of crude oil per day.

TOP • 5 • FIVE

US CRUDE OIL IMPORTS

(January–December 1993)

Country	Barrels 1,000s per day
Saudi Arabia	1,277
Venezuela	999
Canada	903
Mexico	866
Nigeria	720

U.S. Department of Energy

United States The largest refinery in the United States is Amoco Oil Co.'s Texas City, TX refinery, which has a capacity of 433,000 barrels per day.

Oil tanks The largest oil tanks ever constructed are the five ARAMCO 1½ million-barrel storage tanks at Ju'aymah, Saudi Arabia. They are 72 ft tall with a diameter of 386 ft and were completed in March 1980.

Platforms *Heaviest* The world's heaviest oil platform is the *Pampo* in the Campos Basin off Rio de Janeiro, Brazil, built and operated by the Petrobrás company. Opened in the 1970s, the platform weighs 26,560 tons, covering 32,292 ft^2, and processes 30,000 barrels per day. It operates at a height of 377 ft from the seabed.

Tallest In December 1993 the "Auger" tension leg platform was installed in the Gulf of Mexico. Designed and engineered by Shell Oil Company, it set a new water depth record for a drilling and production platform, extending 2,860 ft from seabed to surface.

Oil gushers The greatest wildcat ever recorded blew at Alborz No. 5 well, near Qum, Iran on 26 Aug 1956. The uncontrolled oil gushed to a height of 170 ft at 120,000 barrels per day at a pressure of 9,000 lb/in^2. It was closed after 90 days' work by B. Mostofi and Myron Kinley of Texas.

Spills The world's worst oil spill occurred as a result of a marine blow-out beneath the drilling rig *Ixtoc I* in the Gulf of Campeche, Gulf of Mexico, on 3 Jun 1979. The slick reached 400 miles by 5 Aug 1979. It was capped on 24 Mar 1980 after a loss of 505,600 tons.

The worst single assault ever made on the environment was released on 19 Jan 1991 by the Iraqi president, Saddam Hussein, who ordered the pumping of Gulf crude oil from Kuwait's Sea Island terminal and from seven large tankers into the Persian Gulf. Provisional estimates put the loss at 6–8 million barrels.

The *Exxon Valdez* in Prince William Sound, AK struck a reef on 24 Mar 1989, spilling 10 million gallons of crude. The slick spread over 2,600 $miles^2$.

NATURAL GAS

Production The world's largest producer of natural gas in 1992 was Russia, with 22.62 trillion ft^3. In 1993 the United States produced 18.430 trillion ft^3.

Deposits The largest gas deposit in the world is at Urengoi, Russia, with an eventual production of 261.6 billion yd^3 per year through six pipelines from proved reserves of 9.156 trillion yd^3.

Greatest gas fire The greatest gas fire was the one that burned at Gassi Touil in the Algerian Sahara from noon on 13 Nov 1961 to 9:30 A.M. on 28 Apr 1962. The pillar of flame rose 450 ft and the smoke 600 ft. It was eventually extinguished by Paul Neal ("Red") Adair (b. 1916) of Houston, TX, using 550 lb of dynamite. His fee was reported to be about $1 million plus expenses.

Water wells *Water bore* The world's deepest water bore is the Stensvad

Water Well 11-W1 of 7,320 ft, drilled by the Great Northern Drilling Co. Inc. in Rosebud County, MT in October–November 1961.

Steam well The Thermal Power Co. geothermal steam well, begun in Sonoma County, CA in 1955, is down to 9,029 ft.

TIMEPIECES

CLOCKS

Most accurate The most accurate timekeeping device is a commercially available atomic clock manufactured by Hewlett-Packard of Palo Alto, CA, unveiled in December 1991. Designated the HP 5071A primary frequency standard with cesium II technology, the device, costing $54,000 and about the size of a desktop computer, is accurate to one second in 1.6 million years.

Oldest The oldest surviving working clock in the world is the faceless clock, dating from 1386, or possibly earlier, at Salisbury Cathedral in Great Britain, which was restored in 1956, having struck the hours for 498 years and ticked more than 500 million times.

Largest The world's most massive clock is the astronomical clock in the Cathedral of St-Pierre, Beauvais, France, constructed between 1865 and 1868. It contains 90,000 parts and is 40 ft high, 20 ft wide and 9 ft deep.

Largest clock face The world's largest is that of the floral clock constructed at Matsubara Park, Toi, Japan on 18 Jun 1991. The clock face is 101 ft in diameter.

Highest The highest two-sided clock in the world is at the top of the Morton International Building, Chicago, IL. The clock is 580 ft above street level.

Largest sundial The world's largest sundial has a base diameter of 122 ft and is 120 ft high, with a gnomon (projecting arm) of the same length. Designed by Arata Isozaki of Tokyo, Japan, as the centerpiece of the Walt Disney World Co. headquarters in Orlando, FL, it was unveiled on 1 Mar 1991.

Most expensive The highest price paid for any clock is $1,540,000 for a rare "Egyptian Revival" clock made by Cartier in 1927. Designed as an ancient Egyptian temple gate, with figures and hieroglyphs, the exotic clock is made of mother-of-pearl, coral and lapis lazuli. It was sold at Christie's, New York on 24 Apr 1991 to a private bidder.

Longest pendulum The world's longest pendulum measures 73 ft 9¾ in and is part of the water-mill clock installed by the Hattori Tokeiten Co. in the Shinjuku NS building in Tokyo, Japan in 1983.

Watches

Largest The largest "watch" was a "Swatch" 531 ft 6 in long and 65 ft 7½ in in diameter, made by D. Tomas Feliu, which was set up on the site of the Bank of Bilbao building, Madrid, Spain from 7–12 Dec 1985.

Heaviest The Eta "watch" on the Swiss pavilion at Expo 86 in Vancouver, British Columbia, Canada from May to October weighed 38.5 tons and stood 80 ft high.

Smallest The smallest watches are those produced by Jaeger le Coultre of Switzerland. Equipped with a 15-jeweled movement, they measure just over ½ in long and 3/16 in in width. Movement and case weigh under 0.25 oz.6

Most expensive The record price paid for a watch is SFr4.95 million ($3,315,000) at Habsburg Feldman, Geneva, Switzerland on 9 Apr 1989 for a Patek Philippe "Calibre '89" with 1,728 separate parts.

Astronomical clockface The entirely mechanical Planetarium Copernicus, made by Ulysse Nardin of Switzerland, is the only wristwatch that indicates time of day, date, phases of the moon, and astronomical position of the sun, Earth, the moon and the planets known in Copernicus' day. It also represents the Ptolemaic universe, showing the astrological "aspects" at any given time.

The Patek Philippe "Calibre '89" is the world's most expensive watch. (Patek Philippe)

United States The longest pendulum is a reconstruction of Foucault's experiment. It swings from a cable 90 ft long and 23 ft above the heads of visitors to the Convention Center in Portland, OR and weighs 900 lb.

TELEPHONES & FAXES

Telephones At the end of 1992, the International Telecommunication Union estimated that there were approximately 575 million telephone subscribers in the world. The country with the greatest number was the United States, with 144,056,700. Monaco has the most telephones per head of population, with 1,004 per 1,000. The greatest number of calls made in any country is in the United States, with 502.85 billion per year.

Largest The world's largest operational telephone was exhibited at a festival on 16 Sep 1988 to celebrate the 80th birthday of Centraal Beheer, an insurance company based in Apeldoorn, the Netherlands. It was 8 ft 1 in high and 19 ft 11 in long, and weighed 3.8 tons. The handset, which was 23 ft 5 in long, had to be lifted by crane in order for a call to be made.

Smallest The smallest operational telephone was created by Zbigniew Rózanek of Pleszew, Poland in September 1992 and measured $2^5/_8 \times {}^3/_4 \times 1^1/_8$ in. The smallest operational telephone in the United States was created by Jeff Smith of GTE Northwest, Everett, WA in 1988 and measured $4^1/_8 \times {}^3/_4 \times 1^1/_2$ in.

GUESS WHAT?

Q. How many phone numbers can one person remember?

A. Check "Brains" (Human Being)

Busiest routes The busiest international telephone route is between the United States and Canada. In 1992 there were some 3.7 billion minutes of two-way traffic between the two countries.

Busiest telephone exchange GPT (GEC Plessey Telecommunications Ltd) demonstrated the ability of the "System X" telephone exchange to handle 1,558,000 phone calls in an hour through one exchange in Beeston, Great Britain on 27 Jun 1989.

Largest switchboard The world's biggest switchboard is the one in the Pentagon, Washington, D.C., with 34,500 lines handling over 1 million calls per day through 200,000 miles of telephone cable.

Longest telephone cable The world's longest submarine telephone cable is

ANZCAN, which runs for 9,415 miles from Port Alberni, Canada to Auckland, New Zealand and Sydney, Australia via Fiji and Norfolk Island. It cost some $379 million and was inaugurated by Queen Elizabeth II in November 1984.

Optical fiber The longest distance at which signals have been transmitted without repeaters is 156.3 miles, at the British Telecom (BT) research laboratory at Martlesham Heath, Great Britain in 1985. The longest unspliced ducted optical fiber link, with a capacity of 8,000 telephone lines, was installed by BT in February 1991. The optical fibers, made by Optical Fibres of Deeside, Great Britain, are 8.45 miles long.

Most expensive telephone card The highest price paid for a phone card was for the first card issued in Japan. It changed hands in January 1992 for $42,000.

Morse code The highest recorded speed at which anyone has received Morse code is 75.2 words per minute—over 17 symbols per second. This was achieved by Ted R. McElroy of the United States in a tournament at Asheville, NC on 2 Jul 1939.

The fastest speed recorded for hand-key transmitting is 175 symbols a minute by Harry A. Turner of the US Army Signal Corps at Camp Crowder, MO on 9 Nov 1942.

Fax *Largest* The largest facsimile (fax) machine is manufactured by WideCom Group Inc. of Mississauga, Ontario, Canada. "WIDEFax 36" is able to scan, print and copy documents of up to 36 in.

Smallest The world's smallest fax machine is the Real Time Strategies Inc. hand-held device Pagentry, which combines various functions including the transmission of messages to facsimile machines. It measures just 3 × 5 × 3/4 in and weighs 5 oz.

TELESCOPES

Largest telescope The Keck telescope on Mauna Kea, HI has a 394 in mirror, made up of 36 segments fitted together to produce the correct curve. Each segment is 72 in in aperture. An active support system holds each segment in place and focuses the images. A twin Keck telescope is to be set up close to the first. When completed, Keck I and Keck II will be able to work together as an interferometer. Theoretically they would be able to see a car's headlights separately from a distance of 15,500 miles.

Largest reflector The largest single-mirror telescope now in use is the 19 ft 8 in reflector sited on Mount Semirodriki, near Zelenchukskaya, Russia, at an altitude of 6,830 ft, completed in 1976.

United States The largest single-mirror telescope in the United States is the 200 in Hale reflector at Mount Palomar, CA, completed in 1948.

ON THE RECORD

KECK TELESCOPE

KECK OBSERVATORY, MAUNA KEA, HAWAII

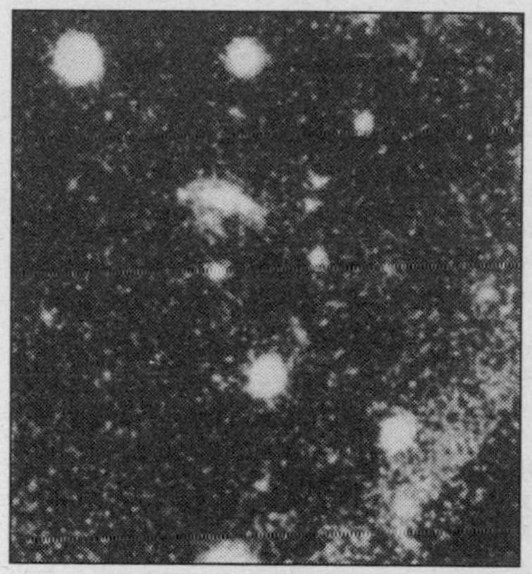

4C41.17, the most distant galaxy. (W.M. Keck Observatory)

Here's what Andy Perala, spokesman for the Keck Observatory, says about why the world needs a giant telescope, on top of a 14,000-ft mountain, under skies so clear the stars don't twinkle:

"If you hold your thumb at arm's length, the patch of sky your thumbnail hides holds 50,000 galaxies. There are billions out there."

The astronomers who use the Keck Telescope hope to spot at least a few of those galaxies. Already they've chalked up some new records.

"We've seen the most distant known galaxy, the most luminous objects, and the farthest away object, a quasar." Just how far away is far? "Ten to 12 to 14 billion light-years away. That's how long the light has been traveling to get here."

If people who work with this telescope tend to get a little cosmic, that's why. "In time, we're looking back into the Stone Age," Perala explains. "A giant telescope is like a time machine. When you look through it, it's like watching the universe evolve over eons and eons."

In the works? A closer view of a previously unknown galactic cluster . . . and interaction with the Hubble Telescope. The Keck's range is 17 times larger than the Hubble's, but because the Hubble is situated above the Earth's atmosphere, it's in a unique position to find things for astronomers to point the Keck at for a closer look.

(W.M. Keck Observatory)

Infrared The largest infrared reflector in the world is the UKIRT (United Kingdom Infrared Telescope) on Mauna Kea, HI, with a 147 in mirror. It is so good that it can be used for visual work as well as infrared.

Metal-mirror A 72 in reflector was made by the third Earl of Rosse, and set up at Birr Castle, Ireland in 1845. The mirror was of speculum metal (an alloy of copper and tin). With it, Lord Rosse discovered the spiral forms of the galaxies. It was last used in 1909.

Largest planned The largest telescope of the century should be the VLT (Very Large Telescope) being planned by the European Southern Observatory. It will consist of four 26 ft 3 in telescopes working together, providing a light-grasp equal to a single 52 ft 6 in mirror. The chosen site is Paranal in northern Chile. It is hoped that the first units will be working by 1995, and the telescope completed by 2000.

Multiple-mirror The MMT (Multiple-Mirror Telescope) at the Whipple Observatory at Mount Hopkins, AZ uses six 72 in mirrors together, giving a light-grasp equal to a single 176 in mirror.

Solar The McMath solar telescope at Kitt Peak, AZ has a 6 ft 11 in primary mirror; the light is sent to it via a 32° inclined tunnel from a coelostat (rotatable mirror) at the top end.

Submillimeter The James Clerk Maxwell telescope on Mauna Kea, HI has a 49 ft 3 in paraboloid primary, and is used for studies of the submillimeter part of the electromagnetic spectrum (0.01– 0.03 in).

Largest refractor A 62 ft long 40 in refractor completed in 1897 is situated at the Yerkes Observatory, Williams Bay, WI and belongs to the University of Chicago, IL. Although nearly 100 years old, it is still in full use on clear nights.

Largest radio dish The world's largest radio telescope is the partially-steerable ionospheric assembly built over the natural bowl at Arecibo, Puerto Rico, completed in November 1963. The reflector dish is 1,000 ft in diameter and covers 18½ acres suspended 426 ft under a 600-ton triangular platform.

Largest radio installation The largest radio installation is the Australia Telescope, which includes dishes at Parkes (210 ft in diameter), Siding Spring (72 ft) and Culgoora (also 72 ft). There are also links with tracking stations at Usuada and Kashima, Japan, and with the TDRS (Tracking and Data Relay Satellite), which is in a geosynchronous orbit. This is equivalent to a radio telescope with an effective diameter of 2.16 Earth diameters (17,102 miles).

United States The VLA (Very Large Array) of the US National Science Foundation is Y-shaped, with each arm 13 miles long and with 27 mobile antennae (each of 82 ft diameter) on rails. It is 50 miles west of Socorro in the Plains of San Augustin, NM. It was completed on 10 Oct 1980.

Largest Schmidt telescope A Schmidt telescope uses a spherical mirror with a correcting plate and can cover a very wide field with a single expo-

A section of the VLA (Very Large Array) radio telescope interferometer. (Science Photo Library/R. Ressmeyer, Starlight)

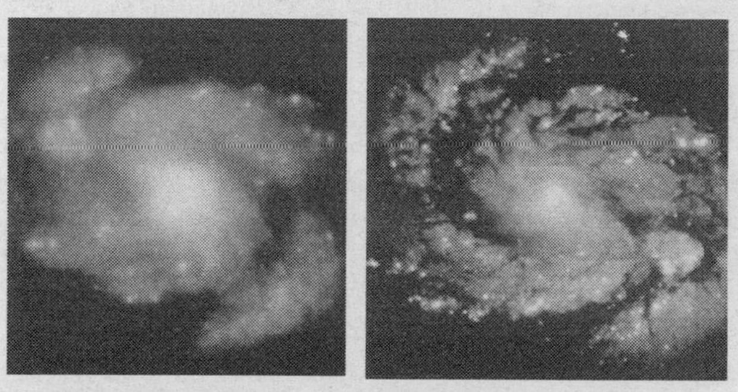

The Hubble Space Telescope repair mission in December 1993 proved a great success, as evidenced by these before and after shots of spiral galaxy M100. (Science Photo Library/Space Telescope Science Inst./NASA)

sure. The largest is the 6 ft 6¾ in instrument at the Karl Schwarzschild Observatory in Tautenberg, Germany. It has a clear aperture of 52¾ in with a 78¾ in mirror, focal length 13 ft. It was brought into use in 1960.

Space telescope Largest The largest is the $2.1 billion NASA Edwin P. Hubble Space Telescope of 12 tons and 43 ft in overall length with a 94½ in reflector. It was placed in orbit at 381 miles altitude aboard a US space shuttle on 24 Apr 1990.

Observatory *Oldest* The oldest observatory building extant is the "Tower of the Winds" used by Andronichus of Cyrrhus in Athens, Greece *c.* 100 B.C., and equipped with sundials and clepsydra (water clock).

Highest The high-altitude observatory at Denver, CO is at 14,100 ft and was opened in 1973. The main instrument is a 24 in reflector. It is slightly higher than the observatory at the summit of Mauna Kea in Hawaii at 13,760 ft.

Lowest The lowest "observatory" is at Homestake Mine, SD, where the "telescope" is a tank of cleaning fluid (perchloroethylene), which contains chlorine, and can trap neutrinos from the sun. The installation is 1.1 miles below ground level, in the shaft of a gold mine; the detector has to be at this depth, as otherwise the experiments would be confused by cosmic rays.

Planetaria The ancestor of the modern planetarium is the rotatable Gottorp Globe, built by Andreas Busch in Denmark about 1660. It was 34 ft 7 in in circumference, and is now preserved in St Petersburg, Russia. The stars were painted on the inside. The first modern planetarium was opened in 1923 in Jena, Germany; it was designed by Walther Bauersfelt of the Carl Zeiss company.

The world's largest planetarium is in Miyazaki, Japan, and was completed on 30 Jun 1987. The dome has a diameter of 88 ft 7 in.

United States The Kelly Space Voyager Planetarium in Charlotte, NC is the largest planetarium in the United States. Completed in October 1991, it has a dome 78½ feet in diameter. The facility has 307 seats.

The American Museum–Hayden Planetarium, New York City has a dome diameter of 75 ft 2 in, but has the largest seating capacity of any planetarium in the United States, with 650 seats.

The Adler Planetarium in Chicago, IL, which opened on 12 May 1930, is

Chicago's Adler Planetarium is the oldest planetarium in the United States. (D. Ontiveros/Adler Planetarium)

the oldest planetarium in the United States. Its dome is 68 ft in diameter and it seats 450 people.

ROCKETRY

Most powerful rocket The NI booster of the former USSR, first launched from the Baikonur Cosmodrome at Tyuratam, Kazakhstan on 21 Feb 1969, had a thrust of 5,200 tons but exploded at takeoff + 70 secs. Its current booster, *Energya*, first launched on 15 May 1987 from the Baikonur Cosmodrome, has a thrust of 3,900 tons. It is capable of placing 116 tons into low Earth orbit. Four strap-on boosters powered by single RD-170 engines burning liquid oxygen and kerosene were used.

Most powerful rocket engine The most powerful rocket engine was built in the former USSR by Scientific Industrial Corporation of Energetic Engineering in 1980. The engine has a thrust of 900 tons in open space and 830 tons at the Earth's surface. The RD-170 burns liquid oxygen and kerosene.

Lunar records The first direct hit on the moon was achieved at 2 min 24 sec after midnight (Moscow time) on 14 Sep 1959, by the Soviet space probe *Lunar II*, near the Mare Serenitatis. The first photographic images of the hidden side of the moon were collected by the Soviet *Lunar III* from 6:30 A.M. on 7 Oct 1959 from a range of up to 43,750 miles, and transmitted to the Earth from a distance of 292,000 miles.

Closest approach to the sun by a rocket The research spacecraft *Helios B* approached within 27 million miles of the sun, carrying both US and German instrumentation, on 16 Apr 1976.

Remotest man-made object *Pioneer 10*, launched from Cape Canaveral, FL, crossed the mean orbit of Pluto on 17 Oct 1986, being then at a distance of 3.67 billion miles from Earth.

DID YOU KNOW?

The fastest escape velocity from Earth was 34,134 mph, achieved by the ESA Ulysses spacecraft, powered by an IUS–PAM upper stage after deployment from the Space Shuttle Discovery on 7 Oct 1990, en route to a solar polar orbit via Jupiter.

The fastest solar system speed of approximately 158,000 mph is reached by the NASA-German Helios B solar probe each time it reaches the perihelion of its solar orbit.

SPACE FLIGHT

The first artificial satellite was successfully put into orbit by an intercontinental ballistic missile from the Baikonur Cosmodrome, Kazakhstan on the night of 4 Oct 1957. It reached an altitude of between 142 miles (perigee or nearest point to Earth) and 588 miles (apogee or furthest point from Earth) and a velocity of more than 17,750 mph. This spherical satellite, called *Sputnik 1* ("Fellow Traveler"), was officially designated "Satellite 1957 Alpha 2." It weighed 184.3 lb, with a diameter of 22¾ in; its lifetime is believed to have been 92 days, ending on 4 Jan 1958.

Earliest manned satellite The earliest manned spaceflight was by Cosmonaut Flight Major (later Col.) Yuri Alekseyevich Gagarin (1934–68) in *Vostok 1* on 12 Apr 1961. Takeoff was from the Baikonur Cosmodrome, Kazakhstan at 6:07 GMT and the landing was near Smelovka, in the Saratov region of Russia, 108 minutes later. Col. Gagarin landed separately from his spacecraft, by parachute. The maximum altitude during *Vostok 1*'s 25,394½ mile flight was listed at 203 miles, with a maximum speed of 17,560 mph.

United States On 5 May 1961, aboard *Mercury 3*, Cdr. Alan B. Shepard, Jr. (USN) became the first American to pilot a spaceflight. The suborbital flight, which lasted 15 min 28 sec, covered 302 miles and reached an altitude of 116.5 miles.

John H. Glenn was the first American to orbit the Earth. His flight aboard *Mercury 6* (*Friendship 7*) was launched at 9:47 A.M. EST on 20 Feb 1962 and splashed down into the Atlantic Ocean at 2:43 P.M. EST that same day. Glenn completed three orbits of the Earth and traveled approximately 81,000 miles.

First woman in space The first woman to orbit the Earth was Junior Lt (now Lt-Col. Eng) Valentina Vladimirovna Tereshkova (b. 6 Mar 1937), who was launched in *Vostok 6* from the Baikonur Cosmodrome, Kazakhstan at 9:30 GMT on 16 Jun 1963, and landed at 8:16 GMT on 19 June, after a flight of 2 days 22 hr 50 min, during which she completed over 48 orbits (1,225,000 miles) and passed momentarily within three miles of *Vostok 5*.

United States The first American woman in space was Sally Ride, who was launched in the US space shuttle *Challenger STS–7* on 18 Jun 1983, and returned to Earth on 24 June.

Astronauts *Oldest* The oldest astronaut of the 307 people in space (to 18 Apr 1994) was Vance DeVoe Brand (USA; b. 9 May 1931), age 59, while on the space shuttle mission aboard the *Columbia STS 35*, 2–10 Dec 1990. The oldest woman was Shannon Lucid (USA), age 50 years 278 days, on takeoff of space shuttle mission *Columbia STS 58* in October 1993.

Youngest The youngest was Major (later Lt-Gen.) Gherman Stepanovich Titov (b. 11 Sep 1935), who was 25 years 329 days when launched in *Vostok*

ON THE RECORD

SPACE FLIGHTS

At age 5, Shannon Lucid decided to become a pilot. She dreamed of exploring space before the word astronaut existed in the English language. Nowadays her dream is a trip to Mars. NASA has tested Lucid (along with other astronauts) to gauge the effects of long-term space travel on the human body.

"There's no limit to the length of time I could spend in space," says Lucid. But space does take some getting used to. "It's never routine." Lucid can feel her heart calming while she's in orbit—and feels the strain it goes through getting up to normal rate back on the ground. Leg muscles suffer from lack of use, too. "I couldn't go for a hike up a mountain right after returning to Earth," she says. "I'd really feel it."

Lucid doesn't feel any ill effects in space, though. She doesn't mind bouncing off the walls in the zero-gravity of the space shuttle. "Back on Earth I feel constrained. Up there we use space more effectively. We use the floors, the ceiling and the walls, and it doesn't take as much effort to move around. Also, in space, body fluid redistributes throughout the body. It doesn't bother me." She explains, "My face gets fuller, but my legs and waist get smaller." She laughs: "Some people have the kind of figure that looks better in space."

Does she have any regrets about spending a long time in space? Just one: "My two weeks in space were the longest time of my entire life without a book to read. Now that's a record!"

Shannon Lucid (NASA)

2 on 6 Aug 1961. The youngest woman in space was Valentina Tereshkova, 26.

The youngest American astronaut was Sally Ride (b. 26 May 1951), who on 18 Jun 1983, aged 32 years 23 days, was launched on *Challenger STS 7*.

Longest and shortest manned spaceflight The longest manned flight was by Col. Vladimir Georgeyevich Titov (b. 1 Jan 1947) and Flight Engineer Musa Khiramanovich Manarov (b. 22 Mar 1951), who were launched to the *Mir* space station aboard *Soyuz TM4* on 21 Dec 1987, and landed, in *Soyuz TM6* (with French spationaut Jean-Loup Chretien), at a secondary recovery site near Dzhezkazgan, Kazakhstan, on 21 Dec 1988, after a spaceflight lasting 365 days 22 hr 39 min 47 sec. The shortest manned flight was made by Cdr. Alan B. Shepard, Jr. (USN; b. 18 Nov 1923) aboard *Mercury Redstone 3* on 5 May 1961. His suborbital mission lasted 15 min 28 sec.

The most experienced space traveler is the Soviet (now Azerbaijani) flight engineer Musa Manarov, who clocked 541 days 31 min 10 sec on two space flights in 1987–88 and 1990–91.

United States Gerald P. Carr, Edward G. Gibson and William R. Pogue manned the longest American flight, aboard *Skylab 4*, which was launched 16 Nov 1973 and splashed down 8 Feb 1974, after 84 days 1 hr 15 min 31 sec in space. They are the most experienced US astronauts. The most experienced space shuttle flier is Daniel Brandenstein, with 32 days 22 hr 10 min.

Shuttle flight The longest space shuttle flight was one of 336 hr 13 min by *Columbia*, 18 Oct–1 Nov 1993. The main purpose of the mission was to test

The Russian space station Mir was the home for Vladimir Titov and Musa Manarov during their year-long space flight. (Science Photo Library/Novosti Press Agency)

the effects of weightlessness on the human body. The seven-person crew (five men and two women) included Shannon Lucid, who was making her record fourth space flight.

Most isolated human being The farthest any human has been removed from his nearest living fellow human is 2,233.2 miles, in the case of the command module pilot Alred M. Worden on the US *Apollo 15* lunar mission of 30 Jul–1 Aug 1971, while David Scott and James Irwin (1930–91) were at Hadley Base exploring the surface.

Most journeys Capt. John Watts Young (USN ret.; b. 24 Sep 1930) completed his sixth spaceflight on 8 Dec 1983, when he relinquished command of *Columbia STS 9/Spacelab* after a space career of 34 days 19 hr 41 min 53 sec. Young flew *Gemini 3, Gemini 10, Apollo 10, Apollo 16, STS 1* and *STS 9*. The greatest number of flights by a Soviet cosmonaut is five, by Vladimir Dzhanibekov (between 1978 and 1985). The most by a woman is four, by Shannon Lucid (USA) (*STS 419*, *31*, *45* and *58*). Lucid is also is the woman with the most space experience, with 34 days 22 hr 52 min.

Largest crew The largest crew on a single space mission was eight. This included one woman and was launched on space shuttle *Challenger 9 STS 61A*, the 22nd shuttle mission, on 30 Oct 1985, carrying the German *Spacelab D1* laboratory. The mission, commanded by Henry Warren "Hank" Hartsfield, lasted 7 days 44 min 51 sec. The greatest number of women in a space crew is three (of seven) on *Columbia STS 40* in June 1991.

Most in space The greatest number of people in space at any one time has been 12, on three occasions. Seven Americans were aboard the space shuttle *Columbia STS 35*; two Soviet cosmonauts were aboard the *Mir* space station; and two cosmonauts and one Japanese journalist were aboard *Soyuz TM11*, on 2–10 Dec 1990.

On 23–24 Mar 1992, six Americans and one Belgian were on space shuttle *Atlantis*, two CIS cosmonauts were on *Mir*, and two CIS cosmonauts and a German were on *Soyuz TM14*. Most recently, on 31 Jul 1992, four CIS cosmonauts and one Frenchman were aboard *Mir* at the same time as five US astronauts, one Swiss and one Italian were on *STS46 Atlantis*.

Lunar conquest Neil Alden Armstrong (b. 5 Aug 1930), command pilot of the *Apollo 11* mission, became the first human to set foot on the moon, on the Sea of Tranquility, at 02:56 and 15 sec GMT on 21 Jul 1969. He was followed out of the lunar module *Eagle* by Col. Edwin Eugene "Buzz" Aldrin, Jr. (USAF; b. 20 Jan 1930) while the command module *Columbia*, piloted by Lt Col. Michael Collins (USAF;b. 31 Oct 1930), orbited above.

Longest spacewalk The longest spacewalk ever made was 8 hr 29 min, by Pierre Thuot, Rick Hieb and Tom Akers of *STS 49 Endeavor* on 13 May 1992. The longest spacewalk by a woman lasted 7 hr 49 min, by Kathryn Thornton (USA) of *STS 49 Endeavor* on 14 May 1992.

Longest in orbit The longest recorded spacewalk in Earth orbit was made outside space shuttle *Discovery STS 51I* in September 1985, lasting 7 hr 20 min, by James van Hoften and Bill Fisher.

Untethered Capt. Bruce McCandless II (USN; b. 8 Jun 1937), from the space shuttle *Challenger*, was the first to engage in untethered EVA, at an altitude of 164 miles above Hawaii, on 7 Feb 1984.

Most spacewalks Russian cosmonaut Aleksandr Serebrov completed a record ninth spacewalk on 22 Oct 1993. The mission was carried out to check the orbiting *Mir* space station.

United States During the 11-day *Endeavor* shuttle mission to repair the Hubble Telescope, Lt Col. Thomas Akers made his fifth space walk. Akers had logged 29 hr 40 min walking in space by 7 Dec 1993. Dave Scott also made five space walks, during *Apollo* missions *9* and *15* in 1969 and 1971.

Space fatalities The greatest published number to perish in any of the 159 attempted spaceflights to 6 Apr 1993 is seven aboard the *Challenger 51L* on 28 Jan 1986, when an explosion occurred 73 sec after liftoff, at a height of 47,000 ft. *Challenger* broke apart under extreme aerodynamic overpressure.

Apollo 17 astronauts Eugene Cernan and Harrison Schmidt spent the longest time on the Moon. Schmidt is seen above beside a lunar boulder—he was a geologist— and (left) next to the US flag at the landing site. (Science Photo Library/NASA)

Farthest from Earth The greatest altitude attained by humans was when the crew of the *Apollo 13* were at apocynthion (i.e., their furthest point) 158 miles above the lunar surface, and 248,655 miles above the Earth's surface, at 1:21 A.M. EST on 14 Apr 1970. The crew were Capt. James Arthur Lovell, Jr. (USN; b. 25 Mar 1928), Fred Wallace Haise, Jr. (b. 14 Nov 1933) and John L. Swigert (1931–82).

The greatest altitude attained by an American woman is 360 nautical miles, by Kathryn Thornton during her flight on space shuttle *Endeavor,* to repair the Hubble Telescope on 4–7 Dec 1993.

Speed The fastest speed at which humans have traveled is 24,791 mph, when the command module of *Apollo 10,* carrying Col. (now Brig. Gen.) Thomas Patten Stafford (USAF; b. 17 Sep 1930), Cdr. Eugene Andrew Cernan (USN; b. 14 Mar 1934) and Cdr. (now Capt.) John Watts Young (USN; b. 24 Sep 1930), reached this maximum value at the 75.7 mile altitude interface on its trans-Earth round-trip flight on 26 May 1969.

Longest flight Under the FAI Category P for aerospacecraft, the *Columbia* is the holder of the current absolute world record for duration—13 days 19 hr 30 min to main touchdown—when it was on its 12th mission, *STS 50,* with five crewmen, on 9 Jan 1992.

First extraterrestrial vehicle The first wheeled vehicle to land on the moon was the unmanned *Lunokhod I,* which began its Earth-controlled travels on 17 Nov 1970. It moved a total of 6.54 miles on gradients up to 30° in the Mare Imbrium and did not break down until 4 Oct 1971. The lunar speed and distance record was set by the manned *Apollo 16* Rover, driven by John Young, at 11.2 mph downhill and 22.4 miles.

Heaviest and largest space objects The heaviest object orbited is the *Saturn V* third stage of the *Apollo 15* spacecraft, which, prior to translunar injection into parking orbit, weighed 310,000 lb. The 440 lb US RAE (Radio Astronomy Explorer) B, or *Explorer 49,* launched on 10 Jun 1973, was, however, larger, with antennae 1,500 ft from tip to tip.

First reusable spacecraft The US space shuttle *Columbia STS 1,* the world's first reusable spacecraft, lifted off from its launch pad at Cape Canaveral, FL, on 12 Apr 1981 at 7 A.M. EST. After 36 orbits and 54 hours in space, the craft glided to a perfect landing on a dry lake bed at Edwards Air Force Base in the Mojave Desert, CA on 14 April at 1:21 P.M. EST. The craft was manned by John W. Young (USN) and Robert L. Crippen. As of 6 May 1994 *Discovery* has flown the most times, with 18 missions.

Duration record on the moon The crew of *Apollo 17* collected a record 253 lb of rock and soil during their three EVAs of 22 hr 5 min. They were Capt. Eugene Cernan (see Speed) and Dr Harrison Hagen "Jack" Schmidt. The crew were on the lunar surface for 74 hr 59 min during this longest of lunar missions, which took 12 days 13 hr 51 min on 7–19 Dec 1972.

BUILDINGS & STRUCTURES

ORIGINS

The earliest human structure may be the footings of a windbreak. It is a rough circle of loosely piled lava blocks associated with artifacts and bones on a work-floor, dating from *c.* 1,750,000 B.C. and found by Dr Mary Leakey in January 1960.

The oldest free-standing structures in the world are now believed to be the megalithic temples at Mgarr and Skorba in Malta. With those at Ggantija in Gozo, Malta, they date from *c.* 3250 B.C., some 3½ centuries earlier than the earliest Egyptian pyramid.

United States It was reported in March 1992 that archeologists had discovered the remains of a circular structure believed to be the oldest man-made structure in North America. Samples taken from the site confirmed it to be a Native American hunting camp in Medina County, near Akron, OH; it has been dated to 11,000 years ago.

Oldest wooden structure The oldest extant wooden buildings in the world are those comprising the Pagoda, Chumanar Gate and Temple of Horyu (Horyu-ji) at Nara, Japan, dating from *c.* A.D. 670 and completed in 715.

The temple of Mnadjra in Malta, one of the oldest free-standing structures in the world. (Spectrum Colour Library)

BUILDINGS FOR LIVING

HABITATIONS

Earliest The earliest evidence of a habitational structure is 21 huts with hearths or pebble-lined pits and delimited by stake-holes found in October 1965 at the Terra Amata site in Nice, France, thought to belong to the Acheulian culture of *c.* 400,000 years ago.

Northernmost The Danish scientific station set up in 1952 in Pearyland, northern Greenland is over 900 miles north of the Arctic Circle and is manned every summer.

Southernmost The most southerly permanent human habitation is the United States' Amundsen–Scott South Polar Station, completed in 1957 and replaced in 1975.

CASTLES

Earliest The castle at Gomdan, Yemen originally had 20 stories and dates from before A.D. 100.

Largest The largest ancient castle in the world is Hradčany Castle, Prague, Czech Republic, originating in the 9th century. It is an oblong irregular polygon with an axis of 1,870 ft and an average transverse diameter of 420 ft for a surface area of 18 acres.

Sand castles The tallest sand castle on record, constructed only with hands, buckets and shovels, was 21 ft 6 in high and was made by a team led by Joe Maize, George Pennock and Ted Siebert at Harrison Hot Springs, British Columbia, Canada on 26 Sep 1993. Their "Christmas Tree" sand castle was made to look even more authentic by the addition of gifts. Joe Maize suffers from a fear of heights, but was still able to help as the sand castle neared completion.

The longest sand castle was 5.2 miles long, and was made by staff and pupils of Ellon Academy, near Aberdeen, Great Britain on 24 Mar 1988.

PALACES

Largest The Imperial Palace (Gugong) in the center of Beijing, China covers a rectangle 3,150 × 2,460 ft, an area of 178 acres. The outline survives from the construction of the third Ming emperor, Yongle (1402–24), but due to constant reconstruction work most of the buildings are from the 18th century. These consist of five halls and 17 palaces.

The Palace of Versailles, 14 miles southwest of Paris, France, has a façade 1,902 ft in length, with 375 windows. The building, completed in 1682 for Louis XIV (1643–1715), occupied over 30,000 workmen under the supervision of Jules Hardouin-Mansert (1646–1708).

The tradition continues. The sand castle builders of Harrison Hot Springs, Canada, have constructed three record-breaking castles since 1990, including the current champion. (Loretta MacMahon/Harrison Hot Springs)

Two thousand sheets of gingerbread and 1,650 lb of icing were required to build the world's largest gingerbread house. (Club Corporation of America)

RIFLING WITH THE SPIRITS

Winchester House in San Jose, California was under construction for 38 years. The original house was an eight-room farmhouse with separate barn on the 161-acre estate of Oliver Winchester, the son of the manufacturer of the Winchester repeating rifle—the most famous rifle used in conquering the West. Sarah Winchester, widowed when Oliver died in 1886, consulted a psychic in Boston, who told her that the spirits of those who had been killed by her family's rifles had placed a curse on her and would haunt her forever. She could apparently escape the curse by moving west and continually rebuilding a house under the direction of the spirits. By this means only could she escape the curse, and perhaps even find the key to eternal life.

One of several staircases leading to nowhere. (Winchester Mystery House)

Mrs. Winchester moved to California and used her $1,000-a-day private income to transform the farmhouse into a mansion, which now has 13 bathrooms, 52 skylights, 47 fireplaces, 10,000 windows, 40 staircases, 2,000 doorways and three $10,000 elevators. She built steadily, 24 hours a day, until her death in 1922. Much of the renovation and rebuilding of the house was intended to confuse the resident ghosts: closets opening onto blank walls, secret passageways, trapdoors, and hundreds of pillars and posts that are upside down.

Windows in the Grand Ballroom contain unexplained quotations from Shakespeare. (Winchester Mystery House)

Unused building materials, including Tiffany glass doors. (Winchester Mystery House)

Residential The palace (Istana Nurul Iman) of HM the Sultan of Brunei in the capital Bandar Seri Begawan, completed in January 1984 at a reported cost of $350 million, is the largest residence in the world, with 1,788 rooms and 257 lavatories. The underground garage accommodates the sultan's 110 cars.

Largest moat From plans drawn by French sources it appears that those that surround the Imperial Palace in Beijing (see Largest palaces) measure 162 ft wide and have a total length of 10,800 ft.

HOUSING

According to the National Association of Realtors, as of 31 Dec 1993, the median price of existing homes sold in the 136 largest metropolitan areas in the United States is $107,000 and for new homes $126,200. The metropolitan area with the highest median price is Honolulu, HI, at $360,000.

Largest The 250-room Biltmore House in Asheville, NC is owned by George and William Cecil, grandsons of George Washington Vanderbilt II (1862–1914). The house was built between 1890 and 1895 in an estate of 119,000 acres, at a cost of $4.4 million; it is now valued at $5.5 million, with 12,000 acres.

Gingerbread house A gingerbread house 52 ft high and 32 ft square was built by David Sunken and Roger A. Pelcher of the Bohemian Club of Des Moines, IA and 100 volunteers on 2 Dec 1988. The house was made of 2,000 sheets of gingerbread and 1,650 lb of icing.

TEEPEE!

The largest teepee in the United States measures 43 ft in height and 42 ft in diameter, and utilizes 42 teepee poles. It belongs to Dr Michael P. Doss of Washington, D.C., a member of Montana's Crow Tribe of Indians. The teepee was exhibited near the Little Bighorn National Cemetery in 1992.

Most expensive The most expensive private house ever built is the Hearst Ranch at San Simeon, CA. It was built from 1922–39 for William Randolph Hearst (1863–1951), at a total cost of more than $30 million. It has more than 100 rooms, a 104-ft-long heated swimming pool, an 83-ft-long assembly hall and a garage for 25 limousines. The house was maintained by 60 servants.

Largest nonpalatial residence St Emmeram Castle, Regensburg, Germany, valued at more than $177 million, contains 517 rooms with a floor space of 231,000 ft^2. Only 95 rooms are personally used by the family of the late Prince Johannes von Thurn und Taxis.

Pole sitting champ Mellissa Sanders in her tiny home, where she spent nearly 1½ years. (Glen Burton and Mauri Rose Sanders)

Camping out The silent Indian *fakir* Mastram Bapu ("contented father") remained on the same spot by the roadside in the village of Chitra for 22 years from 1960–82.

Pole sitting Modern records do not come close to that of St Simeon the Younger (*c.* A.D. 521–97), called Stylites, a monk who spent his last 45 years atop a stone pillar on the Hill of Wonders, near Antioch, Syria. His achievement is the longest-standing record in *The Guinness Book of Records*.

Living standards at the tops of poles can vary widely. Mellissa Sanders lived in a shack measuring 6 ft × 7 ft at the top of a pole in Indianapolis, IN from 26 Oct 1986–24 Mar 1988, a total of 516 days.

Rob Colley stayed in a barrel (maximum capacity 180 gal) at the top of a pole 43 ft high in Dartmoor Wildlife Park, near Plymouth, Great Britain for 42 days 35 min from 13 Aug–24 Sep 1992.

House of cards The greatest number of stories achieved in building free-standing houses of standard playing cards is 81, to a height of 15 ft 8 in, built by Bryan Berg of Spirit Lake, IA on 26 May 1994. No adhesives are allowed in such houses.

Tallest apartment building The 1,127-ft John Hancock Center in Chicago, IL is 100 stories high; floors 44–92 are residential.

The tallest purely residential apartment house is Lake Point Tower,

Chicago, IL, which has 879 units consisting of 70 stories, standing 639 ft high.

HOTELS

Oldest The Hōshi Ryokan at the village of Awazu, Japan dates from A.D. 717, when Garyo Hōshi built an inn near a hot water spring that was said to have miraculous healing powers. The waters are still celebrated for their recuperative effects and the Ryokan now has 100 bedrooms.

Largest The MGM Grand Hotel/Casino/Theme Park in Las Vegas, NV consists of 30-story towers on a 112-acre site. The hotel has 5,009 rooms with suites of up to 6,000 ft^2, and the complex also includes a 15,200-seat movie theater, a 33-acre theme park and the world's largest casino. The complex was started in 1991, topped out in February 1993 and opened officially in December 1993. Its total cost was $1 billion.

Hoteliers With its acquisition of Holiday Inns Worldwide in February 1991, Bass plc, Great Britain's largest brewing company, took ownership of the world's largest hotel chain. The company now owns, manages and franchises 1,645 hotels totaling 327,059 rooms in 52 countries.

United States The largest hotel operator as of 31 Dec 1993, based on number of rooms, was Holiday Inns Worldwide, which operates 279,581.

Largest lobby The lobby at the Hyatt Regency, San Francisco, CA is 350 ft long and 160 ft wide, and with its 170 ft ceiling is the height of a 17-story building.

GUESS WHAT?

Q. WHAT IS THE FASTEST TIME FOR MAKING A BED?

A. SEE "FANTASTIC FEATS" (HUMAN ACHIEVEMENTS)

Tallest Measured from the street level of its main entrance to the top, the 73-story Westin Stamford in Raffles City, Singapore "topped out" in March 1985 at 741.9 ft tall. However, the Westin at the Renaissance Center in Detroit, MI, is 748 ft tall when measured from the rear entrance.

Most expensive room The Galactic Fantasy Suite in the Crystal Palace Resort & Casino in the Bahamas can be rented for $25,000 per night, although the casino's big spenders are likely to be accommodated on a complimentary basis. The price includes a robot named Ursula who explains all the suite's high-tech toys. These include a Lucite piano that produces images as well as music, a rotating sofa and bed, and a thunder and lightning storm sound and light show.

Most mobile The three-story brick Hotel Fairmount (built 1906) in San Antonio, TX, which weighed 1,600 tons, was moved on 36 dollies with

MOBILE HOTEL

"As long as you have a wide enough road, you can move anything," says Terry Emmert of Emmert Construction, Portland, Oregon. His company, Emmert International, manufactures the transportation equipment necessary to move large objects such as yachts and steam generators; they organize the moves as well. But why move a three-story hotel?

The Hotel Fairmount originally stood behind the Alamo in the area now known as the Plaza del Rio Mall. When the mall was being planned, the city had to decide whether to keep the hotel as it was, to refurbish it, or to move it. "It's a landmark, a part of history, and it was worthwhile to save it," say Emmert. "Sure, it was a complicated job, an interesting project. It's something we'd like to do every day, if we could." Emmert, who got his start moving houses and duplexes, likes the challenge of a big job. Recently his company relocated Howard Hughes's enormous plane, the *Spruce Goose*, from Long Beach, California to a town in Oregon. The plane had to be disassembled, then transported over ocean, river and land.

With the Hotel Fairmount, the challenge was to keep it together. Before the move, the hotel's structure was reinforced inside and out. Then it was wrapped in a steel cage of beams and cables. Hydraulic jacks raised the building at 34 points in its foundation, hoisted it 8½ feet high, and moved it five blocks away on 36 dollies. The hotel hung over the sidewalks on both sides of the street, requiring the removal of light poles, traffic lights and parking meters.

Hotel Fairmount, San Antonio, Texas (Emmert International)

pneumatic tires approximately five blocks and over a bridge, which had to be reinforced. The move, by Emmert International of Portland, OR, took six days, 30 Mar–4 Apr 1985, and cost $650,000. See On the Record feature on page 221.

BUILDINGS FOR WORKING

Largest construction project The Madinat Al-Jubail Al-Sinaiyah project in Saudi Arabia is the largest public works project in modern times. Construction started in 1976 for an industrial city covering 250,705 acres. At the peak of construction nearly 52,000 workers were employed, representing 62 nationalities. The total earth dredging and moving volume has reached 953.5 billion ft^3, enough to construct a 3-ft-3-in-high belt around the Earth at the equator seven times.

Largest industrial building The largest multilevel industrial building that is one discrete structure is the container freight station of Asia Terminals Ltd at Hong Kong's Kwai Chung container port. The 15-level building was completed in 1994 and has a total area of 9,320,867 ft^2. The building measures 906 × 958 ft, with a height of 359.25 ft. The entire area in each floor is directly accessible by 46 ft container trucks, and the building has 16.67 miles of roadway and 2,609 container truck parking bays.

Hod carrying Russell Bradley of Worcester, Great Britain carried bricks weighing 361 lb 9 oz up a ladder of the minimum specified length of 12 ft on 28 Jan 1991 at Worcester City Football Club. The hod weighed 94 lb 13 oz and he was therefore carrying a total weight of 456 lb 6 oz.

Brick carrying The greatest distance achieved for carrying a 9-lb brick in a nominated ungloved hand in an uncradled downward pincer grip is 64 miles, by Ashrita Furman of Jamaica, NY, on 13–14 Jun 1993. The women's record for carrying a 9 lb 12 oz brick is 22½ miles, by Wendy Morris of Walsall, Great Britain on 28 Apr 1986.

Largest brickworks The largest brickworks in the world is the London Brick Co. Ltd plant at Stewartby, Great Britain. Established in 1898, the site now covers 221 acres and has a weekly production capacity of 6 million bricks and brick equivalent.

Largest commercial building In terms of floor area, the largest commercial building in the world under one roof is the flower auction building of the Co-operative VBA (Verenigde Bloemenveilingen Aalsmeer), Aalsmeer, Netherlands, with dimensions of 2,546 × 2,070 ft. The original floor surface of 3.7 million ft^2 has now been extended to 5.27 million ft^2.

The world's largest building in terms of volume is the Boeing Company's main assembly plant in Everett, WA, at 196,476,000 ft^3 on completion in 1968. Subsequent expansion programs have increased the volume to 472 million ft^3, with a further increase in volume of 50 percent completed in 1993 to accommodate the new 777 airliner. The site covers 1,025 acres.

Administrative The largest ground area covered by any office building is that of the Pentagon, in Arlington, VA. Built to house the US Defense Department's offices, it was completed on 15 Jan 1943 and cost an estimated $83 million. Each of the outermost sides is 921 ft long and the perimeter of the building is about 4,610 ft. Its five stories enclose a floor area of 149.2 acres. The corridors total 17 miles in length and there are 7,748 windows to be cleaned. There are 29,000 people working in the building.

At 1,454 feet (1,707 feet with its TV antennae), Chicago's Sears Tower is the tallest office building in the world. (Spectrum Colour Library)

OFFICES

Largest The complex with the largest rentable space is the World Trade Center in New York City, with a total of 12 million ft^2 of rentable space available in seven buildings, including 4.37 million ft^2 in each of the twin towers. Each tower has 99 elevators and 43,600 windows comprising 600,000 ft^2 of glass. There are 50,000 people working in the complex and 90,000 visitors daily.

Tallest The tallest office building in the world is the Sears Tower, national headquarters of Sears, Roebuck & Co. on Wacker Drive, Chicago, IL, with 110 stories, rising to 1,454 ft. The addition of two TV antennae brought the total height to 1,707 ft. Construction was started in August 1970 and it was "topped out" on 4 May 1973. The building has a gross area of 4.5 million ft^2, is served by 18 elevators and has 16,100 windows.

Most expensive The highest rentals in the world for prime offices, according to *World Rental Levels* by Richard Ellis of London, Great Britain, were in Tokyo, Japan at $206.68 per ft^2 in June 1991. With added service charges and rates this increased to $225.34.

LEISURE FACILITIES

STADIUMS

Largest The open Strahov Stadium in Prague, Czech Republic was completed in 1934 and could accommodate 240,000 spectators for mass displays of up to 40,000 Sokol gymnasts.

Largest in use The Maracaña Municipal Stadium in Rio de Janeiro, Brazil has a normal capacity of 205,000, of whom 155,000 can be seated. A crowd of 199,854 was accommodated for the World Cup final between Brazil and Uruguay on 16 Jul 1950. A dry moat, 10 ft wide and more than 5 ft deep, separates players from spectators.

The largest stadium in the United States is Michigan Football Stadium, Ann Arbor, MI, which has a seating capacity of 102,501. The largest crowd ever to attend an event there was 106,851 for the Michigan *v* Ohio State game on 11 Sep 1993. Ohio State won 27–23.

Covered The Aztec Stadium, Mexico City, opened in 1968, has a capacity of 107,000 for soccer, although a record attendance of 132,274 was achieved for boxing on 20 Feb 1993. Nearly all seats are under cover.

Indoor The $173-million 273-ft-tall Louisiana Superdome in New Orleans, LA, covering 13 acres, was completed in May 1975. Its maximum seating capacity for conventions is 97,365, or 76,791 for football.

Largest roof The transparent acrylic glass "marquee" roof over the Munich Olympic Stadium, Germany measures 914,940 ft^2 in area, resting on a steel net supported by masts.

The transparent "tent" roof spanning Munich's Olympic Stadium, Germany covers an area of 914,940 ft^2. (Images)

The roof of Mexico City's Aztec Stadium provides cover for the entire official seating capacity of 107,000 people. (Allsport)

The largest roofspan in the world is 787 ft 4 in for the major axis of the elliptical Texas Stadium, completed in 1971 at Irving, TX.

Retractable roof The world's largest covers the SkyDome, Toronto, Ontario, Canada, completed in June 1989. The roof covers 8 acres, spans 674 ft at its widest point and rises to 282 ft.

Largest air-supported building The 80,638-capacity octagonal Pontiac Silverdome Stadium, Pontiac, MI is 522 ft wide and 722 ft long. The 10-acre translucent Fiberglas roof is 202 ft high and is supported by compressed air. Geiger-Berger Associates of New York City were the structural engineers.

RESORTS

Amusement resort *Largest* Disney World is set in 28,000 acres of Orange and Osceola counties, 20 miles southwest of Orlando in central Florida. It was opened on 1 Oct 1971 after a $400 million investment.

Largest recreational beach Virginia Beach, VA has 28 miles of beachfront on the Atlantic and 10 miles of estuary frontage. The area embraces 310 miles^2 with 157 hotels, motels and condos and 2,230 campsites.

Piers Longest The longest entertainment pier in the world is Southend Pier at Southend-on-Sea, Great Britain. The original wooden pier was opened in 1830; the present iron pier is 1.34 miles in length and was opened on 8 Jul 1889. In 1949–50 the pier had a peak 5.75 million visitors.

Most The resort with the most piers was Atlantic City, NJ, with seven, built from 1898 to 1912. Currently only four remain.

Largest casino The casino at the MGM Grand Hotel in Las Vegas, NV covers 171,500 ft^2 and comprises four gaming areas including 3,500 slot machines and 165 gaming tables.

Slot machines The biggest beating handed to a "one-armed bandit" was $6,814,823.48 by Cammie Brewer, 61, at the Club Cal-Neva, Reno, NV on 14 Feb 1988.

Nudist resorts *Largest* The largest nudist site is Domaine de Lambeyran, near Lodève in southern France, at 840 acres. The Helio-Marin Center at Cap d'Agde, also in southern France, is visited by around 250,000 people per year.

United States The largest nudist colony in the United States in terms of total acreage is Oaklake Trails, Tulsa, OK, which covers 418 acres. Club Paradise, Land O'Lakes, FL, had 70,000 visitors in 1993.

FAIRS

Earliest The earliest major international fair was the Great Exhibition of 1851 in the Crystal Palace, London, Great Britain, which in 141 days attracted 6,039,195 admissions.

Largest The site of the Louisiana Purchase Exposition at St Louis, MO in 1904 covered 1,271.76 acres and there was an attendance of 19,694,855. Events of the 1904 Olympic Games were staged in conjunction with the fair.

Largest exhibition center The International Exposition Center in Cleveland, OH, the world's largest, is situated on a 188 acre site adjacent to Cleveland's Hopkins International Airport in a building that measures 2.5 million ft². An indoor terminal provides direct rail access and parking for 10,000 cars.

Ferris wheels The largest wheel now operating is the Cosmoclock 21 at Yokohama City, Japan. It is 344½ ft high and 328 ft in diameter, with 60 eight-seat gondolas. It features illumination by laser beams and acoustic effects by sound synthesizers. The 60 arms holding the gondolas serve as second hands for the 42½-ft-long electric clock mounted at the hub.

United States The tallest Ferris wheel in the United States is the Texas Star at Fair Park in Dallas, TX, built in 1985. It is 212 ft 6 in high, with 44 gondolas and a seating capacity of 244 riders. It operates during the State Fair of Texas.

ROLLER COASTERS

Oldest operating The *Rutschbahnen* (Scenic Railway) Mk.2 was constructed at the Tivoli Gardens, Copenhagen, Denmark, in 1913. This coaster opened to the public in 1914 and has remained open ever since.

Yeee-ow! The world's longest roller coaster, *The Ultimate!* (Barry Norman, WKVL Amusement Research)

United States The oldest operating roller coaster in the United States is the *Zippin Pippin*, constructed at Libertyland Amusement Park, Memphis, TN in 1915.

Longest The longest roller coaster in the world is *The Ultimate* at Lightwater Valley Theme Park in Ripon, Great Britain. The run is 1.42 miles.

United States The longest roller coaster in the United States is *The Beast* at Kings Island near Cincinnati, OH. The run of 1.40 miles includes 800 ft of tunnels and a 540-degree banked helix.

Greatest and fastest drop The *Steel Phantom*, opened in April 1991 at Kennywood Amusement Park, West Mifflin, PA, has a vertical drop of 225 ft into a natural ravine, with a design speed of 80 mph.

Tallest The tallest above-ground super-structure is the *Pepsi Max—The Big One* at Blackpool Pleasure Beach, Great Britain. This non-looping roller coaster has a design height of 222 ft above its footings. It features a first vertical drop of 209 ft, with a speed of 80 mph.

Looping The first loop of the *Viper* at Six Flags Magic Mountain, Valencia, CA is 140 ft above ground. Riders are turned upside-down seven times over a 3,830 ft track.

Greatest number The most roller coasters at any amusement park is 11, at Cedar Point Amusement Park in Sandusky, OH. There is a choice of two wood and nine steel track coasters.

BARS AND RESTAURANTS

Bars *Largest* The largest beer-selling establishment in the world is the "Mathäser," Bayerstrasse 5, Munich, Germany, where daily sales reach 84,470 pints. It was established in 1829, demolished in World War II and rebuilt by 1955. It seats 5,500 people.

Tallest Humperdink's Seafood and Steakhouse Bar in Dallas, TX is 25 ft 3 in high with two levels of shelving containing over 1,000 bottles. The lower level has four rows of shelves approximately 40 ft across and can be reached from floor level. The upper level, which has five rows of shelves, is reached by climbing a ladder.

Longest The world's longest permanent bar is the 405-ft-10-in-long counter in the "Beer Barrel Saloon" at Put-in-Bay, South Bass Island, OH, opened in 1989. The "Bar at Erickson's," on Burnside Street, Portland, OR, in its heyday (1883–1920) possessed a bar measuring 684 ft that ran continuously around and across the main saloon. Beer was five cents for 16 fluid ounces. Temporary bars of greater length have been erected, notably at beer festivals.

Night clubs *Largest* Gilley's Club (formerly Shelly's) on Spencer Highway, Houston, TX, built in 1955, was extended in 1971 and now has a seating capacity of 6,000 under one roof covering 4 acres.

The roller skate-shod staff of the Royal Dragon restaurant, the world's largest, bring a new meaning to the term "meals on wheels." (Gamma)

Lowest The Minus 206 in Tiberias, Israel, on the shores of the Sea of Galilee, is 676 ft below sea level.

Restaurants Largest The Royal Dragon (Mang Gorn Luang) restaurant in Bangkok, Thailand, opened in October 1991, can seat 5,000 potential customers served by a staff of 1,200. In order to cover the large service area—8.35 acres—the employees wear roller skates, which helps to improve their service speed.

Highest The highest restaurant in the world is in the Chacaltaya ski resort, Bolivia, at 17,519 ft.

Restaurateurs The world's largest food service chain is operated by McDonald's Corporation of Oak Brook, IL, founded in 1955 by Ray A. Kroc (1902–84) after buying out brothers Dick and "Mac" McDonald, pioneers of the fast-food drive-in. By 31 Dec 1993 McDonald's licensed and owned 13,993 restaurants in 70 countries. Worldwide sales in 1993 were $23.6 billion.

SHOPPING CENTERS

Largest The world's largest center is the $1.1 billion West Edmonton Mall in Alberta, Canada, which was opened on 15 Sep 1981 and completed four years later. It covers 5.2 million ft^2 on a 121 acre site and encompasses over 800 stores and services as well as 11 major department stores. Parking is provided for 20,000 vehicles for more than 500,000 shoppers per week.

United States The largest shopping center and entertainment complex in

MALL OF AMERICA

At the Mall of America, there's always room for one—or one thousand—more. During the Christmas season, the Mall holds a promotion, offering special low air fares to people from 42 cities who fly in for one brief day of shopping. "It's power shopping," says Mall spokesperson Susan Austin. "They're just there for one Saturday. People bring their suitcases—not for clothes, for their purchases!"

But are they just shopping? Only 2.5 million of the Mall's 4.2 million square feet are devoted to retail. So what's going on in the rest of the Mall of America? There's a theme park, an 18-hole miniature golf course, a LEGO showplace, a 14-screen movie theater, a school (with high school and adult continuing education courses), restaurants, night clubs, a health center… and most of the time there aren't enough people to make the place feel crowded. "Oh, you can tell when it's empty," admits Susan Austin, "but there's never a sense that it's crowded, even on Saturday when there might be 200,000 people here."

Mall of America, Bloomington, Minnesota (Bob Perzel)

Austin compares the Mall to a city under a roof—a city with no snow and no wind chill factor. "The worse the weather is, the better our business," she says. "We've created an experience for people who want to do more than shop. The lines between shopping and entertainment are beginning to blur. The key to our success is the way we've combined the two."

the United States is the Mall of America, located in Bloomington, MN. The mall was opened on 11 Aug 1992 and covers 4.2 million ft². It contains 350 stores, eight night clubs, and a 7-acre amusement park. Parking is provided for 12,750 vehicles for approximately 750,000 weekly shoppers.

Largest wholesale center The world's largest wholesale merchandise mart is the Dallas Market Center on Stemmons Freeway, Dallas, TX, with nearly 9.3 million ft² in six buildings. Together with two additional buildings under separate management, the whole complex covers 175 acres and houses some 2,580 permanent showrooms displaying merchandise of more than 30,000 manufacturers. The center attracts 760,000 buyers each year to its 107 annual markets and trade shows.

Longest mall The longest mall in the world is part of the £40 million ($68 million) shopping center at Milton Keynes, Great Britain. It measures 2,133 ft.

BRIDGES

Oldest The oldest datable bridge in the world still in use is the slab stone single-arch bridge over the River Meles in Izmir (formerly Smyrna), Turkey, which dates from *c.* 850 B.C.

Busiest The world's busiest bridge is the Howrah Bridge across the river Hooghly in Calcutta, India. In addition to 57,000 vehicles per day, it carries an incalculable number of pedestrians across its 1,500-ft-long 72-ft-wide span.

Fastest bridge building A team of British soldiers from 21 Engineer Regiment based at Nienburg, Germany constructed a bridge across a 26 ft gap using a five-bay single-story MGB (medium-girder bridge) in a time of 7 min 12 sec at Hameln, Germany on 3 Nov 1992.

Bridge sale The largest antique ever sold was London Bridge, in Great Britain in March 1968. Ivan F. Luckin (d. 1992) of the Court of Common Council of the Corporation of London sold it to the McCulloch Oil Corporation of Los Angeles, CA for £1,029,000 ($2,469,600). The 11,800 tons of façade stonework were reassembled at a cost of $7.2 million at Lake Havasu City, AZ and rededicated on 10 Oct 1971.

LONGEST

Cable suspension The world's longest bridge span is the main span of the Humber Estuary Bridge, Humberside, Great Britain, at 4,626 ft. The towers are 533 ft 1⅝ in tall and are 1⅜ in out of parallel to allow for the curvature of the Earth. Including the Hessle and the Barton side spans, the bridge stretches 1.37 miles. It was completed on 18 Jul 1980 at a cost of £96 million ($192 million) and was opened by Queen Elizabeth II on 17 Jul 1981.

Cable-stayed The longest cable-stayed bridge span in the world is the 1,739 ft Skarnsundet Bridge over the Trondheim Fjord in Norway, completed in 1991.

The Mackinac Straits Bridge between Mackinac City and St Ignace, MI is the longest suspension bridge between anchorages (1.58 miles), and has an overall length, including approaches, of 5 miles.

United States The longest suspension bridge in the United States is the Verrazano–Narrows Bridge, completed in 1964, which measures 4,260 ft. The bridge spans Lower New York Bay and connects Staten Island to Brooklyn.

Cantilever The Quebec Bridge over the St Lawrence River in Canada has the longest cantilever truss span of any in the world—1,800 ft between the piers and 3,239 ft overall. It carries a railroad track and two carriageways. Begun in 1899, it was finally opened to traffic on 3 Dec 1917 at a cost of Can $22.5 million and 87 lives.

United States The longest cantilever bridge in the United States is the John Barry Bridge, in Chester, PA. It spans the Delaware River and measures 1,644 ft. Work was completed in 1974.

Covered The longest is that at Hartland, New Brunswick, Canada, measuring 1,282 ft overall, completed in 1899.

Floating The longest is the Second Lake Washington Bridge, Evergreen, Seattle, WA, with a total length of 12,596 ft and a floating section that measures 7,518 ft. It was built at a cost of $15 million and completed in August 1963.

Railroad The world's longest railroad bridge is the 43,374-ft-long Seto-Ohashi double-deck road and rail bridge linking Kojima, Honshū with Sakaide, Shikoku, Japan.

United States The longest is the Huey P. Long Bridge, Metairie, LA, with a railroad section 23,235 ft long (4.4 miles), including approach roads. It has a three-span trestle: 529 ft, 790 ft and 531 ft, followed by a single span of 531.5 ft. It was completed on 16 Dec 1935.

Ropeway or téléphérique The longest ropeway in the world is the *Compagnie Minière de l'Ogooué*, or COMILOG, installation built in 1959–62 for the Moanda manganese mine in Gabon, which extends 47 miles. It has 858 towers and 2,800 buckets, with 96 miles of wire rope running over 6,000 idler pulleys.

Cable car The highest and longest passenger-carrying aerial ropeway in the world is the *Teleférico Mérida* in Venezuela, from Mérida City (5,379 ft) to the summit of Pico Espejo (15,629 ft), a rise of 10,250 ft. The ropeway is in four sections, involving three car changes in the eight-mile ascent in one hour. The fourth span is 10,070 ft in length. The two cars have a maximum capacity of 45 persons and travel 3 mph.

Longest bridging The Second Lake Pontchartrain Causeway was completed on 23 Mar 1969, joining Mandeville and Metairie, LA. It has a length of 126,055 ft. It cost $29.9 million and is 228 ft longer than the adjoining First Causeway, completed in 1956.

Concrete arch The longest concrete arch is the Jesse H. Jones Memorial Bridge, which spans the Houston Ship Canal in Texas. Completed in 1982, the bridge measures 1,500 ft.

Steel arch The longest is the New River Gorge Bridge, near Fayetteville, WV, completed in 1977, with a span of 1,700 ft.

Stone arch The longest stone arch bridge is the 3,810 ft-long Rockville Bridge north of Harrisburg, PA, with 48 spans containing 216,050 tons of stone. It was completed in 1901.

Widest The widest long-span bridge is the 1,650 ft Sydney Harbor Bridge, Australia (160 ft wide), officially opened on 19 Mar 1932. It carries two railroad tracks, eight lanes of roadway, and bicycle and pedestrian lanes.

HIGHEST

The highest bridge in the world is 1,053 ft above the Arkansas River in the Royal Gorge in Colorado. It is a suspension bridge with a main span of 880 ft and was constructed in six months, ending on 6 Dec 1929.

Railroad The highest railroad bridge in the world is the Mala Rijeka viaduct of Yugoslav Railways at Kolasin on the Belgrade–Bar line. It is 650 ft high and was opened on 1 Jun 1976. It consists of steel spans mounted on concrete piers.

Road The road bridge at the highest altitude in the world, 18,380 ft, is the 98.4-ft-long Bailey Bridge, built by an Indian Army team in August 1982 near Khardung-La, in Ladakh, India.

TALLEST

The tallest bridge towers in the world are those of the Golden Gate Bridge, which connects San Francisco and Marin Co., CA. The towers of this suspension bridge extend 745 ft above the water. Completed in 1937, the bridge has an overall length of 8,966 ft.

VIADUCTS

The longest railway viaduct is the rock-filled Great Salt Lake Railroad Trestle, carrying the Southern Pacific Railroad 11.85 miles across the Great Salt Lake, UT. It was opened as a pile and trestle bridge on 8 Mar 1904, but converted to rock fill in 1955–60.

AQUEDUCTS

Longest ancient The greatest of ancient aqueducts was the aqueduct of Carthage in Tunisia, which ran 87.6 miles from the springs of Zaghouan to Djebel Djougar. It was built by the Romans during the reign of Publius

Aelius Hadrianus (A.D. 117–138). In 1895, 344 arches still survived. Its original capacity has been calculated at 7 million gal per day.

Longest modern The world's longest aqueduct, in the nonclassical sense of water conduit, excluding irrigation canals, is the California State Water Project aqueduct, completed in 1974, with a length of 826 miles, of which 385 miles is canalized.

Tallest arches The tallest of the 14 arches of the Aguas Livres aqueduct, built in Lisbon, Portugal, in 1784 is 213 ft.

TOWERS & MASTS

TALLEST STRUCTURES

The tallest-ever structure in the world was the guyed Warszawa Radio mast at Konstantynow, 60 miles northwest of Warsaw, Poland. Prior to its fall during renovation work on 10 Aug 1991 it was 2,120⅔ ft tall, or more than four-tenths of a mile. It was completed on 18 Jul 1974 and put into operation on 22 Jul 1974. The mast was designed by Jan Polak and weighed 606 tons.

The tallest structure is now a stayed television transmitting tower 2,063 ft tall, between Fargo and Blanchard, ND. It was built at a cost of about $500,000 for Channel 11 of KTHI-TV in 30 days (2 Oct to 1 Nov 1963) by 11 men of Hamilton Erection, Inc. of York, SC.

TALLEST TOWERS

The tallest self-supporting tower (as opposed to a guyed mast) in the world is the $63 million CN Tower in Metro Center, Toronto, Ontario, Canada, which rises to 1,815 ft 5 in. Excavation began on 12 Feb 1973 for the erection of the 143,300-ton reinforced, post-tensioned concrete structure, which was "topped out" on 2 Apr 1975. The 416-seat restaurant revolves in the Sky Pod at 1,150 ft, from which the visibility extends to hills 74½ miles distant.

Lego tower The world's tallest Lego tower was 70 ft high and was constructed by Lego Belgium n.v./s.a. in Brussels on 26–27 Jun 1993.

GUESS WHAT?

Q. WHERE IS THE WORLD'S LONGEST NATURAL ARCH?

A. SEE "OTHER FEATURES" (EARTH & SPACE)

CANALS

Longest Ancient The longest canal in the ancient world was the Grand Canal of China from Beijing to Hangzhou. It was begun in 540 B.C. and not completed until A.D. 1327, by which time it extended (including canalized river sections) for 1,107 miles. The estimated work force *c.* A.D. 600 was 5 million on the Bian section.

Modern The Beloye More (White Sea) Baltic Canal from Belomorsk to Povenets, Russia is 141 miles long and has 19 locks. It was completed with the use of forced labor in 1933 but cannot accommodate ships of more than 16 ft in draft.

The world's longest big-ship canal is the Suez Canal linking the Red Sea with the Mediterranean, opened on 16 Nov 1869. It is 100.6 miles in length from the Port Said lighthouse to Suez Roads, and 197 ft wide. The work force consisted of 1.5 million people; 120,000 of them died during the construction of the canal.

United States The longest canal in the United States is the Erie Barge Canal, connecting the Hudson River at Troy, NY, with Lake Erie at Buffalo, NY. It is 365 miles long, 150 ft wide and 12 ft in depth.

Longest irrigation The Karakumsky Kanal stretches 745 miles from Haun-Khan to Ashkhabad, Turkmenistan. The navigable length in 1993 was 500 miles.

BUSIEST!

The busiest ship canal is the Kiel Canal linking the North Sea with the Baltic Sea in Germany. Over 40,000 transits are recorded annually. The busiest in terms of tonnage of shipping is the Suez Canal, with nearly 338 million gross registered tons in 1992.

Longest canal system The seawater cooling system associated with the Madinat Al-Jubail Al-Sinaiyah construction project in Saudi Arabia is believed to be the world's largest canal system, bringing 353 million ft^3 of seawater per day to cool the industrial establishment.

Longest artificial seaway The St Lawrence Seaway is 189 miles long along the New York State–Ontario border from Montreal to Lake Ontario. It enables ships up to 728 ft long and 29,100 tons to sail 2,342 miles from the North Atlantic up the St Lawrence estuary and across the Great Lakes to Duluth, MN. The project cost $470 million and was opened on 25 Apr 1959.

LOCKS

Largest The Berendrecht lock, which links the River Scheldt with docks at Antwerp, Belgium, is the largest sea lock in the world. First used in April 1989, it has a length of 1,640 ft, a width of 223 ft and a sill level of 44 ft. Each of its four sliding lock gates weighs 1,770 tons.

Deepest United States The deepest lock in the United States is the John Day dam lock on the River Columbia, in Oregon and Washington State, completed in 1963. It can raise or lower barges 113 ft and is served by a 1,100-ton gate.

Highest rise and longest flight The world's highest lock elevator rises to 225 ft at Ronquières on the Charleroi–Brussels Canal, Belgium. Two 236-wheeled caissons are each able to carry 1,500 tons, and take 22 minutes to cover the 4,698-ft-long inclined plane.

Largest cut The Corinth Canal, Greece, opened in 1893, is 3.93 miles long, 26 ft deep, 81 ft wide at the surface and has an extreme depth of cutting of 259 ft.

DAMS

Most massive Measured by volume, the largest dam is at the Sobradinho hydroelectric power station on the São Francisco River, Bahia, Brazil. Completed in 1983, the dam has a volume of 44.5 billion yd^3, an area of 1,622 miles^2, and is 217 miles long. It was constructed by the Companhia Hidro Elétrica do São Francisco.

Largest concrete The Grand Coulee Dam on the Columbia River, WA was begun in 1933 and was finally completed in 1942 at a cost of $56 million. It has a crest length of 4,173 ft and is 550 ft high. The amount of concrete poured was 285 million ft^3 or 21.5 million tons.

Highest The highest dam is the 1,098-ft-high Rogun earth-filled dam across the river Vakhsh, Tadzhikistan, with a crest length of only 1,975 ft but a volume of 92.9 million yd^3. The dam was constructed between 1981 and 1987.

United States The embankment–earthfill Oroville Dam is the United States' highest dam, reaching 754 ft and spanning the Feather River in California. It was completed in 1968.

Strongest The strongest is the 803-ft-high Sayano-Shushenskaya Dam on the River Yenisey, Russia, which is designed to bear a load of 20 million tons from a fully filled reservoir of 41 billion yd^3 capacity. Although completed, this dam is not yet operational.

Longest The Kiev Dam across the Dnieper, Ukraine, completed in 1964, has a crest length of 25.6 miles.

Largest levees The most massive ever built were the Mississippi levees, begun in 1717 but vastly augmented by the federal government after the disastrous floods of 1927. They extended for 1,732 miles along the main river from Cape Girardeau, MO to the Gulf of Mexico and comprised more than 1 billion yd^3 of earthworks. Levees on the tributaries comprised an additional 2,000 miles. Much of the area suffered from extensive flooding in the summer of 1993, which caused serious damage to the levees.

RESERVOIRS

Largest The most voluminous man-made reservoir is the Bratskoye reservoir, on the Angara River in Siberia, Russia, with a volume of 40.6 $miles^3$ and an area of 2,111 $miles^2$. It extends for 372 miles with a width of 21 miles. It was filled in 1961–67.

The world's largest artificial lake measured by surface area is Lake Volta, Ghana, formed by the Akosombo Dam, completed in 1965. By 1969 the lake had filled to an area of 3,275 $miles^2$, with a shoreline 4,500 miles long.

United States The largest wholly artificial reservoir in the United States is Lake Mead in Nevada. It was formed by the Hoover Dam, which was completed in 1936. The lake has a capacity of 1,241,445 million ft^3 and a surface area of 28,255,000 acre–ft.

TUNNELS

LONGEST

The longest tunnel of any kind is the New York City West Delaware water-supply tunnel, begun in 1937 and completed in 1944. It has a diameter of 13½ ft and runs for 105 miles from the Rondout Reservoir into the Hillview Reservoir, on the border of Yonkers, NY and New York City.

Rail The 33.46-mile-long Seikan Rail Tunnel was bored to 787 ft beneath sea level and 328 ft below the seabed of the Tsugaru Strait between Tappi Saki, Honshū, and Fukushima, Hokkaidō, Japan. It was holed through on 27 Jan 1983. The first test run took place on 13 Mar 1988.

United States The longest main-line tunnel railroad in the United States is the Moffat Tunnel, which cuts through a 6.2 mile section of the Rocky Mountains in Colorado. Tunnel construction was completed in 1928.

Continuous subway The Moscow Metro Kaluzhskaya underground railroad line from Medvedkovo to Bittsevsky Park is 23½ miles long and was completed in early 1990.

Road Longest The 10.14-mile-long two-lane St Gotthard road tunnel from Göschenen to Airolo, Switzerland opened to traffic on 5 Sep 1980.

The longest road tunnel in the United States is the 2.5 mile Lincoln Tunnel, linking New York City and New Jersey. The tunnel was dug beneath the Hudson River and was completed in 1937.

Largest The largest-diameter road tunnel in the world is the one blasted through Yerba Buena Island, San Francisco, CA. It is 77 ft 10 in wide, 56 ft high and 540 ft long. More than 250,000 vehicles pass through on its two decks every year.

Hydroelectric irrigation The 51½-mile-long Orange–Fish Rivers tunnel, South Africa, was bored between 1967 and 1973 at an estimated cost of $144 million. The lining to a minimum thickness of 9 in gave a completed diameter of 17 ft 6 in.

The Majes dam project in Peru involves 60.9 miles of tunnels for hydroelectric and water-supply purposes. The dam is at 13,780 ft altitude.

SEWERAGE!

The Chicago Water Reclamation District Tunnel and Reservoir Project (TARP) in Illinois, also known as the "Deep Tunnel," will involve 131 miles of sewerage tunneling when it is complete. It is divided into a pollution control section and a flood control section. As of March 1994, 60 miles were in operation. The estimated cost of the project, including three 41-billion-gallon total capacity reservoirs, is $3.6 billion.

Bridge-tunnel The Chesapeake Bay Bridge-Tunnel extends 17.65 miles from the Eastern Shore peninsula to Virginia Beach, VA. It cost $200 million and was opened to traffic on 15 Apr 1964. The longest bridged section is Trestle C (4.56 miles long) and the longest tunnel section is the Thimble Shoal Channel Tunnel (1.09 miles).

Longest and largest canal-tunnel The Rove Tunnel on the Canal de Marseille au Rhône in the south of France was completed in 1927 and is 23,359 ft long, 72 ft wide and 37 ft high. Built to be navigated by seagoing ships, it was closed in 1963 following a collapse and has not been reopened.

Oldest navigable The Malpas tunnel on the Canal du Midi in southwest France was completed in 1681 and is 528 ft long. Its completion enabled vessels to navigate from the Atlantic Ocean to the Mediterranean Sea via the river Garonne to Toulouse and the Canal du Midi to Sète.

Tunneling The longest unsupported example of a machine-bored tunnel is the Three Rivers water tunnel, 5.82 miles long with a 10 ft 6 in diameter, constructed for the city of Atlanta, GA, from April 1980 to February 1982.

SPECIALIZED STRUCTURES

Bonfire The largest was constructed in Workington, Great Britain by inhabitants of the town and off-duty firefighters. It was 122 ft 6 in high and had an overall volume of 250,700 ft^3, and was lit on 5 Nov 1993.

Breakwater The world's longest breakwater is the one that protects the Port of Galveston, TX. The granite South Breakwater is 6.74 miles in length.

Cemeteries *Largest* Ohlsdorf Cemetery in Hamburg, Germany is the largest cemetery, covering an area of 990 acres, with 967,774 burials and 397,966 cremations as of 31 Dec 1993. It has been in continuous use since 1877.

The United States' largest cemetery is Arlington National Cemetery, which is situated on the Potomac River in Virginia. It is 612 acres in extent, and more than 200,000 members of the armed forces are buried there.

Tallest The permanently illuminated Memorial Necrópole Ecumênica, located in Santos, near São Paulo, Brazil, is 10 stories high, occupying an area of 4.4 acres. Its construction started in March 1983 and the first burial was on 28 Jul 1984.

Chimneys *Tallest* The Ekibastuz, Kazakhstan coal power plant No. 2 stack, completed in 1987, is 1,377 ft tall. The chimney tapers from 144 ft in diameter at the base to 46 ft 7 in at the top, and it weighs 53,600 tons.

Most massive The world's most massive chimney is one of 1,148 ft at Puentes de Garcia Rodriguez, northwest Spain, built by M.W. Kellogg Co. for Empresa Nacional de Electricidad S.A. It contains 556,247 ft^3 of concrete and 2.9 million lb of steel and has an internal volume of 6.7 million ft^3.

Columns The tallest are the thirty-six 90-ft-tall fluted pillars of Vermont marble in the colonnade of the Education Building, Albany, NY. Their base diameter is 6 ft 6 in.

Cooling towers The largest is that adjacent to the nuclear power plant at Uentrop, Germany. It is 590 ft tall and was completed in 1976.

Crematorium The world's largest crematorium is at the Nikolo-Arkhangelskiy Crematorium, east Moscow, Russia with seven twin cremators, completed in March 1972. It covers an area of 519 acres.

Demolition work The largest building ever demolished by explosives was the 21-story Traymore Hotel, Atlantic City, NJ on 26 May 1972 by Controlled Demolition Inc. of Towson, MD. This 600-room hotel had a volume of 6.5 million ft^3.

The tallest structure ever demolished by explosives was the Matla Power Station chimney, Kriel, South Africa, on 19 Jul 1981. It stood 902 ft and was brought down by the Santon (Steeplejack) Co. Ltd of Greater Manchester, Great Britain.

Fifteen members of the Black Leopard Karate Club demolished a seven-room wooden farmhouse west of Elnora, Alberta, Canada in 3 hr 18 min by foot and unaided hand on 13 Jun 1982.

Domes The largest is the Louisiana Superdome, New Orleans, which has a diameter of 680 ft.

Doors Largest The four doors in the Vehicle Assembly Building near Cape Canaveral, FL have a height of 460 ft.

Heaviest The door of the laser target room at Lawrence Livermore National Laboratory, CA weighs 360 tons and is up to 8 ft thick. It was installed by Overly Manufacturing Company.

Fences Longest The dingo-proof wire fence enclosing the main sheep areas of Australia is 6 ft high, 1 ft underground and stretches for 3,437 miles. The Queensland state government discontinued full maintenance in 1982.

Tallest The world's tallest fences are security screens 65 ft high erected by Harrop-Allin of Pretoria, South Africa in November 1981 to protect fuel depots and refineries at Sasolburg from rocket attack.

Tallest flagpoles The tallest flagpole was erected outside the Oregon Building at the 1915 Panama–Pacific International Exposition in San Francisco, CA. It stood 299 ft 7 in in height, weighed 52 tons, and was cut from a Douglas fir.

The tallest unsupported flagpole in the world is the 282-ft-tall steel pole, weighing 120,000 lb, that was erected on 22 Aug 1985 at the Canadian Expo 86 exhibition in Vancouver, British Columbia and supports a gigantic hockey stick 205 ft in length.

Tallest fountain The tallest is the fountain at Fountain Hills, AZ, built at a cost of $1.5 million for McCulloch Properties Inc. When all three pumps are on, the water column can reach 625 ft if weather conditions are favorable.

Garbage dump Reclamation Plant No. 1, Fresh Kills, Staten Island, NY, opened in March 1947, is the world's largest sanitary landfill. The facility covers 3,000 acres and is estimated to contain 100,000 tons of garbage. In 1993 Fresh Kills processed 14,000 tons of garbage.

Largest gas tanks The largest gas tanks are at Fontaine l'Evêque, Belgium, where disused mines have been adapted to store up to 17.6 billion ft^3 of gas at ordinary pressure.

The largest conventional gas tank is that at Simmering, Vienna, Austria, completed in 1968, with a height of 275 ft and a capacity of 10.6 million ft^3.

Largest revolving globe The largest revolving globe is a 33-ton 33-ft-diameter sphere called "Globe of Peace." It was built in five years, from 1982 to 1987, by Orfeo Bartolucci of Apecchi, Pesaro, Italy.

Largest grain elevator The single-unit elevator operated by the C-G-F Grain Co. at Wichita, KS consists of a triple row of storage tanks, 123 on each side of the central loading tower or "head house." The unit is 2,717 ft long and 100 ft wide. Each tank is 120 ft high, with an inside diameter of 30 ft, giving a total storage capacity of 20 million bushels of wheat.

The world's largest collection of grain elevators are the 23 at Thunder Bay, Ontario, Canada, on Lake Superior, with a total capacity of 103.9 million bushels.

AMAZING MAZES

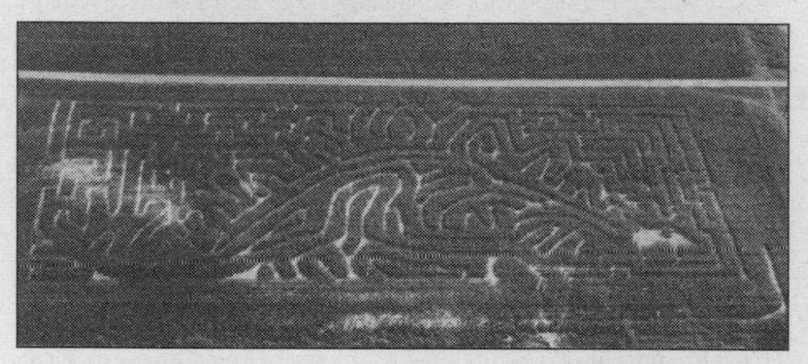

(Dwayne Arehart)

The largest maze ever constructed was the stegosaurus made in a cornfield at Lebanon Valley College, Pennsylvania. It was 500 ft long and covered an area of 126,000 ft^2, and was in existence for two months between September and November 1993.

The stegosaurus, called Cornelius, was the brainchild of Adrian Fisher of Minotaur Designs in St Albans, Great Britain, who has designed over 70 mazes worldwide. He explains how this particular challenge arose.

"It was one of those wonderful occasions when everything came together at once. Former student Don Frantz wanted Lebanon Valley College to help the Red Cross Appeal for Flood Victims of the Midwest, where millions of cornfields had been devastated. How about using a cornfield to raise funds and give everyone a great time? The biggest maze in the world would certainly generate media interest! We brainstormed the idea, and the Amazing Maize Maze was born.

All summer, paths were cut through 6-ft-high rows of corn. Together with creative entertainment specialist Chase Senge, we created a total maze experience, with horse-drawn haywagon rides, an all-day barbecue, a sound and music system throughout the maze, a quiz trail, a free soda fountain within the hedges, and a portatoilet halfway around (it was such a big maze, you might have needed it). A traditional English village turf maze was dug in 24 hours as performance art.

Over a sunny weekend, 6,000 visitors raised over $32,000 for the Red Cross Appeal. It was one of the happiest maze events I have known."

Kitchen An Indian government field kitchen set up in April 1973 at Ahmadnagar, Maharashtra, then a famine area, daily provided 1.2 million subsistence meals.

Lampposts The tallest lighting columns are the four made by Petitjean & Cie of Troyes, France and installed by Taylor Woodrow at Sultan Qaboos Sports Complex, Muscat, Oman. They stand 208 ft 4 in high.

***Lighthouses** Tallest* The 348 ft steel tower near Yamashita Park in Yokohama, Japan has a power of 600,000 candelas and a visibility range of 20 miles.

Greatest range The lights with the greatest range are those 1,089 ft above the ground on the Empire State Building, New York City. Each of the four-arc mercury bulbs is visible 80 miles away on the ground and 300 miles away from aircraft.

Largest marquee A marquee covering an area of 188,350 ft² (4.32 acres) was erected by the firm of Deuter of Augsburg, Germany for the 1958 "Welcome Expo" in Brussels, Belgium.

Maze The largest permanent maze is the hedge maze at Ruurlo, Netherlands, which has an area of 94,080 ft². It was created from beech hedges in 1891.

The maze with the greatest path length is that at Longleat, Warminster, Great Britain, which has 1.69 miles of paths flanked by 16,180 yew trees. It was opened on 6 Jun 1978.

The oldest datable representation of a labyrinth is that on a clay tablet from Pylos, Greece *c.* 1220 B.C.

Menhir The tallest known menhir (prehistoric upright monolith) is the 330 ton Grand Menhir Brisé, now in four pieces, which originally stood 59 ft high at Locmariaquer, France.

***Monuments** Tallest* The stainless-steel Gateway to the West arch in St Louis, MO, completed on 28 Oct 1965 to commemorate the westward expansion after the Louisiana Purchase of 1803, is a sweeping arch spanning 630 ft and rising to the same height of 630 ft. It cost $29 million and was designed in 1947 by the Finnish-American architect Eero Saarinen (1910–61).

Tallest column Constructed from 1936–39, at a cost of $1.5 million, the tapering column that commemorates the Battle of San Jacinto (21 Apr 1836), on the bank of the San Jacinto River near Houston, TX, is 570 ft tall, 47 ft square at the base, and 30 ft square at the observation tower, which is surmounted by a star weighing 220 tons.

Largest trilithons The largest trilithons are at Stonehenge, to the south of Salisbury Plain, Great Britain, with single sarsen blocks weighing over 50 tons. The blocks would have required more than 550 men to drag them up a 9 degree gradient. The earliest stage of the construction of the ditch has been dated to 2800 B.C.

Largest artificial mound The largest artificial mound is the gravel mound built as a memorial to the Seleucid King Antiochus I (r. 69–34 B.C.), that stands on the summit of Nemrud Dagi (8,182 ft), southeast of Malatya, Turkey. It measures 197 ft tall and covers 7.5 acres.

The unfinished obelisk at Aswan, Egypt, probably commissioned by Queen Hatshepsut, is 136 ft long and weighs 1,287 tons. (Spectrum Colour Library)

Obelisks Tallest The world's tallest obelisk is the Washington Monument in Washington, D.C. Situated in a 106 acre site and standing 555 ft 5$^{1}/_{8}$ in high, it was built to honor George Washington (1732–99).

Largest The obelisk of Tuthmosis III brought from Aswan, Egypt, by Emperor Constantius in the spring of A.D. 357 was repositioned in the Piazza San Giovanni in Laterane, Rome on 3 Aug 1588. Once 118 ft 1 in tall, it now stands 107 ft 7 in and weighs 500 tons.

The unfinished obelisk, probably commissioned by Queen Hatshepsut *c.* 1490 B.C., and *in situ* at Aswan, Egypt is 136 ft 10 in in length and weighs 1,287 tons.

DID YOU KNOW?

The largest fumigation ever was carried out during the restoration of the Mission Inn complex in Riverside, CA on 28 Jun–1 Jul 1987 to rid the buildings of termites. The fumigation was performed by Fume Masters Inc. of Riverside. More than 350 tarpaulins were used, and the operation involved completely covering the 70,000 ft² site and buildings—domes, minarets, chimneys and balconies, some of which exceeded 100 ft in height.

Longest piers The Dammam Pier, Saudi Arabia, on the Persian Gulf, with an overall length of 6.79 miles, was begun in July 1948 and completed on 15 Mar 1950. The area was subsequently developed by 1980 into the King Abdul Aziz Port, with 39 deep-water berths. The original causeway, greatly widened, now extends to 7.95 miles including other port structures.

Longest covered promenade The Long Corridor in the Summer Palace in Beijing, China is a covered promenade running for 2,388 ft. It is built entirely of wood and divided by crossbeams into 273 sections.

***Pyramids** Largest* The largest pyramid, and the largest monument ever constructed, is the Quetzalcóatl at Cholula de Rivadabia, 63 miles southeast of Mexico City. It is 177 ft tall and its base covers an area of nearly 45 acres. Its total volume has been estimated at 4.3 million yd³.

Oldest The Djoser step pyramid at Saqqâra, Egypt dates from *c.* 2900 B.C. It was constructed by Imhotep to a height of 204 ft, and originally had a Tura limestone casing.

Refuse electrical generation plants The two biggest refuse electrical generation plants in the United States are the South Meadow, Hartford County, CT plant, and the Refuse and Coal Plant in Franklin County, OH, both with a capacity of 90Mw.

Scaffolding The tallest scaffolding was erected by Regional Scaffolding & Hoisting Co., Inc. of Bronx, NY around the New York City Municipal Building, and was in place from 1988–92. Its total height was 650 ft and its volume 4,800,000 ft². The work required 12,000 scaffold frames and 20,000 aluminum planks.

United States The largest freestanding scaffolding in the United States is believed to be the one erected for the restoration of the Goldstone antenna in California. It was 170 ft high, 70 ft deep and went 180 ft around the circumference of the structure.

Scarecrow The tallest scarecrow ever built was "Stretch II," constructed by the Speers family of Paris, Ontario, Canada and a crew of 15 at the Paris, Ontario Fall Fair on 2 Sep 1989. It measured 103 ft 6¾ in in height.

Largest sewage works The Stickney Water Reclamation Plant (formerly the West–Southwest Sewage Treatment Works), in Stickney, IL began operation in 1939 on a 570-acre site and serves an area containing 2,200,000 people. Its 656 employees treated an average of 825 million gal of waste per day in 1993.

Snow and ice constructions A snow palace 87 ft high, one of four structures that together spanned 702 ft 8 in, was unveiled on 7 Feb 1987 at Asahikawa City, Hokkaidō, Japan.

The world's largest ice construction was the ice palace completed in January 1992, using 18,000 blocks of ice, in St Paul, MN during the Winter Carnival. Built by TMK Construction Specialties, it stood 166 ft 8 inches tall, covered an area the size of a football field, and contained 10.8 million pounds of ice.

Snowman The tallest stood 90 ft 1 in high and was built by a team of eight local residents at Saas-Fee, Switzerland. It took 21 days to build the snowman, which was completed on 6 Nov 1993.

The tallest snowman in the United States stood 76 ft 2 in high and was named Price William. It was built by Philip and Colleen Price, coordinators, with 10 others at Prince William Sound Community College, Valdez, AK. Construction took nearly three weeks, and the snowman was finished on 2 Apr 1992.

Stairways *Longest* The service staircase for the Niesenbahn funicular near Spiez, Switzerland rises to 7,759 ft. It has 11,674 steps and a banister.

Spiral The tallest spiral staircase is on the outside of the chimney Bobila Almirall, located in Terrassa, Barcelona, Spain. Built by Mariano–Masana i Ribas in 1956, it is 207 ft high and has 217 steps.

The longest spiral staircase is one 1,103 ft deep with 1,520 steps installed in the Mapco-White County Coal Mine, Carmi, IL by Systems Control Inc. in May 1981.

Statues *Tallest* A bronze statue of Buddha 394 ft high was completed in Tokyo, Japan in January 1993. It is 115 ft wide and weighs 1,100 tons. The statue took seven years to make, and was a joint Japanese–Taiwanese project.

The Statue of Liberty, originally named Liberty Enlightening the World, is the tallest statue in the United States. Designed and built in France to commemorate the friendship of the two countries, the 152 ft statue was shipped to New York City, where its copper sheets were assembled. President Grover Cleveland accepted the statue for the United States on 28 Oct 1886.

Longest Near Bamiyan, Afghanistan lie the remains of the recumbent Sakya Buddha, built of plastered rubble, which was "about 1,000 ft" long and is believed to date from the third or fourth century A.D.

Largest Lego statue The sculpture of the Indian chief Sitting Bull, at the Legoland Park, Billund, Denmark, measures 25 ft to the top of the feather. The largest statue ever constructed from Lego, it required 1.5 million bricks, individually glued together to withstand the weather.

The bronze Buddha (left) in Tokyo, Japan is the world's largest statue. Below, three inquisitive visitors attempt to discuss what's afoot. (Gamma/Kaku Kurita and Torin Boyd)

Largest swing A glider swing 30 ft high was constructed by Kenneth R. Mack, Langenburg, Saskatchewan, Canada for Uncle Herb's Amusements in 1986. The swing is capable of taking its four riders 25 ft off the ground.

Tidal river barrier The largest tidal river barrier is the Oosterscheldedam, a storm-surge barrier in the southwestern corner of the Netherlands. It has 65 concrete piers and 62 steel gates, and covers a total length of 5½ miles. It was opened by HM Queen Beatrix on 4 Oct 1986.

Tombs *Largest* The Mount Li tomb, the burial place of Qin Shi Huangdi, the First Emperor of Qin, dates to 221 B.C. and is situated 25 miles east of Xianyang, China. The two walls surrounding the grave measure 7,129 × 3,195 ft and 2,247 × 1,896 ft respectively. Several pits in the tomb contained a vast army of an estimated 8,000 life-sized terracotta soldiers.

Largest mass tomb A tomb housing 180,000 World War II dead on Okinawa, Japan was enlarged in 1985 to accommodate another 9,000 bodies thought to be buried on the island.

Grave digging It is recorded that Johann Heinrich Karl Thieme, sexton of Aldenburg, Germany, dug 23,311 graves during a 50-year career. In 1826 his understudy dug *his* grave.

Totem pole A 173-ft-tall pole was raised on 6 Jun 1973 at Alert Bay, British Columbia, Canada. It tells the story of the Kwakiutl tribe and took 36 man-weeks to carve.

Vats *Largest* "Strongbow," used by H. P. Bulmer Ltd, the English cidermakers, measures 64½ ft in height and 75½ ft in diameter, with a capacity of 1.95 million gal.

The largest wooden winecask in the world is the Heidelberg Tun, completed in 1751, in the cellar of the Friedrichsbau, Heidelberg, Germany. Its capacity is 58,570 gal.

Oldest The world's oldest known vat still in use is at Hugel et Fils (founded 1639), Riqueweihr, Haut-Rhin, France. Twelve generations of the family have used it since 1715.

Walls *Longest* The Great Wall of China has a main-line length of 2,150 miles. Completed during the reign of Qin Shi Huangdi (221– 210 B.C.), it has a further 1,780 miles of branches and spurs. Its height varies from 15–39 ft and it is up to 32 ft thick. It runs from Shanhaiguan, on the Gulf of Bohai, to Yumenguan and Yanguan. On 6 Mar 1985 a report from China stated that a five-year survey proved that its total length was once 6,200 miles. In October 1990 it was reported that after two years of exertion Lin Youdian had become the first person to walk its entire length.

Thickest Urnammu's city walls at Ur (now Muqayyar, Iraq), destroyed by the Elamites in 2006 B.C., were 88 ft thick and made of mud brick.

Indoor waterfall The tallest indoor waterfall measures 114 ft in height and is backed by 9,000 ft² of marble. It is situated in the lobby of the International Center Building, Detroit, MI.

In a "glass" above the rest, the world's largest windows fronting the Palace of Industry and Technology in Paris. (Gamma)

Water tower The waterspheroid at Edmond, OK, built in 1986, rises to a height of 218 ft, and has a capacity of 500,000 gal. The tower was manufactured by Chicago Bridge and Iron.

Largest waterwheel The Mohammadieh Noria wheel at Hamah, Syria has a diameter of 131 ft and dates from Roman times.

Largest windows The largest sheet of glass ever manufactured was one of 540 ft^2, or 65 ft 7 in by 8 ft 2¼ in, exhibited by the Saint Gobin Co. in France at the *Journées Internationales de Miroiterie* in March 1958.

The largest single windows in the world are those in the Palace of Industry and Technology at Rondpoint de la Défense, Paris, France, with an extreme width of 715 ft and a maximum height of 164 ft.

Stained glass The tallest stained glass is the 135-ft-high back-lit glass mural installed in 1979 in the atrium of the Ramada Hotel, Dubai.

Window cleaning Keith Witt of Amarillo, TX cleaned three standard 42½ × 47 in office windows with an 11.8-in-long squeegee and 2 gal of water in 10.13 sec on 31 Jan 1992, at the International Window Cleaning Association convention in San Antonio, TX. In this contest smears are not tolerated and are penalized.

Largest wine cellars The cellars at Paarl of the Ko-operative Wijnbouwers Vereeniging, known as KWV, Cape Province, in the center of the wine-growing district of South Africa, cover an area of 25 acres and have a capacity of 36 million gal.

GUESS WHAT?

Q. How old is the oldest wine?

A. Look in "Drink" (Human Achievements)

United States The Cienega Winery of the Almaden Vineyards in Hollister, CA covers 4 acres and can house 37,300 oak barrels containing 1.83 million gallons of wine.

Ziggurat The largest ziggurat (from the Assyrian *ziqqurati*, meaning summit, height) ever built was that of the Elamite King Untas, *c.* 1250 B.C., known as the Ziggurat of Choga Zambil, 18.6 miles from Haft Tepe, Iran. The outer base was 344 × 344 ft and the fifth "box" 92 × 92 ft, nearly 164 ft above.

TRANSPORT

SHIPS

OLDEST BOATS

The earliest surviving "vessel" is a pinewood dugout found in Pesse, Netherlands and dated to *c.* 6315 B.C. ± 275, now in the Provincial Museum, Assen.

An 18-in-long paddle was found in Great Britain in 1948. It has been dated to *c.* 7600 B.C. and is now in the Cambridge Museum of Archaeology, Great Britain.

The oldest surviving boat is a 27-ft-long 2½-ft-wide wooden eel-catching canoe discovered at Tybrind Vig on the Baltic island of Fünen, which is dated to *c.* 4490 B.C.

Oldest paddle wheeler The world's oldest active paddle wheeler is *Skibladner*, which has been continuously operated since 1856. It was built in Motala, Sweden, has had two major refits, and continues to ply Lake Mjøsa in Norway.

WARSHIPS

Largest aircraft carriers The warships with the largest full-load displacement in the world are the Nimitz class US Navy aircraft carriers USS *Nimitz, Dwight D. Eisenhower, Carl Vinson, Theodore Roosevelt, George Washington*, and *Abraham Lincoln*, the last two of which displace

***Skibladner*, the world's oldest active paddle wheeler, has plied Lake Mjøsa, Norway since 1856. (Quadrant Picture Library/A.R. Dalton)**

100,846 tons. They are 1,092 ft in length overall, with 4½ acres of flight deck, and have a speed well in excess of 30 knots. They have to be refueled after about 900,000 miles of steaming. Their full complement of personnel is 5,986.

Most aircraft landings The greatest number of landings on an aircraft carrier in one day was 602, achieved by Marine Air Group 6 of the United States Pacific Fleet Air Force aboard the USS *Matanikau* on 25 May 1945 between 8 A.M. and 5 P.M.

Largest battleships The Japanese battleships *Yamato* (completed on 16 Dec 1941 and sunk southwest of Kyūshū, Japan by US planes on 7 Apr 1945) and *Musashi* (sunk in the Philippine Sea by 11 bombs and 16 torpedoes on 24 Oct 1944) were the largest battleships ever commissioned, each with a full-load displacement of 81,545 tons. With an overall length of 863 ft, a beam of 127 ft and a full-load draft of 35½ ft, they mounted nine 18.1-in guns in three triple turrets. Each gun weighed 181.5 tons and was 75 ft in length, firing a 3,200 lb projectile.

United States The largest battleships were the USS *Missouri*, an Iowa class battleship, and the USS *Wisconsin*, 887 ft long and with a full load displacement of 64,960 tons. Both were first commissioned in 1944 and later recommissioned in 1986 and 1988 respectively, following major refits. Armaments include nine 16-inch guns used in the Gulf War in 1991 and capable of firing 2,700 lb projectiles a distance of 23 miles. Both ships are now in reserve.

Fastest armed vessel A US Navy hovercraft, the 78-ft-long 110-ton test vehicle SES-100B, achieved a speed of 91.9 knots (105.8 mph), on 25 Jan 1980. (See Hovercraft, fastest.)

Fastest destroyers The fastest speed attained by a destroyer was 45.25 knots (51.83 mph) by the 3,120 ton French destroyer *Le Terrible* in 1935. It was built in Blainville, France and was powered by four Yarrow small-tube boilers and two Rateau geared turbines, giving 100,000 shp. It was removed from the active list at the end of 1957.

The fastest destroyers in the US Navy arsenal are the Spruance class and Kidd class ships, which attain a maximum speed of 33 knots (38 mph).

SUBMARINES

Largest The world's largest submarines are of the Russian Typhoon class. The launch of the first at the covered shipyard at Severodvinsk in the White Sea was announced on 23 Sep 1980. They are believed to have a dive displacement of 27,557 tons, to measure 558 ft overall and to be armed with 20 SS-NX-20 missiles with a 4,800-nautical-mile range, each with seven warheads. By late 1987 two others built in St Petersburg, Russia (formerly Leningrad, USSR) were operational, each deploying 140 warheads.

The largest submarines in the US Navy are of the Ohio class. Each of the nine ships in active service has a displacement of 18,700 tons. At 560 ft, they are the longest submarines in the fleet, and also have the largest crew, at 165.

Fastest The Russian Alpha class nuclear-powered submarines have a reported maximum speed of 45 knots plus (51.8 mph). With the use of titanium alloy in the hull, they arc believed to be able to dive to 2,500 ft.

Deepest The US Navy deep submergence vessel *Sea Cliff* (DSV 4), 30 tons, commissioned in 1973, reached a depth of 20,000 ft in March 1985.

Longest submarine patrol The longest submarine patrol that ever dove unsupported (of those that have been made public) is 111 days, by HM Submarine *Warspite* in the South Atlantic from 25 Nov 1982 to 15 Mar 1983. It sailed 30,804 nautical miles.

Fastest underwater human-powered vehicle *Propeller* The fastest speed attained by a human-powered propeller submarine is 5.94 knots, by *F.A.U-Boat*, designed and built by the Florida Atlantic University Ocean Engineering Department, Boca Raton, FL, on 8 Mar 1994. The vessel used a two-blade high aspect ratio propeller propulsion system, and was crewed by Karl Heeb, Charles Callaway and William Fay.

Non-propeller The fastest speed attained by a human-powered non-propeller submarine is 2.9 knots, by *SubDUDE* on 21 Aug 1992. The submarine was designed by the Scripps Institution of Oceanography, University of California, San Diego and used a horizontal oscillating foil propulsion system. The crew consisted of Kimball Millikan, pilot; Ed Trevino, athlete; and team leader, Kevin Hardy.

A starboard view of the nuclear-powered USS *Michigan*, one of the Ohio class submarines that are the largest in the United States fleet. (U.S. Navy)

TANKERS

Largest The *Jahre Viking*, formerly known as the *Happy Giant*, is 622,420 tons deadweight. It is the world's largest oil tanker, and the world's largest ship of any kind, at 1,471 ft long overall, with a beam of 225 ft 11 in, and a draft of 80 ft 9 in. The ship was lengthened by Nippon Kokan in 1980 by adding a 265 ft 8 in midship section.

Largest wreck The 354,043-ton deadweight very large crude carrier (VLCC) *Energy Determination* blew up and broke in two in the Straits of Hormuz on 12 Dec 1979. Its hull value was $58 million.

Removal The largest wreck removal was carried out in 1979 by Smit Tak International, which removed the remains of the French tanker *Betelgeuse*, 120,000 tons, from Bantry Bay, Republic of Ireland, within 20 months.

Most massive collision The closest an irresistible force has come to striking an immovable object was on 16 Dec 1977, 22 miles off the coast of southern Africa, when the tanker *Venoil* (330,954 deadweight tons) struck its sister ship *Venpet* (330,869 deadweight tons).

CARGO VESSELS

Largest The largest ship carrying dry cargo is the Norwegian ore carrier *Berge Stahl*, 402,082.6 tons deadweight, built in South Korea for the Norwegian owner Sig Bergesen. It has a length of 1,125 ft, a beam measuring 208 ft and was launched on 5 Nov 1986.

Largest containership American President Lines has built five ships in Germany—*President Adams*, *President Jackson*, *President Kennedy*, *President Polk* and *President Truman*—that are termed post-Panamax, being the first container vessels too large for the Panama Canal. They are 902.69 ft in length and 129.29 ft abeam; the maximum beam for the Panama transit is 105.97 ft.

GUESS WHAT?

Q. HOW HIGH IS THE WORLD'S TALLEST LIGHTHOUSE?

A. LOOK IN "SPECIALIZED STRUCTURES" (BUILDINGS & STRUCTURES)

Largest propeller The largest propeller ever made is the triple-bladed screw of 36 ft 1 in diameter made by Kawasaki Heavy Industries, Japan, and delivered on 17 Mar 1982 for the 233,787-ton bulk carrier *Hoei Maru* (now renamed *New Harvest*).

Barges The world's largest RoRo (roll-on, roll-off) ships are five 730-ft long barges operated by Crowley American Transport of Jacksonville, FL.

Largest human-powered ship The giant ship *Tessarakonteres*, a three-banked catamaran galley with 4,000 rowers, built for Ptolemy IV *c.* 210 B.C. in Alexandria, Egypt, measured 420 ft, with up to eight men to an oar of 38 cubits (57 ft) in length.

Most powerful tugs The largest and most powerful tugs are the *Nikolay Chiker* (SB-135) and *Fotiy Krylov* (SB-134), commissioned in 1989, and built by Hollming Ltd of Finland for V/O Sudoimport, in the former USSR. They have 24,480 hp and are capable of 250 tons bollard pull at full power. At 324 ft long and 63 ft wide, they are now owned and operated under the names *Tsavliris Titan* and *Tsavliris Giant* by the Tsavliris Group of Companies of Piraeus, Greece.

Car ferries *Largest* The world's largest car and passenger ferry is the 59,914 gross registered tonnage *Silja Europa*, which entered service in 1993 between Stockholm, Sweden and Helsinki, Finland. Operated by the Silja Line, the ferry is 662 ft long and 107 ft abeam, and can carry 3,000 passengers, 350 cars and 60 trucks.

Fastest The fastest car ferries are the twin-hulled, wave-piercing Sea Cats constructed by International Catamarans of Hobart, Tasmania, Australia and first launched in 1990. They have a cruising speed of 35 knots and are capable of 42 knots. Each one can carry 432 passengers and 80 cars.

Rail ferries The operating route of the biggest international rail ferries, *Klaipeda*, *Vilnius*, *Mukran* and *Greifswald*, is in the Baltic Sea, between the ports of Klaipeda, Lithuania and Mukran, Germany. Consisting of two decks 625 ft in length, 301.4 ft in breadth and 13,104 tons deadweight, these ferries were built in Wismar, Germany. Each of them can lift 103 railcars of standard 48.65 ft length and weighing up to 84 tons. The ferries can cover a distance of 273 nautical miles (314.2 miles) in 17 hours.

Largest hydrofoil The 212-ft-long *Plainview* (347 tons full-load) naval hydrofoil was launched by the Lockheed Shipbuilding and Construction Co. at Seattle, WA on 28 Jun 1965. It has a service speed of 57.2 mph.

Most powerful icebreakers The most powerful icebreakers are the *Rossiya* and its sister ships *Sovetskiy Soyuz* and *Oktyabryskaya Revolutsiya*. The 28,000-ton 460-ft-long *Rossiya*, powered by 75,000 hp nuclear engines, was built in Leningrad (now St. Petersburg), Russia and completed in 1985.

Most powerful dredger The 468.4-ft-long *Prins der Nederlanden* of 10,586 gross tons can dredge up 22,400 tons of sand from a depth of 115 ft via two suction tubes in less than an hour.

MESSAGE IN A BOTTLE!

The longest recorded interval between drop and pickup is 73 years. A message thrown from the SS *Arawatta* out of Cairns, Queensland, Australia on 9 Jun 1910 in a lotion bottle was found on Moreton Island, Queensland on 6 Jun 1983.

Wooden ship *Heaviest* The *Richelieu*, 333 2/3 ft long and weighing 9,548 tons, was launched in Toulon, France on 3 Dec 1873.

Longest The longest ever built was the New York-built *Rochambeau* (1867–72), formerly the *Dunderberg*, which measured 377 ft 4 in overall.

PASSENGER VESSELS

Fastest turnaround The largest liner under the British flag, MV *Queen Elizabeth II*, set a "turnaround" record of 3 hr 18 min in New York City on 14 Dec 1993.

Largest passenger liner The largest in current use, and the longest ever, is the *Norway*, 76,049 tons and 1,035 ft 7 1/2 in in overall length, with a capacity of 2,022 passengers and 900 crew. It was built as the *France* in 1960 and renamed after purchase in June 1979 by Norwegian Knut Kloster. It normally cruises in the Caribbean and is based at Miami, FL. Work undertaken during an extensive refit, including two new decks, during the fall of 1990 increased the number of passenger decks to 11. Its draft is 34 1/2 ft and its speed is 18 knots.

The fastest liner is *Queen Elizabeth II*, which set a turnaround record of 3 hr 18 min in New York City on 14 Dec 1993. (Quadrant Picture Library/Matthews)

Largest riverboat The world's largest inland boat is the 382-ft *Mississippi Queen*, designed by James Gardner of London, Great Britain. The vessel was commissioned on 25 Jul 1976 in Cincinnati, OH and is now in service on the Mississippi River.

Largest yacht *Royal* The largest royal yacht in the world is the Saudi Arabian royal yacht *Abdul Aziz*, which is 482 ft long. Built in Denmark and completed in 1984 at Vospers Yard, Southampton, Great Britain, it was estimated in September 1987 to be worth more than $100 million.

Nonroyal The largest private (nonroyal) yacht is the *Alexander*, a former ferry converted to a private yacht in 1986, at 400 ft overall.

Longest canoe The "Snake Boat" *Nadubhagóm*, 135 ft long, from Kerala, southern India, has a crew of 109 rowers and nine "encouragers."

Largest passenger hydrofoil Three 185-ton Supramar PTS 150 Mk III hydrofoils carry 250 passengers at 40 knots across the Öre Sound between Malmö, Sweden and Copenhagen, Denmark. They were built by Westermoen Hydrofoil Ltd of Mandal, Norway.

SAILING SHIPS

Oldest active The oldest active square-rigged sailing vessel in the world is the restored SV *Maria Asumpta* (formerly the *Ciudad de Inca*), built near Barcelona, Spain in 1858. It is 98 ft overall and weighs 142.3 tons. Restored in 1981–82, it is operated by The Friends of *Maria Asumpta* of Lenham, Great Britain.

Largest The largest vessel ever built in the era of sail was the *France II* (5,806 gross tons), launched at Bordeaux, France in 1911. This was a steel-hulled, five-masted barque with a hull measuring 418 ft overall. It was wrecked off New Caledonia on 12 Jul 1922.

Largest in service The largest now in service is the 357-ft-long *Sedov*, built in 1921 in Kiel, Germany. It is 48 ft wide, with a displacement of 6,300 gross registered tons (4,267.2 tons) and a sail area of 45,123 ft^2.

Longest The longest is the 613-ft-long French-built *Club Med I* with five aluminum masts. The 3,013-ft^2 polyester sails are computer-controlled. It is operated as a Caribbean cruise vessel for 425 passengers bound for Club Med. With its small sail area and powerful engines it is really a motor-sailer. A sister ship, *Club Med II*, is now being commissioned.

Largest junks The largest on record was the seagoing *Zheng He*, flagship of Admiral Zheng He's 62 treasure ships, *c.* 1420, with a displacement of 3,472 tons and a length variously estimated up to 538 ft. It is believed to have had nine masts.

Largest sails The largest spars ever carried were those in HM Battleship *Temeraire*, completed at Chatham, Great Britain, on 31 Aug 1877. It was broken up in 1921. The fore and main yards measured 115 ft in length. The foresail contained 5,100 ft of canvas weighing 2.23 tons, and the total sail area was 25,000 ft^2.

The *Sedov* is the largest sailing ship in active service. (Quadrant Picture Library/A.R. Dalton)

Tallest mast The *Velsheda*, a J-class sailing vessel, is the tallest known single-masted yacht in the world. Measured from heel fitting to the mast truck, it is 169¼ ft in height. Built in 1933, it has a displacement of 160 tons and supports a sail area of 7,500 ft².

OCEAN CROSSINGS

Earliest Atlantic The earliest crossing of the Atlantic by a power vessel, as opposed to an auxiliary-engined sailing ship, was a 22-day voyage begun in April 1827, from Rotterdam, Netherlands, to the West Indies, by the *Curaçao*. It was a 127-ft wooden paddle boat of 490.5 tons, built as the *Calpe* in Dover, Great Britain in 1826 and purchased by the Dutch government for a West Indian mail service.

The earliest Atlantic crossing entirely under steam (with intervals for desalting the boilers) was by HMS *Rhadamanthus*, from Plymouth, Great Britain to Barbados in 1832.

The earliest crossing under continuous steam power was by the condenser-fitted packet ship *Sirius* (787 tons) from Queenstown (now Cóbh), Ireland to Sandy Hook, NJ, in 18 days 10 hr, from 4–22 Apr 1838.

Fastest Atlantic Under the rules of the Hales Trophy or "Blue Riband," which recognizes the highest average speed rather than the shortest duration, the record is held by the 222-ft Italian powerboat *Destriero*, with an average speed of 53.09 knots between the Nantucket Light Buoy and Bishop Rock Lighthouse, Isles of Scilly, Great Britain, on 6–9 Aug 1992, in a time of 58 hr 34 min 4 sec.

Fastest Pacific The fastest crossing from Yokohama, Japan to Long Beach, CA—4,840 nautical miles (5,567.64 miles)—took 6 days 1 hr 27 min (30 Jun–6 Jul 1973) by the containership *Sea-Land Commerce* (56,353 tons), at an average speed of 33.27 knots (38.31 mph).

San Francisco to Boston Richard B. Wilson and Bill Biewenga sailed from San Francisco to Boston via Cape Horn in 69 days 19 hr 44 min. They left San Francisco in the 53-ft trimaran *Great American II* on 27 January and arrived in Boston on 1 Apr 1993.

Fastest circumnavigation Peter Blake (New Zealand) and Robin Knox-Johnson (Great Britain) won the Jules Verne Trophy when they arrived back in France on 1 Apr 1994, after circling the globe nonstop in 74 days 22 hr 17 min in the catamaran *Enza*.

Water speed The fastest speed ever achieved on water is an estimated 300 knots (345.48 mph) by Kenneth Peter Warby (b. 9 May 1939) on Blowering Dam Lake, New South Wales, Australia on 20 Nov 1977 in his unlimited hydroplane *Spirit of Australia*.

The official world water speed record is 275.8 knots (511.11 km/h) set on 8 Oct 1978 by Warby on Blowering Dam Lake.

Mary Rife of Flint, TX set a women's unofficial record of 206.72 mph in her blown fuel hydro *Proud Mary* in Tulsa, OK on 23 July 1977. Her official record is 197 mph.

MERCHANT SHIPPING

Shipbuilding Worldwide production completed in 1993 was 20 million gross tonnage of ships, excluding sailing ships, non-propelled vessels and vessels of less than 100 gross tonnage. Japan completed 9.1 million gross tonnage (45 percent of the world total) in 1993.

The world's leading shipbuilder in 1993 was Daewoo Shipbuilding and Heavy Machinery Ltd. of South Korea, which completed 13 ships of 1.55 million gross tonnage.

Biggest owner The largest ship owners are the Japanese NYK Group, whose fleet of owned vessels totaled 11,096,170 gross tonnage on 1 Feb 1994.

United States The largest shipping owner and operator in the United States is Exxon Corporation, whose fleets of owned/managed and chartered tankers in 1987 totaled a daily average of 10.42 million deadweight tons.

Bill Biewenga (left in photo below) and Rich Wilson (right in photo below) aboard *Great American II*. At right, a view of the trimaran during the voyage. (Stephen Rose; Tom Hamilton)

Largest fleet The largest merchant fleet in the world at the end of 1993 was that under the flag of Panama, with a fleet totaling 57,618,623 gross tons.

Fastest shipbuilding The fastest times in which complete ships of more than 10,000 tons were ever built were achieved at Kaiser's Yard, Portland, OR during the wartime program for building 2,742 Liberty ships in 18 shipyards from 27 Sep 1941. In 1942 No. 440, named *Robert E. Peary*, had its keel laid on 8 November, was launched on 12 November and was operational after 4 days 15½ hr on 15 November. It was broken up in 1963.

Fastest riveting The world record for riveting is 11,209 rivets in 9 hr, by John Moir at the Workman Clark Ltd shipyard, Belfast, Northern Ireland in June 1918. His peak hour was his seventh, with 1,409 rivets, an average of nearly 23½ per min.

PORTS

Largest The largest port in the world is the Port of New York and New Jersey. The port has a navigable waterfront of 755 miles (295 miles in New Jersey), stretching over 92 miles^2, with a total berthing capacity of 391 ships at a time. The total warehouse floor space covers 422.4 acres.

Busiest The busiest port and the largest artificial harbor in the world is Rotterdam-Europoort in the Netherlands, which covers 38 miles^2, with 76 miles of quays. It handled 292 million tons of sea-going cargo in 1991.

Although the port of Singapore handles less tonnage than Rotterdam in total seaborne cargo, it handles the greatest number of containers, making it the No. 1 container port in the world, with a record of 7.97 million TEUs in 1992.

United States The busiest port in the United States is New Orleans, LA, which handled 1.775 million tons of cargo in 1989.

Dry dock With a maximum shipbuilding capacity of 1.2 million deadweight tons, the Daewoo Okpo No. 1 Dry Dock, Koje Island in South Korea measures 1,740 ft long by 430 ft wide and was completed in 1979. The dock gates, 46 ft high and 33 ft thick at the base, are the world's most massive.

MODEL BOATS

Duration records Members of the Lowestoft Model Boat Club crewed a radio-controlled scale model boat on 17–18 Aug 1991 at Dome Leisure Park, Doncaster, Great Britain and set a 24-hr distance record of 111.18 miles.

David and Peter Holland of Doncaster, Great Britain, of the Conisbrough and District Modelling Association, crewed a 28-in-long scale model boat of the trawler *Margaret H* continuously on one battery for 24 hours, and recorded a distance of 33.45 miles, at the Dome Leisure Complex, Doncaster, Great Britain on 15–16 Aug 1992.

Crossing the Benue River in Cameroon, the British Trans-African Expedition hovercraft caused river rubbernecking (above). On land, as the turbine roared into action (below), crowds of onlookers panicked and ran from the instant sandstorm. (David Smithers FRGS)

HOVERCRAFT

Fastest The world's fastest hovercraft is the 78-ft-long 110.2-ton US Navy test hovercraft SES-100B. It attained a world record 91.9 knots (105.8 mph) on 25 Jan 1980 on the Chesapeake Bay Test Range, MD.

Largest The SRNY Mk III, a British-built civil hovercraft, weighs 341 tons and can carry 418 passengers and 60 cars. It is 185 ft long and can travel at over 65 knots.

Longest journey The longest hovercraft journey was one of 5,000 miles, by the British Trans-African Hovercraft Expedition, under the leadership of David Smithers, through eight West African countries in a Winchester class SRN6, between 15 Oct 1969 and 3 Jan 1970.

Highest The highest altitude reached by a hovercraft was on 11 Jun 1990 when *Neste Enterprise* and her crew of 10 reached the navigable source of the Yangzi River, China at 16,050 ft.

The greatest altitude at which a hovercraft is operating is on Lake Titicaca, Peru, where since 1975 an HM2 Hoverferry has been hovering 12,506 ft above sea level.

BICYCLES

PRODUCTION

Longest The longest true tandem bicycle ever built (i.e., without a third stabilizing wheel) is one designed and built by Terry Thessman of Pahiatua, New Zealand. It measures 72.96 ft long and weighs 340 lb. It was ridden by four riders a distance of 807 ft on 27 Feb 1988. Turning corners proved to be a problem.

Smallest The world's smallest wheeled ridable bicycle is one with wheels of 0.76 in in diameter that was ridden by its constructor, Neville Patten of Gladstone, Queensland, Australia for a distance of 13 ft 5½ in on 25 Mar 1988.

Jacques Puyoou of Pau, Pyrénées-Atlantiques, France built a tandem 14.1 in long, which has been ridden by him and Madame Puyoou.

Largest The largest bicycle as measured by the front-wheel diameter is "Frankencycle," built by Dave Moore of Rosemead, CA and first ridden by Steve Gordon of Moorpark, CA, on 4 Jun 1989. The wheel diameter is 10 ft and the bicycle itself is 11 ft 2 in high.

Tricycle The largest tricycle is the Dillon Colossal Tricycle. Designed by Arthur Dillon, it has rear wheels 11 ft in diameter, constructed by David Moore, and a front wheel 5 ft 10 in high.

The Dillon Colossal Tricycle (above) being ridden by its designer, Arthur Dillon, and his son Christopher.

The smallest bicycle built for two (left), ridden by Frenchman Jacques Puyoou and his wife. (J.L. Cachou/Galerie Commerciale Baratinau)

RIDING

Wheelie David Robilliard set a record of 5 hr 12 min 33 sec at the Beau Sejour Leisure Center, St Peter Port, Channel Islands on 28 May 1990.

Underwater tricycling A team of 32 divers pedaled a distance of 116.66 miles in 75 hr 20 min on a standard tricycle at Diver's Den, Santa Barbara, CA on 16–19 Jun 1988.

HUMAN-POWERED VEHICLES

Fastest land The world speed records for human-powered vehicles (HPVs) over a 200 m (656.2 ft) flying start are 65.484 mph (single rider) by Fred Markham at Mono Lake, CA on 11 May 1986 and 62.92 mph (multiple riders) by Dave Grylls and Leigh Barczewski at the Ontario Speedway, CA, on 4 May 1980.

The one-hour standing start (single rider) record is held by Pat Kinch, riding *Kingcycle Bean*, averaging 46.96 mph on 8 Sep 1990 at Millbrook Proving Ground, Great Britain.

Water cycle The men's 6,562 ft (single rider) record is 12.84 mph, by Steve Hegg in *Flying Fish* off Long Beach, CA on 20 Jul 1987.

UNICYCLES

Tallest The tallest unicycle ever mastered is one 101 ft 9 in tall ridden by Steve McPeak (with a safety wire suspended by an overhead crane) for a distance of 376 ft in Las Vegas, NV in October 1980.

Smallest Peter Rosendahl (Sweden) of Las Vegas, NV rode a unicycle with a wheel diameter of 1 in, with no attachments or extensions fitted, a distance of 12 ft in Las Vegas on 25 Mar 1994.

One hundred miles Takayuki Koike of Kanagawa, Japan set a unicycle record for 100 miles in 6 hr 44 min 21.84 sec on 9 Aug 1987 (average speed 14.83 mph).

Endurance Akira Matsushima (Japan) unicycled 3,260 miles from Newport, OR to Washington, D.C. from 10 Jul–22 Aug 1992.

Backwards Peter Rosendahl rode his 24-in-wheel unicycle backwards for a distance of 46.7 miles in 9 hr 25 min on 19 May 1990.

Sprint Peter Rosendahl set a sprint record for 100 m (328.1 ft) of 12.11 secs (18.47 mph) in Las Vegas, NV on 25 Mar 1994.

MOTORCYCLES

PRODUCTION

In January 1993 it was estimated that there were 4,001,000 registered motorcycles in the United States.

Longest Gregg Reid of Atlanta, GA designed and built a Yamaha 250 cc motorcycle that measures 15 ft 6 in long and weighs 520 lb. It is street legal and has been insured.

Smallest Simon Timperley and Clive Williams of Progressive Engineering Ltd, Ashton-under-Lyne, Great Britain designed and built a motorcycle with a wheelbase of 4¼ in, a seat height of 3¾ in and a wheel diameter of 0.75 in for the front and 0.95 in for the back. The bike was ridden 3.2 ft.

Fastest production road machine The 151 hp 1-liter Tu Atara Yamaha Bimota 6th edition EI has a road-tested top speed of 186.4 mph.

SPEED

Fastest speeds Dave Campos (USA), riding a 23 ft long streamliner named *Easyriders*, powered by two 91 in^3 Ruxton Harley-Davidson engines, set AMA and FIM absolute records with an overall average of 322.150 mph and completed the faster run at an average of 322.870 mph on Bonneville Salt Flats, UT on 14 Jul 1990.

The fastest time for a single run over 440 yd from a standing start is 7.08 sec by Bo O'Brechta (USA) riding a supercharged 1,200 cc Kawasaki-based machine in Ontario, CA in 1980.

The highest terminal velocity recorded at the end of a 440 yd run from a standing start is 199.55 mph, by Russ Collins (USA) in Ontario, CA on 7 Oct 1978.

RIDING

Duration The longest time a motor scooter has been kept in nonstop motion is 1,001 hr. A Kinetic Honda DX 100 cc, ridden by Har Parkash Rishi, Amarjeet Singh and Navjot Chadha, covered a distance of 19,241 miles at Traffic Park, Pune, Maharashtra, India between 22 Apr and Jun 1990.

Longest ride Jari Saarelainen (Finland; b. 4 Apr 1959) rode his Honda Gold Wing 1,500 cc motorcycle over 67,109 miles through 43 countries. He set off from Helsinki, Finland on 1 Dec 1989 and returned 742 days later on 12 Dec 1991.

Jim Rogers and Tabitha Estabrook traveled 57,022 miles on two motorcycles, covering six continents. They set off from New York in March 1990 and returned in November 1991.

Trans-Americas Kurt Nerlich and Hans Shirmer traveled 67,000 miles (55,400 by motorcycle) around the Americas (North, South and Central) in 27 months from July 1954 to September 1956. Travel to and through Central and South America was much more primitive then than it is today.

Trans-America Ken Hatton of Chicago, IL completed a solo motorcycle trek across the United States, in September 1988, in a record time of 43 hr 17 min.

Biggest pyramid The Dare Devils of the Corps of Signals, Indian Army established a world record with a pyramid of 81 men on nine motorcycles. The pyramid was held together by muscle and determination only, with no straps, harnesses or other aids. It traveled a distance of 328 yd at Shivchhatrapati Stadium, Pune, India on 25 Jan 1994.

Backwards riding Steering a motorcycle facing backwards from the top of a 10 ft ladder, over a continuous period of 1 hr 30 min, Signalman Dewi Jones of the Royal Signals White Helmets covered a distance of 20½ miles at Catterick Airfield, Great Britain on 30 Nov 1988.

Wheelie Distance Yasuyuki Kudō covered 205.7 miles nonstop on the rear wheel of his Honda TLM 220 R 216 cc motorcycle at the Japan Automobile Research Institute, Tsukuba, Japan on 5 May 1991.

The United States record was set by Doug Domokos (USA) on the Alabama International Speedway, Talladega on 27 Jun 1984. He covered 145 miles nonstop on the rear wheel of his Honda XR 500. He stopped only when the gasoline ran out.

Speed The highest speed attained on a rear wheel of a motorcycle is 157.87 mph, by Jacky Vranken (Belgium) on a Suzuki GSXR 1100 at St Truiden Military Airfield, Belgium on 8 Nov 1992.

Wall of death The greatest endurance feat on a "wall of death" was 7 hr 0 min 13 sec, by Martin Blume, Berlin, Germany on 16 Apr 1983. He rode over 12,000 laps on the 33-ft-diameter wall on a Yamaha XS400, averaging 30 mph for the 181½ miles.

Two-wheel sidecar riding Konstantin Matreyev (Russia) rode a distance of 210½ miles on a Ural at Irbit Stadium, Sverdloskaya, Russia on 7–8 Jun 1992.

Most on one machine The record for the most people on a single machine is 46 members of the Illawarra Mini Bike Training Club, New South Wales, Australia. They rode on a 1,000 cc motorcycle and traveled a distance of one mile on 11 Oct 1987.

Ramp jumping The longest distance ever achieved by a motorcycle long-jumping is 251 ft, by Doug Danger on a 1991 Honda CR500 at Loudon, NH on 22 Jun 1991.

AUTOMOBILES

PRODUCTION

The total number of vehicles constructed worldwide in 1992 was a record 47,955,000, of which 34,838,000 were automobiles. The peak year for production of cars only was 1990, when 35,277,986 vehicles were produced.

The world's largest manufacturer of motor vehicles and parts (and the largest manufacturing company) is General Motors Corporation of Detroit, MI. The company has on average 750,000 employees. A peak figure of 948,000 vehicles was produced in 1978. The company's highest annual income was $138.2 billion in 1993.

Largest plant The largest single automobile plant in the world is the Volkswagenwerk at Wolfsburg, Germany, with 60,000 employees and a capacity for producing 4,000 vehicles every week (208,000 per year). The factory buildings cover an area of 371 acres and the whole plant covers 1,878 acres, with 46 miles of rail sidings.

United States The largest automobile plant in the United States is the Nissan Motor Manufacturing Corp.'s Smyrna, TN plant. The plant had a capacity of 450,000 cars and compact pickup trucks at the end of 1993. The plant covers an area of 5.1 million ft^2.

Longest in production Among mass-production models, the Volkswagen "Beetle" dates from 1938. The 21-millionth "Beetle" rolled off the last remaining production line, at Puebla, Mexico, in December 1991.

The Morgan 4/4, built by the Morgan Motor Car Co. of Malvern, Great Britain (founded 1910), celebrated its 58th birthday on 27 Dec 1993. There is still a six- to eight-year waiting list to buy this model.

United States The oldest mass-production model still being made is the Chrysler Imperial, which was in production from 1926–84 and 1990–present. The luxury model Cadillac Fleetwood has been in continuous production since 1936.

Largest cars Of cars produced for private use, the largest was the Bugatti Royale type 41, of which only six were assembled at Molsheim, France by the Italian Ettore Bugatti. First built in 1927, this machine has an eight-cylinder engine of 12.7 liters capacity, and measures over 22 ft in length. The hood is over 7 ft long.

Longest car A 100-ft-long 26-wheeled limo was designed by Jay Ohrberg of Burbank, CA. It has many special features, including a swimming pool, a diving board and a king-sized water bed. It is designed to be driven as one piece, or it can be changed to bend in the middle.

Largest engines The largest engine capacity of a production car is 13.5 liters, for the US Pierce-Arrow 6–66 Raceabout of 1912–18, the US Peerless 6–60 of 1912–14, and the Fageol of 1918.

Most powerful The most powerful current production car is the Bugatti EB110 Super Sports, which develops in excess of 610 bhp.

Heaviest The heaviest car recently in production (up to 25 were made annually) appears to be the Soviet-built Zil–41047 limousine with a 12.72 ft wheelbase. It weighs 7,352 lb (3.3 tons).

A "stretched" Zil (two to three made annually) was used by former USSR President Mikhail Gorbachev until December 1991. It weighed 6.6 tons and was made of three-inch armor-plated steel. The eight-cylinder, 7-liter engine guzzled fuel at a rate of 6 miles to the gallon.

Lightest Louis Borsi of London, Great Britain has built and driven a 21 lb car with a 2.5-cc engine. It is capable of 15 mph.

If you are over 7 feet tall, the smallest street-legal car in the United States (88¾ in long) might not be the car for you. (Jeff Gibson)

Smallest street-legal car The smallest registered street-legal car in the United States has an overall length of 88¾ in and a width of 40½ in. It was built by Arlis Sluder and is now owned by Jeff Gibson.

Most expensive The most expensive car ever built was the US Presidential 1969 Lincoln Continental Executive delivered to the US Secret Service on 14 Oct 1968. It has an overall length of 21 ft 6¼ in with a 13 ft 4 in wheelbase, and with the addition of 2.2 tons of armor plate weighs 6 tons (12,000 lb). The estimated cost of research, development and manufacture was $500,000, but it is rented at $5,000 per year. Even if all four tires were shot out it could travel at 50 mph on inner rubber-edged steel discs.

Used The greatest confirmed price paid is $15 million, including commission, for the 1931 Bugatti Type 41 Royale Sports Coupé by Kellner, sold to the Meitec Corporation of Japan on 12 Apr 1990.

Most inexpensive The cheapest car of all time was the 1922 Red Bug Buckboard, built by the Briggs & Stratton Co. of Milwaukee, WI, listed at $125–$150. It had a 62 in wheelbase and weighed 245 lb. Early models of the King Midget cars were sold in kit form for self-assembly for as little as $100 in 1948.

Car collection The unrivaled collector of Rolls-Royces was Bhagwan Shree Rajneesh (Osho; ne Chandra Mohan Jain [1931–90]), the Indian mystic of Rajneeshpuram, OR. His disciples bestowed 93 of these upon him before his deportation from the United States in November 1985.

Parade of Rolls-Royces A parade of 147 Rolls-Royces, organized by the Rolls-Royce Owners' Club of Australia, drove around Lake Wendouree, Ballarat, Australia on 19 Sep 1992.

Car registrations License plate No. 9 was sold at a Hong Kong government auction for HK$13 million (approximately $1.7 million) in April 1994 to Albert Yeung Sau-Shing. "Nine" sounds like the word "dog" in Chinese, and the purchase was considered lucky because 1994 was the Year of the Dog.

Car wrecking In a career lasting 25 years, from 1968 to 1993, stuntman Dick Sheppard of Gloucester, Great Britain wrecked 2,003 cars.

Tire supporting The greatest number of tires supported in a free-standing lift is 96, by Gary Windebank of Romsey, Great Britain in February 1984. The total weight was 1,440 lb. The tires used were Michelin XZX 155 × 13.

SPEED

Land speed The *official* one-mile land-speed record is 633.468 mph, set by Richard Noble (b. 1946) on 4 Oct 1983 over the Black Rock Desert, NV in his 17,000 lb thrust Rolls-Royce Avon 302 jet-powered *Thrust 2*, designed by John Ackroyd.

Rocket-engined The fastest speed attained by any wheeled land vehicle is 631.367 mph by *The Blue Flame*, a rocket-powered four-wheeled vehicle driven by Gary Gabelich (USA; b. 23 Aug 1940) on the Bonneville Salt

***The Blue Flame*, the fastest-ever rocket-powered vehicle. (Quadrant Picture Library)**

Flats, UT on 23 Oct 1970. Gabelich momentarily exceeded 650 mph. The car was powered by a liquid natural gas/hydrogen peroxide rocket engine developing a thrust of up to a maximum 22,000 lb.

The fastest reputed land speed figure in one direction is 739.666 mph, or Mach 1.0106, by Stan Barrett (USA) in the *Budweiser Rocket*, a rocket-engined three-wheeled car, at Edwards Air Force Base, CA on 17 Dec 1979. *This published speed of Mach 1.0106 is* not *officially sanctioned by the USAF, as the Digital Instrument Radar was not calibrated or certified. The radar information was not generated by the vehicle directly but by an operator aiming a dish by means of a TV screen.*

Piston-engined The fastest speed measured for a wheel-driven car is 432.692 mph by Al Teague in *Speed-O-Motive/Spirit of '76* at Bonneville Salt Flats, UT on 21 Aug 1991 over the final 132 ft of a mile run (av. 425.230 mph for the whole mile).

Diesel-engined The prototype 3-liter Mercedes C 111/3 attained 203.3 mph in tests on the Nardo Circuit, southern Italy on 5–15 Oct 1978, and in April 1978 averaged 195.4 mph for 12 hours, thus covering a world record 2,344.7 miles.

Steam car On 19 Aug 1985 Robert E. Barber broke the 79-year-old record for a steam car driving No. 744, *Steamin' Demon*, built by the Barber-Nichols Engineering Co, which reached 145.607 mph at Bonneville Salt Flats, UT.

Road cars Various revved up track cars have been licensed for road use but are not normal production models.

The fastest speed ever attained by a standard production car is 217.1

mph for a Jaguar XJ220, driven by Martin Brundle at the Nardo Circuit, Italy on 21 Jun 1992.

The highest road-tested acceleration reported for a standard production car is 0–60 mph in 3.275 sec for a Ford RS200 Evolution, driven by Graham Hathaway at the Boreham Proving Ground, Essex, Great Britain on 28 Apr 1993.

Fastest street-legal car The highest road-tested acceleration is 0–60 mph in 3.89 sec for a Jankel *Tempest* driven by Mark Hargreaves at Millbrook Proving Ground, Bedfordshire, Great Britain on 13 Apr 1992.

DRIVING

Six continents The fastest drive taking in the six continents, with a total distance driven of more than an equator's length (24,901 miles), is one of 39 days 7 hr 55 min by Navin Kapila, Man Badahur, and Vijay Raman, driving a Contessa Classic. They left New Delhi on 22 Nov 1991, and returned to the same place on 31 Dec 1991.

Amphibious circumnavigation The only circumnavigation by an amphibious vehicle was by Ben Carlin (Australia; d. 7 Mar 1981) in the amphibious jeep *Half-Safe*. He completed the last leg of the Atlantic crossing (the English Channel) on 24 Aug 1951. He arrived back in Montreal, Canada on 8 May 1958, having completed a circumnavigation of 39,000 miles over land and 9,600 miles by sea and river. He was accompanied on the transatlantic stage by his ex-wife Elinore (USA) and on the long transpacific stage (Tokyo, Japan to Anchorage, AK) by Broye Lafayette De-Mente (USA; b. 1928).

One-year duration record The greatest distance covered in one year is 354,257 miles, by two Opel Rekord 2-liter passenger sedans, both of which covered this distance between 18 May 1988 and the same date in 1989 without any major mechanical breakdowns. The vehicles were manufactured by the Delta Motor Corporation, Port Elizabeth, South Africa, and were driven on tar and gravel roads in the Northern Cape by a team of company drivers from Delta.

Trans-Americas Garry Sowerby (Canada), with Tim Cahill (USA) as co-driver and navigator, drove a 1988 GMC Sierra K3500 four-wheel-drive pickup truck powered by a 6.2-liter V8 Detroit diesel engine from Ushuaia, Tierra del Fuego, Argentina to Prudhoe Bay, AK, a distance of 14,739 miles, in a total elapsed time of 23 days 22 hr 43 min from 29 Sep to 22 Oct 1987. The vehicle and team were surface-freighted from Cartagena, Colombia to Balboa, Panama so as to bypass the Darién Gap.

Trans-America The three-man team of Jeremiah L. Burr (driver/leader), Kurt E. Detlefsen (driver) and Thaddeus E. Burr (navigator) of Connecticut completed the first documented traverse of all the contiguous 48 states of the United States from 13 May to 19 May 1991, in a total elapsed time of 5 days, 7 hours and 15 minutes and a total distance of 7,217.8 miles. They drove a 1990 Chevrolet Astro Van and stopped only for fuel. Dehydrated foods and nine gallons of water made the team self-sufficient.

Gasoline consumption A team of students from Lycée St Joseph La Joliv-

The successful team of French students with their "car," which ran for 7,591 miles on one gallon of gas. (Gamma/A. Le Bot)

erie, Nantes, France achieved 7,591 mpg in the Shell Mileage Marathon at Silverstone, Great Britain on 17 Jul 1992.

Longest fuel range The greatest distance driven without refueling on a single fuel fill in a standard vehicle (38.2 gal carried in factory-optional twin fuel tanks) is 1,691.6 miles, by a 1991 Toyota LandCruiser diesel station wagon. Driven by Ewan Kennedy with Ian Lee (observer) from Nyngan, New South Wales, Australia to Winton, Queensland and back between 18–21 May 1992, the car averaged 37.3 mph, giving 44.2 mpg.

The greatest distance traveled by an unmodified production car on the contents of a standard fuel tank is 1,338.1 miles, giving 75.94 mpg, between 26–28 Jul 1992. Stuart Bladon and Robert Procter drove the length of Great Britain, from John o'Groats to Land's End, and returned to Scotland driving an Audi 100 TD1 diesel car. The fuel of the 17.62-gal fuel tank ran out after 35 hr 18 min.

Driving in reverse Charles Creighton (1908–70) and James Hargis of Maplewood, MO drove their Model A Ford 1929 roadster in reverse from New York 3,340 miles to Los Angeles, CA, from 26 Jul–13 Aug 1930 without once stopping the engine. They arrived back in New York in reverse on 5 September, completing 7,180 miles in 42 days.

Brian "Cub" Keene and James "Wilbur" Wright drove their Chevrolet Blazer 9,031 miles in reverse in 37 days (1 Aug–6 Sep 1984) through 15 American states and Canada. Though the name of the car, "Stuck in Reverse," was prominently displayed, law-enforcement officers in Oklahoma refused to believe it and insisted they drive in reverse reverse—i.e., forward—out of the state.

The highest average speed attained in any nonstop reverse drive exceeding 500 miles was achieved by Gerald Hoagland, who drove a 1969 Chevrolet Impala 501 miles in 17 hr 38 min at Chemung Speed Drome, NY on 9–10 Jul 1976, to average 28.41 mph.

Battery-powered car David Turner and Tim Pickhard of Turners of Boscastle Ltd., Cornwall, Great Britain, traveled 875 miles from Land's End to John o' Groats in a Freight Rover Leyland Sherpa, powered by a Lucas electric motor, from 21–25 Dec 1985.

Two-side-wheel driving Car Bengt Norberg (b. 23 Oct 1951) of Äppelbo, Sweden drove a Mitsubishi Colt GTi-16V on two side wheels nonstop for a distance of 192.873 miles in a time of 7 hr 15 min 50 sec. He also achieved a distance of 27.842 miles in 1 hr at Rattvik Horse Track, Sweden on 24 May 1989.

Sven-Erik Söderman (Sweden; b. 26 Sep 1960) achieved a speed of 102.14 mph over a 100 m (328.1 ft) flying start on the two wheels of an Opel Kadett at Mora Siljan airport, Mora, Sweden on 2 Aug 1990. Söderman achieved a record speed for the flying kilometer at 152.96 km (95.04 mph) at the same venue on 24 Aug 1990.

Truck Sven-Erik Söderman drove a Daf 2800 7.5-ton truck on two wheels for a distance of 6.73 miles at Mora Siljan airport, Mora, Sweden on 19 May 1991.

Bus Bobby Ore (Great Britain; b. Jan 1949) drove a double-decker bus a distance of 810 ft on two wheels at North Weald Airfield, Great Britain on 21 May 1988.

MILEAGE!

The highest recorded mileage for a car was 1,512,755 miles up to 25 Jan 1994 for a 1963 Volkswagen "Beetle" owned by Albert Klein of Pasadena, CA. The highest record mileage for a car with the original gasoline motor without an overhaul is 604,760 miles to 31 May 1994 for a 1979 Cadillac Sedan DeVille owned by Don Champion of Louisville, KY.

Wheelie Steve Murty, driving a Pirelli High Performer, established the record for the longest wheelie in a truck, covering 1,794.9 ft at the National Power Sports Festival in Blackpool, Great Britain on 28 Jun 1991.

Most durable driver Goodyear Tire and Rubber Co. test driver Weldon C. Kocich drove 3,141,946 miles from 5 Feb 1953 to 28 Feb 1986, thus averaging 95,210 miles per year.

Oldest drivers Roy M. Rawlins (b. 10 Jul 1870) of Stockton, CA was given a warning for driving at 95 mph in a 55 mph zone in June 1974. On 25 Aug 1974 he was awarded a California State license valid until 1978, but he died on 9 Jul 1975, one day short of his 105th birthday.

Mrs Maude Tull of Inglewood, CA, who took to driving at the age of 91 after her husband died, was issued a renewal on 5 Feb 1976 when she was 104.

Driving tests The world's easiest tests are those in Egypt, in which the ability to drive 19.64 ft forward and the same in reverse has been deemed sufficient. In 1979 it was reported that an accurate reversing test had been added.

Mrs Fannie Turner (b. 1903) of Little Rock, AR passed the *written* test for drivers on her 104th attempt in October 1978.

Worst driver It was reported that a 75-year-old male driver received 10 traffic tickets, drove on the wrong side of the road four times, committed four hit-and-run offenses and caused six accidents, all within 20 minutes, in McKinney, TX on 15 Oct 1966.

Most parking tickets Mrs Silvia Matos of New York City has set what must be a world record in unpaid parking tickets, totaling $150,000. She collected the 2,800 tickets between 1985 and 1988, but authorities have been unable to collect any money; she registered her car under 19 addresses and 36 license plates and cannot be found.

SPECIALIZED VEHICLES

GENERAL

Largest The most massive automotive land vehicle is "Big Muskie," the 12,004 ton mechanical shovel built by Bucyrus Erie for the Musk mine. It is 487 ft long, 151 ft wide and 222 ft high, with a grab capacity of 364 tons.

Longest The Arctic Snow Train owned by Steve McPeak (USA) has 54 wheels and is 572 ft long. It was built by R.G. Le Tourneau Inc. of Longview, TX for the US Army. Its gross train weight is 441 tons, with a top speed of 20 mph, and it was driven by a crew of six when used as an "overland train" for the military. It generates 4,680 shp and has a fuel capacity of 7,832 gal. McPeak undertook all repairs, including every punctured wheel, single-handedly in often sub-zero temperatures in Alaska.

Heaviest load On 14–15 Jul 1984 John Brown Engineers & Contractors BV moved the Conoco Kotter Field production deck with a roll-out weight of 325 tons for the Continental Netherlands Oil Co. of Leidsenhage, Netherlands.

BUSES

Longest The longest are the articulated DAF Super CityTrain buses of Zaire, with 110 passenger seats and room for 140 "strap-hangers" in the first trailer, and 60 seated and 40 "strap-hangers" in the second, for a total of 350. The buses are 105.64 ft long and weigh 32 tons empty.

Rigid The longest rigid single bus is 49 ft long and carries 69 passengers. It was built by Van Hool of Belgium.

Largest fleet The 10,364 single-deck buses in Sao Paulo, Brazil make up the world's largest bus fleet.

Longest route The longest regularly scheduled bus route is 6,003 miles long. Operated by Expreso Internacional Ormeño S.A., the regular scheduled service between Caracas, Venezuela and Buenos Aires, Argentina takes 214 hr, with a 12-hour stopover in Santiago, Chile and a 24-hour stopover in Lima, Peru.

United States The longest scheduled bus route currently in use in the United States is by Greyhound from Chicago to San Francisco. It runs once per day, is 2,294 miles long, and takes 51 hours 49 minutes to complete, employing seven drivers, with no change of bus.

Greatest passenger volume The city with the greatest passenger volume in the United States as of December 1992 was New York City, with 636.7 million for buses and 1.32 billion for trains and unlinked passenger trips. In 1992 the city with the highest aggregate for passenger miles traveled was also New York City, where riders logged approximately 1.9 billion miles.

CAMPERS

Largest The largest camper is a two-wheeled, five-story vehicle built in 1990 by H.E Sheik Hamad Bin Hamdan Al Nahyan of Abu Dhabi, United Arab Emirates. It is 66 ft long, 39 ft wide and stands 39 ft high. Weighing 120 tons, it comprises eight bedrooms, eight bathrooms, four garages and water storage for 6,340 gal.

Longest journey The continuous motor camper journey of 143,716 miles by Harry B. Coleman and Peggy Larson in a Volkswagen Camper from 20 Aug 1976 to 20 Apr 1978 took them through 113 countries.

Fastest The world speed record for a camper is 126.76 mph, by a Roadster camper towed by a 1990 Ford EA Falcon, driven by Charlie Kovacs, at Mangalore Airfield, Seymour, Victoria, Australia on 18 Apr 1991.

CRAWLERS

Largest The most massive crawler ever constructed is the Marion eight-caterpillar crawler used for conveying Saturn V rockets to their launch pads at Cape Canaveral, FL. It measures 131 ft 4 in × 114 ft, and the two built cost $12.3 million. The loaded train weight is 9,000 tons. The windshield wiper blades are 42 in long and are the world's largest.

FIRE ENGINES

Greatest pumping capacity The fire appliance with the greatest pumping capacity is the 860 hp eight-wheel Oshkosh firetruck, which weighs 66 tons and is used for aircraft and runway fires. The truck can discharge 50,200 gal of foam through two turrets in just 150 sec.

GO-KART RACING

"When I was finished, they had to pick me up out of the car and peel my hands off the steering wheel. My hands hurt, my back hurt, my legs were numb. I had big old bruises on my ribs from going around turns and bumping against the seat." Zack Dawson was 10 years old when he set his record.

He had been ready to stop when he passed the previous record, but his father urged him on. "Dad said for every lap he'd give me a dollar," Zack grins. "I went 50 more laps."

Zack had only been racing go-karts for a year when he and his father spotted the record for mileage. "Dad asked me if I wanted to do it, and I said yes. We started getting information and looking for sponsors, but we didn't get any. Dad sold his truck so we could do it."

Not only would the trip take 15 tanks of gas, but Zack's go-kart needed work. "My old go-kart was under a go-kart cover, and my mom and dad told me to go look at the new repairs they'd done. There was a new go-kart under there!"

Zack hasn't spent a lot of time in his go-kart since his record-breaking drive. "Somebody will try and break it, but I don't know if I'd do it again to stay on top. You look in *The Guinness Book* and see all these people . . . and there I am. Wow! It's really cool. And it was, like, I did it by myself."

Fastest The fastest on record is the Jaguar XJ12 "Chubb Firefighter," which on 2 Nov 1982 attained a speed of 130.57 mph in tests when servicing the *Thrust 2* land-speed record trials.

Fire pumping The greatest gallonage stirrup-pumped by a team of eight in an 80 hr charity pump is 37,898 gal, by firefighters at the Knaresborough Fire Station, Great Britain from 25–28 Jun 1992.

Fire pump handling The longest unaided tow of a fire appliance in excess of 1,120 lb in 24 hr on a closed circuit is 223 miles, by a 32-man team of the Dublin Fire Brigade with a 1,144-lb fire pump on 20–21 Jun 1987.

GO-KARTS

Highest mileage The highest mileage recorded in 24 hours on an outdoor circuit by a four-man team is 1,018 miles, on a one-mile track at the Erbsville Kartway, Waterloo, Ontario, Canada on 4–5 Sep 1983. The 5-hp 140 cc Honda engined kart was driven by Owen Nimmo, Gary Ruddock, Jim Timmins and Danny Upshaw.

The highest mileage in 24 hours on an indoor track by a four-man team driving 160 cc karts is 883.9 miles, at the Welsh Karting Centre, Cardiff, Great Britain on 26 Nov 1993, bye Ian O'Sullivan, Paul Marram, Richard Jenkins and Michael Watts.

Six hours The record distance achieved in six hours in the 100 cc non-gearbox category is 249.117 miles, by Zack Dawson of Ridgecrest, CA at the Mesa Marin Raceway, Bakersfield, CA on 9 Apr 1993. See On the Record feature (p. 277).

MODEL CARS

Duration A Scalextric Jaguar XJ8 ran nonstop for 866 hr 44 min 54 sec and covered a distance of 1,771.2 miles from 2 May to 7 Jun 1989. The event was organized by the Rev. Bryan G. Apps and church members of Southbourne, Great Britain.

24-hour slot car racing On 5–6 Jul 1986 the North London Society of Model Engineers team at the ARRA club in Southport, Great Britain achieved a distance record for a 1:32 scale car of 305.949 miles in 24 hours, 11,815 laps of the track, driving a Rondeau M482C Group C Sports car, built by Ian Fisher. This was under the rules of the BSCRA (British Slot Car Racing Association).

The longest slot car track measures 958 ft and was built at Mallory Park Circuit, Great Britain on 22 Nov 1991 using pieces collected from enthusiasts. One car successfully completed a full lap.

ROCKET-POWERED SLEDS

Fastest The fastest speed recorded on ice is 247.93 mph by *Oxygen*, driven by Sammy Miller (b. 15 Apr 1945) on Lake George, NY on 15 Feb 1981.

The ultimate in shovels is this giant snow plow operating at New York's Kennedy Airport. In one pass it can clear 1,095 ft^3 of snow. (V. Dejana)

The team of John Outzen and the Boucher brothers, Andre, Carl and Dennis, with the snowmobiles that transported them across a continent. (John Outzen)

SNOW PLOWS

Snow-plow blade A blade measuring 50.25 ft long and 4 ft high, with a clearing capacity of 1,095 ft^3 in one pass, was made by Aero Snow Removal Corporation of New York, NY in 1992 for operation at JFK International Airport.

SNOWMOBILES

Longest distance John W. Outzen of Derry, NH (expedition organizer and leader), Andre, Carl and Dennis Boucher, traveled 10,252.3 miles across North America, from Anchorage, AK to Dartmouth, Nova Scotia, Canada, in 62 days (56 riding days) from 2 Jan to 3 Mar 1992 on four Arctic Cat Panther Deluxe Snowmobiles.

Tony Lenzini of Duluth, MN, drove his 1986 Arctic Cat Cougar snowmobile a total of 7,211 miles in 60 riding days between 28 Dec 1985 and 20 Mar 1986.

SOLAR-POWERED

Fastest speed The fastest speed attained by a solely solar-powered land vehicle is 48.71 mph, by Molly Brennan driving the General Motors *Sunraycer* at Mesa, AZ on 24 Jun 1988. The fastest speed of 83.88 mph using solar/battery power was achieved by Star Micronics' solar car *Solar Star*, driven by Manfred Hermann on 5 Jan 1991 at Richmond RAAF Base, Richmond, New South Wales, Australia.

TANKS

Heaviest The heaviest tank ever constructed was the German Panzer Kampfwagen Maus II, which weighed over 210 tons. By 1945 it had reached only the experimental stage and was not developed further.

The heaviest operational tank used by any army was the 83-ton 13-man French Char de Rupture 2C bis of 1922. It carried a 155-mm howitzer and had two 250 hp engines giving a maximum speed of 8 mph. The world's most heavily armed tank since 1972 has been the Soviet T-72, with a 4⁷/₈ in high-velocity gun.

The heaviest tank in the United States Army is the M1A1 Abrams, which weighs 67 tons when combat loaded, is 32 ft 3 in long, and can reach a maximum speed of 41.5 mph.

Fastest The fastest armored reconnaissance vehicle is the British Scorpion, which can reach 50 mph with a 75 percent payload.

The American experimental tank M1936, built by J. Walter Christie, was clocked at 64.3 mph during official trials in Great Britain in 1938.

Most prolific The greatest production of any tank was that of the Soviet T-54/55 series, of which more than 50,000 were built between 1954 and 1980 in the USSR alone, with further production in the one-time Warsaw Pact countries and China.

TAXIS

Largest fleet The largest taxi fleet is that in Mexico City, with 60,000 "normal" taxis, *pesaros* (communal fixed-route taxis) and *settas* (airport taxis).

United States The city with the largest taxi fleet in the United States is New York City, which on 1 Jan 1993 had 11,787 registered yellow medallion cabs and 40,000 licensed drivers serving an estimated 226 million passengers yearly. In addition, there are approximately 30,000 For Hire Vehicle (FHV) cabs serving out of 600 bases stationed throughout the city's five boroughs.

Taxi drivers Carmen Fasanella was continuously licensed as a taxicab owner and driver in the Borough of Princeton, NJ for 68 years 243 days, from 1 Feb 1921 to 2 Nov 1989.

Longest taxicab ride The longest taxicab ride on record is one of 14,414 miles at a cost of 70,000 FIM (approximately $16,000). Mika Lehtonen and Juhani Saramies left Nokia, Finland on 2 May 1991, traveling through Scandinavia down to Spain, and arrived back in Nokia on 17 May 1991.

TRACTORS

Largest The world's largest tractor is a $459,000 US Department of Agriculture Wide Tractive Frame Vehicle completed by Ag West of Sacramento, CA in June 1982. It measures 33 ft between its wheels, which are designed to run on permanent paths, and weighs 24.5 tons.

Tractor-pulling The sport of tractor-pulling was put on a national US championship basis in 1967 at Bowling Green, OH, where the winner was "The Purple Monster" built and driven by Roger E. Varns. Today there are 12 classes, ranging up to "12,200 lb unlimited."

Longest journey The longest journey on record by tractor is 14,500 miles. The Young Farmers Group of Devon, Great Britain left their native country on 18 Oct 1990 in one tractor and supporting trailer, and drove overland to Zimbabwe, arriving on 4 Mar 1991.

TROLLEYS

Oldest The oldest trolleys in continuous service in the world are motor cars 1 and 2 of the Manx Electric Railway, dating from 1893. These run regularly on the 17¾-mile railroad between Douglas and Ramsey, Isle of Man, Great Britain.

Most extensive system By early 1991, St Petersburg, Russia had the most extensive tramway system, with 2,402 cars on 64 routes and 429.13 miles of track.

Longest journey The longest trolley journey now possible is from Krefeld St Tönis to Witten Annen Nord, Germany. With luck at the eight interconnections, the 65.5-mile trip can be completed in 5½ hours.

TRUCKS

Largest The world's largest is the Terex Titan 33–19 manufactured by General Motors Corporation and now in operation at Westar Mine, British Columbia, Canada. It has a loaded weight of 604.7 tons and a capacity of 350 tons. When tipped, its height is 56 ft. The 16-cylinder engine delivers 3,300 hp. The fuel tank holds 1,300 gal.

Most powerful Les Shockley of Galena, KS drove his Jet Truck *Shock-Wave*, powered by three Pratt & Whitney jet engines developing 36,000 hp, to a record speed of 256 mph in 6.36 sec over a quarter-mile from a standing start on 4 Jun 1989 at Autodrome de Monterrey, Mexico. He set a further record for the standing mile at 376 mph at Paine Field, Everett, WA on 18 Aug 1991.

WRECKERS

Most powerful The world's most powerful wrecker is the Twin City Garage and Body Shop's 22.7-ton, 36-ft-long International M6-23 "Hulk" 1969 stationed at Scott City, MO. It can lift in excess of 325 tons on its short boom.

Les Shockley's *ShockWave*, the world's most powerful truck. (Les Shockley)

SERVICES

FILLING STATIONS

Largest The largest concentration of pumps is 204—96 of them Tokheim Unistar (electronic) and 108 Tokheim Explorer (mechanical)—in Jeddah, Saudi Arabia.

Highest The highest filling station in the world is at Leh, Ladakh, India, at 12,001 ft, operated by the Indian Oil Corporation.

GARAGES

Largest The largest private garage is one of two stories built outside Bombay, India for the private collection of 176 cars owned by Pranlal Bhogilal (b. 1939).

The KMB Overhaul Center, operated by the Kowloon Motor Bus Co. (1933) Ltd, Hong Kong, is the world's largest multistory service center. Built expressly for double-decker buses, it has four floors occupying more than 11.6 acres.

PARKING LOTS

Largest The world's largest is the one in the West Edmonton Mall, Edmonton, Alberta, Canada. It holds 20,000 vehicles, with overflow facilities on an adjoining lot for 10,000 more cars.

TIRES

Largest The largest ever manufactured are by Goodyear Tire & Rubber Co. for giant dump trucks. They measure 12 ft in diameter, weigh 12,500 lb and cost $74,000.

Longest skid marks The skid marks made by the jet-powered *Spirit of America*, driven by Norman Craig Breedlove, after the car went out of control at Bonneville Salt Flats, UT, on 15 Oct 1964, were nearly six miles long.

TOWS

Longest The longest on record was one of 4,995 miles from Ascot to Widmerpool, Great Britain conducted by the Automobile Association from 4–12 May 1993. They used a Land Rover to tow a replica Model T Ford van.

ROADS

Road mileages The country with the greatest length of road is the United States (all 50 states), with 3,880,151 miles of graded road. The state with the most miles of road is Texas (305,951), while Hawaii has the least, with 4,099 miles.

Longest driveable road The Pan-American Highway, running from northwest Alaska to Santiago, Chile, then to Buenos Aires, Argentina, and terminating in Brasilia, Brazil, is over 15,000 miles long. There is, however, a small incomplete section in Panama and Colombia known as the Darién Gap.

United States The longest highway solely in the United States is US-20, which runs 3,370 miles from Boston, MA to Newport, OR. The longest highway in the interstate system is I-90, 3,107 miles from Boston, MA to Seattle, WA.

Worst exit to miss The longest distance between controlled access exits in the United States is 51.1 miles from Florida Turnpike exit 193 (Yeehaw Junction, FL) to exit 244 (Kissimee, FL). The longest distance on any interstate highway is 37.7 miles from I-80 exit 41 (Knolls, UT) to exit 4 (Bonneville Speedway, UT).

Highest roads The highest trail in the world is an eight-mile stretch of the Gangdise between Khaleb and Xinji-fu, Tibet, which in two places exceeds 20,000 ft.

The highest road in the world is in Kyardungla Pass, at an altitude of 18,650 ft. This is one of three passes of the Leh-Manali road completed in 1976 by the Border Roads Organization, New Delhi, India; motor vehicles were able to use it from 1988 on.

JAM!

The longest ever reported was that of 16 Feb 1980, which stretched northwards from Lyons 109.3 miles towards Paris, France.

A record traffic jam was reported for 1.5 million cars crawling bumper-to-bumper over the East–West German border on 12 Apr 1990.

Lowest roads The lowest road is along the Israeli shores of the Dead Sea at 1,290 ft below sea level.

The world's lowest named "pass" is Rock Reef Pass, Everglades National Park, FL, which is 3 ft above sea level.

Widest roads The widest road in the world is the Monumental Axis, running for 1½ miles from the Municipal Plaza to the Plaza of the Three Powers in Brasilia, the capital of Brazil. The six-lane boulevard, opened in April 1960, is 820.2 ft wide.

Highest traffic volume The most heavily traveled stretch of road is Interstate 405 (San Diego Freeway), in Orange County, CA, which has a rush-hour volume of 25,500. This volume occurs on a 0.9 mile stretch between Garden Grove Freeway and Seal Beach Boulevard.

Highest traffic density The territory with the highest traffic density in the world is Hong Kong. In 1992 there were 418 vehicles per mile of serviceable road, giving a density of 4.53 yd per vehicle.

Streets Longest The longest designated street in the world is Yonge Street, running north and west from Toronto, Ontario, Canada. The first stretch, completed on 16 Feb 1796, ran 34 miles. Its official length, now extended to Rainy River on the Ontario–Minnesota border, is 1,178.3 miles.

Narrowest The world's narrowest street is in the village of Ripatransone in the Marche region of Italy. It is called *Vicolo della Virilita* ("Virility Alley") and is 16.9 in wide.

Shortest The title for "The Shortest Street in the World" is claimed by the town of Bacup, Great Britain, where Elgin Street, situated by the old market ground, measures just 17 ft.

Founding editor Norris McWhirter verifies Baldwin Street's claim to be the world's steepest street. Located in Dunedin, New Zealand, it has a maximum gradient of 1 in 1.266. (Tessa McWhirter)

Steepest The steepest street in the world is Baldwin Street, Dunedin, New Zealand, which has a maximum gradient of 1 in 1.266.

The crookedest and steepest street in the United States is Lombard Street, San Francisco, CA. It has eight 90-degree turns of 20-ft radius.

RAILROADING

TRAINS

Fastest The fastest speed attained by a railed vehicle is 6,121 mph, or Mach 8, by an unmanned rocket sled over the 9½-mile-long rail track at White Sands Missile Range, NM on 5 Oct 1982.

The fastest speed recorded on any national rail system is 320.2 mph by the French SNCF high-speed train TGV (*Train à Grande Vitesse*) Atlantique between Courtalain and Tours on 18 May 1990. The TGV Sud-Est was brought into service on 27 Sep 1981. By September 1983 it had reduced its scheduled time for the Paris–Lyons run in France of 264 miles to exactly 2 hours, thus averaging 132 mph.

United States The fastest train in the United States is the Amtrak X2000, whch has a maximum speed of 156 mph. The train completed its demonstration run between Washington, D.C. and New York on 1 Feb 1993. The Swedish-built passenger train will travel the New York–Washington corridor and New Haven-to-Boston route in 1997.

Steam locomotive The highest speed ever ratified for a steam locomotive was 125 mph over 1,320 ft, by the LNER 4–6–2 No. 4468 *Mallard* (later numbered 60022), which hauled seven coaches weighing 267.9 tons down Stoke Bank, near Essendine, Great Britain on 3 Jul 1938. Driver Joseph

The TGV zooms across the French countryside at 320.2 mph. (Sipa Press/Chamussy)

Duddington was at the controls with Fireman Thomas Bray. The engine suffered some damage to the middle big-end bearing.

Largest steam locomotive The largest operating steam locomotive is the Union Pacific RR *Challenger* type 4–6–6–4 No. 3985, built by the American Locomotive Co. in 1943. In working order, with tender, it weighs 543.2 tons. It is used on special trips for train buffs in the United States.

Most powerful The world's most powerful steam locomotive, measured by tractive effort, was No. 700, a triple-articulated or triplex six-cylinder 2–8–8–8–4 engine built by the Baldwin Locomotive Works in 1916 for the Virginian Railway. It had a tractive force of 166,300 lb when working compound and 199,560 lb when working simple.

Greatest load The world's strongest rail carrier, with a capacity of 838 tons, is the 36-axle "Schnabel," 301 ft 10 in long, built for a US railroad by Krupp, Germany in March 1981.

The heaviest load ever moved on rails is the 11,971 ton Church of the Virgin Mary (built in 1548 in the village of Most, Czech Republic), in October–November 1975, moved because it was in the way of coal operations. It was moved 2,400 ft at 0.0013 mph over four weeks, at a cost of $17 million.

Freight trains The world's longest and heaviest freight train on record, with the largest number of cars ever recorded, made a run on the 3-ft-6-in-gauge Sishen–Saldanha railroad in South Africa on 26–27 Aug 1989. The train consisted of 660 cars each loaded to 105 tons gross, a tank car and a caboose, moved by nine 50 kV electric and seven diesel-electric locomotives distributed along the train. The train was 4½ miles long and weighed 77,720 tons excluding locomotives. It traveled a distance of 535 miles in 22 hr 40 min.

United States The longest and heaviest freight train on record was about 4 miles in length. It comprised 500 coal motor cars with three 3,600 hp diesels pulling and three more in the middle, on the Iaeger, WV–to–Portsmouth, OH stretch of 157 miles on the Norfolk and Western Railway on 15 Nov 1967. The total weight was nearly 47,040 tons.

Passenger train The longest passenger train was 1,895 yds long, consisted of 70 coaches, and had a total weight of over 2,800 tons. The National Belgium Railway Company's train was powered by one electric locomotive and took 1 hr 11 min 5 sec to complete the 38.5-mile journey from Ghent to Ostend on 27 Apr 1991.

TRACKS

Longest The world's longest run is one of 5,864½ miles on the Trans-Siberian line from Moscow to Nakhodka, Russia, on the Sea of Japan. There are 97 stops on the journey, which is scheduled to take 8 days 4 hr 25 min.

Longest straight The Commonwealth Railways Trans-Australian line over the Nullarbor Plain, from Mile 496 between Nurina and Loongana, Western Australia to Mile 793 between Ooldea and Watson, South Australia, is 297 miles dead straight, although not level.

United States The longest straight track in the United States is 78.86 miles on CSX Railroad, between Wilmington and Hamlet, NC.

Widest and narrowest gauge The widest in standard use is 5 ft 6 in. This width is used in Spain, Portugal, India, Pakistan, Bangladesh, Sri Lanka, Argentina and Chile.

The narrowest gauge on which public services are operated is 10¼ in on the Wells Harbor (0.7 mile) and the Wells–Walsingham Railways (4 miles) in Norfolk, Great Britain.

Highest line At 15,806 ft above sea level, the standard gauge (4 ft 8½ in) track on the Morococha branch of the Peruvian State Railways at La Cima is the highest in the world.

Lowest line The world's lowest line is in the Seikan Tunnel, which crosses the Tsugaro Strait between Honshu and Hokkaido, Japan. It reaches a depth of 786 ft below sea level. The tunnel opened on 13 Mar 1988 and is 33½ miles long.

Steepest railway The world's steepest railway is the Katoomba Scenic Railway in the Blue Mountains of New South Wales, Australia. It is 1,020 ft long with a gradient of 1 in 0.82. A 220 hp electric winding machine hauls the car by twin steel cables of 22 mm diameter. The ride takes about 1 min 40 sec and carries about 420,000 passengers a year.

Greatest length of railroad As of 1992, the country with the greatest length of railroad was the United States, with 169,664 miles operated for all classes of track. There were 126,237 miles of class I track (freight only) and 43,427 miles of non-class I track operated. There was a total of 190,591 miles of track owned, which included sidings and yards.

Spike driving In the World Championship Professional Spike Driving Competition, held at the Golden Spike National Historic Site in Utah, Dale C. Jones, 49, of Lehi, UT, drove six 7-in railroad spikes in a time of 26.4 sec on 11 Aug 1984. He incurred no penalty points under the official rules.

Steepest gradient The world's steepest gradient worked by adhesion is 1:11, between Chedde and Servoz on the meter-gauge SNCF Chamonix line, France.

Busiest system The railroad carrying the largest number of passengers is the East Japan Railway Co. In 1992 it carried 16,306,000 passengers daily.

TRAIN TRAVEL

Most countries in 24 hours The greatest number of countries traveled through entirely by train in 24 hours is 11, by Alison Bailey, Ian Bailey, John English and David Kellie on 1–2 May 1993. Their journey started in Hungary and continued through Slovakia, the Czech Republic, Austria, Germany, back into Austria, Liechtenstein, Switzerland, France, Luxembourg, Belgium and the Netherlands, where they arrived 22 hr 10 min after setting off.

Most miles traveled John E. Ballenger of Dunedin, FL logged 76,485 miles of unduplicated rail routes in North and South America.

United States James J. Brady of Wilmington, OH traveled through 442 out of 498 stations over 21,485 unduplicated miles of track from 11 Feb to 11 Mar 1984.

Most miles in one week Andrew Kingsmell and Sean Andrews of Bromley, Great Britain, together with Graham Bardouleau of Crawley, Great Britain, traveled 13,105 miles on the French National Railway System in 6 days 22 hr 38 min from 28 Nov–5 Dec 1992.

Longest issued train ticket A train ticket 111 ft 10½ in long was issued to Ronald, Norma and Jonathan Carter for journeys traveled on British Rail between 15–23 Feb 1992.

Handpumped railcars A speed of 20.58 mph for a 984-ft course was achieved by a five-man team (one pusher, four pumpers) at Rolvenden, Great Britain on 21 Aug 1989, recording a time of 32.61 sec.

STATIONS

Largest The world's largest is Grand Central Terminal, Park Avenue and 42nd Street, New York City, built from 1903–13. It covers 48 acres on two levels with 41 tracks on the upper level and 26 on the lower. On average there are more than 550 trains and 200,000 commuters daily, in addition to 500,000 who pass through the terminal.

Busiest The busiest railroad junction in the world is Clapham Junction, London, Great Britain, in the Southern Region of British Rail, with an average of 2,200 trains passing through each 24 hours.

Highest Condor station in Bolivia at 15,705 ft on the meter-gauge Rio Mulato-to-Potosi line is the highest in the world.

Waiting rooms The world's largest waiting rooms are the four in Beijing Station, Chang'an Boulevard, Beijing, China, opened in September 1959, with a total standing capacity of 14,000.

Suggestion boxes The most prolific example on record of the use of a suggestion box is that of John Drayton (1907–87) of Newport, Great Britain, who plied the British rail system with a total of 31,400 suggestions from 1924 to August 1987. More than one in seven were adopted, and 100 were accepted by London Transport.

Longest platform The longest railroad platform in the world is the Kharagpur platform, West Bengal, India, which measures 2,733 ft in length.

Freight yard The largest freight yard is Bailey Yard in North Platte, NE,

An aerial view of the massive Bailey Yard freight yard at North Platte, NE. (Union Pacific Railroad)

which covers 2,850 acres and has 260 miles of track. It handles an average of 108 trains and some 8,500 freight cars every day.

MODEL TRAINS

Model trains—nonstop duration A standard Life-Like BL2 HO scale electric train pulled six eight-wheel coaches for 1,207.5 hr, from 4 August to 23 Sep 1990, and covered a distance of 909.5 miles. The event was organized by Ike Cottingham and Mark Hamrick of Mainline Modelers of Akron, OH.

The longest recorded run by a model steam locomotive is 144 miles in 27 hr 18 min by the 7¼ in gauge "Winifred," built in 1974 by Wilf Grove, at Thames Ditton, Great Britain, on 7–9 Sep 1979. "Winifred" works on 80 lb/in^2 pressure and is coal-fired, with cylinders 2⅛ in in diamater and 3⅛ in stroke.

The most miniature model railway ever built is one of 1:1,000 scale by Jean Damery (b. 1923) of Paris, France. The engine runs on a 4½ volt battery and measures 5/16 in overall.

SUBWAY SYSTEMS

Most extensive The most extensive underground or rapid transit railway system of the 94 in the world is the London Underground, Great Britain, with 254 miles of route, of which 85 miles is bored tunnel. The whole system is operated by a staff of 17,000 serving 273 stations. The 4,134 cars, forming a fleet of 570 trains, carried 728 million passengers in 1992–93.

Most stations The subway with the most stations in the world is the New York City Metropolitan Transportation Authority subway (first section opened on 27 Oct 1904). The network covers 238 route miles, comprising 469 subway stations. In 1993, it served an average of 3.4 million passengers per day.

Traveling *New York subway* The record time for traveling the whole system is 26 hr 21 min 08 sec, set by Kevin Foster (USA) on 25–26 Oct 1989.

Busiest The world's busiest metro system has been the Greater Moscow Metro (opened 1935) in Russia, with as many as 3.3 billion passenger journeys per year at its peak—although by 1991 the figure had declined to 2.5 billion. It has 3,500 railcars and a workforce of 25,000. There are 141 stations.

Longest platform The State Street Center subway platform on "The Loop" in Chicago, IL measures 3,500 ft in length.

Worst subway disaster The worst subway accident in the United States occurred on 1 Nov 1918, in Brooklyn, NY when a BRT Line train derailed on a curve on Malbone St. in the Brighton Beach section. There were 97 fatalities on the scene and five more people died later from injuries sustained in the crash. The BRT line went bankrupt on 31 Dec 1918 as a result of the tragedy.

AIRCRAFT & FLIGHT

EARLIEST FLIGHTS

The first controlled and sustained power-driven flight occurred near Kill Devil Hill, Kitty Hawk, NC, at 10:35 A.M. on 17 Dec 1903, when Orville Wright (1871–1948) flew the 12-hp chain-driven *Flyer I* for a distance of 120 ft at an airspeed of 30 mph, a ground speed of 6.8 mph and an altitude of 8–12 ft for about 12 seconds, watched by his brother Wilbur (1867–1912), four men and a boy. The *Flyer* was first exhibited in the National Air and Space Museum at the Smithsonian Institution, Washington, D.C. on 17 Dec 1948.

Jet-engined The first flight by an airplane powered by a turbojet engine was made by the Heinkel He 178, piloted by Flugkapitän Erich Warsitz, at Marienehe, Germany on 27 Aug 1939. It was powered by a Heinkel He

S3b engine weighing 834 lb (as installed with long tailpipe) designed by Dr Hans Pabst von Ohain.

United States The earliest flight of a jet aircraft built in the United States was that of the Bell XP59A, using Whittle-designed engines, at Muroc, CA on 1 October 1942. The first US-built operational jet aircraft was the Lockheed P-80. The P-80's maiden flight was on 8 January 1944. It was first used in combat during the Korean War.

DID YOU KNOW?

The first supersonic flight was achieved on 14 Oct 1947 by Capt. (later Brig. Gen.) Charles "Chuck" Elwood Yeager (b. 13 Feb 1923), over Edwards Air Force Base, Muroc, CA, in a Bell XS-1 rocket plane (*Glamorous Glennis*—named after Yeager's wife) at Mach 1.015 (670 mph) at an altitude of 42,000 ft. The XS-1 is now in the National Air and Space Museum at the Smithsonian Institution, Washington, D.C.

Transatlantic The first crossing of the North Atlantic by air was made by Lt-Cdr (later Rear Admiral) Albert Cushion Read (1887–1967) and his crew (Stone, Hinton, Rodd, Rhoads and Breese) in the 84-knot US Navy/Curtiss flying boat NC-4 from Trepassey Harbor, Newfoundland, Canada, via the Azores, to Lisbon, Portugal from 16–27 May 1919. The whole flight of 4,717 miles, originating from Rockaway Air Station, Long Island, NY on 8 May, required 53 hr 58 min, terminating at Plymouth, Great Britain on 31 May.

Nonstop The first nonstop transatlantic flight was achieved 18 days later. The pilot, Capt. John Williams Alcock (1892–1919), and navigator, Lt Arthur Whitton Brown (1886–1948), left Lester's Field, St John's, Newfoundland, Canada at 4:13 P.M. GMT on 14 Jun 1919, and landed at Derrygimla Bog near Clifden, Republic of Ireland, at 8:40 A.M. GMT, 15 June, having covered a distance of 1,960 miles in their Vickers Vimy, powered by two 360-hp Rolls-Royce Eagle VIII engines.

Solo The first solo transatlantic flight was achieved by Capt. Charles Augustus Lindbergh (USA; 1902–74), who took off in his 220-hp Ryan monoplane *Spirit of St Louis* at 12:52 P.M. GMT on 20 May 1927 from Roosevelt Field, Long Island, NY. He landed at 10:21 P.M. GMT on 21 May 1927 at Le Bourget Airfield, Paris, France. His flight of 3,610 miles lasted 33 hr 29½ min and he won a prize of $25,000. The *Spirit of St Louis* is now in the National Air and Space Museum at the Smithsonian Institution, Washington, D.C.

Transpacific The first nonstop flight across the Pacific was by Major Clyde Pangborn and Hugh Herndon in the Bellanca cabin monoplane *Miss Veedol*. They took off from Sabishiro Beach, Japan and covered the 4,558 miles to Wenatchee, WA in 41 hr 13 min from 3–5 Oct 1931.

Circumnavigational flights Strict circumnavigation of the globe requires the aircraft to pass through two antipodal points, thus covering a minimum distance of 24,859.73 miles.

First without refueling Richard G. "Dick" Rutan and Jeana Yeager, in their specially constructed aircraft *Voyager*, designed by Dick's brother Burt Rutan, flew from Edwards Air Force Base, CA from 14–23 Dec 1986. Their flight took 9 days 3 min 44 sec and they covered a distance of 24,987 miles, averaging 115.65 mph. The plane, with a wingspan of 110.8 ft, was capable of carrying 1,240 gal of fuel weighing 8,934 lb. It took over two years and 22,000 man-hours to construct. The pilot flew from a cockpit measuring 5.6 × 1.8 ft and the off-duty crew member occupied a cabin 7.5 × 2 ft. *Voyager* is now in the National Air and Space Museum at the Smithsonian Institution, Washington, D.C.

First circumpolar Capt. Elgen M. Long, 44, achieved the first circumpolar flight in a Piper PA-31 Navajo from 5 Nov–3 Dec 1971. He covered 38,896 miles in 215 flying hours. The cabin temperature sank to –40°F over Antarctica.

AIRCRAFT

Largest wingspan The aircraft with the largest wingspan is the $40-million Hughes H.4 Hercules flying boat (*Spruce Goose*). It was raised 70 ft into the air in a test run of 3,000 ft, piloted by Howard Hughes (1905–76), off Long Beach Harbor, CA, on 2 Nov 1947, but after this it never flew again. The eight-engined 212-ton aircraft had a wingspan of 319 ft 11 in and a length of 218 ft 8 in.

Among current aircraft, the Ukrainian Antonov An-124 has a span of 240 ft 5³/₄ in. The USAF C-5B cargo plane has a wingspan of 222 ft 8¹/₂ in, which is the greatest for any United States military aircraft.

Heaviest The aircraft with the highest standard maximum takeoff weight is the Ukrainian Antonov An-225 *Mriya* ("Dream") at 660 tons (1,322,750 lb). This aircraft lifted a payload of 344,579 lb to a height of 40,715 ft on 22 Mar 1989. The flight was achieved by Capt. Aleksandr Galunenko and his crew of seven pilots.

Most capacious The Aero Spacelines Super Guppy has a cargo hold with a usable volume of 49,790ft^3 and a maximum takeoff weight of 87.5 tons. Its wingspan is 156 ft 3 in and its length 141 ft 3 in. Its cargo compartment is 108 ft 10 in long with a cylindrical section 25 ft in diameter.

Heaviest commercial cargo movement Ukrainian aircraft designer Antonov and British charter company Air Foyle carried out the heaviest commercial air cargo movement, by taking three transformers weighing 53 tons each and other equipment from Barcelona, Spain to Nouméa, New Caledonia (Pacific) between 10–14 Jan 1991. The total weight carried in the An-124 *Ruslan* was 156.8 tons.

Air Foyle and Antonov also hold the record for carrying the heaviest single piece of cargo, by flying a 145.6-ton power plant generator from Düsseldorf, Germany to New Delhi, India on 22 Sep 1993. Again, the aircraft used was the Ukrainian An-124 *Ruslan*. Because of the huge weight, the plane had to make six refueling stops during the 5,600 mile flight.

Smallest The smallest biplane ever flown is the *Bumble Bee Two*, designed and built by Robert H. Starr of Arizona. It was 8 ft 10 in long, with a wingspan of 5 ft 6 in, and weighed 396 lb empty. The fastest speed it attained was 190 mph. On 8 May 1988, after flying to a height of approximately 400 ft, it crashed, and was totally destroyed.

Ultralight On 3 Aug 1985 Anthony A. Cafaro (b. 30 Nov 1951) flew an ultralight aircraft (ULA; maximum weight 245 lb, maximum speed 65 mph, fuel capacity 4¹/₄ gal) single-seater Gypsy Skycycle for 7 hr 31 min at Dart Field, Mayville, NY. Nine fuel "pickups" were completed during the flight.

Most flights by propeller-driven airliner General Dynamics (formerly Convair) reported in March 1994 that some of its CV-580 turboprop airliners had logged over 150,000 flights, typically averaging no more than 20 minutes, in short-haul operations.

Bombers Heaviest The former Soviet four-jet Tupolev Tu-160 has a maximum takeoff weight of over 606,270 lb.

Longest The Boeing B-52G is the longest bomber in the USAF at 160 ft 11 in. The B-52H has the greatest thrust of a bomber in the US fleet, at 136,000 lbs, and the greatest unrefueled range of over 8,800 miles.

Fastest The world's fastest operational bombers include the French Dassault Mirage IV, which can fly at Mach 2.2 (1,450 mph) at 36,000 ft.

The American variable-geometry or "swing-wing" General Dynamics FB-111A has a maximum speed of Mach 2.5. The Soviet swing-wing Tupolev Tu-22M has an estimated over-target speed of Mach 2.0 but could be as fast as Mach 2.5.

Bumble Bee Two **was the smallest biplane to buzz the skies. Designed and built by Robert Starr, the plane was destroyed in a crash (R.H. Starr)**

JET AIRLINERS

Oldest According to the British-based aviation information and consultancy service company Airclaims, a first-generation Douglas DC-8 airliner built in 1959 was still in service in May 1994 as a flying operating theater.

Largest The first 747-400 entered service with Northwest Airlines on 26 Jan 1989 with a wingspan of 211 ft 5 in, a range exceeding 8,000 miles and a capacity for up to 567 passengers. The highest-capacity jet airliner is the Boeing 747 "Jumbo Jet," which has a capacity of 385 to 560 passengers and a maximum speed of 602 mph. Its wingspan is 195 ft 5 in and its length 231 ft 10 in. It entered service on 22 Jan 1970.

Fastest The supersonic BAC/Aérospatiale Concorde, first flown on 2 Mar 1969, with a designed capacity of 128 (and potentially 144) passengers, cruises at up to Mach 2.2 (1,450 mph). It has a maximum takeoff weight of 408,000 lb. It flew at Mach 1.05 on 10 Oct 1969, exceeded Mach 2 for the first time on 4 Nov 1970, and became the first supersonic airliner used in passenger service on 21 Jan 1976. The New York–London, Great Britain record is 2 hr 54 min 30 sec, set on 14 Apr 1990.

Greatest passenger load The greatest passenger load carried by any single commercial airliner was 1,088 during *Operation Solomon*, which began on 24 May 1991 when Ethiopian Jews were evacuated from Addis Ababa to Israel on a Boeing 747 belonging to El Al airline. This figure includes two babies born during the flight.

Most flights by a jet airliner A survey of aging airliners or so-called "geriatric jets" published in *Flight International* magazine in April 1994 reported a McDonnell Douglas DC-9 still in service that had logged 95,939 flights in less than 28 years.

The most hours recorded by a jet airliner still in service is 94,804 hours in less than 25 years, reported for a Boeing 747 in the same issue of *Flight International*.

AIRLINES

Oldest The oldest airline still in existence is KoninklijkeLuchtvaart-Maatschappij NV (KLM), the national airline of the Netherlands, which was established on 7 Oct 1919. It opened its first scheduled service (Amsterdam– London, Great Britain) on 17 May 1920.

Chalk's International Airline has been flying amphibious planes from Miami, FL to the Bahamas since July 1919. Albert "Pappy" Chalk flew from 1911–75.

Largest The Russian state airline Aeroflot was instituted on 9 Feb 1923 and was the largest airline of all time. In its last complete year of formal existence (1990) it employed 600,000 (more than the top 18 US airlines put together) and flew 139 million passengers, with 20,000 pilots, along 620,000 miles of domestic routes across 11 time zones.

Since the breakup of the Soviet Union, the company that carries the greatest number of passengers is American Airlines, with 86,001,000 in 1993. The German airline Lufthansa has the longest route network, covering 585,000 miles.

1,088 PASSENGERS IN ONE AIRCRAFT

An astounding record was set on 24 May 1991, when 1,086 Ethiopian Jews were evacuated to Israel in one plane. This was more than double the normal capacity of a passenger jumbo jet, and, not surprisingly, never before had so many people flown in a commercial airliner. Two babies were born en route, bringing the total who landed in Israel to 1,088.

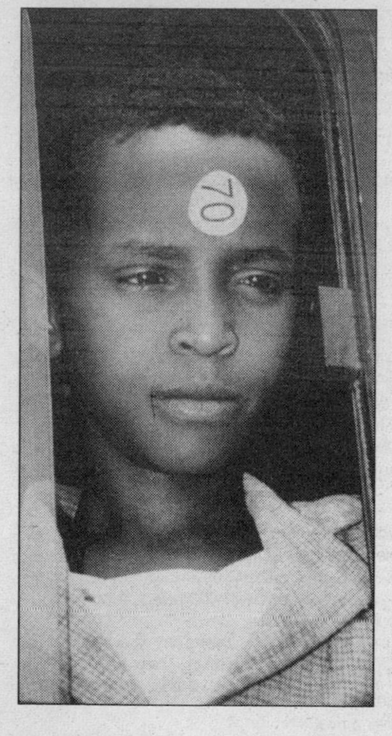

The flight was just one of 40 that were arranged to evacuate a total of 14,200 Jews to their promised land from Addis Ababa, the besieged capital of Ethiopia, all in the space of 24 hours. The exercise, code-named *Operation Solomon*, had been planned over several weeks with US diplomatic assistance, and President Bush personally helped with the request to the Ethiopian government for permission to carry out the airlift. The

Rex Feature/Sipa

Jewish Agency for Israel and El Al, the Israeli national airline, helped coordinate the whole operation.

Following the collapse of the Marxist regime in Ethiopia, and the installation of an interim government, Addis Ababa was under siege by rebels supporting the former president. Because the rebels were Arab-backed and thought to be anti-Jewish, it became increasingly evident that the airlift had to be carried out as quickly as possible; hence the packed conditions on the planes. On the record-breaking flight, some of the rows of 10 seats had as many as 18 people jammed into them. There were no toilets, since the aim was simply to bring the greatest possible number of people to Israel. The flights were operated by El Al and the Israeli Air Force; one Ethiopian plane was also used.

Many of the evacuees had never been close to a plane, let alone actually flown in one. Conditions were unbearable, but this was offset by great anticipation over the new life that was about to begin. Four babies were born during the flights, and the happiness continued as the planes flew into Israeli airspace, with announcements in the immigrants' own language causing spontaneous singing and celebration. The culmination of each flight was of course a safe landing in Israel, with some of the arrivals having to be carried down the gangways. Many people kneeled to kiss the ground in gratitude upon their arrival.

Busiest The country with the busiest airline system is the United States, where the total number of passenger enplanements by large commercial air carriers in domestic operations in 1993 was 441.9 million.

Busiest international route The city-pair with the highest international scheduled passenger traffic is London/Paris. More than 3 million passengers fly between the two cities annually, or more than 4,100 each way each day (although London-bound traffic is greater than that bound for Paris).

SCHEDULED FLIGHTS

Longest The longest nonstop scheduled flight currently operating is one of 7,969 miles by South African Airways for the flight from New York to Johannesburg, South Africa. In terms of time taken, the longest is 15 hr 5 min, for the flight from Heathrow, London, Great Britain to Osaka, Japan with British Airways and also for the flight from Los Angeles, CA to Hong Kong with Delta Air Lines.

The longest nonstop flight by a commercial airliner was one of 11,951 miles from Auckland, New Zealand to Le Bourget, Paris, France in 21 hr 46 min on 17–18 Jun 1993 by the Airbus Industrie A340–200. It was the return leg of a flight that started at Le Bourget the previous day.

Shortest The shortest scheduled flight is by Loganair between the Orkney Islands of Westray and Papa Westray, Great Britain, which has been flown with Britten-Norman Islander twin-engined 10-seat transports since September 1967. Though scheduled for two minutes, in favorable wind conditions it was once completed in 58 sec by Capt. Andrew D. Alsop. The check-in time for the 2 min flight is 20 min.

Alaska Airlines provides the shortest scheduled flight by jet, by McDonnell Douglas MD-80 between San Francisco and Oakland, CA. There is one daily round trip flight six days a week; the time averages 5 minutes for the 12 mile journey. Some 25 minutes are allowed in the airline timetable.

Captain Pierre Baud at the controls of the Airbus Industrie A340-200 that completed the world's longest nonstop commercial flight from Auckland, New Zealand to Paris, France. (Airbus Industrie)

Around the world The fastest time for a circumnavigation on scheduled flights is 44 hr 6 min, by David J. Springbett (b. 2 May 1938) of Taplow, Great Britain. His route took him from Los Angeles, CA eastwards via London, Bahrain, Singapore, Bangkok, Manila, Tokyo and Honolulu from 8–10 Jan 1980 over a 23,069 mile course. A minimum distance of 22,858.8 miles (the length of the Tropic of Cancer or Capricorn) must be flown.

Around the world—antipodal points Brother Michael Bartlett of London, Great Britain traveled around the world on scheduled flights, taking in exact antipodal points, in a time of 67 hr 4 min from 10–13 Jun 1993. Leaving from London, he flew via Tokyo, Japan and Auckland, New Zealand to Palmerston, also in New Zealand, and then traveled by car to Ti Tree Point. He later changed planes at Madrid airport, Spain (exactly opposite Ti Tree Point on the other side of the world). His journey took him a total distance of 25,841 miles.

Most flights in 24 hours Brother Michael Bartlett made 42 scheduled passenger flights with Heli Transport of Nice, France between Nice, Sophia Antipolis, Monaco and Cannes in 13 hr 33 min on 13 Jun 1990.

Stowaway The most rugged stowaway was Socarras Ramirez, who escaped from Cuba on 4 Jun 1969 by stowing away in an unpressurized wheel well in the starboard wing of a Douglas DC-8 from Havana, Cuba to Madrid, Spain in a 5,600-mile Iberian Airlines flight.

SPEED

Official record The airspeed record is 2,193.2 mph, by Capt. Eldon W. Joersz and Major George T. Morgan, Jr., in a Lockheed SR-71A "Blackbird" near Beale Air Force Base, CA over a 15½ mile course on 28 Jul 1976.

Air-launched record The fastest fixed-wing aircraft in the world was the US North American Aviation X-15A-2, which flew for the first time (after modification from the X-15A) on 25 Jun 1964, powered by a liquid oxygen and ammonia rocket-propulsion system. The landing speed was momentarily 242 mph. The fastest speed attained was 4,520 mph (Mach 6.7) when piloted by Major William J. Knight, USAF (b. 1930), on 3 Oct 1967.

The space shuttle *Columbia*, commanded by Capt. John W. Young (USN) and piloted by Capt. Robert L. Crippen (USN), was launched from the Kennedy Space Center, Cape Canaveral, FL on 12 Apr 1981 after expenditure of $9.9 billion since 1972. *Columbia* broke all records in space by a fixed-wing craft, with 16,600 mph at main engine cutoff. After reentry

GUESS WHAT?

Q. WHICH "JET" HAS THE MOST PASS COMPLETIONS IN AN NFL GAME?

A. CHECK "FOOTBALL" (SPORTS & GAMES)

from 75.8 miles, experiencing temperatures of 3,920°F, it glided home weighing 107 tons, and with a landing speed of 216 mph, on Rogers Dry Lake, CA on 14 Apr 1981.

Fastest jet The USAF Lockheed SR-71, a reconnaissance aircraft, was the world's fastest jet. First flown in its definitive form on 22 Dec 1964, it was reportedly capable of attaining an altitude ceiling of close to 100,000 ft. It had a wingspan of 55.6 ft and a length of 107.4 ft and weighed 85 tons at takeoff. Its reported range at Mach 3 was 2,982 miles at 78,750 ft.

Fastest biplane The fastest is the Italian Fiat CR42B, with a 1,010 hp Daimler-Benz DB601A engine, which attained 323 mph in 1941. Only one was built.

Fastest piston-engined aircraft On 21 Aug 1989, in Las Vegas, NV, the *Rare Bear*, a modified Grumman Bearcat F8F piloted by Lyle Shelton, set the FAI-approved world record for a 3 km run of 528.3 mph.

Fastest propeller-driven aircraft The fastest propeller-driven aircraft in use is the former Soviet Tu-95/142 "Bear" with four 14,795 hp engines driving eight blade counter-rotating propellers with a maximum level speed of Mach 0.82 (575 mph).

Fastest coast-to-coast flight The record aircraft time from coast to coast (Los Angeles to Washington, D.C.) is 68 min 17 sec by Lt. Col. Ed Yeilding, pilot, and Lt. Col. J. T. Vida, reconnaissance systems officer, aboard the SR–71 Blackbird spy plane on 6 Mar 1990. The Blackbird was refueled over the Pacific Ocean at 27,000 ft before starting a climb to above 80,000 ft, heading east from the California coastline and crossing the finish line near Salisbury, MD. This is the first (and only) time that a sonic boom has traveled uninterrupted from coast to coast across the United States.

Fastest transatlantic flight The flight record is 1 hr 54 min 56.4 sec by Major James V. Sullivan (USA), 37, and Major Noel F. Widdifield (USA), 33, flying a Lockheed SR-71A "Blackbird" eastwards on 1 Sep 1974. The average speed, slowed by refueling from a KC-135 tanker aircraft, for the New York–London stage of 3,461.53 miles was 1,806.96 mph.

The solo record (Gander, Newfoundland, Canada to Gatwick, Great Britain) is 8 hr 47 min 32 sec, an average speed of 265.1 mph, by Capt. John J.A. Smith in a Rockwell Commander 685 twin-turboprop on 12 Mar 1978, achieving an average speed of 265.214 mph.

London–New York The record time from central London, Great Britain to downtown New York City by helicopter and Concorde is 3 hr 59 min 44 sec, and for the return, 3 hr 40 min 40 sec, both by David J. Springbett and David Boyce on 8–9 Feb 1982.

Time zone parties On 31 Dec 1992 a group of 97 Atlantic "Time Tunnelers" saw the New Year in twice by having a party at Shannon, Republic of Ireland and leaving at 10 minutes past midnight on Concorde for Bermuda, where they arrived at 11:21 P.M. the previous day, in time for a second New Year's celebration. In so doing they achieved the fastest west–east Atlantic crossing for a passenger aircraft, with a time of 2 hr 51 min.

RARING TO GO!

She was a heap of metal when he found her. "Some guy had wrecked her in 1962, in Indiana. I took the fuselage and wings in '68 and shipped them back to California. We've won more air races—12, now—than any other airplane." If planes could talk, what would the *Rare Bear* say about those six years as a wreck? Did she dream that a Navy pilot would come along and take her to the height of air racing?

Lyle Shelton can't answer for the *Rare Bear,* a Bearcat that's one of the last piston fighters the Navy ever built. He will allow, however, that his worst moment came over Reno, Nevada, when the *Bear*'s engine blew at the racing altitude of just 50 feet above the ground. "The engine came apart, with nine out of 18 connecting rods broken. I heard a pop, and a bang, and I just zoomed up." *Up?* "That's what you do to set up to glide in. The engine totally quit. I had a dead stick. But we managed to glide in."

Air racers steel themselves against what seems like the natural response in a situation like this: dropping down, opting out, saving their skins. Instead, these pilots—to whom the frequent crashes and deaths never become routine—train themselves to put others first: the crowd below, and the other pilots. Says Shelton: "Sure, it's demanding to lose your engine at 50 feet, but it's not a scary big deal to me. Maybe it's kind of like combat, which I've never seen. It's just a job for me. It's just what I do."

The Rare Bear *prepares for takeoff. (William S. Romano)*

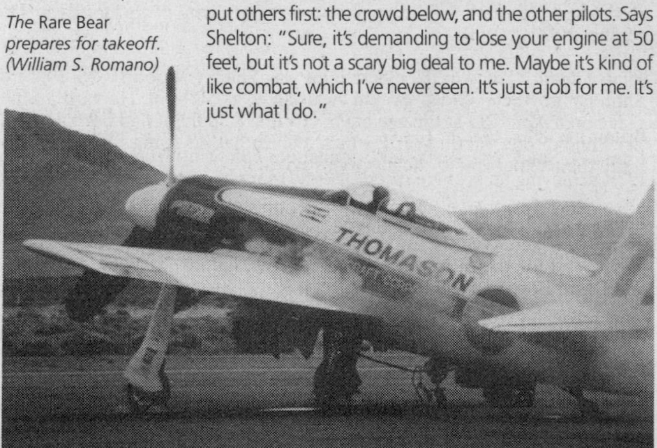

Fastest circumnavigational flight The fastest flight under the FAI rules, which permit flights that exceed the length of the Tropic of Cancer or Capricorn (22,858.8 miles), was that of the westbound flight of 32 hr 49 min by an Air France Concorde (Capts. Claude Delorme and Jean Boyé) from Lisbon, Portugal via Santo Domingo, Acapulco, Honolulu, Guam, Bangkok and Bahrain on 12–13 Oct 1992.

Fastest climb Heinz Frick of British Aerospace took a Harrier GR5 powered by a Rolls-Royce Pegasus 11-61 engine from a standing start to 39,370 ft in 2 min 6.63 sec above the Rolls-Royce flight test center, Filton, Bristol, Great Britain on 15 Aug 1989.

Aleksandr Fedotov (USSR) in a Mikoyan E 266M (MiG-25) aircraft established the fastest time-to-height record on 17 May 1975, reaching 114,830 ft in 4 min 11.7 sec after takeoff from Podmoscovnoe, Russia.

United States The fastest time-to-height record for a United States aircraft is to 62,000 ft in 2 min 2.94 sec, by Major Roger J. Smith (USAF), in an F-15 Eagle on 19 January 1975.

DURATION RECORDS

Longest flight The longest flight on record is 64 days 22 hr 19 min 5 sec, set by Robert Timm and John Cook in the Cessna 172 *Hacienda*. They took off from McCarran Airfield, Las Vegas, NV just before 3:53 P.M. local time on 4 Dec 1958 and landed at the same airfield just before 2:12 P.M. on 7 Feb 1959. They covered a distance equivalent to six times around the world, being refueled without any landings.

PERSONAL AVIATION RECORDS

Oldest and youngest passengers Airborne births are reported every year. The oldest person to fly was Mrs Jessica S. Swift (b. Anna Stewart, 17 Sep 1871), age 110 years 3 months. She flew from Vermont to Florida in December 1981.

***Pilots** Oldest* The world's oldest pilot was Stanley Wood (1896–1994) of Shoreham-by-Sea, Great Britain, who flew a US-built Harvard trainer plane on 6 Apr 1993 at the age of 96. His first solo flight had been an unofficial one during World War I, which means that his flying career spanned more than 80 percent of the history of aviation.

***Most flying hours** Pilot* John Edward Long (USA; b. 10 Nov 1915) between 1 May 1933 and 18 May 1994 logged 59,300 hours of flight time as a pilot—cumulatively more than six years airborne.

Passenger The record for a supersonic passenger is held by Fred Finn, who made his 706th Concorde crossing in October 1993. He commutes regularly from New Jersey to London, Great Britain, and has flown a total distance of 10,959,311 miles.

Most planes flown James B. Taylor, Jr. (1897–1942) flew 461 different types of powered aircraft during his 25 years as an active experimental test and demonstration pilot for the US Navy and a number of American aircraft manufacturers.

Refuel!

The record time for refueling an airplane (with 102.7 gal of 100 octane avgas) is 3 min 42 sec, for a 1975 Cessna 310 (N92HH), by the Sky Harbor Air Service Line Crew. It had landed at Cheyenne Airport, WY, on 5 Jul 1992 during an around-the-world air race.

Most transatlantic flights Between March 1948 and his retirement on 1 Sep 1984, Flight Service Manager Charles M. Schimpf logged a total of 2,880 Atlantic crossings—a rate of 6.4 per month.

Most experienced passenger Edwin A. Shackleton of Bristol, Great Britain has flown as a passenger in 500 different types of aircraft. His first flight was in March 1943 in D.H. Dominie R9548; other aircraft have included helicopters, gliders, microlights, gas and hot air balloons.

Longest airplane ticket A ticket 39 ft $4\frac{1}{2}$ in long was issued for $4,500 to Bruno Leunen of Brussels, Belgium in December 1984 for a 53,203 mile trip on 80 airlines with 109 layovers.

Plane pulling David Huxley single-handedly pulled a Boeing 767 weighing 115 tons a distance of 203 ft 10 in across the tarmac at the Qantas jet base in Sydney, Australia on 9 Mar 1994.

A team of 59 Qantas personnel pulled a Boeing 747 weighing 226 tons a distance of 328 ft in 62.1 sec at Perth Airport, Australia on 22 Oct 1988.

Wing walking Roy Castle, the host of the British Broadcasting Corporation *Record Breakers* television program, flew on the wing of a Boeing Stearman airplane for 3 hr 23 min on 2 Aug 1990. The plane took off from Gatwick, Great Britain and landed at Le Bourget, near Paris, France.

John Long has accumulated more than six years of flying time. He first attempted to fly by strapping an ironing board across his shoulders and biking down a hill as fast as possible. (Paul Robertson Photography)

Not a new form of fuel economy, but the Qantas employees' plane-pulling team during their successful record attempt. Below, jet lag sets in. (Ian Cugley)

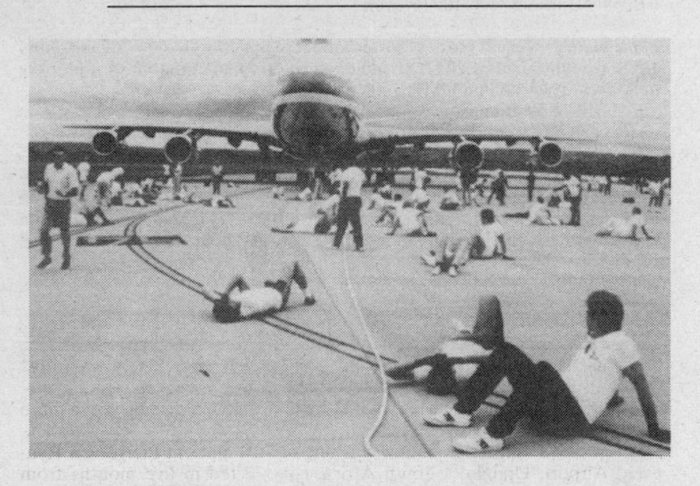

AIRPORTS

Largest The largest is the $3.6 billion King Khalid International Airport outside Riyadh, Saudi Arabia, which covers an area of 87 miles^2 (55,040 acres). It was opened on 14 Nov 1983. It also has the world's largest control tower, 266 ft in height. The Hajj Terminal at the $4.76 billion King Abdul-Aziz Airport near Jeddah, Saudi Arabia is the world's largest roofed structure, covering 370 acres.

The world's largest airport terminal is at Hartsfield Atlanta International Airport, GA, opened on 21 Sep 1980, with floor space covering 2.5 million ft^2 (57½ acres) and still expanding. In 1993 the terminal serviced 47,751,988 passengers using 145 gates, although it has a capacity for 75 million.

Busiest The busiest airport is Chicago International Airport, O'Hare Field, IL, with a total of 65,077,508 passengers and 859,208 aircraft movements in 1993. This represents a takeoff or landing every 37 sec around the clock.

Heathrow Airport, London, Great Britain, handles more international traffic than any other airport, with 40,788,000 international passengers in 1993.

The busiest landing area ever was Bien Hoa Air Base, South Vietnam, which handled approximately 1,000,000 takeoffs and landings in 1970.

Helipad The heliport at Morgan City, LA, one of a string used by helicopters flying energy-related offshore operations into the Gulf of Mexico, has pads for 46 helicopters. The world's largest helipad was at An Khe, South Vietnam, during the Vietnam war. It covered an area of 1¼ × 1¾ miles and could accommodate 434 helicopters.

Landing fields *Highest* The highest is La Sa (Lhasa) Airport, Tibet, People's Republic of China, at 14,315 ft.

Lowest The lowest landing field is El Lisan on the east shore of the Dead Sea, 1,180 ft below sea level, but during World War II BOAC Short C-class flying boats operated from the surface of the Dead Sea at 1,292 ft below sea level.

The lowest international airport is Schiphol, Amsterdam, Netherlands, at 15 ft below sea level.

Longest runways The longest runway in the world is at Edwards Air Force Base on the west side of Rogers dry lakebed at Muroc, CA. It measures 39,104 ft, or 7.4 miles. The *Voyager* aircraft, taking off on its around-the-world unrefueled flight, used 14,200 ft of the 15,000-ft-long main base concrete runway.

The world's longest civil runway is one of 3.04 miles at Pierre van Ryneveld Airport, Upington, South Africa, constructed in five months from August 1975 to January 1976.

Largest hangars Hangar 375 ("Big Texas") at Kelly Air Force Base, San Antonio, TX, completed on 15 Feb 1956, has four doors each 250 ft wide, 60 ft high, and weighing 681 tons. The high bay is 2,000 × 300 × 90 ft in area and is surrounded by a 44 acre concrete apron. It is the largest freestanding hangar in the world.

Largest wooden hangars Between 1942 and 1943, 16 Navy airship wooden blimp hangers were built at various locations throughout the United States. They measure 1,040 ft long, 150 ft 4 in high at the crown and 296 ft 6 in wide at the base. There are only nine remaining—two each at Tillamook, OR, Moffett Field and Santa Ana, CA and Lakehurst, NJ, and one at Elizabeth City, NC.

HELICOPTERS

Fastest Under FAI rules, the world's speed record for helicopters was set by John Trevor Eggington with co-pilot Derek J. Clews, who averaged 249.09 mph over Somerset, Great Britain on 11 Aug 1986 in a Westland Lynx company demonstrator helicopter.

Largest The former Soviet Mil Mi-12 was powered by four 6,500 hp turboshaft engines and had a span of 219 ft 10 in over its rotor tips, with a length of 121 ft 4½ in. It weighed 114 tons. The aircraft was demonstrated in prototype form at the Paris Air Show but never entered formal service.

The largest rotorcraft was the Piasecki Heli-Stat, which used four Sikorsky S-58 airframes attached to a Goodyear ZPG-2 airship. Powered by four 1,525 hp piston engines, it was 343 ft long, 111 ft high and 149 ft wide. It first flew in October 1985 at Lakehurst, NJ, but was destroyed in a crash on 1 Jul 1986.

Smallest The single-seat Seremet WS-8 ultralight helicopter was built in Denmark in 1976. It had a 35 hp engine, a rotor diameter of 14 ft 9 in and an empty weight of 117 lb.

Highest altitude The record for helicopters is 40,820 ft by an Aérospatiale SA315B Lama, over Istres, France on 21 Jun 1972 by Jean Boulet.

The highest recorded landing was at 24,600 ft, during SA315B demonstrations in the Himalayas in 1969.

Longest hover Doug Daigle, Brian Watts and Dave Meyer of Tridair Helicopters, together with Rod Anderson of Helistream, Inc. of California, maintained a continuous hovering flight in a 1947 Bell 47B model for 50 hr 50 sec between 13 and 15 Dec 1989.

Greatest load lifted On 3 Feb 1982 at Podmoscovnoe in the USSR, a Mil Mi-26 heavy-lift helicopter crewed by G.V. Alfeurov and L.A. Indeyev lifted a total mass of 62.5 tons to 6,560 ft.

Longest flight Under FAI rules, the record for the longest unrefueled nonstop flight was set by Robert Ferry, flying a Hughes YOH-6A, over a distance of 2,213.1 miles from Culver City, CA to Ormond Beach, FL in April 1966.

Circumnavigation H. Ross Perot, Jr. and Jay Coburn made the first helicopter circumnavigation in *Spirit of Texas* in 29 days 3 hr 8 min 13 sec on 1–30 Sep 1982 from Dallas, TX.

The first solo around-the-world flight in a helicopter was completed by Dick Smith (Australia) on 22 Jul 1983. Taking off from and returning to the Bell Helicopter Facility at Fort Worth, TX, in a Bell Model 206L,

Autogyro pilot Wing-Cdr Kenneth Wallis has set a whirl of records, including speed, altitude and distance records.

LongRanger III, his unhurried flight began on 5 Aug 1982 and covered a distance of 35,258 miles.

AUTOGYROS

Speed, altitude and distance records Wing-Cdr Kenneth H. Wallis (Great Britain) holds the straight-line distance record of 543.27 miles, set in his WA-116F autogyro on 28 Sep 1975 with a nonstop flight from Lydd to Wick, Great Britain. On 20 Jul 1982, flying from Boscombe Down, Great Britain, he established a new autogyro altitude record of 18,516 ft in his WA-121/Mc.

Wing-Cdr Wallis also flew his WA-116/F/S, with a 60 hp Franklin aero-engine, to a record speed of 120.3 mph over a 1.86 mile straight course at Norfolk, Great Britain, on 18 Sep 1986.

AIRSHIPS

Largest Rigid The largest was the 235-ton German *Graf Zeppelin II* (LZ 130), with a length of 804 ft and a capacity of 7.06 million ft^3. It flew its maiden flight on 14 Sep 1938, and in May and August 1939 made radar spying missions in British air space. It was dismantled in April 1940. Its sister ship, *Hindenburg*, was 5 ft 7 in longer.

Non-rigid The largest ever constructed was the US Navy ZPG 3-W, which

DID YOU KNOW?

The most people ever carried in an airship was 207, in the US Navy *Akron* in 1931. The transatlantic record is 117, by the German Hindenburg in 1937. It exploded into a fireball at Lakehurst, NJ on 6 May 1937.

The largest airship currently certified for the public transport of passengers is the 221 ft 5 in-long Sentinel 1000 of 353,100 ft^3 capacity, built by Westinghouse Airships, Inc. Its maiden flight was on 26 Jun 1991.

had a capacity of 1.5 million ft^3, a length of 403 ft, a diameter of 85.1 ft and a crew of 21. It first flew on 21 Jul 1958 but crashed into the sea in June 1960.

Distance records The FAI-accredited straight-line distance record for airships is 3,967.1 miles, set by the German *Graf Zeppelin* LZ127, captained by Dr Hugo Eckener, between 29 Oct and 1 Nov 1928.

From 21–25 Nov 1917 the German *Zeppelin* L59 flew from Yambol, Bulgaria to a point south of Khartoum, Sudan and returned, covering a minimum of 4,500 miles.

Duration record The longest recorded flight by a non-rigid airship (without refueling) is 264 hr 12 min by a US Navy Goodyear-built ZPG-2 class ship (Cdr J.R. Hunt, USN) that flew 9,448 miles from South Weymouth Naval Air Station, MA to Key West, FL, on 4–15 Mar 1957.

HELIUM BALLOONING

First transatlantic crossing Col. Joe Kittinger (USAF), became the first person to complete a solo transatlantic crossing by balloon. In the 101,000 ft^3 helium-filled balloon *Rosie O'Grady* Kittinger lifted off from Caribou, ME on 14 Sep 1984 and completed a distance of 3,543 miles before landing at Montenotte, near Savóna, Italy 86 hours later on 18 Sep 1984.

Distance record The record distance traveled by a balloon is 5,208.68 miles, by the Raven experimental helium-filled balloon *Double Eagle V* (capacity 399,053 ft^3) from 9–12 Nov 1981. The journey started at Nagashima, Japan and ended at Covello, CA. The crew for this first manned balloon crossing of the Pacific Ocean was Ben L. Abruzzo, 51, Rocky Aoki (Japan), 43, Ron Clark, 41, and Larry M. Newman, 34.

Duration record Richard Abruzzo, 29, together with Troy Bradley, 28, set a duration record of 144 hr 16 min in *Team USA* in crossing the Atlantic Ocean from Bangor, ME to Ben Slimane, Morocco on 16–22 Sep 1992. The previous record had been set by Richard's father, Ben, in *Double Eagle II* in 1978.

Highest Unmanned The highest altitude attained by an unmanned balloon was 170,000 ft, by a Winzen balloon with a 47.8 million ft^3 capacity, launched at Chico, CA in October 1972.

Manned The highest altitude reached in a manned balloon is an unofficial 123,800 ft by Nicholas Piantanida (1933–66) of Bricktown, NJ, from Sioux Falls, SD on 1 Feb 1966. He landed in a cornfield in Iowa but did not survive.

The official record (closed gondola) is 113,740 ft by Cdr Malcolm D. Ross (USNR) and the late Lt Cdr Victor A. Prother (USN), in an ascent from the deck of the USS *Antietam* over the Gulf of Mexico on 4 May 1961 in a balloon of 12 million ft^3 capacity.

Scientists Harold Froelich and Keith Lang of Minneapolis, MN made an unplanned ascent in an open gondola, without pressure suits or goggles, to an altitude of 42,126 ft on 26 Sep 1956. During the 6½-hour flight they measured a temperature of –72°F.

Largest The largest balloon ever built had an inflatable volume of 70 million ft^3 and stood 1,000 ft tall. It was unmanned, and was manufactured by Winzen Research Inc. of Minnesota.

HOT-AIR BALLOONING

Mass ascent The greatest mass ascent of hot-air balloons from a single site took place within one hour on 15 Aug 1987 when 128 participants at the Ninth Bristol International Balloon Festival in Bristol, Great Britain took off.

Atlantic crossing Richard Branson (Great Britain) and his pilot, Per Lindstrand (Great Britain), were the first to cross the Atlantic in a hot-air balloon, on 2–3 Jul 1987. They ascended from Sugarloaf, ME and covered the distance of 3,075 miles to Limavady, Northern Ireland in 31 hours 41 minutes.

Pacific crossing Richard Branson and Per Lindstrand crossed the Pacific in the *Virgin Otsuka Pacific Flyer* from the southern tip of Japan to Lac la Matre, Yukon, northwestern Canada on 15–17 Jan 1991 in a 2.6 million ft^3 capacity hot-air balloon (the largest ever flown) to set FAI records for duration (46 hr 15 min) and distance (great circle 4,768 miles).

Altitude Per Lindstrand (Great Britain) achieved the altitude record of 64,997 ft in a Colt 600 hot-air balloon over Laredo, TX on 6 Jun 1988.

Gas The FAI endurance and distance record for a gas and hot-air balloon is 144 hr 16 min and 3,318.2 miles by *Team USA*, crewed by Richard Abruzzo and Troy Bradley on 16–22 Sep 1992.

Most passengers The balloon *Super Maine*, of 2.6 million ft^3 capacity, was built by Tom Handcock of Portland, ME. Tethered, the balloon rose to a height of 50 ft with 61 passengers on board on 19 Feb 1988.

The Dutch balloonist Henk Brink made an untethered flight of 656 ft in the 850,000 ft^3 capacity Nashua Number One, carrying a total of 50 passengers and crew. The flight, on 17 Aug 1988, began from Lelystad Airport, Netherlands, lasted 25 minutes, and reached an altitude of 228 ft.

BALLOONING
THE ABRUZZO WAY

When Richard Abruzzo set a new ballooning duration record of 144 hr 16 min in September 1992, he beat a record that had stood for 14 years. What was particularly noteworthy, however, and virtually unprecedented in the field of record-breaking, was the fact that the previous record had been held by his father, Ben Abruzzo.

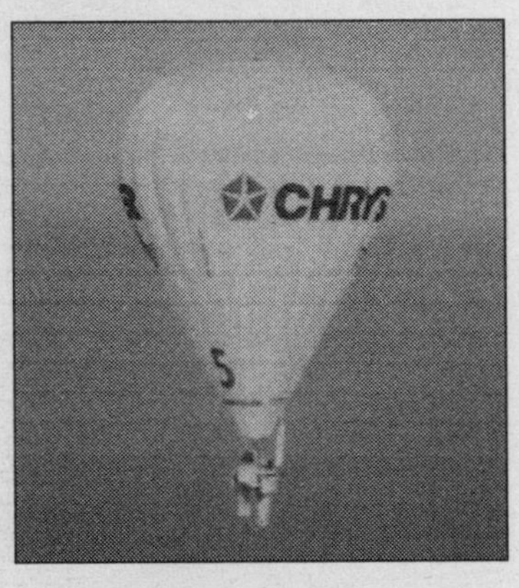

On 12 Aug 1978 Ben Abruzzo, 48, along with Maxie Anderson and Larry Newman, set off from Presque Isle, Maine with the aim of achieving the first-ever crossing of the North Atlantic in their helium-filled balloon *Double Eagle II*. After a journey lasting 137 hr 6 min, during which they experienced icy winds, they landed at Miserey, in northern France, on 17 August. Although they had hoped to travel as far as Le Bourget Airport, just outside Paris, unfavorable winds made them abandon their plan and they came down in a field, where crowds rushed to welcome them as heroes. Richard was just a teenager at the time, but when his parents were tragically killed in a plane crash in 1985, he was already dreaming of making a transoceanic flight. An ideal opportunity arose to

Ben and Richard celebrate Ben's transpacific flight in 1981. This set a new distance (but not duration) record, and the record still stands.

Opposite page, Team USA during its successful flight.

The close-up, below, shows just how cramped it was inside.

test his abilities against the best when an international transatlantic race was organized in 1992 with participants from a number of different countries. Richard, 29, and his flying partner Troy Bradley set off from Bangor, Maine on 16 Sep 1992 in their helium and hot-air balloon *Team USA*. They were not the first to reach Europe, but they were able to keep aloft for a sufficient time to surpass the previous duration record.

Helped by winds that took them in a southeasterly direction, they eventually landed in Africa, at Ben Slimane, not far from Casablanca, Morocco on 22 September after an exhausting flight. As with his father's record flight, they were met by a throng of curious onlookers who came to see them as they landed. Naturally, Richard was a very proud man—as he said, "That we were able to break one of his (Ben's) records made this achievement special."

Most to jump from a balloon On 12 Sep 1992, a record 15 people all parachuted from a hot-air balloon over the Somerset/Devon county line, Great Britain. The same group made a similar ascent on 1 Oct 1992, when a record 10 people jumped simultaneously from a height of 6,000 ft.

First flight over Mount Everest Two balloons—*Star Flyer 1*, piloted by Chris Dewhirst and with cameraman Leo Dickinson, and *Star Flyer 2*, piloted by Andy Elson with cameraman Eric Jones (all British)—achieved the first overflight of the summit of Mt Everest on 21 Oct 1991. The two 240,000 ft^3 balloons had the highest recorded launch of a hot-air balloon at 15,536 ft and the highest recorded touch-down of a hot-air balloon at 16,200 ft.

MODEL AIRCRAFT

Altitude, speed and duration Maynard L. Hill (USA), flying a radio-controlled model, established the world record for altitude of 26,922 ft on 6 Sep 1970.

Gianmaria Aghem (Italy) holds the closed-circuit distance record, with 769.9 miles, achieved on 26 Jul 1986.

The speed record is 242.95 mph, set by Walter Sitar (Austria) on 10 Jun 1977.

The record duration flight is one of 33 hr 39 min 15 sec by Maynard Hill, with a powered model on 1–2 Oct 1992.

An indoor model with a wound rubber motor, designed by James Richmond (USA), set a duration record of 52 min 14 sec on 31 Aug 1979.

Jean-Pierre Schiltknecht flew a solar-driven model aircraft for a duration of 10 hr 43 min 51 sec at Wetzlar, Germany on 10 Jul 1991.

Largest model glider In January 1990 *Eagle III*, a radio-controlled glider weighing 14 lb 8 oz with a wingspan of 32 ft 6 in, was designed and constructed by Carlos René Tschen and Carlos René Tschen Jr. of Colonia San Lázaro, Guatemala.

Smallest model aircraft The smallest to fly is one weighing 0.004 oz, powered by an attached horsefly and designed by insectonaut Don Emmick of Seattle, WA. On 24 Jul 1979 an Emmick flew for 5 minutes at Kirkland, WA.

PAPER AIRPLANE!

A paper plane was reported by "Chick" C.O. Reinhart to have flown 1¼ miles from a tenth-story office window at 60 Beaver Street, New York City across the East River to Brooklyn in August 1933, helped by a thermal from a coffee-roasting plant.

Paper aircraft The level flight duration record for a hand-launched paper aircraft is 16.89 sec, by Ken Blackburn in the Reynolds Coliseum, North Carolina State University, on 29 Nov 1983.

An indoor distance of 193 ft was recorded by Tony Felch at the La Crosse Center, WI on 21 May 1985.

Largest The largest flying paper airplane, with a wingspan of 30 ft 6 in, was constructed by pupils of various schools in Hampton, VA and flown on 25 Mar 1992. It was launched indoors from a 10-ft-high platform and flown for a distance of 114 ft 9 in.

ARTS & ENTERTAINMENT

ART

PAINTINGS

Largest The largest-ever painting measures 72,437 ft^2 after allowing for shrinkage of the canvas. It is made up of brightly colored squares with a "Smiley" face superimposed, and was painted by students of Robb College at Armidale, New South Wales, Australia, aided by local schoolchildren and students from neighboring colleges. The canvas was completed by its designer, Australian artist Ken Done, and unveiled at the University of New England at Armidale on 10 May 1990.

Pablo Picasso was the most prolific of the great masters. (Gamma)

Most valuable The "Mona Lisa" (*La Gioconda*) by Leonardo da Vinci (1452–1519) in the Louvre, Paris, France, was assessed for insurance purposes at $100 million for its move to Washington, D.C. and New York City for exhibition from 14 Dec 1962 to 12 Mar 1963. However, insurance was not purchased because the cost of the closest security precautions was less than that of the premiums. It was painted *c.* 1503–07 and measures 30.5 × 20.9 in.

Most prolific painter Pablo Picasso (1881–1973) was the most prolific of all painters in a career that lasted 78 years. It has been estimated that Picasso produced about 13,500 paintings or designs, 100,000 prints or engravings, 34,000 book illustrations and 300 sculptures or ceramics. The complete body of his work has been valued at over $800 million.

Finest standard paintbrush The finest standard brush sold is the 000 in Series 7 by Winsor and Newton, known as a "triple goose." It is made of 150–200 Kolinsky sable hairs weighing 0.000529 oz.

GALLERIES

Largest The world's largest art gallery is the Winter Palace and the neighboring Hermitage in St Petersburg, Russia. One has to walk 15 miles to cover all of its 322 galleries, which house nearly 3 million works of art and objects of archaeological interest.

Most heavily endowed The J. Paul Getty Museum at Malibu, CA was established with an initial $1.4 billion budget in January 1974 and now has an annual budget of $180 million for acquisitions to stock its 38 galleries.

MOSAICS

Largest The world's largest mosaic is on the walls of the central library of the Universidad Nacional Autónoma de Mexico in Mexico City. Of the four walls, the two largest measure 12,949 ft^2, and the scenes on each represent the pre-Hispanic past.

MURALS

Oldest The oldest known murals on man-made walls are clay relief leopards at Catal Hüyük in southern Anatolia, Turkey, discovered by James Malaart at level VII in 1961 and dating from *c.* 6200 B.C.

Largest *Planet Ocean*, by the artist Wyland, is the largest mural in the world, measuring 105 ft high and 1,220 ft long (128,000 ft^2). It is painted on the Long Beach Arena, CA and was completed on 4 May 1992.

POSTERS

Largest A poster measuring 236,119 ft^2 was made by the Community Youth Club of Hong Kong on 26 Oct 1993. The poster followed the theme of the International Year of the Family, and was displayed at Victoria Park, Hong Kong.

Completed in May 1992, *Planet Ocean* is the largest mural in the world. It adorns the Long Beach Arena. (Gamma/Giboux)

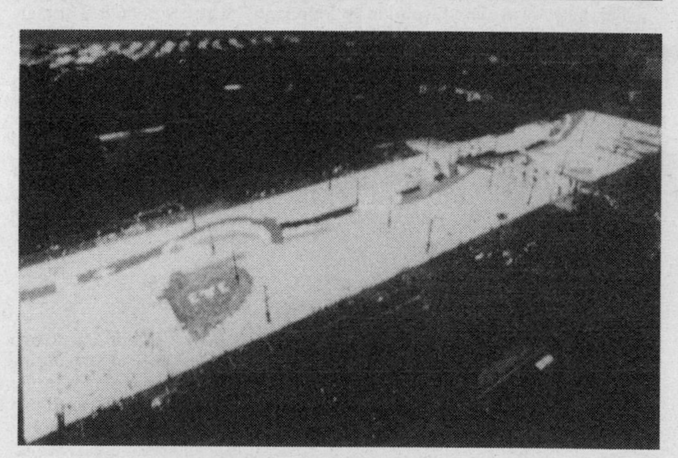

The world's largest poster was made by the Community Youth Club of Hong Kong and displayed in Victoria Park on 26 Oct 1993. (East Asia Pro Photo Lab)

SCULPTURE

Oldest An animal head carved on a woolly rhinoceros vertebra from Tolbaga, Siberia is thought to be 34,860 years old. The oldest stone figurine is a 31,790-year-old serpentine female statuette from Galgenberg, Austria. About 32,000 years ago, several ivory figurines of humans and animals were deposited in Hohler Stein, Geissenklösterle and Vogelherd caves in southern Germany. Remarkably, these are generally more sophisticated and more animated than the sculpture of subsequent periods.

Largest The mounted figures of Jefferson Davis (1808–89), Gen. Robert E. Lee (1807–70) and Gen. Thomas "Stonewall" Jackson (1824–63) cover 1.33 acres on the face of Stone Mountain, near Atlanta, GA. They are 90 ft high. Roy Faulkner was on the mountain face for 8 years 174 days with a thermo-jet torch, working with the sculptor Walker Kirtland Hancock and other helpers, from 12 Sep 1963 to 3 Mar 1972.

The largest scrap-metal sculpture was built by Sudhir Deshpande of Nashik, India and unveiled in February 1990. Named *Powerful*, the colossus weighs 30.24 tons and stands 55¾ ft tall.

Sand sculptures The longest sand sculpture ever made was the 86,535-ft-6-in-long sculpture named "The GTE Directories Ultimate Sand Castle" built by more than 10,000 volunteers at Myrtle Beach, SC on 31 May 1991.

The tallest was the "Invitation to Fairyland," which was 56 ft 2 in high, and was built by 2,000 local volunteers at Kaseda, Japan on 26 Jul 1989 under the supervision of Gerry Kirk (USA) and Shogo Tashiro (Japan).

Largest ground figures In the Nazca Desert, 185 miles south of Lima, Peru, there are straight lines (one more than 7 miles long), geometric shapes, and outlines of plants and animals that were drawn on the ground some time between 100 B.C. and A.D. 600. They were first detected from the air *c*. 1928 and have been described as the world's longest works of art.

Largest hill figures A 330-ft-tall figure was found on a hill above Tarapacá, Chile in August 1968.

HIGHEST PRICES

Painting On 15 May 1990, *Portrait of Dr Gachet* by Vincent Van Gogh (1853–90) was sold for $82.5 million at Christie's, New York. The painting depicts Van Gogh's physician and was completed only weeks before the artist's suicide in 1890. The owner was subsequently identified as Ryoei Saito, Japan's second-largest paper manufacturer.

Miniature The record price is the £352,000 ($621,632) paid by the Alexander Gallery of New York at Christie's, London on 7 Nov 1988 for a 2⅛-in-high miniature of George Washington. It was painted by the Irish-American miniaturist John Ramage (*c*. 1748–1802) in 1789.

Twentieth-century painting The record bid at auction for a 20th-century painting is $47.8 million for a self-portrait by Pablo Picasso (1881–1973), *Yo Picasso* (1901), at Sotheby's, New York on 9 May 1989.

Living artist The highest price paid at auction for a work by a living artist is $20.68 million for *Interchange*, an abstract by the American painter Willem de Kooning (b. 1904) at Sotheby's, New York on 8 Nov 1989. Painted in 1955, it was bought by Japanese dealer-collector "Mountain Tortoise."

Print The record price for a print at auction was £561,600 ($786,000) for a 1655 etching of *Christ Presented to the People* by Rembrandt (1606–69) at Christie's, London on 5 Dec 1985.

Drawing The highest price ever paid for a drawing is $8.36 million for the pen-and-ink scene *Jardin de Fleurs*, drawn by Vincent Van Gogh in Arles, France in 1888 and sold at Christie's, New York on 14 Nov 1990 to an anonymous buyer.

Poster The record price for a poster is £68,200 (*c.* $93,000) for an advertisement for the 1895 Glasgow exhibition by Charles Rennie Macintosh (1868–1928), sold at Christie's, London on 4 Feb 1993.

Sculpture The record price for a sculpture at auction is £6.82 million ($12 million) at Sotheby's, London on 7 Dec 1989 for a bronze garden ornament, *The Dancing Faun*, made by the Dutch-born sculptor Adrien de Vries (1545/6–1626). London dealer Cyril Humpris bought the figure from a couple who had paid £100 ($240) for it in the 1950s and in whose garden it had stood undiscovered for 40 years.

The highest price paid for the work of a sculptor during his lifetime is the $1,265,000 at Sotheby's, New York on 21 May 1982 for the 75-in-long elmwood *Reclining Figure* by Henry Moore (Great Britain; 1898–1986).

United States The highest price paid at auction for a sculpture by an American sculptor is $4.4 million for *Coming Through the Rye*, by Frederic Remington (1861–1909), at Christie's, New York on 25 May 1989.

ANTIQUES

All prices quoted are inclusive of the buyer's premium, and all records were set at public auction unless otherwise stated.

Art nouveau The highest auction price for any piece of art nouveau is $1.78 million for a standard lamp in the form of three lotus blossoms by the Daum Brothers and Louis Majorelle of France, sold at Sotheby's, New York on 2 Dec 1989.

Auctioneering The longest one-man auction on record was one of 60 hr. It was conducted by Reg Coates at Gosport, Great Britain from 9–11 Sep 1988.

Blanket The most expensive blanket was a Navajo Churro hand-spun serape of *c.* 1852 sold for $115,500 at Sotheby's, New York on 22 Oct 1983.

Bottle A rare Korean Punch'ong bottle was sold at Christie's, New York on 17 Nov 1993 for $376,500.

Box A Cartier jeweled vanity case, set with a fragment of an ancient Egyptian stela, was sold at Christie's, New York for $189,500 on 17 Nov 1993.

Carpet On 21 May 1992, a Louis XIV Savonnerie carpet was sold at Sotheby's, New York to a private buyer for $1.21 million.

The most expensive carpet ever made was the Spring carpet of Khusraw, made for the audience hall of the Sassanian palace at Ctesiphon, Iraq. It was about 7,000 ft² of silk and gold thread, and was encrusted with emeralds. The carpet was cut up as booty by looters in A.D. 635, and from the known realization value of the pieces must have had an original value of some $170 million.

Ceramics The highest auction price for any ceramic is £3.74 million ($6.4 million) for a Chinese Tang dynasty (A.D. 618–906) horse sold by the British Rail Pension Fund and bought by a Japanese dealer at Sotheby's, London, on 12 Dec 1989.

Furniture The highest price ever paid for a single piece of furniture is £8.58 million ($15 million) at Christie's, London on 5 Jul 1990 for the 18th-century Italian "Badminton Cabinet" owned by the Duke of Beaufort. It was bought by Barbara Piasecka Johnson of Princeton, NJ.

United States The highest price ever paid for a single piece of American furniture is $12.1 million at Christie's, New York on 3 Jun 1989 for a mahogany desk-cum-bookcase, made in the 1760s. It was bought by dealer Israel Sack.

Glass The auction record is £520,000 ($1,175,200) for a Roman glass cage-cup of *c.* A.D. 300, measuring 7 in in diameter and 4 in in height, sold at Sotheby's, London, on 4 Jun 1979 to Robin Symes.

Guns A .45 caliber Colt single-action army revolver, Serial No. 1 from 1873 was sold for $242,000 at Christie's New York on 14 May 1987.

Helmet The highest price ever paid for an item of headwear is $66,000 by the Alaska State Museum at an auction in New York City in November 1981 for a native North American Tlingit Kiksadi ceremonial frog helmet dating from *c.* 1600.

Jewelry The world's largest jewelry auction, which included a Van Cleef and Arpels 1939 ruby and diamond necklace, realized over $50 million when the collection belonging to the Duchess of Windsor (1896–1986) was sold at Sotheby's, Geneva, Switzerland on 3 Apr 1987.

The highest auction price for individual items of jewelry is $6.2 million for two pear-shaped diamond drop earrings of 58.6 and 61 carats bought and sold anonymously at Sotheby's, Geneva on 14 Nov 1980.

A Harry Winston diamond necklace was bought for $4.40 million at Sotheby's, New York on 14 Apr 1994 by Saudi Arabian businessman Ahmed Fitahi.

Music box The highest price paid for a music box is £20,900 ($22,990) for a Swiss example made for a Persian prince in 1901 and sold at Sotheby's, London on 23 Jan 1985.

Playing cards The highest price for a deck of playing cards is $143,352, paid by the Metropolitan Museum of Art, New York City at Sotheby's, London on 6 Dec 1983.

The highest price paid for a single card was $7,450 for a card used as currency in Canada dated 1717. It was sold by Yasha Beresiner to Lars Karlson (Sweden) in October 1990.

Silver The record for silver is $3,386,440 for a Hanover chandelier from the collection of M. Hubert de Givenchy, sold at Christie's, Monaco on 4 Dec 1993.

Surgical instrument The record price for a surgical instrument was $34,848 for a mid-19th century German mechanical chain saw sold at Christie's, London on 19 Aug 1993.

Tapestry The highest auction price for a tapestry is £638,000 ($1,124,794), paid by Swiss dealer Peter Kleiner at Christie's, London on 3 Jul 1990 for a fragment of a rare Swiss example woven near Basle in the 1430s.

Toy The most expensive antique toy was sold for $231,000 to an anonymous telephone bidder at Christie's, New York on 14 Dec 1991. The work is a hand-painted tinplate replica of the "Charles" hose reel, a piece of fire-fighting equipment pulled by two firemen, measuring 15 × 23 in and built *c*. 1870 by George Brown & Co. of Forestville, CT.

LANGUAGE

Oldest English words The parent language of English and the other Indo-European languages is thought to have been spoken before 3,000 B.C., and to have split into different languages over the period 3,000–2,000 B.C. According to research completed in 1989, about 40 words of a proto–Indo-European substratum survive in English, among them apple (apal), bad (bad), gold (gol) and tin (tin).

Commonest language The language used by more people than any other is Chinese, spoken by an estimated 1 billion people. The so-called "common language" (*pǔtōnghuà*) is the standard form of Chinese, with a pronunciation based on that of Beijing. It is known in Taiwan as *guoyu* ("national speech") and in the West as Mandarin.

The most widespread language is English, with a conservative estimate of 800 million speakers, rising to a more generous estimate of 1.5 billion. Of these, some 350 million are native speakers, of whom 220 million are in the United States.

Most complex The following extremes of complexity have been noted: the

Ample language of Papua New Guinea has the most verb forms, with over 69,000 finite forms and 860 infinitive forms of the verb; Haida, a North American Indian language, has the most prefixes, with 70; Tabassaran, a language of Daghestan, Azerbaijan, uses the most noun cases, 48; and Inuit uses 63 forms of the present tense, and simple nouns have as many as 252 inflections.

Fewest irregular verbs The artificial language Esperanto, with no irregular verbs, was first published by its inventor, Dr Ludwig Zamenhof (1859–1917) of Warsaw, Poland in 1887. It is now estimated (by textbook sales) to have a million speakers worldwide. The even earlier interlanguage Volapük, invented by Johann Martin Schleyer (1831–1912), also has absolutely regular configuration.

Most irregular verbs According to *The Morphology and Syntax of Present-day English* by Prof. Olu Tomori, English has 283 irregular verbs, 30 of which are formed merely by adding prefixes.

Rarest sounds The rarest speech sound is probably that written "ř" in Czech and termed a "rolled post-alveolar fricative." In the southern Bushman language !xo there is a click articulated with both lips, which is written ʘ. This sound, essentially a kiss, is termed a "velaric ingressive bilabial stop." In some contexts the "l" sound in the Arabic word *Allah* is pronounced uniquely in that language.

Dr Harold Williams (right) spoke 58 languages fluently. He was the only person to attend the League of Nations and converse with all the delegates in their own languages.

LANGUAGES!

Papua New Guinea has, because of its many isolated valleys, the greatest concentration of separate languages in the world, with an estimated 869; each language has about 4,000 speakers.

Commonest sound No language is known to be without the vowel "a" (as in the English "father").

Vocabulary The English language contains about 616,500 words plus another 400,000 technical terms, the most in any language, but it is doubtful if any individual speaker uses more than 60,000. William Shakespeare, for instance, employed a vocabulary of only *c.* 33,000 words.

Greatest linguist The world's greatest linguist is believed to have been Dr Harold Williams of New Zealand (1876–1928), a journalist. He was reputed to speak 58 languages and many dialects fluently.

Living The greatest living linguist is Ziad Fazah (Brazil; b. 10 Jul 1954), who speaks and writes 58 languages. He was tested in a live interview in Athens, Greece on 30 Jul 1991, when he surprised members of the audience by talking to them in their various native tongues.

Alexander Schwartz of New York City *worked* with 31 languages as a translator for the United Nations between 1962 and 1986.

Debating Students at St Andrews Presbyterian College in Laurinburg, NC, together with staff and friends, debated the motion "There's no place like home" for 517 hr 45 min from 4–26 Apr 1992. The aim of the debate was to increase awareness of the problems of being homeless.

ALPHABET

Earliest The earliest known example of alphabetic writing was found at Ugarit (now Ras Sharma), Syria, dated to *c.* 1450 B.C. It comprised a clay tablet of 32 cuneiform letters.

Oldest letter The letter "O" is unchanged in shape since its adoption in the Phoenician alphabet *c.* 1,300 B.C.

Newest letters The newest letters to be added to the English alphabet are "j" and "v," which are of post-Shakespearean use (*c.* 1630). Formerly they were used only as variants of "i" and "u."

Longest The language with the most letters in its alphabet is Cambodian, with 74.

Shortest Rotokas of central Bougainville Island, Papua New Guinea has the fewest letters, with 11 (a, b, e, g, i, k, o, p, ř, t and u).

Most and fewest consonants The language with the greatest number of distinct consonantal sounds was Ubykh in the Caucasus, with 80–85. Ubykh speakers migrated from the Caucasus to Turkey in the 19th century and the language is now obsolete. The language with the fewest consonants is Rotokas, which has only six.

Most and fewest vowels The language with the most vowels is Sedang, a central Vietnamese language with 55 distinguishable vowel sounds, and the one with the fewest is the Caucasian language Abkhazian, with two.

Smallest letters Scanning tunneling microscope (STM) techniques pioneered in April 1990 by physicists Donald Eigler and Erhard Schweizer at IBM's Almaden Research Center in San Jose, CA have enabled single atoms of various elements to be manipulated to form characters and pictures.

WORDS

Longest Lengthy concatenations and some compound or agglutinative words or nonce words are or have been written in the closed-up style of a single word. The longest known example is a compound "word" of 195 Sanskrit characters (which transliterates into 428 letters in the Roman alphabet) describing the region near Kanci, Tamil Nadu, India. The word appears in a 16th-century work by Tirumalāmbā, Queen of Vijayanagara.

English The longest word in the *Oxford English Dictionary* is *pneumonoultramicroscopicsilicovolcanoconiosis* (*-koniosis*), which has 45 letters and allegedly means "a lung disease caused by the inhalation of very fine silica dust." It is, however, described as "factitious" by the editors of the dictionary.

Longest scientific name The systematic name for *deoxyribonucleic acid* (DNA) of the human mitochondria contains 16,569 nucleotide residues and is thus *c*. 207,000 letters long. It was published in key form in *Nature* on 9 Apr 1981.

Longest palindromes The longest known palindromic word (a word that reads the same backward or forward) is *saippuakivikauppias* (19 letters), which is Finnish for "a dealer in lye" (caustic soda). The longest in English is *tattarrattat*, with 12 letters, which appears in the *Oxford English Dictionary*.

Some baptismal fonts in Greece and Turkey bear the circular 25-letter inscription NIψON ANOMHMATA MH.M.ONAN OψIN, meaning "wash (my) sins not only (my) face."

Longest anagrams The longest nonscientific English words that can form anagrams are the 17-letter transpositions *representationism* and *misrepresentation*. The longest scientific transposals are *hydroxydesoxycorticosterone* and *hydroxydeoxycorticosterones*, with 27 letters.

Abbreviations *Longest* The initials S.K.O.M.K.H.P.K.J.C.D.P.W.B., which stand for the Syarikat Kerjasama Orang-orang Melayu Kerajaan Hilir Perak Kerana Jimat Cermat Dan Pinjam-meminjam Wang Berhad, are the Malay name for The Cooperative Company of the Lower State of Perak

LONGEST WORDS

Japanese[1] Chi-n-chi-ku-ri-n (12 letters)
a very short person (slang)

Spanish Superextraordinarisimo (22)
extraordinary

French Anticonstitutionnellement (25)
anticonstitutionally

Italian Precipitevolissimevolmente (26)
as fast as possible

Portuguese Inconstitucionalissimamente (27)
with the highest degree of unconstitutionality

Icelandic Haecstaréttarmálaflutningsmaôur (29 Icelandic letters, transliterating as 31)
supreme court barrister

Russian Ryentgyenoelyektrokardiografichyeskogo (33 Cyrillic letters, transliterating as 38)
of the X-ray electrocardiographic

Hungarian Megszentségtelenithetetlenségeskedéseitekért (44)
for your unprofanable actions

Dutch[2] Kindercarnavalsoptochtvoorbereidingswerkzaamheden (49)
preparation activities for a children's carnival procession

Mohawk[3] Tkanuhstasrihsranuhwe'tsraaksahsrakaratattsrayeri' (50)
the praising of the evil of the liking of the finding of the house is right

Turkish[2] Cekoslovakyalılastırabilemediklerimizlerdenmisiniz (50)
"are you not of that group of persons that we were said to be unable to Czechoslovakianize?"

German[2,4] Donaudampfschiffahrtselektrizitaetenhauptbetriebswerkbauunterbeamtengesellschaft (80)
The club for subordinate officials of the head office management of the Danube steamboat electrical services (name of a prewar club in Vienna)

Swedish[2] Nordöstersjökustartilleriflygspaningssimulatoranläggningsmaterielunderhåsuppföljningssystemdiskussionsinläggsförberedelsearbeten (130)
Preparatory work on the contribution to the discussion on the maintaining system of support of the material of the aviation survey simulator device within the northeast part of the coastartillery of the Baltic

[1] *Patent applications sometimes harbor long compound "words." An extreme example is one of 13 kana (Japanese syllabary) which transliterates to the 40-letter Kyūkitsūrohekimenfuchakunenryosekisanryo meaning "the accumulated amount of fuel condensed on the wall face of the air intake passage."*

[2] *Agglutinative words are limited only by imagination and are not found in standard dictionaries. The first 100-letter such word was published in 1975 by the late Eric Rosenthal in Afrikaans.*

[3] *Lengthy concatenations are a feature of Mohawk.*

[4] *The longest dictionary word in everyday usage is Rechtsschutzversicherungsgesellschaften (39) meaning "insurance companies which provide legal protection."*

Government's Malay People for Money Savings and Loans Ltd, in Teluk Anson, Perak, West Malaysia (formerly Malaya). The abbreviation for this abbreviation is Skomk.

Shortest The 55-letter full name of Los Angeles (El Pueblo de Nuestra Señora la Reina de los Angeles de Porciuncula) is abbreviated to L.A., or 3.63 percent of its length.

Longest acronym The longest acronym is NIIOMTPLABOPARMBETZHELBETRABSBOMONIMONKONOTDTEKHSTROMONT with 56 letters (54 in Cyrillic) in the *Concise Dictionary of Soviet Terminology, Institutions and Abbreviations (1969)*, meaning: the Laboratory for Shuttering, Reinforcement, Concrete and Ferroconcrete Operations for Composite-monolithic and Monolithic Constructions of the Department of the Technology of Building-Assembly Operations of the Scientific Research Institute of the Organization for Building Mechanization and Technical Aid of the Academy of Building and Architecture of the USSR.

Commonest words and letters The most frequently used words in written English are, in descending order of frequency: *the, of, and, to, a, in, that, is, I, it, for* and *as*. The most commonly used in conversation is "*I*." The commonest letter is "e." More words begin with the letter "s" than with any other, but the most commonly *used* initial letter is "t" as in "the," "to," "that" or "there."

Most meanings The most overworked word in English is "set," to which Dr Charles Onions (1873–1965) of Oxford University Press gave 58 uses as a noun, 126 uses as a verb and 10 as a participial adjective.

Most synonyms The condition of being inebriated has more synonyms than any other condition or object. *Dickson's Word Treasury*, compiled by Paul Dickson of Garrett Park, MD, and published in 1992, contains a list of 2,660 synonyms for that condition.

PERSONAL NAMES

Oldest The oldest surviving personal name seems to be that of a predynastic king of Upper Egypt *ante* 3,050 B.C., who is represented by the hieroglyphic sign for a scorpion. It has been suggested that the name should be read as Sekhen.

NAME!

The longest name appearing on a birth certificate is that of Rhoshandiatellyneshiaunneveshenk Koyaanfsquatsiuty Williams, born to Mr and Mrs James Williams in Beaumont, TX on 12 Sep 1984. On 5 Oct 1984 the father filed an amendment that expanded his daughter's first name to 1,019 letters and her middle name to 36 letters.

Most first names Laurence Watkins (b. 9 Jun 1965) of Auckland, New Zealand claims a total of 2,310 first names, added by deed poll in 1991 after official opposition by the registrar and a prolonged court battle.

Shortest family names The commonest single-letter surname is "O," which is prevalent in Korea. Every other letter, except "Q," has been traced as a surname in US telephone books by A. Ross Eckler.

Commonest family name The commonest surname in the English-speaking world is Smith. There are an estimated 2,382,509 Smiths in the United States.

Most contrived name In the United States the determination to derive commercial or other benefit from being the last listing in the local telephone book has resulted in self-given names starting with up to nine "Z's"—an extreme example being Zachary Zzzzzzzzzra in the San Francisco book.

PLACE-NAMES

Oldest The world's oldest place-names are pre-Sumerian, e.g., Kish, Ur and the now-lost Attara. These names have survived from before *c.* 3,600 B.C.

Longest The official name for Bangkok, the capital city of Thailand, is Krungthep Mahanakhon. However, the full name is Krungthep Mahanakhon Bovorn Ratanakosin Mahintharayutthaya Mahadilokpop Noparatratchathani Burirom Udomratchanivet mahasathan Amornpiman Avatarnsathit Sakkathattiyavisnukarmprasit (167 letters), which in its most scholarly transliteration emerges with 175 letters.

The longest place-name now in use in the world is Taumatawhakatangihangakoauauotamateaturipukakapikimaungahoronukupokaiwhenuakitanatahu, the unofficial 85-letter version of the name of a hill (1,002 ft above sea level) in the Southern Hawke's Bay district of North Island, New Zealand. The Maori translation means "The place where Tamatea, the man with the big knees, who slid, climbed and swallowed mountains, known as land-eater, played his flute to his loved one."

The longest place-name in the United States is Lake Chargoggu-goggmonchauggagoggchaubunagungamaug near Webster, MA. The 44-letter name of this two-square-mile lake is derived from the Algonquin Indian "You fish on your side, we fish on our side; nobody fish in the middle." The standardized version has been reduced to Lake Chaubunagungamaug by the United States Board on Geographic Names.

Shortest The shortest place-names consist of just single letters, and examples of these can be found in various countries around the world. There was once a town called "6" in West Virginia.

Most spellings The spelling of the Dutch town of Leeuwarden has been recorded in 225 versions since A.D. 1046.

LITERATURE

Oldest Tokens or tallies from Tepe Asiab and Ganji-I-Dareh Tepe in Iran have been dated to 8,500 B.C. The earliest written language discovered is on Yangshao culture pottery from Paa-t'o in the Shaanxi province of China, found in 1962. This bears proto-characters for the numbers 5, 7 and 8 and has been dated to 5,000–4,000 B.C.

Paper dated to between 71 B.C. and A.D. 21, i.e., 100 years earlier than the previous presumed date for paper's invention, has been found in northwest China.

Oldest book The oldest handwritten book, still intact, is a Coptic Psalter dated to about 1,600 years ago, found in 1984 at Beni Suef, Egypt.

Oldest mechanically printed The oldest surviving printed work is the Dharani scroll or *sutra* from wooden printing blocks found in the foundations of the Pulguk Sa pagoda, Kyŏngju, South Korea on 14 Oct 1966. It has been dated to no later than A.D. 704.

It is widely accepted that the earliest mechanically printed full-length book was the 42-line-per-page Gutenberg Bible, printed in Mainz, Germany *c.* 1454 by Johann Henne zum Gensfleisch zur Laden, called "zu Gutenberg" (*c.* 1398–1468). The earliest exactly dated printed work is the Psalter completed on 14 Aug 1457 by Johann Fust (*c.* 1400–66) and Peter Schöffer (1425–1502), who had been Gutenberg's chief assistant.

Smallest book The smallest marketed bound printed book is one printed on 22 gsm paper measuring 1/25 × 1/25 in, comprising the children's story *Old King Cole!* and published in 85 copies in March 1985 by The Gleniffer Press of Paisley, Great Britain. The pages can be turned (with care) only by the use of a needle.

Largest publications The largest publication ever compiled was the *Yongle Dadian* (the great thesaurus of the Yongle reign) of 22,937 manuscript chapters (370 of which still survive) in 11,095 volumes. It was written by 2,000 Chinese scholars in 1403–08.

Dictionaries *Deutsches Wörterbuch*, started by Jacob and Wilhelm Grimm in 1854, was completed in 1971 and consists of 34,519 pages and 33 volumes.

The largest English-language dictionary is the 20-volume *Oxford English Dictionary*, with 21,728 pages. The first edition was published between 1884 and 1928. Published in March 1989, the second edition defines a total of 616,500 word-forms, with 2,412,400 illustrative quotations and approximately 350 million letters and figures. The longest entry in the second edition is that for the verb *set*, with over 75,000 words of text.

The largest English-language dictionary published in the United States is *Webster's Third New International Dictionary Unabridged*, published in 1986 by Merriam-Webster, Inc. It defines 472,300 word-forms, with 9,370 illustrative quotations and approximately 60 million letters and numerics. The longest entry is for the verb *turn*, with over 5,500 words of text.

Encyclopedias Largest The largest encyclopedia ever compiled was the Chinese *Yongle Dadian* (See Largest publications.)

Currently, the largest encyclopedia is *La Enciclopedia Universal Ilustrada Europeo-Americana* (J. Espasa & Sons, Madrid and Barcelona), totaling 105,000 pages, with an annual supplement since 1935. The encyclopedia comprises 165.2 million words. The number of volumes in the set in August 1983 was 104, and the price $2,325.

Fiction The novel *Tokuga-Wa Ieyasu* by Sohachi Yamaoka has been serialized in Japanese daily newspapers since 1951. Now completed, it will require nearly 40 volumes.

MAPS

Oldest A clay tablet depicting the river Euphrates flowing through northern Mesopotamia (Iraq) dates to *c.* 2250 B.C. The earliest printed map in the world is one of western China dated to 1115.

Largest The largest permanent, two-dimensional atlas measures 49,000 ft^2 and was painted by students of O'Hara Park School, Oakley, CA in the summer of 1992.

Relief The Challenger relief map of British Columbia, Canada, measuring 6,080 ft^2, was designed and built in the period 1945–52 by the late George Challenger and his son Robert. It is now on display at the Pacific National Exhibition in Vancouver, British Columbia.

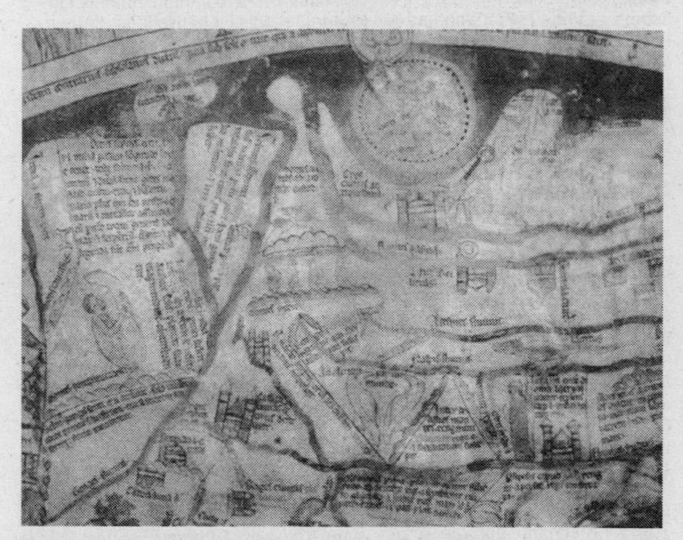

Ptolemy's *Cosmographia* is the most expensive map ever sold at auction. (E.T. Archive/British Library)

Smallest In 1992 Dr Jonathon Mamin of IBM's Zurich laboratory used sudden electrical impulses to create a map of the Western Hemisphere from atoms. The map has a scale of one trillion to one, and a diameter of about one micron or 1/100th of the diameter of a human hair.

Most expensive The highest price paid for an atlas is $1,925,000 for a copy of Ptolemy's *Cosmographia*, which was sold at Sotheby's, New York City on 31 Jan 1990.

HIGHEST PRICES

Book The highest price paid for any book is £8.14 million ($11.9 million) for the 226-leaf manuscript *The Gospel Book of Henry the Lion, Duke of Saxony* at Sotheby's, London on 6 Dec 1983. The book, which measures 13½ × 10 in, was illuminated *c.* 1170 by the monk Herimann at Helmershansen Abbey, Germany with 41 full-page illustrations.

The highest price ever paid for a *printed* book is $5.39 million for an Old Testament (Genesis to the Psalms) Gutenberg Bible printed in 1455 in Mainz, Germany. It was bought by Tokyo booksellers Maruzen Co. Ltd at Christie's New York on 22 Oct 1987.

Broadsheet The highest price ever paid for a broadsheet was $2,420,000 for one of the 24 known copies of the Declaration of Independence, printed by John Dunlap in Philadelphia, PA in 1776, and sold to Donald J. Scheer of Atlanta, GA on 13 Jun 1991.

Manuscript The highest price ever paid for a complete manuscript is £2.97 million ($11.4 million) by London dealers Quaritch at Sotheby's, London on 29 Nov 1990 for the 13th-century *Northumberland Bestiary*, a colorful and heavily illustrated encyclopedia of real and imaginary animals.

United States On 16 Dec 1992, a Lincoln manuscript was sold for $1.54 million. The one-page script was written in preparation for a speech. It is the first surviving formulation of his "house divided" doctrine, written in the winter of 1857 or 1858. The manuscript was bought by Seth Kaller of Kaller Historical Documents.

Musical The auction record for a musical manuscript is $4,394,500 at Sotheby's, London on 22 May 1987 for a 508-page, 8½ × 6½ in bound volume of nine complete symphonies in Mozart's hand. The manuscript is owned by Robert Owen Lehman and is on deposit at the Pierpont Morgan Library in New York City.

The record price paid for a single musical manuscript is £1.1 million (*c.* $2 million), paid at Sotheby's, London on 6 Dec 1991 for the autograph copy of the Piano Sonata in E minor, opus 90, by Ludwig van Beethoven (1770–1827).

DIARIES AND LETTERS

Longest-kept diary Col. Ernest Loftus of Harare, Zimbabwe began his daily diary on 4 May 1896 at the age of 12 and continued it until his death on 7 Jul 1987 at the age of 103 years 178 days. George C. Edler (1889–1987) of Bethesda, MD kept a handwritten diary continuously from 20 Sep 1909, a total of 78 years.

Victor Hugo holds the record for producing the shortest correspondence. He wrote "?" to his publishers in 1862, and received the reply "!" (Archiv für Kunst und Geschichte, Berlin)

Longest and most letters Uichi Noda, from July 1961 until his bedridden wife Mitsu's death in March 1985, wrote her 1,307 letters amounting to 5 million characters during his overseas trips. These letters have been published in 25 volumes totaling 12,404 pages. Rev. Canon Bill Cook and his fiancée/wife Helen of Diss, Great Britain exchanged 6,000 love letters during their 4¼ year separation from March 1942–May 1946.

Shortest correspondence The shortest correspondence on record was that between Victor Marie Hugo (1802–85) and his publisher, Hurst and Blackett, in 1862. The author was on vacation and was anxious to know how his new novel *Les Misérables* was selling. He wrote "?" and received the reply "!"

Pen pals The longest sustained correspondence on record is one of 75 years between Mrs Ida McDougall of Tasmania, Australia and Miss R. Norton of Sevenoaks, Great Britain from 11 Nov 1904 until Mrs McDougall's death on 24 Dec 1979.

Most Christmas cards The greatest number of personal Christmas cards sent by an individual is believed to be 62,824, by Werner Erhard of San Francisco, CA in December 1975.

Bill in Italy in 1944.
Helen in 1942, a year after they met.

MOST LOVE LETTERS

Reverend Canon Bill Cook and Helen Appleton first met in the summer of 1941 when Bill was a 27-year-old Army Chaplain and Helen was a student, aged 21, living with her father in Diss, Great Britain. It was love at first sight. After a courtship lasting two months, and shortly before Bill was due to take up an overseas post, the couple became engaged. Separated by war, they did not even know when they would eventually be able to marry, and they began exchanging letters that fervently expressed their mutual love and devotion. During the course of their 4¼-year separation, from March 1942 to May 1946, they exchanged a record 6,000 love letters. They celebrated their fortieth wedding anniversary on 23 Aug 1985 and have now been married 49 years.

Helen and Bill Cook.

Christmas card exchange Frank Rose of Burnaby, British Columbia, Canada and Gordon Loutet of Lake Cowichan, British Columbia have exchanged the same Christmas card every year since 1929.

Warren Nord of Mesa, AZ and Thor (Tut) Andersen (d. 11 Sep 1988) of Ashtabula, OH exchanged the same Christmas card every year from 1930–87.

AUTOGRAPHS AND SIGNATURES

Oldest The earliest surviving examples of autographs are those made by scribes on cuneiform clay tablets from Tell Abu Salābīkh, Iraq dated to the early Dynastic III A period *c.* 2,600 B.C. A scribe named "a-du" has added "dub-sar" after his name, translating to "Adu, scribe." The earliest surviving signature on a papyrus is that of the scribe Amen-'aa, held in the St Petersburg Museum, Russia and dated to the Egyptian Middle Kingdom, which began *c.* 2,130 B.C.

Most expensive The highest price ever paid on the open market for a single signed autograph letter was $748,000 on 5 Dec 1991 at Christie's, New York for a letter written by Abraham Lincoln on 8 Jan 1863 defending the Emancipation Proclamation. It was sold to Profiles in History of Beverly Hills, CA.

Rarest and most valuable Only one example of the signature of Christopher Marlowe (1564–93) is known. It is in the County Archives in Kent, Great Britain on a will of 1583.

The only known document that bears eleven US presidential signatures is a letter sent by President Franklin Delano Roosevelt to Richard C. Corbyn, then of Dallas (now of Amarillo), TX, dated 26 Oct 1932. It was subsequently signed by Herbert Hoover, Harry S. Truman, Dwight D. Eisenhower, Gerald Ford, Lyndon Johnson, Jimmy Carter, Ronald Reagan, George Bush and Bill Clinton. Richard Nixon's first signature was signed with an auto-pen but he later re-signed it.

AUTHORS

Most prolific A lifetime output of 72–75 million words has been calculated for Charles Harold St John Hamilton, alias Frank Richards (1876–1961), the creator of Billy Bunter. In his peak years (1915–26) he wrote up to 80,000 words a week for the boys' school weeklies *Gem* (1907–39), *Magnet* (1908–40) and *Boys' Friend*, published in Great Britain.

Novels The greatest number of novels published is 904, by Kathleen Lindsay (Mrs Mary Faulkner; 1903–73) of Somerset West, Cape Province, South Africa. She wrote under two other married names and eight pen names.

Baboorao Arnalkar (b. 9 Jun 1907) of Maharashtra State, India published 1,092 short mystery stories in book form and several nonfiction books between 1936 and 1984.

Top-selling The world's top-selling writer of fiction is Dame Agatha Christie (nee Miller, later Lady Mallowan, 1890–1976), whose 78 crime novels have sold an estimated 2 billion copies in 44 languages. Agatha Christie also wrote 19 plays and six romantic novels under the pseudonym

Mary Westmacott. Royalty earnings from her works are estimated to be worth $4.25 million per year.

Highest-paid author per word In 1958 Mrs Deborah Schneider of Minneapolis, MN wrote 25 words to complete a sentence in a competition for the best slogan for Plymouth cars. She beat about 1.4 million other entrants to win a prize of $500 every month for life. Based on normal life expectancy, she should collect $12,000 per word. No known anthology includes Mrs Schneider's deathless prose, but it is in her safe deposit box at her bank, "Only to be opened after death," because the company feared complaints from other disgruntled contestants.

Oldest The oldest author in the world was Alice Pollock (nee Wykeham-Martin, 1868–1971) of Haslemere, Great Britain. Her first book, *Portrait of My Victorian Youth* (Johnson Publications), was published in March 1971, when she was aged 102 years 8 months.

Most pseudonyms The writer with the greatest number of pseudonyms is the minor Russian humorist Konstantin Arsenievich Mikhailov (b. 1868), whose 325 pen names are listed in the *Dictionary of Pseudonyms* by I.F. Masanov, published in Moscow in 1960. The names, ranging from Ab. to Z, were mostly abbreviations of his real name.

Longest poem The longest poem ever published was the Kirghiz folk epic *Manas*, which appeared in printed form in 1958 but has never been translated into English. According to the *Dictionary of Oriental Literatures*, this three-part epic runs to about 500,000 lines.

The longest poem ever written in the English language is one on the life of King Alfred by John Fitchett (1766–1838) of Liverpool, Great Britain, which ran to 129,807 lines and took 40 years to write. His editor, Robert Riscoe, added the concluding 2,585 lines.

Longest literary gestation *Acta Sanctorum*, begun by Jean Bolland in 1643, arranged according to saints' days, reached the month of November in 1925, and an introduction for December was published in 1940.

BEST-SELLING BOOKS

The world's best-selling and most widely distributed book is the Bible, with an estimated 2.5 billion copies sold between 1815 and 1975. By the end of 1993, the whole Bible had been translated into 337 languages; 2,062 languages have translations of at least one book of the Bible. The oldest publisher of bibles is the Cambridge University Press, which began with the Geneva version in 1591.

Excluding versions of the Bible, the world's all-time best-selling book is *The Guinness Book of Records*, first published in October 1955 by the Guinness Brewery and edited by Norris Dewar McWhirter (b. 12 Aug 1925) and his twin brother Alan Ross McWhirter (1925–75). Global sales in 43 languages surpassed 74 million in May 1993.

Best-seller lists The longest duration on the *New York Times* best-seller list (founded 1935) has been for *The Road Less Traveled* by M. Scott Peck, which had its 559th week on the list, as of 24 Jul 1994.

Slowest seller The prize for the world's slowest-selling book (a category known in publishing as slooow sellers) probably belongs to David Wilkins' translation of the New Testament from Coptic into Latin, published by Oxford University Press (OUP) in 1716 in a printing of 500 copies. Selling an average of one copy every 20 weeks, the book remained in print for 191 years.

PRINTERS AND PUBLISHERS

Largest printers The largest printers in the world are Dai Nippon Printing Co. Ltd. of Tokyo, Japan. Net sales as of 31 Mar 1993 were 1.19 trillion yen ($14 billion). The DNP Group employs approximately 35,000 people.

The largest printers in the United States are believed to be R.R. Donnelley & Sons Co. of Chicago, IL. The company, founded in 1864, has 130 manufacturing facilities, offices, service centers and subsidiaries worldwide, turning out $4.4 billion worth of work in 1993.

The largest printer under one roof is the United States Government Printing Office (founded 1861) in Washington, D.C. Encompassing 34.4 acres of floor space, the central office processes an average of 1,464 print orders daily, and uses 93.2 million lb of paper each year.

MOST VALUABLE LITERATURE PRIZE

The Nobel Prize is the most valuable award for literature, and was worth SwKr6.7 million (about $825,000) in 1993. To date 32 different countries (counting Germany as two) have produced winners, the latest being St Lucia, birthplace of poet Derek Walcott, the 1992 literature prize winner. The award has been declined twice, by Boris Pasternak (1890–1960) in 1958 and by Jean-Paul Sartre (1905–80) in 1964.

The table shows those countries with more than one winner.

Country	Winners
France	**12**
United States	**11**
Great Britain	**8**
Sweden	**6**
Germany	**5**
Italy	**5**
Spain	**5**
Denmark	**3**
Netherlands	**3**
Poland	**3**
USSR (former)	**3**
Chile	**2**
Greece	**2**
Republic of Ireland	**2**
Switzerland	**2**

BY THE BOOK

On 5 Aug 1993, the record for the fastest publishing of a book was broken resoundingly at the annual Zimbabwe Book Fair. The book was an anthology of Zimbabwean poetry and prose on the importance of reading and learning. The final production was more than twice as fast as the previous world record.

Before the record attempt began, and in full view of the visitors at the book fair, authors, editors, sub-editors, proofreaders, illustrators and typesetters worked together to produce the required copy on computer by the evening of Thursday 5 August. They completed their work within one day. Then the record-breaker really began: the printers were standing by to print the book against the clock; starting at 4:04 p.m., they completed it in less than five and a half hours. By the end of the evening they had exceeded even their own target, printing a total of 2,000 copies of the publication.

To improve their record even further, the book was also produced in four other formats on the same day: Braille (8 hours 19 min), Large Print (8 hours 18 min), and CD-ROM and audio-tape (11 hours 26 min).

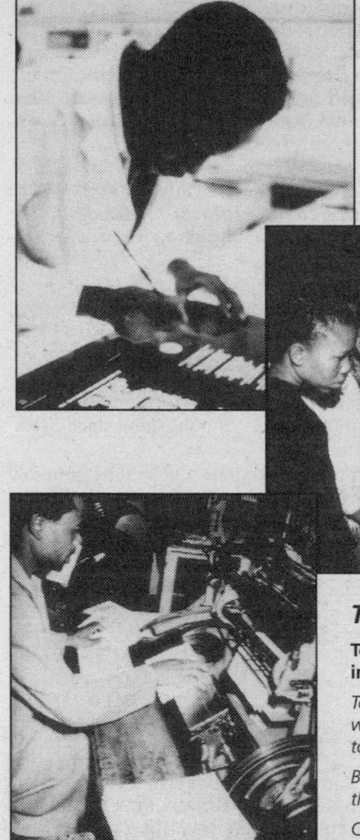

THE CHALLENGE

To print 1,000 books of 100 pages in less than 12 hours.

Text: Printed 1 color throughout with about 8 line drawings from disk to ready copy

Binding: Sections of text folded and thread-sewn into covers

Cover: Printed two colors on one side only from copy

(All photos: Zimbabwe International Book Fair Trust)

Fastest printer The world's fastest printer was the Radiation Inc. electrosensitive system at the Lawrence Radiation Laboratory, Livermore, CA. It printed up to 36,000 lines per minute, each line containing 120 alphanumeric characters, by controlling electronic pulses through chemically impregnated recording paper that moved rapidly under closely spaced fixed styli. The system could print the entire wordage of the Bible (773,692 words) in 65 seconds.

Highest printings It is believed that in the United States, Van Antwerp Bragg and Co. printed some 60 million copies of the 1879 edition of *The McGuffey Reader*, compiled by Henry Vail in the pre-copyright era for distribution to public schools.

Oldest publishers Cambridge University Press has a continuous history of printing and publishing since 1584. The University received a Royal Letters Patent to print and sell all manner of books on 20 Jul 1534.

United States The firm of Williams and Wilkins (formerly Lea and Febiger) of Malvern, PA has a continuous history of publishing since 1785.

Most prolific publisher At its peak in 1989, Progress Publishers (founded in 1931 as the Publishing Association of Foreign Workers in the former USSR) of Moscow, Russia printed over 750 titles in 50 languages annually.

Fastest publishing Two thousand bound copies of *The Book Fair Book*, published by the Zimbabwe International Book Fair Trust and printed by Print Holdings (Pvt) Ltd, were produced from raw disk in 5 hr 23 min at the Zimbabwe International Book Fair in Harare on 5 Aug 1993. The time for 1,000 copies was 4 hr 50 min. Braille, large print, CD-ROM and audiotape formats were produced simultaneously.

BOOKSTORES

The bookstore with the most titles and the longest shelving (30 miles) in the world is W. & G. Foyle Ltd of London, Great Britain. First established in 1904 in a small store, the company now has a site covering 75,825 ft^2.

The most capacious individual bookstore in the world measured by square footage is the Barnes & Noble Bookstore at 105 Fifth Ave at 18th Street, New York City. It covers 154,250 ft^2 and has 12.87 miles of shelving.

LIBRARIES

Earliest One of the earliest known collections of archival material was that of King Ashurbanipal at Nineveh (668–627 B.C.). He had clay tablets referring to events and personages as far back as the Dynasty of Agode *c.* 23rd century B.C.

United States The first library in America was established at Harvard University in 1638. The first subscription library in the country was the Philadelphia Library Company in 1731. The first library in America that meets the definition of a modern public library was in Peterboro, NH, established on 9 Apr 1833. The original collection contained 700 books.

The Library of Congress is the world's largest library. Founded in 1800, it has 575 miles of shelving and stores over 100 million items, including more than 15 million books. (Library of Congress)

Largest The United States Library of Congress (founded on 24 Apr 1800) in Washington, D.C. contains 104,834,652 items, including 16,055,353 books in the classified collections and 88,779,299 items in the nonclassified collections. As of May 1993 there were 575 miles of shelving. The Library of Congress employs 5,050 people.

Nonstatutory The largest nonstatutory library in the world is the New York Public Library (founded 1895) on Fifth Avenue, New York City with a floor space of 525,276 ft^2 and 172 miles of shelving, plus an underground extension with the capacity for an additional 84 miles. Its collection, including 82 branch libraries, embraces 4.6 million volumes and 38 million items of research material.

Public The largest public library in the United States is the Harold Washington Library Center, Chicago, IL, which opened on 7 Oct 1991. The ten-story, 756,640 ft^2 building contains 70.85 miles of bookshelves and cost $144 million. The collection includes 1.6 million books, 9,513 periodical titles, and more than 5 million microforms, recordings and other items.

Overdue books The record for an unreturned and overdue library book was set when a book in German on the Archbishop of Bremen, published in 1609, was borrowed from Sidney Sussex College, Cambridge, Great Britain by Colonel Robert Walpole in 1667–68. It was found by Prof. Sir John Plumb in the library of the then-Marquess of Cholmondeley at Houghton Hall, Norfolk, Great Britain and returned 288 years later. No fine was exacted.

The most overdue book in the United States was a book on febrile diseases (London, 1805, by Dr J. Currie) checked out in 1823 from the University of Cincinnati Medical Library and returned 7 Dec 1968 by the borrower's great-grandson, Richard Dodd. The calculated fine of $2,264 was waived.

GUESS WHAT?

Q. WHAT IS 275 FT TALL AND ANSWERS TO THE NAME "GENERAL SHERMAN"?

A. LOOK IN "TREES" (LIVING WORLD)

MUSEUMS

Oldest The world's oldest extant museum is the Ashmolean in Oxford, Great Britain, built between 1679 and 1683 and named after the collector Elias Ashmole (1617–92).

Largest The Smithsonian Institution comprises 16 museums containing over 140 million items and has over 6,000 employees.

The American Museum of Natural History in New York City was founded in 1869 and comprises 23 interconnected buildings in an 18-acre park. The buildings of the museum and the planetarium contain 1.2

million ft^2 of floor space, accommodating more than 30 million artifacts and specimens. Its exhibits are viewed by more than 3 million visitors each year.

Most popular The highest attendance on a single day for any museum is over 118,437 on 14 April 1984 at the Smithsonian's National Air and Space Museum, Washington, D.C., opened in July 1976. The record-setting day required the doors to be temporarily closed.

NEWSPAPERS

Oldest A copy has survived of a news pamphlet published in Cologne, Germany in 1470. The oldest existing newspaper in the world is the Swedish official journal *Post och Inrikes Tidningar*, founded in 1645 and published by the Royal Swedish Academy of Letters. The oldest existing commercial newspaper is the *Haarlems Dagblad/Oprechte Haarlemsche Courant*, published in Haarlem, Netherlands, first issued as the *Weeckelycke Courante van Europa* on 8 Jan 1656. A copy of issue No. 1 survives.

United States The oldest continuously published newspaper in the United States is the *Hartford Courant*, established by Thomas Greene on 29 Oct 1764. Originally a weekly four-page newspaper, it became a daily newspaper in 1836. Its current circulation figures are 231,922 daily and 323,892 Sunday papers, as of March 1994.

Sir Etienne Dupuch edited the Nassau, Bahamas *Tribune* from 1919 to 1972 and was a contributing editor until his death in 1991—a total of 72 years. (R. Chapman for Guinness Publishing)

Largest The most massive single issue of a newspaper was an edition of the Sunday *New York Times*, which weighed 12 lb and contained 1,612 pages, on 14 Sep 1987.

The largest page size ever used was 55.9 × 39.2 in for the 14 Jun 1993 edition of *Het Volk*, which was published in Gent, Belgium.

Smallest The smallest original page size was the 3 × 3 3/4 in of the *Daily Banner* (25 cents per month) of Roseberg, OR, issues of which, dated 1 and 2 Feb 1876, survive.

Longest editorship Sir Etienne Dupuch (b. 16 Feb 1899) of Nassau, Bahamas was editor-in-chief of *The Tribune* from 1 Apr 1919 to 1972, and a contributing editor until his death on 23 Aug 1991—a total of 72 years.

Most belated apology The *Hartford Courant* issued an apology to Thomas Jefferson, 193 years late. In 1800 the newspaper ran a vehement editorial opposing his election as president, expounding on the ways in which the country would be irrevocably damaged as a result. At the 250th anniversary of his birth, in 1993, the *Courant* finally admitted the error of its judgment with a formal apology, and the words: "It's never too late to admit a mistake."

Most Pulitzer prizes The *New York Times* has won 69 Pulitzer prizes, more than any other news organization.

Most durable feature Mary MacArthur of Port Appin, Scotland has contributed a regular feature to *The Oban Times and West Highland Times* since 1926.

Most durable advertiser The Jos Neel Co., a clothing store in Macon, GA (founded 1880) has run an ad in the *Macon Telegraph* every day in the upper-left-hand corner of page 2 since 22 Feb 1889.

Most syndicated columnist Ann Landers (nee Eppie Lederer, b. 4 Jul 1918) appears in over 1,200 newspapers with an estimated readership of 90 million.

CARTOON STRIPS

Earliest "The Yellow Kid" first appeared in the *New York Journal* on 18 Oct 1896.

Most durable The longest-lived newspaper comic strip is "The Katzenjammer Kids" (Hans and Fritz), created by Rudolph Dirks and first published in the *New York Journal* on 12 Dec 1897.

Most syndicated "Peanuts" by Charles Schulz of Santa Rosa, CA, first published in October 1950, currently appears in 2,300 newspapers in 68 countries and 26 languages.

Political cartoons Ranan R. Lurie (USA; b. 26 May 1932) is the most widely syndicated political cartoonist in the world. As of April 1994 his work was published in 102 countries in 1,098 newspapers with a circulation

The 14 Jun 1993 edition of the Belgian newspaper *Het Volk* was the largest ever published. Its trim size was 55.9 × 39.2 in. (Gamma/Lebrun/Photo News)

of 102 million copies. See also "Heads of State" in Business & Public Affairs (p. 428).

CIRCULATION

The country with the leading number of newspaper readers in the world is Sweden, where 580 newspapers are sold for every 1,000 people.

In 1993 the total number of morning and evening newspapers published in the United States was 1,556, with a total circulation of 59,815,032. There were 889 Sunday newspapers with a circulation of 62,643,379. The peak year for US newspapers was 1910, when there were 2,202.

Highest The highest circulation for any newspaper in the world was that for *Komsomolskaya Pravda* (founded 1925), the youth paper of the former Soviet Communist Party, which reached a peak daily circulation of 21,975,000 copies in May 1990.

The eight-page weekly newspaper *Argumenty i Fakty* (founded 1978) of Moscow, Russia reached a figure of 33,431,100 copies in May 1990, when it had an estimated readership of over 100 million.

The highest circulation for any *currently* published newspaper is that of *The Yomiuri Shimbun*, founded 1874, which publishes morning and evening editions, and had a combined daily circulation of 14,552,000 as of January 1994. These figures imply that 1 out of every 4.3 households in Japan reads *The Yomiuri Shimbun*.

United States The highest-circulation daily newspaper in the United States is the *Wall Street Journal* (founded 1889), published by Dow Jones & Co. As of 31 Mar 1994, circulation was 1,854,901 copies.

PERIODICALS

Oldest The oldest continuing periodical in the world is *Philosophical Transactions of the Royal Society*, published in London, Great Britain, which first appeared on 6 Mar 1665.

United States The oldest continuously published periodical in the United States is *The Old Farmer's Almanac*, started in Massachusetts by Robert Thomas, a teacher and amateur astronomer, in 1792.

Largest circulations The total dispersal through noncommercial channels by Jehovah's Witnesses of *The Truth that Leads to Eternal Life*, published by the Watchtower Bible and Tract Society of New York City on 8 May 1968, reached 107,562,995 in 117 languages by April 1993.

The world's highest-circulation periodical is *TV Guide*, with a circulation of 14.1 million copies as of December 1993. The world's highest-circulation magazine is currently *Modern Maturity*, with a figure as of February 1994 of 22.2 million.

In its 41 basic international editions, *Reader's Digest* (established February 1922) circulates 28.5 million copies monthly in 17 languages, including a US edition of more than 16.3 million copies. *Parade*, the syndicated color magazine, is distributed with a record 352 US newspapers every Sunday, giving a peak circulation in July 1994 of 37.61 million.

Largest The bulkiest consumer magazine ever published was the January 1992 issue of *Hong Kong Toys*, running to 1,356 pages. Published by the Hong Kong Trade Development Council, it retails for HK$100 (about $12.50).

Most advertising pages The greatest number of pages of advertisements sold in a single issue of a periodical is 829.54, by the October 1989 issue of *Business Week*.

CROSSWORD PUZZLES

Largest published In July 1982 Robert Turcot of Québec, Canada compiled a crossword puzzle comprising 82,951 squares. It contained 12,489 clues across, 13,125 down, and covered 38.28 ft^2.

Compilers The most prolific compiler is Roger F. Squires of Ironbridge, Great Britain, who composes 39 published puzzles single-handedly each week. His total output to September 1991 was over 37,500 puzzles.

Fastest crossword puzzle solution The fastest recorded time for completing *The Times* (London) crossword puzzle under test conditions is 3 min 45 sec, by Roy Dean of Bromley, Great Britain, on 19 Dec 1970.

Slowest solution In May 1966 *The Times* of London received an announcement from a Fijian woman that she had just succeeded in completing their crossword puzzle No. 673, published in the issue of 4 Apr 1932. The problem wasn't that the puzzle was so fiendishly difficult—it was just that it was in an edition that had been used to wrap a package, and had subsequently lain uncompleted for 34 years.

MUSIC

Origins Whistles and flutes made from perforated phalange bones (parts of fingers or toes) have been found at Upper Paleolithic sites of the Aurignacian period (*c*. 25,000–22,000 B.C.) at Istallóskö, Hungary and in Moldova.

Musical history can be traced back to the third millennium B.C., when the yellow bell (*huang zhong*) had a recognized standard musical tone in Chinese temple music. The world's earliest surviving musical notation dates from *c*. 1800 B.C. A heptatonic scale deciphered from a clay tablet by Dr Duchesne-Guillemin in 1966–67 was found at a site in Nippur, Sumer, now Iraq.

The human voice Before this century the extremes were a staccato E in *alt altissimo* (e^{iv}) by Ellen Beach Yaw (1869–1947) in Carnegie Hall, New York City on 19 Jan 1896, and an A_1 (55 Hz [cycles per sec]) by Kasper Foster (1617–73).

Madeleine Marie Robin (1918–60), the French operatic coloratura, could produce and sustain the B above high C in the Lucia mad scene in

Ivan Rebroff's vocal range extends over four octaves, from low F to high F, $1\frac{1}{4}$ octaves above C. The effect of a sudden burst of cold water has not been recorded. (Gamma/A. Skopelos)

Donizetti's *Lucia di Lammermoor*. Ivan Rebroff, the German singer, has a voice that extends easily over four octaves, from a low F to a high F, one and a quarter octaves above C. Dan Britton of Branson, MI can produce the note E-O (18.84 Hz).

The highest note put into song is G^{iv}, occurring in Mozart's *Popoli di Tessaglia*. The lowest vocal note in the classical repertoire is in Mozart's *Die Entführung aus dem Serail* in Osmin's aria, which calls for a low D (73.4 Hz).

SONGS

Oldest The *shaduf* chant has been sung since time immemorial by irrigation workers on the Nile water mills (or *saqiyas*) in Egypt.

The oldest known harmonized music performed today is the English song *Sumer is icumen in*, which dates from *c.* 1240.

National anthems The oldest national anthem is the *Kimigayo* of Japan, the words of which date from the ninth century, although the music was written in 1881. The oldest music belongs to the anthem of the Netherlands, *Vilhelmus*, which was written *c.* 1570.

The shortest anthems are those of Japan, Jordan and San Marino, each with only four lines. Of the 11 wordless national anthems, the oldest is that of Spain, dating from 1770.

Longest rendering of a national anthem "God Save the King" was played nonstop 16 or 17 times by a German military band on the platform of Rathenau railroad station, in Brandenburg, Germany on the morning of 9 Feb 1909. The reason was that King Edward VII was struggling inside the train to put on a German field-marshal's uniform before he could emerge.

Most renditions of the national anthem in 24 hours Susan R. Jeske sang the Star-Spangled Banner live at 17 official events in California, attended by approximately 60,000 people, within a 24-hr period on 3–4 Jul 1992. She traveled to the functions by automobile, helicopter and boat.

Top songs The most frequently sung songs in English are *Happy Birthday to You* (based on the original *Good Morning to All*), by Kentucky-born Sunday school teachers Mildred Hill and Patty Smith Hill of New York (written in 1893 and under copyright from 1935 to 2010); *For He's a Jolly Good Fellow* (originally the French *Malbrouk*), known at least as early as 1781; and *Auld Lang Syne* (originally the Strathspey *I Fee'd a Lad at Michaelmass*), some words of which were written by Robert Burns (1759–96). *Happy Birthday* was sung in space by the *Apollo IX* astronauts on 8 Mar 1969.

Songwriters The most successful songwriters in terms of number-one singles are John Lennon (1940–80) and Paul McCartney (b. 18 Jun 1942). McCartney is credited as writer on 32 number-one hits in the United States to Lennon's 26 (with 23 co-written), whereas Lennon authored 29 Great Britain number-ones to McCartney's 28 (25 co-written).

Oldest hymns The music and parts of the text of a hymn in the *Oxyrhynchus Papyri* from the second century are the earliest known hymnody. The earliest exactly datable hymn is the *Heyr Himna Smióur* (*Hear, the Maker of Heaven*) from 1208 by the Icelandic bard and chieftain Kolbeinn Tumason (1173–1208).

Longest hymns The *Hora novissima tempora pessima sunt; vigilemus* by Bernard of Cluny (mid-12th century) runs to 2,966 lines. The longest in English is *The Sands of Time Are Sinking* by Anne Ross Cousin (nee Cundell, 1824–1906), which runs to 152 lines in full, though only 32 lines appear in the Methodist Hymn Book.

Most prolific hymnist Frances (Fanny) Jane van Alstyne (nee Crosby, 1820–1915) of the United States wrote 8,500 hymns.

Oldest choral society The oldest choral society in the United States is the Old Stoughton Musical Society of Stoughton, MA, founded in 1786.

INSTRUMENTS

Oldest piano The earliest pianoforte in existence is one built in Florence, Italy in 1720 by Bartolommeo Cristofori (1655–1731) of Padua, and now kept in the Metropolitan Museum of Art, New York City.

Grandest piano The grandest grand piano was one of 1.4 tons and 11 ft 8 in in length made by Chas H. Challen & Son Ltd of London, Great Britain in 1935. Its longest bass string measured 9 ft 11 in, with a tensile strength of 33 tons.

Most expensive piano The highest price ever paid for a piano was $390,000 at Sotheby Parke Bernet, New York City on 26 Mar 1980 for a Steinway grand of *c*. 1888 sold by the Martin Beck Theater. It was bought by a non-pianist.

Largest organ The largest and loudest musical instrument ever constructed is the now only partially functional Auditorium Organ in Atlantic City, NJ. Completed in 1930, this instrument had two consoles (one with seven manuals and another movable one with five), 1,477 stop controls and 33,112 pipes, ranging in tone from $^{1}/_{5}$ in to the 64 ft tone. It had the volume of 25 brass bands, with a range of seven octaves.

The world's largest fully functional organ is the six manual 30,067 pipe Grand Court Organ installed in the Wanamaker Department Store, Philadelphia, PA in 1911 and enlarged between then and 1930. The organ has a 64 ft tone gravissima pipe.

Loudest organ stop The Ophicleide stop of the Grand Great in the Solo Organ in the Atlantic City Auditorium is operated by a pressure of water $3^{1}/_{2}$ lb/in^2 and has a pure trumpet note of ear-splitting volume, more than six times the volume of the loudest locomotive whistles.

Largest pan pipes The world's largest pan pipes, created by Simon Desorgher and Lawrence Casserley, consist of five contrabass pipes, each 4 in in diameter, with lengths of 19 in, 16 in, 14 in, 12 in and 10 in respectively, and five bass pipes of 2 in diameter with lengths of 9.5 in, 8 in, 7 in, 6 in and 5 in.

ALPHORN!

An alphorn 154 ft 8 in long (excluding mouthpiece) weighing 227 lb was completed by Swiss-born Peter Wutherich, of Boise, ID in December 1989. The diameter at the bell is $24^{1}/_{2}$ in and the sound takes 105.7 milliseconds to emerge from the bowl after entry into the mouthpiece.

Largest brass instrument The largest recorded brass instrument is a tuba standing $7^{1}/_{2}$ ft tall, with 39 ft of tubing and a bell 3 ft 4 in across. This contrabass tuba was constructed for a world tour by the band of American composer John Philip Sousa (1854–1932), *c*. 1896–98.

Largest stringed instrument The largest movable stringed instrument ever constructed was a pantaleon with 270 strings stretched over 50 ft^2 used by George Noel in 1767.

Largest double bass A double bass measuring 14 ft tall was built in 1924 in Ironia, NJ by Arthur K. Ferris. It weighed 1,301 lb with a sound box 8 ft across, and had leather strings totaling 104 ft. Its low notes could be felt rather than heard.

Double bass playing Sixteen musicians from Blandford, Great Britain played a double bass simultaneously (five fingering and eleven bowing) in a rendition of Strauss' *Perpetuum Mobile* at Blandford Town Hall on 6 Jun 1989.

Largest guitar The largest playable guitar in the world is 38 ft 2 in tall, 16 ft wide and weighs 1,865 lb. It was made by students of Shakamak High School in Jasonville, IN, and was unveiled on 17 May 1991 when, powered by six amplifiers, it was played simultaneously by six members of the school.

Acoustic A guitar 28 ft 5 in long and 3 ft 2 in deep is on display at the Stradivarium exhibition in The Exploratory, Bristol, Great Britain. Its dimensions were enlarged from the proportions of a Stradivarius classical guitar. When the guitar is played, its five strings resonate impressively.

The world's largest acoustic guitar is 28 ft 5 in long. The team members instrumental in its creation sit back admiringly on their creation. (The Stradivarium)

Most expensive guitar A Fender Stratocaster belonging to legendary rock guitarist Jimi Hendrix (1942–70) was sold by his former drummer Mitch Mitchell to an anonymous buyer for £198,000 ($338,580) at Sotheby's, London on 25 Apr 1990.

Most valuable violin The highest price paid at auction for a violin is £902,000 ($1.7 million) for the 1720 "Mendelssohn" Stradivarius. It was sold to a mystery buyer at Christie's, London on 21 Nov 1990.

Most valuable cello The highest auction price for a violoncello is £682,000 (approximately $1.2 million) at Sotheby's, London on 22 Jun 1988 for a Stradivarius known as "The Cholmondeley," which was made in Cremona, Italy *c.* 1698.

Largest drum A drum with a 13 ft diameter was built by the Supreme Drum Co., London, Great Britain and played at the Royal Festival Hall, London on 31 May 1987.

Largest drum kit A drum kit consisting of 112 pieces—88 drums, 18 cymbals, 4 hi-hats, a gong and a cowbell, along with various other assorted accessories—was constructed by Jeffrey Carlo of Brentwood, NY, in 1990.

Drumming Four hundred separate drums were played in 20.50 sec by Carl Williams at the Alexander Stadium, Birmingham, Great Britain on 4 Oct 1992.

LARGEST DRUM KIT

"I wanted to be different from every other drummer in the world."

Jeff Carlo's drum kit isn't louder than anyone else's, but it's certainly larger. The black-and-chrome set has as many "keys" as a piano—88—and, says its creator, nearly as many tones. "It's not just for looks," says Carlo, who's been drumming since he was seven and now plays with the rock band Runner. "I play it, and I play it well. I wanted to be appreciated because I'm a musician—not just for my drum set."

Nevertheless, the public doesn't often get a look at Carlo's drums. "They take up a full-size garage," he says. "Most stages aren't adequate." Not surprisingly, drums dominate Carlo's music, and his big set is a striking centerpiece of his music videos and recordings.

Carlo began assembling the set in 1983 and finished it in 1985. The hard part wasn't finding the drums—it was figuring out where to put them. "Nobody's ever made a set like this, so I couldn't just copy things. I had to be able to reach all the drums and play them easily. So I had to invent the set, envision it, before I put it all together." Carlo insists, "I didn't build it to get into *Guinness,* I built it for myself—and for the world."

Highest and lowest notes The extremes of orchestral instruments (excluding the organ) range from a handbell tuned to g^{v} (6,272 cycles/sec) to the sub-contrabass clarinet, which can reach C_{11} or 16.4 cycles/sec. The highest note on a standard pianoforte is c^{v} (4,186 cycles/sec), which is also the violinist's limit. In 1873 a sub-double bassoon able to reach $B_{111} \pm$ or 14.6 cycles/sec was constructed, but no surviving specimen is known.

The extremes for the organ are g^{iv} (the sixth G above middle C) (12,544 cycles/sec) and C_{111} (8.12 cycles/sec), obtainable from 3/4 in and 64 ft pipes respectively.

BELLS

Oldest The world's oldest bell is the tintinnabulum found in the Babylonian Palace of Nimrod in 1849 by Mr (later Sir) Austen Henry Layard (1817–94), dating from *c.* 1100 B.C. The oldest tower bell is one in St Benedict Church, Rome, Italy, that bears the date "anno domini millesimo sexagesimo IX" (1069).

United States The oldest bell in the United States is located at St Stephens Episcopal Church in East Haddam, CT. The bell was cast in Spain in 815 A.D. and shipped to the United States in 1834.

Heaviest The Tsar Kolokol, cast by Russian brothers I.F. and M.I. Motorin on 25 Nov 1735 in Moscow, weighs 222.6 tons, measures 22 ft in diameter and 20 ft high. The bell was cracked in a fire in 1737 and a fragment, weighing about 12.91 tons, was broken from it. The bell has stood, unrung, on a platform in the Kremlin in Moscow since 1836 with the broken section alongside.

The heaviest bell still in use is the Mingun bell, weighing 101 tons, with a diameter of 16 ft 8½ in at the lip, in Mandalay, Myanmar. The bell is struck by a teak boom from the outside. It was cast late in the reign of King Bodawpaya (1782–1819). The heaviest swinging bell in the world is the Petersglocke in the southwest tower of Cologne Cathedral, Germany, cast in 1923, with a diameter of 11 ft 1¾ in, weighing 28 tons.

United States The largest bell in the United States weighs 17 tons and hangs at St Francis de Scelle Church in Cincinnati, OH. It was cast *c.* 1895. The heaviest ring in the United States is that of 10 bells cast in 1963 for the Washington National Cathedral, Washington, D.C. The total bell weight is 13,682 lb—the heaviest bell weighs 3,588 lb.

Peals The heaviest ring in the world is that of 13 bells cast in 1938–39 for the Anglican Cathedral in Liverpool, Great Britain. The total bell weight is 18.5 tons, of which Emmanuel, the tenor bell note A, weighs 9,195 lb.

Bell ringing Eight bells have been rung to their full "extent" (40,320 unrepeated changes) only once without relays. This took place in a bell foundry at Loughborough, Great Britain, beginning at 6:52 A.M. on 27 Jul 1963 and ending at 12:50 A.M. on 28 July, after 17 hr 58 min. The peal was composed by Kenneth Lewis of Altrincham, Great Britain, and the eight ringers were conducted by Robert B. Smith of Marple, Great Britain.

The greatest number of peals (minimum of 5,000 changes, all in tower bells) rung in a year is 303, by Colin Turner of Abingdon, Great Britain in 1989.

As of 1 Jan 1994, both John Mayne of St Albans, Great Britain and Peter Border of Barford, Great Britain had rung in more than 3,000 peals.

George Symonds (1875–1974) of Ipswich, Great Britain was a regular bell-ringer for 89 years. He rang his last peal in 1973 at the age of 98.

Largest carillon The largest carillon (minimum of 23 bells) in the world is the Laura Spelman Rockefeller Memorial Carillon in Riverside Church, New York City, with 74 bells weighing 114 tons. The bourdon, giving the note lower C, weighs 20.5 tons and is the largest tuned bell in the world.

ORCHESTRAS

Oldest The oldest existing symphony orchestra, the Gewandhaus Orchestra of Leipzig, Germany, was established in 1743. Originally known as the Grosses Concert and later as the Musikübende Gesellschaft, its current name dates from 1781.

United States The oldest orchestra in the United States is the Philharmonic-Symphony Society of New York, which was founded by Ureli Corelli Hill in 1842.

Largest On 17 Jun 1872, Johann Strauss the younger (1825–99) conducted an orchestra of 987 pieces supported by a choir of 20,000, at the World Peace Jubilee in Boston, MA. The number of first violinists was 400.

On 14 Dec 1991 the 2,000-piece "Young People's Orchestra and Chorus of Mexico," consisting of 53 youth orchestras from Mexico plus musicians from Venezuela and the former USSR, gave a full classical concert conducted by Fernando Lozano and others at the Magdalena Mixhiuca Sports Center, Mexico City.

Bottle orchestra The Brighton Bottle Orchestra—consisting of Terry Garoghan and Peter Miller—performed a musical medley on 444 Gordon's Gin bottles at the Brighton International Festival, Great Britain on 21 May 1991. It took 18 hours to tune the bottles, and about 10 times the normal rate of puff (90 breaths/min) to play them. There was no risk of intoxication, as the bottles were filled with water.

Largest band The most massive band ever assembled was one of 20,100 players at the Ullevaal Stadium, Oslo, Norway from Norges Musikkorps Forbund bands on 28 Jun 1964.

One-man band Rory Blackwell, of Starcross, Great Britain, aided by his double left-footed perpendicular percussion-pounder, his three-tier right-footed horizontal 22-pronged differential beater, and his 12-outlet bellow-powered horn-blower, played 108 different instruments (19 melody and 89 percussion) simultaneously in Dawlish, Great Britain on 29 May 1989. He also played 314 instruments in a single rendition in 1 min 23.07 sec, also in Dawlish, on 27 May 1985.

Marching band The largest marching band was one of 6,017 people, including 927 majorettes and standard-bearers. On 27 Jun 1993 the band marched 3,084 ft at Stafsberg Airport, Hamar, Norway, under the direction of Odd Aspli, Chairman of Hamar County Council.

The world's largest orchestra, the 2,000-piece Young People's Orchestra and Chorus of Mexico, led by Fernando Lozano, performed in Mexico City on 14 Dec 1991.

Under the direction of Odd Aspli, the world's largest marching band performed in Hamar, Norway on 27 Jun 1993. The band totaled 6,017 players, including 927 majorettes and flag-bearers. (Brox Reklamaphoto)

Austrian maestro Herbert von Karajan was classical music's most prolific conductor. He made more than 800 recordings, the majority with his beloved Berlin Philharmonic. (Deutsche Grammophon/Image Select)

Musical march The longest musical march was one of 46.7 miles, by members of showband Marum, a Dutch marching band, who walked from Assen to Marum, Netherlands on 9 May 1992. Of the 60 people who started, 52 managed to complete the march in 13 hr 50 min.

Musical chairs The largest game on record was one starting with 8,238 participants, ending with Xu Chong Wei on the last chair, which was held at the Anglo-Chinese School, Singapore on 5 Aug 1989.

Conductors The Austrian conductor Herbert von Karajan (1908–89), principal conductor of the Berlin Philharmonic Orchestra for 35 years before his retirement from the position shortly before his death, was the most prolific conductor ever, having made over 800 recordings of all the major works.

The 1991–92 season was the 58th for the Cork Symphony Orchestra (Cork, Republic of Ireland) under the baton of Dr Aloys Fleischmann (1910–92).

United States The Chicago Symphony Orchestra was directed by Frederic Stock from 1905 until his death in 1942, a total of 37 seasons.

Baton twirling The greatest number of complete spins done between tossing a baton into the air and catching it is 10, by Donald Garcia, on 9 Dec 1986. The record for women is seven, shared by Lisa Fedick, set on the same day; Joanne Holloway, at Great Britain National Baton Twirling Association Championships in Paignton, Great Britain on 29 Oct 1987; and Rachel Hayes, on 18 Sep 1988.

CONCERT ATTENDANCES

Classical An estimated record 800,000 attended a free open-air concert by the New York Philharmonic conducted by Zubin Mehta, on the Great Lawn of Central Park, New York City on 5 Jul 1986, as part of the Statue of Liberty Weekend.

Rock/pop festival The best claim is believed to be 725,000 for Steve Wozniak's 1983 US Festival in San Bernardino, CA.

Solo performer The largest *paying* audience ever attracted by a solo performer was an estimated 180,000–184,000 in the Maracaña Stadium, Rio de Janeiro, Brazil to hear Paul McCartney (b. 1942) on 21 Apr 1990. Jean-Michel Jarre, the *son et lumière* specialist, entertained an estimated audience of 2 million in Paris, France at a free Bastille Day concert in 1990.

DID YOU KNOW?

Excluding "singalongs" by stadium crowds, the greatest choir is one of 60,000 that sang in unison as a finale of a choral contest among 160,000 participants in Breslau, Germany on 2 Aug 1937.

Most successful concert tour The Rolling Stones' 1989 "Steel Wheels" North American tour earned an estimated $310 million and was attended by 3.2 million people in 30 cities.

Most durable musicians The Romanian pianist Cual Delavrancea (1887–1991) gave her last public recital, receiving six encores, at the age of 103. The longest international career in the history of Western music is held by Polish pianist Mieczyslaw Horszowski (1892–1993), who played for Emperor Franz-Joseph in Vienna, Austria in 1899 and was still playing in 1989.

The world's oldest active musician is Jennie Newhouse (b. 12 Jul 1889) of High Bentham, Great Britain, who has been the regular organist at the Church of St Boniface in Bentham since 1920.

Most successful concert series Michael Jackson sold out for seven nights at Wembley, London, Great Britain in the summer of 1988. The stadium has a capacity of 72,000, so a total of 504,000 people saw Jackson perform 14–16, 22–23 Jul and 26–27 Aug 1988.

Largest concert On 21 Jul 1990, Potsdamer Platz, straddling East and West Berlin, was the site of the largest single rock concert in terms of participants and organization ever staged. Roger Waters' production of Pink Floyd's "The Wall" involved 600 people performing on a stage measuring

551 × 82 ft at its highest point. An estimated 200,000 people gathered for the symbolic building and demolition of a wall made of 2,500 styrofoam blocks.

Clapping The duration record for continuous clapping (sustaining an average of 160 claps per min, audible at 120 yd) is 58 hr 9 min by V. Jeyaraman of Tamil Nadu, India from 12–15 Feb 1988.

COMPOSERS

Most prolific The most prolific composer of all time was probably Georg Philipp Telemann (1681–1767) of Germany. He composed 12 complete sets of services (one cantata every Sunday) for a year, 78 services for special occasions, 40 operas, 600 to 700 orchestral suites, 44 passions, plus concertos, sonatas and other chamber music.

Longest symphony The longest single classical symphony is the orchestral Symphony No. 3 in D Minor, composed in 1896 by Gustav Mahler (1860–1911) of Austria. A full performance requires 1 hr 40 min, of which the first movement alone takes between 30 and 36 min.

The symphony *Victory at Sea*, written by Richard Rodgers (1902–79) and arranged by Robert Russell Bennett in 1952 for the NBC television series of the same name, lasted 13 hours.

Longest piano composition The longest continuous nonrepetitious piano piece ever published is *The Well-Tuned Piano* by La Monte Young, first presented by the Dia Art Foundation at the Concert Hall, Harrison St, New York City on 28 Feb 1980. The piece lasted 4 hr 12 min 10 sec.

Symphonic Variations, composed in the 1930s for piano and orchestra by the British-born Kaikhosru Shapurji Sorabji (1892–1988) on 500 pages of close manuscript in three volumes, would last for six hours if played at the prescribed tempo.

Longest silence The longest interval between the known composition of a piece by a major composer and its performance in the manner intended is from 3 Mar 1791 until 9 Oct 1982, in the case of Mozart's *Organ Piece for a Clock*, a fugue fantasy in F minor (K 608), arranged by the organ builders Wm Hill & Son and Norman & Beard Ltd at Glyndebourne, Great Britain.

OPERA

Longest *The Heretics* by Gabriel von Wayditch (1888–1969), a Hungarian-American, is orchestrated for 110 pieces and lasts 8½ hr. The longest of commonly performed operas is *Die Meistersinger von Nürnberg* by Wilhelm Richard Wagner (1813–83) of Germany. A normal uncut performance of this opera entails 5 hr 15 min of music.

Shortest The shortest opera published is *The Sands of Time* by Simon Rees and Peter Reynolds, first performed by Rhian Owen and Dominic Burns on 27 Mar 1993 at The Hayes, Cardiff, Great Britain; it lasted for 4 min 9 sec. An even shorter performance, lasting only 3 min 34 sec, was directed by Peter Reynolds at BBC Television Centre, London, Great Britain on 14 Sep 1993.

Longest aria The longest single aria, in the sense of an operatic solo, is Brünnhilde's immolation scene in Wagner's *Götterdämmerung*. It has been timed at 14 min 46 sec.

Oldest opera singers The tenor Giovanni Martinelli sang Emperor Altoum in *Turandot* in Seattle, WA on 4 Feb 1967 when he was 81. Danshi Toyotake (b. Yoshie Yokota, 1891–1989) of Hyogo, Japan sang *Musume Gidayu* (traditional Japanese narrative) for 91 years from the age of seven. Her professional career spanned 81 years.

Most curtain calls On 24 Feb 1988 Luciano Pavarotti (b. 12 Oct 1935) received 165 curtain calls and was applauded for 1 hr 7 min after singing the part of Nemorino in Gaetano Donizetti's *L'elisir d'Amore* at the Deutsche Oper in Berlin, Germany.

Largest opera houses The Metropolitan Opera House, Lincoln Center, New York City, completed in September 1966 at a cost of $45.7 million, has a standing and seating capacity of 4,065 with 3,800 seats in an auditorium 451 ft deep. The stage is 230 ft wide and 148 ft deep.

The Teatro della Scala (La Scala) in Milan, Italy shares with the Bolshoi Theatre in Moscow, Russia the distinction of having the greatest number of tiers—six.

Oldest opera company in US The oldest continuously performing opera company in the United States is the Metropolitan Opera Company of New York City; its first season was in 1883.

Longest operatic encore The longest operatic encore was of the entire opera *Il Matrimonio Segreto* by Cimarosa at its premiere in 1792. This was at the command of the Austro-Hungarian emperor Leopold II (r. 1790–92).

RECORDED SOUND

Oldest recordings The oldest existing recording was made in 1878 by Augustus Stroh, but it remains on the mandrel of his machine and has never been played.

The oldest playable record is believed to be an engraved metal cylinder made by Frank Lambert in 1878 or 1879 and voicing the hours on the clock. The recording is owned by Aaron Cramer of New York City.

Smallest recorder In April 1983 Olympic Optical Industry Co. of Japan marketed a micro-cassette recorder measuring $4\frac{1}{5} \times 2 \times \frac{1}{2}$ in and weighing 4.4 oz.

Smallest cassette The NT digital cassette made by the Sony Corporation of Japan for use in dictating machines measures just $1\frac{1}{5} \times \frac{4}{5} \times \frac{1}{5}$ in.

Smallest functional record Six titles of $1\frac{5}{16}$ in diameter were recorded by

HMV's studio at Hayes, Great Britain on 26 Jan 1923 for Queen Mary's Doll House. Some 92,000 of these miniature records were pressed, including 35,000 of *God Save the King*.

TOP RECORDING ARTISTS

Most successful solo recording artist Although no independently audited figures have ever been published for Elvis Presley (1935–77), he has had over 170 hit singles and over 80 top-selling albums since 1956. Aretha Franklin is the female solo artist with the most million-selling singles, with 14 between 1967 and 1973.

Most successful group The singers with the greatest sales of any group have been the Beatles. This group from Liverpool, Great Britain comprised George Harrison (b. 25 Feb 1943), John Lennon (1940–1980), Paul McCartney (b. 18 Jun 1942) and Richard Starkey, alias Ringo Starr (b. 7 Jul 1940). The all-time Beatles sales up to May 1985 have been estimated by EMI at over one billion discs and tapes. All four ex-Beatles sold many million more records as solo artists.

Most golden discs The only *audited* measure of gold, platinum and multiplatinum singles and albums within the United States is certification by the Recording Industry Association of America (RIAA), introduced on 14 Mar 1958.

The Rolling Stones, with 56 (34 gold, 16 platinum, 6 multiplatinum)

The first gold disc was Glenn Miller's "Chattanooga Choo-Choo." His record company, RCA Victor, presented him with a gold spray-painted copy of the record on 10 Feb 1942. (Hulton-Deutsch Collection)

have the most for any group. The group with the most multiplatinum albums is the Beatles, with 11.

In August 1992, following new audit figures, the estate of Elvis Presley was presented with 110 gold and platinum records, making him the most certified recording artist ever. The female solo artist to receive the most awards is Barbra Streisand, with 57 (7 gold singles, 30 gold albums and 12 platinum albums).

The first platinum album was awarded to the Eagles for *Greatest Hits, 1971–75* in 1976. The group Chicago holds the record for most platinum albums, with 17. Barbra Streisand holds the record for a solo artist, with 19, and the record for most multiplatinum, with 7. Paul McCartney holds the record for a male solo artist, with 12, while Billy Joel holds the record for the most multiplatinum albums for an individual, with 8.

GUESS WHAT?

Q. WHICH COUNTRY HAS THE GREATEST GOLD RESERVES?

A. LOOK IN "ECONOMICS" (BUSINESS & PUBLIC AFFAIRS)

Most recordings A set of 180 compact discs containing the complete authenticated works of Mozart were produced by Philips Classics for release in 1990/91 to commemorate the bicentennial of the composer's death. The complete set comprises over 200 hours of music and would occupy 6½ ft of shelving.

Most Grammy awards An all-time record 31 awards have been won since 1958 by the Hungarian-born British conductor Sir Georg Solti (b. 21 Oct 1912). The most won by a group or orchestra is 46, by the Chicago Symphony. The greatest number won in a year is 8, by Michael Jackson in 1984.

BIGGEST SELLERS

Singles The greatest seller of any phonograph record to date is *White Christmas* by Irving Berlin (b. Israel Bailin, 1888–1989), recorded by Bing Crosby on 29 May 1942. North American sales alone reached 170,884,207 copies by 30 Jun 1987.

The highest claim for any "rock" record is an unaudited 25 million for *Rock Around the Clock*, copyrighted in 1953 by James E. Myers under the name Jimmy De Knight and the late Max C. Freedmann and recorded on 12 Apr 1954 by Bill Haley (1927–1981) and the Comets.

Albums The best-selling album of all time is *Thriller* by Michael Jackson (b. 29 Aug 1958), with global sales of over 47 million copies to date. The best-selling album by a group is Fleetwood Mac's *Rumours* with over 21 million sales by May 1990.

Whitney Houston by Whitney Houston, released in 1985, is the best-selling debut album of all time. It has sold over 14 million copies, including over 9 million in the United States, 1 million in Great Britain, and a further million in Canada.

Whitney Houston (LFI)

Soundtrack The best-selling movie soundtrack is *Saturday Night Fever*, with sales of over 26.5 million by May 1987.

Classical album The best-selling classical album is *In Concert*, with sales of 5 million to date. It was recorded by José Carreras, Placido Domingo and Luciano Pavarotti at the 1990 Soccer World Cup Finals in Rome, Italy.

THE CHARTS

US singles Singles record charts were first published by *Billboard* on 20 Jul 1940, when the No. 1 single was *I'll Never Smile Again* by Tommy Dorsey (1905–56) with vocal by Frank Sinatra. *Near You* by Francis Craig stayed at the No. 1 spot for 17 weeks in 1947.

The Beatles have had the most No. 1's (20), Conway Twitty (1933–93) the most Country No. 1's (40) and Aretha Franklin the most Rhythm and Blues No. 1's (20). Elvis Presley has had the most hit singles on *Billboard*'s Hot 100—149 from 1956 to Jan 1983.

Bing Crosby's *White Christmas* spent a total of 86 weeks on the charts between 1942 and 1962, while *Tainted Love* by Soft Cell stayed on the charts for 43 *consecutive* weeks from January 1982.

Albums *Billboard* first published an album chart on 24 Mar 1945, when the No. 1 was *King Cole Trio* featuring Nat "King" Cole (1919–65). *South Pacific* was No. 1 for 69 weeks (nonconsecutive) from May 1949. *Dark Side of the Moon* by Pink Floyd enjoyed 741 weeks on the *Billboard* charts to October 1988.

TOP 10 TEN

ALL-TIME TOP US SINGLES

Rank	Title	Artist	Year	Weeks at No. 1
1	I Will Always Love You	Whitney Houston	1992	14
2	End of the Road	Boyz II Men	1992	13
3	Physical	Olivia Newton-John	1981	10
4	You Light Up My Life	Debby Boone	1977	10
5	Endless Love	Diana Ross/ Lionel Richie	1981	9
6	Singing the Blues	Guy Mitchell	1956	9
7	Mack the Knife	Bobby Darin	1959	9
8	Bette Davis Eyes	Kim Carnes	1981	9
9	Theme from "A Summer Place"	Percy Faith	1960	9
10	Hey Jude	Beatles	1968	9

Radio Computing Services/Billboard Publications

The Beatles had the most No. 1's (15), Elvis Presley was the most successful male soloist (9), and Simon and Garfunkel the top duo with 3. Elvis Presley has had the most hit albums (92 from 1956 to September 1992).

The woman with the most No. 1 albums (7), and most hit albums in total (43 between 1963 and July 1994), is Barbra Streisand.

Number one in most countries Madonna (b. 16 Aug 1958) reached No. 1 in 28 countries with her album *True Blue*, which sold over 17 million copies.

Boyz II Men (LFI)

Compact discs Developed by Philips and Sony in 1978 and introduced in 1982, the compact disc (CD) increasingly challenges the LP and cassette as a recording medium. The first CD to sell a million copies worldwide was Dire Straits' *Brothers in Arms* in 1986. It subsequently topped a million sales in Europe alone.

Largest record store HMV opened the world's largest record store at 150 Oxford Street, London, Great Britain on 24 Oct 1986. Its trading area measures 36,684 ft^2.

Fastest rapper Rebel X.D. of Chicago, IL rapped 674 syllables in 54.9 sec at the Hair Bear Recording Studio, Alsip, IL on 27 Aug 1992.

DANCING

Largest An estimated 30,000 people took part in a Madison/Electric Slide line dance held during the 1991 Comin' Home African American Holiday Celebration in Columbus, OH on 12 Jul 1991.

Longest The most taxing marathon dance staged as a public spectacle was one by Mike Ritof and Edith Boudreaux, who logged 214 days 12 hr 28½ min to win $2,000 at Chicago's Merry Garden Ballroom, Belmont and Sheffield, IL from 29 Aug 1930 to 1 Apr 1931. Rest periods were progressively cut from 20 to 10 to 5 to zero minutes per hour, with 10-inch steps and a maximum of 15 seconds for closure of eyes.

Cathy McConochie led an ensemble of 18 dancers through the streets of Sacramento, CA on 30 May 1992 during the Sacramento Children's Festival, in a choreographed routine, covering a distance of 8.8 miles.

Ballet *Fastest "entrechat douze"* In the *entrechat*, the starting and finishing position each count as one, so that in an *entrechat douze* there are five crossings and uncrossings. This feat was performed by Wayne Sleep for the British Broadcasting Corporation *Record Breakers* TV program on 7 Jan 1973. He was in the air for 0.71 sec.

Grands jetés On 28 Nov 1988, Wayne Sleep completed 158 grands jetés along the length of Dunston Staiths, Great Britain in 2 min.

Most turns The greatest number of spins called for in classical ballet choreography is 32 *fouettés rond de jambe en tournant* in *Swan Lake* by Piotr Ilyich Tchaikovsky (1840–93). Delia Gray (Great Britain; b. 30 Oct 1975) achieved 166 such turns during the Harlow Ballet School's summer workshop at The Playhouse, Harlow, Great Britain on 2 Jun 1991.

Most curtain calls The greatest recorded number of curtain calls ever received is 89, by Dame Margot Fonteyn (1919–91) and Rudolf Nureyev (1938–93) after a performance of *Swan Lake* at the Vienna Staatsoper, Austria in October 1964.

Ballroom The world's most successful professional ballroom dancing champions are Bill and Bobbie Irvine, who won 13 world titles from 1960 to 1968.

The oldest competitive ballroom dancer was Albert J. Sylvester (1889–1989) of Corsham, Great Britain, who retired at the age of 94.

The oldest competitive ballroom dancer in the United States is Lorna S. Lengfeld, who is still competing at the age of 90.

CONGA!

The longest recorded conga line was the Miami Super Conga, held in conjunction with Calle Ocho—a party to which Cuban-Americans invite the rest of Miami for a celebration of life together. Held on 13 Mar 1988, the conga line consisted of 119,986 people.

Country dancing The largest genuine Scottish country dance ever held was a 512-person reel, held in Toronto, Ontario, Canada on 17 Aug 1991 and organized by the Toronto branch of the Royal Scottish Country Dance Society.

Dancing dragon The longest dancing dragon measured 4,868 ft 2 in from the end of its nose to the tip of its tail. A total of 1,019 people brought the dragon to life, making it dance for 1 minute at the Volksfeest Havelte, a festival held at Havelte, Netherlands on 4 Sep 1993.

Flamenco The fastest flamenco dancer ever measured is Solero de Jerez, age 17, who in Brisbane, Australia in September 1967 attained 16 heel taps per second.

Limbo The lowest height for a bar (flaming) under which a limbo dancer has passed is 6 in off the floor, by Dennis Walston, alias King Limbo, in Kent, WA on 2 Mar 1991.

The record for a performer on roller skates is 4$^{7}/_{10}$ in, achieved by Syamala Gowri in Hyderabad, Andhra Pradesh, India on 10 May 1993.

Square dance calling Alan Covacic called for 26 hr 2 min for the Wheelers and Dealers Square Dance Club at Halton Royal Air Force Base, Aylesbury, Great Britain from 18–19 Nov 1988.

Tap The fastest rate ever measured for tap dancing is 32 taps per second, by Stephen Gare of Sutton Coldfield, Great Britain, at the Grand Hotel, Birmingham, Great Britain on 28 Mar 1990.

The fastest rate measured for a tap dancer in the United States is 28 taps per second, by Michael Flatley of Palos Park, IL on 9 May 1989.

Roy Castle (b. 1933), host of the British Broadcasting Corporation *Record Breakers* TV program, achieved one million taps in 23 hr 44 min at the Guinness World of Records exhibition, London, Great Britain on 31 Oct–1 Nov 1985.

They've got rhythm. Some of the 6,196 record-breaking tap dancers strut their stuff at Macy's Tap-O-Mania. (Macy's Northeast, Inc.)

The longest distance ever tapped by one person was 13.1 miles, by Elizabeth Ursic, who tap-danced the Arizona Half Marathon in Tempe, AZ on 10 Jan 1993.

The greatest assemblage of tap dancers in a single routine numbered 6,196 outside Macy's department store at 34th Street and Sixth Avenue, New York City on 22 Aug 1993.

THEATER

Oldest Theater in Europe has its origins in Greek drama performed in honor of a god, usually Dionysus. Small theaters had been built on several sites in Greece by the fifth century B.C.

Oldest indoor theater The oldest indoor theater in the world is the Teatro Olimpico in Vicenza, Italy. Designed in the Roman style by Andrea di Pietro, alias Palladio (1508–80), it was begun three months before his death and finished in 1583. It is preserved today in its original form.

Largest The theater with the largest capacity is the Perth Entertainment Center, Western Australia, completed in November 1976, with 8,003 seats. The stage area is 12,000 ft^2.

United States The highest-capacity theater currently in use on Broadway is the Gershwin Theater, with 1,933 seats. Designed by Ralph Alswang, the theater opened on 28 Nov 1972.

Smallest The smallest regularly operated professional theater in the world is the Piccolo in Juliusstrasse, Hamburg, Germany. It was founded in 1970 and has a maximum capacity of 30 seats.

Largest amphitheater The Flavian amphitheater or Colosseum of Rome, Italy, completed in A.D. 80, covers five acres and has a capacity of 87,000. It has a maximum length of 612 ft and a maximum width of 515 ft.

Largest stage The largest stage in the world is in the Ziegfeld Room, Reno, NV, with 176 ft passerelle, three main elevators each capable of raising 1,200 show girls (72 tons), two 62½-ft-circumference turntables and 800 spotlights.

Longest runs The longest continuous run of any show in the world is *The Mousetrap* by Dame Agatha Christie (1890–1976). This thriller opened on 25 Nov 1952 at the Ambassadors Theatre, London, Great Britain (capacity 453) and moved after 8,862 performances to the St Martin's Theatre next door on 25 Mar 1974. The 17,256th performance was on 9 May 1994, and the box office total was £20 million ($36 million) from more than 9 million attenders.

The Vicksburg Theater Guild, MS has been playing the melodrama *Gold in the Hills* by J. Frank Davis discontinuously but every season since 1936.

Revue The greatest number of performances of any theatrical presentation is 47,250 (to April 1986) in the case of *The Golden Horseshoe Revue*, a show staged at Disneyland, Anaheim, CA. It started on 16 Jul 1955 and closed on 12 Oct 1986 after being seen by 16 million people.

Most ardent theatergoer Dr H. Howard Hughes (b. 1902), Prof. Emeritus of Texas Wesleyan College, Fort Worth, TX attended 6,136 shows in the period 1957–87.

Musical shows The off-Broadway musical show *The Fantasticks* by Tom Jones and Harvey Schmidt opened on 3 May 1960, and the total number of performances to 24 May 1994 is 14,095 at the Sullivan Street Playhouse, Greenwich Village, New York City.

Greatest loss The greatest loss sustained by a theatrical show was by the American producers of the Royal Shakespeare Company's musical *Carrie*, which closed after five performances on Broadway on 17 May 1988 at a cost of $7 million. *King*, the musical about Martin Luther King, incurred a loss of £3 million ($5.04 million) in a six-week run in London, Great Britain ending on 2 Jun 1990, thus matching the record losses of *Ziegfeld* in 1988 in London.

Tony awards Harold (Hal) S. Prince (b. 1928) has won 16 Tonys—the awards of the American Theater Wing—the most of any individual. Prince has won eight awards as a producer, seven as a director and one special award.

Three plays share the record for most Tonys, with five: *A Man for All Seasons* (1962), *Who's Afraid of Virginia Woolf?* (1963) and *Amadeus* (1981).

The only person to win five Tonys in starring roles is Julie Harris, in *I am a Camera* (1952), *The Lark* (1956), *Forty Carats* (1969), *The Last of Mrs Lincoln* (1973) and *The Belle of Amherst* (1977).

One-man shows The longest run of one-man shows is 849, by Victor Borge (b. Copenhagen, 3 Jan 1909) in his *Comedy in Music* from 2 Oct 1953 to 21 Jan 1956 at the Golden Theater, Broadway, New York City.

The world aggregate record for one-man shows is 1,700 performances of *Brief Lives* by Roy Dotrice (b. Guernsey, 26 May 1923), including 400

Kabuki, the classical Japanese theatrical form, features 25-day-long productions. Kanzaburo Nakamura has performed in 806 Kabuki titles, giving 20,150 performances.

straight at the Mayfair Theatre, London, Great Britain ending on 20 Jul 1974. He was on stage for more than 2½ hr per performance of this 17th-century monologue and required 3 hr for makeup and 1 hr for removal of makeup, thus totaling 40 weeks in the chair.

Most durable performer Kanmi Fujiyama (b. 1929) played the lead role in 10,288 performances by the comedy company Sochiku Shikigeki from November 1966 to June 1983.

Most durable understudy On 12 Mar 1994 Nancy Seabrooke, 79, retired from the company of *The Mousetrap* in London, Great Britain after having understudied the part of "Mrs Boyle" for 15 years and 6,240 performances.

Advance sales The musical *Miss Saigon*, produced by Cameron Mackintosh and starring Jonathan Pryce and Lea Salonga, opened on Broadway in April 1991 after generating record advance sales of $36 million.

Most roles The greatest recorded number of theatrical, film and television roles portrayed is 3,385, from 1951 to March 1989, by Jan Leighton (USA).

Theatrical roles Kanzaburo Nakamura (b. July 1909) performed in 806 Kabuki titles from November 1926 to January 1987. Since each title in this classical Japanese theatrical form lasts 25 days, he therefore gave 20,150 performances.

Shakespeare The longest of the 37 plays written by Shakespeare is *Hamlet* (1604), with 4,042 lines and 29,551 words. Of Shakespeare's 1,277 speaking parts, the longest is the role of Hamlet, with 11,610 words.

Longest chorus lines The longest chorus line in performing history numbered up to 120 in some of the early *Ziegfeld Follies*. In the finale of *A Chorus Line* on the night of 29 Sep 1983, when it broke the record as the longest-running Broadway show ever, 332 top-hatted "strutters" performed on stage.

On 28 Mar 1992 at the Swan Center, Eastleigh, Great Britain, 543 members of the cast of *Showtime News*, a production by Hampshire West Guides, performed a routine choreographed by professional dancer Sally Horsley.

Arts festival The world's largest arts festival is the annual Edinburgh Fringe Festival, Great Britain (instituted in 1947). In 1992, its record year, 540 groups gave 12,132 performances of 1,103 shows between 16 August and 5 September. Prof. Gerald Berkowitz of Northern Illinois University attended a record 145 separate performances at the 1979 Festival from 15 August–8 September.

Fashion shows The greatest distance covered by a model on a catwalk is 83.1 miles, by Eddie Warke at Parke's Hotel, Dublin, Republic of Ireland from 19–21 Sep 1983. The record by female models is 71.1 miles, by Roberta Brown and Lorraine McCourt on the same occasion.

Fastest magician Eldon D. Wigton, alias Dr Eldoonie, performed 225 different tricks in 2 min in Kilbourne, OH on 21 Apr 1991.

CIRCUS

The oldest permanent circus building is Cirque d'Hiver (originally Cirque Napoléon), which opened in Paris, France on 11 Dec 1852.

The largest traveling circus tent was that of Ringling Bros and Barnum & Bailey, which was used on tours in the United States from 1921 to 1924. It covered 91,415 ft^2, consisting of a round top 200 ft in diameter with five middle sections 60 ft wide.

The largest audience for a circus was 52,385 for Ringling Bros and Barnum & Bailey, at the Superdome, New Orleans, LA on 14 Sep 1975. The largest audience in a tent was 16,702 (15,686 paid), also for Ringling Bros and Barnum & Bailey, at Concordia, KS on 13 Sep 1924.

Flexible pole The first and only publicly performed quadruple back somersault on the flexible pole was accomplished by Maxim Dobrovitsky (USSR) at the Egorov Troupe at the International Circus Festival of Monte Carlo in Monaco on 4 Feb 1989.

Corina Colonelu Mosoianu (Romania) is the only person to have performed a triple full twisting somersault, at Madison Square Garden, New York City, on 17 Apr 1984.

DID YOU KNOW?

The greatest number of plates ever spun simultaneously is 108, by Dave Spathaky of London, Great Britain for the Tarm Pai Du television program in Thailand on 23 Nov 1992.

High diving Col. Harry A. Froboess (Switzerland) jumped 394 ft into the Bodensee from the airship *Graf Hindenburg* on 22 Jun 1936.

The greatest height reported for a dive into an air bag is 326 ft, by stuntman Dan Koko, who jumped from the top of Vegas World Hotel and Casino onto a 20 × 40 × 14 ft target on 13 Aug 1948.

Stilt-walking The fastest stilt-walker on record is Roy Luiking, who covered 328 ft on 1-ft-high stilts in 13.01 sec at Didam, Netherlands on 28 May 1992.

Over a long distance, the fastest is M. Garisoain of Bayonne, France, who in 1892 walked the 4.97 miles from Bayonne to Biarritz on stilts in 42 min, an average speed of 7.10 mph.

The greatest distance ever walked on stilts is 3,008 miles, from Los Angeles, CA to Bowen, KY by Joe Bowen from 20 Feb–26 Jul 1980.

The tallest and heaviest stilts ever mastered measured 40 ft 9½ in from ground to ankle and weighed 57 lb each. Eddy Wolf ("Steady Eddy") of Loyal, WI walked a distance of 25 steps without touching his safety handrail wires on 3 Aug 1988 using these stilts.

Illustration: Francis Button. © Guinness Publishing

Human cannonball

The first human cannonball was Eddie Rivers (USA), billed as "Lulu," from a Farini cannon at Royal Cremorne Music Hall, London, Great Britain in 1871. Emanuel Zacchini (Italy) was fired a record 175 ft from a cannon in the United States in 1940.

Human pyramid

The weight record is 1,700 lbs, when Tahar Douis supported 12 members of the Hassani Troupe (three levels in height) at the BBC TV studios, Birmingham, Great Britain on 17 Dec 1979. The height record is 39 ft, when Josep-Joan Martinez Lozano of the Colla Vella dels Xiquets mounted a nine-high pyramid at Valls, Spain on 25 Oct 1981.

Horseback riding

The record for consecutive somersaults on horseback is 23, by James Robinson (USA) at Spalding & Rogers Circus, Pittsburgh, PA in 1856. Willy, Beby and Rene Fredianis (Italy) performed a three-high column at Nouveau Cirque, Paris, France in 1908, a feat not since emulated. "Poodles" Hanneford (Ireland; b. England) holds the record for running leaps on and off, with 26 at Barnum & Bailey Circus, New York in 1915.

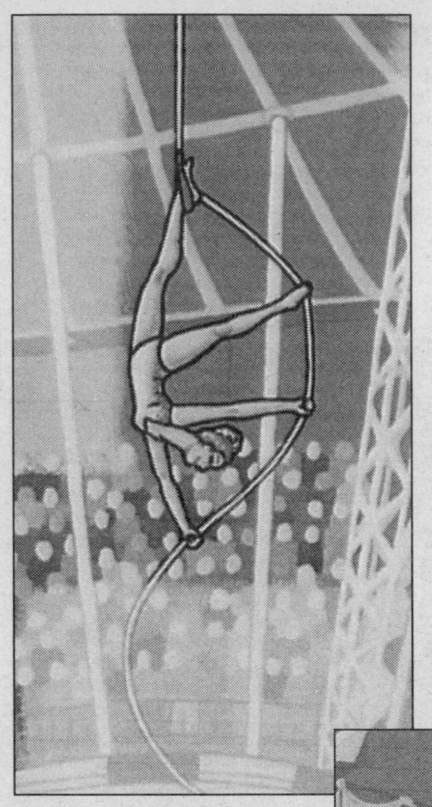

Aerial acts

The highest trapeze act was performed by Ian Ashpole (Great Britain) at a height of 16,420 ft, suspended from a hot-air balloon between St Neots and Newmarket, Great Britain on 16 May 1986. Janet May Klemke (USA) performed 305 one-arm planges at Medina Shrine Circus, Chicago, IL on 21 Jan 1938. Angela Revelle performed the first single-heel hang on a swinging bar in Australia in 1977.

Wild animal presentations

Willy Hagenbeck (Germany) worked with 70 polar bears in a presentation at the Paul Busch Circus, Berlin, Germany in 1904. The greatest number of lions mastered and fed in a cage by an unaided lion-tamer was 40, by "Captain" Alfred Schneider in 1925. Clyde Raymond Beatty (USA) handled 43 "cats" (lions and tigers) simultaneously in 1938, and was the featured attraction at every show he appeared in for more than 40 years.

Flying return trapeze

A flying return trapeze act was first performed by Jules Léotard (France) at Cirque Napoléon, Paris, France on 12 Nov 1859. A triple back somersault on the flying trapeze was first performed by Lena Jordan (Latvia) to Lewis Jordan (USA) in Sydney, Australia in April 1897. The back somersault record is a quadruple back, by Miguel Vasquez (Mexico) to Juan Vasquez at Ringling Bros and Barnum & Bailey Circus, Tucson, AZ on 10 Jul 1982. The greatest number of consecutive triple back somersaults is 135, by Jamie Ibarra (Mexico) to Alejandro Ibarra, between 23 July–12 Oct 1989, at various locations in the United States.

High wire

A seven-person pyramid (three layers) was achieved by the Great Wallendas (Germany) at Wallenda Circus in 1947. The highest high-wire feat (ground supported) was at a height of 1,350 ft by Philippe Petit (France) between the towers of the World Trade Center, New York on 7 Aug 1974.

Teeter board The Kehaiovi Troupe (Bulgaria) achieved a seven-person-high perch pole column at Blackpool Tower Circus, Blackpool, Great Britain on 16 Jul 1986.

Trampoline Marco Canestrelli (USA) performed a septuple twisting back somersault to bed at Ringling Bros and Barnum & Bailey Circus, St Petersburg, FL on 5 Jan 1979. He also managed a quintuple twisting back somersault to a two-high column, to Belmonte Canestrelli at Ringling Bros and Barnum & Bailey Circus, New York City, on 28 Mar 1979. Richard Tison (France) achieved a triple twisting triple back somersault at Berchtesgaden, Germany on 30 Jun 1981.

Traveling amusement park The largest traveling amusement park or carnival in the United States is Amusements of America, which encompasses a route of over 19,000 miles, with a yearly attendance in excess of 8 million people.

PHOTOS & CAMERAS

PHOTOGRAPHS

Oldest photograph The earliest known surviving photograph, by Joseph Niépce (1765–1833), was taken in 1827 using a camera obscura and shows the view from the window of his home. It is now in the Gernsheim Collection at the University of Texas, Austin, TX.

Most expensive photograph A photograph by Alfred Stieglitz of the hands of his wife, Georgia O'Keeffe, called *Georgia O'Keeffe—A Portrait with Symbol*, was sold at Christie's, New York City on 8 Oct 1993 for a record $398,500.

CAMERAS

Largest The largest and most expensive industrial camera ever built is the 30 ton Rolls-Royce camera now owned by BPCC Graphics Ltd of Derby, commissioned in 1956. It measures 8 ft 10 in high, 8¼ ft wide and 46 ft in length. The lens is a 63 in f 16 Cooke Apochromatic.

A pinhole camera was created from a Portakabin unit measuring 34 × 9½ × 9 ft by photographers John Kippen and Chris Wainwright at the National Museum of Photography, Film and Television at Bradford, Great Britain on 25 Mar 1990. The unit produced a direct positive measuring 33 × 4 ft 2 in.

Largest lens The National Museum of Photography, Film and Television, Bradford, Great Britain has the largest lens on display, made by Pilkington Special Glass Ltd, St Asaph, Great Britain. Its dimensions are: focal length 333 in, diameter 54 in, weight 474 lb. Its focal length allows writing on the museum's walls to be read from a distance of 40 ft.

Smallest Apart from cameras built for espionage and intracardiac surgery, the smallest that has been marketed is the circular Japanese "Petal" camera, with a diameter of 1.14 in and a thickness of 0.65 in. It has a focal length of 0.47 in.

Fastest A camera built for research into high-power lasers by The Blackett Laboratory of Imperial College of Science and Technology, London, Great Britain registers images at a rate of 33 billion per sec. The fastest production camera is currently the Imacon 675, made by Hadland Photonics Ltd of Bovington, Great Britain, at up to 600 million frames per sec.

Camera auction The record total for any camera auction is £296,043 ($503,000) for a collection of "spy," subminiature and detective cameras sold at Christie's, London, Great Britain on 9 Dec 1991.

The highest auction price for a camera is $58,727 for a gold camera custom-made for Sultan Abdul Aziz of Morocco in 1901. It was sold at Christie's, London on 25 Nov 1993.

Longest negative On 6 May 1992 Thomas Bleich of Austin, TX produced a negative measuring 23 ft 4½ in × 10½ in using a 10½ in focal length Turner-Reich lens and Kodak No. 10 Cirkut Camera. The photograph was a portrait of about 3,500 attendants at a concert in Austin.

CINEMA

FILMS

Origins The earliest motion pictures were made by Louis Aimé Augustin Le Prince (1842–90), who was attested to have achieved dim moving outlines on a whitewashed wall at the Institute for the Deaf, Washington Heights, New York City as early as 1885–1887. The earliest surviving film (sensitized 2⅛ in wide paper roll) is from his camera, taken in early October 1888, of the garden of his father-in-law, Joseph Whitley, in Roundhay, Great Britain at 10 to 12 frames per second.

Earliest feature film The world's first full-length feature film was *The Story of the Kelly Gang*, made in Melbourne, Victoria, Australia in 1906. Produced on a budget of £450, this biography of the notorious armored bushranger Ned Kelly (1855–80) ran for 60–70 minutes and opened at the Melbourne Town Hall on 26 Dec 1906. It was produced by the local theatrical company J. and N. Tait.

Earliest "talkie" The earliest sound-on-film motion picture was achieved by Eugene-Augustin Lauste (1857–1935), who patented his process on 11 Aug 1906 and produced a workable system using a string galvanometer in 1910 at Benedict Road, London, Great Britain. The earliest public presentation of sound on film was by the Tri-ergon process at the Alhambra Theater, Berlin, Germany on 17 Sep 1922.

United States The earliest screening of a sound-on-picture motion picture in the United States before a paying audience was at the Rivoli Theater in New York City on 15 Apr 1923. The first all-talking motion picture was Warner Brothers' *Lights of New York*, shown at the Strand Theater, New York City on 6 Jul 1928.

Country with largest output India's production of feature-length films was a record 948 in 1990, and its annual output has exceeded 700 every year since 1979.

In the United States, 330 films were produced in 1991; 479 were produced in 1988, the most in a year since 1968.

Most expensive film At the time of its release in July 1991, *Terminator 2: Judgment Day* was reported to have cost Carolco Pictures $95 million, plus print and advertising costs of about $20 million. Its star, Arnold Schwarzenegger, was believed to have received a fee of $15 million for the film.

In terms of real costs adjusted for inflation, the most expensive film ever made was *Cleopatra* (USA, 1963), whose $44 million budget would be equivalent to over $200 million in 1993.

Most expensive film rights The highest price ever paid for film rights was $9.5 million, announced on 20 Jan 1978 by Columbia for *Annie*, the Broadway musical by Charles Strouse.

Longest film The longest film commercially released in its entirety was Edgar Reitz's 25 hr 32 min *Die Zweite Heimat* (Germany, 1992), premiered in Munich on 5–9 Sep 1992.

Highest box office gross The box office gross champion is Universal's *Jurassic Park*. It earned $875.3 million ($345 million in North America; $530.3 million elsewhere) through April 1994.

Batman Returns (Warner Brothers) set an opening-day record of $16.1 million on 19 Jun 1992 and also a single-day record of $16.8 million on 20 June during its US opening weekend at a record 2,644 theaters.

Foreign language The highest-grossing foreign language film in the United States is Alfonso Arau's *Like Water for Chocolate*, which had made $20,380,744 as of May 1994.

Largest film premiere *A Few Good Men*, starring Tom Cruise, Demi Moore and Jack Nicholson, was released simultaneously in over 50 countries by Columbia Pictures in December 1992.

Largest loss *Inchon!*, a film about UN landings in Inchon Bay during the Korean War, starring Laurence Olivier (1907–89), was given limited release in the southwestern United States in 1982. It was withdrawn after four days, having earned less than $5,000. The film had cost in excess of $102 million to make.

Highest earnings Jack Nicholson stood to receive up to $60 million for playing "The Joker" in Warner Brothers' $50 million *Batman*, through a percentage of the film's receipts in lieu of salary.

Most durable series The longest series of films is the 100 features made in

Hong Kong about the 19th century martial arts hero Huang Fei-Hong, starting with *The True Story of Huang Fei-Hong* (1949) and continuing through *Once Upon a Time in China 2* (1992). The most durable continuing series with the same star is Shockiku Studios of Japan's 46 *Tora-San* comedy films, featuring Kiyoshi Atsumi (b. 1929) in a Chaplinesque role from August 1969 to December 1992.

Most profitable series The most successful movie series is the 18 James Bond films, from *Dr No* (1962) starring Sean Connery to *License to Kill* (1989) with Timothy Dalton. The series has grossed over $1 billion worldwide to date.

Fastest film production The feature film *Mohabbat Ka-Mashiba* was filmed by a 90-member production team in 48 hours in 1990. It was written, produced and directed by M. Maroof of Lucknow, India.

Largest studios The largest complex of film studios in the world is the one at Universal City, Los Angeles, CA. The back lot contains 479 buildings and there are 31 sound stages on the 420-acre site.

Largest studio stage The world's largest studio stage is the 007 stage at Pinewood Studios, Buckinghamshire, Great Britain. It was designed by Ken Adam and Michael Brown and built in 1976 for the James Bond film *The Spy Who Loved Me*. It measures 336 × 139 × 41 ft, and accommodates 1.2 million gallons of water, a full-scale 672,000 ton oil tanker and three scaled-down nuclear submarines.

Largest film set The largest film set ever built was the 1,312 × 754 ft Roman Forum designed by Veniero Colosanti and John Moore for Samuel Bronston's production of *The Fall of the Roman Empire* (1964). It was built on a 55 acre site outside Madrid, Spain, where 1,100 workmen spent seven months laying the surface of the Forum with 170,000 cement blocks, erecting 22,000 ft of concrete stairways, 601 columns and 350 statues, and constructing 27 full-size buildings.

Largest number of extras It is believed that over 300,000 extras appeared in the funeral scene of Sir Richard Attenborough's *Gandhi* (1982).

Most expensive prop The highest price paid at auction for a film prop is $275,000 at Sotheby's, New York City on 28 Jun 1986 for James Bond's Aston Martin DB5 from *Goldfinger* (Great Britain, 1964).

Longest directorial career The directorial career of King Vidor (1894–1982) lasted for 67 years, beginning with the two-reel comedy *Hurricane in Galveston* (1913) and culminating in another short, a documentary called *The Metaphor* (1980).

Oldest director The Dutch director Joris Ivens (1898–1989) made the Franco-Italian co-production *Une Histoire de Vent* in 1988 at the age of 89. He made his directorial debut with the Dutch film *De Brug* in 1928. Hollywood's oldest director was George Cukor (1899–1983), who made his 50th and final film, MGM's *Rich and Famous*, in 1981 at the age of 81.

1993's Jurassic Park *reached new heights in special effects technology and box office receipts. (Kobal Collection)*

MOST SUCCESSFUL DIRECTOR

Steven Spielberg is the most successful filmmaker ever, with seven movies in the all-time top ten. Collectively, his films have grossed more than $2.17 billion. *Schindler's List*, Spielberg's masterful and moving portrayal of the Holocaust, won him his first "Best Director" Oscar.

(David James/Universal Studios Inc.)

Spielberg's Top-Grossing Movies

Movie	Year	North American Gross ($ millions)
E.T. The Extra-Terrestrial[1]	1982	399.0
Jurassic Park[2]	1993	345.0
Jaws	1975	260.0
Raiders of the Lost Ark	1981	242.0
Indiana Jones and the Last Crusade	1989	197.0
Indiana Jones and the Temple of Doom	1984	180.0
Close Encounters of the Third Kind	1977	165.0
Hook	1991	116.0
The Color Purple	1985	94.0
Schindler's List[3]	1993	74.7

[1] Includes 1985 re-release.

[2] *Jurassic Park* is the biggest-grossing movie worldwide, with receipts of $875.3 million through April 1994. *E.T.* is the North American Champ, but is only second worldwide, earning $640.5 million during its first release.

[3] As of 3 Apr 1994.

Amblin Entertainment

Spielberg-directed movies dominated the 1994 Academy Awards. Jurassic Park *and* Schindler's List *won 10 Oscars between them. (Gamma/B. King/Liaison)*

In 1975 Jaws *crossed $260 million at the box office and created the summer blockbuster movie phenomenon. (Kobal Collection Universal)*

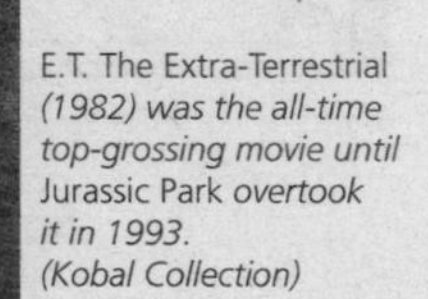

E.T. The Extra-Terrestrial *(1982) was the all-time top-grossing movie until* Jurassic Park *overtook it in 1993. (Kobal Collection)*

The Color Purple *(1986) earned Spielberg the Directors' Guild of America Award and was nominated for 11 Academy Awards. (Kobal Collection/ Warner Brothers)*

GUESS WHAT?

Q. Where is the world's largest casino?

A. See "Resorts" (Buildings & Structures)

Youngest director The film *Lex the Wonderdog*, a thriller of canine detection, was written, produced, and directed by Sydney Ling (b. 1959) when he was 13 years old. Ling was therefore the youngest-ever director of a professionally made feature-length film.

Oldest performer The oldest screen performer in a speaking role was Jeanne Louise Calment (b. 1875–*fl.* April 1994), who portrayed herself in the 1990 Canadian film *Vincent and Me*. She is the last living person to have known Vincent van Gogh.

Most durable performers The record for the longest screen career is 83 years, held by German actor Curt Bois (1900–91), who made his debut in *Der Fidele Bauer* at the age of eight and whose most recent films include *Wings of Desire* (1988). American actress Helen Hayes (1900–93) first appeared on screen at the age of 10 in *Jean and the Calico Doll*, with much of her later work being for television. Her last screen role was in *Divine Mercy, No Escape* (1988) in a career lasting 78 years. The most enduring star of the big screen was Lillian Gish (1893–1993—although her birthdate is usually given as 1896). She made her debut in *An Unseen Enemy* (1912), and her last film in a career spanning 75 years was *The Whales of August* (1987).

Most generations of screen actors in a family There are four generations of screen actors in the Redgrave family. Roy Redgrave (1872–1922) made his screen debut in 1911 and continued to appear in Australian films until 1920. His son, Sir Michael Redgrave, married actress Rachel Kempson, and their two daughters Vanessa and Lynn and son Corin are all actors. Vanessa's two daughters, Joely and Natasha, and Corin's daughter Jemma, are also actresses.

Most portrayed character The character most frequently recurring on the screen is Sherlock Holmes, created by Sir Arthur Conan Doyle (1859–1930). The Baker Street sleuth has been portrayed by some 75 actors in over 211 films since 1900.

In horror films the character most often portrayed is Count Dracula, created by the Irish writer Bram Stoker (1847–1912). Representations of the Count or his immediate descendants outnumber those of his closest rival, Frankenstein's monster, by 160 to 115.

Most films seen Gwilym Hughes of Dolgellau, Great Britain had seen 20,064 films by March 1991. He saw his first film in 1953 while in the hospital.

Albert E. van Schmus (b. 1921) saw 16,945 films in 32 years (1949–1982) as a rater for the Motion Picture Association of America Inc.

Welshman Gwilym Hughes has seen more than 20,000 movies. He's lost track of how much popcorn he's eaten. (Gwilym Hughes)

Costumes The largest number of costumes used for any one film was 32,000 for the 1951 film *Quo Vadis*.

Most changes Elizabeth Taylor changed costume 65 times in *Cleopatra* (1963). The costumes were designed by Irene Sharaff and cost $130,000.

Most expensive Constance Bennett's sable coat in *Madame X* was valued at $50,000. The most expensive costume designed and made specially for a film was Edith Head's mink and sequins dance costume worn by Ginger Rogers in *Lady in the Dark*. It cost Paramount $35,000. The ruby slippers, a personal prop worn by Judy Garland in the 1939 film *The Wizard of Oz*, were sold on 2 Jun 1988 to a mystery buyer at Christie's, New York for $165,000.

Highest-paid stunt performer Stuntman Dar Robinson was paid $100,000 for the 1,000 ft leap from the CN Tower, Toronto, Canada in November 1979 for *High Point*. His parachute opened just 300 ft above ground.

Oscar winners Walter (Walt) Elias Disney (1901–66) won more Oscars—the awards of the Academy of Motion Picture Arts and Sciences, instituted on 16 May 1929—than any other person. The physical count comprises 20 statuettes and 12 other plaques and certificates, including posthumous awards.

The only person to win four Oscars in starring roles is Katharine Hepburn (b. 8 Nov 1909), for *Morning Glory* (1932/33), *Guess Who's Coming to Dinner* (1967), *The Lion in Winter* (1968) and *On Golden Pond* (1981). She has been nominated 12 times. Edith Head (1907–81) won eight individual awards for costume design.

The film with the most awards is *Ben Hur* (1959) with 11. The film with the most nominations was *All About Eve* (1950) with 14. It won 6 awards.

Youngest winners The youngest winner in competition was Tatum O'Neal (b. 5 Nov 1963), who was 10 when she received the award in 1974 for Best Supporting Actress in *Paper Moon* (1973). Shirley Temple (b. 23 Apr 1928) was awarded an honorary Oscar at the age of five in 1934.

Oldest winners The oldest recipients, George Burns (b. 20 Jan 1896) for *The Sunshine Boys* in 1976 and Jessica Tandy (b. 7 Jun 1909) for *Driving Miss Daisy* in 1990, were both 80 at the time of the presentation, although Miss Tandy was the elder by five months.

MOVIE THEATERS

Largest The largest movie theater in the world is the Radio City Music Hall, New York City, opened on 27 Dec 1932, with 5,945 (now 5,874) seats. Kinepolis, the first eight screens of which opened in Brussels, Belgium in 1988, is the world's largest theater complex. It has 24 screens and a total seating capacity of 7,000.

Highest attendance The largest movie theater audience is that of China, with mainland attendance figures of 14 billion in 1991, compared with a peak of 21.8 billion in 1988.

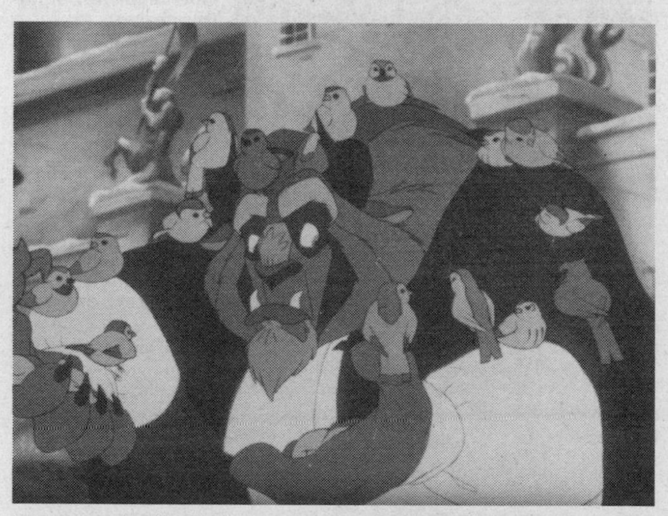

The Disney animated classics have dominated the best-selling video categories. *The Jungle Book, Beauty and the Beast* (above), and *Aladdin* have all set records. The 1994 release of *Snow White and the Seven Dwarfs* is expected to eclipse the marks of these movies. (Walt Disney Co.)

Nashville's legendary theater, the Grand Ole Opry, is the backdrop for one of radio's longest-running shows. Every country star has appeared on the show, including Garth Brooks (top), Vince Gill (middle) and Johnny Cash (bottom). (Gaylord Entertainment/Donnie Beauchamp)

Biggest screen The largest permanently installed theater screen, with an area of 96 × 70½ ft, is located at the Keong Emas Imax Theatre, Taman Mini Park, Jakarta, Indonesia, opened on 20 Apr 1984. The Six Flags Great America Pictorium, Gurnee, IL, opened in 1979, has a screen of equal size, but it is 3D. A temporary screen measuring 297 × 33 ft was used at the 1937 Paris Exposition in France.

Highest box office gross In 1993, domestic gross box office receipts (USA only) were $5 billion, an all-time high.

VIDEO

Best-selling video The world's best-selling video is Walt Disney's *Aladdin*. Released in North America in October 1993, it had sold over 24 million copies in the United States and Canada by April 1994.

Fastest video production Tapes of the Royal Wedding of HRH Prince Andrew and Miss Sarah Ferguson on 23 Jul 1986 were produced by Thames Video Collection. Live filming ended with the departure of the honeymoon couple from Chelsea Hospital by helicopter at 4:42 P.M. The first fully edited and packaged VHS tapes were purchased 5 hr 41 min later at the Virgin Megastore in Oxford Street, London, Great Britain at 10:23 P.M.

RADIO

Origins The authentic first patent for a system of communication by means of electromagnetic waves, numbered No. 12039, was granted on 2 Jun 1896 to the Italian-Irish Marchese Guglielmo Marconi (1874–1937). A public demonstration of wireless transmission of speech was, however, given in Murray, KY in 1892 by Nathan B. Stubblefield.

The first permanent wireless installation was constructed on the Isle of Wight, Great Britain, by Marconi's Wireless Telegraph Co. Ltd, in November 1897.

Most durable programs *Rambling with Gambling*, the early morning program on WOR, New York City, was first broadcast in March 1925 and celebrated its 21,569th show on 30 Apr 1994. The show has been hosted by three generations of the Gambling family: John B. Gambling (1925–59), John A. Gambling (1959–present) and John R. Gambling (1985–present). The show currently airs six days a week, year round.

The Grand Ole Opry has broadcast continuously from November 1925 to May 1994, a total of more than 68 years.

The weekly sports report "The Tenpin Tattler" was first broadcast on WCFL, Chicago, IL on 24 Aug 1935. Fifty-eight years and more than 2,900 broadcasts later, it continues on WGN, Chicago with the original host, Sam Weinstein, who is the longest continuing host of a program.

Longest continuous radio broadcast Radio Telefis Éireann transmitted an

BROADCASTING

"Henry Aaron told me that he never thought about Babe Ruth's record until he looked up one day and saw he had 650 homers," recalls the King of broadcasting. "When I heard the number of hours I'm on, and realized that I had interviewed over 40,000 people, it was like, wow!"

If Larry King thinks and talks like Everyman, he figures that's part of his charm. "I'm very curious, and I read a lot. I tend to work impromptu." That means going on the air without a list of carefully researched and studied questions to ask his guests. "Sometimes I don't even know who the guest is till I get in. If I had to do a lot of preparation, I couldn't do this."

King got his start as a kid, play-announcing the cars that drove through his Brooklyn neighborhood. At 23, he had his own radio show. Now in his sixties, King has become a powerful voice in American broadcasting, so influential that a presidential campaign wouldn't be complete without an appearance on his show. Still, King holds no special brief for celebrities. "It has been fascinating to meet so many people, but I don't get nervous anymore. They put their pants on one leg at a time."

Even First Ladies don't intimidate him. Hillary Rodham Clinton spent her interview interviewing her interviewer about Eleanor Roosevelt. With a sigh, King recalls interviewing Roosevelt when he was 24. "She was beyond anyone else." The guest who made him most nervous? Quick response: "Sinatra. I used to sit in the Paramount Theater and watch him as a kid. There I was, interviewing him. Wow."

unedited reading of *Ulysses* by James Joyce (1881–1941) for 29 hr 38 min 47 sec on 16–17 Jul 1982.

Most hours broadcast per week Larry King's radio and television programs were broadcast a combined 36 hours per week from 1985 through 27 May 1994 in 131 countries. From 30 May 1994 onward, King's television and radio shows aired simultaneously for one hour nightly.

Most stations The country with the greatest number of radio broadcasting stations is the United States, where there were 11,608 authorized broadcast stations as of 31 Mar 1994, made up of 4,933 AM stations, 5,001 FM stations and 1,674 FM educational stations.

Largest audience Surveys carried out in 90 countries showed that, in 1993, the global estimated audience for the British Broadcasting Corporation World Service, broadcast in 39 languages, was 130 million regular listeners—greater than the combined listenership of Voice of America, Radio Moscow and *Deutsche Welle*.

Largest response The largest recorded response to a radio show occurred on 21–27 Jun 1993, when FM Osaka 85.1 in Osaka, Japan received a total of 8,091,309 calls in response to a phone-in lottery. The prize was 100,000 yen (around $1,500), and a chance to win it was offered for a twenty-minute period every hour, for 10 hours each day. The maximum call count in one day of phone-ins (3 hours 20 minutes) was 1,540,793 on 23 Jun 1993.

Biggest radio prize Mary Buchanan, 15, on WKRQ Cincinnati won a prize of $25,000 for 40 years (or $1 million) on 21 Nov 1980.

Most assiduous radio ham The late Richard C. Spenceley of KV4AA at St Thomas, VI built his contacts (QSOs) to a record level of 48,100 in 365 days in 1978.

TELEVISION

At the end of 1992 there were 1,125 commercial television stations in the United States.

Origins A.A. Campbell Swinton (1863–1930) published the fundamentals of television transmission on 18 Jun 1908 in a brief letter to the publication *Nature* entitled "Distant Electric Vision."

The earliest public demonstration of television was given on 27 Jan 1926 by John Logie Baird (1888–1946) of Scotland, using a development of the mechanical scanning system patented by Paul Gottlieb Nipkow (1860–1940) on 6 Jan 1884.

Most durable shows The world's most durable TV show is NBC's *Meet the*

Press, first transmitted on 6 Nov 1947 and broadcast weekly since 12 Sep 1948. As of 22 May 1994, 2,344 shows had been broadcast.

The last televised broadcast of the Joe Franklin Show aired in August 1993. Starting in 1951, Franklin hosted 31,015 episodes of the show and conducted 309,136 interviews.

Stock Market Observer is the longest-running television show in terms of total hours of air time. Since August 1967 it has broadcast more than 39,779 hours of New York Stock Exchange floor trading.

Most episodes Since 1949 over 150,000 individual episodes of the TV show *Bozo the Clown*, by Larry Harmon Pictures, have been aired daily on 150 stations in the United States and abroad.

Most hours on camera The greatest number of hours on camera on US national television is 10,347 hr by the TV personality Hugh Downs in over 47 years up to 19 May 1994.

Greatest audience The highest-ever TV viewership was 134.8 million, watching Super Bowl XXVIII on NBC on 30 Jan 1994.

The program that attracted the highest-ever rating share was the "Goodbye, Farewell and Amen" final episode of *M*A*S*H*, transmitted by CBS on 28 Feb 1983 to 60.3 percent of all households in the United States. It was estimated that some 125 million people tuned in, taking a 77 percent share of all viewing.

The *Muppet Show* is the most widely viewed program in the world, with an estimated audience of 235 million in 106 countries as of August 1989.

Most expensive television rights In November 1991 it was reported that a group of US and European investors, led by CBS, had paid $8 million for the television rights to *Scarlett*, the sequel to Margaret Mitchell's *Gone With the Wind*, written by Alexandra Ripley.

Most Emmy Awards The most Emmys won by any individual is 16, by television producer Dwight Arlington Hemion (b. 14 Mar 1926). He also holds the record for most nominations, with 37. *The Mary Tyler Moore Show* (CBS) has won the most awards for a series, with 29. *Cheers* has received the most nominations, with 117 (winning 27) between 1983 and 1993. The most Emmys awarded to a miniseries was 9, to *Roots* (ABC) in 1977. In 1977 *Eleanor and Franklin: The White House Years* (ABC) received the most Emmys, 11, for a television movie. Columbia Broadcasting System (CBS) holds the record for most Emmys won by a network in a single season, with 44 in 1973–74.

Most expensive production *War and Remembrance* was the most expensive TV production ever, costing $110 million. This 14-episode miniseries was aired by ABC in two parts in November 1988 and Mar 1989, and won the 1989 Emmy Award for best miniseries. Shooting took three years to complete.

Most successful telethon The world record for a telethon is $78,438,573 in pledges in 21½ hours by the 1989 Jerry Lewis Labor Day Telethon on 4 September.

Biggest sale The greatest number of episodes of any TV program ever sold was 1,144 episodes of *Coronation Street* by Granada Television to CBKST Saskatoon, Saskatchewan, Canada, on 31 May 1971. This constituted 20 days 15 hr 44 min of continuous viewing. A further 728 episodes (January 1974–January 1981) were sold to CBC in August 1982.

Most prolific scriptwriter The most prolific television writer in the world was the Rt Hon Lord Willis (1918–92). He created 41 series, 37 stage plays and 39 feature films, and had 29 plays produced. His total output since 1942 was estimated to be 20 million words.

TV producers The most prolific producer in television history was game show producer Mark Goodson (1915-92). Goodson produced over 39,000 episodes totaling more than 21,240 hours of airtime. Since February 1950, a Mark Goodson-produced show has appeared on national television at least once every week.

Aaron Spelling (b. 1928) has produced more than 2,993.5 TV episodes totaling 2,576.5 hours of air time.

TV's most frequent clapper It has been estimated that *Wheel of Fortune* hostess Vanna White claps 720 times per show, or 28,080 times in one year.

Largest sets The Sony Jumbo Tron color TV screen at the Tsukuba International Exposition '85 near Tokyo, Japan in March 1985 measured 80 ft × 150 ft.

Smallest sets The Seiko TV-Wrist Watch, launched on 23 Dec 1982 in Japan, has a 1.2 in screen and weighs only 2.8 oz. Together with the receiver unit and headphones, the entire black and white system, costing 108,000 yen ($1,038), weighs only 11.3 oz.

The smallest single-piece set is the Casio-Keisanki TV-10, weighing 11.9 oz with a 2.7 in screen, launched in Tokyo in July 1983.

The smallest and lightest color set is the Casio CV-1, launched by the Casio Computer Co. Ltd of Japan in 1992, with dimensions of 2.4 × 0.9 × 3.6 in, weighing, with batteries, only 6 oz. It has a screen size of 1.4 in and retails in Japan for 40,000 yen (about $350).

ADVERTISING

TELEVISION

Highest TV advertising rates The highest TV advertising rate was $1,700,000 per minute for NBC network prime time during the transmission of Super Bowl XXVI on 26 Jan 1992, watched by over 120 million viewers.

Shortest commercial An advertisement lasting only four frames (there are 30 frames in a second) was aired on KING-TV's *Evening Magazine* on 29 Nov 1993. The ad was for Bon Marche's Frango candies, and cost $3,780 to make.

A four-frame TV commercial, lasting less than one second, was aired on a Seattle station on 29 Nov 1993. It was over before you could say "Bon Marche's Frango Candies," the subject of the ad.

Fastest production A 30-second TV advertisement for Reebok Insta-PUMP shoes, starring Emmitt Smith of the Dallas Cowboys, was created, filmed and aired during SuperBowl XXVII on 31 Jan 1993. Filming continued until the beginning of the fourth quarter, editing began in the middle of the third quarter, and the finished product was aired during the commercial break at the 2-minute warning of the fourth quarter.

Longest-running commercial characters in TV history The longest-running characters in TV commercials in American television history are Dick Wilson, alias "Mr Whipple," from 1964 to 1989, and Jan Miner as "Madge the Manicurist" from 1965 to 1991.

Most takes The greatest number of takes for a TV commercial is 28, in 1973 by Pat Coombs, the British comedienne. Her explanation was "Every time we came to the punch line I just could not remember the name of the product."

SIGNS

Highest The highest advertising sign is the logo "I" at the top of the 73-story 1,017-ft-tall First Interstate World Center building, Los Angeles, CA.

Most visible The most conspicuous sign ever erected was the electric Citroën sign on the Eiffel Tower, Paris, France. It was switched on on 4 Jul 1925, and could be seen 24 miles away. It was in six colors with 250,000 lamps and 56 miles of electric cables. The letter "N" that terminated the name "Citroën" between the second and third levels measured 68 ft 5 in in height. The whole apparatus was dismantled in 1936.

Largest The largest advertisement on a building measured 41,756 ft^2 and was erected to promote Emirates, the international airline of the United Arab Emirates. It was located along the M4 motorway, near Chiswick, Great Britain, and was displayed from November 1992 to January 1993.

Airborne Reebok International Ltd of Massachusetts flew a banner from a single-seater plane that read "Reebok Totally Beachin." The banner measured 50 ft in height and 100 ft in length, and was flown from 13–16 and 20–23 Mar 1990 for four hours each day at Daytona Beach, FL.

Animated The world's most massive is the one outside the Circus Circus Hotel, Reno, NV, which is named Topsy the Clown. It is 127 ft tall and weighs over 45 tons, with 1.4 miles of neon tubing. Topsy's smile measures 14 ft across.

Billboard The world's largest billboard is that of the Bassat Ogilvy Promotional Campaign for Ford España, measuring 475 ft 9 in in length and 49 ft 3 in in height. It is sited at Plaza de Toros Monumental de Barcelona, Barcelona, Spain, and was installed on 27 Apr 1989.

Illuminated *Longest* The world's longest illuminated sign measures 197 ft × 66 ft. It is lit by 62,400 W metal-halide projectors and was erected by Abudi Signs Industry Ltd of Israel. A larger such sign, measuring 171 × 138 ft, was displayed throughout 1988 on the Australian Mutual Provident Building in Sydney, New South Wales, Australia. The sign, reading "1788–1988," consisted of 4.26 miles of LUMENYTE fiber optics.

Neon The longest neon sign is the letter "M" installed on the Great Mississippi River Bridge, Old Man River at Memphis, TN. It is 1,800 ft long and comprises 200 high-intensity lamps.

The largest measures 210 × 55 ft and was built for Marlboro cigarettes at Hung Hom, Kowloon, Hong Kong in May 1986. It contains 35,000 ft of neon tubing and weighs approximately 126 tons.

An interior-lit fascia advertising sign in Clearwater, FL completed by the Adco Sign Corp. in April 1983 measured 1,168 ft 6½ in in length.

BUSINESS & PUBLIC AFFAIRS

COMMERCE

Oldest industry The oldest known industry is flint knapping, involving the production of chopping tools and hand axes, dating from 2.5 million years ago in Ethiopia. The earliest evidence of trading in exotic stone and amber dates from *c.* 28,000 B.C. in Europe.

Oldest company The oldest existing documented company is Stora Kopparbergs Bergslags of Falun, Sweden, which has been in continuous operation since the 11th century. It is first mentioned in historical records in the year 1288, when a bishop bartered an eighth share in the enterprise, and it was granted a charter in 1347.

Family business The Hōshi Ryokan, a hotel in Japan, dates back to A.D. 717 and has been run as a family business for 46 generations.

Largest company The largest manufacturing company in the world is General Motors Corporation of Detroit, MI, with operations throughout the world and a workforce of 710,000. Its assets in 1993 were $188.2 billion, with sales totaling $138.2 billion and a net profit of $2.465 billion.

Company names The longest company name on the Index registered under the British Companies Acts is "The Only Ordinary People Trying to Impress the Big Guys with Extra Ordinary Ideas, Sales, Management, Creative Thinking and Problem Solving Consultancy Company Ltd," Company number 2660603.

An automotive assembly plant of General Motors Corporation, the largest manufacturing company in the world. (Gamma/Caputo/Liaison)

The shortest names on the Index are D Ltd, E Ltd, H Ltd, Q Ltd, X Ltd and Y Ltd.

Largest employer The world's largest employer is Indian Railways, with 1,654,066 employees on 31 Mar 1992.

Greatest sales The *Fortune 500* list of leading industrial corporations in April 1994 is headed by the General Motors Corporation of Detroit, MI, with sales of $138.2 billion for 1993.

Greatest profit The greatest net profit ever made by a corporation in 12 months is $7.6 billion, by American Telephone and Telegraph Co. (AT&T) from 1 Oct 1981 to 30 Sep 1982.

Greatest loss The world's worst annual net trading loss is $23.5 billion, reported by General Motors for 1992. The bulk of this figure was, however, due to a single charge of some $21 billion for employees' health costs and pensions and was disclosed because of new US accounting regulations.

Takeover The highest bid in a corporate takeover was $21 billion, for RJR Nabisco Inc., the tobacco, food and beverage company, by the Wall Street leveraged buyout firm Kohlberg Kravis Roberts (KKR), which offered $90 a share on 24 Oct 1988. By 1 Dec 1988 the bid, led by Henry Kravis, had reached $109 per share, to total $25 billion.

Bankruptcies On 3 Sep 1992 Kevin Maxwell, son of the former press magnate Robert Maxwell (1923–91), became the world's biggest bankrupt, with debts of £406.8 million (*c.* $813.6 million).

Corporate The biggest corporate bankruptcy in terms of assets was $35.9 billion, filed by Texaco in 1987.

Greatest auction The world's largest-ever public auction took place in Dallas, TX on 1–2 Dec 1992, organized by the Federal Deposit Insurance Corporation (FDIC). Bidders in five other US cities were able to participate via satellite. The 4,000 participants in attendance purchased $418,836,100 in foreclosed, commercial and multifamily property consisting of hotels, residential properties and office buildings. Lots were put on the block every two minutes.

Greatest barter deal The biggest barter in trading history was 30 million barrels of oil, valued at $1,710 million, exchanged for 10 Boeing 747s for the Royal Saudi Airline in July 1984.

Banks The world's biggest commercial bank is the Dai-Ichi Kangyo Bank Ltd of Japan, with assets on 31 Mar 1993 of $427.1 billion.

The largest commercial bank in the United States is Citibank, N.A., located in New York City, with total assets of $216.574 billion and deposits of $145.1 billion for the fiscal year 1993.

The world's largest multilateral development bank is the International Bank of Reconstruction and Development, founded on 27 Dec 1945 and known as the World Bank. Based in Washington, D.C., the bank had an authorized share capital of $167.8 billion on 30 Jun 1993.

Newspaper heir Kevin Maxwell became the world's biggest bankrupt, following the mysterious death of his father, Robert Maxwell, and the subsequent collapse of his father's media empire. (Rex Features/Today Newspaper)

Most branches The bank with most branches is the State Bank of India, which had 12,704 outlets on 31 Dec 1993.

Oldest The oldest bank in the United States in continuous operation is The Bank of New York, founded in 1834 by Alexander Hamilton.

Largest piggy bank The largest piggy bank in the United States measures 6 ft 11 in high × 10 ft × 17 ft 2 in and answers to the name of Penny the Pig. Created by Mary Ann Spanagel and Coldwell Banker Real Estate of Pittsburgh, PA, Penny is used to raise money for the homeless in Pennsylvania.

Penny the Pig, the largest piggy bank in the United States. (Mary Ann Spanagel/Coldwell Banker)

Department stores Woolworth Corporation operates 8,368 general stores worldwide. Frank Winfield Woolworth opened his first store, "The Great Five Cent Store," in Utica, NY on 22 Feb 1879. The corporation's net loss as of 30 Jan 1993 was $495 million.

Drug stores The largest chain of drug stores in the world is Rite Aid Corporation of Shiremanstown, PA, which in 1993 had 2,439 branches throughout the United States. The Walgreen Co. of Deerfield, IL has fewer stores, but a larger volume of sales, totaling $8.3 billion in 1993.

Grocery stores The largest grocery chain in the United States is Kroger Co. of Cincinnati, OH, with sales of $22.38 billion as of 1 Jan 1994. The company also has the most stores in the United States, with 2,217.

Insurance The company with the highest volume of insurance in force in the world is the Metropolitan Life Insurance Co. of New York City, with $1.24 trillion at year end 1993. The Prudential Insurance Company of America of Newark, NJ has the greatest volume of consolidated assets, totaling $218 billion in 1993.

The largest single insurance association in the world is the Blue Cross and Blue Shield Association. It had a membership of 65.8 million in 1993, and benefits paid out totaled $62 billion.

Policies The largest life insurance policy ever issued was for $100 million, bought by a major American entertainment corporation on the life of a leading American entertainment industry figure. The policy was sold in July 1990 by Peter Rosengard of London, Great Britain and was placed by Shel Bachrach of Albert G. Ruben & Co. Inc. of Beverly Hills, CA and Richard Feldman of the Feldman Agency, East Liverpool, OH with nine insurance companies to spread the risk.

The highest payout on a single life was reported on 14 Nov 1970 to be some $18 million to Linda Mullendore, widow of an Oklahoma rancher. Her murdered husband had paid $300,000 in premiums in 1969.

Marine insurance The largest-ever marine insurance loss was approximately $836 million for the Piper Alpha Oil Field in the North Sea. On 6 Jul 1988 a leak from a gas compression chamber underneath the living quarters ignited and triggered a series of explosions that blew Piper Alpha apart. Of the 232 people on board, only 65 survived.

The largest sum claimed for consequential losses was approximately $1.7 trillion against owning, operating and building corporations and Claude Phillips, resulting from the 55-million-gallon oil spill from MT *Amoco Cadiz* on the Brittany coast, France on 16 Mar 1978.

Longest pension Miss Millicent Barclay was born on 10 Jul 1872, three months after the death of her father, Col. William Barclay, and became eligible for a Madras Military Fund pension to continue until her marriage. She died unmarried on 26 Oct 1969, having drawn the pension every day for 97 years 3 months.

Real estate *Landowners* The world's largest landowner is the United States government, with a holding of 728 million acres, which is more than 31 times larger than Indiana.

Most expensive land The most expensive piece of property ever recorded was the land around the central Tokyo retail food store Mediya Building in the Ginza district, which was quoted in October 1988 by the Japanese National Land Agency at 358.5 million yen ($248,000) per ft^2.

Retailer The largest retailer in the United States is Wal-Mart, Inc. of Bentonville, AR, with unaudited sales of $67.3 billion and an unaudited net income of $2.3 billion, as of 31 Jan 1994. Wal-Mart was founded by Samuel Moore "Sam" Walton (1918–92) in Rogers, AR in 1962, and as of 16 May 1994 Wal-Mart had more than 2,700 retail locations, employing 528,000 people.

Rummage sale The Cleveland Convention Center, OH White Elephant Sale (instituted 1933) on 18–19 Oct 1983 raised $427,935.21. The greatest amount of money raised at a one-day sale was $203,247.12 at the 61st one-day rummage sale organized by the Winnetka Congregational Church, IL on 13 May 1993.

Savings and loan association The world's biggest lender is the Japanese-government-controlled House Loan Corporation.

The largest savings and loan association (S&L) in the United States is Home Savings of America, FA in Irwindale, CA. As of 31 Dec 1993 the company had total assets of $50.5 billion and total deposits of $38.02 billion.

ECONOMICS

MONETARY AND FINANCIAL

Largest budget The greatest governmental expenditure ever made by any country was $1.408 trillion by the United States government for the fiscal year 1993. The highest-ever revenue figure was $1.154 trillion in the same fiscal year.

The greatest fiscal surplus ever was $8,419,469,844 in the United States in 1947/48. The worst deficit was $290 billion in the US fiscal year 1992.

Foreign aid The greatest donor of foreign aid has been the United States—the total net foreign aid given by its government between 1 Jul 1945 and 30 Sep 1992 was $406.8 billion.

The country receiving most US aid in 1991 was Israel, with $3.65 billion for both economic and military aid.

Least taxed The sovereign countries with the lowest income tax in the world are Bahrain and Qatar, where the rate is zero, regardless of income. No tax is levied on the Sarkese (inhabitants of Sark), in the Channel Islands, Great Britain.

United States The lowest income tax rate in United States history was 1 percent between 1913 and 1915.

Highest taxation rates The country with the highest taxation is Norway, where the highest rate of income tax in 1992 was 65 percent, although additional personal taxes make it possible to be charged in excess of 100 percent.

In Denmark the highest rate of income tax is 68 percent, but a net wealth tax of 1 percent can result in tax of over 100 percent on income in extreme situations.

United States The highest income tax rate in United States history was implemented in 1944 by the Individual Tax Act with a 91 percent bracket. The current highest income tax bracket is 31 percent.

Highest personal tax levy The highest recorded personal tax levy is one for $336 million on 70 percent of the estate of Howard Hughes.

Balance of payments (current account) The record balance of payments deficit for any country for a calendar year is $167.3 billion in 1987 by the United States. The record surplus was Japan's $136.1 trillion in 1992.

National debt The largest national debt of any country in the world is that of the United States. By the end of 1993, it reached $4.351 trillion, with net interest payments on the debt of $213 billion.

Most foreign debt The country most heavily in overseas debt at the end of

Death and taxes are widely reported to be inevitable—except in Bahrain and Qatar, where income tax is zero. (Gamma/K. Arell/Spooner; Gamma/Y. Gellie)

fiscal year 1992 was the United States, with $449 billion, although the size of its debt is small relative to its economic strength.

Gross national product The country with the largest gross national product is the United States. Having reached $3 trillion in 1981, the GNP was running at $6.38 trillion in the fourth quarter of 1993.

National wealth The richest country in the world, according to the United Nations Statistical Division, is Liechtenstein, which in 1992 had an average

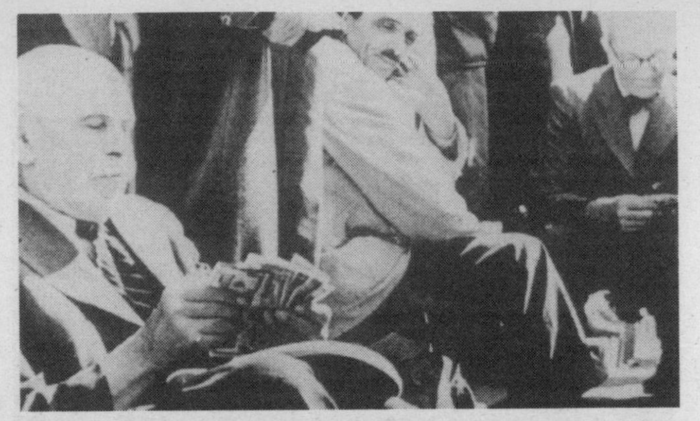

The worst example of hyperinflation occurred after Hungary issued the 10 million pengö banknote in April 1945. Two of these notes were worth $1 on the Budapest black market; before World War II, $1 was worth less than 6 pengös. (Hulton Deutsch Collection)

gross national product (GNP) per capita of $54,607. As of 31 Dec 1993 the per capita income for the United States was $23,332.

According to figures released by the Commerce Department's Bureau of Economic Analysis, in 1993 Connecticut enjoyed the highest per capita income level of any state ($28,110), while Mississippi continued to have the lowest ($14,894). Personal income in the United States totaled $20,817 per person for 1993. Personal income set a record high of $5.37 trillion in 1993.

The median household income in the United States in 1992 was $30,786. Hawaii enjoyed the highest level, at $42,171, and West Virginia had the lowest, at $20,301.

Poorest country Mozambique had the lowest GNP per capita in 1991, with $70, although there are several countries for which the *World Bank Atlas* is not able to include data.

Gold reserves The country with the greatest monetary gold reserves is the United States, whose Treasury held 262 million fine troy oz as of 30 Sep 1993. At $355.10 per fine oz (30 Sep 1993, NY COMEX price), their value was $93.04 billion. The highest price for gold in 1993 was $409 per fine oz.

The United States Bullion Depository at Fort Knox, 30 miles southwest of Louisville, KY, has been the principal federal depository of US gold since December 1936. Gold is stored in 446,000 standard mint bars of 400 troy ounces measuring $7 \times 3^5/_8 \times 1^5/_8$ in. Gold's peak price was $875 per fine oz on 21 Jan 1980.

Inflation The United States Department of Labor measures changes in the Consumer Price Index (CPI) in 12-month periods ending in December. The Bureau of Labor Statistics first began keeping the CPI in 1913. Since that time the change of the greatest magnitude was a 20.4 percent increase for the 12-month period ending December 1918, and the largest decline was –10.8 percent in December 1921. The largest peacetime increase, recorded in December 1979, was 13.3 percent. Figures are based on the United States city average CPI for all urban consumers.

Worst The world's worst inflation occurred in Hungary in June 1946, when the 1931 gold pengö was valued at 130 million trillion (1.3×10^{20}) paper pengös. Notes were issued for "Egymillard billion" (one sextillion or 10^{21}) pengös on 3 June and withdrawn on 11 Jul 1946. Vouchers for 1 billion trillion (10^{27}) pengös were issued for taxation payment only.

The best-known and most frequently analyzed hyperinflationary episode occurred in Germany in 1923. The circulation of the Reichsbank mark on 6 November of that year reached 400,338,326,350,700,000,000 and inflation was 755,700 millionfold at 1913 levels.

The country with the worst inflation in 1993 was Moldova, where prices rose by 2,707 percent.

WEALTH AND POVERTY

Comparisons and estimates of extreme personal wealth present intractable difficulties. Quite apart from reticence and the element of approximation in the valuation of assets, as Jean Paul Getty (1892–1976) once said: "If you can count your millions, you are not a billionaire." The term millionaire was invented *c.* 1740, and the term billionaire in 1861.

Richest men Much of the wealth of the world's monarchs represents national rather than personal assets. The least fettered and most monarchical is HM Sir Muda Hassanal Bolkiah Mu'izzaddin Waddaulah (b. 15 Jul 1946) of Brunei. *Fortune* magazine reported in June 1993 that his fortune was $37 billion.

The richest private individual is Warren Buffett of Omaha, NE, who owns 42 percent of Berkshire Hathaway. *Forbes* magazine listed his net worth as $8.3 billion in October 1993. Taikichiro Mori of Japan (1904–93) was estimated to have assets of $10 billion during 1991.

Richest women Her Majesty Queen Elizabeth II is asserted by some to be the wealthiest woman in the world, and *The Sunday Times* of London, Great Britain estimated in April 1993 that she had assets worth £6.75 billion ($11.7 billion). However, few of her assets under the perpetual succession of the Crown are either personal or disposable, and her personal wealth was estimated at £500 million ($900 million). An alternative estimate published by the British magazine *The Economist* in January 1992 placed her personal wealth at much closer to £150 million ($270 million).

Richest families It has been tentatively estimated that the combined value of the assets nominally controlled by the Du Pont family, of some 1,600 members, may be on the order of $150 billion. The family arrived in the United States from France on 1 Jan 1800.

A more conclusive claim is for the Walton retailing family, worth an estimated $23.5 billion.

Youngest millionaire The youngest self-made millionaire was the American child film actor Jackie Coogan (1914–84), who co-starred with Charlie Chaplin (1889–1977) in *The Kid*, made in 1921.

Bill Gates, the youngest billionaire (above). (Rex Features)

The Sultan of Brunei, the man who has it all (including a reported 153 cars). Here he is seated with his two wives: Princess Salaha (left) and Mariam Bell (right), a former flight attendant now known as Pengiram Isteri Hajjah Mariam. (Photo: Gamma)

"IF YOU CAN COUNT YOUR MILLIONS, YOU ARE NOT A BILLIONAIRE."

JEAN PAUL GETTY

Nubar Gulbenkian in earnest conversation with J. Paul Getty (right). (George Hales/Hulton Deutsch Collection)

Youngest billionaire The youngest of the 101 billionaires reported in the United States in 1992 was William Gates, 36, cofounder of Microsoft of Seattle, WA, whose *MS/DOS* operating system runs on an estimated 72 million of the United States' 90 million personal computers. Gates was 20 when he set up his company in 1976 and was a billionaire by 31.

Highest incomes The largest incomes derive from the collection of royalties per barrel by rulers of oil-rich sheikhdoms who have not formally revoked personal entitlement. Sheikh Zayid ibn Sultan an-Nuhayan (b. 1918), head of state of the United Arab Emirates, arguably has title to some $9 billion of the country's annual gross national product.

Largest dowry The largest recorded dowry was that of Elena Patiño, daughter of Don Simón Iturbi Patiño (1861–1947), the Bolivian tin millionaire, who in 1929 bestowed $39 million from a fortune at one time estimated to be worth $607.5 million.

Largest return of cash The largest amount of cash ever found and returned to its owners was $500,000, discovered by Lowell Elliott, 61, on his farm in Peru, IN. It had been dropped in June 1972 by a parachuting hijacker.

Jim Priceman, 44, assistant cashier at Doft & Co. Inc., returned an envelope containing $37.1 million in *negotiable* bearer certificates found outside 110 Wall Street to A.G. Becker Inc. of New York on 6 Apr 1982. In announcing a reward of $250, Becker was acclaimed as being "all heart."

Charity fund-raising Profits from the single *Do They Know It's Christmas*, recorded by *Band Aid* in 1984, and other related projects in support of the Ethiopian Famine Relief Fund raised $170 million at the close of the account in 1992.

The greatest recorded amount raised by a charity walk or run is $Cdn24.7 million by Terry Fox (1958–81) of Canada who, with an artificial leg, ran from St John's, Newfoundland to Thunder Bay, Ontario in 143 days from 12 Apr–2 Sep 1980. He covered 3,339 miles.

Greatest bequests The largest single bequest in the history of philanthropy was of the art collection belonging to the American publisher Walter Annenberg, which was worth $1 billion. He announced on 12 Mar 1991 that he would be leaving the collection to the Metropolitan Museum of Art in New York City.

The largest single cash bequest was the $500 million gift, announced on 12 Dec 1955, to 4,157 educational and other institutions by the Ford Foundation (established 1936) of New York.

Highest salary It was reported by the US government that Michael Milken, the "junk bond king" at Drexel Burnham Lambert Inc., was paid $550 million in salary and bonuses in 1987. (See Judicial, Fines.)

Largest golden handshake *Business Week* magazine reported in May 1989 that the largest "golden handshake" ever given was one of $53.8 million, to F. Ross Johnson, who left RJR Nabisco as chairman in February 1989.

A 1,000-muhur coin (left) from 17th century India. It weighs 32 troy pounds. (Habsburg)

No false moves! Coin balancing champion Mohammad Irshadullah Hamidi (right) hovers over his record-breaking creation. (M.I. Hamidi)

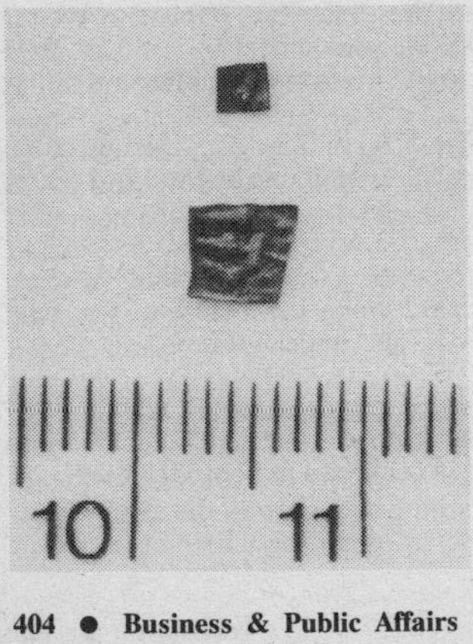

The Nepalese silver 1/4 jawa (left) weighs 14,000 to the ounce. (British Museum)

PAPER MONEY

Earliest Paper money was an invention of the Chinese, first tried in A.D. 812 and prevalent by A.D. 970. The world's earliest bank notes (*banco-sedler*) were issued in Stockholm, Sweden in July 1661, the oldest survivor being one of five dalers dated 6 Dec 1662.

Largest The largest paper money ever issued was the one-guan note of the Chinese Ming Dynasty issue of 1368–99, which measured 9 × 13 in.

Smallest The smallest national note ever issued was the 10-bani note of the Ministry of Finance of Romania, in 1917. It measured (printed area) 1¹/₁₆ × 1¹/₂ in.

Highest values The highest value ever issued by the US Federal Reserve System is a note for $100,000, bearing the head of Woodrow Wilson (1856–1924), which is only used for transactions between the Federal Reserve and the Treasury Department.

The highest-value notes in circulation are US Federal Reserve $10,000 bank notes, bearing the head of Salmon P. Chase (1808–73). It was announced in 1969 that no further notes higher than $100 would be issued, and only 345 $10,000 bills remain in circulation or unretired.

Most expensive The record price paid for a single lot of bank notes was £240,350 ($478,900 including buyer's premium) by Richard Lobel, on behalf of a consortium, at Phillips, London, Great Britain on 14 Feb 1991. The lot consisted of a cache of British military notes that were found in a vault in Berlin, Germany, and contained more than 17 million notes.

Largest collection Chris Boyd of New Malden, Great Britain has accumulated bank notes from 204 different countries, since he started collecting in 1990.

CHECKS AND COINS

Largest An internal US Treasury check for $4,176,969,623.57, was drawn on 30 Jun 1954.

Most expensive collection The highest price ever paid for a coin collection was $25,235,360 for the Garrett collection of US and colonial coins, which had been donated to Johns Hopkins University, Baltimore, MD. The sales were made at a series of four auctions held on 28–29 Nov 1979 and 25–26 Mar 1981 at the Bowers & Ruddy Galleries in Wolfeboro, NH. The collection was put together by members of the Garrett family between 1860 and 1942.

Column of coins The most valuable column of coins was worth 39,458 Irish pounds ($55,063) and was 6 ft 2 in high. It was built by St Brigid's Family and Community Centre in Waterford, Ireland on 20 Nov 1993.

Coin snatching The greatest number of new British 10p pieces clean-caught from being flipped from the back of a forearm into the same downward palm is 328, by Dean Gould of Felixstowe, Great Britain on 6 Apr 1993.

PILE OF COINS

The coins were piled, the money was counted, and there was nothing to do but wait for the armored truck. "The ceremony was over," Seattle–King County YWCA Director of Community Affairs Kerry Coughlin recalls. "The media drifted away, and the attending policeman left to go on duty." It was just Coughlin, Director of Development Carolee Danz, and a pile of coins worth more than $100,000. "We put another tarp on, sat on the coins, and tried to act casual."

The smiles were as shiny as the coins. (YWCA)

Family Village (YWCA)

The truck came at last, and the pile of coins became the cornerstone of a fund-raising effort that was anything but casual. The goal was $3.2 million, and the plan was to build Family Village, a combined unit of housing, employment services, and daycare for homeless families. Now it's built, and several families have already moved in.

Where did the rest of the money come from? "It was really terrific!" smiles Coughlin. "The community pulled together in a unique collaboration of government, private and corporate donors. We had government donations from every level—from a small municipality in east King County to the federal government, and business donations all the way from small stores to Microsoft. People even had parties and asked for contributions to Family Village instead of presents."

"It's been a dream project for us," Coughlin says, noting that contrary to public perception, less than one percent of her Y's budget goes for health and fitness. "Family Village has been open for over a year. It's so good to hear clients saying, 'This is exactly what I needed. We're doing great.'"

Coin balancing Mohammad Irshadullah Hamidi of Muzaffarpur, India stacked a pyramid of 870 coins on the edge of a coin free-standing vertically on the base of another coin that was on a table on 16 Mar 1993.

The tallest single column of coins ever stacked on the edge of a coin was made up of 253 Indian one-rupee pieces on top of a vertical five-rupee coin, by Dipak Syal of Yamuna Nagar, India on 3 May 1991. He also balanced 10 one-rupee coins and 10 ten-paise coins alternately horizontally and vertically in a single column on 1 May 1991.

Hoards The most valuable hoard of coins was one of about 80,000 aurei found in Brescello near Modena, Italy in 1714, and believed to have been deposited *c.* 37 B.C.

Mints Largest The largest mint in the world is that of the US Treasury. It was built from 1965–69 on Independence Mall, Philadelphia and covers 11½ acres, with an annual production capacity on a three-shift seven-day week of 12 billion coins.

COINS

Oldest

Electrum staters of King Gyges of Lydia, Turkey, *c.* 670 B.C.[1]

Earliest Dated

Samian silver tetradrachm struck in Zankle (now Messina), Sicily, dated year 1, viz. 494 B.C.

Heaviest

Swedish 10-daler copper plate, 1644, 43 lb 7¼ oz.
Gold: Islamic 1,000-muhur, 32 lb, minted in Agra, 1613.[2]

Lightest

Nepalese silver ¼ jawa *c.* 1740, 14,000 to the oz.

Most Expensive

Set: $3,190,000 for the King of Siam Proof Set, a set of 1804 and 1834 US coins that had once been given to the King of Siam, purchased by Iraj Sayah and Terry Brand at Superior Galleries, Beverly Hills, CA on 28 May 1990. Included in the set of nine coins was the 1804 silver dollar, which had an estimated value of about $2,000,000.

Individual: $1,500,000 for the US 1907 Double Eagle Ultra High Relief $20 gold coin, sold by MTB Banking Corporation of New York to a private investor on 9 Jul 1990.

[1] *Chinese uninscribed "spade" money of the Zhou dynasty has been dated to* c. *770* B.C.
[2] *The largest coinlike medallion was completed on 21 Mar 1986 for the World Exposition in Vancouver, British Columbia, Canada, Expo 86—a $1,000,000 gold piece. Its dimensions were 37.5 in diameter and ¾ in thick and it weighed 365 lb 15 oz, or 5,337 oz (troy) of gold.*

Fastest The Graebner Press high-speed stamping machine can produce coins at a rate of 42,000 per hour. The record production for coins was in 1982, when 19.5 billion were produced between the Philadelphia and Denver mints.

Smallest The smallest issuing mint in the world belongs to the Sovereign Military Order of Malta, the City of Rome. Its single-press mint is housed in one small room and has issued proof coins since 1961.

Line of coins The most valuable line of coins was made up of 1,724,000 quarters with a value of $431,000. It was 25.9 miles long, and was laid at the Atlanta Marriott Marquis Hotel, GA by members of the National Exchange Club on 25 Jul 1992.

The longest line of coins on record had a total length of 30.38 miles and was made using 1,886,975 two-pence coins. It was laid by the Friends of the Samaritans at the Great Park, Windsor, Great Britain on 16 Aug 1992.

Pile of coins The most valuable pile of coins had a total value of $126,463.61 and consisted of 1,000,298 coins of various denominations. It was constructed by the YWCA of Seattle, King County, WA in Redmond, WA on 28 May 1992. See On the Record feature (p. 406).

EMPLOYMENT

Largest labor union The world's largest union is Professionalniy Soyuz Rabotnikov Agro-Promyshlennogo Kompleksa (Agro-Industrial Complex Workers' Union) in the former Soviet Union, with 15.2 million members in January 1993.

United States As of January 1994 the largest union in the United States was the National Education Association (NEA), which has 2.1 million members.

Smallest labor union The ultimate in small unions was the Jewelcase and Jewelry Display Makers Union (JJDMU), founded in 1894. It was dissolved on 31 Dec 1986 by its general secretary, Charles Evans. The motion was seconded by Fergus McCormack, its only other surviving member.

Longest name The union with the longest name is the International Association of Marble, Slate and Stone Polishers, Rubbers and Sawyers, Tile and Marble Setters' Helpers and Marble, Mosaic and Terrazzo Workers' Helpers, or the IAMSSPRSTMSHMMTWH, based in Washington, D.C.

Earliest labor dispute A labor dispute concerning monotony of diet and working conditions was recorded in 1153 B.C. in Thebes, Egypt. Workers wanted sesame and onions to go with their steady diet of bread and okra.

The earliest recorded strike was one by an orchestra leader named Aristos from Greece, in Rome *c.* 309 B.C. The musicians wanted to eat their midday meal in the temple where they were playing.

Longest strike The world's longest recorded strike ended on 4 Jan 1961, after 33 years. It concerned the employment of barbers' assistants in Copenhagen, Denmark.

Unemployment *Lowest* In December 1973 in Switzerland (population 6.6 million), the total number of unemployed was reported to be 81.

United States The highest annual unemployment average in United States history was 24.9 percent, or 12,830,000 people, in 1933 during the Great Depression, and the lowest average was 1.2 percent, or 670,000 people, in 1944 during World War II, based on a labor force aged 14 and older.

Longest working career The longest working life was one of 98 years, by Mr Izumi (see Human Beings, Oldest authentic centenarian), who began work goading draft animals at a sugar mill at Isen, Tokunoshima, Japan in 1872. He retired as a sugar cane farmer in 1970 at the age of 105.

STOCK EXCHANGES

The oldest stock exchange in the world is that of Amsterdam, Netherlands, founded in 1602 with dealings in printed shares of the United East India Company of the Netherlands in the Oude Zijds Kapel. The largest in trading volume in 1993 was the New York Stock Exchange, with $2,283.4 billion, ahead of London, Great Britain with $1,567.5 billion and the Federation of German Stock Exchanges with $1,336 billion.

New York Stock Exchange The market value of stocks listed on the New York Stock Exchange reached an all-time high of $3.2 trillion in January 1994. The record day's trading was 608,148,710 shares on 20 Oct 1987.

The largest stock trade in the history of the New York Stock Exchange was a 48,788,800-share block of Navistar International Corporation stock at $10 in a $487,888,000 transaction on 10 Apr 1986.

The highest price paid for a seat on the New York Stock Exchange was $1.15 million in 1987. The lowest 20th-century price was $17,000, in 1942.

Closing prices The highest index figure on the Dow Jones Industrial average (instituted 8 Oct 1896) of selected stocks at the close of a day's trading was 3,794.33 on 29 Dec 1993.

The Dow Jones Industrial average, which reached 381.71 on 3 Sep 1929, plunged 30.57 points on 29 Oct 1929, on its way to the Depression's lowest point of 41.22 on 2 Jul 1932. The largest decline in a day, 508 points (22.6 percent), occurred on 19 Oct 1987.

The total lost in security values from 1 Sep 1929 to 30 Jun 1932 was $74 billion. The greatest paper loss in a year was $210 billion in 1974.

The record daily increase, on 21 Oct 1987, was 186.84 points, to 2,027.85.

Largest flotation The largest-ever flotation in stock market history was the £5.2 billion ($9.9 billion) sale of the 12 British regional electricity companies to 5.7 million stockholders at the end of 1990.

The earlier flotation of British Gas plc in 1986 had an equity offer that produced the higher sum of £7.75 billion ($10.85 billion), but to only 4.5 million stockholders.

Longest-listed company Consolidated Edison Company of New York (ConEd) is reported to be the longest continually listed company on the New York Stock Exchange. First traded under the name New York Gas

Light Company in 1824, it formed a merger to create the Consolidated Gas Company of New York in 1884. ConEd took its current name in 1936.

The longest-listed company traded under the same name is the Brooklyn Union Gas Company. Originally listed as the Brooklyn Gas Light Company in the late 1830s, it has been traded under its current name since the mid-1860s.

Most valued company The greatest aggregate market value of any corporation in April 1993 was $120 billion for Exxon of Irving, TX.

Stockholders attendance, greatest A total of 20,109 stockholders attended the annual general meeting in April 1961 of the American Telephone and Telegraph Co. (AT&T), thereby setting a world record.

Longest-serving current member As of 16 May 1994, the longest-serving current member of the New York Stock Exchange was David Granger. He became a member on 4 Feb 1926.

Largest rights issue The largest recorded rights issue was one of £921 million ($1.57 billion) by Barclays Bank, Great Britain, announced on 7 Apr 1988.

Gold prices The highest closing spot price for gold on the Commodities Exchange (COMEX) in New York City was $875 per fine oz on 21 Jan 1980.

Silver prices The highest closing spot price for silver on the Commodities Exchange (COMEX) in New York City was $50.35 per fine oz on 18 Jan 1980.

Highest par value The highest denomination of any share quoted in the world is a single share in Moeara Enim Petroleum Corporation, worth 165,000 Dutch florins ($75,500) on 22 Apr 1992.

POSTAL SERVICES

Largest mail service The country with the largest mail service in the world is the United States. Its population mailed 171 billion letters and packages during the fiscal year 1993, when the US Postal Service employed 710,000 people, with the world's largest civilian vehicle fleet of 198,000 cars and trucks. The average number of letters and packages per capita was 675. There are 39,595 post offices in the US.

Oldest mailboxes The first organized system of roadside mailboxes was es-

GUESS WHAT?

Q. HOW LONG WAS THE LONGEST LETTER?

A. SEE "DIARIES & LETTERS" (ARTS & ENTERTAINMENT)

POSTAGE STAMPS

Earliest

Put on sale 6 May 1840. 1 d Penny Black of Great Britain, Queen Victoria, 68,158,080 printed.

USA

Put on sale in New York City 1 Jul 1847. 5-cent red-brown Benjamin Franklin, 3,712,200 issued, and 10-cent black George Washington, 891,000 issued.

Earliest Adhesive Stamp

Earliest adhesive stamps were those used for local delivery by the City Dispatch Post established in New York City 15 Feb 1842.

Highest Price (Auction)

SFr 3,400,000 ($2,400,000), including buyer's premium. Penny Black, 2 May 1840 cover, bought at Harmers, Lugano, Switzerland, on behalf of a Japanese buyer on 23 May 1991.

£203,500 ($350,000), including buyer's premium, for a philatelic item. Bermuda 1854 Perot Postmasters' Stamp affixed to a letter, 1d red on bluish wove paper, sold by Christie's Robson Lowe, London, Great Britain on 13 Jun 1991.

USA

$1.1 million (including buyer's premium). "Curtiss Jenny" plate block of four 24-cent stamps from 1918 with inverted image of an airplane, bought by an unnamed American executive at Christie's, New York on 12 Oct 1989.

Largest Purchase

$11 million. Marc Haas collection of 3,000 US postal and pre-postal covers to 1869 by Stanley Gibbons International Ltd of London, Great Britain in August 1979.

Largest (Special)

$9^3/_4 \times 2^3/_4$ in. Express Delivery of China, 1913.

USA

$3^3/_4 \times 2$ in. 1865 newspaper stamps.

Largest (Standard)

6.3 × 4.33 in. Marshall Islands 75-cent issued 30 Oct 1979.

USA

$^1/_{11} \times 1^5/_{11}$ in. 5-cent blue and carmine Air Beacon issued 25 Jul 1928, and 2-cent black and carmine George Rogers Clark issued 25 Feb 1929.

Smallest

0.31 × 0.37 in. 10-cent and 1-peso Colombian State of Bolivar, 1863–66.

Highest Denomination

$10,000. Documentary and Stock Transfer stamps, 1952–58.

USA

$100. Indian Maiden, 1895–97

Lowest Denomination

3,000 pengö of Hungary. Issued 1946 when 604.5 trillion pengö = 1 cent.

USA

$^1/_2$ cent. Earliest sepia Nathan Hale, 1925; George Washington, 1932; Benjamin Franklin, 1938 and 1954.

tablished in 1653 in Paris, France, to facilitate the interchange of correspondence in the city. The mailboxes were erected at the intersections of main thoroughfares and were emptied three times a day.

Post offices The country with the greatest number of post offices is India, with 144,829 in 1988.

Stamp licking John Kenmuir of Hamilton, Great Britain licked and affixed 393 stamps in 4 min at the BBC TV studios on 26 Sep 1990.

POLITICAL & SOCIAL

COUNTRIES

The world is made up of 191 sovereign countries and 65 nonsovereign or other territories (dependencies of sovereign states, territories claimed in Antarctica and disputed territories), making a total of 256 as of April 1994.

Largest The country with the greatest area is Russia, with a total area of 6,592,800 miles², or 11.5 percent of the world's total land area. It is 1.8 times the size of the United States, but with 149.47 million people in 1991 has a population about 60 percent the size of the United States population.

The United States covers 3,787,425 miles², with a land area of 3,536,342 miles² and a water area of 251,083 miles². It ranks fourth in the world in area behind Russia, Canada, and China.

Smallest The smallest independent country in the world is the State of Vatican City or Holy See (Stato della Città del Vaticano), which was made an enclave within the city of Rome, Italy on 11 Feb 1929. The enclave has an area of 108.7 acres. The world's smallest republic is Nauru, just south of the equator in the western Pacific, which became independent on 31 Jan 1968. It has an area of 5,263 acres and a population of 9,600 (latest estimate 1992).

Colony Until it was forcibly incorporated into Dahomey (now Benin) in 1961, the smallest colony was the Portuguese enclave of Ouidah, consisting of the Fort of St John the Baptist of Ajuda, with an area of just 5 acres. The smallest colony in the world is now Gibraltar (since 1969, the City of Gibraltar), with an area of 1,440 acres. However, Pitcairn Island, the only inhabited island (55 people in late 1993) of a group of four (total area 18½ miles²), has an area of 960 acres.

Flattest and most elevated The country with the lowest "high point" is Maldives, at 8 ft above sea level. The country with the highest "low point" is Lesotho, where the egress of the Senqu (Orange) riverbed is 4,530 ft above sea level.

Largest political division The Commonwealth, a free association of 50 independent states and their dependencies, covers an area of 11,323,906 miles^2 with a population estimated to be 1,506,517,000. Almost all member countries once belonged to the former British Empire.

National boundaries There are 319 national land boundaries in the world. The continent with the greatest number is Africa, with 109. Of the estimated 420 maritime boundaries, only 140 have so far been ratified. The ratio of boundaries to area of land is greatest in Europe.

The frontier which is crossed most frequently is that between the United States and Mexico. In the fiscal year 1993 (to September 1993) there were 452,657,133 crossings.

Longest boundaries The longest *continuous* boundary in the world is that between Canada and the United States, which (including the Great Lakes boundaries) extends for 3,987 miles (excluding the frontier of 1,538 miles with Alaska). If the Great Lakes boundary is excluded, the longest land boundary is that between Chile and Argentina, which is 3,265 miles in length.

Shortest boundaries The land frontier between Gibraltar and Spain at La Linea, closed between June 1969 and February 1985, measures 1 mile. The "frontier" of the Holy See in Rome measures 2.53 miles. Zambia, Zimbabwe, Botswana and Namibia, in Africa, almost meet at a single point on the Zambezi River.

Most boundaries China has the most land frontiers, with 16—Mongolia, Russia, North Korea, Hong Kong, Macau, Vietnam, Laos, Myanmar (Burma), India, Bhutan, Nepal, Pakistan, Afghanistan, Tajikistan, Kyrgyzstan and Kazakhstan. These extend for 14,900 miles. The country with the largest number of maritime boundaries is Indonesia, with 19. The longest maritime boundary is that between Greenland and Canada at 1,676 miles.

Coastlines Canada has the longest coastline of any country in the world, with 152,100 miles including islands. The sovereign country with the shortest coastline is Monaco, with 3½ miles, excluding piers and breakwaters.

Capital cities The nearest capitals of two neighboring countries are the Vatican City and Rome (Italy), as the Vatican is actually surrounded by Rome. The greatest distance between the capitals of countries that share a common border is 2,600 miles, in the case of Moscow (Russia) and Pyongyang (Democratic People's Republic of Korea).

POPULATIONS

World The world's population in 1993 was 5.5 ± 0.6 billion. The average daily increase is approximately 256,000 or an average of 178 per minute. There are, however, seasonal variations in the numbers of births and deaths throughout the year.

Most populous country The most populous country is China, which had an estimated population of 1,165,888,000 in mid-1992 and had a rate of natural increase of about 14.6 million per year or just over 40,000 per day. Its population is more than that of the whole world 200 years ago.

Least populous country The independent state with the smallest population is Vatican City or the Holy See, with 750 inhabitants in 1992 and no births.

Most densely populated The most densely populated territory in the world is the Portuguese province of Macau, on the southern coast of China. It has an estimated population of 367,000 (1992) in an area of 6.9 $miles^2$, giving a density of $53{,}188/mile^2$.

Most sparsely populated Antarctica became permanently occupied by relays of scientists from 1943 on. The population varies seasonally and reaches 2,000 at times.

Worst housing crisis In 1959, at the peak of the housing crisis in Hong Kong, it was reported that in one house designed for 12 people the number of occupants was 459, including 104 in one room and four living on the roof.

STRIKE!

The longest recorded industrial strike in the world was that at the plumbing fixtures factory of the Kohler Co. in Sheboygan, WI, between April 1954 and October 1962. The strike is alleged to have cost the United Automobile Workers' Union about $12 million to sustain.

Most houses For comparison purposes, a dwelling unit is defined as a structurally separated room or rooms occupied by a private household of one or more people and having separate access or a common passageway to the street.

The country with the greatest number of dwelling units is China, with 276,947,962 in 1990.

Emigration More people emigrate from Mexico than from any other country, mainly to the United States (see also Immigration, below). Wars or droughts periodically cause large upheavals in population; in late 1992 there were some 27 million refugees worldwide.

Immigration The country that regularly receives the most legal immigrants is the United States. During fiscal year 1993 (October 1992–September 1993) an estimated 980,014 people legally entered the United States.

In fiscal year 1993 a total of 1,327,259 people were apprehended for immigration violations. The largest group by nationality were 1,269,294 from Mexico.

Tourism The most popular tourist destination is France, which in 1992 received 59,590,000 foreign tourists. The country with the greatest receipts from tourism is the United States, with $53.9 billion in 1992. The biggest spenders on foreign tourism are Americans, who in the same year spent $39.9 billion abroad.

Death rate The crude death rate—the number of deaths per 1,000 population of all ages—for the whole world was an estimated 9.7 per 1,000 in the period 1985–90. East Timor had a peak rate of 45.0 per 1,000 from 1975–80. The lowest estimated rate for 1985–90 was 3.5 deaths per 1,000 for Bahrain.

Most psychiatrists The country with the most psychiatrists is the United States. The registered membership of the American Psychological Association was 124,000 in 1994, and the membership of the American Psychiatric Association was 38,285.

Suicide The country with the highest suicide rate is Sri Lanka, with a rate of 47 per 100,000 population in 1991. The country with the lowest recorded rate is Jordan, with just a single case in 1970 and hence a rate of 0.04 per 100,000.

Marriage The world's highest marriage rate is for the Northern Mariana Islands, in the Pacific Ocean, where the rate is 31.2 per 1,000 population.

Divorce The country with the most divorces is the United States, with a total of 1,215,000 in 1992—a rate of 4.7 per 1,000 population. The all-time high rate was 5.4 per 1,000 population in 1979. The all-time low was 2.0 per 1,000 population in 1940.

Gender ratio There were estimated to be 1,014 males in the world for every 1,000 females in 1990. The country with the largest recorded shortage of males is the Ukraine, with an estimated 1,153 females to every 1,000 males. The country with the largest recorded shortage of women in 1990 was the United Arab Emirates, with an estimated 493 females to every 1,000 males.

Infant mortality The world infant mortality rate—the number of deaths at ages under one year per 1,000 live births—in 1985–90 was 68 per 1,000 live births. The lowest of the latest recorded rates is 5 per 1,000 in Japan for the period 1985–90. The highest rate recently estimated is 172 per 1,000 in Afghanistan (1985–90).

United States The infant mortality rate for the United States in 1993 was estimated to be 8.5 per 1,000 live births, or 33,000. Washington, D.C. had the highest infant mortality rate in 1993, with 18.5 percent, while Vermont had the lowest, with 4.9 percent.

Life expectancy World life expectancy has risen from 46.4 years (1950–55) to 63.3 years (1985–90).

The highest average life expectancy at birth is in Japan, with 82.1 years for women and 76.1 years for men in 1991. The lowest life expectancy at birth for the period 1985–90 is 39.4 years for males in Ethiopia and Sierra Leone, and 42.0 years for females in Afghanistan.

In 1952 thick smog caused the deaths of about 4,000 people in London, Great Britain. Here, one of London's famed buses inches its way along its route. (Hulton-Deutsch Collection)

WORST DISASTERS IN THE WORLD

Type of Disaster	Number killed	Location	Date
Atomic Bomb	155,200	Hiroshima, Japan (including radiation deaths within year)	6 Aug 1945
Conventional Bombing[1]	*c.* 140,000	Tokyo, Japan	10 Mar 1945
Marine (Single Ship)	*c.* 7,700	*Wilhelm Gustloff* (28,542.1 tons) German liner torpedoed off Danzig by USSR submarine S-13 (only 903 survivors)	30 Jan 1945
Dam Burst[2]	*c.* 5,000	Machhu River Dam, Morvi, Gujarat, India	11 Aug 1979
Panic	*c.* 4,000	Chongquig, China, air raid shelter	6 Jun 1941
Smog	3,500–4,000	London, Great Britain	4–9 Dec 1952
Industrial (Chemical)	3,350	Union Carbide methylisocyanate plant, Bhopal, India	2–3 Dec 1984
Tunneling (Silicosis)	*c.* 2,500	Hawk's Nest hydroelectric tunnel, West Virginia	1931–35
Fire (Single building)[3]	1,670	The Theatre, Canton, China	May 1845
Explosion[4]	1,635	Halifax, Nova Scotia, Canada	6 Dec 1917
Mining[5]	1,549	Honkeiko Colliery, (Benxihu) China (coal dust explosion)	26 Apr 1942
Tornado	*c.* 1,300	Shaturia, Bangladesh	26 Apr 1989
Riot	*c.* 1,400	Riots following arrest of woman selling contraband cigarettes, Taiwan	March 1947
Mass Suicide[6]	960	Jewish Zealots, Masada, Israel	A.D. 73
Railway	>800	Bagmati River, Bihar, India	6 Jun 1981
Fireworks	>800	Dauphin's wedding, Seine, Paris, France	16 May 1770
Aircraft (Civil)[7]	583	KLM-Pan Am Boeing 747 ground crash, Tenerife, Canary Islands, Spain	27 Mar 1977
Man-eating Animal	436	Champawat district, India, tigress shot by Col. Jim Corbett (died 1955)	1902–07
Terrorism	329	Bomb aboard Air-India Boeing 747, crashed into Atlantic southwest of Ireland. Sikh extremists suspected	23 Jun 1985
Road[8]	176	Gas tanker explosion inside Salang Tunnel, Afghanistan	3 Nov 1982
Offshore Oil Platform	167	Piper Alpha oil production platform, North Sea	6 Jul 1988
Submarine	130	*Le Surcouf* rammed by US merchantman Thomas Lykes in Caribbean	18 Feb 1942
Helicopter	61	Russian military helicopter carrying refugees shot down near Lata, Georgia	14 Dec 1992

Mountaineering	43	Lenin Peak, Tajikistan/Kyrgyzstan border (then USSR)	13 Jul 1990
Ski Lift (Cable car)	42	Cavalese resort, northern Italy	9 Mar 1976
Nuclear Reactor[9]	31	Chernobyl No. 4, Ukraine (then USSR)	26 Apr 1986
Elevator (Lift)	31	Gold mine lift at Vaal Reefs, South Africa fell 1.2 miles	27 Mar 1980
Yacht Racing	19	28th Fastnet Race—23 boats sunk or abandoned in Force 11 gale	13–15 Aug 1979
Space Exploration[10]	7	US *Challenger 51L* Shuttle, Cape Canaveral, FL	28 Jan 1986
Nuclear Waste Accident[11]	high but undisclosed	Venting of plutonium extraction wastes, Kyshtym, Russia (then USSR)	*c.* Dec 1957

[1] The number of civilians killed by the bombing of Germany has been put variously at 593,000 and "over 635,000," including some 35,000 deaths in the raids on Dresden, Germany from 13–15 Feb 1945. Total Japanese fatalities were 600,000 (conventional) and 220,000 (nuclear).
[2] The dynamiting of a Yangtze Kiang dam at Huayuan Kou by the Kuomintang during the Sino-Japanese war in 1938 is reputed to have resulted in 900,000 deaths.
[3] >200,000 were killed in the sack of Moscow, as a result of fires started by the invading Tartars in May 1571. In the worst-ever hotel fire, 162 were killed in the Hotel Daeyungak, Seoul, South Korea, 25 Dec 1971. The worst circus fire killed 168 in Hartford, CT 6 Jul 1944.
[4] Some sources maintain that the final death toll was over 3,000 on 6–7 December.
[5] The worst gold-mining disaster in South Africa was when 182 were killed in Kinross gold mine on 16 Sep 1986.
[6] As reported by the historian Flavius Josephus (c. 37–100). In modern times, the greatest mass suicide was on 18 Nov 1978 when 913 members of the People's Temple cult died of mass cyanide poisoning near Port Kaituma, Guyana. In June 1943, 22,000 Japanese jumped off a cliff during the US Marines' assault on the island of Tarawa (now in Kiribati).
[7] The crash of JAL's Boeing 747, flight 123, near Tokyo on 12 Aug 1985, in which 520 passengers and crew perished, was the worst crash involving a single plane in aviation history.
[8] Western estimates gave the number of deaths at c. 1,100. Latvia has the highest fatality rate in road accidents, with 34.7 deaths per 100,000 population, and Malta the lowest, with 1.6 per 100,000. The worst year for road deaths in the United States was 1972 (56,278).
[9] Explosion at 0123 hrs local time. Thirty-one was the official Soviet total of immediate deaths. It is not known how many of the c. 200,000 people involved in the cleanup died in the five-year period following the disaster since no systematic records were kept. The senior scientific officer, Vladimir Chernousenko, who gave himself two to four years to live due to his exposure to radiation, put the death toll at between 7,000 and 10,000 in a statement on 13 Apr 1991.
[10] In the greatest space disaster on the ground, 91 people were killed when an R-16 rocket exploded during fueling at the Baikonur Space Center, Kazakhstan, on 24 Oct 1960.
[11] More than 30 small communities in a 460 mile^2 area were eliminated from maps of the USSR in the years after the accident, with 17,000 people evacuated. It was possibly an ammonium nitrate-hexone explosion. A report released in 1992 indicated that 8,015 people had died over a 32-year period of observation as a direct result of discharges from the complex.

POLITICAL UNREST

Biggest demonstration A figure of 2.7 million was reported from China for a demonstration against the USSR in Shanghai on 3–4 Mar 1969 following border clashes.

Saving of life The greatest number of people saved from extinction by one person is estimated to be nearly 100,000 Jews in Budapest, Hungary from July 1944 to January 1945, by the Swedish diplomat Raoul Wallenberg (b. 4 Aug 1912). After escaping an assassination attempt by the Nazis, he was imprisoned without trial in the Soviet Union. Although officials claimed that Wallenberg died in Lubyanka Jail, Moscow on 16 Jul 1947, sighting reports within the Gulag system persisted for years after his disappearance. He was made an Honorary Citizen of the United States on 5 Oct 1981.

Mass killings *Cambodia* As a percentage of a nation's total population the worst genocide appears to have been that in Cambodia during the Khmer Rouge regime of Saloth Sar, alias Pol Pot. According to the Foreign Minister, Ieng Sary, more than a third of the 8 million Khmers were killed between 17 Apr 1975, when the Khmer Rouge captured Phnom Penh, and January 1979, when they were overthrown.

China The greatest massacre ever imputed by the government of one sovereign nation to the government of another is that of 26.3 million Chinese during the regime of Mao Zedong (Tse-tung) (1893–1976) between 1949 and May 1965. This accusation was made by an agency of the Soviet government in a radio broadcast on 7 Apr 1969.

The Walker Report, published by the US Senate Committee of the Judiciary in July 1971, placed the parameters of the total death toll within China since 1949 between 32.25 and 61.7 million. An estimate of 63.7 million was published by *Le Figaro* Magazine, 19–25 Nov 1978.

Nazi Germany Reliable estimates of the number of victims of the Holocaust, the genocidal "Final Solution" (*End-lösung*) ordered by Adolf Hitler, starting at the latest by the fall of 1941 and continuing into May 1945, range from 5.1 to 6 million Jews. At the SS death camp at Auschwitz-Birkenau in southern Poland, it is estimated that over a million Jews and up to 2 million others were murdered from 14 Jun 1940 to 18 Jan 1945. The greatest number killed in a day was 6,000.

STATES

Most populous The most populous state in the United States as of 1 Jul 1992 was California, with an estimated 30,867,000 people.

Least populous The least populous state, as of 1 Jul 1992, was Wyoming, with 466,000 people as of 1 Jul 1992.

COUNTIES

As of year end 1992 there were 3,142 counties in the United States (in Alaska, counties are known as divisions, and in Louisiana they are called parishes). The largest in the lower 48 states is San Bernardino County, CA, with an area of 20,062 miles^2. The biggest legally established county is the

North Slope Borough of Alaska at 87,860 acres. The state with the most counties is Texas, with 254, and the state with the fewest is Delaware, with three (Kent, New Castle and Sussex).

Most counties visited Allen F. Zondlak visited all 3,142 counties and county equivalents in the United States, completing his travels in 1991.

TOWNS AND CITIES

Oldest The oldest walled town in the world is Arihā (Jericho), which was inhabited by perhaps 2,700 people as early as 7800 B.C. The settlement of Dolní Věstonice, Czech Republic has been dated to the Gravettian culture *c.* 27,000 B.C. The oldest capital city in the world is Damascus, Syria. It has been continuously inhabited since *c.* 2500 B.C.

Most populous The most populous urban agglomeration in the world, as listed in the United Nations *Prospects of World Urbanization 1992*, is Tokyo, Japan, with a population of 25,000,000 in 1990. By the year 2000 this is expected to have increased to 28,000,000.

United States The largest metropolitan area in the United States is that of New York City, with 18,087,251 residents.

Smallest incorporated place The smallest incorporated place in the United States in 1990 was Valley Park, OK, with one resident.

Largest in area The world's largest city (defined as a densely populated settlement), in area, is Mount Isa, Queensland, Australia. The area administered by the City Council is 15,822 miles^2.

Highest The new town of Wenzhuan, founded in 1955 on the Qinghai–Tibet road north of the Tangla range, is the highest city in the world at 16,730 ft above sea level.

The highest incorporated city in the United States is Leadville, CO, at an elevation of 10,152 ft. Founded in 1878, Leadville has a current population of 2,629.

Capital city The highest capital in the world, before the domination of Tibet by China, was Lhasa, at an elevation of 12,087 ft above sea level. La Paz, administrative and *de facto* capital of Bolivia, stands at an altitude of 11,916 ft above sea level. The city was founded in 1548 by Capt. Alonso de Mendoza on the site of an Indian village named Chuquiapu. Sucre, the legal capital of Bolivia, stands at 9,301 ft above sea level.

Most remote from the sea The large town most remote from the sea is Urumqi (Wu-lu-mu-ch'i) in Xinjiang, the capital of China's Xinjiang Uygur Autonomous Region, at a distance of about 1,500 miles from the nearest coastline. Its population was estimated to be 1,160,000 in 1990.

Greatest altitude The settlement on the T'e-li-mo trail in southern Tibet is sited at an altitude of 19,800 ft.

The highest inhabited buildings in the world are those in the Indo-Tibetan border fort of Bāsisi by the Māna Pass (Lat. 31°04′N, Long. 79°24′E) at *c.* 19,700 ft.

In April 1961 a three-room dwelling was discovered at 21,650 ft on Cerro Llullaillaco (22,057 ft), on the Argentina–Chile border, believed to date from the late pre-Columbian period *c.* 1480.

Lowest The Israeli settlement of Ein Bokek on the shores of the Dead Sea is the lowest in the world, at 1,291 ft below sea level.

United States The lowest incorporated city in the United States is Calipatria, CA, founded on 28 Feb 1919, at 184 ft below sea level. The flagpole outside city hall is exactly 184 ft tall, allowing "Old Glory" to fly at sea level.

Northernmost The northernmost village is Ny Ålesund (78°55′N), a settlement on King's Bay, Vest Spitsbergen, in the Norwegian territory of Svalbard. Its population varies from around 25 in winter to approaching 100 in summer. The northernmost capital is Reykjavik, Iceland (64°08′N). Its population was 99,623 in 1991.

United States The northernmost city in the United States is Barrow, AK (71°17′N).

Southernmost The world's southernmost village is Puerto Williams (population about 1,000) on the north coast of Isla Navarino, Tierra del Fuego, Chile, 680 miles north of Antarctica. Wellington, New Zealand, with a 1989 population of 324,600, is the southernmost capital city (41°17′S). The world's southernmost administrative center is Port Stanley, Falkland (Malvinas) Islands (51°43′S), with a population of 1,643 in 1991.

United States The southernmost city in the United States is Hilo, HI (19°43′N).

DID YOU KNOW?

The oldest town of European origin in the United States is St Augustine, St John's County, FL (present population 12,000), founded on 8 Sep 1565, on the site of Seloy, by Pedro Menendez de Aviles.

The oldest incorporated city is York, ME (present population 14,000), which received an English charter in March 1642, and was incorporated under the name Georgiana.

HEADS OF STATE & ROYALTY

Forty-six of the world's 191 sovereign states are not republics. They are headed by 1 emperor, 14 kings, 3 queens, 2 sultans, 1 grand duke, 2 princes, 3 emirs, an elected monarch, the Pope, a president chosen from and by 7 hereditary sheiks, a head of state currently similar to a constitutional monarch, and 2 nominal nonhereditary "princes" in one country. Queen Elizabeth II is head of state of Great Britain and 15 other commonwealth countries.

Oldest ruling house The Emperor of Japan, Akihito (b. 23 Dec 1933), is the 125th in line from the first Emperor, Jimmu Tenno or Zinmu, whose reign was traditionally from 660 to 581 B.C., but more probably dates from *c.* 40 B.C. to *c.* 10 B.C.

***Reigns** Longest all-time* The longest recorded reign of any monarch is that of Phiops II (also known as Pepi II), or Neferkare, a Sixth Dynasty pharaoh of ancient Egypt. His reign began *c.* 2281 B.C., when he was 6 years of age, and is believed to have lasted *c.* 94 years. Musoma Kanijo, chief of the Nzega district of western Tanganyika (now part of Tanzania), reputedly reigned for more than 98 years, from 1864, when he was 8 years old, until his death on 2 Feb 1963.

Longest current The King of Thailand, Bhumibol Adulyadej (Rama IX; b. 5 Dec 1927), is currently the world's longest-reigning monarch, having succeeded to the throne on 9 Jun 1946. The longest-reigning queen is Queen Elizabeth II of the United Kingdom, who succeeded to the throne on 6 Feb 1952 on the death of her father.

Shortest Crown Prince Luis Filipe of Portugal was mortally wounded at the same time that his father was assassinated in the streets of Lisbon on 1 Feb 1908. He was thus technically King of Portugal (Dom Luis III) for about 20 minutes.

Youngest king and queen The country with the youngest king is Swaziland, where King Mswati III was crowned on 25 Apr 1986 at the age of 18 years 6 days. He was born Makhosetive, the 67th son of King Subhusa II. The country with the youngest queen is Denmark, with Queen Margrethe II (b. 16 Apr 1940).

Most prolific royalty The most prolific monogamous "royal" was Prince Hartmann of Liechtenstein (1613–86), who had 24 children, of whom 21 were born alive, by Countess Elisabeth zu Salm-Reifferscheidt (1623–88). HRH Duke Roberto I of Parma (1848–1907) also had 24 children, but by two wives.

Highest post-nominal numbers The highest post-nominal number ever used to designate a member of a royal house was 75, briefly enjoyed by

Count Heinrich LXXV Reuss zu Schleiz (1800–1801). All male members of this branch of the German family are called Heinrich and are successively numbered from I upwards in three sequences. The first began in 1695 (and ended with Heinrich LXXV), the second began in 1803 (and ended with Heinrich XLVII) and the third began in 1910.

Heaviest monarch The world's heaviest monarch is the 6-ft-3-in-tall King Taufa'ahau of Tonga, who in September 1976 was weighed on the only adequate scales in the country, at the airport, recording 462 lb. By 1985 he was reported to have slimmed down to 308 lb, and in early 1993 he weighed 280 lb.

Heads of state *Oldest and youngest* The oldest head of state in the world is Joaquín Balaguer (b. 1 Sep 1907), President of the Dominican Republic. The oldest monarch is King Taufa'ahau of Tonga (b. 4 Jul 1918). The youngest is King Mswati III of Swaziland (b. 19 Apr 1968).

First female presidents Isabel Perón (b. 4 Feb 1931) of Argentina became the world's first female president when she succeeded her husband on his death on 1 Jul 1974. She held office until she was deposed on 24 Mar 1976. President Vigdis Finnbogadottir (b. 15 Apr 1930) of Iceland became the world's first democratically elected female head of state on 30 Jun 1980.

Largest meeting The summit segment of the United Nations Conference on Environment and Development, on 12–13 Jun 1992, was attended by 92 heads of state and heads of government—the largest gathering of world leaders. The summit had 103 participants altogether and was one of the meetings at the "Earth Summit," which was held in Rio de Janeiro, Brazil from 3–14 Jun 1992.

UNITED STATES GOVERNMENT

PRESIDENTS

Oldest The oldest president was Ronald Wilson Reagan, who was 69 years 349 days old when he took the oath of office. He was reelected at age 73.

Youngest The youngest president to assume office was Theodore Roosevelt. Vice-President Roosevelt became president at the age of 42 years, 10 months when President William McKinley was assassinated in 1901. The youngest president ever elected was John Fitzgerald Kennedy, who took the oath of office at age 43 years 236 days in 1961.

Term of office Franklin D. Roosevelt served the longest term—12 years 39 days (1933–45). The shortest term in office was 32 days (4 Mar–4 Apr 1841) by William Henry Harrison.

Inaugural speeches William Henry Harrison's inaugural speech of 1841

HANDSHAKING!

The record number of hands shaken by a public figure at an official function was 8,513, by President Theodore Roosevelt (1858–1919) at a New Year's Day White House presentation in Washington, D.C. in 1907.

lasted for two hours, making it the longest one ever. George Washington's second inaugural speech of 4 Mar 1793 was the shortest, lasting only 90 seconds.

Largest gathering The largest gathering of men who had been or would become president was eight, on 30 Dec 1834 in the old House Chamber of the Capitol: ex-president John Quincy Adams; ex-president Andrew Jackson; Vice-President Martin Van Buren; Senator John Tyler; Senator James Buchanan; and Representatives James K. Polk, Millard Fillmore and Franklin Pierce.

ELECTIONS

Largest popular majority Since the introduction of the popular vote in presidential elections in 1872, the greatest majority won was 17,994,460 votes in 1972 when President Richard M. Nixon (Republican) defeated George S. McGovern (Democrat) with 47,165,234 votes to 29,170,774.

Smallest popular majority The smallest popular majority was 7,023 votes in 1880 when President James A. Garfield (Republican) defeated Winfield Scott Hancock (Democrat) with 4,449,053 votes to 4,442,030.

Largest electoral college majority Since 1872, the greatest electoral college majority was 515 votes in 1936 when President Franklin D. Roosevelt (Democrat) defeated Alfred M. Landon (Republican) with 523 votes to 8.

VICE-PRESIDENTS

Longest term of office Only five vice-presidents have served two full four-year terms in office: John Adams (1789–97), Thomas R. Marshall (1913–1921), John Nance Garner (1933–41), Richard Nixon (1953–61) and George Bush (1981–89).

Youngest to hold office The youngest man to become vice-president was John Cabell Breckinridge (Democrat; b. 21 Jan 1821), who took office on 4 Mar 1857 at the age of 36 years 1 month.

Oldest to hold office Alben William Barkley (Democrat; b. 24 Nov 1877) took office on 20 Jan 1949 at the age of 71 years 40 days. He served a full four-year term.

Longest-lived The longest-lived vice-president was John Nance Garner, who served under Franklin D. Roosevelt from 1933 to 1941. He was born in 1868 and died on 7 Nov 1967 at the age of 98.

GOVERNORS

Oldest Walter S. Goodland became governor of Wisconsin in 1943, at the age of 84.

Youngest Stevens T. Mason was 24 years old when he was elected governor of Michigan in 1835.

CONGRESS

Most expensive election The Federal Election Commission reported on 30 Dec 1992 that the 1992 congressional campaign was the most expensive in history. Candidates spent a total of $504 million. Senate candidates spent $190 million and House candidates $314 million.

Congressional service Carl Hayden (1877–1972; D-Arizona) holds the record for the longest congressional service, a total of 57 consecutive years (1912–69), of which 42 years were spent as a senator and the remainder as a representative.

Speaker of the House of Representatives James K. Polk is the only person to have held the offices of both speaker (1835–39) and president (1845–49).

Longest service The longest time served by any speaker was 17 years, by Sam Rayburn (1882–1961; D-Texas). Rayburn served three terms: 1940–47, 1949–53, 1955–61.

Shortest term The shortest term of any speaker was one day, 3 Mar 1869, served by Theodore Medad Pomeroy (1824–1905; R-New York).

Oldest speaker The oldest speaker was Sam Rayburn (D-Texas), who was reelected speaker for the 87th Congress on 3 Jan 1961 at age 78 years 11 months.

Youngest speaker The youngest speaker was Robert Mercer Taliaferro Hunter (1809–87; D-Virginia), who was chosen speaker for the 26th Congress on 2 Dec 1839 at age 30 years 7 months.

House of Representatives *Longest service* The longest any representative has ever served is 52 years 6 months (as of June 1994), by Rep. Jamie L. Whitten (D-Mississippi). He began his career on 4 Nov 1941.

Youngest elected The youngest man ever to serve in the House was William Charles Cole Claiborne (1775–1817; Jeffersonian Democrat-Tennessee), who, in contravention of the 25-year age requirement of the Constitution, was elected in August 1797 at the age of 22.

Oldest elected The oldest man ever elected representative was Claude Denson Pepper (1900–89; D-Florida), who was reelected on 8 Nov 1988 at age 88 years 2 months.

Senate *Longest service* The longest any senator has ever served is 42 years, by Carl Trumbull Hayden (1877–1972; D-Arizona). Hayden served in the Senate from 1927–69. The current longest-serving member of the Senate is James Strom Thurmond (b. 5 Dec 1902; R-South Carolina). As of June 1994 Thurmond had served for 39 years. He was originally elected as a Democrat in December 1954, but changed to the Republican Party in 1964.

Oldest elected The greatest age at which anyone has been returned as a senator is 87 years 11 months, the age at which Strom Thurmond (R-South Carolina) was reelected in November 1990.

Youngest elected The youngest person ever elected senator was Brig. Gen. Armistead Thomson Mason (1787–1819; D-Virginia), who was elected on 3 Jan 1816 and was sworn in on 22 January at the age of 28 years 5 months 18 days. The youngest-ever senator was John Henry Eaton (1790–1856; D-Tennessee), who was appointed on 5 Sep 1818 and sworn in on 16 November at age 28 years 4 months 29 days.

Most expensive seats In 1992 Rep. Barbara Boxer (D-California) spent a record $10,289,773 in her successful attempt to win the California senate seat vacated by the retirement of Sen. Alan Cranston (D). This election was the most expensive in congressional history, with Boxer's Republican opponent, Bruce Herschensohn, spending $7,408,101. Herschensohn also gained the dubious distinction of becoming the biggest-spending losing candidate in Senate history.

Most roll calls Senator William Proxmire (D-Wisconsin) did not miss a single one of the 9,695 roll calls from April 1966 to 27 Aug 1987. Rep. William H. Natcher (D-Kentucky; 1909–94) cast 18,401 consecutive roll call votes from 6 Jan 1954 to 3 Mar 1994.

Filibusters The longest continuous speech in the history of the Senate was that of Senator Wayne Morse (1900–74; D-Oregon) on 24–25 Apr 1953, when he spoke on the Tidelands oil bill for 22 hr 26 min without resuming his seat.

Interrupted only briefly by the swearing-in of a new senator, Senator Strom Thurmond (b. 5 Dec 1902) (R-South Carolina) spoke against a civil rights bill for 24 hr 19 min on 28–29 Aug 1957. The record on a state level is 43 hr, by Texas State Senator Bill Meier, who spoke against nondisclosure of industrial accidents, in May 1977.

Fastest amendment The constitutional amendment that took the shortest time to ratify after congressional approval was the 26th Amendment, which gave 18-year-olds the right to vote. It was approved by Congress 23 Mar 1971, and ratified 1 Jul 1971.

HEADS OF STATE

The record for the most presidents of the United States alive at one time is six; this has occurred twice.* Here, Ranan R. Lurie, the world's most widely syndicated political cartoonist, depicts the latest group of record-breakers "living it up."

** 4 Mar 1861–18 Jan 1862 (Abraham Lincoln's inauguration to John Tyler's death): Martin Van Buren, John Tyler, Millard Fillmore, Franklin Pierce, James Buchanan, and Abraham Lincoln; 20 Jan 1993–22 Apr 1994 (Bill Clinton's inauguration to Richard Nixon's death): Richard Nixon, Gerald Ford, Jimmy Carter, Ronald Reagan, George Bush, and Bill Clinton.*

MOST WIDELY SYNDICATED POLITICAL CARTOONIST

As of April 1994, Lurie's daily political analysis was published in 102 countries and territories, in 1,098 newspapers with a total circulation of 102,000,000 copies. The countries are shown below.

Country	No.	Country	No.	Country	No.	Country	No.
American Samoa	1	Egypt	1	Lithuania	4	Serbia	1
Argentina	7	Estonia	5	Luxembourg	1	Singapore	1
Australia	3	Finland	2	Macao	1	Slovakia	1
Austria	2	France	1	Malawi	1	Slovenia	1
Bahamas	1	Gambia	1	Malaysia	3	South Africa	5
Bangladesh	2	Georgia	1	Malta	1	South Korea	7
Barbados	1	Germany	6	Mexico	86	Spain	18
Belgium	3	Great Britain	2	Netherlands	2	St Lucia	1
Bolivia	2	Greece	2	New Zealand	4	Swaziland	1
Brazil	3	Grenada	1	Nicaragua	1	Sweden	2
British W. Indies	1	Guatemala	4	Norway	1	Switzerland	1
Bulgaria	5	Hong Kong	6	Oman	1	Tahiti	1
Canada	18	Hungary	1	Pakistan	2	Taiwan	3
Chile	1	India	13	Panama	1	Tanzania	1
China	2	Indonesia	6	Paraguay	1	Thailand	3
C.I.S.*	479	Israel	2	Peru	2	Trinidad	1
Colombia	4	Italy	7	Philippines	2	Tunisia	2
Costa Rica	3	Jamaica	1	Poland	10	Turkey	2
Cyprus	2	Japan	3	Portugal	4	U.A.E.	1
Czech Republic	2	Jordan	2	Puerto Rico	1	Uruguay	2
Denmark	2	Kenya	3	Qatar	1	U.S.A.	279
Dominican Rep.	1	Kuwait	1	Romania	9	U.S. Virgin Is.	1
Ecuador	1	Latvia	3	Saudi Arabia	1	Venezuela	3

** Former USSR*   *Source: Cartoonews International*

World watchdogs: Lurie and Annie. Flags represent Lurie's newspaper clients. (Andreas Aquino)

During his career, 46 heads of state have sat for Lurie, among them Idi Amin, Jimmy Carter, Mikhail Gorbachev, Lyndon Johnson, Yitzhak Rabin, Ronald Reagan, Anwar Sadat and Lech Walesa. Lurie's favorite subject is Walesa: "He is amazed and amused at his success. It shows all the time."

A typical sitting takes 30 to 45 minutes (the actual drawing requires at least 5 hours). So why do leaders hold up their busy schedules to have their caricatures drawn? Lurie sees a common link. "They all have a very strong desire to impress and communicate with the international community, whether democrats or dictators."

Reactions to caricatures vary. George Bush described his as "fantastic" but noted that his wife said he "looked mean and sour." President Georges Pompidou (France) was furious, writing a personal letter objecting to the emphasis on his weak nose and chin. Is the possibility of upsetting the world's most powerful people a strain? Lurie remains unmoved. "The pressure is extremely nice."

WORLD LEGISLATURES

PARLIAMENTS

Oldest The oldest recorded legislative body is the Althing of Iceland, founded in A.D. 930. This body was abolished in 1800, but restored by Denmark to a consultative status in 1843 and a legislative status in 1874. The legislative assembly with the oldest *continuous* history is the Isle of Man Tynwald, Great Britain, which may have its origins in the late ninth century and possibly predates the Althing.

Largest The largest legislative assembly in the world is the National People's Congress of the People's Republic of China, which has 2,978 single-party members who are indirectly elected for a five-year term.

Highest-paid legislators The most highly paid of all the world's legislators are the Japanese. The prime minister has an annual salary of 38,463,360 yen ($343,000) including monthly allowances and bonuses. Members of the House of Representatives and the House of Councilors have annual salaries of 23,633,565 yen ($211,000) including bonuses.

Smallest quorum The House of Lords in Great Britain has the smallest quorum, expressed as a percentage of members eligible to vote, of any legislative body in the world—less than one-third of 1 percent of 1,205 members. To transact business, there need be only three peers present, including the lord chancellor or his deputy.

Greatest petitions The greatest petition on record was signed by 13,078,935 people in South Korea between 11 Nov–23 Dec 1991. They were protesting against efforts by advanced agricultural exporting countries to open their country's rice market to foreign imports.

Longest membership The longest span as a legislator was 83 years, by József Madarász (1814–1915). He first attended the Hungarian Parliament from 1832–38 as *oblegatus absentium* (i.e., on behalf of an absent deputy). He was a full member from 1848–50 and from 1861 until his death on 31 Jan 1915.

Longest speeches The longest speech made was one by Chief Mangosuthu Buthelezi, the Zulu leader, when he gave an address to the KwaZulu legislative assembly between 12 and 29 Mar 1993. He spoke on 11 of the 18 days, averaging nearly 2½ hours on each of the 11 days.

The longest continuous speech made in the United Nations was one of 4 hr 29 min on 26 Sep 1960 by President Fidel Castro Ruz (b. 13 Aug 1927) of Cuba.

Oldest treaty The oldest treaty still in force is the Anglo-Portuguese Treaty, which was signed in London, Great Britain over 621 years ago on 16 Jun 1373. The text was confirmed "with my usual flourish" by John de Banketre, Clerk.

Zulu political leader Chief Buthelezi gave the longest speech in history in an address that started on 12 Mar 1993 and finished 18 days later. (Gamma/T. Selwyn)

Constitutions The world's oldest national constitution still in uninterrupted use is that of the United States of America, ratified by the necessary ninth state (New Hampshire) on 21 Jun 1788 and declared to be in effect on 4 Mar 1789.

Woman's suffrage As far back as 1838 the Pitcairn Islands incorporated female suffrage in its constitution, although this was only *de facto* and not legally binding. The earliest legislature with female voters was that of the Territory of Wyoming in 1869, followed by that of the Isle of Man, Great Britain in 1881. The first country to have universal woman's suffrage was New Zealand in 1893.

United States In 1920 the 19th Amendment to the Constitution granted nationwide suffrage to women.

ELECTIONS

Largest The largest elections in the world were thosc beginning on 20 May 1991 for the Indian Lower House, which has 543 elective seats. A total of 315,439,908 people cast their votes out of an eligible electorate of 488,678,993. The elections were contested by 359 parties, and there were nearly 565,000 polling stations manned by 3 million people. As a result of the election a new government was formed under the leadership of P.V. Narasimha Rao of the Congress (I) Party.

Closest The ultimate in close general elections occurred in Zanzibar (now part of Tanzania) on 18 Jan 1961, when the Afro-Shirazi Party won by a single seat, after the seat of Chake-Chake on Pemba Island had been gained by a single vote.

The narrowest recorded percentage win in an election was for the office of Southern District Highway Commissioner in Mississippi on 7 Aug 1979. Robert E. Joiner was declared the winner over W.H. Pyron, with 133,587 votes to 133,582. The loser thus obtained more than 49.999 percent of the votes.

Most decisive North Korea recorded a 100 percent turnout of electors and a 100 percent vote for the Workers' Party of Korea in the general election of 8 Oct 1962. An almost unanimous vote occurred in Albania on 14 Nov 1982, when a single voter spoiled national unanimity for the official (and only) candidates, who consequently obtained 99.99993 percent of the vote in a reported 100 percent turnout of 1,627,968.

Most crooked In the Liberian presidential election of 1927, President Charles D.B. King (1875–1961) was returned with an officially announced majority of 234,000 over his opponent, Thomas J.R. Faulkner of the People's Party. President King thus claimed a "majority" more than 15½ times greater than the entire electorate.

Longest in power In Mongolia the Communists (Mongolian People's Revolutionary Party) have been in power since 1924, although only in the last four years within a multiparty system. In February 1992 the term "People's Republic" was dropped from the official name of Mongolia.

Highest personal majority The highest-ever personal majority for any politician was 4,726,112 by Boris Yeltsin, in the parliamentary elections held in the former Soviet Union on 26 Mar 1989. Yeltsin received 5,118,745 votes out of the 5,722,937 that were cast in the Moscow constituency, his closest rival obtaining 392,633 votes. Benazir Bhutto achieved 96.71 percent of the vote in the Larkana-III constituency in the 1988 general election in Pakistan, with 82,229 votes. The next-highest candidate obtained just 1,979 votes.

Largest political party The largest political party is the Chinese Communist Party, formed in 1920, with a membership estimated to be 50,320,000 in 1991.

Largest field of candidates There were 301 candidates running to represent one seat, that of Belgaum City, in the State Assembly (Vidhan Sabha) elections in Karnataka, India held on 5 Mar 1985.

Most coups Statisticians contend that Bolivia, since it became a sovereign country in 1825, has had 191 coups. The latest was on 30 Jun 1984, when the president, Hernan Siles Zuazo, age 70, was temporarily kidnapped from his official residence by more than 60 armed men masquerading as police officers.

PRIME MINISTERS AND HEADS OF STATE

Oldest The longest-lived prime minister of any country was Naruhiko Higashikuni (Japan), who was born on 3 Dec 1887 and died on 20 Jan 1990, at age 102 years 48 days. He was his country's first prime minister after

El Hadji Muhammad el Mokri, Grand Vizier of Morocco, was the oldest person to hold office in a capacity equivalent to prime minister. He is seen here wearing the hooded cape of his office, as he waits with other officials outside the Sultan's palace. (Popperfoto)

The changing of the generations in politics has been a widely noted trend in recent years. This is perhaps best highlighted by one politician who has received little publicity: Liechtenstein's Dr Mario Frick, the world's youngest prime minister at age 28. (Presse- und Informationsamt)

Indira Gandhi holds the record for greatest length of service for a woman prime minister. She served 15 years during two terms as India's leader. (Popperfoto)

World War II, but held office for less than two months, resigning in October 1945.

El Hadji Muhammad el Mokri, Grand Vizier of Morocco, died on 16 Sep 1957 at a reputed age of 116 Muslim (*Hijri*) years, equivalent to 112½ years.

The oldest age at first appointment was 81, in the case of Morarji Ranchhodji Desai of India (b. 29 Feb 1896) in March 1977. Philippe Pétain (1856–1951), although not prime minister, became "chief of state" of the French state on 10 Jul 1940 at the age of 84.

Currently the oldest prime minister is Andreas Papandreou of Greece (b. 5 Feb 1919), who is now in his second term of office.

Youngest Currently the youngest head of government is Dr Mario Frick (b. 8 May 1965), who became Prime Minister of Liechtenstein at the age of 28 on 15 Dec 1993.

Longest term of office The longest-serving prime minister of a sovereign state is Khalifa bin Sulman al-Khalifa (b. 3 Jul 1933) of Bahrain, who took office 1½ years before Bahrain became independent in August 1971.

Marshall Kim Il Sung (ne Kim Sung Chu; 1912–1994) was head of government or head of state of the Democratic People's Republic of Korea from 25 Aug 1948 until his death on 8 Jul 1994.

Woman Indira Gandhi (1917–84) of India was prime minister for a record 15 years in two spans, from 1966 to 1977 and from 1980 to 1984. Eugenia Charles (b. 15 May 1919) of Dominica is the current living record-holder, having taken office when her Dominica Freedom Party won the elections in July 1980.

Most women in a cabinet The greatest representation of women in a cabinet is in Norway, where there are currently eight women ministers, including Prime Minister Gro Harlem Brundtland.

JUDICIAL

LEGISLATION AND LITIGATION

***Statutes** Oldest* The earliest surviving judicial code was that of King Ur-Nammu during the third dynasty of Ur, Iraq, *c.* 2250 B.C.

Most inexplicable legislation Certain pieces of legislation have always defied interpretation, and the most inexplicable must be a matter of opinion. A judge of the Court of Session of Scotland once nominated the following law as his candidate for most confusingly worded law: *"In the Nuts (unground), (other than ground nuts) Order, the expression nuts shall have reference to such nuts, other than ground nuts, as would but for this amending Order not qualify as nuts (unground) (other than ground nuts) by reason of their being nuts (unground)."*

Most protracted litigation A controversy over the claim of the Prior and Convent (now the Dean and Chapter) of Durham Cathedral in Great Britain to administer the diocese during a vacancy in the See grew fierce in 1283. The dispute, with the Archbishop of York, flared up again in 1672 and 1890; an attempt in November 1975 to settle the issue, then 692 years old, was unsuccessful. Neither side admits the legitimacy of writs of appointment issued by the other, even though identical persons are named.

Greatest mass arrest The greatest mass arrest reported in a democratic country was of 15,617 demonstrators on 11 Jul 1988, rounded up by South Korean police to ensure security in advance of the 1988 Olympic Games in Seoul.

Longest trial The longest civil case heard before a jury is *Kemner* v. *Monsanto Co.,* which concerned an alleged toxic chemical spill in Sturgeon, MO in 1979. The trial started on 6 Feb 1984, at St Clair County Court House, Belleville, IL before Circuit Judge Richard P. Goldenhersh, and ended on 22 Oct 1987. The testimony lasted 657 days, following which the jury deliberated for two months. The residents of Sturgeon were awarded $1 million nominal compensatory damages and $16,280,000 punitive damages, but these awards were overturned by the Illinois Appellate Court on 11 Jun 1991 because the jury in the original trial had not found that any damage had resulted from the spill.

***Greatest damages** Personal injury* The greatest personal injury damages ever awarded were $78,183,000, to model Marla Hanson, 26, on 29 Sep 1987. Her face was slashed with razors in Manhattan, NY in June 1987. The award was uncontested and included $4 million in punitive damages. The three men convicted and now serving 5–15 years have no assets, but Miss Hanson is entitled to 10 percent of their post-prison earnings.

The compensation for the disaster on 2–3 Dec 1984 at the Union Carbide Corporation plant in Bhopal, India was set at $470 million. The Supreme Court of India passed the order for payment on 14 Feb 1989 after a settlement between the corporation and the Indian government, which represented the interests of more than 500,000 claimants. On 27 Mar 1992 the Bhopal Court put the death toll at more than 4,000, with 20,000 injured and the number of claimants rising to 600,000.

Civil damages The largest damages awarded in legal history were $11.12 billion to Pennzoil Company against Texaco Inc. concerning the latter's allegedly unethical tactics in January 1984 in attempting to break up a merger between Pennzoil and Getty Oil Company. The verdict was handed down in Houston, TX on 10 Dec 1985. An out-of-court settlement of $5.5 billion was reached after a 48-hour negotiation on 19 Dec 1987.

The largest damages awarded against an individual were $2.1 billion. On 10 Jul 1992 Charles H. Keating, Jr., the former owner of Lincoln Savings and Loan of Los Angeles, CA, was ordered by a federal jury to pay this sum to 23,000 small investors who were defrauded by his company. On 8 Jul 1993, Keating was sentenced to 12½ years in prison.

Best-attended trial The greatest attendance at any trial was at that of Major Jesús Sosa Blanco, age 51, for an alleged 108 murders. At one point in the 12½-hr trial (5:30 P.M. to 6 A.M., 22–23 Jan 1959), 17,000 people were present in the Havana Sports Palace, Cuba. He was executed on 18 Feb 1959.

Greatest compensation for wrongful imprisonment Robert McLaughlin, 29, was awarded $1,935,000 in October 1989 for wrongful imprisonment as a result of a murder in New York City in 1979 which he did not commit. He had been sentenced to 15 years in prison and had actually served six years, from 1980 to 1986, when he was released after his foster father succeeded in showing the authorities that he had had nothing to do with the crime.

Largest divorce settlement The largest publicly declared settlement, achieved in 1982 by the lawyers for Soraya Khashóggi, was £500 million ($950 million) plus property from her husband Adnan. Mrs Anne Bass, former wife of Sid Bass of Texas, was reported to have rejected a settlement of $535 million as inadequate to live in the style to which she had become accustomed.

Largest alimony suit Belgian-born Sheika Dena Al-Fassi, 23, filed the highest-ever alimony claim of $3 billion against her former husband, Sheik Mohammed Al-Fassi, 28, of the Saudi Arabian royal family, in Los Angeles, CA in February 1982. Attorney Marvin Mitchelson, explaining the size of the settlement claim, alluded to the Sheik's wealth, which included 14 homes in Florida alone and numerous private aircraft. On 14 Jun 1983 the claimant was awarded $81 million and declared she would be "very very happy" if she were able to collect.

Largest patent case Litton Industries Inc. was awarded $1.2 billion in damages from Honeywell Inc. on 31 Aug 1993. A jury in Los Angeles, CA decided that Honeywell had violated a Litton patent covering airline navigation systems.

Most patents Thomas Alva Edison (1847–1931) had the most patents, with 1,093 either on his own or jointly. They included the microphone, the motion-picture projector and the incandescent electric lamp.

Largest suit The highest amount of damages ever sought to date is $675 trillion in a suit by Mr I. Walton Bader brought in the US District Court, New York City on 14 Apr 1971 against General Motors and others for polluting all 50 states.

Highest costs The Blue Arrow trial, involving the illegal support of the company's shares during a rights issue in 1987, is estimated to have cost approximately £35 million (*c.* $60 million). The trial at the Old Bailey, London, Great Britain, lasted a year and ended on 14 Feb 1992 with four of the defendants being convicted. Although they received suspended prison sentences, they were later cleared on appeal.

United States The McMartin Preschool case in Los Angeles, CA is estimated to have cost $15 million. The trial, concerning the alleged abuse of children at the school in Manhattan Beach, CA, had begun with jury selection on 20 Apr 1987 and resulted in the acquittal on 18 Jan 1990 of the two defendants on 52 counts of child molestation and conspiracy.

Longest lease There is a lease concerning a plot for a sewage tank adjoining Columb Barracks, Mullingar, Ireland, which was signed on 3 Dec 1868 for 10 million years. It is to be assumed that a future civil servant will bring up the matter for review early in A.D. 10,001,868.

Wills *Shortest* The shortest valid will in the world consists of the words "Vše zene," the Czech for "All to wife," written and dated 19 Jan 1967 by Herr Karl Tausch of Langen, Germany.

Longest The longest will on record was that of Mrs Frederica Evelyn Stilwell Cook (b. USA), proved in London, Great Britain on 2 Nov 1925. It consisted of four bound volumes containing 95,940 words, primarily concerning some $100,000 worth of property.

Oldest The oldest written will dates from 2061 B.C. and is that of Nek'ure, the son of the Egyptian pharaoh Khafre. The will was carved onto the walls of his tomb, and indicated that he would bequeath 14 towns, two estates and other property to his wife, another woman and three children.

Codicils The largest number of codicils (supplements modifying the details) to a will admitted to probate is 21, in the case of the will of J. Paul Getty. The will was dated 22 Sep 1958 and it had 21 codicils dating from 18 Jun 1960 through 11 Mar 1976. Getty died on 6 Jun 1976.

Most durable judge The oldest recorded active judge was Judge Albert R. Alexander (1859–1966) of Plattsburg, MO. He was enrolled as a member of the Clinton County Bar in 1926, and was later the magistrate and probate judge of Clinton County until his retirement at the age of 105 years 8 months on 9 Jul 1965.

Narrowest margin Judge Clarence Thomas was elected to the Supreme Court in 1991 by the narrowest margin ever recorded, 52 votes to 48.

Youngest judge No collated records on the ages of judicial appointments exist. However, David Elmer Ward had to await the legal age of 21 before taking office after nomination in 1932 as judge of the County Court in Fort Myers, FL.

Muhammad Ilyas passed the examination enabling him to become a civil judge in July 1952 at the age of 20 years 9 months, although formalities such as medicals meant that it was not until eight months later that he started work as a civil judge in Lahore, Pakistan.

Most judges Lord Balmerino (Great Britain) was found guilty of treason by 137 of his peers on 28 Jul 1746.

Most lawyers In the United States there were 846,000 resident and active lawyers in December 1993, or one lawyer for every 300 people.

Oldest lawyer The oldest lawyer was Cornelius Van de Steeg (1889–1994) of Perry, IA. He was still practicing as a lawyer until April 1991, when he was 101 years 11 months old.

CRIME

Largest criminal organizations There are believed to be more than 250,000 members of Chinese triad societies worldwide, but they are fragmented into many groups that often fight each other and compete in disputed areas. Hong Kong alone has some 100,000 triads.

In terms of profit, the largest syndicate in organized crime is the Mafia or La Cosa Nostra. The Mafia consists of some 3,000 to 5,000 individuals in 25 "families" federated under "The Commission," with an annual turnover in illegal activities that was estimated by *US News & World Report* in December 1982 at $200 billion, and a profit estimated in Mar 1986 by US District Attorney Rudolph Giuliani at $75 billion.

In terms of numbers, the Yamaguchi-gumi gang of the *yakuza* in Japan is the largest, with 30,000 members. There are some 90,000 *yakuza* or gangsters altogether, in more than 3,000 groups. On 1 Mar 1992 Japan instituted new laws to combat their activities, which include drug trafficking, smuggling, prostitution and gambling.

Assassinations The most frequently assassinated heads of state in modern times have been the Tsars of Russia. In the two hundred years from 1718 to 1918, four Tsars and two heirs apparent were assassinated, and there were many other unsuccessful attempts.

The target of the highest number of *failed* assassination attempts on an individual head of state in modern times was Charles de Gaulle (1890–1970), President of France from 1958 to 1969. He was reputed to have survived no fewer than 31 plots against his life between 1944 and 1966 (although some plots were foiled before culminating in actual physical attacks).

Most successful murderers It was established at the trial of Behram, the Indian Thug, that he had strangled at least 931 victims with his yellow and white cloth strip or *ruhmal* in the Oudh district between 1790 and 1840. It has been estimated that at least 2 million Indians were strangled by Thugs during the reign of the Thugee (pronounced tugee) cult from 1550 until its final suppression by the British raj in 1853.

Reportedly the world's largest criminal organization is the Mafia. Recent crackdowns by the Italian police have led to a series of trials of Mafia leaders, requiring construction of specially built courts to ensure security. (P. Guerrin)

Robbery!

The greatest robbery on record was that of the Reichsbank following Germany's collapse in April–May 1945. The Pentagon in Washington described the event as "an unverified allegation." The book *Nazi Gold* by Ian Sayer and Douglas Botting, published in 1984, however, finally revealed full details and estimated the total haul at what were then current values as £2.5 billion ($3.75 billion).

Twentieth century A total of 592 deaths was attributed to one Colombian bandit leader, Teófilo ("Sparks") Rojas, between 1948 and his death in an ambush near Armenia, Colombia on 22 Jan 1963. Some sources attribute 3,500 slayings to him during *La Violencia* of 1945–62.

United States The greatest mass murder committed in the United States was the Happy Land fire, which resulted in the deaths of 87 individuals. The fire was set by 36-year-old Julio Gonzalez, on 25 Mar 1990 at an illegal New York City social club, The Happy Land, in revenge for being thrown out of the club after an argument with a former girlfriend, Lydia Feliciano, who worked at the club. Ms Feliciano was one of six survivors.

Lynching The worst year in the 20th century for lynchings in the United States was 1901, with 130 lynchings, of which 125 were of blacks and five were of whites. The first year with no reported cases was 1952. The date on which lynchings were last reported was 21 Jun 1964, in Philadelphia, Mississippi. Three men, two white (Michael Schwerner and Andrew Goodman) and one black (James Chaney), were lynched in the Neshoba County town.

Mass poisoning On 1 May 1981 an eight-year-old boy became the first of more than 600 victims of the Spanish cooking oil scandal. On 12 June it was discovered that the cause of his death was the use of "denatured" industrial oil from rape-seed. The trial of 38 defendants, including the manufacturers, Ramón and Eli´as Ferrero, lasted from 30 Mar 1987 to 28 Jun 1988. The 586 counts on which the prosecution demanded jail sentences totaled 60,000 years.

Robbery The government of the Philippines announced on 23 Apr 1986 that it had succeeded in identifying $860.8 million salted away by former President Ferdinand Edralin Marcos (1917–89) and his wife Imelda. The total since November 1965 was believed to be $5–$10 billion.

Art It is arguable that the *Mona Lisa*, though never appraised, is the most valuable object ever stolen. It disappeared from the Louvre, Paris, France on 21 Aug 1911. It was recovered in Italy in 1913, when Vincenzo Perugia was charged with its theft.

Bank During the extreme civil disorder prior to 22 Jan 1976 in Beirut,

Lebanon, a guerrilla force blasted the vaults of the British Bank of the Middle East in Bab Idriss and cleared out safe deposit boxes with contents valued by former Finance Minister Lucien Dahdah at $50 million and by another source at an "absolute minimum" of $20 million.

Jewels The greatest recorded theft of jewels was from the Knightsbridge Safety Deposit Center, London, Great Britain on 12 Jul 1987, when jewels with an estimated value of $40 million were stolen as part of an even larger robbery.

Largest object stolen by a single person On a moonless night at dead calm high water on 5 Jun 1966, at Wolfe's Cove, St Lawrence Seaway, Canada, N. William Kennedy, armed with only a sharp ax, slashed free the mooring lines of the 10,640-ton SS *Orient Trader*, owned by Steel Factors Ltd of Ontario. The vessel drifted to a waiting blacked-out tug, thus escaping the ban on any shipping movements during a violent wildcat waterfront strike. It then sailed for Spain.

DID YOU KNOW?

The highest amount ever paid to aircraft hijackers was $6 million, by the Japanese government, in the case of a JAL DC-8 at Dacca Airport, Bangladesh on 2 Oct 1977, with 38 hostages. Six convicted criminals were also exchanged. The Bangladesh government had refused to sanction any retaliatory action.

Greatest kidnapping ransom Historically the greatest ransom paid was that for Atahualpa by the Incas to Francisco Pizarro in 1532–33 at Cajamarca, Peru, which constituted a hall full of gold and silver, worth some $170 million on today's market. Pizarro did not keep his end of the bargain; he murdered Atahualpa instead of returning him.

The greatest ransom ever reported in modern times was 1,500 million pesos ($60 million) for the release of the brothers Jorge Born, 40, and Juan Born, 39, of the firm Bunge and Born, paid to the left-wing urban guerrilla group Montoneros in Buenos Aires, Argentina on 20 Jun 1975.

Largest narcotics haul The greatest haul in a drug seizure in terms of value was on 28 Sep 1989, when cocaine with an estimated street value of $6–7 billion was seized in a raid on a warehouse in Los Angeles, CA. The haul of 22 tons was prompted by a tip-off from a local resident who had complained about heavy truck traffic and people leaving the warehouse "at odd hours and in a suspicious manner."

Largest narcotics operation The bulkiest haul was 3,200 tons of Colombian marijuana in the 14-month-long "Operation Tiburon," carried out by the US Drug Enforcement Administration and Colombian authorities. The arrest of 495 people and the seizure of 95 vessels was announced on 5 Feb 1982.

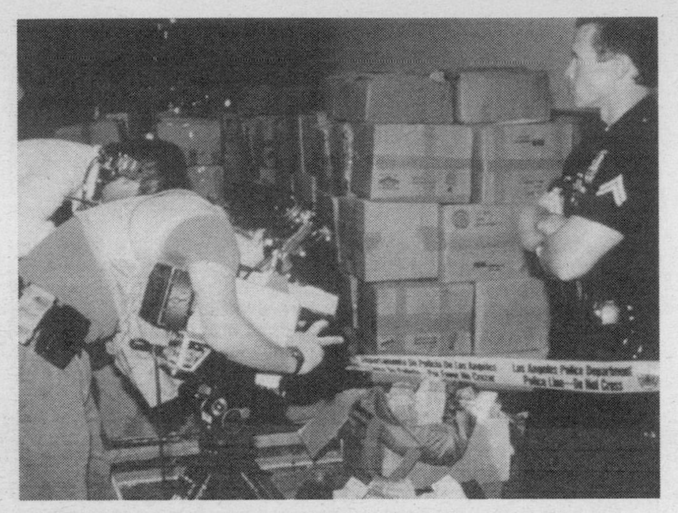

The scene at a Los Angeles warehouse in 1989 after the seizure of cocaine worth $6–$7 billion, the most valuable haul on record. (Gamma/Biggins)

Greatest bank note forgery The greatest forgery was the German Third Reich's forging operation, code name "Operation Bernhard," engineered by Major Bernhard Krüger during World War II. It involved more than £130 million worth of British notes, which were produced by 140 Jewish prisoners at Sachsenhausen concentration camp.

Biggest bank fraud The Banca Nazionale del Lavoro, Italy's leading bank, admitted on 6 Sep 1989 that it had been defrauded of a huge sum, later estimated to be in the region of $5 billion, with the disclosure that its branch in Atlanta, GA had made unauthorized loan commitments to Iraq. Both the bank's chairman, Nerio Nesi, and its director general, Giacomo Pedde, resigned following the revelation.

Computer fraud Between 1964 and 1973, 64,000 fake insurance policies were created on the computer of the Equity Funding Corporation in the United States, involving $2 billion.

Stanley Mark Rifkin (b. 1946) was arrested in Carlsbad, CA by the FBI on 6 Nov 1978 and charged with defrauding a Los Angeles bank of $10.2 million by manipulation of a computer system. He was sentenced to eight years' imprisonment in June 1980.

Maritime fraud A cargo of 198,414 tons of Kuwaiti crude oil on the supertanker *Salem* at Durban was sold without title to the South African government in December 1979. The ship mysteriously sank off Senegal on 17 Jan 1980, leaving the government to pay £148 million ($318.2 million) to Shell International, which owned the shipment.

Crowds look on with grim anticipation at the last public hanging in the United States. More than 10,000 people attended the execution in Owensboro, KY in 1936. (Popperfoto)

CAPITAL PUNISHMENT

Largest hanging The Nazi Feldkommandant simultaneously hanged 50 Greek resistance fighters as a reprisal measure in Athens, Greece on 22 Jul 1944.

The most people hanged from one gallows were 38 Sioux Indians by William J. Duly outside Mankato, MN on 26 Dec 1862 for the murder of unarmed citizens.

Last public hangings The last public hanging in the United States occurred at Owensboro, KY on 14 Aug 1936, when Rainey Bethea was hung in a field by the banks of the Ohio River. He was executed in the presence of a crowd of between 10,000 and 15,000.

Death row The longest sojourn on death row was the 39 years of Sadamichi Hirasawa (1893–1987) in Sendai Jail, Japan. He was convicted in 1948 of poisoning 12 bank employees with potassium cyanide to effect a theft of $403, and died in prison at the age of 94.

United States Howard Virgil Lee Douglas spent 17½ years on death row, longer than any other person in American penal history. On 15 May 1991 he was resentenced to life in prison.

PRISON SENTENCES

Longest sentences Chamoy Thipyaso, a Thai woman known as the queen of underground investing, and seven of her associates were each sentenced to serve 141,078 years in jail by the Bangkok Criminal Court, Thailand on 27 Jul 1989 for swindling the public through a multimillion-dollar deposit-taking business.

The longest sentence imposed on a mass murderer was 21 consecutive life sentences and 12 death sentences in the case of John Wayne Gacy, Jr., who killed 33 boys and young men between 1972 and 1978 in Illinois. He was sentenced by a jury in Chicago, IL on 13 Mar 1980, and executed on 10 May 1994.

Longest time served Paul Geidel (1894–1987) was convicted of second-degree murder on 5 Sep 1911 when he was a 17-year-old porter in a hotel in New York. He was released from the Fishkill Correctional Facility, Beacon, NY at the age of 85 on 7 May 1980, having served 68 years, 8 months and 2 days—the longest recorded term in US history. He first refused parole in 1974.

Oldest Bill Wallace (1881–1989) was the oldest prisoner on record, spending the last 63 years of his life in Aradale Psychiatric Hospital, at Ararat, Victoria, Australia. He had shot and killed a man at a restaurant in Melbourne, Victoria in December 1925, and having been found unfit to plead, was transferred to the responsibility of the Mental Health Department in February 1926. He remained at Aradale until his death on 17 Jul 1989, shortly before his 108th birthday.

FINES

Heaviest The largest fine ever was one of $650 million, which was imposed on the US securities firm of Drexel Burnham Lambert in December 1988 for insider trading. This figure represented $300 million in direct fines, with the balance to be put into an account to satisfy claims of parties who could prove they were defrauded by Drexel's actions.

The record for an individual is $200 million, which Michael Milken agreed to pay on 24 Apr 1990. He also agreed to settle civil charges filed by the Securities and Exchange Commission. The payments were in settlement of a criminal racketeering and securities fraud suit brought by the US government. On appeal Milken's sentence was reduced to 33 months and 26 days (5 Aug 1992). He was released from prison on 2 Mar 1993, but was required to give 1,800 hours of community service.

PRISONS

Most expensive prison Spandau Prison, Berlin, originally built in 1887 for 600 prisoners, was used solely for the Nazi war criminal Rudolf Hess (26 Apr 1894–17 Aug 1987) for the last 20 years of his life. The cost of maintenance of the staff of 105 was estimated in 1976 to be $415,000 per year.

Longest escape The longest recorded escape by a recaptured prisoner was that of Leonard T. Fristoe, 77, who escaped from Nevada State Prison on 15 Dec 1923 and was turned in by his son on 15 Nov 1969 at Compton, CA. He had had 46 years of freedom under the name of Claude R. Willis. He had killed two sheriff's deputies in 1920.

Greatest jail breaks In February 1979 a retired US Army colonel, Arthur "Bull" Simons, led a band of 14 to break into Gasre Prison, Tehran, Iran to rescue two fellow Americans. Some 11,000 other prisoners took advantage of this, and of the Islamic revolution, in what became history's largest-ever jailbreak.

In September 1971, Raúl Sendic and 105 other Tupamaro guerrillas, plus five nonpolitical prisoners, escaped from a Uruguayan prison through a tunnel 298 ft long.

Highest prison population Some human rights organizations have estimated that there are 20 million prisoners in China, which would be equal to 1,715 per 100,000 population, although this figure is not officially acknowledged. Among countries for which statistics are available, the country with the highest per capita prison population is the United States, with 455 prisoners per 100,000 population.

HONORS, DECORATIONS & AWARDS

Oldest order The earliest known honor was the "Gold of Honor" for extraordinary valor awarded in the 18th Dynasty *c.* 1440–1400 B.C. A representative statuette was found at Qan-el-Kebri, Egypt. The oldest true order was the Order of St John of Jerusalem (the direct descendant of which is the Sovereign Military Order of Malta), legitimized in 1113.

Youngest awardees Kristina Stragauskaite of Skirmantiskes, Lithuania was awarded a medal "for courage in fire" when she was just 4 years 8 months old. She had saved the lives of her younger brother and sister when a fire broke out on 7 Apr 1989 in the family's home while her parents were out. The award was decreed by the Presidium of the Lithuanian Soviet Socialist Republic.

The youngest age at which an official gallantry award has ever been won is eight years, in the case of Anthony Farrer, who was given the Albert Medal on 23 Sep 1916 for fighting off a cougar at Cowichan Lake, Vancouver Island, Canada to save Doreen Ashburnham. She was also awarded the Albert medal, which she exchanged in 1974 for the George Cross.

Most titles The most titled person in the world is the 18th Duchess of Alba (Alba de Tormes), Doña Maria del Rosario Cayetana Fitz-James Stuart y Silva (b. 28 Mar 1926). She is six times a duchess, once a viscountess, 18 times a marchioness, 19 times a countess and 17 times a Spanish grandee.

Most valuable annual prize The most valuable annual prize is the Louis Jeantet Prize for Medicine, which in 1994 was worth SFr 2.1 million (equivalent to approximately $1,421,000). It was first awarded in 1986 and is intended to "provide substantial funds for the support of biomedical research projects."

Most statues The world record for raising statues to oneself was set by

Joseph Stalin (1879–1953), the leader of the Soviet Union from 1924–53. It is estimated that during the Stalin era there were *c.* 6,000 statues to him throughout the USSR and in many cities in Eastern Europe.

The man to whom the most statues have been raised is Buddha. The 20th-century champion is Vladimir Ilyich Ulyanov, alias Lenin (1870–1924), busts of whom have been mass-produced.

Most honorary degrees The greatest number of honorary degrees awarded to any individual is 129, given to Rev. Father Theodore M. Hesburgh (b. 25 May 1917), president of the University of Notre Dame, IN. These have been accumulated since 1954.

MILITARY & DEFENSE

WAR

Oldest weapon The oldest known offensive weapon is a broken wooden spear found in April 1911 at Clacton-on-Sea, Great Britain by S. Hazzledine Warren. It is much beyond the limit of radiocarbon dating but is estimated to have been fashioned before 200,000 B.C.

Longest The longest war that can be described as continuous was the Thirty Years' War, between various European countries, from 1618 to 1648. The *Reconquista*—the series of campaigns in the Iberian Peninsula to recover the region from the Islamic Moors—began in the year 718 and continued intermittently until 1492, when Granada, the last Moorish stronghold, was finally conquered.

Bloodiest By far the most costly war in terms of human life was World War II (1939–45), in which the total number of fatalities, including battle deaths and civilians of all countries, is estimated to have been 54.8 million, assuming 25 million Soviet fatalities and 7.8 million Chinese civilians killed. The country that suffered most was Poland, with 6,028,000 or 17.2 percent of its population of 35.1 million killed.

In the Paraguayan war of 1864–70 against Brazil, Argentina and Uruguay, Paraguay's population was reduced from 1.4 million to 220,000 survivors.

Civil The bloodiest civil war in history was the *Taiping* ("Great Peace") rebellion, which was a revolt against the Chinese Qing Dynasty between 1851 and 1864. According to the best estimates, the loss of life was some 20 million, including more than 100,000 killed by government forces in the sack of Nanjing on 19–21 Jul 1864.

Most costly The material cost of World War II far transcended that of all the rest of history's wars put together and has been estimated at $1.5 trillion.

Bloodiest battles It is difficult to compare the major battles of World Wars I and II because of the different time scales. The 142-day-long first battle of the Somme, France (1 Jul–19 Nov 1916) produced an estimated total number of casualties of over 1.22 million; of these, 623,907 were Allied and the rest German. The greatest death toll in a battle has been estimated at *c.* 1,109,000 in the Battle of Stalingrad, USSR, ending with the German surrender on 31 Jan 1943 by Field Marshal Friedrich von Paulus (1890–1957). The Germans suffered 200,000 losses. The Soviet garrison commander was Gen. Vasiliy Chuikov; *c.* 650,800 soldiers from the Soviet army were injured but survived. Additionally, only 1,515 civilians from a pre-war population of more than 500,000 were found alive after the battle. The final drive on Berlin, Germany by the Soviet Army, and the battle for the city that followed, from 16 Apr–2 May 1945, involved 3.5 million men, 52,000 guns and mortars, 7,750 tanks and 11,000 aircraft on both sides.

United States The American Civil War (1861–65) is the bloodiest war fought on American soil. The bloodiest battles between the Northern (Union) and the Southern (Confederate) forces were at Shiloh Church, near Pittsburg Landing in Hardin County, TN on 6–7 Apr 1862, when each side reported casualties of over 10,000; at Fredericksburg, VA on 13 Dec 1862, when Union losses were over 12,000, more than double those of the Confederacy; and at Gettysburg, PA on 1–3 Jul 1863, when the Union reported losses of 23,000 and the Confederacy 25,000 (a disputed figure).

Greatest naval battles *Modern* The greatest number of ships and aircraft ever involved in a sea–air action was 231 ships and 1,996 aircraft in the Battle of Leyte Gulf, in the Philippines, during World War II. It raged from 22–27 Oct 1944, with 166 Allied and 65 Japanese warships engaged, of which 26 Japanese and 6 US ships were sunk. In addition, 1,280 US and 716 Japanese aircraft were engaged. The greatest purely naval battle of modern times was the Battle of Jutland on 31 May 1916, during World War I, in which 151 British Royal Navy warships were involved against 101 German warships. The Royal Navy lost 14 ships and 6,097 men, and the German fleet lost 11 ships and 2,545 men.

Greatest invasion *Seaborne* The greatest invasion in military history was the Allied land, air and sea operation against the Normandy coast of France on D-Day, 6 Jun 1944. Thirty-eight convoys of 745 ships moved in during the first three days, supported by 4,066 landing craft, carrying 185,000 men, 20,000 vehicles and 347 minesweepers. The air assault comprised 18,000 paratroopers from 1,087 aircraft. The 42 available divisions had air support from 13,175 aircraft. Within a month 1.1 million troops, 200,000 vehicles and 840,000 tons of stores were landed. The Allied invasion of Sicily from 10–12 Jul 1943 involved the landing of 181,000 men in three days.

Airborne The largest airborne invasion was the Anglo-American assault of three divisions (34,000 men), with 2,800 aircraft and 1,600 gliders, near Arnhem, in the Netherlands, on 17 Sep 1944.

Longest-range attacks The longest-range attacks in air history were those undertaken by seven B-52G bombers, which took off from Barksdale Air Force Base, LA on 16 Jan 1991 to deliver air-launched cruise missiles against targets in Iraq shortly after the start of the Gulf War. Each bomber flew a distance of 14,000 miles, refueling four times in flight, with the round-trip mission lasting some 35 hours.

Greatest evacuation The greatest evacuation in military history was that carried out by 1,200 Allied naval and civilian craft from the beachhead at Dunkerque (Dunkirk), France between 27 May and 4 Jun 1940. A total of 338,226 British and French troops were evacuated.

Largest civilian evacuation Following the Iraqi invasion of Kuwait in August 1990, Air India evacuated 111,711 of its nationals who were working in Kuwait. Beginning on 13 August, 488 flights took the expatriates back to India over a two-month period.

Longest march The longest march in military history was the famous Long March by the Chinese Communists in 1934–35. In 368 days, of which 268 were days of movement, from October to October, their force of some 100,000 covered 6,000 miles from Ruijin, in Jiangxi, to Yan'an, in Shaanxi. They crossed 18 mountain ranges and 24 rivers, and eventually reached Yan'an with only about 8,000 survivors, following continual rearguard actions against nationalist Kuomintang (KMT) forces.

Flt Sgt Chris Chandler set an individual record in the RAF Swinderby Marathon at Swinderby, Great Britain on 25 Sep 1992, with a pack weighing 40 lbs. His time was 3 hr 56 min 10 sec.

Army drill On 8–9 Jul 1987 a 90-man squad of the Queen's Color Squadron, Royal Air Force (RAF) performed a total of 2,722,662 drill movements (2,001,384 rifle and 721,278 foot) at RAF Uxbridge, Great Britain from memory and without a word of command in 23 hr 55 min.

MUTINY!

The biggest mutiny was in World War I, when 56 French divisions, comprising some 650,000 men and their officers, refused orders on the Western front sector of General Robert Nivelle in April 1917 after the failure of his offensive

Worst sieges The worst siege in history was the 880-day siege of Leningrad, USSR (now St Petersburg, Russia) by the German Army from 30 Aug 1941 until 27 Jan 1944. The best estimate is that between 1.3 and 1.5 million defenders and citizens died. This included 641,000 people who died of hunger in the city and 17,000 civilians killed by shelling. More than 150,000 shells and 100,000 bombs were dropped on the city.

The longest recorded siege was that of Azotus (now Ashdod), Israel, which according to Herodotus was besieged by Psamtik I of Egypt for 29 years, during the period 664–610 B.C.

Chemical warfare The greatest number of people killed through chemical warfare were the estimated 4,000 Kurds who died at Halabja, Iraq in March 1988 when President Saddam Hussein used chemical weapons against Iraq's Kurdish minority in revenge for the support it had given to Iran in the Iran–Iraq war.

ARMED FORCES

Largest China's People's Liberation Army's strength in 1992 was estimated to be 3,030,000 (comprising land, sea and air forces), with reductions continuing. Its reserves number around 1.2 million. The military forces of the United States for 1993 totaled 1,731,287. There were 586,401 active duty personnel in the United States Army as of 30 Mar 1993. The total number of reservists in the United States was 1,901,905 as of 30 Sep 1992.

Navies Largest The largest navy in the world in terms of personnel is the United States Navy, with a total of 481,066 servicemen and women, plus 174,816 Marines as of June 1994. The active strength in 1992 included 6 nuclear-powered aircraft carriers, 6 conventionally powered aircraft carriers, 25 ballistic missile submarines, 48 nuclear attack submarines, 1 diesel attack submarine, 46 cruisers, 45 destroyers, 83 frigates and 65 amphibious warfare ships.

The world's largest-ever fleet, the navy of the former USSR, had a larger submarine fleet, comprising 250 vessels (including 55 ballistic missiles). It also had 4 aircraft carriers, 33 cruisers, 26 destroyers, 129 frigates and 80 amphibious warfare ships. This excludes the Black Sea Fleet, which has 18 submarines (none with ballistic missiles), and 36 surface combatants. The Black Sea Fleet will be split among Ukraine, Russia and Georgia. The rest of the Navy is based at Russian ports.

Armies Oldest The oldest army in the world is the 80–90 strong Pontifical Swiss Guard in Vatican City, founded 21 Jan 1506. Its origins, however, predate 1400.

Largest Numerically, the world's largest army is that of the People's Republic of China, with a total strength of some 2.3 million in mid-1992. The total size of the former USSR's army in mid-1991 was estimated at 1,400,000, believed to be organized into 139 divisions (tank, motor rifle and airborne).

Oldest soldier The oldest "old soldier" of all time was probably John B. Salling of the Army of the Confederate States of America and the last accepted survivor of the Civil War (1861–65). He died in Kingsport, TN on 16 Mar 1959, aged 113 years 1 day.

Youngest soldier Luís Alves de Lima e Silva, Marshal Duke of Caxias (25 Aug 1803–7 May 1880), Brazilian military hero and statesman, entered his infantry regiment at the age of five in 1808. He was promoted to captain in 1824 and made Duke in 1869.

Fernando Inchauste Montalvo (b. 18 Jun 1930), the son of a major in the Bolivian air force, went to the front with his father on his fifth birthday during the war between Bolivia and Paraguay (1932–35). He had received military training and was subject to military discipline.

Youngest conscripts President Francisco Macias Nguema of Equatorial Guinea (deposed in August 1979) in March 1976 decreed compulsory military service for all boys between the ages of 7 and 14. The edict stated that any parent refusing to hand over his or her son "will be imprisoned or shot."

The D-Day invasion of the Normandy coast was the largest seaborne invasion in military history. The invasion strategy was top secret and the final plans took months to complete. During the spring of 1944, southeastern England became a huge military camp awaiting the attack. On 6 June 1944, the first troops finally landed on the Normandy beaches and stepped into history. (Gamma Archives)

Tallest soldier The tallest soldier of all time was Väinö Myllyrinne (1909–63), who was conscripted into the Finnish Army when he was 7 ft 3 in and who later grew to 8 ft 3 in.

Air forces *Oldest* The earliest autonomous air force is the Royal Air Force, which can be traced back to 1878, when the British War Office commissioned the building of a military balloon. Balloons had been used for military observation by both sides during the American Civil War (1861–65).

Largest The largest air force of all time was the United States Army Air Corps (now the US Air Force), which had 79,908 aircraft in July 1944 and 2,411,294 personnel in March 1944. The US Air Force, including strategic missile forces, had 431,053 personnel as of June 1994.

BOMBS

Heaviest The heaviest conventional bomb ever used operationally was the Royal Air Force's *Grand Slam*, weighing 22,000 lb and measuring 25 ft 5 in long, dropped on Bielefeld railroad viaduct, Germany on 14 Mar 1945.

In 1949 the United States Air Force tested a bomb weighing 42,000 lb at Muroc Dry Lake, CA. The heaviest known nuclear bomb was the MK 17, carried by US B-36 bombers in the mid-1950s. It weighed 42,000 lb and was 24 ft 6 in long.

Thermonuclear The most powerful thermonuclear device so far tested is one with a power equivalent to that of 57 megatons of TNT, detonated by the former USSR in the Novaya Zemlya area at 8:33 GMT on 30 Oct 1961. The shock-wave circled the world three times, taking 36 hr 27 min for the first circuit. The largest US H-bomb tested was the 18–22 megaton *Bravo* at Bikini Atoll, Marshall Islands on 1 Mar 1954.

Largest nuclear weapons The most powerful ICBM (intercontinental ballistic missile) is the former USSR's SS–18 (Model 5), believed to be armed with ten 750-kiloton MIRVs (multiple independently targetable reentry vehicles). SS–18 ICBMs are located on both Russian and Kazakhstan territory—they are now controlled by the Commonwealth of Independent States. The US Titan II, carrying a W-53 warhead, was rated at 9 megatons but has now been withdrawn, leaving the 1.2 megaton W-56 as the most powerful US weapon.

Largest "conventional" explosion The largest use of conventional explosives was by a team of Chinese army engineers who blew up a mountain to allow for the expansion of an airport in Zhuhai, an economic development zone near Macau. A total of nearly 12,460 tons of TNT were detonated on 28 Dec 1992, after 1,000 technicians spent several months preparing for the explosion.

GUNS

Largest The largest gun ever constructed was used by German forces in the siege of Sevastopol, USSR (now Russia) in July 1942. It was of a caliber of 31 in with a barrel 94 ft 8½ in long. The whole gun was 141 ft long and weighed 1,481.5 tons, with a crew of 1,500. The range for an 8.9-ton projectile was 29 miles.

Heaviest The heaviest gun in the US Army is the MK19-3 40mm automatic grenade launcher, which weighs 72.5 lb and has both the greatest caliber and range of any US Army weapon: about 1,650 yd at point targets, over 2,400 yd at area targets. The bullets can penetrate 2 in into armor at 2,400 yd.

Greatest range The greatest range ever attained by a gun was achieved by the HARP (High Altitude Research Project) gun, consisting of two 16½-in caliber barrels in tandem 119 ft 5 in long and weighing 165 tons, at Yuma, AZ. On 19 Nov 1966 an 185-lb projectile was fired to an altitude of 112 miles or 590,550 ft.

Mortars The largest mortars ever constructed were Mallet's mortar (Woolwich Arsenal, London, Great Britain, 1857); and the *Little David* of World War II, made in the United States. Each had a caliber of 36 in, but neither was ever used in action.

Largest cannon The highest-caliber cannon ever constructed is the *Tsar Pushka* (*King of Cannons*), now housed in the Kremlin, Moscow, Russia. It was built in the 16th century with a bore of 35 in and a barrel 17 ft 6 in long. It weighs 44 tons.

Armor The highest auction price paid for a suit of armor was £1,925,000 ($3,657,000), by B.H. Trupin (USA) on 5 May 1983 at Sotheby's, London, Great Britain for a suit made in Milan by Giovanni Negroli in 1545 for Henri II of France. It came from the Hever Castle Collection in Kent, Great Britain.

EDUCATION

Universities Oldest The oldest educational institution in the world is the University of Karueein, founded in A.D. 859 in Fez, Morocco.

The oldest college in the United States is Harvard College in Cambridge, MA, founded in 1636 as Newtowne College and renamed in 1638 after its first benefactor, John Harvard.

Largest The largest university building in the world is the M.V. Lomonosov State University, south of Moscow, Russia. It stands 787 ft 5 in tall, and has 32 stories and 40,000 rooms. It was constructed from 1949–53.

Greatest enrollment The university with the greatest enrollment in the world is the State University of New York, which had 397,637 students at 64 campuses throughout the state in the fall of 1993. The greatest enrollment at a university centered in one city is at the University of Rome (*La Sapienza*), in Italy, which had 184,000 students in 1993. It was built in the 1920s as a single-site campus, and still is mainly based there.

THE YOUNGEST COLLEGE PRESIDENT

"When I was a kid, I didn't know what I wanted to be," says Ellen Futter. "I played a lot of sports. I wasn't always an A student. I always knew I wanted to do *something*."

It's hard to find something that Ellen Futter, now in her forties, *hasn't* done. The self-proclaimed "Prime Primate" of the American Museum of Natural History, Futter is the institution's first woman president and has an office amid the ape exhibit.

Indeed, everything about Futter seems prime; her resume is chock-full of directorships and memberships in everything from the Helsinki Watch to the Academy of American Poets. "I was on the Board of Trustees at Barnard when they asked me to be acting president. I was 29. The college did a full search, then asked me to stay on. By then I was a known quantity. I was no longer thought of in terms of my age." Under Futter Barnard went co-ed, became fully residential, and tripled its endowment.

Besides chimps, Futter shares office space with the largest meteorite, the Western Hemisphere's largest natural history library, and the world's largest mammal fossil collection. "Nature is the answer," she says vehemently. "What do I feel called to do? I love running institutions that are concerned with causes and issues I feel passionate about. At Barnard it was women's education. Here it's science education. I like being the spokesperson for groups that will help society by having a voice."

Most graduates in family Mr and Mrs Harold Erickson of Naples, FL saw all of their 14 children—11 sons and 3 daughters—obtain university or college degrees between 1962 and 1978.

Youngest university students Michael Tan (b. 4 Apr 1984) of Christchurch, New Zealand took and passed his New Zealand bursary examination in mathematics (equivalent to high school graduation exams in the United States) in November 1991 at the age of 7 years 7 months. He started studying for a BSc degree in mathematics at Canterbury University, New Zealand in March 1992 at the age of 7 years 11 months.

United States Adragon Eastwood De Mello (b. 5 Oct 1976) of Santa Cruz, CA obtained his BA in mathematics from the University of California in Santa Cruz on 11 Jun 1988 at the age of 11 years 8 months.

Youngest doctorate On 13 Apr 1814 the mathematician Carl Witte of Lochau was made a Doctor of Philosophy of the University of Giessen, Germany at the age of 12.

Youngest college president The youngest president of a major college was Ellen Futter, who was appointed to head Barnard College, New York City in May 1981 at the age of 31.

Schools *Most* The country with the greatest number of primary schools is China, with 938,394 in 1990. San Marino has the lowest pupil-to-teacher ratio, with 5.5 children per teacher.

At general secondary level, India has the most schools, with 214,380 in 1990, while the Australian external territory of Cocos (Keeling) Islands has the best pupil-to-teacher ratio, with 5.5 children per teacher.

Most expensive The annual cost of keeping a pupil at the most expensive school in the United States for the academic year 1994/95 will be $32,500 at the Oxford Academy (founded 1906), in Westbrook, CT.

Largest In 1992/93 Rizal High School, Pasig, Manila, Philippines had an enrollment of 16,535 regular students, although the numbers slightly declined for 1993/94.

Most schools attended The greatest documented number of schools attended by a pupil is 265, by Wilma Williams, now Mrs R.J. Horton, from 1933–43 when her parents were in show business traveling around the United States.

Most durable teacher Medarda de Jesús León de Uzcátegui, alias La Maestra Chucha, has been teaching in Caracas, Venezuela for a total of 83 years. In 1911, when she was 12, she and her two sisters set up a school there which they named *Modelo de Aplicación*. Since marrying in 1942, she has run her own school, which she calls the *Escuela Uzcátegui*, from her home in Caracas.

Highest endowment The greatest single gift in the history of education was $500 million, to the US public education system by Walter Annenberg in December 1993. The gift was intended to help fight violence in schools.

RELIGION

Largest Christianity is the world's most widely practiced religion, with some 1,833 million adherents in 1992, or 33.4 percent of the world's population. There were 1,026 million Roman Catholics in the same year. The largest non-Christian religion is Islam (Muslim), with some 971 million followers in 1992.

Oldest church The oldest standing Protestant edifice in the United States is the Newport Parish Church, commonly known as St Luke's, in Isle of Wight County, VA, four miles south of Smithfield, VA. The church was built *c.* 1632 and was originally called Warrisquioke Parish Church. In 1637 it was renamed the Isle of Wight Parish Church, and its present name was instituted in 1957.

Synagogue The oldest synagogue in the United States is Touro Synagogue, Newport, RI. Construction was started in 1759 and completed in 1763. Originally called the Jewish Synagogue of Newport, the synagogue was closed in 1820, but reopened in 1883, renamed Touro Synagogue.

Largest temple The largest religious structure ever built is Angkor Wat ("City Temple"), enclosing 402 acres in Cambodia. It was built to the Hindu god Vishnu by the Khmer King Suryavarman II in the period A.D. 1113–50. Its curtain wall measures 4,199 × 4,199 ft and its population, before it was abandoned in 1432, was 80,000. The whole complex of 72 major monuments, begun *c.* A.D. 900, extends over 15 × 5 miles.

Largest cathedral The world's largest cathedral is the cathedral church of the Diocese of New York, St John the Divine, in New York City, with a floor area of 121,000 ft^2 and a volume of 16,822,000 ft^3. The cornerstone was laid on 27 Dec 1892, and work on the building was stopped in 1941. Work was restarted in July 1979, but is still not finished. The nave is the longest in the world at 601 ft, with a vaulting 124 ft in height.

The cathedral covering the largest area is that of Santa Mariá de la Sede in Sevilla (Seville), Spain. It was built in Spanish Gothic style between 1402 and 1519, and is 414 ft long, 271 ft wide and 100 ft high to the vault of the nave.

Smallest cathedral The smallest church in the world designated as a cathedral (the seat of a diocesan bishop) is the Christ Catholic Church, Highlandville, MO, consecrated in July 1983. It measures 14 × 17 ft and seats 18 people.

Largest church The largest church in the world is the Basilica of Our Lady of Peace (Notre Dame de la Paix) in Yamoussoukro, Ivory Coast, completed in 1989 at a cost of $180 million. It has a total area of 100,000 ft^2, with seating for 7,000 people. Including its golden cross, it is 519 ft high.

The elliptical Basilica of St Pio X at Lourdes, France, completed in 1957 at a cost of $5.6 million, has a capacity of 20,000 under its giant span arches and a length of 660 ft.

Part of the world's largest group of stained glass windows. Adorning the Basilica of Our Lady of Peace, Yamoussoukro, Ivory Coast, the windows cover 80,000 ft². (Gamma/G. Bassignac)

Longest The crypt of the underground Civil War Memorial Church in the Guadarrama Mountains, 28 miles from Madrid, Spain, is 853 ft in length. It took 21 years (1937–58) to build, at a reported cost of $392 million, and is surmounted by a cross 492 ft tall.

Largest synagogue The largest synagogue in the world is Temple Emanu-El on Fifth Avenue at 65th Street, New York City. The temple, completed in September 1929, has a frontage of 150 ft on Fifth Avenue and 253 ft on 65th Street. The sanctuary proper can accommodate 2,500 people, and the adjoining Beth-El Chapel seats 350. When all the facilities are in use, more than 6,000 people can be accommodated.

Largest mosque The largest mosque is Shah Faisal Mosque, near Islamabad, Pakistan. The total area of the complex is 46.87 acres, with the covered area of the prayer hall being 1.19 acres. It can accommodate 100,000 worshippers in the prayer hall and the courtyard, and a further 200,000 people in the adjacent grounds.

Tallest minaret The tallest minaret in the world is that of the Great Hassan II Mosque, Casablanca, Morocco, measuring 656 ft. The cost of construction of the mosque was $540 million.

Tallest spire Cathedral The tallest cathedral spire in the world is that of the Protestant Cathedral of Ulm in Germany. The building is early Gothic and was begun in 1377. The tower, in the center of the west façade, was not finally completed until 1890 and is 528 ft high.

Church The world's tallest church spire is that of the Chicago Temple of the First Methodist Church on Clark Street, Chicago, IL. The building consists of a 22-story skyscraper (erected in 1924) surmounted by a parsonage at 330 ft, a "Sky Chapel" at 400 ft and a steeple cross at 568 ft above street level.

Stained glass *Oldest* Pieces of stained glass dated before A.D. 850, some possibly even to the seventh century, excavated by Prof. Rosemary Cramp, were set into a window of that date in the nearby St Paul's Church, Jarrow, Ireland. The oldest complete stained-glass window in the world represents the Prophets in a window of the Cathedral of Augsburg, Germany, dating from the second half of the 11th century.

The oldest figured stained-glass window in the United States is in Christ Church, Pelham Manor, NY and was designed by William Jay Bolton and John Bolton in 1843.

Largest The largest stained-glass window is that of the Resurrection Mausoleum in Justice, IL, measuring 22,381 ft^2 in 2,448 panels, completed in 1971.

Although not one continuous window, the Basilica of Our Lady of Peace (Notre Dame de la Paix) at Yamoussoukro, Ivory Coast contains a number of stained-glass windows covering a total area of 80,000 ft^2.

HUMAN ACHIEVEMENTS

FANTASTIC FEATS

Barrel rolling The record for rolling a full 36-gallon metal beer barrel over a measured mile is 8 min 7.2 sec, by Phillip Randle, Steve Hewitt, John Round, Trevor Bradley, Colin Barnes and Ray Glover of Haunchwood Collieries Institute and Social Club, Nuneaton, Great Britain on 15 Aug 1982.

A team of 10 rolled a 140-lb barrel 150 miles in 30 hr 31 min in Chlumčany, Czech Republic, on 27–28 Oct 1982.

Barrow pushing The heaviest loaded one-wheeled barrow pushed for a minimum 200 level feet was one loaded with bricks weighing a gross 8,275 lb. It was pushed a distance of 243 ft by John Sarich at London, Ontario, Canada on 19 Feb 1987.

Barrow racing The fastest time attained in a 1-mile wheelbarrow race is 4 min 48.51 sec, by Piet Pitzer and Jaco Erasmus at the Transvalia High School, Vanderbijlpark, South Africa on 3 Oct 1987.

Bathtub racing The record for a 36-mile bathtub race is 1 hr 22 min 27 sec, by Greg Mutton at the Grafton Jacaranda Festival, New South Wales, Australia on 8 Nov 1987. Tubs are limited to 75 in and 6 hp motors. The greatest distance for paddling a hand-propelled bathtub in still water in 24 hr is 90½ miles, by 13 members of Aldington Prison Officers Social Club, near Ashford, Great Britain on 28–29 May 1983.

TWANG!

The greatest recorded distance for a catapult shot is 1,362 ft, by James M. Pfotenhauer, using a patented 17 ft 1½ in Monarch IV Supershot and a 53-caliber lead musket ball on Ski Hill Road, Escanaba, MI on 10 Sep 1977.

Bed making The pair record for making a bed with one blanket, two sheets, an undersheet, an uncased pillow, one bedspread and "hospital" corners is 14.0 sec, by Sister Sharon Stringer and Nurse Michelle Benkel of the Royal Masonic Hospital, London, Great Britain on 26 Nov 1993 at Canary Wharf, London, Great Britain.

The record time for one person to make a bed is 28.2 sec, by Wendy Wall, 34, of Hebersham, Sydney, Australia on 30 Nov 1978.

Bed pushing The longest recorded push of a normally stationary object is of 3,233 miles, in the case of a wheeled hospital bed, by a team of nine employees of Bruntsfield Bedding Center, Edinburgh, Great Britain from 21 Jun–26 Jul 1979.

Bed race The course record for a 10-mile bed race is 50 min, as established by the Westbury Harriers' three-man bed team at Chew Valley, Avon, Great Britain.

Beer coaster flipping Dean Gould of Felixstowe, Great Britain flipped a pile of 111 coasters (0.047 in wood pulp board) through 180 degrees and caught them all on 13 Jan 1993.

Beer keg lifting Carl Fentham raised a keg of beer weighing 137 lb 13 oz above his head 676 times in the space of six hr at Dudley, Great Britain on 12 Jun 1993.

Beer stein carrying Duane Osborn covered a distance of 49 ft 2½ in in 3.65 sec with five full steins in each hand in a contest in Cadillac, MI on 10 Jul 1992.

Brick balancing John Evans of Marlpool, Great Britain balanced 66 bricks (weighing a total of 296 lb 4 oz) on his head for 10 sec in Cannock, Great Britain on 12 Feb 1994.

Brick laying Sammy Wingfield of Arlington, TN laid 1,048 bricks in 60 min on 20 May 1994 in the everyday working conditions of an average bricklayer.

Brick lifting Russell Bradley of Worcester, Great Britain lifted 31 bricks laid side by side off a table, raising them to chest height and holding them there for 2 sec, on 14 Jun 1992. The greatest weight of bricks lifted was by Fred Burton of Cheadle, Great Britain, who lifted 20 bricks weighing a total of 195 lb on 21 Jan 1994, holding them for 3 sec.

Bubble David Stein of New York City created a 50-ft-long bubble on 6 Jun 1988. He made the bubble using a bubble wand, dishwashing liquid and water.

Bubble-gum blowing The greatest reported diameter for a bubble-gum bubble under the strict rules of this highly competitive activity is 23 in, by Susan Montgomery Williams of Fresno, CA on 19 Jul 1994.

Car washing Students from Carroll High School, Yakima, WA washed 3,844 cars in 8 hr on 7 May 1983.

Carriage pushing The greatest distance covered in pushing a baby carriage in 24 hr is 350.23 miles, by 60 members of the Oost-Vlanderen branch of Amnesty International at Lede, Belgium on 15 Oct 1988. A 10-man team from the Royal Marines School of Music, Deal, Great Britain, with an adult "baby," covered a distance of 271.7 miles in 24 hr from 22–23 Nov 1990.

Cigar box balancing Terry Cole of London, Great Britain balanced 220 unmodified cigar boxes on his chin for 9 sec on 24 Apr 1992.

BEER KEG LIFTING

Most iron pumpers work out, then grab a beer, but on 12 Jun 1993, Carl Fentham raised a 137-lb 13-oz beer keg above his head 676 times in six hours.

Our roving reporter went to Dudley, Great Britain to meet the man who likes to drink his beer and lift it, too.

(**G** = *Guinness Book of Records*, **CF** = Carl Fentham)

G: Why did you choose this record?

CF: The record was set by the manager of the gymnasium where I train in 1989, but unfortunately he didn't make the book because the record was broken again before it was published. I promised him I'd get the record back for the gym.

G: How much training did you have to do before the attempt?

CF: I began beer keg lifting in March 1992, but as I was approaching peak condition around September I pulled a back muscle and was unable to train for three months. When I started again in January I added weights, swimming and hill running to my program, along with lifting kegs.

G: So how did the attempt go? Were you confident?

CF: No. I really didn't know how it would go, but by the time the day came I wanted that record—bad! The record had started off as a bit of a joke, but before long everyone was asking me when I was going to do it, and soon I had pressured myself into it. I got the book as a Christmas present when I was a child. That made it even more of a challenge.

G: How did you know if you were at record pace?

CF: Two of my support crew had been with me throughout every practice session, and they'd worked out a program that was accurate down to the second.

G: How did you feel when you knew that you had beaten the record?

CF: Excited and relieved—both at once!

G: So did you pop open a keg to celebrate?

CF: Well, for two weeks after the event I couldn't even grip the handbrake on my car.

Ouch! The editorial team raises a glass to you, Carl—we'll leave the keg lifting to the champ.

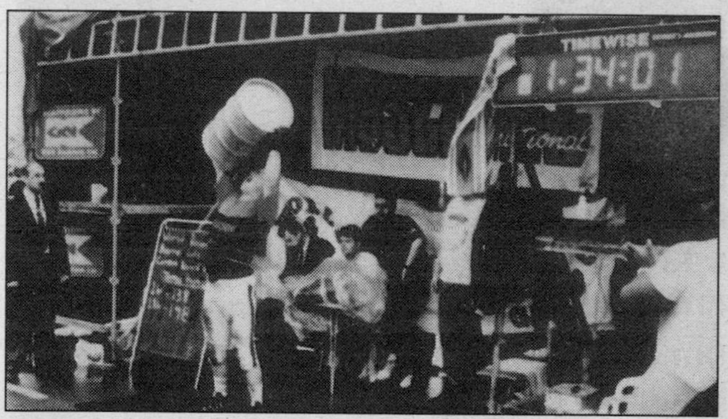

(Carl Fentham) (Mick Williams)

ASHRITA FURMAN EIGHT WORLD RECORDS

He walks. He dribbles. He somersaults. He pogos. He holds the record for holding the most records—and sets them all over the world, from Queens, NY to Zurich, Switzerland to Mount Fuji, Japan. What does he do it for? For Guinness. . . and for inner harmony.

Ashrita Furman has at one time or another held over 30 Guinness records since he first beat the somersault record on 19 Nov 1980. He uses meditation and relaxation to help him in his efforts.

Ashrita's impressive collection of currently published records shows his ability to excel in a wide range of activities:

Ashrita has also been known to skip long distances at great speed and yodel for hours on end, and may soon be attempting a backwards unicycling or roller skating record.

"I feel that *The Guinness Book* is a very positive source of inspiration for people to recognize their unlimited potential, and of course it has revolutionized my life!"

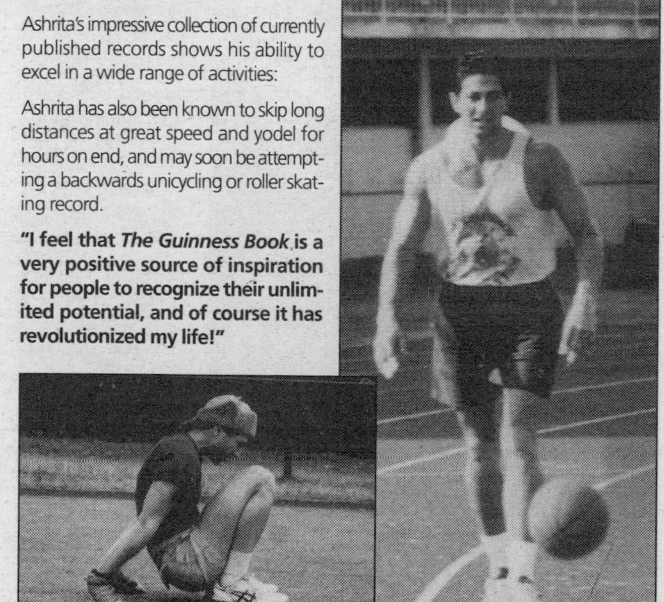

Milk bottle balancing He covered a record distance of 70.16 miles balancing a milk bottle on his head on 1–2 Aug 1993. It took him 18 hr 46 min to complete the walk.

Brick carrying He carried a 9-lb brick in one hand a record distance of 64 miles on 13–14 Jun 1993.

Basketball dribbling He dribbled a basketball a distance of 83 miles in 24 hours on 6–7 Jan 1994.

Somersaults He performed a record 8,341 consecutive forward rolls on 30 Apr 1986. It took him 10 hr 30 min and he covered 12 miles 390 yards.

Joggling (juggling and running at the same time) He completed the marathon —26 miles 385 yards —in 3 hr 22 min 32.5 sec on 4 Jul 1988.

Joggling He also holds the record for 50 miles, with a time of 8 hr 52 min 7 sec on 12 Mar 1989.

Pogo stick jumping He set a distance record of 14.99 miles on 25 May 1991.

Hopscotch He successfully completed a record 307 games of hopscotch in 24 hours on 5–6 Apr 1991.

Crawling The longest continuous voluntary crawl (progression with one or the other knee in unbroken contact with the ground) on record is 31½ miles, by Peter McKinlay and John Murrie, who covered 115 laps of an athletic track at Falkirk, Great Britain on 28–29 Mar 1992. Over a space of 15 months ending on 9 Mar 1985, Jagdish Chander, 32, crawled 870 miles from Aligarh to Jamma, India to propitiate his revered Hindu goddess, Mata.

Crocheting Barbara Jean Sonntag (b. 1938) of Craig, CO crocheted 330 shells plus five stitches (equivalent to 4,412 stitches) in 30 min at a rate of 147 stitches per min on 13 Jan 1981.

Ria van der Honing of Wormerveer, Netherlands completed a crochet chain 38.83 miles long on 14 Jul 1986.

Egg and spoon racing Dale Lyons of Meriden, Great Britain ran 26 miles 385 yd (the classic marathon distance) while carrying a dessert spoon with a fresh egg on it in 3 hr 47 min on 23 Apr 1990.

United States Chris Riggio of San Francisco, CA took 4 hr 9 min 45 sec to run 26 miles 385 yd in a fresh-egg-and-dessert-spoon marathon on 7 Oct 1979.

Egg hunt The greatest egg hunt on record in the United States involved 120,000 plastic and candy eggs at a community Easter egg hunt at Coquina Beach in Manatee, FL on 23 Mar 1991. The event, hosted by Meals on Wheels PLUS of Manatee, Inc., involved more than 40,000 children.

GUESS WHAT?

Q. HOW BIG IS THE BIGGEST EGG?

A. LOOK IN "DINOSAURS" (LIVING WORLD)

Fire bucket brigade The longest fire company bucket brigade stretched over 11,471 ft, with 2,271 people passing 50 buckets along the complete course, at the Centennial Parade and Muster held at Hudson, NY on 11 Jul 1992.

Four-leaf clover collection Norman W. Bright of Heber Springs, AR had collected 6,558 4-leaf clovers as of 26 Apr 1994.

Largest garbage can The world's largest garbage can was made by Natsales of Durban, South Africa for "Keep Durban Beautiful Association Week" from 16–22 Sep 1991. The 19-ft-9-in-tall fiberglass can is a replica of Natsales' standard model and has a capacity of 11,493 gal.

Garbage collection The greatest number of volunteers involved in collecting garbage in one location in one day is 50,405, along the coastline of California on 2 Oct 1993, in conjunction with the International Coastal Cleanup.

Glass balancing John Elliot succeeded in balancing 40 pint glasses on his chin for 10 sec at Tidworth, Great Britain on 16 Dec 1993.

Gold panning The fastest time for "panning" eight planted gold nuggets in a 10-in diameter pan is 7.55 sec, by Don Roberts of Diamond Bar, CA in the 27th World Gold Panning Championship on 16 Apr 1989 at Dahlonega, GA.

The women's record is 10.03 sec, by Susan Bryeans of Fullerton, CA at the 23rd World Gold Panning Championship on 6 Mar 1983 at Knott's Berry Farm, Buena Park, CA.

Grape catching The greatest distance at which a grape thrown from level ground has been caught in the mouth is 327 ft 6 in, by Paul J. Tavilla at East Boston, MA on 27 May 1991. The grape was thrown by James Deady.

Gum wrapper chain The longest gum wrapper chain on record measured 12,105 ft in length, and was made by Gary Duschl of Ontario, Canada between 1965 and 1994.

United States The longest gum wrapper chain in the United States is 7,400 ft long, and was made by Cathy Ushler of Redmond, WA between 1969 and 1992.

Hopscotch The greatest number of games of hopscotch successfully completed in 24 hr is 307, by Ashrita Furman of Jamaica, NY in Zürich, Switzerland on 5–6 Apr 1991.

Hula-hooping, simultaneous The record for simultaneous hula-hooping is 2,010 participants, at the St John Labatt's Lite 24 Hour Relay in St John, New Brunswick, Canada on 21 Sep 1990.

Human centipede The largest "human centipede" to move 98 ft 5 in (30 meters), with ankles firmly tied together, consisted of 1,537 students from Great Barr School, Birmingham, Great Britain on 11 Mar 1994. Nobody fell over in the course of the walk.

Kissing Alfred A.E. Wolfram of New Brighton, MN kissed 8,001 people in 8 hr at the Minnesota Renaissance Festival on 15 Sep 1990—one every 3.6 sec.

Kite flying The following records are all recognized by *Kite Lines* Magazine.

Longest The longest kite flown was 3,394 ft in length. It was made and flown by Michel Trouillet and a team of helpers at Nîmes, France on 18 Nov 1990.

Largest The largest kite flown was 5,952 ft^2. It was first flown by a Dutch team on the beach at Scheveningen, Netherlands on 8 Aug 1991.

Highest A record height of 31,955 ft was reached by a train of eight kites over Lindenberg, Germany on 1 Aug 1919.

The altitude record for a single kite is 12,471 ft, in the case of a kite

Open wide! Grape catching champ Paul Tavilla demonstrates his skills. (Paul Tavilla)

Gary Duschl beside his record-breaking gum wrapper chain—all 12,105 ft of it! (Gary Duschl/Hamilton)

flown by Henry Helm Clayton and A.E. Sweetland at the Blue Hill Weather Station, Milton, MA on 28 Feb 1898.

Fastest The fastest speed attained by a kite was 120 mph for a kite flown by Pete Di Giacomo at Ocean City, MD on 22 Sep 1989.

Greatest number of figure-eights The greatest number of figure-eights achieved with a kite in an hour is 2,911, by Stu Cohen at Ocean City, MD on 25 Sep 1988.

Most on a single line The greatest number of kites flown on a single line is 11,284, by Sadao Harada and a team of helpers at Sakurajima, Kagoshima, Japan on 18 Oct 1990.

Longest duration The longest recorded flight is one of 180 hr 17 min by the Edmonds Community College team at Long Beach, WA from 21–29 Aug 1982. Managing the flight of this J-25 parafoil was Harry N. Osborne.

Knitting The world's most prolific hand-knitter has been Mrs Gwen Matthewman of Featherstone, Great Britain. She attained a speed of 111 stitches per min in a test at Phildar's Wool Shop, Leeds, Great Britain on 29 Sep 1980.

The Exeter Spinners—Audrey Felton, Christine Heap, Eileen Lancaster, Marjorie Mellis, Ann Sandercock and Maria Scott—produced a sweater by hand from raw fleece in 1 hr 55 min 50.2 sec on 25 Sep 1983 at British Broadcasting Corporation Television Centre, London, Great Britain.

Knot-tying The fastest recorded time for tying the six Boy Scout Handbook knots (square knot, sheet bend, sheepshank, clove hitch, round turn and two half hitches, and bowline) on individual ropes is 8.1 sec, by Clinton R. Bailey, Sr., 52, of Pacific City, OR on 13 Apr 1977.

Ladder-climbing A team of 10 firefighters from WR67 Derbyshire Fire & Rescue Service climbed a vertical height of 31.8 miles up a standard fire department ladder in 24 hours in Derby, Great Britain on 1–2 Apr 1994.

Land rowing The greatest distance covered on a land rowing machine is 3,280 miles, by Rob Bryant of Fort Worth, TX, who "rowed" across the United States. He left Los Angeles, CA on 2 Apr 1990, reaching Washington, D.C. on 30 July.

Log rolling *Most championships* The record number of International Championships won is 10, by Jubiel Wickheim of Shawnigan Lake, British Columbia, Canada, between 1956 and 1969.

Mantle of bees Jed Shaner was covered by a mantle of an estimated 343,000 bees weighing an aggregate of 80 lb at Staunton, VA on 29 Jun 1991.

Milk bottle balancing The greatest distance walked by a person continuously balancing a milk bottle on the head is 70.16 miles, by Ashrita Furman in Jamaica, NY on 1–2 Aug 1993. It took him 18 hr 46 min to complete the walk.

Milk crate balancing Terry Cole of Walthamstow, Great Britain managed to balance 29 crates on his chin for the minimum specified 10 sec on 16 May 1994. John Evans of Marlpool, Great Britain balanced 90 crates (weighing a total of 284 lb) on his head for 10 sec on 27 Oct 1993 for the British Broadcasting Corporation's *Record Breakers* program.

Needle threading The record number of times that a strand of cotton has been threaded through a number 13 needle (eye $^1/_2 \times ^1/_{16}$ in) in 2 hr is 20,675, achieved by Om Prakash Singh of Allahabad, India on 25 Jul 1993.

United States The United States record is 5,370, set by Diane Sharp on 1 Aug 1987 at the Charitable Union's centennial event, Battle Creek, MI.

Oyster opening The record for opening oysters is 100 in 2 min 20.07 sec, by Mike Racz in Invercargill, New Zealand on 16 Jul 1990.

Paper chain A paper chain 36.69 miles long was made by 60 students from University College Dublin, Republic of Ireland, as part of UCD Science Day in Dublin on 11–12 Feb 1993. The chain consisted of nearly 400,000 links and was made over a period of 24 hours.

Paper clip chain A chain of 190,400 paper clips was made by 60 students from Nanyang Technological University, Singapore on 12 Jul 1992. The chain was completed in 5 hr 35 min and measured 18,087.3 ft in length.

Pass the parcel The largest game of pass the parcel involved 3,464 people who removed 2,000 wrappers in 2 hr from a parcel measuring 5 × 3 × 3 ft at Alton Towers, Great Britain on 8 Nov 1992. The event was organized by Parcelforce International, and the final prize was an electronic keyboard, won by Sylvia Wilshaw.

Pedal-boating Kenichi Horie of Kobe, Japan set a pedal-boating distance record of 4,660 miles, leaving Honolulu, HI on 30 Oct 1992 and arriving in Naha, Okinawa, Japan on 17 Feb 1993.

Pogo stick jumping The greatest number of jumps achieved is 177,737, by Gary Stewart at Huntington Beach, Los Angeles, CA on 25–26 May 1990. Ashrita Furman of Jamaica, NY set a distance record of 16 miles in 6 hr 40 min on 8 Oct 1993 in Gotemba, Japan.

TOP • 5 • FIVE

MILK BOTTLE BALANCING

Name	Distance	Place	Date
Ashrita Furman	70.16 miles	Jamaica, NY	1–2 Aug 1993
Milind Deshmukh	64.75 miles	Pune, India	14–15 May 1993
Dhirendra Tomar	52.19 miles	Bhopal, India	29 Sep 1991
Willie Hollingsworth	18.50 miles	New York City	24 Mar 1979
William Charlton	15.33 miles	Davenport, Australia	4 Jun 1972

MANTLE OF BEES

"The normal thing people do when a bee comes around is start waving their arms," says the Bee Man. "The body gives off a fear pheromone, and the bee is naturally alerted to your fear. Then her concern (all worker bees are she) is to get you."

(Chuck Haggard)

Well, if that's the normal thing, is there anything normal about setting yourself up to have 80 lb of bees (that's 80 pounds, not 80 bees) buzzing around you? To Jed Shaner, 34, there's nothing more normal. "I'm a fifth-generation bee-keeper," he says. His company, Black Gold's Shaner Honey, produces 385,000 lb of honey annually. "As a kid I was fascinated by our bees. The little creatures used to crawl over me and suddenly sting me." That would be sort of off-putting to most people, but to Jed, stings are "just one of those things. The first couple of times each spring it hurts. After that I don't notice."

To make his bee beard, Jed attached 18 vials of queen bee pheromone (a scented hormone) to a cotton suit. "I draped additional queen bees all over me. Then they dumped bees at my waist, and they started to crawl up." It took an hour and ten minutes to set the record—in 110-degree heat. To Jed it was well worth it. "My sponsor was PULSAR, a police group that helps teens at risk. And I just wanted to show people that bees are not bad. There are 134 crops a year—food on our table—that need to be pollinated by bees. Without them, we'd have nothing."

The ups and downs of record-breaking are highlighted by Gary Stewart's record 177,737 pogo stick jumps. (Photo: S. Seal/K. Taylor)

Quizzes The greatest number of participants was 80,799 in the All-Japan High School Quiz Championship, televised by NTV on 31 Dec 1983.

Rope slide The greatest distance recorded in a rope slide is from near the top of Blackpool Tower, Lancashire, Great Britain—at a height of 416 ft—to a fixed point 1,128 ft from the base of the tower. Set up by the Royal Marines, the rope was descended on 8 Sep 1989 by Sgt. Alan Heward and Cpl. Mick Heap of the Royal Marines, John Herbert of Blackpool Tower, and TV show hosts Cheryl Baker and Roy Castle. The total length descended was 1,202 ft.

Spitting The greatest recorded distance for a cherry stone is 88 ft $5\frac{1}{2}$ in, by Horst Ortmann at Langenthal, Germany on 29 Aug 1992. The record for projecting a watermelon seed is 68 ft $9\frac{1}{8}$ in by Lee Wheelis at Luling, TX on 24 Jun 1989.

United States Rick Krause of Flint, MI spat a cherry stone 72 ft $7\frac{1}{2}$ in on 2 Jul 1988 at the International Cherry Pit Spitting Championship in Eau Claire, MI.

Randy Ober of Bentonville, AR spat a tobacco wad 47 ft 7 in at the Calico 5th Annual Tobacco Chewing and Spitting Championships, held north of Barstow, CA on 4 Apr 1982.

Standing The longest period on record that anyone has continuously stood is more than 17 years in the case of Swami Maujgiri Maharaj when performing the *Tapasya* or penance from 1955 to November 1973 in Shahjahanpur, Uttar Pradesh, India. When sleeping he would lean against a plank. He died at the age of 85 in September 1980.

Step-ups Gareth Morris of Perton, Great Britain completed 1,873 step-ups in one hour on 30 Jan 1993 using a 15 in high exercise bench.

Stone skipping The video-verified stone skipping record is 38 skips, achieved by Jerdone at Wimberley, TX on 20 Oct 1991.

Tailoring The fastest speed in which the manufacture of a three-piece suit has been executed from sheep to finished article is 1 hr 34 min 33.42 sec, by 65 members of the Melbourne College of Textiles, Pascoe Vale, Victoria, Australia on 24 Jun 1982. Catching and fleecing took 2 min 21 sec, and carding, spinning, weaving and tailoring occupied the remaining time.

Tightrope walking The oldest tightrope walker was "Professor" William Ivy Baldwin (1866–1953), who crossed the South Boulder Canyon, CO on a 320-ft wire with a 125-ft drop on his 82nd birthday on 31 Jul 1948.

The world tightrope endurance record is 205 days, by Jorge Ojeda-Guzman of Orlando, FL, on a wire 36 ft long and 35 ft above the ground. He was there from 1 Jan–25 Jul 1993 and entertained onlookers by walking, balancing on a chair and dancing.

Ashley Brophy of Neilborough, Victoria, Australia walked 7.18 miles on a wire 147.64 ft long and 32.81 ft above the ground in Adelaide, Australia on 1 Nov 1985 in 3½ hr.

The greatest drop over which anyone has walked on a tightrope is 10,335 ft, above the French countryside, by Michel Menin of Lons-le-Saunier, France, on 4 Aug 1989.

Typewriting The highest recorded speeds attained with a 10-word penalty per error on a manual machine are—five minutes: 176 wpm by Mrs Carole Forristall Waldschlager Bechen at Dixon, IL on 2 Apr 1959; one hour: 147 wpm by Albert Tangora (USA) on an Underwood Standard, 22 Oct 1923.

The official hour record on an electric typewriter is 9,316 words (40 errors) on an IBM machine, giving a net rate of 149 words per min, by Margaret Hamma, now Mrs Dilmore (USA), in Brooklyn, NY on 20 Jun 1941. In an official test in 1946, Stella Pajunas, now Mrs Garnand, attained a rate of 216 words in a minute on an IBM machine.

Gregory Arakelian of Herndon, VA set a speed record of 158 wpm, with two errors, on a personal computer in the Key Tronic World Invitational Type-off, which attracted some 10,000 entrants worldwide. He recorded this speed in the semifinal on 24 Sep 1991.

Mikhail Shestov of Fredriksberg, Denmark set a numerical record by typing spaced numbers from 1 to 795 in 5 min on 14 Oct 1993.

Les Stewart of Mudjimba Beach, Queensland, Australia has typed the numbers 1 to 820,000 in *words* on 16,290 quarto sheets as of 26 Mar 1994. His target is to become a "millionaire."

Unsupported circle The highest recorded number of people who have demonstrated the physical paradox of all being seated without a chair is an unsupported circle of 10,323 employees of the Nissan Motor Co. at Komazawa Stadium, Tokyo, Japan on 23 Oct 1982.

Whip cracking The longest whip ever "cracked" is one of 184 ft 6 in (excluding the handle), wielded by Krist King of Pettisville, OH on 17 Sep 1991.

Writing, minuscule In 1926 an account was published of Alfred McEwen's pantograph record, in which the 56-word version of the Lord's Prayer was written in diamond point on glass in a space measuring 0.0016 × 0.0008 in.

Surendra Apharya of Jaipur, India wrote 10,056 characters (speeches by Nehru) within the size of an Indian postage stamp, measuring 0.78 × 0.70 in, in December 1990, and also wrote 1,749 characters (names of various countries, towns and regions) on a single grain of rice on 19 May 1991. Chang Shi-Qi of Wuhan, China wrote 308 characters ("God bless you" 28 times) on a human hair 0.8 in long at the Guinness World of Records Exhibition, Singapore on 2 Jun 1992.

Yo-yo "Fast" Eddy McDonald of Toronto, Canada completed 21,663 loops in 3 hr on 14 Oct 1990 in Boston, MA, having previously set a 1 hr speed record of 8,437 loops in Cavendish, Prince Edward Island, Canada

The fastest yo-yo exponent is "Fast" Eddy McDonald. His repertoire includes *Shoot the Moon* and *Monkey up the Tree*.

GUESS WHAT?

Q. What letter did the largest neon sign display?

A. See "Signs" (Arts & Entertainment)

on 14 Jul 1990. Dr Allen Bussey completed 20,302 loops in 3 hr in Waco, TX on 23 Apr 1977.

A yo-yo measuring 10 ft 4 in in diameter and weighing 897 lb was devised by J.N. Nichols (Vimto) Ltd and made by engineering students at Stockport College, Great Britain. It was suspended from a 187-ft crane in Wythenshawe, Great Britain on 1 Aug 1993, and "yo-yoed" about four times.

ADVENTURE

Most traveled The world's most traveled man is John D. Clouse of Evansville, IN. He has visited all of the sovereign countries and all but six of the nonsovereign or other territories that existed in early 1994.

The most traveled couple is Dr Robert and Carmen Becker of East Northport, NY, both of whom have visited all of the sovereign countries and all but nine of the nonsovereign or other territories.

Most isolated The farthest any human has been removed from his nearest living fellow human is 2,233.2 miles in the case of the command module pilot Alfred M. Worden on the US *Apollo 15* lunar mission of 30 Jul–1 Aug 1971, while David Scott and James Irwin were at Hadley Base exploring the surface.

Longest walks The first person reputed to have "walked around the world" is George Matthew Schilling (USA) from 3 Aug 1897 to 1904, but the first *verified* achievement in this category was by David Kunst (USA; b. 1939) from 20 Jun 1970 to 5 Oct 1974. He wore out 21 pairs of shoes in the process.

Tomás Carlos Pereira (Argentina; b. 16 Nov 1942) spent 10 years, from 6 Apr 1968 to 8 Apr 1978, walking 29,800 miles around five continents. Steven Newman of Bethel, OH spent four years, from 1 Apr 1983 to 1 Apr 1987, walking 22,500 miles around the world, covering 20 countries and five continents.

Rick Hansen (Canada; b. 1957), who was paralyzed from the waist down in 1973 as a result of an auto accident, wheeled his wheelchair 24,901.55 miles through four continents and 34 countries. He started his journey from Vancouver, British Columbia on 21 Mar 1985 and arrived back there on 22 May 1987.

George Meegan (b. 2 Oct 1952) of Rainham, Great Britain walked 19,019 miles from Ushuaia, in the southern tip of South America, to Prudhoe Bay in northern Alaska, taking 2,426 days from 26 Jan 1977 to 18 Sep 1983. He thus completed the first traverse of the Americas and the Western Hemisphere on foot.

Sean Eugene McGuire (USA; b. 15 Sep 1956) walked 7,327 miles from the Yukon River, north of Livengood, AK to Key West, FL in 307 days, from 6 Jun 1978 to 9 Apr 1979. The trans-Canada (Halifax to Vancouver) record walk of 3,764 miles is 96 days, by Clyde McRae, age 23, from 1 May to 4 Aug 1973. John Lees (b. 23 Feb 1945) of Brighton, Great Britain walked 2,876 miles across the United States from City Hall, Los Angeles to City Hall, New York City in 53 days 12 hr 15 min (averaging 53.75 miles a day) between 11 April and 3 Jun 1972.

MOUNTAINEERING

Mount Everest Everest (29,078 ft) was first climbed at 11:30 A.M. on 29 May 1953, when the summit was reached by Edmund Percival Hillary (b. 20 Jul 1919), of New Zealand, and Sherpa Tenzing Norgay (1914–86, formerly called Tenzing Khumjung Bhutia). The successful expedition was led by Col. (later Hon. Brigadier) Henry Cecil John Hunt (b. 22 Jun 1910).

Most conquests Ang Rita Sherpa (b. 1947), with ascents in 1983, 1984, 1985, 1987, 1988, 1990, 1992 and 1993, has scaled Everest eight times, all without the use of bottled oxygen.

Solo Reinhold Messner (Italy; b. 17 Sep 1944) was the first to make the entire climb solo, on 20 Aug 1980. Also, Messner, with Peter Habeler (Austria; b. 22 Jul 1942), made the first entirely oxygenless ascent, on 8 May 1978.

First woman Junko Tabei (Japan; b. 22 Sep 1939) reached the summit on 16 May 1975.

Oldest Ramon Blanco (Spain) was 60 years old when he reached the summit on 7 Oct 1993.

Most successful expedition The Mount Everest International Peace Climb, a team of American, Russian and Chinese climbers, led by James W. Whittaker (USA), in 1990 succeeded in putting the greatest number of people on the summit, 20, from 7–10 May 1990.

Most in a day On 12 May 1992, 40 climbers (32 men and 8 women) from the USA, Canada, Australia, Great Britain, Russia, New Zealand, Finland, Lithuania, India and Nepal, from nine separate expeditions, reached the summit.

Sea level to summit Timothy John Macartney-Snape (Australia; b. 1956) traversed Mt Everest's entire altitude from sea level to summit. He set off on foot from the Bay of Bengal near Calcutta, India on 5 Feb 1990 and reached the summit on 11 May, having walked approximately 745 miles.

POLAR CONQUEST

The first person to walk to both the North and South Poles was Robert Swan (Great Britain; b. 28 Jul 1956). He led the three-man Footsteps of Scott expedition, which reached the South Pole on 11 Jan 1986, and three years later he headed the eight-man Icewalk expedition, which arrived at the North Pole on 14 May 1989. Below are listed a selection of other firsts in polar conquest.

Both Poles

Category	Adventurers	Date
First to see both poles	Capt. Engeburth Gravning Amundsen and Oskar Wisting	12 May 1926
First to visit both poles	Dr Albert Paddock Crary (USA; 1911–87), by aircraft and Sno Cat	12 Feb 1961
First Pole to Pole circumnavigation[1]	Sir Ranulph Fiennes and Charles Burton	2 Sep 1979–29 Aug 1982

South Pole

Category	Adventurers	Date
First to cross Antarctic Circle	Capt. James Cook, Lt. Tobias Furneaux and 193 crewmen, British Royal Navy	17 Jan 1773
First to sight antarctic ice shelf	Capt. Fabian Gottlieb Benjamin von Bellinshausen	27 Jan 1820
First to sight continent mainland	Capt. William Smith and Master Edward Bransfield, British Royal Navy	27 Jan 1820
First to reach the South Pole	Capt. Roald Engeburth Gravning Amundsen (Norway) and four others	11 A.M., 14 Dec 1911
First to reach the South Pole solo	Erling Kagge (Norway)	7 Jan 1993
First crossing of continent	Dr Vivian Ernest Fuchs (Great Britain; b. 11 Feb 1908) in a party of 12	1:47 P.M., 2 Mar 1958
First crossing in a single season	Sir Ralph Fiennes and Charles Burton	28 Oct–15 Dec 1980

North Pole

Category	Adventurers	Date
First to reach the north pole[2]	Ralph Plaisted (USA), Walter Pederson, Gerald Pitzl, Jean Luc Bombardier	3 P.M. EST, 19 Apr 1968
First to reach the North Pole solo[3]	Naomi Uemura (Japan; 1941–84)	4:45 A.M. GMT, 1 May 1978
First to ski to the North Pole	Dmitry Shparo and six members of a Soviet expedition	31 May 1979
First to motorcycle to North Pole	Shinji Kazama (Japan) on a 200-cc motorcycle	20 Apr 1987
First crossing of continent	Wally Herbert, Maj. Ken Hedges, Allan Gill, Dr Roy Kerner	21 Feb 1968–29 May 1969

[1] *Fiennes and Burton reached the South Pole on 15 Dec 1980 and the North Pole on 10 Apr 1982. In all, they covered over 35,000 miles.*
[2] *The claims of the two Arctic explorers Dr Frederick Albert Cook (1865–1940) and Cdr Robert Edwin Peary (1856–1920) of the US Naval Civil Engineering branch, to have reached the North Pole are not subject to irrefutable proof, and several recent surveys have produced conflicting conclusions.*
[3] *Dr Jean-Louis Etienne was the first to reach the Pole solo and without dogs, on 11 May 1986 after 63 days.*

Most summits Reinhold Messner was the first person to successfully scale all 14 of the world's mountains of over 26,250 ft, all without oxygen. With his ascent of Kanchenjunga in 1982, he became the first person to climb the world's three highest mountains, having earlier reached the summits of Everest and K2.

Oldest mountain climber Teiichi Igarashi (Japan; b. 21 Sep 1886) climbed Mt Fuji (Fujiyama) (12,388 ft) at the age of 99 years 302 days on 20 Jul 1986.

Greatest walls The highest final stage in any wall climb is the one on the south face of Annapurna I (26,545 ft). It was climbed by the British expedition led by Christian John Storey Bonington (b. 6 Aug 1934) when from 2 Apr to 27 May 1970, using 18,000 ft of rope, Donald Whillans (1933–85) and Dougal Haston scaled to the summit. The longest wall climb is on the Rupal-Flank from the base camp, at 11,680 ft, to the South Point, at 26,384 ft, of Nanga Parbat—a vertical ascent of 14,704 ft. This was scaled by the Austro-German-Italian expedition led by Dr Karl Maria Herrligkoffer (b. 13 Jun 1916) in April 1970.

The most demanding free climbs in the world are those rated at 5.13, the premier location for these being in the Yosemite Valley, CA.

Highest bivouac Four Nepalese summiters bivouacked at more than 28,870 ft in their descent from the summit of Everest on the night of 23 Apr 1990. They were Ang Rita Sherpa, on his record-breaking sixth ascent of Everest; Ang Kami Sherpa (b. 1952); Pasang Norbu Sherpa (b. 1963); and Top Bahadur Khatri (b. 1960).

Highest unclimbed mountain The highest unclimbed mountain is Kankar Punsum (24,741 ft), on the Bhutan/Tibet border. It is the 67th highest mountain in the world. The highest unclimbed summit is Lhotse Middle (27,605 ft), one of the peaks of Lhotse, in the Khumbu district of the Nepal Himalaya. It is the tenth highest individually recognized peak in the world, Lhotse being the fourth highest mountain.

Human fly The longest climb on the vertical face of a building occurred on 25 May 1981, when Daniel Goodwin, 25, of California climbed a record 1,454 ft up the outside of the Sears Tower in Chicago, using suction cups and metal clips for support.

POLAR EXPLORATION

Longest sled journeys *Antarctic* The longest polar sled journey was undertaken by the International Trans-Antarctica Expedition (six members), who traveled a distance of about 3,750 miles by sled in 220 days, from 27 Jul 1989 (Seal Nunataks) to 3 Mar 1990 (Mirnyy). The expedition was accompanied by a team of 40 dogs, but a number of the dogs were flown out from one of the staging posts for a period of rest before returning to the Antarctic. The expedition was supported by aircraft throughout its duration.

The longest *totally self-supporting* polar sled journey ever made was one of 1,350 miles from Gould Bay to the Ross Ice Shelf by Sir Ranulph Fiennes and Dr Michael Stroud from 9 Nov 1992 to 11 Feb 1993.

Arctic crossing The first crossing of the Arctic sea-ice was achieved by the British Trans-Arctic Expedition, which left Point Barrow, AK on 21 Feb 1968 and arrived at the Seven Island archipelago northeast of Spitzbergen, Svalbard, Norway 464 days later, on 29 May 1969. This involved a haul of 2,920 statute miles with a drift of 700 miles, compared with the straight-line distance of 1,662 miles. The team was made up of Wally Herbert (leader), 34, Major Ken Hedges, RAMC, 34, Allan Gill, 38, Dr Roy Koerner (glaciologist), 36, and 40 huskies. The only crossing achieved in a single season was that by Fiennes and Burton from Alert via the North Pole to the Greenland Sea in open snowmobiles.

Antarctic crossing The first surface crossing of the Antarctic continent was completed at 1:47 P.M. on 2 Mar 1958, after a trek of 2,158 miles lasting 99 days from 24 Nov 1957, from Shackleton Base to Scott Base via the Pole. The crossing party of 12 was led by Dr (now Sir) Vivian Ernest Fuchs (Great Britain; b. 11 Feb 1908).

The 2,600-mile trans-Antarctic leg from Sanae to Scott Base of the 1980–82 British Trans-Globe Expedition was achieved in 67 days and eight rest days, from 28 Oct 1980 to 11 Jan 1981, the expedition having reached the South Pole on 15 Dec 1980. The three-man party on snowmobiles comprised Sir Ranulph Fiennes, Oliver Shepard and Charles Burton.

OCEAN EXPLORATION

Greatest ocean descent The record ocean descent was achieved in the Challenger Deep of the Mariana Trench, 250 miles southwest of Guam in the Pacific Ocean, when the Swiss-built US Navy bathyscaphe *Trieste*, manned by Dr Jacques Piccard (Switzerland; b. 28 Jul 1922) and Lt Donald Walsh (USN), reached a depth of 35,813 ft on 23 Jan 1960. The descent took 4 hr 48 min and the ascent 3 hr 17 min.

Deep-diving records The record depth for the dangerous (and ill-advised) activity of breath-held diving is 351 ft, by Angela Bandini (Italy) on a marked cable off Elba, Italy on 3 Oct 1989. She was underwater for 2 min 46 sec.

The record dive with scuba (self-contained underwater breathing apparatus) is 437 ft, by John J. Gruener and R. Neal Watson (USA) off Freeport, Grand Bahama on 14 Oct 1968.

The record dive utilizing gas mixtures was a simulated dive to a depth of 2,300 ft of sea-water by Théo Mavrostomos as part of the HYDRA 10 operation at the Hyperbaric Center of Comex in Marseilles, France on 20 Nov 1992, during a 43-day dive. He was breathing "hydreliox" (hydrogen, oxygen and helium).

Arnaud de Nechaud de Feral performed a saturation dive of 73 days from 9 Oct–21 Dec 1989 in a hyperbaric chamber simulating a depth of 985 ft, as part of the Comex HYDRA 9 operation. He was breathing "hydrox," a mixture of hydrogen and oxygen.

Richard Presley spent 69 days 19 min in a module underwater at a lagoon in Key Largo, FL from 6 May to 14 Jul 1992. The test was carried out as part of a mission entitled Project Atlantis that had as its aim to explore the human factors of living in an undersea environment.

Submergence The *continuous* duration record (no rest breaks) with scuba

Théo Mavrostomos (right) reaching his record simulated dive depth of 2,300 ft, and with the colleagues who joined him on the Comex HYDRA 10 operation (above). (Gamma)

gear is 212 hr 30 min, by Michael Stevens of Birmingham, Great Britain in a Royal Navy tank at the National Exhibition Center, Birmingham from 14–23 Feb 1986.

Deepest underwater escapes The deepest underwater rescue ever achieved was of the *Pisces III*, in which Roger R. Chapman (28) and Roger Mallinson (35) were trapped for 76 hours when their vessel sank to 1,575 ft, 150 miles southeast of Cork, Ireland on 29 Aug 1973. It was hauled to the surface on 1 September by the cable ship *John Cabot* after work by *Pisces V*, *Pisces II* and the remote-control recovery vessel *Curv* (Controlled Underwater Recovery Vehicle).

The greatest depth from which an actual escape without any equipment has been made is 225 ft, by Richard A. Slater from the rammed submersible *Nekton Beta* off Catalina Island, CA on 28 Sep 1970.

The record for an escape with equipment was by Norman Cooke and Hamish Jones on 22 Jul 1987. During a naval exercise they escaped from a depth of 601 ft from the submarine HMS *Otus* in Bjornefjorden, off Bergen, Norway. They were wearing standard suits with a built-in life jacket, from which air expanding during the ascent passes into a hood over the escaper's head.

Deepest salvage The greatest depth at which salvage has been successfully carried out is 17,251 ft, in the case of a helicopter that crashed into the Pacific Ocean in August 1991 with the loss of four lives. The crew of the USS *Salvor* and personnel from East Port International managed to raise the wreckage to the surface on 27 Feb 1992 so that the authorities could try to determine the cause of the accident.

The deepest salvage operation ever achieved with divers was on the wreck of HM cruiser *Edinburgh*, sunk on 2 May 1942 in the Barents Sea off northern Norway, inside the Arctic Circle, in 803 ft of water. Over 32 days (from 7 Sep–7 Oct 1981), 12 divers worked on the wreck in pairs, using a bell from the *Stephaniturm* (1,594 tons), under the direction of former British Royal Navy officer Michael Stewart. All of the 460 gold ingots on board were recovered, John Rossier being the first person to touch the gold.

Longest survival at sea Tabwai Mikaie and Arenta Tebeitabu, two fishermen from the island of Nikunau in Kiribati, were found alive on 12 May 1992 after surviving for a record 177 days adrift at sea in their fishing boat, a 13-ft open dinghy.

Longest on a raft The longest recorded survival alone on a raft is 133 days (4½ months) by Second Steward Poon Lim (b. Hong Kong) of Great Britain's Merchant Navy, whose ship, the SS *Ben Lomond*, was torpedoed in the Atlantic 565 miles west of St Paul's Rocks at Lat. 00°30′N, Long. 38°45′W at 11:45 A.M. on 23 Nov 1942. He was picked up by a Brazilian fishing boat off Salinópolis, Brazil on 5 Apr 1943 and was able to walk ashore.

Greatest penetration into the Earth The deepest penetration made into the ground by human beings is in the Western Deep Levels Mine at Carletonville, Transvaal, South Africa, where a record depth of 11,749 ft was attained on 12 Jul 1977. The virgin rock temperature at this depth is 131°F.

Shaft-sinking record The one-month (31 days) world record is 1,251 ft for a standard shaft 26 ft in diameter at Buffelsfontein Mine, Transvaal, South Africa, in March 1962.

MARRIAGES

Longest engagement The longest engagement on record was between Octavio Guillen and Adriana Martinez. They finally took the plunge after 67 years in June 1969 in Mexico City. Both were then 82 years old.

Most marriages The greatest number of marriages contracted by one person in the monogamous world is 27, by former Baptist minister Glynn "Scotty" Wolfe (b. 1908) of Blythe, CA, who first married in 1927. He believed that he had a total of 41 children.

The greatest number of monogamous marriages by a woman is 22, by Linda Lou Essex of Anderson, IN. She has been married to 15 different men since 1957, her most recent marriage being in October 1991. However, that also ended in divorce.

The record for bigamous marriages is 104, by Giovanni Vigliotto—one of many aliases used by either Fred Jipp (USA; b. 3 Apr 1936) or Nikolai Peruskov (Italy; b. 3 Apr 1929) during 1949–81 in 27 states and 14 foreign countries. Four victims were aboard one ship in 1968 and two were in London, Great Britain. On 28 Mar 1983 in Phoenix, AZ he received a sentence of 28 years for fraud and six for bigamy, and was fined $336,000. He died in February 1991.

SPLITSVILLE!

The oldest aggregate age of a couple being divorced is 188. On 2 Feb 1984 a divorce was granted in Milwaukee, WI to Ida Stern, age 91, and her husband Simon, 97.

Oldest bride and bridegroom The oldest recorded bridegroom was Harry Stevens, age 103, who married Thelma Lucas, 84, at the Caravilla Retirement Home, WI on 3 Dec 1984.

The oldest recorded bride is Minnie Munro, age 102, who married Dudley Reid, 83, at Point Clare, New South Wales, Australia on 31 May 1991.

Youngest married It was reported in 1986 that an 11-month-old boy was married to a 3-month-old girl in Bangladesh to end a 20-year feud between two families over a disputed farm.

Longest marriages The longest recorded marriages were both of 86 years. Sir Temulji Bhicaji Nariman and Lady Nariman, who were married from 1853 to 1940, were cousins, and the marriage took place when both were age five. Sir Temulji (b. 3 Sep 1848) died, at the age of 91 years 11 months, in August 1940 in Bombay, India. Lazarus Rowe (b. Greenland, NH in 1725) and Molly Webber were recorded as marrying in 1743. He died first, in 1829, also after 86 years of marriage.

Golden weddings The greatest number of golden weddings in a family is 10. The six sons and four daughters of Joseph and Sophia Gresl of Manitowoc, WI all celebrated golden weddings between April 1962 and September 1988; the six sons and four daughters of George and Eleonora Hopkins of Patrick County, VA all celebrated their golden weddings between November 1961 and October 1988; and the five sons and five daughters of

Alonzo and Willie Alpharetta Cagle of McLennan County, TX all celebrated golden weddings between December 1971 and December 1993.

Wedding ceremonies The largest mass wedding ceremony was one of 20,825 couples officiated over by Sun Myung Moon (b. 1920) of the Holy Spirit Association for the Unification of World Christianity in the Olympic Stadium in Seoul, South Korea on 25 Aug 1992. An additional 9,800 couples around the world took part in the ceremony through a satellite link.

Most ceremonies Richard and Carole Roble of South Hempstead, NY have married each other 53 times, with their first wedding being in 1969. They have chosen a different location each time, including ceremonies in all the states of the USA.

Most expensive The wedding of Mohammed, son of Shaik Rashid Bin Saeed Al Maktoum, to Princess Salama in Dubai in May 1981 lasted seven days and cost an estimated $44 million. The wedding was held in a stadium built especially for the occasion, accommodating 20,000 wedding guests.

Greatest attendance At the wedding of Aharon Mordechai Rokeah and Sara Lea Lemberger in Jerusalem, Israel on 4 Aug 1993, the attendance of the Belz Hasidic community was estimated to be 30,000.

United States At the wedding of cousins Menachem Teitelbaum and Brucha Sima Meisels in Uniondale, Long Island, NY on 4 Dec 1984, the attendance of the Satmar sect of Hasidic Jews was estimated to be 17,000–20,000.

All together now . . . I do. The largest mass wedding ceremony was performed at Seoul's Olympic Stadium, with 20,825 couples being married. (Gamma)

Best man The world champion "best man" is Ting Ming Siong, from Sibu, Sarawak, in Malaysia, who in March 1994 officiated at a wedding for the 891st time since 1976.

JUGGLING

Most objects aloft Eight hundred and twenty-one jugglers kept 2,463 objects in the air simultaneously, each person juggling at least three objects, in Seattle, WA in 1990.

Pirouettes with 3 cigar boxes Kris Kremo (Switzerland) performed a quadruple turn with 3 boxes in mid-air in 1977.

12 rings (flashed) Albert Lucas (USA), 1985; Anthony Gatto (USA), 1993.

8 clubs (flashed) Anthony Gatto (USA), 1989.

11 bean bags (flashed) Bruce Serafian (USA), 1992.

10 balls (flashed) Enrico Rastelli (Italy), 1920s; Albert Lucas (USA), 1984.

French juggler François Chotard displays his one-handed nine-ball spin.

10 balls (bounce juggled) Tim Nolan (USA), 1988.

8 plates (juggled) Enrico Rastelli (Italy), 1920s; Albert Lucas (USA), 1984.

7 flaming torches (juggled) Anthony Gatto (USA), 1989.

7 ping-pong balls with mouth (flashed) Tony Ferko (Czechoslovakia), 1987; Wally Eastwood (USA), 1987.

5 balls inverted Bobby May (USA), 1953.

Ball spinning (on one hand) François Chotard (France), 9 balls, 1990.

Basketball spinning Bruce Crevier (USA), 18 basketballs (whole body), 1993.

Duration: 5 clubs without a drop 45 min 2 sec, Anthony Gatto (USA), 1989.

Duration: 3 objects without a drop Jas Angelo (Great Britain), 8 hr 57 min 31 sec, 1989.

FOOD

Food company The world's leading food company is the Swiss-based Nestlé, with sales in 1993 totaling SFr57.5 billion ($40.7 billion). The biggest seller among its famous confectionery products is KitKat, with 11.3 billion fingers sold worldwide during the year. Every second, 360 KitKat fingers are consumed throughout the world.

Apple pie The largest apple pie ever baked was made by chef Glynn Christian in a 40 × 23 ft dish at Hewitts Farm, Chelsfield, Great Britain from 25–27 Aug 1982. Over 600 bushels of apples were included in the pie, which weighed 30,115 lb.

Banana split The longest banana split ever created measured 4.55 miles in length, and was made by residents of Selinsgrove, PA on 30 Apr 1988.

Burrito The Wilmington Chamber of Commerce and the Wilmington Coordinating Council constructed the world's longest burrito, 2,012.9 ft long, on 11 Apr 1992 in Wilmington, CA. The burrito was made with 738.5 lb of tortillas, 761.3 lb of refried beans and 156.4 lb of cheese.

La Caseta Restaurant of Fallbrook, CA constructed the world's *largest* burrito, weighing 2,237 lb.

Cakes Largest The largest cake ever created weighed 128,238 lb 8 oz, including 16,209 lb of icing. It was made to celebrate the 100th birthday of Fort Payne, AL, and was in the shape of Alabama. The cake was prepared by a local bakery, EarthGrains, and the first cut was made by 100-year-old resident Ed Henderson on 18 Oct 1989.

Tallest The tallest cake was 101 ft 2 1/2 in high, created by Beth Cornell Trevorrow and her team of helpers at the Shiawassee County Fairgrounds, MI. It consisted of 100 tiers, and work was completed on 5 Aug 1990.

Oldest The Alimentarium, a museum of food in Vevey, Switzerland, has on display the world's oldest cake, which was sealed and "vacuum-packed" in the grave of Pepionkh, who lived in ancient Egypt around 2200 B.C. The 4.3-in-wide cake has sesame on it and honey inside, and was possibly made with milk.

Candy The largest candy was a marzipan chocolate weighing 4,078 lb 8 oz, made at the Ven International Fresh Market, Diemen, Netherlands on 11–13 May 1990.

Cheese The largest cheese ever created was a cheddar weighing 40,060 lb, made on 13–14 Mar 1988 at Simon's Specialty Cheese, Little Chute, WI. It was subsequently taken on tour in a specially designed, refrigerated "Cheesemobile."

Cherry pie The largest cherry pie on record weighed 37,740 lb 10 oz and contained 36,800 lb of cherry filling. It measured 20 ft in diameter, and was baked by members of the Oliver Rotary Club in Oliver, British Columbia, Canada on 14 Jul 1990.

Chocolate model The largest chocolate model was one weighing 8,818 lb 6 oz in the shape of a traditional Spanish sailing ship. It was made by Gremi Provincial de Pastissería, Confitería i Bollería school, Barcelona in February 1991 and measured 42 ft 8 in × 27 ft 10 1/2 in × 8 ft 2 1/2 in.

Cookie The largest cookie ever made was a chocolate chip cookie with an area of 1,001 ft^2, made at Santa Anita Fashion Park in Arcadia, CA on 15 Oct 1993. It was 35 ft × 28 ft 7 in and contained more than 3 million chocolate chips.

Crepe The largest crepe was 41 ft 2 in in diameter and 1 1/4 in deep, and weighed 5,908 lb. It was baked by Jos van Achter and flipped at Bloemfontein, South Africa on 7 Mar 1992.

Crepe tossing The greatest number of times a crepe has been tossed in 2 min is 307, by Philip Artingstall in Durban, South Africa on 23 Feb 1993.

COCKTAIL!

The largest cocktail on record was a margarita of 2,133.76 gal, made at the Holiday Inn in Mechanicsburg, PA on 14 Jul 1994. It consisted of sour mix, lime juice, tequila and triple sec.

Dish The largest item on any menu in the world is roasted camel, prepared occasionally for Bedouin wedding feasts. Cooked eggs are stuffed into fish, the fish stuffed into cooked chickens, the chickens stuffed into a roasted sheep's carcass and the sheep stuffed into a whole camel.

Doughnut The largest ever made was a jelly doughnut weighing 3,739 lb. It was 16 ft in diameter and 16 in high in the center. It was made by representatives from Hemstrought's Bakeries, Donato's Bakery and radio station WKLL-FM at Utica, NY on 21 Jan 1993.

The Easter Bunny's worst nightmare, this record-setting chocolate egg was built by a team led by Philip Masters. Here, he and his family admire his creation. (Bert Banner)

Easter egg The heaviest Easter egg on record, and also the tallest, was one weighing 10,482 lb 14 oz, 23 ft 3 in high, made by the staff of Cadbury Red Tulip, led by Philip Masters, at their factory at Ringwood, Victoria, Australia, and completed on 9 Apr 1992.

Most expensive food The most expensive food is saffron powder, which is sold at Harrods, London, Great Britain, for £1,985.49 (*c.* $3,000) per 1 lb.

Gum drop The world's largest gum drop was created by employees of E.J. Brach Corp. of Chicago, IL in December 1993. Made in a starch mold and then sugared, the gum drop weighed 11 lbs, was 9 in tall and had a base diameter of 6 in. It contained 15,250 calories.

Hamburger The largest hamburger on record was one of 5,520 lb, made at the Outagamie County Fairgrounds, Seymour, WI on 5 Aug 1989. It was 21 ft in diameter.

Ice-cream sundae The largest ice-cream sundae was one weighing 54,914 lb 13 oz, made by Palm Dairies Ltd under the supervision of Mike Rogiani in Edmonton, Alberta, Canada on 24 Jul 1988. It consisted of 44,689 lb 8 oz of ice cream, 9,688 lb 2 oz of syrup and 537 lb 3 oz of topping.

Jell-O The world's largest Jell-O, a 9,246 gal watermelon-flavored pink Jell-O made by Paul Squires and Geoff Ross, worth $14,000, was set at Roma Street Forum, Brisbane, Queensland, Australia on 5 Feb 1981 in a tank supplied by Pool Fab.

Jelly bean jar The largest jar of jelly beans was 96 in high and contained 378,000 jelly beans weighing a total of 2,910 lb. The Disney Channel sponsored the jar, which was unveiled on 14 Oct 1992 at Westside Pavilion, Los Angeles, CA.

Kebab The longest kebab ever was one 2,066 ft 11 in long, made by the Namibian Children's Home at Windhoek, Namibia on 21 Sep 1991.

Lasagne The largest lasagne was one weighing 8,188 lb 8 oz and measuring 70 × 7 ft. It was made by the Food Bank for Monterey County in Salinas, CA on 14 Oct 1993.

Loaf The longest loaf on record was a Rosca de Reyes 3,491 ft 9 in long, baked at the Hyatt Regency Hotel in Guadalajara, Mexico on 6 Jan 1991. If a consumer of the "Rosca," or twisted loaf, finds the embedded doll, that person has to host the Rosca party (held annually at Epiphany) the following year.

The largest pan loaf ever baked weighed 3,163 lb 10 oz and measured 9 ft 10 in × 4 ft 1 in × 3 ft 7 in, by the staff of Sasko in Johannesburg, South Africa on 18 Mar 1988.

United States The longest loaf on record in the United States was one 2,357 ft 10 in long, baked by the Northlands Job Corps, Vergennes, VT on 3 Nov 1987. Some 35,840 lb of dough were required in the preparation of the loaf, and over 4,480 lb of charcoal and 4,700 ft of aluminum foil were used to bake it.

Guess how many jelly beans are in this jar! The record breaking jar has more than 378,300 beans. (Disney Channel)

Lollipop The largest candy lollipop was a peppermint-flavored one that weighed 3,011 lb. It was made by the staff of BonBon in Holme Olstrup, Denmark on 22 April 1994.

Meat pie The largest meat pie on record weighed 19,908 lb and was the ninth in the series of pies baked in Denby Dale, Great Britain. It was baked on 3 Sep 1988 to mark the bicentennial of Denby Dale pie-making, the first one having been made in 1788 to celebrate King George III's return to sanity.

Milk shake The largest milk shake was a chocolate one of 1,891.69 gal, made by the Smith Dairy Products Co. of Orrville, OH on 20 Oct 1989.

Noodle making Mark Pi of Hilliard, OH made 4,096 noodle strings from a single piece of noodle dough in 41.34 sec on the *Vicki* NBC television show on 15 Dec 1993. This is nearly 100 noodles per second.

Omelet The largest omelet in the world had an area of 1,383 ft^2 and contained 160,000 eggs. It was cooked by representatives of Swatch at Yokohama, Japan on 19 Mar 1994.

United States The largest omelet in the United States was one with an area of 706 ft 8 in^2, made with 54,763 eggs and 531 lb cheese in a skillet 30 ft in diameter. It was cooked by Michael McGowan, assisted by his staff and the Sunrise Jaycees of Las Vegas, NV on 25 Oct 1986.

Omelet making The greatest number of two-egg omelets made in 30 min is 427, by Howard Helmer at the International Poultry Trade Show held at Atlanta, GA on 2 Feb 1990.

Paella The largest paella measured 65 ft 7 in in diameter and was made by Juan Carlos Galbis and a team of helpers in Valencia, Spain on 8 Mar 1992. It was eaten by 100,000 people.

Pastry The longest pastry in the world was a millefeuille (cream puff pastry) 3,403 ft in length, made by employees of Pidy, a company based in Ypres, Belgium, on 4–5 Sep 1992.

United States The longest pastry in the United States was a blueberry strudel of 2,040 ft, made by employees of the Hotel Fredonia and friends of the city of Nacogdoches, Texas, on 5 Jun 1992.

Pecan pie A pecan pie weighing 40,266 lb and measuring 40 ft in diameter was baked on 16 Jun 1989 for the Pecan Festival in Okmulgee, OK.

Pizza The largest pizza ever baked was one measuring 122 ft 8 in in diameter with an area of 11,816 ft^2, made at Norwood Hypermarket, Norwood, South Africa on 8 Dec 1990.

United States The largest pizza in the United States was one with an area of 10,057 ft^2. Baking was organized by L. Amato and L. Piancone and completed at Highway 27, Havana, FL on 13 Oct 1991.

Popcorn The largest container full of popcorn was one with 5,979.33 ft^3 of popped corn. It was just over 19 ft 6 in in diameter and 19 ft 1 in in height. It took the staff of United Cinemas International in Derby, Great Britain three days to achieve the record, beginning their attempt on 23 Aug 1991 and completing it on 26 August.

United States The largest box of popcorn in the United States contained 5,438.16 ft^3 of popped corn. It measured 52 ft 7¼ in × 10 ft 1½ in and was filled by Stanly Community College, Albermarle, NC from 6–8 Aug 1991. The average depth was 10 ft 2½ in.

Popsicle The world's largest popsicle was a sweet lemon and chocolate one of 14,027 lb, made by the Police Children's and Youth Club at Sisimiut, Greenland and completed on 21 May 1993.

United States The largest popsicle in the United States was 7,080 lb, constructed by students and staff at Lawrence University, Appleton, WI on 17 Feb 1990.

Rice pudding The New York Guild of Chefs made a pot of rice pudding weighing 2,146.6 lb at Manorhaven Park, NY on 11 Sep 1993. The finished pudding was enjoyed by 2,600 people.

Salami The longest salami on record was one 68 ft 9 in long with a circumference of 25 in, weighing 1,492 lb 5 oz, made by employees of A/S Svindlands Pølsefabrikk at Flekkefjord, Norway from 6–16 Jul 1992.

An appropriate location—and appropriate weather conditions—for the world's largest popsicle. (Lind)

United States The longest salami made in the United States was one 61 ft $3^{1}/_{2}$ in long with a circumference of 24 in, weighing 1,202 lb 8 oz, made by the Kutztown Bologna Co., PA and displayed at the Lebanon Bologna Fest in Kutztown on 11–13 Aug 1989.

Sausage The longest continuous sausage on record was one of $13^{1}/_{8}$ miles, made at the premises of Keith Boxley at Wombourne, Great Britain in 15 hr 33 min on 18–19 Jun 1988.

Soda float The largest soda float ever made was produced in a 2,000-gallon container and consisted of 1,800 lb of Ampi skim milk and 1,404 gal of Jolly Good Cola. It was created by Wisconsin Tourism Development Inc. at World Dairy Expo, Madison, WI on 2 Oct 1993.

Spice, "hottest" The hottest of all spices is believed to be the red "Savina" habanero, belonging to the genus *capiscum*, developed by GNS Spices of Walnut, CA. A single dried gram will produce detectable "heat" in 719 lb of bland sauce.

Strawberry bowl The largest bowl of strawberries ever picked had a net weight of 5,266 lb. The strawberries were picked at Joe Moss Farms near Embro, Ontario, Canada and the bowl was filled at the Kitchener-Waterloo Hospital, also in Ontario, on 29 Jun 1993.

Strawberry shortcake A strawberry shortcake measuring 45 ft × 8 ft was made for the Downtown Block Party in Alpena, MI on 30 Jun 1990.

LARGEST RICE PUDDING

There are so many stories associated with the world's largest rice pudding that it's hard to know which one to tell. There's the story of Michael Granata, a third-generation Italian chef whose business serves prune danish, hero sandwiches, teriyaki and vegetarian lasagna to business folks all over Manhattan. There's the story of the New York Guild of Chefs, who got together with the New York Stock Exchange to raise cash for handicapped children through a one-day picnic featuring—you guessed it—rice pudding. There's the engineer who designed the pot, the metalworker who built it, the carpenter who built the scaffolding around it, and the cooking table (heated with propane) under it . . . and then there's the pot itself, still sitting on Granata's front porch.

Let's stick (so to speak) with the pudding itself. "We started at seven A.M. and finished in the late afternoon," says Chef Granata. "Four people stood on the scaffolding at all times, stirring. We worked in 45-minute shifts. It was too hot up there to stay longer." Every single one of the 2,600 picnickers took a taste, "and there were still tons of leftovers." The pudding was constructed of 1,400 lb of milk and heavy cream, as well as rice, sugar, vanilla, cinnamon, and an incredible quantity of raisins.

"I'm not sure why I picked rice pudding," reflects Granata. "The Stock Exchange members aren't big rice pudding eaters." The dessert of choice on Wall Street? "Jell-O," grins Granata. "Cherry Jell-O." Same time, next year? Probably not. Granata, a native of Port Washington, NY, favors Long Island seafood chowder as his next record-breaking food.

(Michael Granata)

The largest teddy bear picnic ever staged, in Christchurch, New Zealand. The bears were all accompanied by humans, who had a great time as well. (Christchurch Press Co. Ltd)

FEASTS AND CELEBRATIONS

***Banquets** Largest* The largest feast was attended by 150,000 guests on the occasion of the renunciation ceremony of Atul Dalpatlal Shah, when he became a monk, at Ahmedabad, India on 2 Jun 1991.

Indoors The greatest number of people served indoors at a single sitting was 18,000 municipal leaders at the Palais de l'Industrie, Paris, France on 18 Aug 1889.

Barbecue The record attendance at a one-day barbecue was 44,158 at Warwick Farm Racecourse, Sydney, Australia on 10 Oct 1993. The record attendance at a one-day barbecue in the United States was 35,072, at the Iowa State Fairgrounds, Des Moines, IA on 21 Jun 1988. The greatest meat consumption ever recorded at a one-day barbecue was at the same event—20,130 lb of pork consumed in 5 hr. The greatest quantity of meat consumed at any barbecue was 21,112 lb of beef at the Sertoma Club Barbecue, New Port Richey, FL, from 7–9 Mar 1986.

Dining out The world champion for eating out was Fred E. Magel of Chicago, IL, who over a period of 50 years dined out 46,000 times in 60 countries as a restaurant grader. He claimed that the restaurant that served the largest helpings was Zehnder's Hotel, Frankenmuth, MI. Mr Magel's favorite dishes were South African rock lobster and mousse of fresh English strawberries.

Highest The greatest altitude at which a formal meal has been held is 22,205 ft, at the top of Mt Huascaran, Peru, when nine members of the

Ansett Social Climbers from Sydney, Australia scaled the mountain on 28 Jun 1989 with a dining table, chairs, wine and a three-course meal. At the summit they put on top hats and thermal evening attire for their dinner party, which was marred only by the fact that the wine turned to ice.

Party!

The world's biggest birthday party was attended by 75,000 people in Buffalo, NY on 4 Jul 1991 as part of the 1991 Friendship Festival, an annual event held every July to celebrate the national birthdays of the United States and Canada.

Party-giving The International Year of the Child children's party in Hyde Park, London, Great Britain on 30–31 May 1979 was attended by 160,000 children.

The largest Christmas party ever staged was the one thrown by the Boeing Co. in the 65,000-seat Kingdome, Seattle, WA. The party was held in two parts on 15 Dec 1979, and a total of 103,152 people attended.

The largest teddy bear picnic ever staged was attended by 16,837 bears together with their owners in Christchurch, New Zealand, on 16 Jan 1994.

DRINK

Alcohol consumption Poland has the highest consumption of hard liquor per person, with 9.5 pints of pure alcohol in 1991. Germany is the leading beer consumer, with 301.7 pints per person, also in 1991, and France heads the list for wine, with 141.2 pints per person.

***Beer** Oldest* Written references to beer have been found dating from as far back as *c.* 5000 B.C., as part of the daily wages of workers at the Temple of Erech in Mesopotamia. Physical evidence of beer dating from as far back as *c.* 3500 B.C. has been detected in the remains of a jug found at Godin Tepe, Iran in 1973 during an expedition by the Royal Ontario Museum, Canada. It was only in 1991 that the remains were analyzed, establishing that residues in deep grooves in the jug were calcium oxalate, also known as beerstone and still created in barley-based beers.

Strongest Uncle Igor's Famous Falling Over Water, brewed by the Ross Brewing Company and sold at The Bristol Brewhouse, Bristol, Great Britain, has an alcohol volume of 21.0 percent.

United States Samuel Adams Triple Bock, brewed by the Boston Beer Company, is 17.7 percent alcohol by volume.

Beer tankard The largest tankard was made by the Selangor Pewter Co. of Kuala Lumpur, Malaysia and unveiled on 30 Nov 1985. It measures 6$^1/_2$ ft in height and has a capacity of 615 gal.

Bottles Largest A bottle 10 ft 2 in tall and 11 ft 6 in in circumference was filled with Schweppes Lemonade in Melbourne, Australia on 17 Mar 1994 to celebrate 200 years of Schweppes.

Smallest The smallest bottles of liquor now sold are of White Horse Scotch Whisky; they stand just over 2 in high and contain 22 minims. A mini case of 12 bottles costs about £8 ($12), and measures 2$^1/_{16}$ × 1$^7/_8$ × 1 $^5/_{16}$ in. The distributor is Cumbrae Supply Co., Linwood, Scotland.

Brewers The oldest brewery in the world is the Weihenstephan Brewery, Freising, near Munich, Germany, founded in A.D. 1040.

The largest single brewing organization in the world is Anheuser-Busch Inc. of St Louis, MO, with 13 breweries in the United States. In 1993 the company sold 2.71 billion gallons, the greatest annual volume ever produced by a brewing company in a year. One of its brands, Budweiser, is the top-selling beer in the world, with 1.271 billion gal sold in 1993.

The company's St Louis plant covers 100 acres, and has an annual capacity of 403 million gallons. The completion of modernization projects in 1993 gave the plant an annual capacity of 416.6 million gallons.

The largest brewery on a single site is Coors Brewing Co. of Golden, CO, where 595 million gallons were produced in 1993. At the same location is the world's largest aluminum can manufacturing plant, with a capacity of more than 5 billion cans annually.

Champagne cork flight The longest flight of a cork from an untreated and unheated bottle 4 ft from level ground is 177 ft 9 in, reached by Prof. Emeritus Heinrich Medicus, RPI, at the Woodbury Vineyards Winery, NY on 5 Jun 1988.

Champagne fountain The greatest number of stories achieved in a champagne fountain, successfully filled from the top and using traditional long-stem glasses, is 47 (height 25 ft 9 in), achieved by Moet et Chandon Champagne with 23,642 glasses at Caesars Palace, Las Vegas, NV from 19–23 Jul 1993.

Distillers The world's largest distilling company is United Distillers, the spirits company of Guinness plc, which sells 56 million cases of "owned" distilled spirits brands per year. It is also the most profitable spirits company, having made £701 million ($1.05 billion) in 1993.

The largest blender and bottler of Scotch whiskey is also United Distillers, at their Shieldhall plant in Glasgow, Great Britain, which has the capacity to fill an estimated 144 million bottles of Scotch a year. This is equivalent to approximately 28.82 million gal, most of which is exported. The world's best-selling brands of Scotch and gin, Johnnie Walker Red Label and Gordon's, are both products of United Distillers.

Most alcoholic drinks When Estonia was independent, between the two World Wars, the Estonian Liquor Monopoly marketed 98 percent alcohol distilled from potatoes (196 percent proof US). In 31 states, Everclear, 190 percent proof or 95 percent volume alcohol, is marketed by the American Distilling Co. "primarily as a base for home-made cordials."

Soft drinks The largest beverage company in the world is Pepsico of Purchase, NY, with total sales for 1993 of $25 billion, compared with $13.957 billion for the Coca-Cola Company of Atlanta, GA. Coca-Cola is, however, the world's most popular soft drink, with sales in 1993 of over 705 million drinks per day, representing an estimated 44 percent of the world market.

Mineral water The world's largest mineral water firm is Source Perrier, near Nîmes, France, with an annual production of more than 2.5 billion bottles. The highest average consumption is in Italy, with 185 pints per person per year.

***Spirits** Most expensive* A bottle of 50-year-old Glenfiddich Scotch was sold for a record price of 99,999,999 lire (approximately $71,200) to an anonymous Italian businessman at a charity auction in Milan, Italy. The postal auction was held over a two-month period from October to December 1992.

Vintners The world's oldest champagne firm is Ruinart Père et Fils, founded in 1729. The oldest cognac firm is Augier Frères & Cie, established in 1643.

***Wine** Oldest* It is thought that New Stone Age people may have been cultivating wine as early as *c.* 8000 B.C. Physical evidence of wine dating from *c.* 3500 B.C. has been detected in remains of a Sumerian jar found at Godin Tepe, Iran in 1973 during an expedition by the Royal Ontario Museum, Canada. In 1989 a large red stain in the jar was analyzed and found to contain tartaric acid, a chemical naturally abundant in grapes.

Most expensive £105,000 ($131,250) was paid for a bottle of 1787 Château Lafite claret, sold to Christopher Forbes (USA) at Christie's, London, Great Britain on 5 Dec 1985. The bottle was engraved with the initials of Thomas Jefferson (1743–1826), "Th J"—a factor that greatly affected the bidding. In November 1986 its cork, dried out by exhibition lights, slipped, making the wine undrinkable.

The record price for a glass of wine is Fr8,600 ($1,447), for the first glass of Beaujolais Nouveau 1993 released in Beaune (from Maison Jaffelin), in the wine region of Burgundy, France. It was bought by Robert Denby at Pickwick's, a British pub in Beaune, on 18 Nov 1993.

Wine tasting The largest ever reported was that staged by WQED on 22 Nov 1986 in San Francisco, CA. Some 4,000 tasters consumed 9,360 bottles of wine.

BIG DEALS

Because of the infinite number of objects it is possible to collect, we can include only a small number of claims, those that in our experience reflect proven widespread interest.

We are more likely to consider claims for items accumulated on a personal basis over a significant period of time, made through appropriate organizations, established and recognized, as these organizations are often in a better position to comment authoritatively in record terms.

Ax A steel ax measuring 60 ft long, 23 ft wide and weighing 7.7 tons was designed and built by BID Ltd of Woodstock, New Brunswick, Canada. The ax was presented to the town of Nackawic, also in New Brunswick, on 11 May 1991 to commemorate the town's selection as Forestry Capital of Canada for 1991. Although calculations suggested it would take a 154-ton lumberjack to swing the ax, a crane was used to lift it into its concrete "stump."

United States The largest ax in the United States was 36 ft long with a 10 ft 1 in × 5 ft 2 in blade. It was designed and built by Moran Iron Works in May 1992.

Balloon sculpture The largest balloon sculpture was a reproduction of Van Gogh's *Fishing Boats on the Beach of Les Saintes Maries*, made out of 25,344 colored balloons on 28 Jun 1992. Students from Haarlem Business School created the picture at a harbor in Ouddorp in the Netherlands.

Basket The world's biggest basket measures 48 × 23 × 19 ft. It is a hand-woven maple example made by the Longaberger Company of Dresden, OH in 1990.

Beer cans William B. Christiensen of Madison, NJ has a collection of over 75,000 different beer cans from 125 different countries, colonies and territories.

Most expensive A Rosalie Pilsner can sold for $6,000 in the United States in April 1981.

Beer labels Jan Solberg of Oslo, Norway has amassed 353,500 different labels from around the world.

Belt buckles Charles J. Odenbrett of Gardena, CA had a collection of 4,538 belt buckles as of 11 Mar 1994.

Bench The longest bench in the world, called "Big Benn," was made by Norimasa Yabuyamada of Toyama, Japan, between April and September 1991. It was 24.93 ft long, 2.43 ft wide and 1.97 ft high.

Blanket A hand-knitted, machine-knitted and crocheted blanket measuring a record 186,107.8 ft^2 was made by members of the Knitting and Cro-

The world's longest bench, dubbed "Big Benn," was built by Norimasa Yabuyamada of Toyama, Japan.

Anyone who wants to challenge Charles Odenbrett's belt buckle collection will have to notch up more than 4,538 buckles.

Breaking this record could drive you "knits."
The largest blanket in the world covers 186,107.8 ft^2.

chet Guild worldwide, coordinated by Gloria Buckley of Bradford, Great Britain, and assembled at Dishforth Airfield, Thirsk, Great Britain on 30 May 1993.

Bottle caps Since 1950 Helge Friholm of Søborg, Denmark has amassed 73,823 different bottle caps from 179 countries.

Pyramid A pyramid consisting of 362,194 bottle caps was constructed by a team of 11 led by Yevgeniy Lepechov at Chernigov, Kiev, Ukraine from 17–22 Nov 1990.

Bottle collections George E. Terren of Southboro, MA has collected 31,804 miniature and distilled spirit and liquor bottles on 31 May 1992.

The record for beer is 3,080 unduplicated full bottles from 102 countries collected by Ted Shuler of Germantown, TN.

Ron Werner of Bothell, WA has a collection of 4,414 different bottles from 71 countries, but some 2,000 are empty.

David L. Maund of Upham, Great Britain had a collection of unduplicated miniature Scotch whiskey bottles amounting to 9,847 as of April 1993.

Christopher Weide of Jacksonville, FL had collected 6,510 different soda bottles as of August 1993.

Bowl, wooden The largest one-piece wooden bowl was made by Dan Cunningham, David Tarleton and Scott Hare in Kamuela, HI in September 1990. The bowl took 2,978 man-hours to complete, and was constructed of monkey-pod wood. It stands 6 ft 7 in tall, and its widest diameter is 5 ft $9^5/_8$ in with a circumference of 18 ft 1 in.

Can construction A 1:4 scale model of the Basilica di Sant'Antonio di Padova was built from 3,245,000 empty beverage cans in Padova (Padua), Italy by the charities AMNIUP, AIDO, AVIS and GPDS. The model, measuring 96 × 75 × 56 ft, was completed on 20 Dec 1992 after 20,000 hours.

Can pyramid Ten girls from Cedar Girls Secondary School in Singapore produced a can pyramid of 3,795 cans in 28 minutes and 53 seconds at Marina City Park, Singapore on 10 Nov 1993.

Carpets and rugs *Largest* Of ancient carpets, the largest was a gold-enriched silk carpet of Hashim (dated A.D. 743) of the Abbasid caliphate in Baghdad, Iraq. It is reputed to have measured 180 × 300 ft (54,000ft^2). A 52,225-ft^2, 31.4-ton red carpet was laid on 13 Feb 1982, by the Allied Corporation, from Radio City Music Hall to the New York Hilton along the Avenue of the Americas, in New York City.

Most finely woven The most finely woven carpet known is a silk hand-knotted example with 4,224 knots per in^2, measuring 14 × 22 in. It was made over a period of 22 months by the Kapoor Rug Corporation of Jaipur, India and completed in May 1993.

Chair The largest is the Washington Chair, a 53-ft-4-in high replica of the chair George Washington sat in when he presided over the Constitutional Convention in Philadelphia in 1787. Built by NSA and first displayed in

The world's largest wooden bowl was made from a Hawaiian monkeypod tree. It took 2,978 hours to carve.

Not creative recycling gone too far, but the can pyramid speed record, set by a 10-girl team from Singapore using 3,795 cans. They took 28 min 53 sec to construct the pyramid. (Marina Jaycees)

Los Angeles, CA on 9 Dec 1988, the chair was designed to withstand earthquakes and 70-mph winds.

Chandelier The world's largest chandelier was created by the Kookje Lighting Co. Ltd of Seoul, South Korea. It is 39 ft high, weighs 11.8 tons and has 700 bulbs. Completed in November 1988, it occupies three floors of the Lotte Chamshil Department Store in Seoul.

Check The world's physically largest check measured 70 × 31 ft. It was presented by InterMortgage of Leeds, Great Britain to Yorkshire Television's 1992 Telephone Appeal on 4 Sep 1992, with a value of £10,000 (*c.* $19,000).

GUESS WHAT?

Q. WHAT IS THE GREATEST DOLLAR AMOUNT PAID OUT BY CHECK?

A. SEE "CHECKS AND COINS" (BUSINESS & PUBLIC AFFAIRS)

Christmas cracker The largest functional Christmas cracker ever constructed was 150 ft long and 10 ft in diameter. It was made by Ray Price for Markson Sparks! of New South Wales, Australia and pulled at Westfield Shopping Town, Chatswood, Sydney, Australia on 9 Nov 1991.

Coasters The world's largest collection of coasters is owned by Leo Pisker of Vienna, Austria, who has collected 140,100 different coasters from 159 countries to date.

Credit cards The largest collection of valid credit cards to date is one of 1,384 (all different) by Walter Cavanagh of Santa Clara, CA. The cost of acquisition for "Mr Plastic Fantastic" was zero, and he keeps them in the world's longest wallet—250 ft long, weighing 38 lb 4 oz and worth more than $1.6 million in credit.

Doll, rag The largest rag doll in the United States is one 41 ft 11 in in total length, created by Apryl Scott at Autoworld in Flint, MI on 20 Nov 1990.

Dress A wedding outfit created by Hélène Gainville with jewels by Alexander Reza is believed to be worth $7,301,587.20 precisely. The dress is embroidered with diamonds mounted on platinum and was unveiled in Paris, France on 23 Mar 1989.

Dress train The world's longest wedding dress train measured 515 ft and was made by the Hansel and Gretel bridal outfitters of Guriskirchen, Germany in 1992.

The longest wedding dress train in the United States measured 412 ft 11 in and was worn by Ann Margaret Boehlke on the occasion of her marriage to Mackinlay Polhemus on 14 Nov 1992 in Bolinas, CA.

Earrings Carol McFadden of Oil City, PA has collected 17,122 different pairs of earrings since 1951. She had her ears pierced just two years ago.

Egg The largest and most elaborate jeweled egg stands 2 ft tall and was fashioned from 37 lb of gold, studded with 20,000 pink diamonds. Designed by British jeweler Paul Kutchinsky, the Argyle Library Egg took six British craftsmen 7,000 hours to create and has a price tag of £7 million ($12 million). It was unveiled on 30 Apr 1990 before going on display at the Victoria and Albert Museum, London, Great Britain.

Fabrics Oldest The oldest surviving fabric, radiocarbon dated to 7000 B.C., was reported in July 1993 to have been discovered in southeastern Turkey. The semi-fossilized cloth, measuring roughly 3 × 1½ in, was believed to be linen.

Most expensive The most expensive wool fabric is one manufactured by Fujii Keori Ltd of Osaka, Japan that retailed at 3 million yen ($30,000) per meter in January 1989.

Fan A handpainted Spanish fan made of fabric and wood, measuring 15.45 ft when unfolded and 8 ft high, was completed by D. Juan Reolid González of Torrent, Valencia, Spain in June 1991.

Fireworks Largest The largest firework ever produced was *Universe I Part II*, exploded for the Lake Toya Festival, Hokkaido, Japan on 15 Jul 1988. The 1,543 lb shell was 54.7 in in diameter and burst to a diameter of 3,937 ft.

Catherine wheel A self-propelled horizontal firework wheel measuring 47 ft 4 in diameter, built by Florida Pyrotechnic Arts Guild, was displayed at the Pyrotechnics Guild International Convention in Idaho Falls, ID on 14 Aug 1992. It functioned for 3 min 45 sec.

Display The longest firecracker display was produced by the Johor Tourism Department, the United Malaysian Youth Movement and Mr Yap Seng Hock, and took place on 20 Feb 1988 at Pelangi Garden, Johor Bahru, Johor, Malaysia. The total length of the display was 18,777 ft and consisted of 3,338,777 firecrackers and 1,468 lb of gunpowder. It burned for 9 hr 27 min.

Flags Oldest The oldest flag is one dated to *c*. 3000 B.C. found in 1972 at Khabis, Iran. It is of metal and measures 9 × 9 in and depicts an eagle, two lions and a goddess, three women and a bull.

The oldest Stars and Stripes in existence is that preserved in Bennington Historical Museum in Old Bennington, VT, dating from the 18th century.

Largest The largest flag in the world, measuring 505 × 255 ft and weighing 1.36 tons, is the American "Superflag," owned by "Ski" Demski of Long Beach, CA. It was made by Humphrey's Flag Co. of Pottstown, PA and was unfurled on Flag Day, 14 Jun 1992, in Washington, D.C.

The largest flag *flown* from a flagpole is a Brazilian national flag measuring 229 ft 8 in × 328 ft 1 in in Brasilia.

Float The world's largest float was 184 ft 8 in long. It was produced by the World of Dreams Foundation for the 169th St Patrick's Day parade, Montreal, Quebec, Canada on 14 Mar 1993.

United States The largest float in the United States was the 155-ft-long, 24-ft-wide "Merry Christmas America" float bearing three double arches, a 17-ft Christmas tree, two 15-ft peppermint candy sticks and 5,380 ft^2 of wrapping paper, used at the 40th Annual Christmas Parade, Baton Rouge, LA on 5 Dec 1986.

Greeting cards Craig Shergold of Carshalton, Great Britain was reported to have collected a record 33 million get-well cards by May 1991, when his mother pleaded for no more.

Jigsaw puzzles Largest The world's largest jigsaw puzzle measures 51,484 ft^2 and consists of 43,924 pieces. Assembled on 8 Jul 1992, it was devised by Centre Socio-Culturel d'Endoume in Marseilles, France and was designed on the theme of the environment.

A puzzle consisting of 204,484 pieces was made by BCF Holland b.v. of Almelo, Netherlands and assembled by students of the local Gravenvoorde School on 25 May–1 Jun 1991. The completed puzzle measured 1,036 ft^2.

Kettle The largest antique copper kettle was one standing 3 ft high with a 6 ft girth and a 20 gal capacity, built in Taunton, Great Britain, for the hardware merchants Fisher and Son *c*. 1800.

Knife The penknife with the greatest number of blades is the Year Knife, made by cutlers Joseph Rodgers & Sons, of Sheffield, Great Britain, whose trademark was granted in 1682. The knife was made in 1822 with 1,822 blades, and a blade was added every year until 1973, when there was no further space. It was acquired by Stanley Works (Great Britain) Ltd of Sheffield, Great Britain, in 1970.

Matchstick model Joseph Sciberras of Malta constructed an exact replica, including the interior, of St Publius Parish Church, Floriana, Malta, consisting of over 3 million matchsticks. The model, made to scale, is $6\frac{1}{2}$ ft^2 × $6\frac{1}{2}$ × 5 ft.

Needles The longest needle is one 6 ft 1 in long made by George Davies of Thomas Somerfield, Bloxwich, Great Britain for stitching on mattress buttons lengthwise. One of these is preserved in the National Needle Museum at Forge Mill, Great Britain.

Pens Vilma Valma Turpeinen from Tampere, Finland had collected 14,492 different pens as of 29 Apr 1992.

The most expensive writing pen is the 5003.002 Caran D'Ache 18-carat solid gold Madison slimline ballpoint pen, incorporating white diamonds of 6.35 carats, exclusively distributed by Jakar International Ltd of London, Great Britain. Its recommended retail price, including tax, in 1993 is £25,995 ($40,000).

A Japanese collector paid 1.3 million French francs ($2,340,000) in February 1988 for the "Anémone" fountain pen made by Réden, France. It was encrusted with 600 precious stones, including emeralds, amethysts, rubies, sapphires and onyx, and took skilled craftsmen over a year to complete.

Piñata The biggest piñata made in the United States measured 27 ft high with a diameter of 30 ft, a circumference of 100 ft and a weight of 10,000 lb. It was built in March 1990 during the celebrations for Carnaval Miami in Miami, FL.

Pottery The largest thrown vase on record is one measuring 17 ft 6 in in height (including a 4 ft 3 in tall lid), weighing 1,322 lb 12 oz. It was completed on 1 Jun 1991 by Faiarte Ceramics of Rustenberg, South Africa. The Chinese ceramic authority Chingwah Lee of San Francisco was reported in August 1978 to have appraised a unique 39-in Kangxi 4-sided vase at $60 million.

Quilt The world's largest quilt was made by 7,000 citizens of North Dakota for the 1989 centennial of North Dakota. It measured 85 × 134 ft.

Refrigerator magnets Louise J. Greenfarb of Spanaway, WA has 8,500 refrigerator magnets, the largest collection in the United States.

Rubber band ball Philip J. Johns of Doncaster, Great Britain had constructed a rubber band ball that weighed 850 lb as of 16 May 1988.

Scarf The longest scarf ever knitted measured 20 miles 13 ft long. It was knitted by residents of Abbeyfield Houses for the Abbeyfield Society in Potters Bar, Great Britain and was completed on 29 May 1988.

Shoes Emperor Field Marshal Jean Fedor Bokassa of the Central African Empire (now Republic) commissioned pearl-studded shoes at a cost of $85,000 from the House of Berluti, Paris, France for his self-coronation on 4 Dec 1977.

The most expensive manufactured shoes are mink-lined golf shoes with 18-carat gold embellishments and ruby-tipped spikes made by Stylo Matchmakers International of Northampton, Great Britain, which retail for $23,000 per pair.

Silver The largest single pieces of silver are a pair of water jugs of 10,408 troy oz (4.77 cwt) made in 1902 for the Maharaja of Jaipur (1861–1922). They are 5 ft 3 in tall, with a circumference of 8 ft 1½ in, and have a capacity of 2,160 gal. They are now in the City Palace, Jaipur, India. The silversmith was Gorind Narain.

Sofa In April 1990 a 21-ft-9-in-long jacquard fabric sofa was specially manufactured by Mountain View Interiors of Collingwood, Ontario, Canada, with an estimated value of $8,000.

The longest standard sofa manufactured is the Augustus Rex Sofa, 12 ft 3 in long, made by Dodge & Son of Sherborne, Great Britain.

String ball The largest ball of string on record is one 13 ft 2½ in in diameter, 41 ft 6 in in circumference, amassed by J.C. Payne of Valley View, TX between 1989 and 1991.

J.C. Payne (wearing the cap) with his huge ball of string—the sign says it all! (Gamma)

Stuffed toy A stuffed snake measuring 1,023.95 ft was completed in October 1993 by students, parents and staff of Bucknell C.E. Primary School, Great Britain.

Table The longest table was set up in Pesaro, Italy on 20 Jun 1988 by the US Libertas Scavolini Basketball team. It was 10,072 ft in length and was used to seat 12,000 people.

Tablecloth The world's largest tablecloth is 1,502 ft long and 4½ ft wide, and was made by the Sportex division of Artex International in Highland, IL on 17 Oct 1990.

Tapestry and embroidery The largest tapestry ever woven is the *History of Iraq*, with an area of 13,370.7 ft². It was designed by the Yugoslavian artist Frane Delale and produced by the Zivtex Regeneracija Workshop in Zabok, Yugoslavia. The tapestry was completed in 1986 and it now adorns the wall of an amphitheater in Baghdad, Iraq.

Longest The famous Bayeux tapestry, *Telle du Conquest, dite tapisserie de la reine Mathilde*, a hanging tapestry 19½ in × 23 ft, depicts events of 1064–66 in 72 scenes and was probably worked in Canterbury, Great Britain, *c*. 1086. The tapestry was "lost" for 2½ centuries, from 1476 until 1724.

Embroidery An 8-in-deep, 1,338-ft-long embroidery of scenes from C.S. Lewis's *Narnia* children's stories has been worked by Margaret S. Pollard of Truro, Great Britain to the order of Michael Maine. Its total area is about 937 ft².

Ties A collection of 10,453 ties accumulated by Bill McDaniel of Santa Maria, CA was sold to a museum in St Augustine, FL in 1992.

Time capsule The world's largest time capsule is the Tropico Time Tunnel of 10,000 ft^3 in a cave in Rosamond, CA, sealed by the Kern Antelope Historical Society on 20 Nov 1966 and intended for opening in A.D. 2866.

Wallet The most expensive wallet ever made is a platinum-cornered, diamond-studded crocodile creation made by Louis Quatorze of Paris, France and Mikimoto of Tokyo, selling in September 1984 for $84,000.

Zipper The world's longest zipper was laid around the center of Sneek, Netherlands on 5 Sep 1989. The brass zipper, made by Yoshida (Netherlands) Ltd, is 9,353.56 ft long and consists of 2,565,900 teeth.

SPORTS & GAMES

GENERAL RECORDS

Fastest The fastest projectile speed in any moving ball game is *c.* 188 mph, in jai alai. This compares with 170 mph (electronically timed) for a golf ball driven off a tee.

Slowest In wrestling, before the rules were modified to favor "brighter wrestling," contestants could be locked in holds for so long that a single bout once lasted for 11 hr 40 min.

In the extreme case of the 2 hr 41 min pull in the regimental tug o' war in Jubbulpore, India, on 12 Aug 1889, the winning team moved a net distance of 12 ft at an average speed of 0.00084 mph.

World record breakers Youngest The youngest age at which anybody has broken a nonmechanical world record is 12 yr 298 days for Gertrude Ederle (USA; b. 23 Oct 1906), with 13 min 19.0 sec for women's 880 yd freestyle swimming, at Indianapolis, IN on 17 Aug 1919.

Oldest Gerhard Weidner (Germany; b. 15 Mar 1933) set a 20-mile walk record on 25 May 1974, at age 41 yr 71 days, the oldest to set an official world record recognized by an international governing body.

Most prolific Between 24 Jan 1970 and 1 Nov 1977, Vasiliy Alekseiev (USSR) broke 80 official world records in weightlifting.

Champions Youngest The youngest successful competitor in a world title event was a French boy, whose name is not recorded, who coxed the Netherlands' Olympic pair in the rowing competition at Paris, France on 26 Aug 1900. He was not more than ten and may have been as young as seven.

Fu Mingxia (China) won the women's world title for platform diving at Perth, Australia on 4 Jan 1991, at the age of 12.

The youngest individual Olympic winner was Marjorie Gestring (USA; b. 18 Nov 1922), who took the springboard diving title at the age of 13 yr 268 days at the Olympic Games in Berlin, Germany on 12 Aug 1936.

Oldest Fred Davis (Great Britain; b. 14 Feb 1913) won the world professional billiards title in 1980, at age 67.

Heaviest sportsman Professional wrestler William J. Cobb of Macon, GA, who in 1962 was billed as "Happy Humphrey," weighed 802 lb. The heaviest player of any ball game was Bob Pointer, the 487-lb football tackle on the 1967 Santa Barbara High School team, CA.

Longest reign Jacques Barre (France; 1802–73) was a world champion for 33 years (1829–62) at court tennis.

Largest crowds It is estimated that more than 10 million people see the annual Tour de France cycling race, which is spread over three weeks. The greatest number of live spectators for any one-day sporting spectacle is the estimated 2.5 million who have lined the route of the New York City Marathon.

Stadium A crowd of 199,854 attended the Brazil *v* Uruguay World Cup Finals deciding soccer game, in the Maracaña Municipal Stadium, Rio de Janeiro, Brazil on 16 Jul 1950.

Most participants On 15 May 1988 an estimated 110,000 (including unregistered athletes) ran in the *Examiner* Bay-to-Breakers 7.6-mile race in San Francisco, CA.

Worst disaster In modern history, the stands at the Hong Kong Jockey Club racetrack collapsed and caught fire on 26 Feb 1918, killing an estimated 604 people.

AEROBATICS

World Championships The former USSR has won the men's team competition a record six times. The most victories in the men's individual championship is two, by Petr Jirmus (Czechoslovakia), 1984 and 1986. In the women's event the record is also two titles, by Betty Stewart (USA), 1980 and 1982.

Inverted flight The duration record is 4 hr 38 min 10 sec by Joann Osterud (USA) from Vancouver to Vanderhoof, Canada on 24 Jul 1991.

Loops Joann Osterud achieved 208 outside loops in a "Supernova" Hyperbipe over North Bend, OR on 13 Jul 1989. On 9 Aug 1986, David Childs performed 2,368 inside loops in a Bellanca Decathalon over North Pole, Alaska.

AIR RACING

The first international airplane racing competition, the Bennett Trophy, was held at Rheims, France from 22–28 Aug 1909. In 1964 the sport was revived in the United States by Bill Stead, who staged the first National Championship Air Races (NCAR) at Reno, NV; this is now the premier air racing event in the United States.

NATIONAL CHAMPIONSHIP AIR RACES

Unlimited class In this class the aircraft must use piston engines, be propeller-driven and be capable of pulling six g's. The planes race over a pylon-marked 9.128 mile course.

Most titles Darryl Greenmyer has won seven NCAR titles in the unlimited class, the top level of the sport: 1965–69, 1971 and 1977.

Fastest average speed (race) Lyle Shelton won the 1991 NCAR title recording the fastest average speed at 481.618 mph, in his "Rare Bear."

Fastest qualifying speed The one-lap NCAR qualifying record is 482.892 mph, by Lyle Shelton in 1992.

ARCHERY

World Championships The most titles won is seven, by Janina Spychajowa-Kurkowska (Poland; 1901–79) in 1931–34, 1936, 1939 and 1947. The most

WORLD ARCHERY RECORDS

Events	Points	Possible	Name & Country	Year
Men (Single FITA rounds)				
FITA	1,354	1,440	Han Seung-Hoon (South Korea)	1994
90 m	330	360	Vladimir Yesheyev (USSR)	1990
70 m	344	360	Hiroshi Yamamoto (Japan)	1990
50 m	345	360	Rick McKinney (USA)	1982
30 m	360	360	Han Seung-Hoon (South Korea)	1994
Final	345	360	Vladimir Yesheyev (USSR)	1990
Team	3,963	4,320	USSR (Stanislav Zabrodskiy, Vadim Shikarev, Vladimir Yesheyev)	1989
Final	1,005	1,080	South Korea (Kim Sun-Bin, Yang Changhoon, Park Jae-Pyo)	1990
Women (Single FITA rounds)				
FITA	1,375	1,440	Cho Youn-Jeong (South Korea)	1992
70 m	338	360	Cho Youn-Jeong (South Korea)	1992
60 m	347	360	Kim Soo-Nyung (South Korea)	1989
50 m	340	360	Lim Jung (South Korea)	1994
30 m	357	360	Joanne Edens (Great Britain)	1990
Final	346	360	Kim Soo-Nyung (South Korea)	1990
Team	4,025	4,320	South Korea (Kim Soo-Nyung, Wang Hee-Nyung, Kim Kyung-Wook)	1989
Final	1,030	1,080	South Korea (Kim Soo-Nyung, Lee Eun-Kyung, Lee Seon-Hee)	1991
Indoor Double FITA rounds at 25 meters				
Men	591	600	Erwin Verstegen (Netherlands)	1989
Women	592	600	Petra Ericsson (Sweden)	1991
Indoor FITA rounds at 18 meters				
Men	591	600	Vladimir Yesheyev (USSR)	1989
Women	587	600	Denise Parker (USA)	1989

titles won by a man is four, by Hans Deutgen (Sweden; 1917–89) in 1947–50. The USA has won a record 14 men's and eight women's team titles.

The most individual world titles by a US archer is three, by Rick McKinney: 1977, 1983 and 1985. Jean Lee, 1950 and 1952, is the only US woman to have won two individual world titles.

Olympic Games Hubert van Innis (Belgium; 1866–1961) won six gold and three silver medals at the 1900 and 1920 Olympic Games. The most successful US archer at the Olympic Games has been Darrell Pace, gold medalist in 1976 and 1984.

US Championships The US National Championships were first held in Chicago, IL from 12–14 Aug 1879, and are staged annually. The most US archery titles won is 17, by Lida Howell (nee Scott; 1859–1939), from 20 contested between 1883 and 1907. The most men's titles is nine (three individual, six pairs), by Rick McKinney, 1977, 1979–83, 1985–87. The greatest span of title winning is 29 years, by William Henry Thompson (1848–1918), who was the first US champion in 1879, and won his fifth and last men's title in 1908.

Twenty-four hours—target archery The highest recorded score over 24 hours by a pair of archers is 76,158, during 70 Portsmouth Rounds (60 arrows per round at 20 yd at 2 ft FITA targets) by Simon Tarplee and David Hathaway at Evesham, Great Britain on 1 Apr 1991. During this attempt Tarplee set an individual record of 38,500.

Greatest draw on a longbow Gary Sentman of Roseberg, OR drew a longbow weighing a record 176 lb to the maximum draw on the arrow of 28¼ in at Forksville, PA on 20 Sep 1975.

AUTO RACING

Oldest race The oldest auto race in the world still regularly run is the Royal Automobile Club (RAC) Tourist Trophy, first staged on 14 Sep 1905, in the Isle of Man, Great Britain.

Fastest circuits The highest average lap speed attained on any closed circuit is 250.958 mph, in a trial by Dr Hans Liebold (Germany), who lapped the 7.85 mile high-speed track at Nardo, Italy in 1 min 52.67 sec in a Mercedes-Benz C111-IV experimental coupé on 5 May 1979. It was powered by a V8 engine with two KKK turbochargers, with an output of 500 hp at 6,200 rpm.

Fastest race The fastest race is the Busch Clash at Daytona, FL over 50 miles on a 2½-mile 31-degree banked track. In 1987 Bill Elliott (USA) averaged 197.802 mph in a Ford Thunderbird.

500 miles Al Unser, Jr. (USA) set the world record for a 500 mile race when he won the Michigan 500 on 9 Aug 1990 at an average speed of 189.727 mph.

NASCAR

The NASCAR (National Association for Stock Car Auto Racing, Inc.) championship, now called the Winston Cup Championship, has been won a record seven times by Richard Petty (USA)—1964, 1967, 1971–72, 1974–75 and 1979. Petty won 200 NASCAR Winston Cup races in 1,185 starts from 1958–1992, and his best season was 1967, with 27 wins.

TOP 10 TEN

NASCAR WINS*

Driver	Wins
Richard Petty	200
David Pearson	105
Bobby Allison	84
Darrell Waltrip	84
Cale Yarborough	83
Dale Earnhardt	62
Lee Petty	54
Ned Jarrett	50
Junior Johnson	50
Herb Thomas	49

** Through 12 Jul 1994*
Source: NASCAR

In NASCAR racing nothing comes easily. From his name alone, let alone his driving skill, it is appropriate that Dale Earnhardt is the career earnings leader. (Daytona International Speedway)

POLE POSITION

When Mario Andretti looks behind him, he's used to seeing competitors, smoke, dust and one hot trail. Nowadays Andretti is looking back on a career that's chock full of records. Andretti retired at the end of the 1994 season. Just before his retirement Mario reflected that by the time he walks away from racing "I should be up to 400 Indy car starts. We're pulling away in that division."

At 53, Andretti would like to think he'll always be a part of racing, through ownership, through watching his sons Michael and Jeffrey and his nephew John tearing up the track, or even through continuing driving. "I don't know when to let go, you see," Andretti shakes his head. "It's very important to me to walk away while I'm still competitive. There are many people in different walks of life who have been successful and are happy with it for a short stint. I'm in it truly for the love of it."

The Andretti "kids"—including Andretti's daughter Barbra Dee, who rides horses at the national level and does stunt work on the side—may earn their own places in the record books, and that's okay by Mario. "Their eyes are wide open," he says. "I'm always concerned about the risks, but it would be hypocritical to say, it was good enough for me, but not good enough for you."

"All these records don't mean anything until you actually reach them. Part of setting up records is just being able to still be around," Andretti says with a laugh. "I thank the man upstairs for looking after me."

(Allsport/Pascal Rondeau)

Most consecutive titles Cale Yarborough is the only driver to "threepeat" as NASCAR champion, winning in 1976–78.

The NASCAR career money record is $20,085,061 to 5 Jun 1994, by Dale Earnhardt (USA). Earnhardt won a season record $3,353,789 in 1993.

Daytona 500 The Daytona 500 has been held at the 2½ mile oval Daytona International Speedway in Daytona, FL since 1959. Richard Petty has a record seven wins—1964, 1966, 1971, 1973–74, 1979 and 1981. The record average speed for the race is 177.602 mph, by Buddy Baker in an Oldsmobile in 1980. The qualifying speed record is 210.364, by Bill Elliott in a Ford Thunderbird in 1987.

INDIANAPOLIS 500

The Indianapolis 500 mile race (200 laps) was inaugurated in the United States on 30 May 1911. Three drivers have four wins: A.J. Foyt, Jr. (USA) in 1961, 1964, 1967 and 1977; Al Unser (USA) in 1970–71, 1978 and 1987; and Rick Mears (USA) in 1979, 1984, 1988 and 1991. The record time is 2 hr 41 min 18.404 sec (185.981 mph) by Arie Luyendyk (Netherlands) driving a Lola-Chevrolet on 27 May 1990. The record average speed for four laps qualifying is 232.482 mph by Roberto Guerrero (Colombia) in a Lola-Buick (including a one-lap record of 232.618 mph) on 9 May 1992. A.J. Foyt, Jr. has started a record 35 races, 1958–92, and Rick Mears has started from pole position a record six times, 1979, 1982, 1986, 1988–89, and 1991. The record prize fund is $7,864,800, awarded in 1994. The individual prize record is $1,373,813 by Al Unser, Jr., in 1994.

Closest finish The closest margin of victory was 0.043 sec in 1992 when Al Unser, Jr. edged Scott Goodyear.

INDY CAR

Most wins National Championships The most successful driver in Indy car history is A. J. Foyt, Jr., who has won 67 races and seven championships (1960–61, 1963–64, 1967, 1975 and 1979). The record for the most victories in a season is 10, shared by two drivers: A.J. Foyt, Jr. (1964) and Al Unser (1970).

Mario Andretti (USA) has the most laps led (7,587) in Indy championships as of 6 Jun 1994; he also holds the record for most pole positions at 64.

FORMULA ONE GRAND PRIX

Most successful drivers The World Drivers' Championship, inaugurated in 1950, has been won a record five times by Juan-Manuel Fangio (Argentina), in 1951 and 1954–57. He retired in 1958, after having won 24 Grand Prix races (two shared) from 51 starts.

The following records stand for Formula One Grand Prix auto racing. Alain Prost (France) holds the records for both the most Grand Prix points in a career, 798.5, and the most Grand Prix victories, 51 from 200 races, 1980–93. The most Grand Prix victories in a year is nine, by Nigel Mansell

(Great Britain) in 1992. The most Grand Prix starts is 255, by Ricardo Patrese (Italy) from 1977–93.

The greatest number of pole positions is 65, by Ayrton Senna (Brazil; 1960-94) from 161 races (41 wins), 1985–94.

Two US drivers have won the World Drivers' Championship—Phil Hill in 1961, and Mario Andretti (USA) in 1978. Andretti has the most Grand Prix wins by a US driver: 12 in 128 races, 1968–82.

Fastest race The fastest overall average speed for a Grand Prix race on a circuit in current use is 146.284 mph, by Nigel Mansell (Great Britain) in a Williams-Honda at Zeltweg in the Austrian Grand Prix on 16 Aug 1987. The qualifying lap record was set by Keke Rosberg (Finland) at 1 min 05.59 sec, an average speed of 160.817 mph, in a Williams-Honda at Silverstone in the British Grand Prix on 20 Jul 1985.

Closest finish The closest finish to a World Championship race was when Ayrton Senna (Brazil) in a Lotus beat Nigel Mansell (Great Britain) in a Williams by 0.014 sec in the Spanish Grand Prix at Jerez de la Frontera on 13 Apr 1986.

Three-time Formula 1 world champion Ayrton Senna died in a crash at the 1994 San Marino Grand Prix. He set many records during his remarkable career, including most pole positions, 65, and most Monaco Grand Prix wins, 6. (Allsport/Pascal Rondeau and Mike Hewitt)

LE MANS

The greatest distance ever covered in the 24-hour *Grand Prix d'Endurance* (first held on 26–27 May 1923) on the old Sarthe circuit at Le Mans, France is 3,315.203 miles, by Dr Helmut Marko (Austria) and Gijs van Lennep (Netherlands; b. 16 Mar 1942) in a 4,907-cc flat-12 Porsche 917K Group 5 sports car, on 12–13 Jun 1971.

The record for the greatest distance ever covered for the current circuit is 3,313.150 miles (average speed 137.047 mph) by Jan Lammers (Netherlands), Johnny Dumfries and Andy Wallace (both from Great Britain) in a Jaguar XJR9 on 11–12 Jun 1988.

The race lap record (now 8.411 mile lap) is 3 min 21.27 sec (average speed 150.429 mph) by Alain Ferté (France) in a Jaguar XRJ-9 on 10 Jun 1989. Hans Stück (West Germany) set the practice lap speed record of 156.377 mph.

Most Le Mans wins The race has been won by Porsche cars 12 times, in 1970–71, 1976–77, 1979, 1981–87. The most wins by one man is six, by Jacky Ickx (Belgium), 1969, 1975–77 and 1981–82.

RALLYING

Longest The longest-ever rally was the *Singapore Airlines* London–Sydney Rally over 19,329 miles from Covent Garden, London, Great Britain on 14 Aug 1977 to Sydney Opera House, Australia, won on 28 Sep 1977 by Andrew Cowan, Colin Malkin and Michael Broad in a Mercedes 280E.

Monte Carlo The Monte Carlo Rally (first run in 1911) has been won a record four times by Sandro Munari (Italy; b. 27 Mar 1940), in 1972, 1975, 1976 and 1977; and by Walter Röhrl (West Germany) (with co-driver Christian Geistdorfer) in 1980, 1982–84, each time in a different car.

Ignoring speed bumps is routine procedure for rally drivers. Four-time world champion Juha Kankkunen is no exception. (Allsport/Chris Cole)

World Championship The World Drivers' Championships (instituted 1979) have been won by Juha Kankkunen (Finland) on a record four occasions, 1986–87, 1991 and 1993. The most wins in a season is six, by Didier Auriol (France) in 1992. The most wins in World Championship races is 21, by Juha Kankkunen.

DRAG RACING

Piston-engined The lowest official elapsed time recorded by a piston-engined dragster from a standing start for 440 yd is 4.726 sec, by Scott Kalitta (USA) in Baytown, TX on 6 Mar 1994. Kalitta set the highest terminal velocity mark at 305.18 mph on 20 Mar 1994 in Gainesville, FL.

In the Funny Car category, John Force (USA) has the quickest run at 4.996 sec on 16 Oct 1993, in Ennis, TX. A top speed of 300.40 mph was achieved by Jim Epler (USA) in Topeka, KS on 3 Oct 1993.

For a gasoline-driven piston-engined car, the lowest elapsed time is 6.998 sec, by Kurt Johnson (USA) on 20 May 1994 in Englishtown, NJ, while the highest terminal velocity is 197.17 mph by Warren Johnson on 23 Apr 1994, in Commerce, GA.

The lowest elapsed time for a gasoline-driven piston-engined motorcycle is 7.542 sec by David Schultz on 20 May 1994, in Englishtown, NJ, and the highest terminal velocity is 180.00 mph, by John Myers on 4 Mar 1994, in Baytown, TX.

NHRA titles The NHRA World Championship Series was inaugurated in 1951. Since 1975 the series has been known as the NHRA Winston Drag Racing Series.

Top Fuel Joe Amato has won a record five national titles: 1984, 1988 and 1990–92.

Funny Car Two drivers have won a record four national titles: Don Prudhomme, 1975–78, and Kenny Bernsein, 1985–88.

Pro Stock Bob Glidden has won a record 10 national titles, in 1974–75, 1978–80 and 1985–89.

Most race wins The greatest number of wins in National Hot Rod Association national events as of 18 Jun 1993 is 83, by Bob Glidden in Pro Stock, 1973–93.

BADMINTON

World Championships *Individual* In this competition, instituted in 1977 and staged biennially, a record five titles have been won by Park Joo-bong (South Korea)—men's doubles, 1985 and 1991, and mixed doubles, 1985, 1989 and 1991.

Three Chinese players have won two individual world titles—men's singles: Yang Yang, 1987 and 1989; women's singles: Li Lingwei in 1983 and 1989; Han Aiping in 1985 and 1987.

Team The most wins at the men's International Team Badminton Championship for the Thomas Cup (instituted 1948) is nine, by Indonesia (1958, 1961, 1964, 1970, 1973, 1976, 1979, 1984 and 1994).

The most wins at the women's International Team Badminton Championship for the Uber Cup (instituted 1956) is five; by Japan (1966, 1969, 1972, 1978 and 1981) and China (1984, 1986, 1988, 1990 and 1992).

United States Championships The first competition was held in 1937 and has since been staged annually.

Asian players dominate the badminton record books. Indonesia's Susi Susanti won the 1993 women's world championship. (Allsport/Mike Cooper)

DID YOU KNOW?

Badminton is a descendant of the children's game of battledore and shuttlecock. It is believed that a similar game was played in China more than 2,000 years ago. The sport of badminton takes its name from Badminton House, the seat of the Duke of Beaufort. The Duke's family and guests popularized the game in England during the 19th century, and it was spread worldwide by British soldiers. The modern rules of the game were set by a group of Army officers stationed in India in 1876.

Most titles Judy Hashman won a record 31 US titles: 12 women's singles, 1954, 1956–63, 1965–67; 12 women's doubles, 1953–55, 1957–63, 1966–67 (11 with her sister Susan); and seven mixed doubles, 1956–59, 1961–62, 1967. David Freeman won seven singles titles: 1939–42, 1947–48, 1953.

Winning streak The longest continuous winning streak achieved by an American badminton team is 338 wins to 20 Jun 1994, by Miller Place High School, Miller Place, NY.

Longest badminton rallies In the men's singles final of the 1987 All-England Championships between Morten Frost (Denmark) and Icuk Sugiarto (Indonesia), there were two successive rallies of over 90 strokes.

Shortest badminton game In the 1992 Olympic Games at Barcelona, Spain, Christine Magnusson (Sweden) beat Martine de Souza (Mauritius) 11–1, 11–0 in 8 min 30 sec.

BASEBALL

MAJOR LEAGUE

Most games played Pete Rose played in a record 3,562 games with a record 14,053 at-bats, for the Cincinnati Reds (NL), 1963–78 and 1984–86, the Philadelphia Phillies (NL), 1979–83, and the Montreal Expos (NL), 1984. Lou Gehrig (1903–41) played in 2,130 successive games for the New York Yankees (AL) from 1 Jun 1925 to 30 Apr 1939.

Most home runs Career Hank Aaron holds the major league career record with 755 home runs—733 for the Milwaukee (1954–65) and Atlanta (1966–74) Braves (NL) and 22 for the Milwaukee Brewers (AL) 1975–76. On 8 Apr 1974 he bettered the previous record of 714 by Babe Ruth (1895–1948). Ruth hit his home runs from 8,399 times at bat, achieving the highest home run percentage of 8.5 percent.

Josh Gibson (1911–47) of the Homestead Grays and Pittsburgh Crawfords, Negro League clubs, hit an estimated 900 home runs in his career, including an unofficial season record of 84 in 1931. These totals are believed to include exhibition games.

Season The major league record for home runs in a season is 61, by Roger Maris (1934–85) for the New York Yankees (AL) in 162 games in 1961. The most official home runs in a minor league season is 72, by Joe Bauman of the Roswell Rockets of the Longhorn League in 1954.

Game The most home runs in a major league game is four, first achieved by Bobby Lowe (1868–1951) for Boston *v* Cincinnati on 30 May 1894. The feat has been achieved a further 11 times since then.

Consecutive games The most home runs hit in consecutive games is eight, set by Dale Long for the Pittsburgh Pirates (NL), 19–28 May 1956, and tied by Don Mattingly for the New York Yankees (AL), on 18 Jul 1987, and by Ken Griffey Jr., Seattle Mariners (AL) on 28 Jul 1993.

Grand slams Seven players have hit two grand slams in a single game. They are: Tony Lazzeri (1903–46) for the New York Yankees (AL) on 24 May 1936; Jim Tabor (1916–53) for the Boston Red Sox (AL) on 4 Jul 1939; Rudy York (1913–70) for the Boston Red Sox (AL) on 27 Jul 1946; Diamond Jim Gentile for the Baltimore Orioles (AL) on 9 May 1961; Tony Cloninger for the Atlanta Braves (NL) on 3 Jul 1966; Jim Northrup for the Detroit Tigers (AL) on 24 Jun 1968; and Frank Robinson for the Baltimore Orioles (AL) on 26 Jun 1970.

Don Mattingly of the New York Yankees (AL) hit six grand slams in 1987. Lou Gehrig hit 23 grand slams during his 16 seasons with the New York Yankees (AL), 1923–39.

Fastest base runner The fastest time for circling bases is 13.3 sec, by Ernest Swanson (1902–73) at Columbus, OH in 1932, at an average speed of 18.45 mph.

Most career hits The career record for most hits is 4,256, by Pete Rose. Rose's record hits total came from a record 14,053 at-bats, which gave him a career batting average of .303.

Most consecutive hits Pinky Higgins (1909–69) had 12 consecutive hits for the Boston Red Sox (AL) in a four-game span, 19–21 Jun 1938. This was equaled by Moose Dropo for the Detroit Tigers (AL), 14–15 Jul 1952. Joe DiMaggio hit in a record 56 consecutive games for the New York Yankees (AL) in 1941; he went to bat 223 times, with 91 hits, totaling 56 singles, 16 doubles, 4 triples and 15 home runs.

Largest baseball bat The largest wooden baseball bat in the United States measures 5 ft 8¼ in high and 22¾ in wide, and weighs 57½ lb. The bat, owned by Stephen Koschal of Boynton Beach, FL, has genuine autographs of all living members of the Baseball Hall of Fame.

Home runs and stolen bases The only player to have hit 40 or more home runs and have 40 stolen bases in a season was José Canseco for the Oakland Athletics (AL) in 1988. His totals were 42 and 40 respectively.

MAJOR LEAGUE RECORDS
American League (AL), National League (NL)

Career Batting Records			
Batting average	.367	Ty Cobb (Detroit–AL, Philadelphia–AL)	1905–28
Runs scored	2,245	Ty Cobb	1905–28
Runs batted in (RBI's)	2,297	Hank Aaron (Milwaukee, Atlanta–NL, Milwaukee–AL)	1954–76
Base hits	4,256	Pete Rose (Cincinnati–NL, Philadelphia–NL, Montreal–NL)	1963–86
Total bases	6,856	Hank Aaron (Milwaukee, Atlanta–NL, Milwaukee–AL)	1954–76

Season Batting Records			
Batting average	438	Hugh Duffy (Boston–NL; 236 hits in 539 at-bats)	1894
modern record (1900–present)	424	Rogers Hornsby (St Louis–NL; 227 hits in 536 at-bats)	1924
Runs scored	196	Billy Hamilton (Philadelphia–NL; in 131 games)	1894
modern record (1900–present)	177	Babe Ruth (New York–AL; in 152 games)	1921
Runs batted in (RBI's)	190	Hack Wilson (Chicago–NL; in 155 games)	1930
Base hits	257	George Sisler (St Louis–AL; 631 times at bat, 143 games)	1920
Singles	202	"Willie" Keeler (Baltimore–NL; in 128 games)	1898
modern record (1900–present)	198	Lloyd Waner (Pittsburgh–NL; in 150 games)	1927
Doubles	67	Earl Webb (Boston–AL; in 151 games)	1931
Triples	36	Owen Wilson (Pittsburgh–NL; in 152 games)	1912
Total bases	457	Babe Ruth (New York–AL); 85 singles, 44 doubles, 16 triples, 59 home runs	1921

Single-game Batting Records

Record		Holder	Date
Runs batted in (RBI's)	12	Jim Bottomley (St Louis–NL) *v* Brooklyn	16 Sep 1924
	12	Mark Whiten (St Louis–NL) *v* Cincinnati	7 Sep 1993
Base hits	9	Johnny Burnett (Cleveland–AL; in 18 innings)	10 Jul 1932
Total bases	18	Joe Adcock (Milwaukee–AL); 1 double, 4 home runs	31 Jul 1954

Career Pitching Records

Record		Holder	Years
Games won	511	Cy Young (in 906 games; Cleveland, St Louis, Boston–NL and Cleveland, Boston–AL)	1890–1911
Shutouts	110	Walter Johnson (Washington–AL; in 802 games)	1907–27
Strikeouts	5,714	Nolan Ryan (New York–NL, California–AL, Houston–NL, Texas–AL)	1968–93

Season Pitching Records

Record		Holder	Year
Games won	60	"Old Hoss" Radbourn (Providence–NL; and 12 losses)	1884
modern record (1900–present)	41	Jack Chesbro (New York–AL)	1904
Shutouts	16	George Bradley (St Louis–NL; in 64 games)	1876
modern record (1900–present)	16	Grover Alexander (Philadelphia–NL; 48 games)	1916
Strikeouts	513	Matt Kilroy (Baltimore–AL)	1886
modern record (1900–present)	383	Nolan Ryan (California–AL)	1973

Single-game Pitching Records

Record		Holder	Date
Strikeouts (9 innings)	20	Roger Clemens (Boston–AL) *v* Seattle	29 Apr 1986
Strikeouts in extra innings	21	Tom Cheney (Washington–AL) *v* Baltimore (16 innings)	12 Sep 1962

Longest home run The longest measured home run in a major league game was 643 ft, by Mickey Mantle for the New York Yankees *v* Detroit Tigers on 10 Sep 1960 at Briggs Stadium in Detroit.

Stolen bases As of 13 Jun 1994, Rickey Henderson of the Oakland Athletics (AL) had stolen a record 1,101 bases. Henderson also holds the mark for most stolen bases in a season, which he set in 1982 when he stole 130 bases.

Walks Babe Ruth holds the record for career walks, 2,056, and the single-season record, 170 in 1923.

Two players share a record six walks for a single game: Jimmie Foxx (1907–67) of the Boston Red Sox (AL) set the mark on 16 Jun 1938, and Andre Thornton of the Cleveland Indians (AL) tied the record on 2 May 1984 in a game that went 18 innings.

GUESS WHAT?

Q. HOW LONG DID THE MOST PROTRACTED LABOR STRIKE LAST?

A. SEE "STRIKE" (BUSINESS & PUBLIC AFFAIRS)

Strikeouts The batter with the career strikeout record is Reggie Jackson, who struck out 2,597 times in 21 seasons with four teams. The season record is 189, by Bobby Bonds, right fielder for the San Francisco Giants in 1970. The longest run of games without striking out is 115, by Joe Sewell while playing third base for the Cleveland Indians (AL) in 1929.

Most games won by a pitcher Cy Young (1867–1955) had a record 511 wins and a record 750 complete games from a total of 906 games and 815 starts in his career for the Cleveland Spiders (NL) 1890–98, the St Louis Cardinals (NL) 1899–1900, the Boston Red Sox (AL) 1901–08, the Cleveland Indians (AL) 1909–11 and the Boston Braves (NL) 1911. He pitched a record total of 7,356 innings.

The career record for most pitching appearances is 1,070, by Hoyt Wilhelm for a total of nine teams between 1952 and 1969; he set the career record with 143 wins by a relief pitcher. The season's record is 106 appearances, by Mike Marshall for the Los Angeles Dodgers (NL) in 1974.

Most consecutive games won by a pitcher New York Giants (NL) pitcher Carl Hubell (1903–88) won a record 24 consecutive games—16 in 1936 and eight in 1937.

Longest throw of a baseball Glen Gorbous (Canada) threw a baseball 445 ft 10 in on 1 Aug 1957. Babe Didrikson (USA; 1914–56) threw a baseball 296 ft at Jersey City, NJ on 25 Jul 1931.

Shutouts The record for the most shut-outs in a career is 110, pitched by Walter Johnson (1887–1946) in his 21-season career with the Washington

The only pitcher to win back-to-back Cy Young awards is Greg Maddux. He won the 1992 award starring for the Chicago Cubs, and the 1993 with the Atlanta Braves. (Allsport USA)

Senators (AL), 1907–27. Don Drysdale (1936–93) pitched six consecutive shutouts for the Los Angeles Dodgers (NL) between 14 May and 4 Jun 1968. Orel Hershiser pitched a record 59 consecutive shutout innings for the Los Angeles Dodgers (NL) from 30 Aug to 28 Sep 1988.

No-hitters Nolan Ryan, playing for the Texas Rangers (AL) against the Toronto Blue Jays (AL), pitched his record seventh no-hitter on 1 May 1991. Ryan also holds the record for greatest number of walks, giving up 2,795, 1968–93. Johnny Vandcr Meer of the Cincinnati Reds (NL) is the only player in baseball history to have pitched consecutive no-hitters, 11–15 Jun 1938.

Perfect game A perfect nine-inning game, in which the pitcher allowed the opposition no hits, no runs and did not allow a man to reach first base, was first achieved by John Lee Richmond (1857–1929) for Worcester, MA against Cleveland in the NL on 12 Jun 1880. There have been 14 subsequent perfect games over nine innings, but no pitcher has achieved this feat more than once.

Barry Bonds demonstrates the skills that earned his record-tying three National League MVP awards. The left-fielder won two awards with the Pirates (seen here) and 1993 honors with the Giants. (Allsport USA/Otto Gruele)

On 26 May 1959 Harvey Haddix, Jr. for Pittsburgh pitched a perfect game for 12 innings against Milwaukee in the National League, but lost in the 13th.

Saves Bobby Thigpen saved a record 57 games for the Chicago White Sox (AL) in 1990. The career record for saves is 425 through 13 Jun 1994, by Lee Smith in his 15th season, playing for the Chicago Cubs (NL) 1980–87; the Boston Red Sox (NL) 1988–90; the St Louis Cardinals (NL) 1990–93; the New York Yankees (AL) 1993; and the Baltimore Orioles (AL) 1994.

Youngest player The youngest major league player of all time was the Cincinnati Reds (NL) pitcher Joe Nuxhall (b. 30 Jul 1928), who played one game in June 1944, age 15 yr 314 days. He did not play again in the National League until 1952.

Oldest player Satchel Paige (1906–82) pitched for the Kansas City A's (AL) at 59 yr 80 days on 25 Sep 1965.

Shortest and tallest players The shortest major league player was Eddie Gaedel, a 3 ft 7 in, 65 lb midget, who pinch-hit for the St Louis Browns (AL) *v* the Detroit Tigers (AL) on 19 Aug 1951. Wearing number 1/8, the batter with the smallest-ever major league strike zone walked on four pitches. The tallest major leaguers of all time are two 6-ft-10-in pitchers: Randy Johnson, who played in his first game for the Montreal Expos (NL) on 15 Sep 1988, and Eric Hillman, who debuted for the New York Mets (NL) on May 18, 1992.

Most Valuable Player Award The most selections in the annual vote (instituted in 1931) of the Baseball Writers' Association for Most Valuable Player of the Year (MVP) in the major leagues is three, won by: *National League*: Stan Musial (St Louis), 1943, 1946, 1948; Roy Campanella (1921–93; Brooklyn), 1951, 1953, 1955; Mike Schmidt (Philadelphia), 1980–81, 1986; Barry Bonds (Pittsburgh, San Francisco), 1990, 1992–93; *American League*: Jimmie Foxx (1907–67; Philadelphia), 1932–33, 1938; Joe DiMaggio (New York), 1939, 1941, 1947; Yogi Berra (New York), 1951, 1954–55; Mickey Mantle (b. 20 Oct 1931; New York), 1956–57, 1962.

Cy Young Award In the competition for this prize, awarded annually from 1956 on to the outstanding pitcher in the major leagues, the most wins is four, by Steve Carlton (Philadelphia Phillies), 1972, 1977, 1980 and 1982.

Dwight Gooden (b. 16 Nov 1964) of the New York Mets became the youngest pitcher to win the Cy Young Award in 1985 by unanimous vote of the 24 sportswriters who make the selection.

PLAY THREE!

On August 19, 1992, Bret Boone made his major league debut for the Seattle Mariners (AL), making the Boone family the first three-generation family in major league histroy. Boone's father Bob Boone played 18 seasons in the majors, 1972–89, and his grandfather Ray Boone played from 1948–60.

Longest and shortest games The longest game was a minor league game in 1981 that lasted 33 innings. At the end of nine innings the score was tied, 1–1, with the Rochester (NY) Red Wings battling the home team Pawtucket (RI) Red Sox. At the end of 21 innings it was tied 2–2, and at the end of 32 innings, the score was still 2–2, at which point the game was suspended. Two months later, play was resumed, and 18 minutes later, Pawtucket scored one run and won. The winning pitcher was the Red Sox's Bob Ojeda.

The Chicago White Sox (AL) played the longest major league ballgame in elapsed time—8 hours 6 min—beating the Milwaukee Brewers, 7–6, in the 25th inning on 9 May 1984 in Chicago. The game started on Tuesday night and was still tied at 3–3 when the 1 A.M. curfew caused suspension until Wednesday night. The most innings in a major league game were 26, when the Brooklyn Dodgers (NL) and the Boston Braves (NL) played to a 1–1 tie on 1 May 1920.

In the shortest major league game on record, the New York Giants (NL) beat the Philadelphia Phillies (NL), 6–1, in nine innings in 51 min on 28 Sep 1919. (A minor league game, Atlanta *v* Mobile in the Southern Association on 19 Sep 1910, took 33 min.)

WORLD SERIES RECORDS
American League (AL), National League (NL)

Record		Holder	Years
Most wins	22	New York Yankees–AL	1923–78
Most series played	14	Yogi Berra (New York Yankees–AL)	1947–63
Most series played by pitcher	11	Whitey Ford (New York Yankees–AL)	1950–64

World Series Career Records

Record		Holder	Years
Batting average (min. 75 at-bats)	.391	Lou Brock (St Louis Cardinals–NL; 34 hits in 87 at-bats, 3 series)	1964–68
Runs scored	42	Mickey Mantle (New York Yankees–AL)	1951–64
Runs batted in (RBI's)	40	Mickey Mantle (New York Yankees–AL)	1951–64
Base hits	71	Yogi Berra (New York Yankees–AL)	1947–63
Home runs	18	Mickey Mantle (New York Yankees–AL)	1951–64
Victories pitching	10	Whitey Ford (New York Yankees–AL)	1950–64
Strikeouts	94	Whitey Ford (New York Yankees–AL)	1950–64

World Series Single Series Records

Record		Holder	Year
Batting average (4 or more games)	.750	Billy Hatcher (Cincinnati Reds–NL; 9 hits in 12 at-bats in four-game series)	1990
Runs scored	10	Reggie Jackson (New York Yankees–AL)	1977
Runs batted in (RBI's)	12	Bobby Richardson (New York Yankees–AL)	1960

Record		Holder	Date
Base hits (7-game series)	13	Bobby Richardson (New York Yankees–AL)	1960
	13	Lou Brock (St Louis Cardinals–NL)	1968
	13	Marty Barrett (Boston Red Sox–AL)	1986
Home runs	5	Reggie Jackson (New York Yankees–AL; in 20 at-bats)	1977
Victories pitching	3	Christy Matthewson (New York Yankees–AL; in five-game series)	1905
	3	Jack Coombs (Philadelphia A's–AL; in five-game series	1910
		Ten other pitchers have won three games in more than five games.	
Strikeouts	35	Bob Gibson (St Louis Cardinals–NL; in 7 games)	1968
	23	Sandy Koufax (Los Angeles Dodgers–NL; in 4 games)	1963
World Series Game Records			
Home runs	3	Babe Ruth (New York Yankees–AL) *v* St Louis Cardinals	6 Oct 1926
	3	Babe Ruth (New York Yankees–AL) *v* St Louis Cardinals	9 Oct 1928
	3	Reggie Jackson (New York Yankees–AL) *v* Los Angeles Dodgers	18 Oct 1977
Runs batted in (RBI's) in a game	6	Bobby Richardson (New York Yankees–AL) *v* Pittsburgh Pirates	8 Oct 1960
Strikeouts by pitcher in a game	17	Bob Gibson (St Louis Cardinals–NL) *v* Detroit Tigers	2 Oct 1968
Perfect game (9 innings)		Don Larsen (New York Yankees–AL) *v* Brooklyn Dodgers	8 Oct 1956

The Colorado Rockies' rookie season attracted 4,483,350 people, setting baseball's home attendance mark. (Allsport USA/Tim Defrisco)

Record attendances The all-time season record for attendance for both leagues is 70,257,938 in 1993. The record for an individual league is 36,924,573, for the National League in 1993. The record for an individual team is 4,483,350 for the home games of the Colorado Rockies (NL) at Mile High Stadium, Denver, CO in 1993.

Around the majors Wayne Zumwalt of Colorado Springs, CO attended a major league baseball game at all 28 major league stadiums in 28 consecutive days, from 10 Jun–7 Jul 1993.

Managers Connie Mack (b. Cornelius Alexander McGillicuddy; 1862–1956) managed in the major leagues for a record 53 seasons and achieved a record 3,731 regular-season victories (and a record 3,948 losses)—139 wins and 134 losses for the Pittsburgh Pirates (NL) 1894–96, and 3,592 wins and 3,814 losses for the Philadelphia Athletics (AL), a team he later owned, 1901–50.

The most successful in the World Series was Casey Stengel (1890–1975), who managed the New York Yankees (AL) to seven wins in 10 World Series, winning in 1949–53, 1956 and 1958, and losing in 1955, 1957 and 1960.

Joe McCarthy (1887–1978) also coached the New York Yankees to seven wins, 1932, 1936–39, 1941, 1943, and his teams lost in 1929 (Chicago) and 1942 (New York). He had the highest win percentage of managers who achieved at least 1,500 regular-season wins, with .614—2,126 wins and 1,335 losses in his 24-year career with the Chicago Cubs (NL) 1926–30, the New York Yankees (AL) 1931–46, and the Boston Red Sox (AL) 1948–50, during which he never had an overall losing season.

Baseball card The most valuable card is one of the six known baseball series cards of Honus Wagner, which was sold at Sotheby's, New York for $451,000 on 22 Mar 1991. The buyers were Bruce McNall, owner of the Los Angeles Kings hockey club, and team member Wayne Gretzky.

WORLD SERIES

Most wins The most wins in the World Series is 22, by the New York Yankees between 1923 and 1978, during a record 33 Series appearances. The most wins in the National League is 19, by the Dodgers—Brooklyn 1890–1957, Los Angeles 1958–88.

Most Valuable Player The only players to have won the award twice are Sandy Koufax (Los Angeles, NL, 1963, 1965), Bob Gibson (St Louis, NL, 1964, 1967) and Reggie Jackson (Oakland, AL, 1973; New York, AL, 1977).

LEAGUE CHAMPIONSHIP SERIES

Most series played Reggie Jackson has played in 11 series, with the Oakland Athletics (AL), 1971–75; New York Yankees (AL), 1977–78 and 1980–81; California Angels (AL), 1982, 1986.

Most games played The record for most games played is 45, by Reggie Jackson. Jackson played for the Oakland Athletics (AL) from 1971–75; the New York Yankees (AL) from 1977–78 and 1980–81; and the California Angels (AL) during the 1982 and 1986 seasons.

Batting average (minimum 50 at-bats) Mickey Rivers of the New York Yankees (AL) had a batting average of .386 in 1976–78. Rivers collected 22 hits in 57 at-bats in 14 games.

Most series pitched Bob Welch has pitched in eight, with the Los Angeles Dodgers (NL), 1978, 1981, 1983, 1985; and the Oakland Athletics (AL), 1988–90 and 1992.

Most games pitched The record for most games pitched is 15, held by two pitchers: Tug McGraw, New York Mets (NL), 1969, 1973, Philadelphia Phillies (NL), 1976–78, 1980; and Dennis Eckersley, Chicago Cubs (NL), 1984, Oakland Athletics (AL), 1988–90, 1992.

COLLEGE BASEBALL

NCAA Division I regular season *Hitting records* The most career home runs was 100, by Pete Incaviglia for Oklahoma State in three seasons, 1983–85. The most career hits was 418, by Phil Stephenson for Wichita State in four seasons, 1979–82.

Pitching records Don Heinkel won 51 games for Wichita State in four seasons, 1979–82. John Powell struck out 602 batters for Auburn University in five seasons, 1990–94.

College World Series The first College World Series was played in 1947 in

Kalamazoo, MI. Since 1950 the College World Series has been played annually at Rosenblatt Stadium in Omaha, NE.

Most championships The most wins in Division I is 11, by the University of Southern California (USC) in 1948, 1958, 1961, 1963, 1968, 1970–74 and 1978.

Hitting records The record for most home runs in a College World Series is four, shared by five players: Bud Hollowell (University of Southern California), 1963; Pete Incaviglia (Oklahoma State), 1983–85; Ed Sprague (Stanford University), 1987–88; Gary Hymel (Louisiana State University), 1990–1991; and Lyle Mouton (Louisiana State University), 1990–91.

Keith Moreland of the University of Texas holds the record for the most hits in a College World Series career, with 23 hits in three series, 1973–75.

Pitching records The record for most wins in the College World Series is four games, shared by nine players: Bruce Gardner (University of Southern California), 1958, 1960; Steve Arlin (Ohio State), 1965–66; Bert Hooten (University of Texas at Austin), 1969–70; Steve Rogers (University of Tulsa), 1969, 1971; Russ McQueen (University of Southern California), 1972–73; Mark Bull (University of Southern California), 1973–74; Greg Swindell (University of Texas), 1984–85; Kevin Sheary (University of Miami of Florida), 1984–85; Greg Brummett (Wichita State), 1988–89.

Carl Thomas of the University of Arizona struck out 64 batters in three College World Series, 1954–56.

BASKETBALL

Highest score In a senior international match, Iraq scored 251 points against Yemen (33) at New Delhi, India, in November 1982 at the Asian Games.

Highest points Mats Wermelin, 13 years old (Sweden), scored all 272 points in a 272–0 win in a regional boys' basketball tournament in Stockholm, Sweden on 5 Feb 1974.

The record score by a woman is 156 points by Marie Boyd (now Eichler) of Central High School, Lonaconing, MD in a 163–3 defeat of Ursaline Academy, Cumbria on 25 Feb 1924.

Largest attendance The largest crowd for a basketball game was 80,000 for the final of the European Cup Winners' Cup between AEK Athens (89) and Slavia Prague (82) at the Olympic stadium, Athens, Greece on 4 Apr 1968.

Dribbling Jamie Borges (USA) dribbled a basketball without "traveling" from Barrington to Boston, MA, a distance of 284.9 miles, from 21–28 Oct 1993.

Longest goal Christopher Eddy scored a field goal measured at 90 ft

ON THE RECORD

LONGEST FIELD GOAL

"I had tried the shot just the day before, and my coach yelled at me. 'You're never going to shoot that shot in a game!'" The next day Nikki Fierstos's girls' high school varsity team, from North Manchester, IN, took on the number seven ranked team in the state.

(Dan Fierstos)

"We weren't even ranked, because our school is so small," laughs Nikki, 18. "It was the very end of the game, and we were 55 points down. I thought, 'Might as well try it. No loss here.' And the ball found the net."

"The first person to stand up was my dad. Then they all came and picked me up and carried me around the court. I was in shock. I didn't know what had happened. But luckily a local cameraman got it on video. He won an award for that shot, and it went all the way to ESPN."

Nikki shoots an average 29 points per game, using skills learned playing one-on-one with a brother seven years older and 12 inches taller. "I began to beat him when I was in fifth grade," Nikki says. "The only way to go was to beat him from the outside." Now Nikki's name and number are painted on the floor of the gym in the spot where she stood when she took her best shot.

$2^1/_4$ in for Fairview High School *v* Iroquois High School at Erie, PA on 25 Feb 1989. The shot was made as time expired in overtime and it won the game for Fairview, 51–50.

Nikki Fierstos scored a field goal of approximately 79 ft, the longest by a woman, on 2 Jan 1993 at Huntington North High School, Huntington, IN.

Shooting speed The greatest goal-shooting demonstration was by Ted St Martin of Jacksonville, FL who, on 25 Jun 1977, scored 2,036 consecutive free throws. On 11 Jun 1992 Jeff Liles scored 231 out of 240 free throws in 10 minutes at Southern Nazarene University, Bethany, OK. He repeated this total of 231 (241 attempts) on 16 June. This speed record is achieved using one ball and one rebounder.

In 24 hours Fred Newman scored 20,371 free throws from a total of 22,049 taken (92.39 percent) at Caltech, Pasadena, CA on 29–30 Sep 1990.

Steve Bontrager (USA) of the British team Polycell Kingston scored 21 points in one minute from seven positions in a demonstration on 29 Oct 1986.

Vertical dunk height record Joey Johnson of San Pedro, CA successfully dunked a basketball at a rim height of 11 ft 7 in at the One-on-One Collegiate Challenge on 25 Jun 1990 at Trump Plaza Hotel and Casino in Atlantic City, NJ.

Most valuable basket Don Calhoun, a spectator at a Chicago Bulls home game on 14 Apr 1993, sank a basket from the opposite foul line—a distance of 75 feet—and won $1 million. He was randomly picked from the crowd to try his luck as part of a promotional stunt.

NATIONAL BASKETBALL ASSOCIATION

Most championships The Boston Celtics have won a record 16 NBA titles—1957, 1959–66, 1968–69, 1974, 1976, 1981, 1984 and 1986.

Most games Kareem Abdul-Jabbar played in a record 1,560 NBA regular-season games over 20 seasons, totaling 57,446 minutes played, for the Milwaukee Bucks, 1969–75, and the Los Angeles Lakers, 1975–89.

The most successive games is 906, by Randy Smith for the Buffalo Braves, the San Diego Clippers, the Cleveland Cavaliers and the New York Knicks from 18 Feb 1972 to 13 Mar 1983.

The record for most complete games played in one season is 79, by Wilt Chamberlain for Philadelphia in 1962, when he was on court for a record 3,882 minutes. Chamberlain went through his entire career of 1,045 games without fouling out. Moses Malone played his 1,195th consecutive game without fouling out to the end of the 1993/94 season. In his career, Malone has played 1,312 games, fouling out on only five occasions.

Most minutes The career record for minutes played in the NBA is 57,446 by Kareem Abdul-Jabbar, Milwaukee Bucks, 1969–75, and Los Angeles Lakers, 1975–89. The season record is 3,882 minutes by Wilt Chamberlain for the Philadelphia Warriors, 1961–62. The single game record is 69 minutes by Dale Ellis for the Seattle SuperSonics *v* Milwaukee Bucks on 9 Nov 1989 in a 5-overtime game.

NBA career three-point leader Dale Ellis rarely travels, but he does love to go "downtown from three-point land." (Allsport/Tim Defrisco)

Highest scoring average The highest career average for players exceeding 10,000 points is 32.3 points per game, by Michael Jordan, 21,541 points in 667 games for the Chicago Bulls, 1984–93. The season record is 50.4 per game, set by Wilt Chamberlain, Philadelphia Warriors, 1961–62.

Playoffs The career scoring average record for the playoffs is held by Michael Jordan, at 34.7 points per game. He scored 3,850 points in 111 games, 1984–93.

Blocked shots The record for most blocked shots in an NBA game is 17, by Elmore Smith for Los Angeles *v* Portland at Los Angeles on 28 Oct 1973. The season record is 456, by Mark Eaton, Utah Jazz during the 1984–85 season. The career mark is held by Kareem Abdul-Jabbar, at 4,657.

Personal fouls The career record for ejections (for a player) is 127, by Vern Mikkelsen, Minneapolis Lakers, 1950–59. The season mark is 26, by Don Meineke, Fort Wayne Pistons, 1952–53.

The most personal fouls in a career was the 4,657 called on Kareem Abdul-Jabbar. The single-season record is 386, by Darryl Dawkins, New Jersey Nets, 1983–84. The NBA record for most fouls in a game is eight, committed by Don Otten, Tri-Cities *v* Sheboygan on 24 Nov 1949.

Most Valuable Player Kareem Abdul-Jabbar was elected the NBA's most valuable player a record six times, 1971–72, 1974, 1976–77 and 1980.

Youngest and oldest player The youngest NBA player has been Bill Willoughby (b. 20 May 1957), who made his debut for the Atlanta Hawks on 23 Oct 1975 at 18 yr 156 days. The oldest NBA regular player was Kareem Abdul-Jabbar (b. 16 Apr 1947), who made his last appearance for the Los Angeles Lakers at age 42 yr 59 days in 1989.

NBA RECORDS

Career Records			
Points	38,387	Kareem Abdul-Jabbar: Milwaukee Bucks, Los Angeles Lakers	1970–89
Field-goal percentage	.599	Artis Gilmore: Chicago Bulls, San Antonio Spurs, Boston Celtics; min. 2,000 field goals	1977–88
Free throws made	8,509	Moses Malone: Buffalo Braves, Houston Rockets, Philadelphia 76ers, Washington Bullets, Atlanta Hawks, Milwaukee Bucks	1976–93
Free-throw percentage	.900	Rick Barry: San Francisco / Golden State Warriors, Houston Rockets; 3,818 from 4,243 attempts (technically .89983)	1965–80
Field goals	15,837	Kareem Abdul-Jabbar	1970–89
Rebounds	23,924	Wilt Chamberlain: Philadelphia / San Francisco Warriors, Philadelphia 76ers, Los Angeles Lakers	1960–73
Assists	9,921	Magic Johnson: Los Angeles Lakers	1980–91
Steals	2,310	Maurice Cheeks: Philadelphia 76ers, San Antonio Spurs, New York Knicks, Atlanta Hawks, New Jersey Nets	1979–93

Season Records			
Points	4,029	Wilt Chamberlain: Philadelphia Warriors	1962
Field-goal percentage	.727	Wilt Chamberlain: Los Angeles Lakers; 426 of 586 attempts	1972
Free throws made	840	Jerry West: Los Angeles Lakers; from 977 attempts	1966
Free-throw percentage	.958	Calvin Murphy: Houston Rockets; 206 of 215 attempts	1981
Field goals	1,597	Wilt Chamberlain: Philadelphia Warriors	1962
Rebounds	2,149	Wilt Chamberlain: Philadelphia Warriors	1961
Assists	1,164	John Stockton: Utah Jazz	1991
Steals	301	Alvin Robertson: San Antonio Spurs	1986

Single-Game Records			
Points	100	Wilt Chamberlain: Philadelphia Warriors *v* New York Knicks	2 Mar 1962
Field goals	36	Wilt Chamberlain	2 Mar 1962
Free throws made	28	Wilt Chamberlain	2 Mar 1962
	28	Adrian Dantley: Utah Jazz *v* Houston Rockets	5 Jan 1984
Rebounds	55	Wilt Chamberlain: Philadelphia Warriors *v* Boston Celtics	24 Nov 1960

Assists	30	Scott Skiles: Orlando Magic *v* Denver Nuggets	30 Dec 1990
Steals	11	Larry Kenon: San Antonio Spurs *v* Kansas City Kings	26 Dec 1976

NBA PLAYOFF RECORDS

Career Records

Most games played	237	Kareem Abdul-Jabbar: Milwaukee Bucks, Los Angeles Lakers	1970–89
Points	5,762	Kareem Abdul-Jabbar (in 237 playoff games)	1970–89
Field goals	2,356	Kareem Abdul-Jabbar	1970–89
Free throws made	1,213	Jerry West: Los Angeles Lakers; from 1,507 attempts	1961–74
Assists	2,142	Magic Johnson: Los Angeles Lakers	1980–91
Rebounds	4,104	Bill Russell: Boston Celtics	1957–69

Series Records

Points	284	Elgin Baylor: Los Angeles Lakers (*v* Boston Celtics); in 7 games	1962
Field goals	113	Wilt Chamberlain: San Francisco (*v* St Louis); in 6 games	1964
Free throws made	86	Jerry West: Los Angeles Lakers (*v* Baltimore); in 6 games	1965
Rebounds	220	Wilt Chamberlain: Philadelphia 76ers (*v* Boston Celtics); in 7 games	1965
Assists	115	John Stockton: Utah Jazz (*v* Los Angeles Lakers); in 7 games	1988

Single-Game records

Points	63	Michael Jordan: Chicago Bulls (*v* Boston Celtics); includes two overtime periods	20 Apr 1986
	61	Elgin Baylor: Los Angeles Lakers (*v* Boston Celtics)	14 Apr 1962
Field goals	24	Wilt Chamberlain: Philadelphia 76ers *v* Syracuse Nationals; in 42 attempts	14 Mar 1960
	24	John Havlicek: Boston Celtics (*v* Atlanta Hawks); in 36 attempts	1 Apr 1973
	24	Michael Jordan: Chicago Bulls (*v* Cleveland Cavaliers); in 45 attempts	1 May 1988
Free throws made	30	Bob Cousy: Boston Celtics (*v* Syracuse Nationals); includes four overtime periods and 32 attempts	21 Mar 1953
	23	Michael Jordan: Chicago Bulls (*v* New York Knicks); in 28 attempts	14 May 1989
Rebounds	41	Wilt Chamberlain: Philadelphia 76ers (*v* Boston Celtics)	5 Apr 1967
Assists	24	Magic Johnson: Los Angeles Lakers (*v* Phoenix Suns)	15 May 1984
	24	John Stockton: Utah Jazz (*v* Los Angeles Lakers)	17 May 1988

Tallest basketball player Tallest in NBA history has been Gheorge Muresan (Romania) of the Washington Bullets, at 7 ft 7 in. He made his pro debut in 1994.

Highest score The highest aggregate score in an NBA game is 370, when the Detroit Pistons (186) beat the Denver Nuggets (184) at Denver, CO on 13 Dec 1983. Overtime was played after a 145–145 tie in regulation time. The record in regulation time is 320, when the Golden State Warriors beat Denver 162–158 at Denver on 2 Nov 1990. The most points in a half is 107, by the Phoenix Suns in the first half *v* the Denver Nuggets on 11 Nov 1990. The most points in a quarter is 58, in the fourth quarter, by Buffalo *v* Boston on 20 Oct 1972.

Winning margin The greatest winning margin in an NBA game is 68 points, by which the Cleveland Cavaliers, 148, beat the Miami Heat, 80, on 17 Dec 1991.

Winning streak The Los Angeles Lakers won a record 33 NBA games in succession from 5 Nov 1971 to 7 Jan 1972, as during the 1971/72 season they won a record 69 games with 13 losses.

Coaches The most successful coach in NBA history has been Red Auerbach with 938 wins (1,037 including playoffs), with the Washington Capitols 1946–49, the Tri-Cities Blackhawks 1949–50, and the Boston Celtics 1950–66. He led the Boston Celtics to a record nine NBA titles, including eight in succession in 1959–66.

Pat Riley has won a record 131 playoff games, 102 with the Los Angeles Lakers (1981– 90) and 29 with the New York Knicks (1992– 94), to set the NBA all-time mark.

The most games coached is 1,722, by Bill Fitch: Cleveland Cavaliers, 1970–79; Boston Celtics, 1979–83; Houston Rockets, 1983–88; New Jersey Nets, 1989–92. Fitch's career totals 845 wins and 877 losses.

NCAA RECORDS

Most wins In this competition, first held in 1939, the record for most Division I titles is 10, by the University of California at Los Angeles (UCLA), 1964–65, 1967–73, 1975.

Most valuable player The only player to have been voted the most valuable player in the NCAA final three times has been Lew Alcindor of UCLA in 1967–69. He subsequently changed his name to Kareem Abdul-Jabbar.

Highest score The NCAA aggregate record is 399, when Troy State (258) beat De Vry Institute, Atlanta (141) at Troy, AL on 12 Jan 1992. Troy's total was also the highest individual team score in a game.

NCAA scoring records The most points scored in an NCAA game is 113, by Clarence "Bevo" Francis, Rio Grande (Div. II), *v* Hillsdale on 2 Feb 1954. Pete Maravich, Louisiana State (Div. I) holds the season record. He scored 1,381 points in 1970 (522 field goals and 337 free throws). The career scoring record is 4,045 points, held by Travis Grant, Kentucky State (Div. II), 1969–72.

Pat Riley has won the most NBA playoff games. (Allsport/Tim Defrisco)

The single game field goal record is 41, by Frank Selvy, Furman (Div. I) *v* Newberry on 13 Feb 1954. The season record is 539, by Travis Grant, Kentucky State in 1972. Grant also holds the career mark, at 1,760.

The most assists in a game is 26, by Robert James, Kean (Div. III) *v* New Jersey Tech on 11 Mar 1989. The season mark is 406, by Mark Wade, UNLV (Div. I) in 1987. The career record is 1,076, by Bobby Hurley, Duke (Div. I), 1990–93.

Consecutive records (Division I) Individual The record for scoring 10 or more points in consecutive games is 115, by Lionel Simmons for La Salle, 1987–90. The consecutive 50-plus points tally is 3 games, by Pete Maravich, Louisiana State, 10–15 Feb 1969.

The longest field goal streak is 25 swishes, by Ray Voelkel, American, over nine games from 24 Nov–16 Dec 1978. The single-game mark is 16 field goals hit by Doug Grayson, Kent *v* North Carolina on 6 Dec 1967.

The record for consecutive 3-point shots made is 15, by Todd Leslie, Northwestern, over four games from 15–28 Dec 1990.

Team UCLA set the NCAA mark for consecutive victories (including the playoffs) at 88 games. The streak started on 30 Jan 1971 and ended on 19 Jan 1974, when the Bruins were defeated by Notre Dame, 71–70.

NCAA MEN'S DIVISION I RECORDS
Through 1992/93 Season

Record	Number	Holder	Date
Career Records			
Points	3,667	Pete Maravich: Louisiana State	1968–70
Field goals	1,387	Pete Maravich: Louisiana State	1968–70
Best percentage	.690	Ricky Need: Appalachian State	1991–94
Rebounds	2,243	Tom Gola: La Salle	1952–55
Assists	1,076	Bobby Hurley: Duke	1990–93
Season Records			
Points	1,381	Pete Maravich: Louisiana State	1970
Field goals	522	Pete Maravich: Louisiana State (from 1,168 attempts)	1970
Best percentage	.749	Steve Johnson: Oregon State	1981
Three-point goals	158	Darrin Fitzgerald: Butler (in 362 attempts)	1987
Free throws	355	Frank Selvy: Furman (in 444 attempts)	1954
Best percentage	.959	Craig Collins: Penn State	1985
Rebounds	734	Walt Dukes: Seton Hall (in 33 games)	1953
Assists	406	Mark Wade: Nevada–Las Vegas	1987
Blocked shots	207	David Robinson: Navy (in 35 games)	1986
Game Records			
Points	100	Frank Selvy: Furman (*v* Newberry)	13 Feb 1954
Field goals	41	Frank Selvy: Furman	13 Feb 1954
Three-point goals	14	Dave Jamerson: Ohio (*v* Charleston)	21 Dec 1989
	14	Askia Jones: Kansas State (*v* Fresno State)	24 Mar 1994
Free throws	30	Pete Maravich: Louisiana State (*v* Oregon State)	22 Dec 1969
Rebounds	51	Bill Chambers: William and Mary (*v* Virginia)	14 Feb 1953
Assists	22	Tony Fairly: Baptist (*v* Armstrong State)	9 Feb 1987
	22	Avery Johnson: Southern–B.R. (*v* Texas Southern)	25 Jan 1988
	22	Sherman Douglas: Syracuse (*v* Providence)	28 Jan 1989
Blocked shots	14	David Robinson: Navy (*v* North Carolina–Wilmington)	4 Jan 1986
	14	Shawn Bradley: BYU (*v* Eastern Kentucky)	7 Dec 1990

NCAA WOMEN'S DIVISION I CHAMPIONSHIP GAME RECORDS
Through 1993/94 Season

Team Records

Record		Team	Year
Most championships	3	Tennessee	1987, 1989, 1991
Most points	97	Texas (*v* USC)	1986
Most field goals	40	Texas (*v* USC)	1986
Highest field-goal percentage	.588	Texas (*v* USC; 40–68)	1986
Most 3-point field goals	11	Stanford (*v* Auburn)	1990
Rebounds	57	Old Dominion (*v* Georgia)	1985
Assists (since 1985)	22	Texas (*v* USC)	1986
Blocked shots (since 1988)	7	Tennessee (*v* Auburn)	1989
Steals (since 1988)	12	Louisiana Tech (*v* Auburn)	1988
	12	Louisiana Tech (*v* North Carolina)	1994

Individual Records

Record		Player	Year
Most points	47	Sheryl Swoopes: Texas Tech (*v* Ohio State)	1993
Most field goals	16	Sheryl Swoopes: Texas Tech (*v* Ohio State)	1993
Highest field-goal percentage	.889	Jennifer White: Louisiana Tech (*v* USC; 8–9)	1983
Most 3-point field goals (since 1988)	6	Katy Steding: Stanford (*v* Auburn)	1990
Rebounds	23	Charlotte Smith: Norht Carolina (*v* Louisiana Tech)	1994
Assists (since 1985)	10	Kamie Ethridge: Texas (*v* USC)	1986
	10	Melissa McCray: Tennessee (*v* Auburn)	1989
Blocked shots (since 1988)	5	Sheila Frost: Tennessee (*v* Auburn)	1989
Steals (since 1988)	6	Erica Westbrooks: Louisiana Tech (*v* Auburn)	1988

Coaches The man to have coached most victories in NCAA Division I competition is Adolph Rupp (1901–77) at Kentucky, with 876 wins (and 190 losses), 1931–72. The highest winning percentage for any Division I coach is .837, by Jerry Tarkanian, Long Beach State, 1969–73; UNLV, 1974–92. The shark's career record was 625 wins, 122 losses. John Wooden (b. 1910) coached UCLA to all its 10 NCAA titles.

Henry Iba (1904–93) coached the most games, 1,105, with Northwest Missouri State 1930–33, Colorado 1934, and Oklahoma State 1935–70. Iba's career record was 767 wins and 338 losses.

Longest career span The longest coaching career was Phog Allen's 48 years. He coached four teams: Baker, 1906–08; Kansas, 1908–09, 1920–56; Haskell, 1909; and Central Missouri State, 1913–19.

Record attendances The highest paid attendance for a college game is 66,144, for Louisiana State's 82–80 victory over Georgetown at the Louisiana Superdome, New Orleans, LA on 28 Jan 1989.

Women's The record for a women's college game is 24,563, in Knoxville, TN for a game between the University of Tennessee and the University of Texas on 9 Dec 1987.

In leading Texas Tech to the 1993 NCAA title, Sheryl Swoopes set scoring records for most points and most field goals in the championships game. (Allsport/Jim Grund)

WOMEN'S BASKETBALL

Women's championships In this competition, first held in 1982, the record for most Division I titles is three, by Tennessee, 1987, 1989 and 1991. The regular-season game aggregate record is 261, when St Joseph's (Indiana) beat North Kentucky 131–130 on 27 Feb 1988.

Coaches Jody Conradt of the University of Texas has won the most games in Women's NCAA Division I competition, with 642 victories through the 1993/94 season.

Most points The women's record for most points scored in a college career is 4,061, by Pearl Moore. She scored 177 points in eight games for Anderson Junior College, Anderson, SC, and 3,884 points for Francis Marion College, Florence, SC, 1975–79. Francis Marion was a member of the Association of Intercollegiate Athletics for Women (AIWA) during Moore's career.

NCAA DIVISION I SCORING RECORDS

Points The career points leader in NCAA Division I competition is Patricia Hoskins of Mississippi Valley State, with 3,122 points (1985–89). The season record is 974 points, by Cindy Brown, Long Beach State in 1987. Brown also hold the single-game mark. She scored 60 points *v* San Jose State on 16 Feb 1987.

Assists The most helpful player in NCAA history is Suzie McConnell, Penn State. She holds the career mark, at 1,307, 1984–88, and the single-season mark, with 355 assists in 1987. Michelle Burden, Kent, has the most assist in a game, 23, *v* Ball State on 6 Feb 1991.

Rebounds Drake's Wanda Ford is the chairwoman of the boards, holding career and season bests, at 1,887 and 534 rebounds respectively. Her career spanned 1983–86, and she set the season mark in 1985. The outstanding game record is 40 rebounds, by Deborah Temple, Delta State *v* Alabama–Birmingham, 14 Feb 1983.

Field goals The all-time leader for field goals is Joyce Walker, Louisiana State, with 1,259, 1981–84. The season mark was set by Clemson's Barbara Kennedy in 1982, when she hit 392 goals. The game record is 27, by Lorri Bauman, Drake *v* Southwest Missouri State, 6 Jan 1984.

DUNK!

On 21 December, 1984, 6-foot 7-inch Georgeann Wells became the first, and so far, only woman to dunk the ball in a NCAA game. Wells, playing for West Virginia, performed the historic slam vs. Charleston at Randolph County Armory, Elkins, W.VA.

Team records *Most points scored* The highest-scoring game was Virginia's defeat of North Carolina State, 123–120, for an aggregate of 243 points. Played on 12 Jan 1991, the game went to three overtimes.

The most points scored by a team in one game is 149, by Long Beach State, in their defeat of San Jose State (69 points) on 16 Feb 1987.

OTHER RECORDS

Olympic Games Six men and two women have won two Olympic gold medals: Bob Kurland in 1948 and 1952; Bill Houghland in 1952 and 1956; Michael Jordan, Patrick Ewing, and Chris Mullin, all in 1984 and 1992; Burdette Eliele Haldorson in 1956 and 1960; Anne Theresa Donovan and Theresa Edwards, both in 1984 and 1988.

Most titles *Olympic* The United States has won 10 men's Olympic titles. From the time the sport was introduced to the Games in 1936 until 1972, the USA won 63 consecutive matches in the Olympic Games, until it lost 51–50 to the USSR in the disputed final match in Munich, Germany. Since then it has won a further 29 matches and has had another loss to the USSR (in 1988).

The women's title has been won a record three times by the USSR, in 1976, 1980 and 1992 (by the Unified team from the republics of the former USSR). The USA team won the title in 1984 and 1988.

World The USSR has won most titles at both the men's World Championships (instituted 1950) with three (1967, 1974 and 1982) and women's (instituted 1953), with six (1959, 1964, 1967, 1971, 1975 and 1983). Yugoslavia has also won three men's world titles: 1970, 1978 and 1990.

BIATHLON

Most titles *Olympic* The most Olympic individual titles is two, won by Magnar Solberg (Norway), in 1968 and 1972; and Franz-Peter Rötsch (East Germany) at both 10 km and 20 km in 1988. The USSR has won all six 4 × 7.5 km relay titles, from 1968 to 1988. Aleksandr Tikhonov, who was a member of the first four teams, also won a silver in the 1968 20 km.

World Frank Ullrich (East Germany) has won a record six individual world titles—four at 10 km, 1978–81, including the 1980 Olympics, and two at 20 km, 1982–83. Aleksandr Tikhonov was on 10 winning Soviet relay teams, 1968–80, and won four individual titles. The Biathlon World Cup (instituted 1979) was won four times by Frank Ullrich, 1978 and 1980–82; and Franz-Peter Rötsch (East Germany), 1984–85 and 1987–88.

Women The first World Championships were held in 1984. The most individual titles is three, by Anne-Elinor Elvebakk (Norway), 10 km 1988, 7.5 km 1989–90. Kaya Parve (USSR) has won six titles, two individual and four relay, 1984–86, 1988. A women's biathlon was included at the 1992

Olympics. Myriam Bédard (Canada) is the only double Olympic champion. She won the 7.5 km and 15 km events in 1994.

United States National Championships In this competition, first held in 1965 in Rosendale, NY, men's events have been staged annually. Women's events were included in 1985.

Most titles Lyle Nelson has won seven National Championships: five in the 10 km, 1976, 1979, 1981, 1985 and 1987; two in the 20 km, 1977 and 1985. Anna Sonnerup holds the women's record with five titles: two in the 10 km, 1986–87; two in the 15 km, 1989 and 1991; and one in the 7.5 km in 1989.

Double Olympic champion Myriam Bédard celebrates her record-breaking success at the Lillehammer Games. (Allsport/Clive Brunskill)

BILLIARDS

Most titles The greatest number of World Championships (instituted 1870) won by one player is eight, by John Roberts, Jr. (Great Britain; 1847–1919), in 1870 (twice), 1871, 1875 (twice), 1877 and 1885 (twice). The record for world amateur titles is four, by Robert James Percival Marshall (Australia), in 1936, 1938, 1951 and 1962.

Youngest champion The youngest winner of the world professional title is Mike Russell (b. 3 Jun 1969), age 20 yr 49 days, when he won at Leura, Australia on 23 Jul 1989.

Highest breaks The highest certified break made by the anchor cannon is 42,746, by William Cook (England) from 29 May to 7 Jun 1907.

The official world record under the then balkline rule is 1,784, by Joe Davis in the United Kingdom Championship on 29 May 1936.

Under the "two pot" rule, restored on 1 Jan 1983, the highest break is Michael Ferreira's (India) 962 unfinished, in a tournament at Bombay, India on 29 Apr 1986.

Fastest century Walter Lindrum made an official 100 break in 46.0 sec, set in Sydney, Australia in 1941.

THREE CUSHION

Most titles Willie Hoppe (USA; 1887–1959) won 51 billiards championships in all forms, spanning the pre- and post-international era, from 1906 to 1952.

Union Mondiale de Billiard (UMB) Raymond Ceulemans (Belgium) has won 20 UMB world three-cushion championships (1963–73, 1975–80, 1983, 1985 and 1990).

BOARD GAMES

Shortest backgammon game Alan Malcolm Beckerson devised a game of 16 throws in 1982.

Domino toppling The greatest number set up single-handedly and toppled is 281,581 out of 320,236, by Klaus Friedrich, 22, at Fürth, Germany on 27 Jan 1984. The dominoes fell within 12 min 57.3 sec, having taken 31 days (10 hr daily) to set up.

Thirty students at Delft, Eindhoven and Twente Technical Universities in the Netherlands set up 1,500,000 dominoes representing all the European Community countries. Of these, 1,382,101 were toppled by one push on 2 Jan 1988.

Domino stacking The record for domino stacking is held by Ralf Laue, who successfully stacked 296 dominoes on a single supporting domino on 11 Jul 1993 in Leipzig, Germany.

Biggest board game The world's biggest board game was a version of the game "Goose," and was organized by "Jong Nederland." It stretched for 2,090 ft and was played by 1,631 participants at Someren, Netherlands on 16 Sep 1989.

Solitaire The shortest time taken to complete the game of solitaire is 10.0 sec, by Stephen Twigge in Scissett Baths, Great Britain on 2 Aug 1991.

BINGO

Largest house The largest "house" in bingo sessions was 15,756, at the Canadian National Exhibition, Toronto on 19 Aug 1983, staged by the Variety Club of Ontario Tent Number 28. There was total prize money of $Cdn250,000 with a record one-game payout of $Cdn100,000.

Earliest and latest full house A "full house" call occurred on the 15th number by Norman A. Wilson at Guide Post Working Men's Club, Bedlington, Great Britain on 22 Jun 1978; by Anne Wintle of Brynrethin, Great Britain, on a bus trip to Bath, Great Britain on 17 Aug 1982; and by Shirley Lord at Kahibah Bowling Club, New South Wales, Australia on 24 Oct 1983.

"House" was not called until the 86th number at the Hillsborough Working Men's Club, Sheffield, Great Britain on 11 Jan 1982. There were 32 winners.

CHECKERS

World champions Walter Hellman (USA; 1916–75) won a record eight world titles during his tenure as world champion, 1948–75.

Youngest and oldest national champion Asa A. Long (b. 20 Aug 1904) became the youngest US national champion, at age 18 yr 64 days, when he won in Boston, MA on 23 Oct 1922. He became the oldest, age 79 yr 334 days, when he won his sixth title in Tupelo, MS on 21 Jul 1984. He was also world champion from 1934 to 1938.

GUESS WHAT?

Q. WHAT CITY HAS THE MOST TAXIS?

A. LOOK IN "TAXIS" (TRANSPORT)

"King" of the checker board is Dr Marion Tinsley. He never lost a match during his international career, 1947–91. (Gamma/A. Berg)

Most opponents Charles Walker played a record 296 games simultaneously, winning 294 and drawing the other two, in Kenosha, WI on 6 Jun 1993.

The largest number of opponents played without a defeat or draw is 172, by Nate Cohen of Portland, ME at Portland on 26 Jul 1981. This was not a simultaneous attempt, but consecutive play over a period of four hours.

Newell W. Banks (1887–1977) played 140 games simultaneously, winning 133 and drawing 7, in Chicago, IL in 1933. His total playing time was 145 min, thus averaging about one move per sec. In 1947 he played blindfolded for 4 hr per day for 45 consecutive days, winning 1,331 games, drawing 54 and losing only 2, while playing six games at a time.

Longest game In competition the prescribed rate of play is not less than 30 moves per hour, with the average game lasting about 90 min. In 1958 a game between Dr Marion Tinsley (USA) and Derek Oldbury (Great Britain) lasted 7 hr 30 min (played under the 5-minutes-a-move rule).

CHESS

World Championships World champions have been officially recognized since 1886. The longest undisputed tenure was 26 yr 337 days, by Dr Emanuel Lasker (1868–1941) of Germany, from 1894 to 1921.

The women's world championship title was held by Vera Francevna

Stevenson-Menchik (USSR, later Great Britain; 1906–44) from 1927 until her death, and was successfully defended a record seven times.

The first American to be regarded as world champion was Paul Charles Morphy (1837–89) in 1858.

Team The USSR has won the biennial men's team title (Olympiad) a record 18 times between 1952 and 1990. The women's title has been won 11 times by the USSR from its introduction in 1957 to 1986, with Georgia winning in 1992.

The USA has won the men's title five times: 1931, 1933, 1935, 1937 and 1976.

Youngest Gary Kasparov (USSR; b. 13 Apr 1963) won the title on 9 Nov 1985 at age 22 yr 210 days. Maya Chiburdanidze (USSR; b. 17 Jan 1961) won the women's title in 1978 when only 17.

Oldest Wilhelm Steinitz (Austria, later USA; 1836–1900) was 58 yr 10 days when he lost his title to Lasker on 26 May 1894.

Most active Anatoly Karpov (USSR) in his tenure as champion, 1975–85, averaged 45.2 competitive games per year, played in 32 tournaments and finished first in 26.

Grand Masters The youngest individual to qualify as an International Grand Master is Judit Polgar (Hungary; b. 23 Jul 1976), aged 15 yr 150 days on 20 Dec 1991.

United States The youngest US Grand Master was Bobby Fischer (b. 9 Mar 1943) in 1958.

Masters In August 1981, Stuart Rachels of Birmingham, AL became the youngest person in the history of the United States Chess Foundation to achieve a master rating, at the age of 11 yr 10 months.

Highest rating The highest rating ever attained on the officially adopted Elo System (devised by Arpad E. Elo [1903–92]) is 2,805, by Gary Kasparov (USSR) at the end of 1992.

The highest-rated woman player is Judit Polgar, who achieved a peak rating of 2,630 at the end of 1993.

Fewest games lost by a world champion José Raúl Capablanca (Cuba; 1888–1942) lost only 34 games (out of 571) in his adult career, 1909–39. He was unbeaten from 10 Feb 1916 to 21 Mar 1924 (63 games) and was world champion 1921–27.

US Championships The most wins since the US Championships became determined by match play competition in 1888 is eight, by Bobby Fischer, 1958–66.

Most opponents The record for most consecutive games played is 663, by Vlastimil Hort (Czechoslovakia, later Germany; b. 12 Jan 1944) over 32½ hours at Porz, Germany on 5–6 Oct 1984. He played 60–120 opponents at a time, scoring over 80 percent wins and averaging 30 moves per game. He also holds the record for most games played simultaneously, 201 during 550 consecutive games of which he lost only 10, in Seltjarnes, Iceland on 23–24 Apr 1977.

Eric G.J. Knoppert (Netherlands; b. 20 Sep 1959) played 500 games of 10-minute chess against opponents, averaging 2,002 on the Elo scale, on 13–16 Sep 1985. He scored 413 points (1 for win, ½ for draw), a success rate of 82.6 percent.

Most moves The Master chess game with the most moves on record was one of 269 moves, when Ivan Nikolić drew with Goran Arsović in a Belgrade, Yugoslavia tournament, on 17 Feb 1989. The game took a total of 20 hr 15 min.

Slowest and longest chess games The slowest reported moving (before time clocks were used) in an official event is reputed to have been by Louis Paulsen (Germany; 1833–91) against Paul Charles Morphy (USA; 1837–84) at the first American Chess Congress, NY on 29 Oct 1857. The game ended in a draw on move 56 after 15 hours of play, of which Paulsen used *c.* 11 hours.

Grand Master Friedrich Sämisch (Germany; 1896–1975) ran out of the allotted time (2 hr 30 min for 45 moves) after only 12 moves, in Prague, Czechoslovakia, in 1938.

The slowest move played, since time clocks were introduced, was at Vigo, Spain in 1980 when Francisco R. Torres Trois took 2 hr 20 min for his seventh move *v* Luis M.C.P. Santos (b. 30 Jun 1955).

Oldest chess pieces The oldest pieces identified as chess pieces were found in Nashipur, dated to *c.* A.D. 900.

SCRABBLE

Highest scores The highest competitive game score is 1,049 by Phil Appleby in June 1989. His opponent scored 253, and the margin of victory, 796 points, is also a record. His score included a single turn of 374 for the word "OXIDIZERS."

The highest competitive single-turn score recorded, however, is 392, by Dr Saladin Karl Khoshnaw (of Kurdish origin) in Manchester, Great Britain in April 1982. He laid down "CAZIQUES," which means "native chiefs of West Indian aborigines."

The highest score in a tournament game (American-style competitive) is 770 points, by game inventor Mark Lansberg of Los Angeles, at the Scrabble tournament in Eagle Rock, CA on 13 Jun 1993. His opponent, Alan Stern, scored 338 points, and their combined total of 1,108 points is also a record for American-style competitive tournament play.

Most tournaments Chuck Armstrong, a hospital worker from Saline, MI, has won the most tournaments—65 to the end of 1989.

TWISTER

Most participants The greatest number of participants in a game of Twister is 4,160 people, at the University of Massachusetts at Amherst on 2 May 1987. Allison Culler won the game.

BOBSLED & LUGE

BOBSLEDDING

Most titles The Olympic four-man bob title (instituted 1924) has been won five times by Switzerland (1924, 1936, 1956, 1972 and 1988).

The Olympic two-man bob title (instituted 1932) has been won four times by Switzerland (1948, 1980, 1992 and 1994).

The most gold medals won by an individual is three, by Meinhard Nehmer (East Germany) and by Bernhard Germeshausen (East Germany) in the 1976 two-man, 1976 and 1980 four-man events.

The most medals won is six (two gold, two silver, two bronze) by Eugenio Monti (Italy), 1956 to 1968.

World and Olympic The world four-man bob title (instituted 1924) has been won 20 times by Switzerland (1924, 1936, 1939, 1947, 1954–57, 1971–73, 1975, 1982–83, 1986–90, 1993), including its five Olympic victories. Switzerland won the two-man title 17 times (1935, 1947–50, 1953, 1955, 1977–80 and 1982–83, 1987, 1990, 1992 and 1994), including its four Olympic successes.

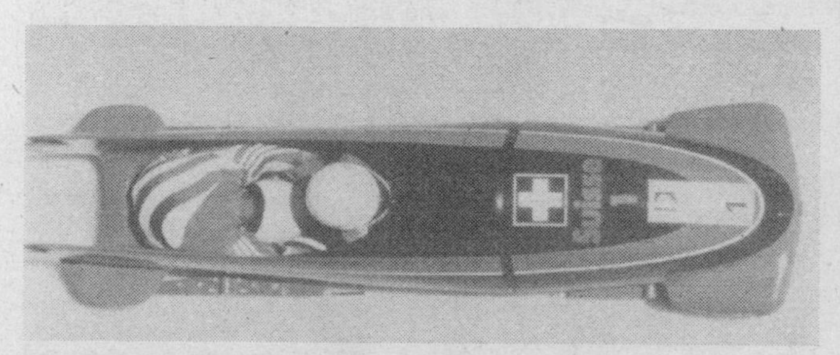

Switzerland has dominated the Olympic bobsled events. Gustav Weder and Donat Acklin won the 1994 2-man event, their second title and the fourth success for a Swiss sled. (Allsport/Pascal Rondeau)

OLDEST!

The oldest and most famous sled run in the world is the Cresta Run in St. Moritz, Switzerland. The oldest person to successfully travel the complete length of the course is Robin Todhunter (Great Britain). He made the run at age 83 yr. 239 days on 2 Feb. 1987.

The luge is one of the simplest sporting events: just lie back on the sled and slide feet first. Georg Hackl (above), the Olympic champion, would recommend going as fast as possible, but that is optional. (Allsport/Pascal Rondeau)

Eugenio Monti was a member of 11 world championship crews, eight two-man and three four-man, in 1957–68.

United States Two American bobsledders have won two gold medals: driver Billy Fiske (1911–40) and crewman Clifford Grey (1887–1941) in 1928 and 1932. At age 16 yr 260 days in 1928, Fiske was America's youngest-ever Winter Games gold medalist.

Oldest gold medalist The oldest age at which a gold medal has been won at any sport at the Winter Olympics is 49 yr 7 days, for James Jay O'Brien (USA; 1883–1940) at four-man bob in 1932.

LUGEING

Most titles The most successful rider in the World Championships was Thomas Köhler (East Germany), who won the single-seater title in 1962, 1964 (Olympic) and 1967, and shared the two-seater title in 1965, 1967 and 1968 (Olympic). Georg Hackl (GDR/Germany) has won four single-seater titles, 1989, 1990, 1992 (Olympic) and 1994 (Olympic). Margit Schumann (East Germany) won five women's titles, 1973–75, 1976 (Olympic) and 1977.

United States No American Luger has won a medal at the Olympic Games. Jennison Heaton won a gold at the 1928 single skeleton sled event.

United States National Championships *Most titles* Frank Masley has won a record six men's championships, 1979, 1981–83 and 1987–88. Bonny Warner, 1983–84, 1987–88 and 1990, and Cammy Miller, 1985, 1989, and 1991–93, have both won a record five women's titles.

Fastest speed in lugeing The fastest recorded photo-timed speed is 85.38 mph, by Asle Strand (Norway) at Tandådalens Linbana, Sälen, Sweden on 1 May 1982.

BOWLING

Highest bowling score—24 hours A team of six scored 217,969 at Strykers Pleasure Bowl, Bushbury, Great Britain on 15–16 Oct 1993. During this attempt a member of the team, Dan Steeles, set an individual record of 48,969.

The American record is held by a team of six called the Brunswick Thursday Nite Stars, who scored 209,072 at Brunswick Sharptown Lanes, Houston, TX on 20–21 Jun 1991.

Largest bowling center The Fukuyama Bowl, Osaka, Japan has 144 lanes. The Tokyo World Lanes Center, Japan, now closed, had 252 lanes.

Consecutive strikes, spares and splits The record for most consecutive strikes is 40, by Jeanne Maiden. Mabel Henry of Winchester, KY had 30 consecutive spares in the 1986/87 season. Shirley Tophigh of Las Vegas, NV holds the unenviable record of rolling 14 consecutive splits in 1968/69.

World Championships The World (*Fédération Internationale des Quilleurs*) Championships were instituted for men in 1954 and for women in 1963.

The highest pinfall in the individual men's event is 5,963 (in 28 games) by Ed Luther (USA) in Milwaukee, WI on 28 Aug 1971.

For the current schedule of 24 games the men's record is 5,261, by Richard Clay "Rick" Steelsmith, and the women's record is 4,894, by Sandra Jo Shiery (USA), both at Helsinki, Finland in June 1987.

The World Cup (instituted 1965) is contested annually by the national champions of each member of FIQ. The most wins is three, by Paeng Nepomuceno (Philippines), 1976, 1980 and 1992.

STRIKE!

The oldest woman to bowl a 300 game is Evelyn Culbert of Austin, MN. She performed the perfect feat at Eden Lanes, Austin, MN, on 4 April 1993 when aged 66 years old.

Of all the women who have rolled a perfect game, the one with the lowest average was Diane Ponza of Santa Cruz, CA, who had a 112 average in the 1977–78 season.

Highest scores The highest individual score for three sanctioned games (out of a possible 900) is 899, by Thomas Jordan (USA) at Union, NJ on 7 Mar 1989. He followed with a 299, setting a four-game series record of 1,198 pins.

The record by a woman is 864, by Jeanne Maiden of Tacoma, WA at Sodon, OH on 23 Nov 1986. This series includes a record 40 consecutive strikes.

Youngest and oldest 300 bowlers The youngest bowler to score 300 is said to be Matthew Gilman of Davie, FL, who performed this feat at age 11 yr 2 mth on 17 Jul 1993. The oldest bowler to score 300 is Jerry Whelman of Port St. Lucie, FL, who performed the feat on 15 Apr. 1992 when aged 81 years old.

PROFESSIONAL BOWLERS ASSOCIATION

Most titles Earl Anthony (USA) has won a lifetime total of 41 PBA titles. The record number of titles won in one PBA season is eight, by Mark Roth of Lake Heights, NJ, in 1978.

Consecutive titles Only three bowlers have ever won three consecutive professional tournaments—Dick Weber (three times), in 1959, 1960 and 1961; Johnny Petraglia in 1971; and Mark Roth in 1977.

PBA TOUR SCORING RECORDS

Games	Score	Bowler	Site	Year
6	1,615	Walter Ray WIlliams Jr.	Beaumont, TX	1991
8	2,165	Billy Hardwick	Tokyo, Japan	1968
12	3,052	Walter Ray WIlliams Jr.	Beaumont, TX	1991
16	4,015	Carmen Salvino	Sterling Heights, MI	1980
18	4,515	Earl Anthony	New Orleans, LA	1977
24	5,826	Kelly Coffman	Riverside, CA	1993

PBA Tour

Perfect games A total of 197 perfect (300-pin) games were bowled in PBA tournaments in 1993, the most ever for one year.

Walter Ray Williams Jr. bowled four perfect games in one tournament, in Mechanicsburg, PA in 1993. He also rolled seven perfect games on the 1993 tour, tying Amleto Monacelli's record, set in 1989.

Triple Crown The first bowler to accumulate the three legs of the triple crown was Billy Hardwick: National Championship (1963); Firestone Tournament of Champions (1965); US Open (1969). Hardwick's feat was matched by Johnny Petraglia: Firestone (1971); US Open (1977); National (1980); and by Pete Weber: Firestone (1987); US Open (1988); National (1989).

US Open The most wins in this tournament is four, by two bowlers: Don Carter in 1953–54 and 1957–58, and Dick Weber in 1962–63 and 1965–66.

PBA National Championship The most wins in this tournament is six, by Earl Anthony in 1973–75 and 1981–83.

Tournament of Champions The most wins in this tournament is three, by Mike Durbin in 1972, 1982 and 1984.

Highest earners Pete Weber has won a record $1,820,987 in PBA competitions through 17 Jun 1994.

Mike Aulby of Indianapolis, IN holds the single-season earnings mark of $298,237, reached in 1989.

AMERICAN BOWLING CONGRESS

Highest score The highest individual score for three games is 899, by Thomas Jordan at Union, NJ on 7 Mar 1989 (see Bowling—Highest scores). The highest three-game team score is 3,868, by Hurst Bowling Supplies of Luzerne, PA on 23 Feb 1994.

The highest season average attained in sanctioned competition is 247.9, by Jeff Phipps of Salem, OR in the 1992/93 season.

The all-time ABC-sanctioned two-man single-game record is 600, held jointly by the teams of John Cotta (300) and Steve Larson (300) on 1 May 1981, at the Manteca, CA, Bowling Association Tournament; Jeff Mraz and Dave Roney of Canton, OH on 8 Nov 1987 in the Ann Doubles Classic in Canton, OH; William Gruner and Dave Conway of Oceanside, CA on

27 Feb 1990; Scott Williams and Willie Hammar of Utica, MI on 7 Jan 1990; and Darrell Guertin and George Tignor of Rutland, VT on 20 Feb 1993.

Perfect scores The highest number of sanctioned 300 games is 45, by Mike Whalin of Cincinnati, OH.

Two perfect games were rolled back-to-back *twice* by two bowlers: Al Spotts of West Reading, PA, on 14 Mar 1982 and again on 1 Feb 1985; and Gerry Wright of Idaho Falls, ID, on 9 Jan 1992 and again on 26 Feb 1992.

WOMEN'S INTERNATIONAL BOWLING CONGRESS (WIBC)

Highest scores Elizabeth Johnson of Niagara Falls, NY had a record 234 one-season average in the 1993/94 season. Patty Ann of Appleton, WI had a record five-year composite average of 227 through the 1985/86 season.

The highest five-woman team score for a three-game series is 3,509, by Goebel Beer, Detroit, MI in the 1993/94 season.

Perfect games Jeanne Nacarrato (nee Maiden) of Tacoma, WA has rolled 20 perfect games to set the WIBC career record. She also set a record of 40 consecutive strikes in 1986 and rolled an 864 on games of 300–300–264. The most 300 games rolled in a career is 20, by Jeanne Nacarrato.

BOXING

Lightest heavyweight Robert James "Bob" Fitzsimmons (1863–1917) of Great Britain weighed 165 lb when he won the title by knocking out James J. Corbett at Carson City, NV on 17 Mar 1897.

Heaviest Primo Carnera (Italy; 1906–67), the "Ambling Alp," who won the title from Jack Sharkey in New York City on 29 Jun 1933, scaled $260\frac{1}{2}$ lb for this fight, but his peak weight was 269 lb. He had an expanded chest measurement of 54 in and the longest reach at $85\frac{1}{2}$ in (fingertip to fingertip).

Most knockdowns in title fight Vic Toweel (South Africa) knocked down Danny O'Sullivan of London, Great Britain 14 times in 10 rounds in their world bantamweight fight at Johannesburg, South Africa on 2 Dec 1950, before the latter retired.

Longest fight The longest recorded fight with gloves was between Andy Bowen of New Orleans (1867–94) and Jack Burke at New Orleans, LA on 6–7 Apr 1893. It lasted 110 rounds, 7 hr 19 min (9:15 P.M.–4:34 A.M.), and was declared a no-contest (later changed to a draw).

Most fights without loss Of boxers with complete records, Packey McFarland (USA; 1888–1936) had 97 fights (five draws) in 1905–15 without a defeat.

Pedro Carrasco (Spain) won 83 consecutive fights from 22 April 1964 to 3 Sep 1970, drew once and had a further nine wins before his loss to Armando Ramos in a WBC lightweight contest on 18 Feb 1972.

Most knockouts The greatest number of finishes classed as "knockouts" in a career (1936–63) is 145 (129 in professional bouts), by Archie Moore (ne Archibald Lee Wright; USA).

***Attendances** Highest* The greatest paid attendance at any boxing match is 132,274 for four world title fights at the Aztec Stadium, Mexico City on 20 Feb 1993, headed by the successful WBC light-welterweight defense by Julio César Chavez (Mexico) over Greg Haugen (USA).

The indoor record is 63,350, at the Muhammad Ali *v* Leon Spinks fight in the Superdome, New Orleans, LA on 15 Sep 1978.

The highest nonpaying attendance is 135,132, at the Tony Zale *v* Billy Pryor fight at Juneau Park, Milwaukee, WI on 16 Aug 1941.

Lowest The smallest attendance at a world heavyweight title fight was 2,434, at the Cassius Clay (Muhammad Ali) *v* Sonny Liston fight at Lewiston, ME on 25 May 1965.

Eight fighters have won an Olympic gold medal and a heavyweight title. Lennox Lewis (above) is the only non-American among the octet. (Allsport/S. Bruty)

WORLD HEAVYWEIGHT

***Reign** Longest* Joe Louis (USA; b. Joseph Louis Barrow, 1914–81) was champion for 11 years 252 days, from 22 Jun 1937, when he knocked out James Joseph Braddock in the eighth round at Chicago, IL, until announcing his retirement on 1 Mar 1949. During his reign Louis made a record 25 defenses of his title.

Shortest Tony Tucker (USA) was IBF champion for 64 days, 30 May–2 Aug 1987, the shortest duration of a title won and lost in the ring.

Most recaptures Muhammad Ali is the only man to have regained the heavyweight championship twice. Ali first won the title on 25 Feb 1964, defeating Sonny Liston. He defeated George Foreman on 30 Oct 1974, after having been stripped of the title by the world boxing authorities on 28 Apr 1967. He won the WBA title from Leon Spinks on 15 Sep 1978, having previously lost to him on 15 Feb 1978.

Undefeated Rocky Marciano (USA; b. Rocco Francis Marchegiano, 1923–69) is the only world champion at any weight to have won every fight of his entire professional career from 17 Mar 1947 to 21 Sep 1955 (he announced his retirement on 27 Apr 1956); 43 of his 49 fights were by knockouts or stoppages.

Oldest heavyweight "Jersey Joe" Walcott (USA; b. Arnold Raymond Cream; 1914–1994) was 37 yr 168 days when he knocked out Ezzard Charles (1921–75) on 18 Jul 1951 in Pittsburgh, PA. He was also the oldest holder, at 38 yr 236 days, losing his title to Rocky Marciano on 23 Sep 1952.

Youngest heavyweight Mike Tyson (USA; b. 30 Jun 1966) was 20 yr 144 days when he beat Trevor Berbick (USA) to win the WBC version at Las Vegas, NV on 22 Nov 1986. He added the WBA title when he beat James "Bone-crusher" Smith on 7 Mar 1987 at 20 yr 249 days. He became undisputed champion on 2 Aug 1987 when he beat Tony Tucker (USA) for the IBF title.

Greatest weight difference When Primo Carnera (Italy), 269 lb, fought Tommy Loughran (USA), 183 lb, for the world heavyweight title at Miami, FL on 1 Mar 1934, there was a weight difference of 86 lb between the two fighters. Carnera won the fight on points.

WORLD CHAMPIONS ANY WEIGHT

***Reign** Longest* The Joe Louis heavyweight duration record of 11 yr 252 days stands for all divisions.

Shortest Tony Canzoneri (USA; 1908–59) was world light-welterweight champion for 33 days, 21 May to 23 Jun 1933, the shortest period for a boxer to have won and lost the world title in the ring.

Youngest Wilfred Benitez (b. 12 Sep 1958) of Puerto Rico was 17 yr

176 days when he won the WBA light-welterweight title in San Juan, Puerto Rico on 6 Mar 1976.

Oldest Archie Moore, who was recognized as a light-heavyweight champion up to 10 Feb 1962 when his title was removed, was then believed to be between 45 and 48 years old.

Longest fight The longest world title fight (under Queensberry Rules) was that between the lightweights Joe Gans (1874–1910), of the USA, and Oscar Matthew "Battling" Nelson (1882–1954), the "Durable Dane," at Goldfield, NV on 3 Sep 1906. It was terminated in the 42nd round when Gans was declared the winner on a foul.

Most recaptures The only boxer to win a world title five times at one weight is "Sugar Ray" Robinson (USA; b. Walker Smith, Jr., 1921–89), who beat Carmen Basilio (USA) in Chicago Stadium, IL on 25 Mar 1958 to regain the world middleweight title for the fourth time.

Most title bouts The record number of title bouts in a career is 37, of which 18 ended in "no decision," by three-time world welterweight champion Jack Britton (USA; 1885–1962) in 1915–22. The record for most contests without a "no decision" is 27 (all heavyweight), by Joe Louis between 1937–50.

Greatest "tonnage" The highest aggregate weight recorded in any fight is 699 lb, when Claude "Humphrey" McBride (Oklahoma), 339½ lb, knocked out Jimmy Black (Houston, TX), 359½ lb, in the third round at Oklahoma City, OK on 1 Jun 1971.

AMATEUR

Olympic titles Only two boxers have won three Olympic gold medals: southpaw László Papp (Hungary; b. 25 Mar 1926), middleweight winner 1948, light-middleweight winner 1952 and 1956; and Teofilo Stevenson (Cuba), heavyweight winner 1972, 1976 and 1980.

The only man to win two titles in one Olympic celebration was Oliver L. Kirk (USA), who won both bantam and featherweight titles in St Louis, MO in 1904, but he needed only one bout in each class.

The youngest Olympic boxing champion was Jackie Fields (ne Finkelstein [USA]; b. 9 Feb 1908), who won the 1924 featherweight title at age 16 yrs 162 days. The minimum age for Olympic boxing competitors is now 17.

Oldest gold medalist Richard Gunn (Great Britain; 1871–1961) won the Olympic featherweight gold medal on 27 Oct 1908 in London, Great Britain at the age of 37 yr 254 days.

World Championships A record of four world titles (instituted 1974) have been won by Félix Savon (Cuba), heavyweight winner 1986, 1989, 1991, and 91 kg 1993.

Most US titles The most titles won is five, by middleweight W. Rodenbach, 1900–04.

CANOEING

Most titles Olympics Gert Fredriksson (Sweden) won a record six Olympic gold medals, 1948–60. He added a silver and a bronze, for a record eight medals.

The most by a woman is four, by Birgit Schmidt (nee Fischer; Germany, formerly GDR), 1980–92.

The most gold medals won at one Games is three, by Vladimir Parfenovich (USSR) in 1980 and by Ian Ferguson (New Zealand; b. 20 Jul 1952) in 1984.

World Including the Olympic Games, a record 25 titles have been won by Birgit Schmidt, 1978–93.

The men's record is 13, by Gert Fredriksson, 1948–60; Rüdiger Helm (East Germany), 1976–83; and Ivan Patzaichin (Romania; b. 26 Nov 1949), 1968–84.

United States The only American canoeist to have won two Olympic gold medals is Greg Barton, who won at K1 and K2 1,000 m events in 1988. He also has a US record three medals, as he took bronze at K1 1,000 m in 1984.

Most US titles Marcia Smoke won 35 US national titles between 1962 and 1981. The men's record is 33 US titles, by Ernest Riedel between 1930 and 1948, mostly at kayak events.

PADDLE!

The fastest time to paddle the length of the River Rhine is 10 days 12 hr 9 min by Frank Palmer, 15-25 May 1988.

The supported team record is 7 days 23 hr 31 sec by the RAF Laarbruch Canne Club, led by Andy Goodsell, 17–24 May 1989.

Fastest speed The German four-man kayak Olympic champions in 1992 in Barcelona, Spain covered 1,000 m in 2 min 52.17 sec in a heat on 4 August. This represents an average speed of 12.98 mph.

At the 1988 Olympics in Seoul, South Korea the Norwegian four achieved a 250 m split of 42.08 sec between 500 m and 750 m for a speed of 13.29 mph.

Longest journey Father and son Dana and Donald Starkell paddled from Winnipeg, Manitoba, Canada by ocean and river to Belem, Brazil, a distance of 12,181 miles, from 1 Jun 1980 to 1 May 1982. All portages were human-powered.

Without portages or aid of any kind, the longest is one of 6,102 miles, by Richard H. Grant and Ernest "Moose" Lassy, circumnavigating the eastern United States via Chicago, New Orleans, Miami, New York City and the Great Lakes from 22 Sep 1930 to 15 Aug 1931.

24 hours Zdzislaw Szubski paddled 157.1 miles in a Jaguar K1 canoe on the Vistula River, Wockawek to Gdansk, Poland, on 11–12 Sep 1987.

Flat water Marinda Hartzenberg (South Africa) paddled, without benefit of current, 137.13 miles on Loch Logan, Bloemfontein, South Africa on 31 Dec 1990–1 Jan 1991.

Open sea Randy Fine (USA) paddled 120.6 miles along the Florida coast on 26–27 Jun 1986.

Greatest lifetime distance in a canoe Fritz Lindner of Berlin, Germany, totaled 64,278 miles of canoeing from 1928 to 1987.

Eskimo rolls Ray Hudspith achieved 1,000 rolls in 34 min 43 sec at the Elswick Pool, Newcastle-upon-Tyne, Great Britain on 20 Mar 1987. He completed 100 rolls in 3 min 7.25 sec at Killingworth Leisure Center, Great Britain on 3 Mar 1991.

Randy Fine (USA) completed 1,796 continuous rolls at Biscayne Bay, Miami, FL on 8 Jun 1991.

"Hand rolls" Colin Brian Hill achieved 1,000 rolls in 31 min 55.62 sec at Consett, Great Britain on 12 Mar 1987. He also achieved 100 rolls in 2 min 39.2 sec in London, Great Britain on 22 Feb 1987. He completed 3,700 continuous rolls at Durham City Swimming Baths, Great Britain on 1 May 1989.

Canoe raft A raft of 568 kayaks and canoes, organized by the Nottinghamshire County Scout Council with the help of scouts from other counties, was held together by hands only, while free floating for 30 seconds on the River Trent, Nottingham, Great Britain on 30 Jun 1991.

Longest race The Canadian Government Centennial Voyageur Canoe Pageant and Race from Rocky Mountain House, Alberta to the Expo 67 site at Montreal, Quebec was 3,283 miles. Ten canoes represented Canadian provinces and territories. The winner of the race, which took from 24 May to 4 Sep 1967, was the Province of Manitoba canoe *Radisson*.

CARD GAMES

Card holding Ralf Laue held 326 standard playing cards in a fan in one hand, so that the value and color of each one was visible, at Leipzig, Germany, on 18 Mar 1994.

Card throwing Jim Karol of Catasauqua, PA threw a standard playing card 201 ft at Mount Ida College, Newton Centre, MA on 18 Oct 1992.

CONTRACT BRIDGE

Biggest tournament The Epson World Bridge Championship, held on 20–21 Jun 1992, was contested by more than 102,000 players playing the same hands, at over 2,000 centers worldwide.

Most world titles The World Championship (Bermuda Bowl) has been won a record 13 times by Italy's Blue Team (*Squadra Azzura*), 1957–59, 1961–63, 1965–67, 1969, 1973–75; and by the USA, 1950–51, 1953–54, 1970–71, 1976–77, 1979, 1981, 1983, 1985, 1987. Italy also won the team Olympiad in 1964, 1968 and 1972 and the USA won in 1988. Giorgio Belladonna was on all the Italian winning teams.

The USA has a record six wins in the women's world championship for the Venice Trophy, 1974, 1976, 1978, 1987, 1989 and 1991, and three women's wins at the World Team Olympiad, 1976, 1980 and 1984.

Most world championship hands In the 1989 Bermuda Bowl in Perth, Australia, Marcel Branco and Gabriel Chagas, both of Brazil, played a record 752 out of a possible 784 boards.

Perfect deals in bridge The mathematical odds against dealing 13 cards of one suit are 158,753,389,899 to 1, while the odds against a named player receiving a "perfect hand" consisting of all 13 spades are 635,013,559,599 to 1. The odds against each of the four players' receiving a complete suit (a "perfect deal") are 2,235,197,406,895,366,368,301,559,999 to 1.

Possible bridge auctions The number of possible auctions with North as dealer is 128,745,650,347,030,683,120,231,926,111,609,371,363,122,697,557.

CRIBBAGE

Rare hands Five maximum 29-point hands have been achieved by Sean Daniels of Astoria, OR, 1989–92. Paul Nault of Athol, MA had two such hands within eight games in a tournament on 19 Mar 1977.

Most points in 24 hours The most points scored by a team of four, playing singles in two pairs, is 126,414, by Mark Fitzwater, Eddie Pepper, Mark Perry and Gary Watson at The Green Man, Potton, Great Britain on 8–9 May 1993.

GUESS WHAT?

Q. HOW HIGH IS THE TALLEST HOUSE OF CARDS?

A. LOOK IN "HOUSING" (BUILDINGS & STRUCTURES)

CRICKET

TEST CRICKET

Career records The most runs scored by an individual is 11,174, by Allan Border (Australia) in 156 Tests, 1978–94. The most wickets taken by a bowler is 434, by Kapil Dev (India) in 131 Tests, 1978–94. The most dismissals by a wicket-keeper is 355, by Rodney Marsh (Australia), in 96 Tests, 1970–84. The most catches by a fielder is 155, by Allan Border in 156 Tests, 1978–94.

The best all-round Test career record is that of Kapil Dev, with 5,248 runs, 434 wickets and 64 catches in 131 matches, 1978–94.

ONE-DAY CRICKET

World Cup The West Indies are the only double winners, in 1975 and 1979.

International records *Team* The highest innings scored by a team is 363–7 (55 overs) by England *v* Pakistan at Nottingham, Great Britain on 20 Aug 1992. The lowest completed innings total is 43 by Pakistan *v* the West Indies at Cape Town, South Africa on 25 Feb 1993. The largest victory margin is 232 runs by Australia *v* Sri Lanka (323–2 to 91), at Adelaide, Australia on 28 Jan 1985.

Individual The highest individual score is 189 not out by Viv Richards for the West Indies *v* England at Manchester, Great Britain on 31 May 1984. The best bowling analysis is 7–37 by Aqib Javed for Pakistan *v* India at Sharjah, UAE on 25 Oct 1991. The best partnership is 263 by Aamir Sohail (134) and Inzamam-ul-Haq (137 not out) for Pakistan *v* New Zealand at Sharjah on 20 Apr 1994.

Career The most matches played is 273 by Allan Border (Australia), 1979–93. The most runs scord is 8,649 (av. 41.38) by Desmond Haynes (West Indies) in 238 matches, 1977–94; this total includes a record 17 centuries. The most wickets taken is 251 (av. 27.22) by Kapil Dev (India) in 220 matches, 1978–94. The most dismissals is 204 (183 catches, 21 stumpings) by Jeff Dujon (West Indies) in 169 matches, 1981–91. The most catches by a fielder is 127 by Border.

Women's World Cup Five women's World Cups have been staged. Australia has won three times, in 1978, 1982 and 1988. The highest individual score in this competition is 143 not out by Lindsay Reeler for Australia *v* Netherlands at Perth, Australia on 29 Nov 1988.

NATIONAL CRICKET CHAMPIONSHIPS

Australia The premier event in Australia is the Sheffield Shield, an interstate competition contested since 1891–92. New South Wales has won the title a record 42 times.

In 1994 West Indian batsman Brian Lara rewrote the cricket record book. Among his achievements were the highest score in an international game (375 runs), above, and the highest score in a major league game (501). (Allsport/Ben Radford)

England The major championship in England is the County Championships, an intercounty competition officially recognized since 1890. Yorkshire has won the title a record 30 times.

India The Ranji Trophy is India's premier cricket competition. Established in 1934 in memory of K. S. Ranjitsinhji, it is contested on a zonal basis, culminating in a playoff competition. Bombay has won the tournament a record 31 times.

New Zealand Since 1975, the major championship in New Zealand has been the Shell Trophy. Otago, Wellington and Auckland have each won the competition four times.

Pakistan Pakistan's national championship is the Quaid-e-Azam Trophy, established in 1953. Karachi has won the trophy a record eight times.

South Africa The Currie Cup, donated by Sir Donald Currie, was first contested in 1889. Transvaal has won the competition a record 28 times.

West Indies The Red Stripe Cup, established in 1966, is the premier prize played for by the association of Caribbean islands (plus Guyana) that form the West Indies Cricket League. Barbados has won the competition a record 13 times.

CROQUET

International trophy The MacRobertson Shield (instituted 1925 and held every three years) has been won a record nine times by Great Britain, in 1925, 1937, 1956, 1963, 1969, 1974, 1982, 1990 and 1993.

A record seven appearances have been made by John G. Prince (New Zealand), in 1963, 1969, 1975, 1979, 1982, 1986 and 1990; on his debut he was the youngest-ever international, at 17 yr 190 days.

World Championships The first World Championships were held at the Hurlingham Club, London, Great Britain in 1989 and have been held annually since. The only double winner is Robert Fulford (Great Britain), 1990 and 1992.

USCA National Championships The first United States Championships were played in 1977. J. Archie Peck has won the singles title a record four times, 1977, 1979–80 and 1982. Ted Prentis has won the doubles title four times with three different partners, 1978, 1980–81 and 1988. The teams of Ted Prentis and Ned Prentis (1980–81), Dana Dribben and Ray Bell (1985–86), and Reid Fleming and Debbie Cornelius (1990–91) have each won the doubles title twice. The New York Croquet Club has won a record six National Club Championships, 1980–83, 1986 and 1988.

Double croquet world champion Robert Fulford demonstrates his mallet technique. (Allsport/Tom Hevezi)

CROSS-COUNTRY RUNNING

World Championships The greatest margin of victory is 56 sec or 390 yd by Jack Holden (England) at Ayr Racecourse, Strathclyde, Great Britain on 24 Mar 1934.

Since 1973 the events have been official World Championships under the auspices of the International Amateur Athletic Federation.

United States The USA has never won either of the men's team races, but Lynn Jennings has won the women's individual title three times, 1990–92, and Craig Virgin won the men's individual race twice, in 1980–81.

Most wins The greatest number of team victories has been by England, with 45 for men. The USA and the USSR each have a record eight women's team victories.

The greatest team domination was by Kenya at Auckland, New Zealand on 26 Mar 1988. Kenya's senior men's team finished eight men in the first nine, with a low score of 23 (six to score), and its junior men's team set a record low score, 11 (four to score) with six in the first seven.

The greatest number of individual victories is five, by John Ngugi (Kenya), 1986–89 and 1992; by Doris Brown-Heritage (USA), 1967–71; and by Grete Waitz (nee Andersen; Norway), 1978–81 and 1983.

Most appearances Marcel van de Wattyne (Belgium) ran in a record 20 races, 1946–65. The women's record is 16, by Jean Lochhead (Wales), 1967–79, 1981, 1983–84.

US championship In this competition, first staged in 1890, the most wins in the men's race is eight, by Pat Porter, 1982–89. The most wins in the women's championships is seven, by Lynn A. Jennings, 1985, 1987–90, 1992 and 1993.

Largest cross-country field The largest recorded field in any cross-country race was 11,763 starters (10,810 finished), in the 18.6-mile Lidingöloppet, near Stockholm, Sweden on 3 Oct 1982.

CURLING

Most titles Canada has won the men's World Championships 22 times, 1959–64, 1966, 1968–72, 1980, 1982–83, 1985–87, 1989–90, and 1993–94.

The most women's World Championships (instituted 1979) is eight, by Canada (1980, 1984–87, 1989, 1993–94).

United States The USA has won the men's world title four times, with Bud Somerville skip on the first two winning teams, 1965 and 1974.

United States National Championship Men In this competition, first held in 1957, two curlers have been skips on five championship teams: Bud Somerville (Superior Curling Club, WI in 1965, 1968–69, 1974, 1981), and Bruce Roberts (Hibbing Curling Club, MN in 1966–67, 1976–77, 1984). Bill Strum of the Superior Curling Club has been a member of five title teams, in 1965, 1967, 1969, 1974 and 1978.

Women In this competition, first held in 1977, Nancy Langley, Seattle, WA has been the skip of a record four championship teams, 1979, 1981, 1983 and 1988.

The Labatt Brier (formerly the Macdonald Brier 1927–79) The Brier is the Canadian Men's Curling championship. The competition was first held at the Granite Club, Toronto in 1927. The most wins is 23, by Manitoba (1928–32, 1934, 1936, 1938, 1940, 1942, 1947, 1949, 1952–53, 1956, 1965, 1970–72, 1979, 1981, 1984 and 1992). Ernie Richardson (Saskatchewan) has been winning skip a record four times (1959–60, 1962–63). His brothers Arnold and Sam Richardson were also members of each championship team.

Fastest game in curling Eight curlers from the Burlington Golf and Country Club curled an eight-end game in 47 min 24 sec, with time penalties of 5 min 30 sec, at Burlington, Ontario, Canada on 4 Apr 1986, following rules agreed on with the Ontario Curling Association. The time is taken from when the first rock crosses the near hogline until the game's last rock comes to a complete stop.

Largest bonspiel The largest bonspiel (curling tournament) in the world is the Manitoba Curling Association Bonspiel, held annually in Winnipeg, Canada. In 1988 there were 1,424 teams of four men, a total of 5,696 curlers, using 187 sheets of curling ice.

Longest curling throw The longest throw of a curling stone was a distance of 576 ft 4 in, by Eddie Kulbacki (Canada) at Park Lake, Neepawa, Manitoba, Canada on 29 Jan 1989. The attempt took place on a specially prepared sheet of curling ice on frozen Park Lake, a record 1,200 ft long.

Largest rink The world's largest curling rink was the Big Four Curling Rink, Calgary, Alberta, Canada, opened in 1959 and closed in 1989. Ninety-six teams and 384 players were accommodated on two floors, each with 24 sheets of ice.

CYCLING

Fastest speed The fastest speed ever achieved on a bicycle is 152.284 mph, by John Howard (USA) behind a windshield at Bonneville Salt Flats, UT on 20 Jul 1985. It should be noted that considerable help was provided by the slipstreaming effect of the lead vehicle.

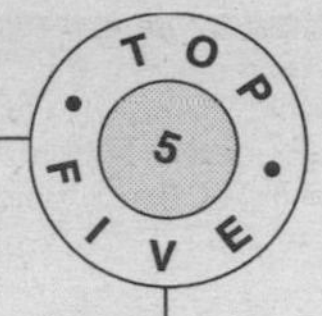

TOUR DE FRANCE STAGE WINS

Rider	Stages
Eddy Merckx (Belgium)	35
Bernard Hinault (France)	28
André Leducq (France)	25
André Darrigade (France)	22
Nicolas Frantz (Luxemburg)	20

The 24 hr record behind pace is 1,216.8 miles, by Michael Secrest at Phoenix International Raceway, AZ on 26–27 Apr 1990.

Fastest rollercycling speed James Baker (USA) achieved a record speed of 153.2 mph at El Con Mall, Tucson, AZ on 28 Jan 1989.

Most titles Olympic The most gold medals won is three, by Paul Masson (France; 1874–1945) in 1896; Francisco Verri (Italy; 1885–1945) in 1906; Robert Charpentier (France; 1916–66) in 1936; and Daniel Morelon (France) in 1968 and 1972.

Burton Cecil Down (USA; 1885–1929) won a record six medals at the 1904 Games—two gold, three silver and one bronze. The only American woman to win a cycling gold medal is Connie Carpenter-Phinney, who won the individual road race in 1984. She became the first woman to compete in both the Winter and the Summer Olympics, as she had competed as a speed skater in 1972.

World World Championships are contested annually. They were first staged for amateurs in 1893 and for professionals in 1895.

The most wins at a particular event is 10, by Koichi Nakano (Japan), professional sprint 1977–86.

The most world titles won by a US cyclist is four, at women's 3 kilometers pursuit, by Rebecca Twigg, 1982, 1984–85 and 1987. The most successful man has been Greg LeMond, winner of the individual road race in 1983 and 1989.

United States National cycling championships have been held annually since 1899. Women's events were first included in 1937.

Leonard Nitz has won the most titles, 16: five pursuit (1976 and 1980–83); eight team pursuit (1980–84, 1986 and 1988–89); two 1-km time-trial (1982 and 1984); and one criterium (1986). Rebecca Twigg has won 14 titles in women's events: five time trials (1982, 1984, 1986, 1993–94); one points race (1984); one match sprint (1984); five pursuits (1981–82, 1984, 1986, 1992); one criterium (1993); and one road race (1983).

Tour de France The greatest number of wins in the Tour de France is five, by Jacques Anquetil (France; 1934–1987), 1957, 1961–64; Eddy Merckx (Belgium), 1969–72 and 1974; and Bernard Hinault (France), 1978–79,

On his home-built bicycle Graeme Obree set the one-hour world record in 1994. His distinctive skiing-style crouch was subsequently banned for use in further attempts, but the record was confirmed. (Vandystat/Bruno Bade)

1981–82 and 1985. Greg LeMond (USA) became the first American winner in 1986, and returned from serious injury to win again in 1989 and 1990.

The closest race ever was in 1989, when after 2,030 miles over 23 days (1–23 July) Greg LeMond, who completed the Tour in 87 hr 38 min 35 sec, beat Laurent Fignon (France) in Paris, France by only 8 sec.

The fastest average speed was 24.547 mph, by Miguel Induráin (Spain) in 1992.

Women The inaugural women's Tour de France was staged in 1984. Jeannie Longo (France) has won the event a record four times, 1987–90.

Longest one-day race The longest single-day "massed start" road race is the 342–385 mile Bordeaux–Paris, France event. Paced over all or part of the route, the highest average speed was 29.32 mph, by Herman van Springel (Belgium) for 363.1 miles in 13 hr 35 min 18 sec, in 1981.

Cross-America The trans-America solo record recognized by the Ultra-Marathon Cycling Association for men is 8 days 8 hr 45 min, by Paul Selon at age 35 from Costa, CA to New York, in the 1989 Race Across AMerica. The women's record is 9 days 9 hr 9 min, by Susan Notorangelo at age 35, also in the 1989 Race Across AMerica. She clipped 16 hr 55 min off the previous women's record.

WORLD CYCLING RECORDS

These records are those recognized by the Union Cycliste Internationale (UCI). *From 1 Jan 1993 their severely reduced list no longer distinguished between those set by professionals and amateurs, indoor and outdoor, or at altitude and at sea level.*

Distance	min : sec	Name and Country	Venue	Date
Men				
Unpaced Standing Start				
1 km	1:02.091	Maic Malchow (East Germany)	Colorado Springs,CO	28 Aug 1986
4 km	4:20.894	Graeme Obree (Great Britain)	Hamar, Norway	19 Aug 1993
4 km team	4:03.822	Australia	Hamar, Norway	20 Aug 1993
Unpaced Flying Start				
200 meters	0:10.099	Vladimir Adamashvili (USSR)	Moscow, USSR	6 Aug 1990
500 meters	0:26.649	Aleksandr Kirichenko (USSR)	Moscow, USSR	29 Oct 1988
Women				
Unpaced Standing Start				
500 m	0:33.438	Galina Yenyukhina (Russia)	Moscow, Russia	29 Apr 1993
3 km	3:37.347	Rebecca Twigg (USA)	Hamar, Norway	20 Aug 1993
Unpaced Flying Start				
200 meters	0:10.831	Olga Slyusareva (Russia)	Moscow, Russia	6 Aug 1990
500 meters	0:29.655	Erika Salumäe (USSR)	Moscow, USSR	6 Aug 1987
Unpaced—One Hour				
1 hour (men)	52.713 km	Graeme Obree	Bordeaux, France	27 Apr 1994
1 hour (women)	46.353 km	Jeannie Longo (France)	Mexico City, Mexico	1 Oct 1989

Most wins Five cyclists have won two titles: Lon Haldeman, 1982–83; Pete Penseyres, 1984, 1986; and Bob Fourney, 1990–91, in the men's division; Susan Notorangelo, 1985, 1989; and Seana Hogan, 1992–93, in the women's division.

Cycling the length of the Americas Daniel Buettner, Bret Anderson, Martin Engel and Anne Knabe cycled the length of the Americas, from Prudhoe Bay, AK to the Beagle Channel, Ushuaia, Argentina from 8 Aug 1986 to 13 Jun 1987. They cycled a total distance of 15,266 miles.

Cross-Canada The trans-Canada record is 13 days 9 hr 6 min, by Bill Narasnek of Lively, Ontario, cycling 3,751 miles from Vancouver, British Columbia to Halifax, Nova Scotia on 5–18 Jul 1991.

Endurance Thomas Godwin (Great Britain; 1912–75), cycling every day during the 365 days of 1939, covered 75,065 miles, or an average of 205.65 miles per day. Continuing his effort, he went on to complete 100,000 miles in 500 days to 14 May 1940.

Jay Aldous and Matt DeWaal cycled 14,290 miles on an around-the-world trip from Place Monument, Salt Lake City, UT in 106 days, from 2 Apr–16 Jul 1984.

Tal Burt (Israel) circumnavigated the world (13,523 road miles) from Place du Trocadero, Paris, France in 77 days 14 hr, from 1 Jun–17 Aug 1992.

Greatest distance in one hour The greatest distance covered in one hour is 122.28 km, by Leon Vanderstuyft (Belgium; 1890–1964) on the Montlhéry Motor Circuit, France, on 30 Sep 1928, achieved from a standing start paced by a motorcycle.

Cycle touring The greatest mileage amassed in a cycle tour was more than 402,000 miles, by Walter Stolle from 24 Jan 1959 to 12 Dec 1976. Starting from Romford, Great Britain, he visited 159 countries. From 1922 to 25 Dec 1973, Tommy Chambers (1903–84) of Glasgow, Great Britain rode a verified total of 799,405 miles.

Visiting every continent, John W. Hathaway (Great Britain) of Vancouver, British Columbia, Canada covered 50,600 miles from 10 Nov 1974 to 6 Oct 1976.

Ronald and Sandra Slaughter hold the US record for tandem bicycling, having traveled 18,077.5 miles around the world from 30 Dec 1989 to 28 Jul 1991.

The most participants in a bicycle tour were 31,678, in the 56-mile London–to–Brighton Bike Ride (Great Britain) on 19 Jun 1988. However, it is estimated that 45,000 cyclists took part in the 44-mile Tour de l'Ile de Montréal, Canada on 7 Jun 1992. The most participants in a tour in excess of 1,000 km is 2,037 (from 2,157 starters) for the Australian Bicentennial Caltex Bike Ride from Melbourne to Sydney, from 26 Nov–10 Dec 1988.

Highest altitude cycling Canadians Bruce Bell, Philip Whelan and Suzanne MacFadyen cycled at an altitude of 22,834 ft on the peak of Mt Aconcagua, Argentina on 25 Jan 1991. This feat was matched by Mozart Hastenreiter Catão (Brazil) on 11 Mar 1993 and by Tim Sumner (Great Britain) and Jonathan Greene (Great Britain) on 6 Jan 1994.

CYCLO-CROSS

The greatest number of World Championships (instituted 1950) has been won by Eric de Vlaeminck (Belgium), with the Amateur and Open in 1966 and six Professional titles in 1968–73.

DARTS

PROFESSIONAL DARTS

Most titles Eric Bristow (Great Britain) has the most wins in the World Masters Championship (instituted 1974) with five, 1977, 1979, 1981 and 1983–84; the most in the World Professional Championship (instituted 1978) with five, 1980–81 and 1984–86; and the most in the World Cup Singles (instituted 1977) with four, 1983, 1985, 1987 and 1989.

SCORING RECORDS

Fewest darts The lowest number of darts thrown for a score of 1,001 is 19, by Cliff Inglis (Great Britain) (160, 180, 140, 180, 121, 180, 40) at the Bromfield Men's Club, Devon, Great Britain on 11 Nov 1975; and by Jocky Wilson (Great Britain) (140, 140, 180, 180, 180, 131, Bull) at The London Pride, Bletchley, Great Britain on 23 Mar 1989.

A score of 2,001 in 52 darts was achieved by Alan Evans (Great Britain) at Ferndale, Great Britain on 3 Sep 1976.

A score of 3,001 in 73 darts was thrown by Tony Benson at the Plough Inn, Gorton, Great Britain on 12 Jul 1986. Linda Batten set a women's 3,001 record of 117 darts at the Old Wheatsheaf, London, Great Britain on 2 Apr 1986.

A score of 100,001 was achieved in 3,579 darts by Chris Gray at the Dolphin, Cromer, Great Britain on 27 Apr 1993.

Roy Blowes (Canada) was the first person to achieve a 501 in nine darts, "double-on, double-off," at the Widgeons Pub, Calgary, Canada on 9 Mar 1987. His scores were: bull, treble 20, treble 17, five treble 20s and a double 20 to finish.

Highest score Team The highest score in 24 hr is 1,722,249, by the Broken Hill Darts Club (eight players) at Broken Hill, New South Wales, Australia on 28–29 Sep 1985.

DOUBLES!

The highest score by a two-man team retrieving their own darts, in six hours is 465,919 by Jon Archer and Neil Rankin on 17 Nov. 1990. They performed their record-breaking feat at the Royal Oak, Cossington, Great Britain.

The women's record is 744,439 by a team of eight players from the Lord Clyde, London, Great Britain on 13–14 Oct 1990.

Individual The highest score in 24 hr by an individual is 566,175, by Russell Locke in Hugglescote, Great Britain on 17–18 Sep 1993.

Bulls and 25s An 8-member team scored 510,625 points at the Kent and Canterbury Hospital Sports and Social Club, Canterbury, Great Britain on 20–21 Oct 1989.

Million and One Up Men (8 players): 36,583 darts by a team at Buzzy's Pub and Grub, Lynn, MA on 19–20 Oct 1991.

Women (8 players): 70,019 darts by The Delinquents darts team at the Top George Pub, Combe Martin, Great Britain on 11–13 Sep 1987.

***10-hour Bulls** (individual)* 1,261, by Glenn Silva (USA) at Thee London Pub One, Margate, FL on 13 Feb 1994.

10-hour trebles 3,056, by Paul Taylor (Great Britain) at the Woodhouse Tavern, Leytonstone, Great Britain on 19 Oct 1985.

10-hour doubles 3,265, by Paul Taylor at the Lord Brooke, Walthamstow, Great Britain on 5 Sep 1987.

SPEED RECORDS

The fastest time taken to complete three games of 301, finishing on doubles, is 1 min 38 sec, by Ritchie Gardner on the British TV show *Record Breakers*, on 12 Sep 1989.

The record time for going around the board clockwise in "doubles" at arm's length is 9.2 sec, by Dennis Gower at the Millers Arms, Hastings, Great Britain on 12 Oct 1975

The record for around-the-board in numerical order is 14.5 sec by Jim Pike (1903–60) at the Craven Club, Newmarket, Great Britain in March 1944.

The record for this feat at the 9-ft throwing distance, retrieving own darts, is 2 min 13 sec by Bill Duddy at The Plough, London, Great Britain on 29 Oct 1972.

EQUESTRIAN SPORTS

CARRIAGE DRIVING

World Championships were first held in 1972. Three team titles have been won by Great Britain, 1972, 1974 and 1980; by Hungary, 1976, 1978 and 1984; and by the Netherlands, 1982, 1986 and 1988.

Most titles Two individual titles have been won by György Bárdos (Hun-

Oncoming traffic need not be alarmed—Floyd Zopfi regularly drives his record 52-hitch llama team. (Satinwood Photography/ Floyd Zopfi)

gary), 1978 and 1980; by Tjeerd Velstra (Netherlands), 1982 and 1986; and by Ijsbrand Chardon (Netherlands), 1988 and 1992.

Most horses in a hitch The only man to drive 48 horses in a single hitch is Dick Sparrow of Zearing, IA, between 1972 and 1977. The lead horses were on reins 135 ft long.

Floyd Zopfi of Stratford, WI has driven 52 llamas in a hitch on several occasions since 1990, with the lead llamas (four abreast) on reins 150 ft long.

Coaching The longest horse-drawn procession was a cavalcade of 68 carriages that measured 3,018 ft "nose to tail," organized by the Spies Traveling Company of Denmark on 7 May 1986. It carried 810 people through the woods around Copenhagen to celebrate the coming of spring.

SHOW JUMPING

Olympic Games The most Olympic gold medals won by a rider is five, by Hans-Günter Winkler (West Germany)—four team wins in 1956, 1960,

1964 and 1972 and the individual Grand Prix in 1956. He also won team silver in 1976 and team bronze in 1968, for a record seven medals overall.

The most team wins in the Prix des Nations is six, by Germany in 1936, 1956, 1960, 1964 and as West Germany in 1972 and 1988.

The lowest score obtained by a winner is no faults, by Frantisek Ventura (Czechoslovakia; 1895–1969) on Eliot, 1928; Alwin Schockemöhle (West Germany) on Warwick Rex, 1976; and Ludger Beerbaum (Germany) on Classic Touch, 1992.

Pierre Jonquères d'Oriola (France) uniquely won the individual gold medal twice, in 1952 and 1964.

United States Two US riders have won individual gold medals: Bill Steinkraus won in 1968 and also won two silver and a bronze medal, 1952–68; and Joe Fargis won both individual and team gold medals in 1984 as well as team silver in 1988.

World Championships The men's World Championships (instituted 1953) have been won twice by Hans-Günter Winkler (1954–55) and Raimondo d'Inzeo (Italy) (1956 and 1960).

The women's title (1965–74) was won twice by Janou Tissot (nee Lefebvre; France) on Rocket (1970 and 1974). A team competition was introduced in 1978, and the most wins is two, by France, 1982 and 1990.

GUESS WHAT?

Q. HOW HIGH IS THE TALLEST FENCE?

A. SEE "SPECIALIZED STRUCTURES" (BUILDING & STRUCTURES)

President's Cup Instituted in 1965 for Nations Cup teams, it has been won a record 14 times by Great Britain, in 1965, 1967, 1970, 1972–74, 1977–79, 1983, 1985–86, 1989 and 1991.

World Cup In this competition, instituted in 1979, double winners have been Conrad Homfeld (USA), 1980 and 1985; Ian Millar (Canada), 1988 and 1989; and John Whitaker (Great Britain), 1990–91.

Jumping records The official *Fédération Equestre Internationale* records are: high jump, 8 ft 1¼ in, by Huasó, ridden by Capt. Alberto Larraguibel Morales (Chile) at Viña del Mar, Santiago, Chile on 5 Feb 1949; long jump over water, 27 ft 6¾ in, by Something, ridden by André Ferreira (South Africa) at Johannesburg, South Africa on 25 Apr 1975.

THREE-DAY EVENT

Olympic Games and World Championships Charles Pahud de Mortanges (Netherlands; 1896–1971) won a record four Olympic gold medals—team 1924 and 1928, individual (riding Marcroix) 1928 and 1932; he also won a team silver medal in 1932.

Bruce Davidson (USA) is the only rider to have won two world titles (instituted 1966), on Irish Cap in 1974 and on Might Tango in 1978.

United States The most medals won for the USA is six, by J. Michael Plumb: team gold 1976 and 1984, and four silver medals, team 1964, 1968 and 1972, and individual 1976. Tad Coffin is the only US rider to have won both team and individual gold medals in 1976.

Badminton Horse Trials The Badminton Three-Day Event, instituted in 1949, is the premier annual competition in the sport. British horsewoman Lucinda Green (nee Prior-Palmer) has won the event a record six times, 1973 (on Be Fair), 1976 (Wide Awake), 1977 (George), 1979 (Killaire), 1983 (Regal Realm), and 1984 (Beagle Bay).

DRESSAGE

Olympic Games and World Championships Germany (West Germany 1968–90) has won a record eight team Olympic gold medals, 1928, 1936, 1964, 1968, 1976, 1984, 1988, and 1992, and has the most team wins, six, at the World Championships (instituted 1966). Dr Reiner Klimke (West Germany) has won a record six Olympic golds (team 1964–88, individual, 1984). He won individual bronze in 1976, for a record seven medals overall, and is the only rider to have won two world titles, on Mehmed in 1974 and on Ahlerich in 1982. Henri St Cyr (Sweden; 1904–79) won a record two individual Olympic gold medals, in 1952 and 1956. This was equaled by Nicole Uphoff (Germany) in 1992; she had previously won in 1988.

World Cup Instituted in 1986, this competition has had only one double winner: Christine Stückelberger (Switzerland) on Gauguin de Lully in 1987–88.

FENCING

Most titles *Olympic* The most individual Olympic gold medals won is three, by Ramón Fonst (Cuba; 1883–1959) in 1900 and 1904 (two); and by Nedo Nadi (Italy; 1894–1952) in 1912 and 1920 (two). Nadi also won three team gold medals in 1920, making five gold medals at one celebration, the record for fencing. Aladár Gerevich (Hungary) won seven golds—one individual and six team.

Edoardo Mangiarotti (Italy), with six gold, five silver and two bronze, holds the record of 13 Olympic medals in fencing. He won them for foil and épée from 1936 to 1960.

The most gold medals won by a woman is four (one individual, three team) by Yelena Novikova (nee Belova; USSR) from 1968 to 1976, and the women's record for all medals is seven (two gold, three silver, two bronze) by Ildikó Sági (formerly Ujlaki, nee Retjö; Hungary) from 1960 to 1976.

United States The only US Olympic champion was Albertson Van Zo Post (1866–1938), who won the men's single sticks and team foil (with two Cubans) at the 1904 Games.

FOILED!

Danish fencer Ivan Osiier is one of five athletes to have competed in the Olympic Games over a span of 40 years, 1908–48. During this span he won only one medal—a silver at épée in 1930. Happily his wife Ellen put the family atop the Olympic podium when she won the women's foil in 1924. No doubt a case of all for one and one for all.

World The greatest number of individual world titles won is five, by Aleksandr Romankov (USSR), at foil 1974, 1977, 1979, 1982 and 1983. Christian d'Oriola (France) won four world foil titles, 1947, 1949, 1953–54, as well as two individual Olympic titles (1952 and 1956).

Four women foilists have won three world titles: Helene Mayer (Germany; 1910–53), 1929, 1931, 1937; Ilona Schacherer-Elek (Hungary; 1907–88), 1934–35, 1951; Ellen Müller-Preis (Austria), 1947, 1949–50; and

Cornelia Hanisch (West Germany), 1979, 1981, 1985. Of these only Ilona Schacherer-Elek also won two individual Olympic titles (1936 and 1948).

The longest time span for winning an individual world or Olympic title is 20 years, by Aladár Gerevich (Hungary) at saber, 1935–55.

United States National Championships The most US titles won at one weapon is 12 at saber, by Peter J. Westbrook, in 1974, 1975, 1979–86, 1988 and 1989. The women's record is 10 at foil, by Janice Romary in 1950–51, 1956–57, 1960–61, 1964–66 and 1968.

The most men's individual foil championships won is eight, by Michael Marx in 1977, 1979, 1982, 1985–87, 1990 and 1993. L. G. Nunes won the most épée championships, with six—1917, 1922, 1924, 1926, 1928 and 1932. Vincent Bradford won a record number of women's épée championships with four in 1982–84 and 1986.

NCAA Championship Division I *(Men)* Inaugurated in 1941, this event was discontinued in 1989. It was won a record 12 times by New York University (1947, 1954, 1957, 1960–61, 1966–67, 1970–71, 1973–74, 1976). Since 1989 it has been replaced by a combined team title.

Michael Lofton, New York University, has won the most titles in a career, with four victories in saber, 1984–87. Abraham Balk, New York University, is the only man to win two individual titles in one year, 1947 (foil and épée).

(Women) Inaugurated in 1982, Wayne State (MI) has won the most titles: three (1982, 1988–89).

Caitlin Bilodeaux (Columbia-Barnard) and Molly Sullivan (Notre Dame) have both won the individual title twice—Bilodeaux in 1985 and 1987; Sullivan in 1986 and 1988.

(Team) In 1990, the NCAA team competition was combined for the first time. Two teams have won two titles: Penn State (1990–91); and Columbia-Barnard (1992–93).

FIELD HOCKEY

Most Olympic medals India was Olympic champion from the reintroduction of Olympic hockey in 1928 until 1960, when Pakistan beat India 1–0 in Rome. India had its eighth win in 1980.

A women's tournament was added in 1980, and there have been four separate winners: Zimbabwe, Netherlands, Australia and Spain.

United States US men won the bronze medal in 1932, but only three teams played that year; US women won the bronze in 1984.

Field hockey World Cup The World Cup for men was first held in 1971, and for women in 1974. The most wins are: (*men*) three by Pakistan, 1971, 1978 and 1982; (*women*) five by the Netherlands, 1974, 1978, 1983, 1986 and 1990.

MEN

Highest international score The highest score was achieved when India defeated the USA 24–1 at Los Angeles, CA in the 1932 Olympic Games.

Most international appearances Heiner Dopp represented West Germany 286 times between 1975 and 1990, indoors and out.

Greatest scoring feats The greatest number of goals scored in international hockey is 267, by Paul Litjens (Netherlands) in 177 games.

Best goalkeeping Richard Allen (India) did not concede a goal during the 1928 Olympic tournament and gave up a total of only three in 1936.

Fastest goal in an international field hockey game John French scored 7 sec after the bully-off for England *v* West Germany at Nottingham, Great Britain on 25 Apr 1971.

WOMEN

Most international appearances Alison Ramsay has made a record 234 international appearances, 127 for Scotland and 107 for Great Britain, 1982–94.

United States Sheryl Johnson made a record 137 appearances for the USA from 1978 to 1989.

Highest scores The highest score in an international game was when England beat France 23–0 at Merton, London, Great Britain on 3 Feb 1923.

NCAA Division I In this competition, inaugurated in 1981, Old Dominion University, Norfolk, VA has won the most championships with seven titles: 1982–84, 1988 and 1990–92.

FISHING

Largest single catch The largest officially ratified fish ever caught on a rod was a man-eating great white shark (*Carcharodon carcharias*) weighing 2,664 lb and measuring 16 ft 10 in long, caught on a 130 lb test line by Alf Dean at Denial Bay, near Ceduna, South Australia on 21 Apr 1959. A great white shark weighing 3,388 lb was caught by Clive Green off Albany, Western Australia on 26 Apr 1976 but will remain unratified, as whale meat was used as bait.

In June 1978 a great white shark measuring 20 ft 4 in in length and weighing over 5,000 lb was harpooned and landed by fishermen in the harbor of San Miguel, Azores.

The largest marine animal killed by *hand* harpoon was a blue whale 97 ft in length, by Archer Davidson in Twofold Bay, New South Wales, Australia in 1910. Its tail flukes measured 20 ft across and its jawbone 23 ft 4 in.

The largest fish ever taken underwater was an 804 lb giant black grouper by Don Pinder of the Miami Triton Club, FL in 1955.

Longest fight The longest recorded individual fight with a fish is 37 hr, by Bob Ploeger (USA) with a King salmon on 12–13 Jul 1989.

World Freshwater Championship France won the European title in 1956 and 12 world titles between 1959 and 1990. Robert Tesse (France) took the individual title a record three times, 1959–60 and 1965.

The record weight (team) is 76.52 lb in 3 hr by West Germany on the Neckar at Mannheim, Germany on 21 Sep 1980. The individual record is 37.45 lb by Wolf-Rüdiger Kremkus (West Germany) at Mannheim on 20 Sep 1980. The most fish caught is 652, by Jacques Isenbaert (Belgium) at Danaújváros, Hungary on 27 Aug 1967.

IGFA World Records The heaviest freshwater category recognized by the IGFA is for the sturgeon; the record weight in this category is 468 lb, caught by Joey Pallotta III on 9 Jul 1983 off Benicia, CA.

Fly fishing World fly fishing championships were inaugurated by the CIPS in 1981. The most team titles is five, by Italy, 1982–84, 1986, 1992. The most individual titles is two, by Brian Leadbetter (Great Britain), 1987 and 1991.

Casting The longest freshwater cast ratified under ICF (International Casting Federation) rules is 574 ft 2 in, by Walter Kummerow (Germany), for the Bait Distance Double-Handed 30 g event held at Lenzerheide, Switzerland in the 1968 Championships.

At the currently contested weight of 17.7 g, known as 18 g Bait Distance, the longest Double-Handed cast is 457 ft 1/2 in, by Kevin Carriero (USA) at Toronto, Ontario, Canada on 24 Jul 1984.

The longest Fly Distance Double-Handed cast is 319 ft 1 in, by Wolfgang Feige (Germany) at Toronto, Ontario, Canada on 23 Jul 1984.

FOOTBAG

This sport originated in Oregon in 1972. Its inventor was John Stalberger (USA).

Men's singles The world record for keeping a footbag airborne is 51,155 consecutive kicks or hacks, by Ted Martin (USA) at Mount Prospect, IL on 29 May 1993.

Women's singles The women's record is held by Francine Beaudry (Canada), with 15,458 on 28 Jul 1987 at Golden, CO.

Men's doubles The record is 100,001 hacks, by Andy Linder and Ted Martin (both USA) on 9 Apr 1994 in Mount Prospect, IL. The pair kept the footbag aloft for 15 hr 38 min 40 sec.

Women's doubles The record is 21,025 hacks, by Constance Reed and Marie Elsner (both USA) on 31 Jul 1986. The pair kept the footbag aloft for 3 hr 6 min 37 sec.

Five minutes The greatest number of kicks in five minutes is 912, by Kenny Shults (USA) at Golden, CO on 30 Jul 1991, and for women the record is 747 by Tricia George (USA) on 29 Aug 1993, at Seaside, OR.

Footbag circle The largest continuous circle of people playing footbag was 862. This gathering of well-rounded people was staged at Colorado State University in Fort Collins on 24 Jun 1986.

FOOTBALL

NATIONAL FOOTBALL LEAGUE (NFL) RECORDS

Most championships The Green Bay Packers have won a record 11 NFL titles, 1929–31, 1936, 1939, 1944, 1961–62, 1965–67.

Most consecutive wins (regular season and playoffs) The Chicago Bears have won 18 consecutive games twice, in 1933–34 and 1941–42. This was matched by the Miami Dolphins in 1972–73 and by the San Francisco 49ers in 1989–90. The most consecutive games without defeat is 25, by the Canton Bulldogs (22 wins and 3 ties) in 1921–23.

Most games played George Blanda played in a record 340 games in a record 26 seasons in the NFL, for the Chicago Bears (1948–58), the Baltimore Colts (1950), the Houston Oilers (1960–66), and the Oakland Raiders (1967–75).

The most consecutive games played is 282, by Jim Marshall for the Cleveland Browns (1960) and the Minnesota Vikings (1961–79).

Longest run from scrimmage Tony Dorsett completed a touchdown after a run of 99 yards for the Dallas Cowboys *v* the Minnesota Vikings on 3 Jan 1983.

Longest field goal 63 yards by Tom Dempsey for the New Orleans Saints *v* the Detroit Lions, 8 Nov 1970.

Longest pass completion Pass completions for a touchdown of 99 yards were achieved by Frank Filchok (to Andy Farkas), Washington Redskins *v* Pittsburgh Steelers, 15 Oct 1939; George Izo (to Bobby Mitchell), Washington Redskins *v* Cleveland Browns, 15 Sep 1963; Karl Sweetan (to Pat Studstill), Detroit Lions *v* Baltimore Colts, 16 Oct 1966; Sonny Jurgensen (to Gerry Allen), Washington Redskins *v* Chicago Bears, 15 Sep 1968; Jim

NFL RECORDS

Most Points

Career 2,002, George Blanda (Chicago Bears, Baltimore Colts, Houston Oilers, Oakland Raiders), 1949–75. **Season** 176, Paul Hornung (Green Bay Packers), 1960. **Game** 40, Ernie Nevers (Chicago Cardinals), 28 Nov 1929.

Most Touchdowns

Career 126, Jim Brown (Cleveland Browns), 1957–65. **Season** 24, John Riggins (Washington Redskins), 1983. **Game** 6, Ernie Nevers (Chicago Cardinals), 28 Nov 1929; William "Dub" Jones (Cleveland Browns) 25 Nov 1951; Gale Sayers (Chicago Bears), 12 Dec 1965.

Most Yards Gained Rushing

Career 16,726, Walter Payton (Chicago Bears), 1975–87. **Season** 2,105, Eric Dickerson (Los Angeles Rams), 1984. **Game** 275, Walter Payton (Chicago Bears), 20 Nov 1977. **Highest career average** 5.22 yds per game (12,352 yds from 2,359 attempts), Jim Brown (Cleveland Browns), 1957–65.

Most Yards Gained Receiving

Career 14,020, James Lofton (Green Bay Packers, Los Angeles Raiders, Buffalo Bills, Los Angeles Rams, Philadelphia Eagles), 1978–93. **Season** 1,746, Charley Hennigan (Houston Oilers), 1961. Game 336, Willie "Flipper" Anderson (Los Angeles Rams), 26 Nov 1989.

Most Yards Gained Passing

Career 47,003, Fran Tarkenton (Minnesota Vikings, New York Giants), 1961–78. **Season** 5,084, Dan Marino (Miami Dolphins), 1984. **Game** 554, Norm Van Brocklin (Los Angeles Rams), 28 Sep 1951.

Passing Attempts

Career 6,467, Fran Tarkenton (Minnesota Vikings, New York Giants), 1961–78. **Season** 655, Warren Moon (Houston Oilers), 1991. **Game** 68, George Blanda (Houston Oilers), 1 Nov 1964.

Most Passes Completed

Career 3,686, Fran Tarkenton (Minnesota Vikings, New York Giants), 1961–78. **Season** 404, Warren Moon (Houston Oilers), 1991. **Game** 42 (from 59 attempts), Richard Todd (New York Jets), 21 Sep 1980. **Consecutive** 22, Joe Montana (San Francisco 49ers), 29 Nov 1987 *v* Cleveland Browns (5); 6 Dec 1987 *v* Green Bay Packers (17).

Pass Receptions

Career 888, Art Monk (Washington Redskins), 1980–93. **Season** 112, Sterling Sharpe (Green Bay Packers), 1993. **Game** 18, Tom Fears (Los Angeles Rams), 3 Dec 1950.

Field Goals

Career 373, Jan Stenerud (Kansas City Chiefs, Green Bay Packers, Minnesota Vikings), 1967–85. **Season** 35, Ali Haji-Sheikh (New York Giants), 1983. **Game** 7, Jim Bakken (St Louis Cardinals), 24 Sep 1967; Rich Karlis (Minnesota Vikings), 5 Nov 1989.

Punting

Career 1,154, Dave Jennings (New York Giants, New York Jets), 1974–87. **Season** 114, Bob Parsons (Chicago Bears), 1981. **Game** 15, John Teltschik (Philadelphia Eagles *v* New York Giants), 6 Dec 1987.

Sacks

Career 137, Reggie White (Philadelphia Eagles, Green Bay Packers), 1985–93. **Season** 22, Mark Gastineau (New York Jets), 1984. **Game** 7, Derrick Thomas (Kansas City Chiefs *v* Seattle Seahawks), 11 Nov 1990.

Most Interceptions

Career 81, Paul Krause (Washington Redskins, Minnesota Vikings), 1964–79. **Season** 14, Dick "Night Train" Lane (Los Angeles Rams), 1952. **Game** 4; 16 players have achieved this feat.

Plunkett (to Cliff Branch), Los Angeles Raiders *v* Washington Redskins, 2 Oct 1983; and Ron Jaworski (to Mike Quick), Philadelphia Eagles *v* Atlanta Falcons, 10 Nov 1985.

Longest punt 98 yards by Steve O'Neal for the New York Jets *v* the Denver Broncos, 21 Sep 1969.

Interception return The longest interception return is 103 yd, by two players: Vencie Glenn, San Diego Chargers *v* Denver Broncos, 29 Nov 1987; and Louis Oliver, Miami Dolphins *v* Buffalo Bills, 4 Oct 1992, both for touchdowns.

Kickoff return Three players share the record for a kickoff return at 106 yd: Al Carmichael, Green Bay Packers *v* Chicago Bears, 7 Oct 1956; Noland Smith, Kansas City Chiefs *v* Denver Broncos, 17 Dec 1967; and Roy Green, St Louis Cardinals *v* Dallas Cowboys, 21 Oct 1979. All three players scored touchdowns.

Punt return Four players share the record for the longest punt return at 98 yd: Gil LeFebvre, Cincinnati Reds *vs* Brooklyn Dodgers, 3 Dec 1933; Charlie West, Minnesota Vikings *v* Washington Redskins, 3 Nov 1968; Dennis Morgan, Dallas Cowboys *v* St Louis Cardinals, 13 Oct 1974; and Terance Mathis, New York Jets *v* Dallas Cowboys, 4 Nov 1990. All four players rumbled all the way to the end zone for touchdowns.

Consecutive games *Scoring* 186, by Jim Breech for the Oakland Raiders, 1979, and the Cincinnati Bengals, 1980–92.

Scoring touchdowns 18, by Lenny Moore for the Baltimore Colts, 1963–65.

Touchdown passes 47, by Johnny Unitas, Baltimore Colts, 1956–60.

Touchdown rushes 13, by two players: John Riggins, Washington Redskins, 1982–83; George Rogers, Washington Redskins, 1985–86.

Touchdown receptions 13, by Jerry Rice, San Francisco 49ers, 1986–87.

Pass receptions 177, by Steve Largent for the Seattle Seahawks, 1977–89.

Field goals 29, by John Carney, San Diego Chargers, 1992–93.

Largest deficit overcome On 3 Jan 1993 the Buffalo Bills, playing at home in the AFC Wild Card game, trailed the Houston Oilers 35–3 with 28 minutes remaining. The Bills rallied to score 35 unanswered ponts and take the lead with 3:08 left. The Bills eventually won the game in overtime, overcoming a deficit of 32 points—the largest in NFL history.

Coaches The winningest coach in NFL history is Don Shula, with 327 victories—73 with the Baltimore Colts (1963–69) and 254 with the Miami Dolphins (1970–present). The highest winning percentage was .740, achieved by Vince Lombardi (1913–70): 105 wins, 35 losses and 6 ties with the Green Bay Packers, 1959–67, and the Washington Redskins, 1969.

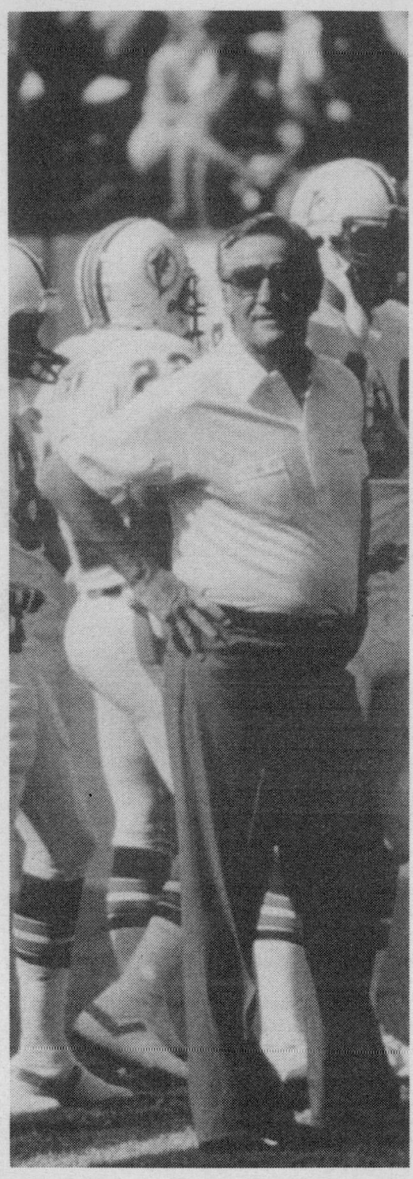

DID YOU KNOW?

The only team to win all its games in one season was the 1972 Miami Dolphins. The Dolphins won 14 regular-season games and then won three playoff games. The only perfect season in NFL history concluded when the Dolphins defeated the Washington Redskins 14–7 in Super Bowl VII.

Don Shula has won more NFL games than any other coach. It's safe to say that his Dolphins are well schooled. (Allsport/Caryn Levy)

Most seasons 40, George Halas, with the Decatur/Chicago Staleys/ Chicago Bears (1920–29, 1933–42, 1946–55, 1958–67).

THE SUPER BOWL

The Super Bowl was first held in 1967 between the winners of the NFL and AFL championships. Since 1970 it has been contested by the winners of the National and American Conferences of the NFL. The most wins is four, by the Pittsburgh Steelers in 1974–75, 1978–79; the San Francisco 49ers in 1981, 1984, 1988–89; and the Dallas Cowboys in 1972, 1978, 1992–93.

Most appearances The Dallas Cowboys have played in seven Super Bowls: V, VI, X, XII, XIII, XXVII and XXVIII. The Cowboys have won four and lost three.

Don Shula has coached six Super Bowls to set the all-time mark: Baltimore Colts, 1968; Miami Dolphins, 1971–73, 1982, 1984. He won two games and lost four.

Highest scores The highest aggregate score was 69 points, when the Dallas Cowboys beat the Buffalo Bills 52–17 on 31 Jan 1993, in Super Bowl XXVII. The highest team score and record victory margin was when the San Francisco 49ers beat the Denver Broncos 55–10 in New Orleans, LA on 28 Jan 1990.

Smallest margin of victory The narrowest margin of victory was one point, when the New York Giants defeated the Buffalo Bills 20–19 on 27 Jan 1991.

Individual game records Points The most points scored is 18 by two players: Roger Craig, San Francisco 49ers (*v* Denver Broncos, 1989) and Jerry Rice, San Francisco 49ers (*v* Denver Broncos, 1989).

Touchdowns The most touchdowns thrown is 5 by Joe Montana, San Francisco 49ers (*v* Denver Broncos, 1989). The most touchdowns scored is 3 by two players: Roger Craig, San Francisco 49ers (*v* Miami Dolphins, 1984) and Jerry Rice, San Francisco 49ers (*v* Denver Broncos, 1989).

Yards gained The most yards gained rushing is 204 by Timmy Smith, Washington Redskins (*v* Denver Broncos, 1987). The most yards gained passing is 357 by Joe Montana, San Francisco 49ers (*v* Cincinnati Bengals, 1988). The most yards gained receiving is 215 by Jerry Rice, San Francisco 49ers (*v* Cincinnati Bengals, 1988).

Completions The most completions thrown is 31 by Jim Kelly, Buffalo Bills (*v* Dallas Cowboys, 1994). The highest pass completion mark is 88 percent (22–25) by Phil Simms, New York Giants (*v* Denver Broncos, 1986).

Receptions The most receptions is 11 by two players: Dan Ross, Cincinnati Bengals (*v* San Francisco 49ers, 1981) and Jerry Rice, San Francisco 49ers (*v* Cincinnati Bengals, 1988).

49ers receiver Jerry Rice holds several NFL and Super Bowl records for receptions and touchdowns. (Allsport/Otto Gruele Jr.)

COLLEGE FOOTBALL (NCAA)

Team records Most wins Michigan has won 739 games out of 1,017 played, 1879–1993.

Highest winning percentage The highest winning percentage in college football history is .762, by Notre Dame. The Fighting Irish have won 723, lost 211 and tied 41 out of 975 games played, 1887–1993.

Career records (Divisions 1-A, 1-AA, II and III) *Points scored* 474, Joe Dudek, Plymouth State (Div. III), 1982–85.

Rushing (yards) 6,320, Johnny Bailey, Texas A&I (Div. II), 1986–89.

Passing (yards) 15,031, Ty Detmer, Brigham Young (Div. I-A), 1988–91.

Receptions (yards) 4,693, Jerry Rice, Mississippi Valley (Div. 1-AA), 1981–84.

Receptions (most) 301, Jerry Rice, Mississippi Valley (Div. 1-AA), 1981–84.

Field goals (game) 8, Goran Lingmerth, Northern Arizona (Div. 1-AA). Booting 8 out of 8 kicks, Lingmerth set the record on 25 Oct 1986 *v* Idaho.

Consecutive games *Scoring touchdowns* 23, by Bill Burnett, Arkansas. Burnett amassed 47 touchdowns during his 23-game streak, which ran from 5 Oct 1968 to 31 Oct 1970.

Touchdown passes 35, by Ty Detmer, Brigham Young, 7 Sep 1989–23 Nov 1991.

Touchdown receptions 12, by two players: Desmond Howard, Michigan, 1990–91; and Aaron Turner, Pacific (Cal.), 1990–91.

Consecutive touchdown passes 6, by Brooks Dawson, UTEP *v* New Mexico, 28 Oct 1967. Dawson completed his first six passes for touchdowns, which must rank as the greatest start to a game ever!

Longest streak The University of Oklahoma won 47 successive games from 1953 to 1957, when they were beaten 7–0 by Notre Dame. The longest unbeaten streak is 63 (59 won, 4 tied) by Washington from 1907 to 1917, ended by a 27–0 loss to California.

Coaches In Division 1-A competition, Paul "Bear" Bryant (1913–83) won more games than any other coach, with 323 wins over 38 years: Maryland 1945, Kentucky 1946–53, Texas A&M 1954–57 and Alabama 1958–82. He led Alabama to five national titles and 15 bowl wins, including seven Sugar Bowls. The best win percentage in Division 1-A was 0.881, by Knute Rockne (1888–1931), with 105 wins, 12 losses and 5 ties, 12,847 points for and 667 against, at Notre Dame 1918–30. In overall NCAA competition, Eddie Robinson, Grambling (Division 1-AA) holds the mark for most victories, with 388 through 1993.

NCAA DIVISION 1-A INDIVIDUAL RECORDS

Record	Value	Holder	Date
Points			
Game	48	Howard Griffith (Illinois *v* Southern Illinois; 8 touchdowns)	22 Sep 1990
Season	234	Barry Sanders (Oklahoma State; 39 touchdowns in 11 games)	1988
Career	423	Roman Anderson (Houston; 70 field goals, 213 point-after-touchdowns)	1988–91
Total yardage			
Game	732	David Klingler (Houston *v* Arizona State; 716 passing, 16 rushing)	1 Dec 1990
Season	5,221	David Klingler (Houston; 5,140 passing, 81 rushing)	1990
Career	14,665	Ty Detmer (Brigham Young; 15,031 passing, 366 rushing)	1988–91
Yards gained rushing			
Game	396	Tony Sands (Kansas *v* Missouri)	23 Nov 1991
Season	2,628	Barry Sanders (Oklahoma State; 344 rushes in 11 games, record av. 238.9)	1988
Career	6,082	Tony Dorsett (Pittsburgh)	1973–76
Yards gained passing			
Game	716	David Klingler (Houston *v* Arizona State)	1 Dec 1990
Season	5,188	Ty Detmer (Brigham Young)	1990
Career	15,031	Ty Detmer (Brigham Young; completed 958 of 1,530)	1988–91
Pass completions			
Game	48	David Klingler (Houston *v* SMU)	20 Oct 1990
Season	374	David Klingler (Houston)	1990
Career	958	Ty Detmer (Brigham Young; 1,530 attempts)	1988–91
Touchdown passes			
Game	11	David Klingler (Houston *v* Eastern Washington)	17 Nov 1990
Season	54	David Klingler (Houston)	1990
Career	121	Ty Detmer (Brigham Young)	1988–91

Category	Record	Holder	Date
Pass receptions			
Game	22	Jay Miller (Brigham Young *v* New Mexico; 263 yards)	3 Nov 1973
Season	142	Emmanuel Hazard (Houston)	1989
Career	266	Aaron Turner (Pacific)	1989–92
Yards gained receiving			
Game	349	Chuck Hughes (UTEP *v* North Texas; caught 10)	18 Sep 1965
Season	1,779	Howard Twilley (Tulsa; caught 134 in 10 games)	1965
Career	4,345	Aaron Turner (Pacific)	1989–92
Pass interceptions			
Game	5	Dan Rebsch (Miami [Ohio] *v* Western Michigan; 88 yards; three others with less yards)	4 Nov 1972
Season	14	Al Worley (Washington; 130 yards, in 10 games)	1968
Career	29	Al Brosky (Illinois; 356 yards, 27 games)	1950–52
Touchdowns (receiving)			
Game	6	Tim Delaney (San Diego State *v* New Mexico State)	15 Nov 1969
Season	22	Emmanuel Hazard (Houston)	1989
Career	43	Aaron Turner (Pacific)	1989–92
Field goals			
Game	7	Mike Prindle (West Michigan *v* Marshall)	29 Sep 1984
	7	Dale Klein (Nebraska *v* Missouri)	19 Oct 1985
Season	29	John Lee (UCLA)	1984
Career	80	Jeff Jaeger (Washington)	1983–86
Consecutive	30	Chuck Nelson (Washington)	1981–82
Touchdowns			
Game	8	Howard Griffith (Illinois *v* Southern Illinois)	22 Sep 1990
Season	39	Barry Sanders (Oklahoma State)	1988
Career	65	Anthony Thompson (Indiana)	1986–89

Record attendances The highest attendances at college football games were estimated crowds of 120,000 at Soldier Field, Chicago, IL on 26 Nov 1927 when Notre Dame beat Southern California 7–6, and on 13 Oct 1928 when Notre Dame beat Navy 7–0. The highest average attendance for home games was 105,867 for the six games played by Michigan in 1992.

National College Football Champions The most wins in the national journalists' poll, established in 1936, to determine the college team of the year is eight by Notre Dame, 1943, 1946–47, 1949, 1966, 1973, 1977 and 1988.

Bowl games The oldest college bowl game is the Rose Bowl. It was first played on 1 Jan 1902 at Tournament Park, Pasadena, CA, when Michigan beat Stanford 49–0. The University of Southern California (USC) has a record 19 wins in the Rose Bowl. The University of Alabama has made a record 46 bowl appearances and had 26 wins. Most wins in the other "big four" bowl games: Orange Bowl: 11, Oklahoma; Sugar Bowl: 8, Alabama; Cotton Bowl: 9, Texas. Alabama, Georgia, Georgia Tech and Notre Dame are the only four teams to have won each of the "big four" bowl games.

Gaelic football action at Croke Park, site of the annual All-Ireland championship. (Allsport/Billy Strickland)

Heisman Memorial Trophy The only double winner has been Archie Griffin of Ohio State, 1974–75. The University of Notre Dame has had more Heisman Trophy winners than any other school, with seven selections.

GAELIC FOOTBALL

All-Ireland Championships The greatest number of All-Ireland Championships won by one team is 30, by Ciarraidhe (Kerry) between 1903 and 1986. The greatest number of successive wins is four, by Wexford (1915–18) and Kerry twice (1929–32, 1978–81).

The most finals contested by an individual is 10, including eight wins by the Kerry players Pat Spillane, Paudie O'Shea and Denis Moran, 1975–76, 1978–82, 1984–86.

The highest team score in a final was when Dublin, 27 (5 goals, 12 points), beat Armagh, 15 (3 goals, 6 points), on 25 Sep 1977. The highest combined score was 45 points, when Cork (26) beat Galway (19) in 1973. A goal equals three points.

The highest individual score in an All-Ireland final has been 2 goals, 6 points by Jimmy Keaveney (Dublin) *v* Armagh, in 1977, and by Michael Sheehy (Kerry) *v* Dublin in 1979.

Largest crowd The record crowd was 90,556 for the Down *v* Offaly final at Croke Park, Dublin in 1961.

GOLF

Oldest club The oldest club of which there is written evidence is the Gentlemen Golfers (now the Honourable Company of Edinburgh Golfers) formed in March 1744. The Royal Burgess Golfing Society of Edinburgh, Great Britain claims to have been founded in 1735.

United States Two golf clubs claim to be the first established in the United States: the Foxburg Golf Club, Clarion Co., PA (1887) and St Andrews Golf Club of Yonkers, NY (1888).

Largest tournament The Volkswagen Grand Prix Open Amateur Championship in Great Britain attracted a record 321,778 (206,820 men and 114,958 women) competitors in 1984.

Longest course The world's longest course is the par-77 8,325 yd International Golf Club in Bolton, MA from the "Tiger" tees, remodeled in 1969 by Robert Trent Jones.

Floyd Satterlee Rood used the entire United States as a course, when he played from the Pacific surf to the Atlantic surf from 14 Sep 1963 to 3 Oct 1964 in 114,737 strokes. He lost 3,511 balls on the 3,397.7 mile trail.

Largest green Probably the largest green in the world is that of the par-6 695 yd fifth hole at International Golf Club, Bolton, MA with an area greater than 28,000 ft^2.

BIRDIE!

The official PGA Tour record for consecutive birdies is 8, recorded by three players: Bob Goalby, during the 4th round of the 1961 St Petersburg Open; Fuzzy Zoeller, during the opening round of the 1976 Quad Cities Open; and Dewey Arnette, during the opening round of the 1987 Buick Open. Goalby was the only one to win his event.

Biggest bunker The world's biggest bunker is Hell's Half Acre on the 585 yd seventh hole of the Pine Valley course, Clementon, NJ, built in 1912 and generally regarded as the world's most trying course.

Longest hole The longest hole in the world is the sixth hole (par-7) of the Koolan Island Golf Course, Western Australia, which measures 948 yd.

United States The longest hole in the United States is the twelfth hole at Meadows Farm Golf Course in Locust Grove, VA, at a distance of 841 yd.

Longest drives The greatest recorded drive on a standard course is one of 515 yd, by Michael Hoke Austin of Los Angeles, CA, in the US National Seniors Open Championship at Las Vegas, NV on 25 Sep 1974. Austin drove the ball to within a yard of the green on the par-4 450 yd fifth hole of the Winterwood course and it rolled 65 yd past the flagstick. He was aided by an estimated 35 mph tailwind.

A drive of 2,640 yd (1½ miles) across ice was achieved by an Australian meteorologist named Nils Lied at Mawson Base, Antarctica in 1962.

Most balls hit in one hour The most balls driven in one hour, over 100 yds and into a target area, is 1,536, by Noel Hunt at Shrigley Hall, Pott Shrigley, Great Britain on 2 May 1990.

Longest putt The longest recorded holed putt in a professional tournament is 110 ft, by Jack Nicklaus in the 1964 Tournament of Champions; and by Nick Price in the 1992 United States PGA Championship.

Bob Cook (USA) sank a putt measured at 140 ft 2¾ in on the 18th at St Andrews, Great Britain in the International Fourball Pro Am Tournament on 1 Oct 1976.

SCORES

Lowest 18 holes Men At least four players have played a long course (over

6,561 yd) in a score of 58—most recently Monte Carlo Money (USA), at the par-72, 6,607 yd Las Vegas Municipal Golf Club, NV on 11 Mar 1981.

The PGA tournament record for 18 holes is 59 (30 + 29), by Al Geiberger in the second round of the Danny Thomas Classic, on the 72-par 7,249 yd Colonial Golf Club course, Memphis, TN on 10 Jun 1977; and by Chip Beck in the third round of the Las Vegas Invitational, on the 72-par 6,979 yd Sunrise Golf Club course, Las Vegas, NV on 11 Oct 1991.

Women The lowest score on an 18-hole course over 5,000 yd is 60 (31 + 29) by Wanda Morgan, on the Westgate and Birchington Golf Club course, Kent, Great Britain, on 11 Jul 1929.

The lowest recorded score in an LPGA tour event on an 18-hole course (over 5,600 yd) is 62 (30 + 32) by Mickey Wright (USA) on the Hogan Park Course (par-71, 6,286 yd) at Midland, TX, in November 1964; Vicki Fergon at the 1984 San Jose Classic, San Jose, CA; Laura Davies (Great Britain) (32 + 30) at the Rail Golf Club, Springfield, IL on 31 Aug 1991; and Hollis Stacy (USA) (30 + 32) at the Meridian Valley CC, Seattle, WA on 18 Sep 1992.

Lowest 72 holes *Men* Horton Smith scored 245 (63, 58, 61 and 63) for 72 holes on the 4,700 yd course (par-64) at Catalina Country Club, CA to win the Catalina Open on 21–23 Dec 1928.

The lowest 72 holes in a PGA tour event is 257 (60, 68, 64, 65), by Mike Souchak in the 1955 Texas Open at San Antonio.

Women Trish Johnson (Great Britain) scored 242 (64, 60, 60, 58; 21 under par) in the Bloor Homes Eastleigh Classic at the Fleming Park Course (4,402 yd) at Eastleigh, Great Britain on 22–25 Jul 1987.

The lowest score in an LPGA tour event is 267 (68, 66, 67, 66), by Betsy King in the 1992 Mazda LPGA championship.

Most shots under par 35, by Tom Kite at the 90-hole 1993 Bob Hope Chrysler Classic, 11–14 Feb 1993.

Fastest rounds *Individual* With wide variations in the lengths of courses, speed records, even for rounds under par, are of little comparative value. The fastest round played with the golf ball coming to rest before each new stroke is 27 min 9 sec, by James Carvill at Warrenpoint Golf Course, County Down, Northern Ireland (18 holes, 6,154 yd) on 18 Jun 1987.

Team The 35 members of the Team Balls Out Diving completed the 18-hole 5,516 meter John E. Clark course at Point Micu, CA in 9 min 39 sec on 16 Nov 1992. They scored 71.

Most holes in 24 hours *On foot* Ian Colston, 35, played 22 rounds plus five holes (401 holes in all) at Bendigo Golf Club, Victoria, Australia (par-73, 6,061 yd) on 27–28 Nov 1971.

Using golf carts David Cavalier played 846 holes at Arrowhead Country Club, North Canton, OH (9 holes, 3,013 yd) on 6–7 Aug 1990.

Most holes in 12 hours Doug Wert played 440 holes in 12 hours on the 6,044-yd course at Tournament Players Club, Coral Springs, FL on 7 Jun 1993.

PGA TOUR ALL-TIME SCORING RECORDS*

Record	Score	Player, Tournament	Year
Lowest score (9 holes)	27	Mike Souchak, Texas Open (back nine)	1955
	27	Andy North, B.C. Open (back nine)	1975
Lowest score (18 holes)	59	Al Geiberger, Danny Thomas Memphis Classic (2nd round)	1977
	59	Chip Beck, Las Vegas Invitational (3rd round)	1991
Lowest score (36 holes)	125	Gay Brewer, Pensacola Open (2nd and 3rd rounds)	1967
	125	Ron Streck, Texas Open (3rd and 4th rounds)	1988
	125	Blaine McCallister, Hardee's Golf Classic (2nd and 3rd rounds)	1988
Lowest score (54 holes)	189	Chandler Harper, Texas Open (2nd, 3rd and 4th rounds)	1954
Lowest score (72 holes)	257	Mike Souchak, Texas Open	1955
Most shots under par	27	Ben Hogan, Portland Invitational	1945
	27	Mike Souchak, Texas Open	1955
Fewest putts (18 holes)	18	Sam Trahan, IVB-Philadelphia Golf Classic (4th round)	1979
	18	Mike McGee, Federal Express St Jude Classic (1st round)	1987
	18	Kenny Knox, MCI Heritage Classic (1st round)	1989
	18	Andy North, Anheuser Busch Golf Classic (2nd round)	1990
	18	Jim McGovern, Federal Express St. Jude Classic (2nd round)	1992
Fewest putts (72 holes)	93	Kenny Knox, MCI Heritage Classic	1989

Source: PGA Tour

* *All records listed are for 72-hole tournaments.*

Most holes played in a week Steve Hylton played 1,128 holes at the Mason Rudolph Golf Club (6,060 yd), Clarksville, TN from 25–31 Aug 1980. Using a golf cart for transport, Colin Young completed 1,260 holes at Patshull Park Golf Club (6,412 yd), Pattingham, Great Britain from 2–9 Jul 1988.

World one-club record Thad Daber (USA), with a six-iron, played the 6,037 yd Lochmore Golf Club course, Cary, NC in 70 to win the 1987 World One-Club Championship.

MEN'S CHAMPIONSHIP RECORDS

Grand Slam The four grand slam events are, in order of play, the Masters, the US Open, the British Open and the PGA Championship. No player has won all four events in one calendar year. Ben Hogan came closest to succeeding in 1951, when he won the first three legs, but he could not return to the United States from Britain in time for the PGA Championship.

Jack Nicklaus has won the most major championships, with 18 professional titles (6 Masters, 4 US Opens, 3 British Opens and 5 PGA Championships). Additionally, Nicklaus has won two US Amateur titles, which are often included in calculating major championship victories.

Lee Janzen celebrating his 1993 US Open victory. He shot 272 to tie the tournament lowest score mark. (Allsport/David Cannon)

The Masters (played on the 6,980 yd Augusta National Golf Course, GA, first in 1934)

Most wins Jack Nicklaus has won six green jackets (1963, 1965–66, 1972, 1975, 1986). Two players have won consecutive Masters: Jack Nicklaus (1965–66) and Nick Faldo (Great Britain; 1989–90).

Lowest total aggregate 271, by Jack Nicklaus (67, 71, 64, 69) in 1965, and by Raymond Loran Floyd (65, 66, 70, 70) in 1976.

US Open (inaugurated 1895)

Most wins Four players have won the title four times: Willie Anderson (1901, 1903–05), Bobby Jones (1923, 1926, 1929–30), Ben Hogan (1948, 1950–51, 1953) and Jack Nicklaus (1962, 1967, 1972, 1980). The only player to gain three successive titles was Willie Anderson, from 1903 to 1905.

Lowest total aggregate The lowest 72-hole score is 272, achieved by two players: Jack Nicklaus, 272 (63, 71, 70, 68) on the lower course (7,015 yd) at Baltusrol Country Club, NJ, 12–15 Jun 1980; and Lee Janzen (67, 67, 69, 69), also at Baltusrol, 17–20 Jun 1993.

British Open (inaugurated 1860)

Most wins Harry Vardon won a record six titles, in 1896, 1898–99, 1903, 1911 and 1914. Tom Morris, Jr. is the only player to have won four successive British Opens, from 1868 to 1872 (the event was not held in 1871).

Lowest total aggregate 267 (66, 68, 69, 64) by Greg Norman (Australia) at Royal St George's, in July 1993.

Professional Golfers Association (PGA) Championship (inaugurated 1916)

Most wins Two players have won the title five times: Walter Hagen (1921, 1924–27) and Jack Nicklaus (1963, 1971, 1973, 1975, 1980). Walter Hagen won a record four consecutive titles from 1924 to 1927.

Lowest total aggregate 271, by Bobby Nicholls (64, 71, 69, 67) at Columbus Country Club, OH in 1964.

WOMEN'S CHAMPIONSHIP RECORDS

Grand Slam The Grand Slam of women's golf has consisted of four tournaments since 1955. The format has changed many times. Since 1983, the US Open, LPGA Championship, du Maurier Classic and Nabisco Dinah Shore have been the major events. Patty Berg has won 15 professional Grand Slam events: US Open (1), Titleholders (7), Western Open (7); the latter two are now defunct. She also won one US Amateur title.

US Open (inaugurated 1946)

Most wins The most wins is four, by Betsy Rawls, 1951, 1953, 1957 and 1960, and by Mickey Wright, in 1958–59, 1961 and 1964.

The Johnnie Walker World Championship, staged annually n Jamaica, offers golf's biggest purse. Larry Mize (above) won the 1993 event. He shot a record 17 under par, mesmerizing the rest of the field. (Allsport/David Cannon)

Lowest total aggregate The lowest 72-hole aggregate is 279, by Pat Bradley in 1981.

Ladies Professional Golfers Association (LPGA) Championship (inaugurated 1955)

Most wins The most wins is four, by Mickey Wright in 1958, 1960–61 and 1963.

Lowest total aggregate The lowest score for 72 holes is 267, by Betsy King at the Bethesda Country Club, MD in 1992.

Du Maurier Classic (inaugurated 1973)

Most wins Pat Bradley holds the record for most wins, with three titles won in 1980, 1985–86.

Lowest total aggregate Pat Bradley and Ayako Okamoto share the record for the lowest score for 72 holes, 276, at the Board of Trade Country Club, Toronto, Ontario, Canada in 1986. Cathy Johnson matched this in 1990 at Westmount Golf and Country Club, Kitchener, Ontario, Canada.

Nabisco Dinah Shore (inaugurated 1972)

Most wins The most wins is three, by Amy Alcott (1983, 1988 and 1991).

Lowest total aggregate The lowest score for 72 holes is 273, by Amy Alcott in 1991.

INDIVIDUAL RECORDS

Richest prize The greatest first place prize money ever won is $1 million, awarded in the Sun City Challenge, 1987–91. Bophuthatswana, South Africa. The greatest total prize money is $2.7 million (including a $550,000 first prize) for the Johnnie Walker World Championship at Tryall Golf Course, Montego Bay, Jamaica in both 1992 and 1993.

***Highest earnings** PGA and LPGA circuits* The all-time top professional money-winner is Tom Kite (USA) with $8,963,804 to 12 Jun 1994. Nick Price holds the earnings record for a year on the US PGA circuit, with $1,478,557 in 1993.

The record career earnings for a woman is $4,641,047 to 13 Jun 1994, by Pat Bradley. The season record for a woman is $863,578, by Beth Daniel in 1990.

Greatest prize money On 1 Nov 1992, Jason Bohn (USA) won $1 million when he made a hole in one during a charity contest. He aced the 136 yard second hole at the Harry S. Pritchett Gold Course in Tuscaloosa, AL using a ninc-iron, having paid $10 to enter the event. The odds of making a hole in one are 1 in 12,000.

Most times leading money winner Jack Nicklaus has been the PGA tour leading money winner eight times—1964–65, 1967, 1971–73, 1975–76. Kathy Whitworth headed the LPGA list eight times—1965–68, 1970–73.

In 1993 not even bunkers were hazardous for Nick Price (above), as he won a PGA tour season record $1,478,557. The LPGA all-time earnings leader is Pat Bradley (right). (Allsport/David Cannon)

Most tournament wins Byron Nelson (USA) won a record 18 tournaments (plus one unofficial) in one year, including a record 11 consecutively from 8 Mar to 4 Aug 1945.

The LPGA record for one year is 13, by Mickey Wright (1963). She also holds the record for most wins in scheduled events, with four between August and September 1962 and between May and June 1963, a record matched by Kathy Whitworth between March and April 1969.

Successive wins Between May and June 1978, Nancy Lopez won all five tournaments that she entered; however, these events did not follow each other and are therefore not considered consecutive tournament victories.

Career wins Sam Snead, who turned professional in 1934, won 84 official PGA tour events, 1936–65. The ladies' PGA record is 88, by Kathy Whitworth from 1962 to 1985.

Oldest winner Sam Snead (b. 27 May 1912) won a PGA tournament at the age of 52 years 312 days at the 1965 Greater Greensboro Open.

Greatest winning margin The greatest margin of victory in a professional tournament is 21 strokes, by Jerry Pate (USA), who won the Colombian Open with 262, from 10–13 Dec 1981.

Bobby Locke (South Africa; 1917–87) achieved the greatest winning margin in a PGA tour event by 16 strokes in the Chicago Victory National Championship in 1948.

NCAA Championships Two golfers have won three NCAA titles: Ben Daniel Crenshaw of the University of Texas in 1971–73, tying with Tom Kite in 1972; and Phil Mickelson of Arizona State University in 1989–90, 1992.

Highest shot on Earth Gerald Williams (USA) played a shot from the summit of Mt Aconcagua (22,834 ft), Argentina on 22 Jan 1989.

Oldest player to score his age The oldest player to achieve a score equal to his age is C. Arthur Thompson (1869–1975) of Victoria, British Columbia, Canada, who scored 103, on the Uplands course of 6,215 yd in 1973.

Golf ball balancing Lang Martin balanced seven golf balls vertically without adhesive at Charlotte, NC on 9 Feb 1980.

Throwing a golf ball The lowest recorded score for throwing a golf ball around 18 holes (over 6,000 yd) is 82, by Joe Flynn (USA), 21, at the 6,228 yd Port Royal course, Bermuda on 27 Mar 1975.

HOLES IN ONE

Longest The longest hole ever holed in one shot was the "dog-leg" 480 yd fifth at Hope Country Club, AR by L. Bruce on 15 Nov 1962.

The women's record is 393 yd, by Marie Robie on the first hole of the Furnace Brook Golf Club, Wollaston, MA on 4 Sep 1949.

Consecutive There are at least 19 cases of "aces" being achieved in two consecutive holes, of which the greatest was Norman L. Manley's unique "double albatross" on the par-4 330 yd seventh and par-4 290 yd eighth holes on the Del Valle Country Club course, Saugus, CA on 2 Sep 1964.

The first woman to record consecutive "aces" was Sue Prell, on the 13th and 14th holes at Chatswood Golf Club, Sydney, Australia on 29 May 1977.

Youngest and oldest The youngest golfer recorded to have shot a hole-in-one is Coby Orr (5 years) of Littleton, CO on the 103 yd fifth at the Riverside Golf Course, San Antonio, TX in 1975. The youngest girl is Nicola Mylonas (10 yr 64 days) on the 133 yd 1st at South Course, Nudgee, Australia on 18 Sep 1993.

The youngest American girl to score an ace was Kimberly C. Smith, at the Skaneateles Country Club, Skaneateles, NY on 14 Jun 1992, at age 12.

The oldest golfers to have performed this feat are: *(men)* 99 yr 244 days, Otto Bucher (Switzerland) on the 130 yd 12th at La Manga Golf Club, Spain on 13 Jan 1985; *(women)* 95 yr 257 days, Erna Ross on the 112 yd 17th at The Everglades Club, Palm Beach, FL on 23 Apr 1986.

TEAM COMPETITIONS

Ryder Cup The USA has won 23 to 5 (with 2 ties) to 1993.

Arnold Palmer has won the most Ryder Cup matches, with 22 out of 32 played, with 2 halved and 8 lost, in six contests from 1963 to 1973. Christy O'Connor, Sr. (Ireland) played in a record 10 contests, 1955–73. Three players have played in eight US Ryder Cup teams: Billy Casper (1965–75), Raymond Floyd (1969–93) and Lanny Wadkins (1977–93).

Walker Cup The series was instituted in 1921 (for the Walker Cup since 1922 and now held biennially). The USA has won 30 matches, Great Britain and Ireland 3 (in 1938, 1971 and 1989), and the 1965 match was tied.

Jay Sigel (USA) has won a record 18 matches, with 5 halved and 10 lost, 1977–93. Joseph Boynton Carr (Great Britain & Ireland) played in 10 contests, 1947–67.

Curtis Cup The biennial ladies' Curtis Cup match between the USA and Great Britain and Ireland was first held in 1932. The USA has won 20 to 1992, GB & Ireland Six (1952, 1956, 1986, 1988, 1992 and 1994).

GREYHOUND RACING

Oldest club St Petersburg Kennel Club, located in St Petersburg, FL, which opened on 3 Jan 1925, is the oldest greyhound track in the world still in operation on its original site.

Derby Two greyhounds have won the American Derby twice, at Taunton, MA: Real Huntsman in 1950–51, and Dutch Bahama in 1984–85.

Fastest greyhound The fastest speed at which any greyhound has been timed is 41.83 mph (400 yd in 19.57 sec) by Star Title on the straightaway track at Wyong, New South Wales, Australia on 5 Mar 1994.

United States Tiki's Ace ran a distance of 5/16 mile in 29.61 sec in Naples, Ft Myers, FL in 1988. The fastest 3/8 mile time was 36.43 sec by P's Rambling in Hollywood, FL in 1987. Old Bill Drozd ran a 7/16 mile track in 42.83 sec in Tucson, AZ in 1973.

Most wins The most career wins is 143, by JR's Ripper of Multnomah, Fairview, OR and Tucson, AZ in 1982–86. The most wins in a year is 61, by Indy Ann in Mexico and the United States in 1966.

The most consecutive victories is 36 by Pat C Rendezvous, owned by Pat Collins, from 29 Dec 1993 to 25 Jun 1994, all at Palm Beach Kennel Club, Palm Beach, FL.

Highest earnings The career earnings record is held by Homespun Rowdy with $297,000 in the United States, 1984–87.

The richest first prize for a greyhound race is $125,000, won by Ben G Speedboat in the Great Greyhound Race of Champions at Seabrook, NH on 23 Aug 1986.

Most stakes victories Real Huntsman achieved 10 wins in 1949–51, including the American Derby twice.

Longest odds Apollo Prince won at odds of 250–1 at Sandown Greyhound Race Course, Springvale, Victoria, Australia on 14 Nov 1968.

GYMNASTICS

Gymnastics/aerobics display The largest number of participants was 15,017 for the 1993 Boots Aerobathon at the Earls Court Exhibition Centre, London, Great Britain on 9 May 1993.

World Championships *Women* The greatest number of titles won in the World Championships (including Olympic Games) is 12 individual wins and six team, by Larisa Latynina (nee Diriy; USSR) between 1954 and 1964.

The USSR won the team title on 21 occasions (11 world and 10 Olympic).

Men Vitaliy Scherbo (Belarus) won 11 individual titles and one team title between 1992 and 1994. Boris Shakhlin (USSR) won 10 individual titles and three team titles, 1954–64.

The USSR won the team title a record 13 times (eight World Championships, five Olympics) between 1952 and 1992.

Three US gymnasts have won three gold medals: Kurt Thomas, floor exercise, 1978 and 1979, horizontal bar, 1979; Kim Zmeskal, all-around,

Vitaliy Scherbo (above) has won a record 12 gymnastics world titles. Shannon Miller (right) was the second American gymnast to win an all-around title. (Allsport/Bob Martin; Vandystadt/Yann Guichaoua)

EXERCISES SPEED AND STAMINA

Records are accepted for the most repetitions of the following activities within the given time span.

Chins–consecutive 370, Lee Chin-yong (South Korea; b. 15 Aug 1925) at Backyon Gymnasium, Seoul, South Korea on 14 May 1988.

Chins–consecutive, one arm, from a ring 22, Robert Chisnall (b. 9 Dec 1952) at Queen's University, Kingston, Ontario, Canada on 3 Dec 1982. (Also 18 two-finger chins, 12 one-finger chins.)

Parallel bar dips–1 hour 3,726, Kim Yang-ki (South Korea) at the Rivera Hotel, Seoul, South Korea on 28 Nov 1991.

Sit-ups–24 hours 70,715, Lou Scripa, Jr. at Beale Airforce Base, Marysville, CA on 1–2 Dec 1992.

Push-ups–24 hours 46,001, Charles Servizio (USA) at Fontana City Hall, Fontana, CA on 24–25 Apr 1993.

Push-ups–one arm, 5 hours 8,151, Alan Rumbell (Great Britain) at the Gym 'N' Slym, St Albans, Great Britain on 26 Jun 1993.

Push-ups–fingertip, 5 hours 7,011, Kim Yang-ki (South Korea) at the Swiss Guard Hotel, Seoul, South Korea on 30 Aug 1990.

Push-ups–consecutive, one finger 124, Paul Lynch (Great Britain) at the Hippodrome, London, Great Britain on 21 Apr 1992.

Push-ups in a year Paddy Doyle (Great Britain) achieved a documented 1,500,230 push-ups from October 1988 to October 1989.

Leg lifts–12 hours 41,788, Lou Scripa, Jr. at Jack La Lanne's American Health & Fitness Spa, Sacramento, CA on 2 Dec 1988.

Somersaults Ashrita Furman performed 8,341 forward rolls in 10 hr 30 min over 12 miles 390 yd from Lexington to Charleston, MA on 30 Apr 1986.

Somersaults–backwards Shigeru Iwasaki somersaulted backwards 54.68 yd in 10.8 sec in Tokyo, Japan on 30 Mar 1980.

Squats–1 hour 4,289, Paul Wai Man Chung at the Yee Gin Kung Fu of Chung Sze Health (HK) Association, Kowloon, Hong Kong on 5 Apr 1993.

Squat thrusts–1 hour 3,552, Paul Wai Man Chung at the Yee Gin Kung Fu of Chung Sze Kung Fu (HK) Association, Kowloon, Hong Kong on 21 Apr 1992.

Burpees–1 hour 1,840, Paddy Doyle at the Bull's Head, Polesworth, Great Britain on 6 Feb 1994.

Pummel horse double circles–consecutive 97, Tyler Farstad (Canada) at Surrey Gymnastic Society, Surrey, British Columbia on 27 Nov 1993.

1991, beam and floor exercise, 1992; Shannon Miller, all-around, floor exercise, uneven bars, 1993.

Youngest champions Aurelia Dobre (Romania; b. 6 Nov 1972) won the women's overall world title at age 14 yr 352 days on 23 Oct 1987. Daniela Silivas (Romania) revealed in 1990 that she was born on 9 May 1971, a year later than previously claimed, so that she was age 14 yr 185 days when she won the gold medal for balance beam on 10 Nov 1985.

The youngest male world champion was Dmitriy Bilozerchev (USSR), at 16 yr 315 days at Budapest, Hungary on 28 Oct 1983.

Olympics The USSR won the women's title 10 times (1952–80, 1988 and 1992). The successes in 1992 were by the Unified Team from the republics of the former USSR. The men's title has been won a record five times, by Japan (in 1960, 1964, 1968, 1972 and 1976) and the USSR (1952, 1956, 1980, 1988 and 1992).

Vera Cáslavská-Odlozil (Czechoslovakia) has won the most individual gold medals, with seven, three in 1964 and four (one shared) in 1968.

The most men's individual gold medals is six, by Boris Shakhlin, one in 1956, four (two shared) in 1960 and one in 1964; and by Nikolay Yefimovich (USSR), one in 1972, four in 1976 and one in 1980.

Larisa Latynina won six individual gold medals and was on three winning teams from 1956–64, earning nine gold medals. She also won five silver and four bronze, 18 in all—an Olympic record.

The most medals for a male gymnast is 15, by Nikolay Andrianov (USSR)—seven gold, five silver and three bronze, from 1972–80.

Aleksandr Dityatin (USSR) is the only man to win a medal in all eight categories in the same Games, with three gold, four silver and one bronze at Moscow in 1980.

Vitaliy Scherbo (Belarus) won a record six golds at one Games in 1992, adding four individual titles to the all-around and team gold that he had won with the Unified Team.

United States The best US performances were in the 1904 Games, when there was only limited international participation. Anton Heida won five gold medals and a silver, and George Eyser, who had a wooden leg, won

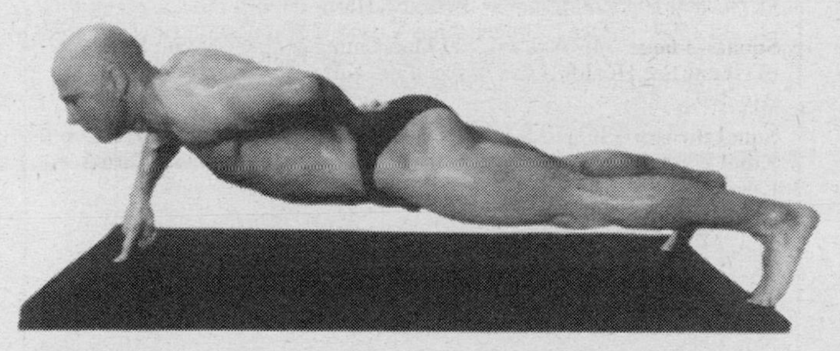

Adhering to the convention that it is rude to point, Paul Lynch found another use for his index finger. (Neil Fenwick)

three gold, two silver and a bronze medal. Mary Lou Retton won a women's record five medals in 1984—gold at all-around, two silver and two bronze.

Highest score Hans Eugster (Switzerland) scored a perfect 10.00 in the compulsory parallel bars at the 1950 World Championships. Nadia Comaneci (Romania) was the first to achieve a perfect score (10.00) in the Olympics, and achieved seven perfect scores in all at Montreal, Canada in July 1976.

World Cup Four gymnasts who won two World Cup (instituted 1975) overall titles; three men: Nikolay Andrianov, 1975, 1977; Aleksandr Ditiatin, 1978, 1979; and Li Ning (China), 1982, 1986; and one woman: Maria Filatova (USSR), 1977, 1978.

US Championships Alfred A. Jochim (1902–81) won a record seven men's all-around US titles, 1925–30 and 1933, and a total of 34 at all exercises, between 1923 and 1934. The women's record is six all-around, 1945–46 and 1949–52, and 39 at all exercises, including 11 in succession at balance beam, 1941–51, by Clara Marie Schroth Lomady.

NCAA Championships Men The men's competition was first held in 1932. The most team championships won is nine, by two colleges: University of Illinois, 1939–42, 1950, 1955–56, 1958, 1989; and Pennsylvania State University, 1948, 1953–54, 1957, 1959–61, 1965, 1976.

The most individual titles in a career is seven, by Joe Giallombardo, University of Illinois, tumbling, 1938–40, all-around title, 1938–40, and floor exercise, 1938; and by Jim Hartung, University of Nebraska, all-around title, 1980–81, rings, 1980–82, and parallel bar, 1981–82.

Women The women's competition was first held in 1982. The most team championships is seven, by the University of Utah, 1982–86, 1990 and 1992.

The most individual titles in a career is five, by Missy Marlowe, University of Utah—all-around title, 1992, balance beam, 1991–92, uneven bars, 1992, floor exercise, 1992.

Modern rhythmic gymnastics The most overall individual world titles in modern rhythmic gymnastics is three, by Maria Gigova (Bulgaria) in 1969, 1971 and 1973 (shared). Bulgaria has a record seven team titles, in 1969, 1971, 1981, 1983, 1985, 1987 and 1989 (shared). Bianka Panova of Bulgaria won all four apparatus gold medals, all with maximum scores, and won a team gold in 1987.

Lilia Ignatova (Bulgaria) has won both of the individual World Cup titles that have been held, in 1983 and 1986. Marina Lobach (USSR) won the 1988 Olympic title with perfect scores for all six disciplines.

HARNESS RACING

Most successful horse The trotter Goldsmith Maid won an all-time record 350 races (including dashes and heats) from 1864 to 1877. The career record tally for a pacer is 262 wins (including dashes and heats) by Single G, 1918–26. The season record is 65 races, by the pacer Victory Hy in 1950. The record for a trotter is 53 victories, by Make Believe in 1949.

Most successful driver The most successful sulky driver in North American harness racing history has been Herve Filion of Québec, Canada, who had achieved 14,235 wins and prize earnings of $81,514,296 through 19 Jun 1994. The most wins in a year is 843, by Walter Case (USA) in 1992. The most wins in a day is 12, by Mike Lechance at Yonkers Raceway, NY on 23 Jun 1987.

John D. Campbell (USA) has the highest career earnings, $122,280,760 through 19 Jun 1994. This includes a season record of $11,620,878 in 1990, when he won 543 races.

Triple Crown Trotters The Triple Crown consists of three races: Hambletonian, Kentucky Futurity, and Yonkers Trot. Six trotters have won the Triple Crown. Stanley Dancer is the only driver to win two Triple Crowns, 1968 and 1972.

Hambletonian The record time is 1 min 53 1/5 sec, by American Winner, driven by Ron Pierce in 1993.

Kentucky Futurity The race record time is 1 min 52 3/5 sec, by Pine Chip, driven by John Campbell in 1993.

Yonkers Trot The race record time is 1 min 56 2/5 sec, by American Winner, driven by Ron Pierce, in 1993.

Triple Crown Pacers The Triple Crown consists of three races: Cane Pace, Little Brown Jug, and Messenger Stakes. Seven horses have won the Triple Crown, each with different drivers.

HARNESS RACING MILE RECORDS

Trotting		**Horse (driver)**	**Place**	**Date**
World	1:52 1/5	*Mack Lobell* (John Campbell)	Springfield, IL	21 Aug 1987
Pacing				
World	1:46 1/5	*Cambest* (Bill O'Donnell)	Springfield, IL	16 Aug 1993
Race	1:48 2/5	*Staying Together* (Bill O'Donnell)	East Rutherford, NJ	19 Jun 1993

Cane Pace The race record time is 1 min 51 2/5 sec, by Riyadh, driven by Jim Morrill Jr., in 1993.

Little Brown Jug The race record time is 1 min 52 sec, by Life Sign, driven by John Campbell, in 1993.

Messenger Stakes The race record time is 1 min 51 1/5 sec, by Die Laughing driven by Richard Silverman, in 1991.

Highest price The highest price paid was $19.2 million for Nihilator (a pacer), who was syndicated by Wall Street Stable and Almahurst Stud Farm in 1984.

Greatest winnings For any harness horse the record amount is $4,907,307, by the trotter Peace Corps, 1988–92.

The single-season record is $2,222,166 by the pacer Presidential Ball in 1993.

The largest-ever purse was $2,161,000, for the Woodrow Wilson two-year-old race over one mile at The Meadowlands, East Rutherford, NJ on 16 Aug 1984. Of this sum a record $1,080,500 went to the winner, Nihilator, driven by William O'Donnell.

HOCKEY

NATIONAL HOCKEY LEAGUE (NHL)

Team records The Montreal Canadiens won a record 60 games and 132 points (with 12 ties) in 80 games played in 1976/77; their eight losses were also a record, the least ever in a season of 70 or more games. The highest percentage of wins in a season was .875, achieved by the Boston Bruins, with 30 wins in 44 games in 1929/30.

The longest undefeated run during a season, 35 games (25 wins and 10 ties), was established by the Philadelphia Flyers from 14 Oct 1979 to 6 Jan 1980.

The most goals scored in a season is 446, by the Edmonton Oilers in 1983/84, when they also achieved a record 1,182 points.

The most assists recorded in a season was the 737 by the Edmonton Oilers during the 1985–86 season.

The most power-play goals scored in a season is 119, by the Pittsburgh Penguins during the 1988–89 season. The most shorthanded goals scored in a season is 36, by the Edmonton Oilers during the 1983–84 season.

The most shutouts in a season is 22, in 1928/29 by the Montreal Canadiens, in just 44 games, all by George Hainsworth, who also achieved a record low for goals against percentage of .98 that season.

Most goals in a game The NHL record is 21 goals, when the Montreal Canadiens beat Toronto St Patrick's, 14–7, at Montreal on 10 Jan 1920, and the Edmonton Oilers beat the Chicago Blackhawks, 12–9, at Chicago on 11 Dec 1985. The NHL single-team record is 16, by the Montreal Canadiens *v* the Québec Bulldogs (3), at Québec City on 3 Nov 1920.

Longest hockey game The longest game, and the longest single shutout, was 2 hr 56 min 30 sec (playing time) when the Detroit Red Wings beat the Montreal Maroons 1–0 in the sixth period of overtime at the Forum, Montreal, at 2:25 A.M. on 25 Mar 1936.

Fastest goals Toronto scored eight goals in 4 min 52 sec *v* the New York Americans on 19 Mar 1938.

INDIVIDUAL RECORDS

Most games played Gordie Howe played in a record 1,767 NHL regular-season games (and 157 playoff games) over a record 26 seasons, from 1946 to 1971, for the Detroit Red Wings and in 1979/80 for the Hartford Whalers.

Fastest goals The fastest goal was after 4 sec by Joseph Antoine Claude Provost (Montreal Canadiens) *v* Boston Bruins in the second period at Montreal on 9 Nov 1957, and by Denis Joseph Savard (Chicago Blackhawks) *v* Hartford Whalers in the third period at Chicago on 12 Jan 1986. From the opening whistle, the fastest is 5 sec, by Doug Smail (Winnipeg Jets) *v* St Louis Blues at Winnipeg on 20 Dec 1981, and by Bryan John Trottier (New York Islanders) *v* Boston Bruins at Boston on 22 Mar 1984. Bill Mosienko (Chicago Blackhawks) scored three goals in 21 sec *v* New York Rangers on 23 Mar 1952.

Most goals, assists and points *Career* "The Great One," Wayne Gretzky, holds the NHL's three most coveted records, all-time leader in goals, assists and points. During his career (Edmonton Oilers 1979–88, Los Angeles Kings 1988–94) he has scored 803 goals, 1,655 assists and 2,658 points.

Season The most goals scored in a season in the NHL is 92, in the 1981/82 season by Wayne Gretzky for the Edmonton Oilers. He scored a record 215 points, including a record 163 assists, in 1985/86.

Game The most goals in an NHL game is seven, by Michael Joe Malone in Québec's 10–6 win over Toronto St Patricks at Québec City on 31 Jan 1920.

The most assists in an NHL game is seven, by Billy Taylor for Detroit, 10–6 *v* Chicago on 16 Mar 1947, and three by Wayne Gretzky for Edmonton, 8–2 *v* Washington on 15 Feb 1980, 12–9 *v* Chicago on 11 Dec 1985, and 8–2 *v* Québec on 14 Feb 1986.

The record number of assists in one period is five, by Dale Hawerchuk, for the Winnipeg Jets *v* the Los Angeles Kings on 6 Mar 1984.

Consecutive games Harry Broadbent scored in 16 consecutive games for Ottawa in the 1921/22 season.

Most hat tricks The most hat tricks (three or more goals in a game) in a career is 49, by Wayne Gretzky through the 1992/93 season for the Edmonton Oilers and the Los Angeles Kings. Gretzky also holds the record for

Canadiens goalie Patrick Roy is one of five players to be awarded the Conn Smythe trophy twice. (William S. Romano)

Paul Coffey holds several of the NHL and Stanley Cup records for scoring by a defenseman, among them: all-time goals, assists and points in the regular season, and the playoff records for most points in a game and a season. (Allsport/Harry Scull)

most hat tricks in a season, 10, in both the 1982 and 1984 seasons for the Oilers.

Most points in one game The NHL record for most points scored in one game is 10, by Darryl Sittler—six goals, four assists for the Toronto Maple Leafs *v* the Boston Bruins in an NHL game at Toronto on 7 Feb 1976.

Period The most points in one period is six, by Bryan Trottier—three goals and three assists in the second period, for the New York Islanders *v* the New York Rangers (9–4) on 23 Dec 1978. Nine players have a record four goals in one period.

Most consecutive games played A record of 962 consecutive games played was achieved by Doug Jarvis for the Montreal Canadiens, the Washington Capitals and the Hartford Whalers from 8 Oct 1975–5 Apr 1987.

Most consecutive 50-or-more-goal seasons Mike Bossy (New York Islanders) scored at least 50 goals in nine consecutive seasons from 1977/78 through 1985/86. Wayne Gretzky (Edmonton Oilers, Los Angeles Kings) has also scored at least 50 goals in one season nine times, but his longest streak is eight seasons.

Most consecutive points The most consecutive games scoring points was 51, by Wayne Gretzky from 5 Oct 1983–27 Jan 1984 for the Edmonton Oilers.

Goaltending Terry Gordon Sawchuk (1929–70) played a record 971 games as a goaltender, for the Detroit Red Wings, the Boston Bruins, the Toronto Maple Leafs, the Los Angeles Kings and the New York Rangers, from 1949 to 1970. He achieved a record 435 wins (to 337 losses, and 188 ties). Jacques Plante (1929–86), with 434 NHL wins, surpassed Sawchuk's figure by adding 15 wins in his one season in the WHA, for a total of 449 in 868 games.

Bernie Parent achieved a record 47 goals in a season, with 13 losses and 12 ties, for Philadelphia in 1973/74.

Most successful goaltending The most shutouts played by a goaltender in an NHL career is 103, by Terry Sawchuck of Detroit, Boston, Toronto, Los Angeles and New York Rangers, between 1949 and 1970. Gerry Cheevers (Boston Bruins) went a record 32 successive games without a defeat in 1971/72. George Hainsworth completed 22 shutouts for the Montreal Canadiens in 1928/29. Alex Connell played 461 min 29 sec without conceding a goal for Ottawa in the 1928/29 season. Roy Worters saved 70 shots for the Pittsburgh Pirates *v* the New York Americans on 24 Dec 1925.

Defensemen Paul Coffey (Edmonton Oilers 1980–87, Pittsburgh Penguins 1988–92, Los Angeles Kings 1992–93, Detroit Red Wings 1993) holds the record for most goals (344), assists (934) and points (1,278) by a defenseman. He scored a record 48 goals in 1985/86. Bobby Orr (Boston Bruins) holds the single-season marks for assists (102) and points (139), both of which were set in 1970/71.

Player awards The Hart Trophy, awarded annually starting with the 1923/24 season by the Professional Hockey Writers Association as the

Most Valuable Player award of the NHL, has been won a record nine times by Wayne Gretzky, 1980–87, 1989. Gretzky has also won the Art Ross Trophy a record nine times, 1981–87 and 1990–91; this has been awarded annually since 1947/48 to the NHL season's leading scorer. Bobby Orr of Boston won the James Norris Memorial Trophy, awarded annually starting with the 1953/54 season to the league's leading defenseman, a record eight times, 1968–75.

Coaches Scotty Bowman holds the records for most victories, highest winning percentage and most games coached by an NHL coach. He won 880 games (110, St Louis Blues 1967–71; 419, Montreal Canadiens 1971–79; 210, Buffalo Sabres 1979–87; 95, Pittsburgh Penguins, 1991–93; 46, Detroit Red Wings, 1993–94). His career record is 880 wins, 410 losses, 234 ties for a record .654 winning percentage from a record 1,524 games.

STANLEY CUP

The Stanley Cup has been won most often by the Montreal Canadiens, with 24 wins in 1916, 1924, 1930–31, 1944, 1946, 1953, 1956–60, 1965–66, 1968–69, 1971, 1973, 1976–79, 1986, 1993 from a record 33 finals. The longest Stanley Cup final game was settled after 115 min 13 sec, in the third period of overtime, when the Edmonton Oilers beat the Boston Bruins 3–2 on 15 May 1990.

Henri Richard played on a record 11 winning teams for the Montreal Canadiens between 1956 and 1973.

Most games played Larry Robinson played in 227 Stanley Cup playoff games, for the Montreal Canadiens (1973–89) and the Los Angeles Kings (1990–92).

Scoring records Wayne Gretzky (Edmonton Oilers, Los Angeles Kings) has scored a record 346 points in Stanley Cup games, a record 110 goals and a record 236 assists. Gretzky scored a playoff record 47 points (16 goals, record 31 assists) in 1985. The most goals in a season is 19, by Reggie Leach for Philadelphia in 1976 and by Jari Kurri (Finland) for Edmonton in 1985.

Five goals in a Stanley Cup game were scored by Maurice Richard in Montreal's 5–1 win over the Toronto Maple Leafs on 23 Mar 1944; by Darryl Glen Sittler for Toronto's 8–5 victory over Philadelphia on 22 Apr 1976; by Reggie Leach for Philadelphia's 6–3 victory over the Boston Bruins on 6 May 1976; and by Mario Lemieux for the Pittsburgh Penguins' 10–7 victory over Philadelphia on 25 Apr 1989. Reggie Leach (Philadelphia) scored at least one goal in nine consecutive playoff games in 1976. The streak started on 17 April *v* the Toronto Maple Leafs, and ended on 9 May when he was shut out by the Montreal Canadiens. Overall, Leach scored 14 goals during his record-setting run.

A record six assists in a game were achieved by Mikko Leinonen (Finland) for the New York Rangers in their 7–3 victory over Philadelphia on 8 Apr 1982, and by Wayne Gretzky for Edmonton's 13–3 victory over Los Angeles on 9 Apr 1987, when his team set a Stanley Cup game record of 13 goals. The most points in a game is eight, by Patrik Sundström (Sweden), three goals and five assists, for the New Jersey Devils (10) *v* the Washington Capitals (4) on 22 Apr 1988, and by Mario Lemieux, five goals and

Even the great ones need a breather. No one, however, could stop Wayne Gretzky from becoming the NHL's all-time leading goal scorer in 1994. (Allsport USA/Harry Scull)

three assists, for the Pittsburgh Penguins (10) *v* the Philadelphia Flyers (7) on 25 Apr 1989.

Point-scoring streak Bryan Trottier (New York Islanders) scored a point in 27 playoff games over three seasons (1980–82), scoring 16 goals and 26 assists for 42 points.

Goal-scoring streak Reggie Leach, Philadelphia Flyers scored at least one goal in nine consecutive playoff games in 1976. The streak started on 17 April *v* the Toronto Maple Leafs and ended on 9 May, when Leach was shut out by the Montreal Canadiens. Overall, Leach scored 14 goals during his record-setting run.

GOLDEN FAMILY

The only father and son to play on gold medal-winning hockey teams are Bill and David Christian. Bill was on the victorious US team in 1960, and David was a member of the 1980 "miracle on ice" team. Bill's brother Roger (David's uncle), was also on the 1960 team.

Goaltending Jacques Plante holds the record for most shutouts in a playoff career, with 14, with the Montreal Canadiens (1953–63) and the St Louis Blues (1969–1970). The record for most victories in a playoff career is 88, by Billy Smith for the New York Islanders (1975–88).

Defensemen During his career with the Edmonton Oilers, 1980–87, Paul Coffey set marks for the most points in a playoff game (6) and in a season (37)—both set in 1985. Also in 1985, Coffey set the record for most goals by a defenseman in a playoff season, with 12 in 18 games. The record for most goals in a game by a defenseman is three, shared by eight players: Bobby Orr (Boston Bruins *v* Montreal Canadiens, 11 Apr 1971); Dick Redmond (Chicago Blackhawks *v* St. Louis Blues, 4 Apr 1973); Denis Potvin (New York Islanders *v* Edmonton Oilers, 17 Apr 1981); Paul Reinhart twice (Calgary Flames *v* Edmonton Oilers, 14 Apr 1983; *v* Vancouver Canucks, 8 Apr 1984); Doug Halward (Vancouver Canucks *v* Calgary Flames, 7 Apr 1984); Al Iafrate (Washington Capitals *v* New York Islanders, 26 Apr 1993); Eric Desjardins (Montreal Canadiens *v* Los Angeles Kings, 3 Jun 1993); and Gary Suter (Chicago Blackhawks *v* Toronto Maple Leafs, 24 Apr 1994).

Most valuable player The Conn Smythe Trophy for the most valuable player in the playoffs has been awarded annually since 1965. It has been won twice by five players: Bobby Orr (Boston), 1970 and 1972; Bernie Parent (Philadelphia), 1974 and 1975; Wayne Gretzky (Edmonton), 1985 and 1988; Mario Lemieux (Pittsburgh), 1991 and 1992; and Patrick Roy (Montreal), 1986 and 1993.

Coaches "Toe" Blake coached the Montreal Canadiens to eight championships (1956–60, 1965–66, 1968), the most of any coach. Scotty Bowman holds the record for most playoff wins at 140: 26, St Louis Blues, 1967–71; 70, Montreal Canadiens, 1971–79; 18, Buffalo Sabres, 1979–87; 23, Pittsburgh Penguins, 1991–93; 3, Detroit Red Wings, 1993–94.

WORLD CHAMPIONSHIPS AND OLYMPIC GAMES

World Championships were first held for amateurs in 1920 in conjunction with the Olympic Games, which were also considered world championships up to 1968. Since 1976, the World Championships have been open to professionals. The USSR won 22 world titles between 1954 and 1990, including the Olympic titles of 1956, 1964 and 1968. It has a record eight Olympic titles with a further five in 1972, 1976, 1984, 1988 and 1992 (as the Unified Team). The longest Olympic career is that of Richard Torriani (Switzerland; 1911–88) from 1928 to 1948. The most gold medals won by any player is three, achieved by Soviet players Vitaliy Davydov, Anatoliy Firsov, Viktor Kuzkin and Aleksandr Ragulin in 1964, 1968 and 1972, and by Vladislav Tretyak in 1972, 1976 and 1984.

Women The first two world championships were won by Canada, in 1990 and 1992.

Most goals The greatest number of goals recorded in a world championship match was when Australia beat New Zealand 58–0 at Perth on 15 Mar 1987.

Fastest goals In minor leagues, Per Olsen scored two seconds after the start of the match for Rungsted against Odense in the Danish First Division at Hørsholm, Denmark on 14 Jan 1990. Three goals in 10 seconds was achieved by Jørgen Palmgren Erichsen for Frisk *v.* Holmen in a junior league match in Norway on 17 Mar 1991. The Skara Ishockeyclubb, Sweden, scored three goals in 11 seconds against Örebro IK at Skara on 18 Oct 1981. The Vernon Cougars scored five goals in 56 seconds against the Salmon Arm Aces at Vernon, British Columbia, Canada on 6 Aug 1982. The Kamloops Knights of Columbus scored seven goals in 2 min 22 sec *v* the Prince George Vikings on 25 Jan 1980.

HORSE RACING

Highest prizes The highest prize money won for a day's racing is $10 million, for the Breeders' Cup series of seven races staged annually since 1984. Included each year is a record $3 million for the Breeders' Cup Classic.

Breeders' Cup Two jockeys have won seven Breeders' Cup races: Laffit Pincay, Jr.; Juvenile (1985, 1986, 1988), Classic (1986), Distaff (1989, 1990), Juvenile Fillies (1993); and Eddie Delahoussaye, Distaff (1984, 1993), Turf (1989), Juvenile Fillies (1991), Sprint (1992, 1993).

MAJOR RACING RECORDS

Race (instituted)	Record Time	Most Wins Jockey	Trainer	Owner	Largest Field
Triple Crown					
Kentucky Derby (1875) **1¼ miles** Churchill Downs, Louisville, KY	1 min 59.4 sec *Secretariat* 1973	5-Eddie Arcaro 1938, 41, 45, 48, 52 5-Bill Hartack 1957, 60, 62, 64, 69	6-Ben Jones 1938, 41, 44, 48, 49, 52	8-Calumet Farm 1941, 44, 48, 49, 52, 57, 58, 68	23 (1974)
Preakness Stakes (1873) **1 mile 1½ furlongs** Pimlico, Baltimore, MD	1 min 53.2 sec *Tank's Prospect* 1985	6-Eddie Arcaro 1941, 48, 50, 51, 55, 57	7-Robert Wyndham Walden 1875, 78, 79, 80, 81, 82, 88	5-George Lorillard 1878, 79, 80, 81, 82	18 (1928)
Belmont Stakes (1867) **1½ miles** Belmont Park, NY	2 min 24.0 sec *Secretariat* 1973 (By a record 31 lengths)	6-Jimmy McLaughlin 1882, 83, 84, 86, 87, 88 6-Eddie Arcaro 1941, 42, 45, 48, 52, 55	8-James Rowe Sr 1883, 84, 1901, 04, 07, 08, 10, 13	5-Dwyer Bros 1883, 84, 86, 87, 88 5-James R. Keene 1901, 04, 07, 08, 10 5-William Woodward Sr (Belair Stud) 1930, 32, 35, 36, 39	15 (1983)

Famous International Races

Derby (1780) **1½ miles** Epsom Downs, Great Britain	2 min 33.8 sec *Mahmoud* 1936 2 min 33.84 sec *Kahyasi* 1988 (Electronically timed)	9-Lester Piggott 1954, 57, 60, 68, 70, 72, 76, 77, 83	7-Robert Robson 1793, 1802,09, 10, 15, 17, 23 7-John Porter 1868, 82, 83, 86, 90, 91, 99 7-Fred Darling 1922, 25, 26,31, 38, 40, 41	5-3rd Earl of Egremont 1782, 1804, 05, 07, 26 5-HH Aga Khan III 1930, 35, 36, 48, 52	34 (1862)
Prix de l'Arc de Triomphe (1920) **1 mile 864 yd** Longchamp, France	2 min 26.3 sec *Trempolino* 1987	4-Jacques Doyasbère 1942, 44, 50, 51 4-Frédéric "Freddy" Head 1966, 72, 76, 79 4-Yves Saint-Martin 1970, 74, 82, 84 4-Pat Eddery 1980, 85, 86, 87	4-Charles Semblat 1942, 44,46, 49 4-Alec Head 1952, 59, 76, 81 4-François Mathet 1950, 51, 70, 82	6-Marcel Boussac 1936, 37, 42, 44, 46, 49	30 (1967)
VRC Melbourne Cup (1861) 1 mile 1739 yd Flemington, Victoria, Australia	3 min 16.3 sec *Kingston Rule* 1990	4-Bobby Lewis 1902, 15, 19, 27 4-Harry White 1974, 75, 78, 79	9-Bart Cummings 1965, 66, 67, 74, 75, 77, 79, 90, 91	4-Etienne de Mestre 1861, 62, 67, 78	39 (1890)
Grand National (1839) **4½ miles** Aintree, Liverpool, Great Britain	8 min 47.8 sec *Mr Frisk* 1990	5-George Stevens 1856, 63, 64, 69, 70	4-Fred Rimell 1956, 61, 70, 76	3-James Machell 1873, 74, 76 3-Sir Charles Assheton-Smith 1893, 1912, 13 3-Noel LeMore 1973, 74, 77	66 (1929)

Highest earnings Pat Day has won a record $9,551,000 in Breeders' Cup racing, 1984–93.

Biggest payout Anthony A. Speelman and Nicholas John Cowan (both Great Britain) won $1,627,084.40, after federal income tax of $406,768.00 was withheld, on a $64 nine-horse accumulator at Santa Anita Racetrack, CA on 19 Apr 1987. Their first seven selections won, and the payout was for a jackpot accumulated over 24 days.

HORSES

Most valuable The most valuable animals are racehorses. The most ever paid for a yearling was $13.1 million on 23 Jul 1985 at Keeneland, KY by Robert Sangster and partners for Seattle Dancer.

Oldest thoroughbred The greatest age recorded for a thoroughbred racehorse is 42 years, in the case of the chestnut gelding Tango Duke (foaled 1935), owned by Carmen J. Koper of Barongarook, Victoria, Australia. The horse died on 25 Jan 1978.

Most successful The horse with the best win–loss record was Kincsem, a Hungarian mare foaled in 1874, who was unbeaten in 54 races (1876–79) throughout Europe, including the Goodwood Cup (Great Britain) of 1878.

Longest winning sequence Camarero, foaled in 1951, was undefeated in 56 races in Puerto Rico from 19 Apr 1953 to his first defeat on 17 Aug 1955 (in his career to 1956, he won 73 of 77 races).

Career Chorisbar (foaled 1935) won 197 of his 325 races in Puerto Rico, 1937–47. Lenoxbar (foaled 1935) won 46 races in one year, 1940, in Puerto Rico from 56 starts.

The most career wins in the United States is 89, by Kingston in 138 starts, 1886–94. This included 33 in stakes races, but the horse with the most wins in stakes races in the USA is Exterminator (foaled 1915), with 34 between 1918 and 1923. John Henry (foaled 1975) won a record 25 graded stakes races, including 16 at Grade 1, 1978–84. On his retirement in 1984, his career prize money was $6,597,947, nearly twice as much as the next best. Of 83 races, he won 39, was second 15 times and third 9 times.

Same race Doctor Syntax (foaled 1811) won the Preston Gold Cup on seven successive occasions, 1815–21.

Triple Crown winners The Triple Crown (Kentucky Derby, Preakness Stakes, Belmont Stakes) has been achieved 11 times, most recently by Affirmed in 1978. Eddie Arcaro is the only jockey to board two Triple Crown winners, Whirlaway in 1941 and Citation in 1948. Two trainers have schooled two Triple Crown winners: James Fitzsimmons, Gallant Fox in 1930 and Omaha in 1935; Ben A. Jones, Whirlaway in 1941 and Citation in 1948.

Greatest winnings The career earnings record is $6,679,242, by the 1987 Kentucky Derby winner Alysheba (foaled 1984), from 1986–88. Alysheba's career record was 11 wins, 8 seconds and 2 thirds from 26 races. The most prize money earned in a year is $4,578,454, by Sunday Silence (foaled 1986) in 1989. The record was set in nine races, Sunday Silence winning seven times and finishing second twice.

The leading money-winning mare is Dance Smartly (foaled 1988), with $3,263,346 in North America, 1990–92.

The one-race record is $2.6 million, by Spend a Buck (foaled 1982), for the Jersey Derby, Garden State Park, NJ on 27 May 1985, of which $2 million was a bonus for having previously won the Kentucky Derby and two preparatory races at Garden State Park.

World speed records The fastest race speed recorded is 43.26 mph, by Big Racket, 20.8 sec for 1/4 mile, at Mexico City, Mexico on 5 Feb 1945. The four-year-old carried 114 lb. The record for 1 1/2 miles is 37.82 mph, by three-year-old Hawkster (carrying 121 lb) at Santa Anita Park, Arcadia, CA on 14 Oct 1989, with a time of 2 min 22.8 sec.

JOCKEYS

Most successful Willie Shoemaker (USA), whose racing weight was 97 lb at 4 ft 11 in, rode a record 8,833 winners out of 40,350 mounts from his first ride on 19 Mar 1949 and first winner on 20 Apr 1949 to his retirement on 3 Feb 1990. Laffit Pincay, Jr. (USA) has earned a career record $180,831,683 from 1964 to 27 Jul 1994.

The most races won by a jockey in a year is 598, in 2,312 rides, by Kent Jason Desormeaux (USA) in 1989. The greatest amount won in a year is 2,356,280,400 yen (*c.* $16,250,000) by Yutaka Take (Japan) in Japan in 1990. The greatest amount won in the United States in a year is $14,877,298, by José Adeon Santos (USA) in 1988. Mike Smith (USA) rode a season record 61 stakes race winners in 1993.

Wins *One day* The most winners ridden in one day is nine, by Chris Antley (USA) on 31 Oct 1987. They consisted of four in the afternoon at Aqueduct, NY and five in the evening at The Meadowlands, NJ.

One card The most winners ridden on one card is eight, by six riders, most recently (and in fewest rides) by Pat Day, in only nine rides at Arlington, IL on 13 Sep 1989.

Consecutive The longest winning streak is 12, by Sir Gordon Richards (Great Britain; 1904–86)—one race at Nottingham, Great Britain on 3 October, six out of six at Chepstow on 4 October, and the first five races next day at Chepstow, in 1933; and by Pieter Stroebel at Bulawayo, Southern Rhodesia (now Zimbabwe), 7 Jun–7 Jul 1958.

The longest consecutive winning streak for an American jockey is nine

GUESS WHAT?

Q. How big is the largest silk carpet?

A. Look in "Big Deals" (Human Achievements)

races, by Albert Adams (USA) at Marlboro Racetrack, MD over three days, 10–12 Sep 1930. He won the last two races on 10 September, all six races on 11 September and the first race on 12 September.

TRAINERS

Jack Charles Van Berg (USA) has the greatest number of wins in a year, 496 in 1976. The career record is 6,362, by Dale Baird (USA) from 1962 to the end of 1993. The greatest amount won in a year is $17,842,358, by D. Wayne Lukas (USA) in 1988; he has won a record $140,024,750 in his career.

OWNERS

The most lifetime wins by an owner is 4,775, by Marion H. Van Berg (1895–1971), in North America, in 35 years. The most wins in a year is 494, by Dan R. Lasater (USA) in 1974. The greatest amount won in a year is $6,881,902, by Sam-Son Farm in North America in 1991.

HORSESHOE PITCHING

World Championships *Most titles (men)* Ted Allen (USA) has won 10 world titles: 1933–35, 1940, 1946, 1953, 1955–57 and 1959.

Most titles (women) Vicki Winston (née Chapelle) has won a record 10 women's titles: 1956, 1958–59, 1961, 1963, 1966–67, 1969, 1975 and 1981.

SHOE-IN!

At the 1968 World Championship, Elmer Hohl, Canada, threw 56 consecutive ringers. This was the longest perfect game ever in a horseshoe-pitching contest.

In world championship play only three pitchers have thrown perfect games: Guy Zimmerman (USA), 1948; Elmer Hohl (above) and Jim Walters (USA) in 1993.

HURLING

***Most titles** All-Ireland* The greatest number of All-Ireland Championships won by one team is 27, by Cork, between 1890 and 1990. The greatest number of successive wins is four, by Cork (1941–44).

Most appearances The most appearances in All-Ireland finals is 10, shared by Christy Ring (Cork and Munster) and John Doyle (Tipperary). They also share the record of All-Ireland medals, won with eight each. Ring's appearances on the winning side were in 1941–44, 1946 and 1952–54, while Doyle's were in 1949–51, 1958, 1961–62 and 1964–65. Ring also played in a record 22 interprovincial finals (1942–63), and was on the winning side 18 times.

Highest and lowest scores The highest score in an All-Ireland final (60 min) was in 1989, when Tipperary, 41 (4 goals, 29 points) beat Antrim, 18 (3 goals, 9 points). The record aggregate score was when Cork, 39 (6 goals, 21 points) defeated Wexford, 25 (5 goals, 10 points), in the 80-minute final of 1970. A goal equals three points.

The highest recorded individual score was by Nick Rackard (Wexford), who scored 7 goals and 7 points against Antrim in the 1954 All-Ireland semifinal. The lowest score in an All-Ireland final was when Tipperary (1 goal, 1 point) beat Galway (zero) in the first championship at Birr in 1887.

Largest crowd The largest crowd was 84,865 for the All-Ireland Final between Cork and Wexford at Croke Park, Dublin in 1954.

ICE & SAND YACHTING

***Fastest speeds** Ice* The fastest speed officially recorded is 143 mph, by John D. Buckstaff in a Class A stern-steerer on Lake Winnebago, WI in 1938. Such a speed is possible in a wind of 72 mph.

Sand The official world record for a sand yacht is 66.48 mph, set by Christian-Yves Nau (France) in *Mobil* at Le Touquet, France on 22 Mar 1981, when the wind speed reached 75 mph. A speed of 88.4 mph was attained by Nord Embroden (USA) in *Midnight at the Oasis* at Superior Dry Lake, CA on 15 Apr 1976.

Largest ice yacht The largest ice yacht was *Icicle*, built for Commodore John E. Roosevelt for racing on the Hudson River, NY in 1869. It was 68 ft 11 in long and carried 1,070 ft^2 of canvas.

ICE SKATING

Largest rink The world's largest indoor ice rink is in the Moscow Olympic Arena, which has an ice area of 86,800 ft^2. The five rinks at Fujikyu Highland Skating Center in Japan total 285,243 ft^2.

Barrel jumping on ice skates The official distance record is 29 ft 5 in over 18 barrels, by Yvon Jolin at Terrebonne, Quebec, Canada on 25 Jan 1981. The women's record is 20 ft 4¼ in over 11 barrels, by Janet Hainstock in Wyandotte, MI on 15 Mar 1980.

FIGURE SKATING

***Most titles** Olympic* The most Olympic gold medals won by a figure skater is three: by Gillis Grafström (Sweden; 1893–1938) in 1920, 1924 and 1928 (also silver medal in 1932); by Sonja Henie (Norway; 1912–69) in 1928, 1932 and 1936; and by Irina Konstantinovna (USSR) with two different partners in the pairs in 1972, 1976 and 1980.

Triple Crown Karl Schäfer (Austria; 1909–76) and Sonja Henie achieved double "Triple Crowns" (world, Olympic and European or US titles won in the same year), both in the years 1932 and 1936. This feat was repeated by Katarina Witt (East Germany) in 1984 and 1988.

World The greatest number of men's individual world figure skating titles (instituted 1896) is 10, by Ulrich Salchow (Sweden; 1877–1949) in 1901–05 and 1907–11. The women's record (instituted 1906) is also 10 individual titles, by Sonja Henie between 1927 and 1936. Irina Rodnina won 10 pairs titles (instituted 1908), four with Aleksey Ulanov, 1969–72, and six with her former husband Aleksandr Zaitsev, 1973–78. The most ice dance titles (instituted 1952) won is six, by Lyudmila Pakhomova (1946–86) and her husband Aleksandr Gorshkov (USSR), 1970–74 and 1976. They also won the first-ever Olympic ice dance title in 1976.

Dick Button set US records with two Olympic gold medals, 1948 and 1952, and five world titles, 1948–52. Five women's world titles were won by Carol Heise, 1956–60, as well as the 1960 Olympic gold.

United States The US Championships were first held in 1914. The most titles won by an individual is nine, by Maribel Y. Vinson (1911–61), 1928–33 and 1935–37. She also won six pairs titles, and her aggregate of 15 titles is equaled by Therese Blanchard (nee Weld; 1893–1978), who won six individual and nine pairs titles between 1914 and 1927. The men's individual record is seven, by Roger Turner, 1928–34, and by Dick Button, 1946–52.

Highest marks The highest tally of maximum six marks awarded in an international championship was 29, to Jayne Torvill and Christopher Dean (both Great Britain) in the World Ice Dance Championships at Ottawa, Canada on 22–24 Mar 1984. This comprised seven in the compulsory dances, a perfect set of nine for presentation in the set pattern dance, and 13 in the free dance, including another perfect set from all nine judges for

In 1994, nearly 10 years after posting record marks in ice dancing, Jayne Torvill and Christopher Dean returned to Olympic competition. The marks were not as high, but the crowd response was just the same: ecstatic. (Allsport/Chris Cole)

Five speedskating records were set at the Lillehammer Winter Olympics. Gracious hosts, Norwegians joyously celebrated the trio of records set by national hero Johann Olav Koss (left), and the triumph of Dan Jansen (above). (Allsport/Clive Brunskill; Allsport/Simon Bruty)

artistic presentation. In their career Torvill and Dean received a record total of 136 sixes.

The most by a soloist is seven: by Donald Jackson (Canada) in the World Men's Championship at Prague, Czechoslovakia in 1962; and by Midori Ito (Japan) in the World Women's Championships at Paris, France in 1989.

Greatest jump Robin Cousins (Great Britain) achieved 19 ft 1 in in an axel jump and 18 ft with a back flip at Richmond Ice Rink, Great Britain on 16 Nov 1983.

SPEED SKATING

Most titles *Olympic* The most Olympic gold medals ever won in speed skating is six, by Lidiya Skoblikova (USSR) in 1960 (two) and 1964 (four).

The men's record is five, by Clas Thunberg (Finland; 1893–1973), in 1924 and 1928 (including one tied); and by Eric Heiden (USA), uniquely at one Games at Lake Placid, NY in 1980.

The most medals won is seven, by Clas Thunberg, who won a silver and a bronze in addition to his five gold medals, and by Ivar Ballangrud (Norway; 1904–69), four gold, two silver and a bronze, 1928–36.

World The greatest number of world overall titles (instituted 1893) won by any skater is five—by Oscar Mathisen (Norway; 1888–1954) in 1908–09 and 1912–14; by Clas Thunberg in 1923, 1925, 1928–29 and 1931; and by Karin Kania (nee Enke; East Germany) in 1982, 1984, 1986–88. Kania also won a record six overall titles at the World Sprint Championships, 1980–81, 1983–84, 1986–87. A record six men's sprint overall titles have been won by Igor Zhelezovskiy (USSR/Belarus), 1985–86, 1989 and 1991–93.

United States Eric Heiden won a US record three overall world titles, 1977–79. His sister Beth Heiden became the only US women's overall champion in 1979.

World Short-track Championships The most successful skater in these championships (instituted 1978) has been Sylvie Daigle (Canada), women's overall champion in 1979, 1983 and 1989–90.

Longest race The "Elfstedentocht" ("Tour of the Eleven Towns"), which originated in the 17th century, was held in the Netherlands from 1909–63, and again in 1985 and 1986, covering 200 km (124 miles 483 yd). As the weather does not permit an annual race in the Netherlands, alternative "Elfstedentocht" have taken place at Lake Vesijärvi, near Lahti, Finland; Ottawa River, Canada; and Lake Weissensee, Austria. The record time for 200 km is: (men) 5 hr 40 min 37 sec, by Dries van Wijhe (Netherlands); and (women) 5 hr 48 min 8 sec, by Alida Pasveer (Netherlands), both at Lake Weissensee (altitude 3,609 ft), Austria on 11 Feb 1989. Jan-Roelof Kruithof (Netherlands) won the race nine times—1974, 1976–77, 1979–84. An estimated 16,000 skaters took part in 1986.

Twenty-four hours Martinus Kuiper (Netherlands) skated 339.67 miles in 24 hr in Alkmaar, Netherlands on 12–13 Dec 1988.

WORLD RECORDS
SPEED SKATING

Meters	min : sec	Name and Country	Place	Date
MEN				
500	35.76	Dan Jansen (USA)	Calgary, Canada	30 Jan 1994
1,000	1:12.43	Dan Jansen	Hamar, Norway	18 Feb 1994
1,500	1:51.29	Johann-Olav Koss (Norway)	Hamar, Norway	16 Feb 1994
3,000	3:56.16	Thomas Bos (Netherlands)	Calgary, Canada	3 Mar 1992
5,000	6:34.96	Johann-Olav Koss	Hamar, Norway	13 Feb 1994
10,000	13:30.55	Johann-Olav Koss	Hamar, Norway	20 Feb 1994
WOMEN				
500	38.99	Bonnie Blair (USA)	Calgary, Canada	26 Mar 1994
1,000	1:17.65	Christa Rothenburger (now Luding) (East Germany)	Calgary, Canada	26 Feb 1988
1,500	1:59.30†	Karin Kania (East Germany)	Medeo, USSR	22 Mar 1986
3,000	4:09.32	Gunda Niemann (nee Kleeman) (Germany)	Calgary, Canada	25 Mar 1994
5,000	7:03.26	Gunda Niemann	Calgary, Canada	26 Mar 1994

† *Set at high altitude.*

SHORT TRACK

MEN

500	43.08	Mirko Vuillermin (Italy)	Beijing, China	27 Mar 1993
1,000	1:28.47	Mike McMillen (New Zealand)	Denver, CO	4 Apr 1992
1,500	2:22.36	Eric Flaim (USA)	Beijing, China	21 Mar 1993
3,000	5:00.83	Chae Ji-hoon (South Korea)	Lake Placid, NY	16 Jan 1993
5,000 relay	7:10.95	New Zealand	Beijing, China	28 Mar 1993

WOMEN

500	45.60	Zhang Yanmei (China)	Beijing, China	27 Mar 1993
1,000	1:35.83	Chun Lee-kyung (South Korea)	Asahikawa, Japan	6 Dec 1993
1,500	2:28.26	Eden Donatelli (Canada)	Seoul, South Korea	31 Mar 1991
3,000	5:17.59	Won Hye-kyung (South Korea)	Asahikawa, Japan	6 Dec 1993
3,000 relay	4:26.56	Canada	Beijing, China	28 Mar 1993

ON THE RECORD

SPEED SKATING

"Why Bonnie Blair?" That's a question this skater asks herself when she discusses the question of speed. And she falters over the answer. "Some people look at me in awe. That's very flattering to me, but I don't want to think that I'm different from anyone else. I feel fortunate, but I don't really know. Why me, and not someone else?"

Known as one of speed skating's best technicians, Blair is all too able to see flaws. "I'm not perfect. There are still things I need to work on. Because of that, there is a possibility of going faster. As long as there's that possibility, I want to try." But what's the point of beating your own records? Is it, as some climbers say of Mount Everest, just because it's there? "I hope that people with high goals do it for the love of it, so they can say 'Hey, I did that.' That's my feeling. Back in Calgary in 1988 when I won the world record and the gold, people said 'Why do you keep doing this? You've done the ultimate.' I love to compete. There's a passion inside me for it, a fire that keeps burning bright."

(Allsport/Bob Martin)

For Blair, there's always just one more goal. "At Lillehammer I crossed the 39-second mark in the 500 meters. If I hadn't kept going I wouldn't have done that. I think especially in our sport, where everything is related to the clock, time is a point of self-satisfaction. In the 1,500 meters (at the 1994 Olympics) I came in fourth. I missed the bronze by .03 seconds. But it was my personal best by half a second. That was great for me. I felt like I had won."

What gives Bonnie Blair her greatest joy? "Competition, yes. But I also love speed. The satisfaction of beating myself just puts me on top of the world."

JAI ALAI (Pelota Vasca)

World Championships The *Federacion Internacional de Pelota Vasca* stages World Championships every four years (the first in 1952). The most successful pair have been Roberto Elias and Juan Labat (Argentina), who won the *Trinquete Share* four times, 1952, 1958, 1962 and 1966. Labat won a record seven world titles in all between 1952 and 1966. Riccardo Bizzozero (Argentina) also won seven world titles in various *Trinquete* and *Frontón corto* events, 1970–82. The most wins in the long court game *Cesta Punta* is three, by José Hamuy (Mexico; 1934–83), with two different partners, 1958, 1962 and 1966.

Fastest speed An electronically measured ball velocity of 188 mph was recorded by José Ramon Areitio (Spain) at the Newport Jai Alai, RI on 3 Aug 1979.

Longest domination The longest domination as the world's No. 1 player was enjoyed by Chiquito de Cambo (né Joseph Apesteguy [France]; 1881–1955) from the beginning of the century until succeeded in 1938 by Jean Urruty (France).

Largest frontón The world's largest frontón (enclosed stadium) is the Palm Beach Jai Alai, West Palm Beach, which has a seating capacity of 6,000 and covers three acres. The record attendance for a jai alai contest was 15,052 people at the World Jai Alai in Miami, FL on 27 Dec 1975. The frontón, which is the oldest in the United States (1926), has seating capacity for only 3,884.

JUDO

Most titles *World and Olympic* World Championships were inaugurated in Tokyo, Japan in 1956. Women's championships were first held in 1980 in New York. Yashiro Yamashita won nine consecutive Japanese titles from 1977 to 1985: four world titles—Over 95 kg in 1979, 1981 and 1983; Open in 1981; and the Olympic Open category in 1984. He retired undefeated after 203 successive wins between 1977 and 1985. Two other men have won four world titles—Shozo Fujii (Japan), Under 80 kg 1971, 1973 and 1975, Under 78 kg 1979; and Naoya Ogawa (Japan), Open 1987, 1989, 1991 and Over 95 kg 1989.

The only men to have won two Olympic gold medals are Wilhelm Ruska, Over 93 kg and Open in 1972; Peter Seisenbacher (Austria), 86 kg 1984 and 1988; Hitoshi Saito (Japan), Over 95 kg 1984 and 1988; and Waldemar Legien (Poland), 78 kg 1988 and 86 kg 1992. Ingrid Berghmans (Belgium) has won a record six women's world titles (first held 1980):

Open 1980, 1982, 1984 and 1986 and Under 72 kg in 1984 and 1989. She has also won four silver medals and a bronze. She won the Olympic 72 kg title in 1988, when women's judo was introduced as a demonstration sport.

The only US judo players to win world titles have been Michael Swain, at men's 71 kg class in 1987, and Ann-Maria Bernadette Burns at women's 56 kg in 1984.

Highest grades The efficiency grades in judo are divided into pupil (*kyu*) and master (*dan*) grades. The highest awarded is the extremely rare red belt *judan* (10th dan), given to only 13 men so far. The Judo protocol provides for an 11th dan (*juichidan*) who also would wear a red belt, a 12th dan (*junidan*) who would wear a white belt twice as wide as an ordinary belt, and the highest of all, *shihan* (ductor), but these have never been bestowed, except for the 12th dan, to the founder of the sport, Dr Jigoro Kano.

Most throws Greg Foster and Lee Finney completed 27,083 judo throwing techniques in a 10-hour period at the Forest Judo Club, Leicester, Great Britain on 25 Sep 1993.

Jiu-Jitsu The World Council of Jiu-Jitsu Organization has staged World Championships biennially since 1984. The Canadian team has been the winner on each occasion.

JUMP ROPE

Ten mile skip-run Vadivelu Karunakaren (India) skipped rope 10 miles in 58 min at Madras, India, 1 Feb 1990.

Most turns of the rope *One hour* 14,628, by Park Bong Tae (South Korea) at Pusan, South Korea, 2 Jul 1989. Robert Commers holds the US record, with 13,783, at Woodbridge, NJ, 13 May 1989.

On a single rope, team of 90 160, by students from the Nishigoshi Higashi Elementary School, Kumamoto, Japan, 27 Feb 1987.

On a tightrope 358 (consecutive), by Julian Albulet (USA) at Las Vegas, NV, 2 Jul 1990.

Most on a rope (minimum 12 turns obligatory) 260, by students of the Yorkton Regional High School, Yorkton, Saskatchewan, Canada, on 28 May 1992.

KARATE

World Championships Great Britain has won a record six world titles (instituted 1970) at the kumite team event, in 1975, 1982, 1984, 1986, 1988 and 1990. Two men's individual kumite titles have been won by Pat McKay (Great Britain) at Under 80 kg, 1982 and 1984; Emmanuel Pinda (France) at Open, 1984, and Over 80 kg, 1988; Theirry Masci (France) at Under 70 kg, in 1986 and 1988; and José Manuel Egea (Spain) at Under 80 kg, 1990 and 1992. Four women's kumite titles have been won by Guus van Mourik (Netherlands) at Over 60 kg, in 1982, 1984, 1986 and 1988. Three individual kata titles have been won by: *(men)* Tsuguo Sakumoto (Japan) in 1984, 1986 and 1988; *(women)* Mie Nakayama (Japan) in 1982, 1984 and 1986.

"Tokey" Hill is the only American ever to win a gold medal at the Karate World Championships in Madrid, Spain. He won the 80-kilogram division on 27 Nov 1980.

LACROSSE

MEN

Most titles World The USA has won six of the seven World Championships, in 1967, 1974, 1982, 1986, 1990 and 1994. Canada won the other world title in 1978, beating the USA 17–16 in overtime; this was the first tied international match.

NCAA National champions were determined by committee from 1936; since 1971 they have been decided by NCAA playoffs. Johns Hopkins University has the most wins overall: seven NCAA titles between 1974 and 1987, and six wins and five ties between 1941 and 1970.

Most points The record for most points in the NCAA lacrosse tournament is 25, by Eamon McEneaney (Cornell) in 1977 and Tim Goldstein (Cornell) in 1987. Both players played in three games. Ed Mullen scored the most points in an NCAA championship game, with 12, for Maryland *v* Navy in the 1976 championship game.

Highest score The highest score in an international lacrosse match was the USA's 32–8 win over England in Toronto, Ontario, Canada in 1986.

WOMEN

The first reported playing of lacrosse by women was in 1886. The women's game has evolved separately from the men's game, so the rules now differ considerably.

World Championships/World Cup The first World Cup was held in 1982, replacing the world championships that had been held three times since 1969. The USA has won four times, in 1974, 1982, 1989 and 1993.

NCAA The NCAA first staged a women's national championship in 1982.

Most titles Four teams have won two titles: Temple, 1984 and 1988; Penn State, 1987 and 1989; Maryland, 1986 and 1992; and Virginia, 1991 and 1993.

MICROLIGHTING

The *Fédération Aéronautique Internationale* has established two classes of aircraft for which records are accepted, C1 a/o and R 1-2-3, and the following are the overall best of the two classes (all in the C1 a/o class).

World records *Distance in a straight line* 1,011.45 miles, Wilhelm Lischak (Austria), Volsau, Austria to Brest, France, 8 Jun 1988.

Distance in a closed circuit 1,679.04 miles, Wilhelm Lischak (Austria), Wels, Austria, 18 Jun 1988.

A relatively unknown sport, microlighting can offer participants a magnificent view of Africa. (Vandystadt/Y. Arthus-Bertrand)

Altitude 30,147 ft, Eric S. Winton (Australia), Tyagarah Aerodrome, New South Wales, Australia, 8 Apr 1989.

Speed over a 500 km closed circuit 182 mph, C.T. Andrews (USA), 3 Aug 1982.

Endurance From 1 Dec 1987 to 29 Jan 1988, Brian Milton (Great Britain) flew from London, Great Britain to Sydney, Australia, covering 13,650 miles in a flying time of 241 hr 20 min.

Eve Jackson flew from Biggin Hill, Great Britain to Sydney, Australia from 26 Apr 1986 to 1 Aug 1987. Flying time was 279 hr 55 min and the flight covered 13,639 miles.

MODERN PENTATHLON

Most titles *World* András Balczó (Hungary) won the record number of world titles (instituted 1949), six individual and seven team. He won the

Michael switched sports. Bo and Deion doubled up. Modern Pentathletes? . . . They play five: fencing, riding, running, shooting and swimming. (Allsport/Howard Boylan)

world individual title in 1963, 1965–67 and 1969 and the Olympic title in 1972. His seven team titles (1960–70) comprised five world and two Olympic.

The USSR has won a record 14 world and four Olympic team titles. Hungary has also won a record four Olympic team titles and 10 world titles.

Women's World Championships were first held in 1981, replacing the World Cup, which began in 1978. Poland has won a record five women's world team titles: 1985, 1988–91; Great Britain won three world titles, 1981–83, and three World Cups, 1978–80. Eva Fjellerup (Denmark), has won the individual title three times, 1990–91, 1993.

The only US modern pentathletes to win world titles have been Robert Nieman, 1979, when the men's team also won, and Lori Norwood (women's) in 1989.

Olympic The greatest number of Olympic gold medals won in pentathlon is three, by András Balczó, a member of the winning team in 1960 and 1968 and the 1972 individual champion.

Lars Hall (Sweden) has uniquely won two individual championships (1952 and 1956). Pavel Serafimovich Lednyev (USSR) won a record seven medals (two team gold, one team silver, one individual silver, three individual bronze), 1968–80.

The only US individual Olympic medalist has been Robert Lee Beck, who won the bronze in 1960.

US National Championships The women's championship was first held in 1977; Kim Dunlop (nee Arata) has won a record nine titles (1979–80, 1984–89 and 1991). The men's championship was inaugurated in 1955. Mike Burley has won a record four titles (1977, 1979, 1981, 1985).

MOTORCYCLE RACING

Oldest race The oldest continuous motorcycle races in the world are the Auto-Cycle Union Tourist Trophy (TT) series, first held on the 15.81 mile "Peel" (St John's) course in the Isle of Man, Great Britain on 28 May 1907, and still run in the island on the "Mountain" circuit.

Earliest race The first reported race in the United States was won by George Holden of Brooklyn, NY in 1903, recording 14 min 57.2 sec for 10 miles.

Fastest circuits The highest average lap speed attained on any closed circuit is 160.288 mph, by Yvon du Hamel (Canada) on a modified 903 cc four-cylinder Kawasaki Z1 at the 31-degree banked 2.5 mile Daytona International Speedway, FL in Mar 1973. His lap time was 56.149 sec.

The fastest road circuit used to be Francorchamps circuit near Spa, Belgium, then 8.77 miles in length. It was lapped in 3 min 50.3 sec (average speed 137.150 mph) by Barry Sheene (Great Britain) on a 495 cc 4-cylinder Suzuki during the Belgian Grand Prix on 3 Jul 1977. On that occasion he

If you suffer from car-sickness, don't ever try sidecar racing. Should the temptation prove irresistible, make sure six-time world champion Rolf Biland is your partner. (Allsport/Mike Hewitt)

Jordi Tarres, winner of five world trials titles, in action. (Vandystadt//Y. Guchaqua)

set a record time for this ten-lap (87.74 mile) race of 38 min 58.5 sec (average speed 135.068 mph).

Longest circuit The 37.73-mile "Mountain" circuit on the Isle of Man, over which the Tourist Trophy (TT) races have been run since 1911, has 264 curves and corners and is the longest used for any motorcycle race.

Most successful riders Giacomo Agostini (Italy) won 122 races (68 at 500 cc, 54 at 350 cc) in the World Championship series between 24 Apr 1965 and 25 Sep 1977, including a record 19 in 1970, a season's total also achieved by Mike Hailwood (Great Britain) in 1966.

The record number of career wins for any one class is 70 by Rolf Biland at sidecar.

Angel Roldan Nieto (Spain) won a record seven 125 cc titles, 1971–72, 1979, 1981–84, and he also won a record six titles at 50 cc, 1969–70, 1972, 1975–77. Phil Read (Great Britain) won a record four 250 cc titles, 1964–65, 1968, 1971.

Sidecar Klaus Enders (Germany) won six world sidecar titles, 1967, 1969–70, 1972–74. This was equaled in 1993 by Rolf Biland (Switzerland), who had previously won in 1978–79, 1981, 1983 and 1992.

World Championships The most World Championship titles (instituted by the *Fédération Internationale Motocycliste* in 1949) won is 15, by Giacomo Agostini—seven at 350 cc, 1968–74, and eight at 500 cc in 1966–72, 1975. He is the only man to have won two World Championships in five consecutive years (350 cc and 500 cc titles, 1968–72).

The most world titles won by an American motorcyclist is four, by Eddie Lawson, at 500 cc in 1984, 1986, 1988–89.

Trials A record five World Trials Championships have been won by Jordi Tarrés (Spain), 1987, 1989–91 and 1993.

Most successful machines Japanese Yamaha machines won 45 World Championships between 1964 and 1992.

Youngest and oldest world champions Loris Capirossi (Italy) is the youngest to win a World Championship. He was 17 yr 165 days when he won the 125 cc title on 16 Sep 1990. The oldest was Hermann-Peter Müller (1909–76) of West Germany, who won the 250 cc title in 1955 at the age of 46.

GUESS WHAT?

Q. HOW FAR DID THE LONGEST WHEELIE TRAVEL?

A. SEE "MOTORCYCLES" (TRANSPORT)

MOTO-CROSS

World Championships Joël Robert (Belgium) won six 250 cc Moto-cross World Championships (1964, 1968–72). Between 25 Apr 1964 and 18 Jun 1972 he won a record fifty 250 cc Grand Prix. Eric Geboers (Belgium) has uniquely won all three categories of the Moto-cross World Championships, at 125 cc in 1982 and 1983, 250 cc in 1987 and 500 cc in 1988 and 1990.

Youngest champion The youngest moto-cross world champion was Dave Strijbos (Netherlands), who won the 125 cc title at the age of 18 yr 296 days on 31 Aug 1986.

NETBALL

Most titles World Australia has won the World Championships (instituted 1963) a record six times—1963, 1971, 1975, 1979, 1983 and 1991.

Highest scores On 9 Jul 1991, during the World Championships in Sydney, Australia, the Cook Islands beat Vanuatu 120–30. The record number of goals in the World Tournament is 402, by Judith Heath (England) in 1971.

Most international appearances The record number of appearances is 102, by Kendra Slawinski of England, 1981–93.

OLYMPICS

Most participants The greatest number of competitors at a Summer Games celebration was 9,369 (6,659 men, 2,710 women), who represented a record 169 nations, at Barcelona, Spain in 1992. The greatest number at the Winter Games was 1,737 (1,216 men, 521 women) representing 67 countries, at Lillehammer, Norway in 1994.

Largest crowd The largest crowd at any Olympic site was 104,102 at the 1952 ski-jumping competition at the Holmenkøllen, outside Oslo, Norway. Estimates of the number of spectators of the marathon race through Tokyo, Japan on 21 Oct 1964 ranged from 500,000 to 1.5 million. The total attendance at the Los Angeles games in 1984 was 5,797,923.

Olympic torch relay The longest journey of the torch within one country was for the XV Olympic Winter Games in Canada in 1988. The torch arrived from Greece at St John's, Newfoundland on 17 Nov 1987 and was transported 11,222 miles (5,088 miles on foot, 4,419 miles by aircraft/ferry, 1,712 miles by snowmobile and 3 miles by dogsled) until its arrival at Calgary on 13 Feb 1988.

Most medals In the ancient Olympic Games, Leonidas of Rhodos won 12 running titles 164–152 B.C. The most individual gold medals won by a male competitor in the modern Games is 10, by Raymond Ewry (USA; 1874–1937) (see Track and Field). The female record is seven, by Vera Cáslavská-Odlozil (Czechoslovakia) (see Gymnastics).

The most gold medals won by an American woman is five, by speed skater Bonnie Blair, 1988–94. The most medals won by an American woman is eight, by swimmer Shirley Babashoff—gold at 4 × 100 meters freestyle relay 1972 and 1976, and six silver medals 1972–76, a record for any competitor in Olympic history.

Gymnast Larisa Latynina (USSR;) won a record 18 medals, and the men's record is 15, by Nikolay Andrianov (see Gymnastics). The record at one celebration is eight, by gymnast Aleksandr Dityatin (USSR) in 1980.

The most medals won by an American Olympian is 11, at shooting, by Carl Osburn (1884–1966) from 1912 to 1924—five gold, four silver, two bronze; by Mark Spitz, at swimming, from 1968 to 1972—nine gold, one silver, one bronze; and by Matt Biondi, at swimming, 1984–92—eight gold, two silver, one bronze.

The only Olympian to win four consecutive individual titles in the same event has been Al Oerter (USA), who won the discus in 1956–68. However, Raymond Ewry (USA) won both the standing long jump and the standing high jump at four games in succession, 1900, 1904, 1906 (the Intercalated Games) and 1908. Also, Paul B. Elvström (Denmark) won four successive gold medals at monotype yachting events, 1948–60, but there was a class change (1948 Firefly class, 1952–60 Finn class).

Swimmer Mark Spitz (USA) won a record seven golds at one celebration, at Munich in 1972, including three in relays. The most won in individual events at one celebration is five, by speed skater Eric Heiden (USA) at Lake Placid, NY in 1980.

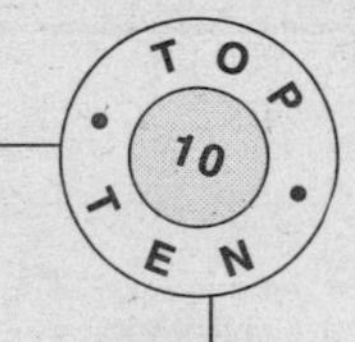

MOST MEDALS WINTER GAMES (1924–94)

	Gold	Silver	Bronze	Total
USSR[1]	99	71	71	241
Norway	73	77	64	214
USA	53	55	39	147
Austria	36	48	44	128
Germany[2]	45	43	37	125
Finland	36	45	42	123
GDR[3]	39	36	35	110
Sweden	39	26	34	99
Switzerland	27	29	29	85
Italy	25	21	21	67

[1] Includes Czarist Russia to 1912, CIS 1992, Russia 1994.

[2] Includes West Germany 1968–88.

A record 67 nations participated in the Lillehammer Winter Olympics. The Norwegian hosts displayed their rich winter culture during the opening ceremony. (Allsport/Mike Powell)

The only man to win a gold medal in both the Summer and Winter Games is Edward Eagan (USA; 1898–1967), who won the 1920 light-heavyweight boxing title and was a member of the winning four-man bob in 1932.

Christa Luding (nee Rothenburger; East Germany) became the first woman to win a medal at both the Summer and Winter Games when she won a silver in the cycling sprint event in 1988. She had previously won medals for speed skating—500 meter gold in 1984, and 1,000 meter gold and 500 meter silver in 1988.

Youngest and oldest gold medalist The youngest-ever winner was a French boy (whose name is not recorded) who coxed the Netherlands pair in rowing in 1900. He was 7–10 years old and he substituted for Dr Hermanus Brockmann, who coxed in the heats but proved too heavy. The youngest-ever female champion was Kim Yoon-mi (South Korea; b. 1 Dec 1980), age 13 yr 83 days, in the 1994 women's 3,000 m short-track speed skating relay event.

The oldest American Olympic champion was retired minister Galen Carter Spencer (1840–1904), who assisted the Potomac Archers to an archery team medal two days after his 64th birthday in 1904. The youngest American gold medalist was Jackie Fields, who won the 1924 featherweight boxing title at 16 yrs 161 days.

Oldest and youngest medalist The oldest person to win an Olympic medal is Oscar Swahn (Sweden), who won a silver medal in running deer shooting at 72 yr 280 days in 1920.

The youngest American medalist and participant was Dorothy Poynton (b. 17 Jul 1915), who won the springboard diving bronze medal at 13 yr 23 days in 1928. The youngest American male medalist was Donald Wills Douglas, Jr. (b. 3 Jul 1917) with silver at 6-meter yachting in 1932, at 15 yr 40 days.

The oldest American medalist and Olympic participant was Samuel Harding Duvall (1836–1908), who was 68 yrs 194 days when he was a member of the Cincinnati Archers silver medal team in 1904.

Longest span The longest span of an Olympic competitor is 40 years, by Dr Ivan Osiier (Denmark; 1888–1965) in fencing, 1908–32 and 1948; Magnus Konow (Norway; 1887–1972) in yachting, 1908–20, 1928 and 1936–48; Paul Elvström (Denmark) in yachting, 1948–1960, 1968–72 and 1984–88; and Durward Knowles (Great Britain 1948, then Bahamas) in yachting, 1948–72 and 1988. Brothers Piero and Raimondo d'Inzeo (Italy) competed in equestrian events at a record eight celebrations from 1948–76. Raimondo won one gold, two silver and three bronze medals. Piero won two silver and four bronze medals. This was equaled by Paul Elvström and Durward Knowles in 1988, and by Hubert Raudaschl (Austria), 1964–92. The longest span by a woman is 28 years, by Anne Ransehousen (nee Newberry; USA) in dressage, 1960, 1964 and 1988. Fencer Kerstin Palm (Sweden) competed in a women's record seven competitions, 1964–88.

TOP 10 TEN

MOST MEDALS SUMMER GAMES (1896–92)*

	Gold	Silver	Bronze	Total
USA	789	603	518	1,910
USSR[1]	442	361	333	1,136
Germany[2]	186	227	236	649
Great Britain	177	224	218	619
France	161	175	191	527
Sweden	133	149	171	453
GDR[3]	154	131	126	411
Italy	153	126	131	410
Hungary	136	124	144	404
Finland	98	77	112	287

** Excludes medals won in Official Art competitions in 1912–1948.*

[1] *Includes Czarist Russia to 1912, CIS 1992, Russia 1994.*

[2] *Germany 1896–1964 and 1992, West Germany 1968–88.*

[3] *GDR (East Germany) 1968–88.*

The US record for longest span of Olympic competition by a man is 32 years, by equestrian J. Michael Plumb, who competed in seven Olympics. The women's record is six competitions, by fencer Janice Romary.

ORIENTEERING

Most titles Sweden has won the women's relay 10 times—1966, 1970, 1974, 1976, 1981, 1983, 1985, 1989, 1991 and 1993. The men's relay has been won a record seven times by Norway—1970, 1978, 1981, 1983, 1985, 1987 and 1989. Three women's individual titles have been won by Annichen Kringstad (Sweden), in 1981, 1983 and 1985. The men's title has been won twice by Åge Hadler (Norway), in 1966 and 1972; Egil Johansen (Norway), in 1976 and 1978; and Øyvin Thon (Norway), in 1979 and 1981.

Most competitors The most competitors at a one-day orienteering event was 38,000, in the Ruf des Herbstes held in Sibiu, Romania in 1982. The largest event is the five-day Swedish O-Ringen at Småland, which attracted 120,000 competitors in July 1983.

US National Championships This competition was first held on 17 Oct 1970. Sharon Crawford, of the New England Orienteering Club, has won a record 11 overall women's titles, 1977–82, 1984–87, 1989. Mikell Platt, of the Blue Star Komplex Orienteering Club, has won a record six overall men's titles, 1985 and 1988–92.

Ski orienteering The World Championships in ski orienteering were instituted in 1975. Sweden has won the men's relay five times (1977, 1980, 1982, 1984 and 1990) and Finland has won the women's relay five times (1975, 1977, 1980, 1988 and 1990). The most individual titles is four, by Ragnhild Bratberg (Norway), Classic 1986, 1990, Sprint 1988, 1990. The men's record is three, by Anssi Juutilainen (Finland), Classic 1984, 1988, Sprint 1992.

PARACHUTING

World championships *Team* The USSR won the men's team title in 1954, 1958, 1960, 1966, 1972, 1976 and 1980, and the women's team title in 1956, 1958, 1966, 1968, 1972 and 1976.

Individual Nikolay Ushamyev (USSR) has won the individual title twice, in 1974 and 1980.

Greatest accuracy At Yuma, AZ, in March 1978, Dwight Reynolds scored a record 105 daytime dead centers, and Bill Wenger and Phil Munden tied with 43 night-time dead centers, competing as members of the US Army Golden Knights.

With electronic measuring, the official *Fédération Aeronautique Internationale* (FAI) record is 50 dead centers, by Linger Abdurakhmanov (USSR) at Fergana in 1988, when the women's record was set at 41, by Natalya Filinkova (USSR) in 1988.

The Men's Night Accuracy Landing record on an electronic score pad is 31 consecutive dead centers, by Vladimir Buchenev (USSR) on 30 Oct 1986. The women's record is 21, by Inessa Stepanova (USSR) at Fergana on 18 Oct 1988.

PARACHUTE RECORDS

First *Tower*[1] • Louis-Sébastien Lenormand (1757–1839), quasi-parachute, Montpellier, France, 1783.

Balloon • André-Jacques Garnerin (1769–1823), 2,230 ft, Monceau Park, Paris, France, 22 Oct 1797.

Aircraft • *Man:* "Captain" Albert Berry, an aerial exhibitionist, St Louis, MO, 1 Mar 1912. Woman: Mrs Georgina "Tiny" Broadwick (b. 1893), Griffith Park, Los Angeles, CA, 21 Jun 1913.

Longest Duration Fall • Lt. Col. Wm H. Rankin, USMC, 40 min due to thermals, North Carolina, 26 Jul 1956.

Longest Delayed Drop *Man* • Capt Joseph W. Kittinger,[2] 84,700 ft (16.04 miles), from balloon at 102,800 ft, Tularosa, NM, 16 Aug 1960.

Woman • E. Fomitcheva (USSR), 48,556 ft over Odessa, USSR, 26 Oct 1977.

Mid Air Rescue *Earliest* • Miss Dolly Shcphcrd (1886 1983) brought down Miss Louie May on her single 'chute from balloon at 11,000 ft, Longton, Great Britain, 9 Jun 1908.

Lowest • Andy Peckett saved Maurizio Brambilla (unconscious), injured when jumping out of aircraft at 15,000 ft, by pulling his ripcord at 2,000 ft—7 secs from impact, Vichy, France, 11 Aug 1993.

Escape *Highest* • Flt. Lt. J. de Salis, RAF and Fg. Off. P. Lowe, RAF, 56,000 ft, Monyash, Derby, Great Britain, 9 Apr 1958.

Lowest • S/Ldr. Terence Spencer DFC, RAF, 30–40 ft, Wismar Bay, Baltic, 19 Apr 1945.

Landing *Highest* • Ten USSR parachutists,[3] 23,405 ft, Lenina Peak, USSR, May 1969.

Cross-Channel (Lateral Fall) • Sgt. Bob Walters with three soldiers and two British Royal Marines, 22 miles from 25,000 ft, Dover, Great Britain to Sangatte, France, 31 Aug 1980.

Total Sport Parachuting Descents *Man* • Don Kellner (USA), 20,000, various locations up to 14 Nov 1993.

Woman • Valentina Zakoretskaya

Paragliding The greatest distance flown is 176.4 miles by Alex François Louw (South Africa) from Kuruman, South Africa on 31 Dec 1992. The women's distance record is 79.8 miles, by Judy Leden (Great Britain) from Vryburg, South Africa on 9 Dec 1992. The height gain record is 14,849 ft by Robby Whittal (Great Britain), at Brandvlei, South Africa on 6 Jan 1993. All these records were tow launched.

Nigel Horder scored four successive dead centers at the Dutch Open, Flevhof, Netherlands on 22 May 1983.

(USSR), 8,000, over USSR, 1964–September 1980.

24-Hour Total *Man* • Dale Nelson (USA), 301 (in accordance with United States Parachute Association rules), PA, 26–27 May 1988.

Woman • Cheryl Stearns (USA), 255 at Lodi, CA, 26–27 Nov 1987.

Most Traveled • Kevin Seaman from a Cessna Skylane (pilot Charles E. Merritt), 12,186 miles, jumps in all 50 US states, 26 Jul–15 Oct 1972.

Heaviest Load • US Space Shuttle *Columbia*, booster rocket retrieval, 80 ton capacity, triple array, each 120 ft diameter, Atlantic, off Cape Canaveral, FL, 12 Apr 1981.

Highest Canopy Formation • 37, a team of French parachutists at Brienne le Chateau, Troyes, France, held for 13 secs on 16 Aug 1992.

Largest Free-fall Duration *Men* • 150, from 21 countries, held for 5.47 sec from 19,192 ft, Koksijde military base, Belgium, 4 Jul 1992.

Women • 100, from 20 countries, held for 5.97 sec, from 17,000 ft, Aéreodrome du Cannet des Maures, France, 14 Aug 1992.

USA: 144, held for 8.8 sec, from 16,000 ft, Quincy, IL, 11 Jul 1988.

Oldest *Man* • Edwin C. Townsend (d. 7 Nov 1987), 89 years, Vermillion Bay, LA, 5 Feb 1986.

Woman • Mrs Sylvia Brett (Great Britain), 80 years 166 days, Cranfield, Great Britain, 23 Aug 1986.

Oldest Tandem *Man* • George Salyer (USA), 91 years, Snohomish, WA, 18 Jun 1992

Woman • Corena Leslie (USA) 89 years 326 days, Buckeye Airport, Sun Valley, AZ, 11 Jun 1992.

Survival from Longest Fall without Parachute • Vesna Vulovic (Yugoslavia), air hostess in DC–9 that blew up at 33,330 ft over Srbská Kamenice, Czechoslovakia (now Czech Republic), 26 Jan 1972.

[1] *The king of Ayutthaya, Siam in 1687 was reported to have been amused by an ingenious athlete parachuting with two large umbrellas. Faustus Verancsis is reputed to have descended in Hungary with a framed canopy in 1617.*
[2] *Maximum speed in rarefied air was 625.2 mph at 90,000 ft—marginally supersonic.*
[3] *Four were killed.*

A breathtaking view of the largest free-fall parachute record. (Gamma/P. Passe)

POLO

Oldest The oldest existing polo club in the United States is Meadow Brook Polo Club, Jericho, NY, founded in 1879.

World Championships The first World Championships were held in Berlin, Germany in 1989. The USA won the title, defeating Great Britain 7–6 in the final.

The United States Open Championship has been won 28 times by the Meadow Brook Polo Club, in 1916, 1920, 1923–41, 1946–51 and 1953.

Highest score The highest aggregate number of goals scored in an international polo match is 30, when Argentina beat the USA 21–9 at Meadowbrook, Long Island, NY in September 1936.

Highest handicap The highest handicap based on six $7^{1}/_{2}$-min "chukkas" is

Although the dimensions of the polo field are the largest of any sport, the ball always attracts a crowd. (Allsport/Simon Bruty)

10 goals, introduced in the USA in 1891. A total of 56 players have received 10-goal handicaps.

A match of two 40-goal teams has been staged on three occasions—in Argentina in 1975, in the United States in 1990, and in Australia in 1991.

Most chukkas The greatest number of chukkas played on one ground in a day is 43. This was achieved by the Pony Club on the Number 3 Ground at Kitlington Park, Great Britain on 31 Jul 1991.

POOL

14.1 CONTINUOUS POOL (AMERICAN STRAIGHT POOL)

World Championship The two most dominant 14.1 players have been Ralph Greenleaf (USA; 1899–1950), who won the "world" professional title six times and defended it 13 times (1919–37), and William "Willie" Mosconi (USA; 1913–93), who dominated the game from 1941 to 1956, and also won the title six times and defended it 13 times.

Longest consecutive run The longest consecutive run in 14.1 recognized by the Billiard Congress of America (BCA) is 526 balls, by Willie Mosconi in March 1954 during an exhibition in Springfield, OH.

Michael Eufemia is reported to have pocketed 625 balls at Logan's Billiard Academy, Brooklyn, NY on 2 Feb 1960, but this run has never been ratified by the BCA.

Most balls pocketed The greatest number of balls pocketed in 24 hr is 16,125, by James Abel at White Plains, NY on 17–18 Dec 1991.

Pool pocketing speed The record times for pocketing all 15 balls in a speed competition are: *(men)* 37.9 sec, by Rob McKenna at Blackpool, Great Britain on 7 Nov 1987; *(women)* 44.5 sec, by Susan Thompson at Shrublands Community Centre, Gorleston, Great Britain on 20 Apr 1990.

POWERBOAT RACING

APBA Gold Cup The American Power Boat Association (APBA) Gold Cup race has been won a record nine times by Chip Hanauer (USA), 1982–88, 1992–93.

The highest average speed for the race is 145.269 mph by Mark Tate, piloting *Smokin' Joe's* in 1994.

Longest races The longest offshore race was the Port Richborough London, Great Britain to Monte Carlo Marathon Offshore international event. The race extended over 2,947 miles in 14 stages from 10–25 Jun 1972. It was won by *H.T.S.* (Great Britain), driven by Mike Bellamy, Eddie Chater and Jim Brooker, in 71 hr 35 min 56 sec, for an average of 41.15 mph. The longest circuit race is the 24-hour race held annually since 1962 on the River Seine at Rouen, France.

PROJECTILES

Throwing The greatest distance that any object has been propelled by human power is 6,141 ft 2 in, in the case of an arrow shot by Harry Drake (USA), using a crossbow at the "Smith Creek" Flight Range near Austin, NV on 30 Jul 1988.

The longest independently authenticated throw of any inert object heavier than air is 1,257 ft, for a flying ring, by Scott Zimmerman on 8 Jul 1986 at Fort Funston, CA.

Records achieved with other miscellaneous objects:

Boomerang juggling Consecutive catches with two boomerangs, keeping at least one boomerang aloft at all times, 502, by Chet Snouffer (USA) at Geneva, Switzerland on 5 Jul 1992.

Boomerang throwing Consecutive two-handed catches, 801, by Stéphane Marguerite (France) on 26 Nov 1989 at Lyons, France.

Longest out-and-return distance, 489 ft 3 in, by Michel Dufayard (France) on 5 Jul 1992 at Shrewsbury, Great Britain.

Longest flight duration (with self-catch), 2 min 59.94 sec by Dennis Joyce (USA) at Bethlehem, PA on 25 Jun 1987.

Brick ....146 ft 1 in (standard 5-lb building brick), Geoff Capes at Braybrook School, Orton, Great Britain on 19 Jul 1978.

Cow chip tossing The greatest distance achieved under the "non-sphericalization and 100 percent organic" rule (established in 1970) is 266 ft, by Steve Urner at the Mountain Festival, Tehachapi, CA on 14 Aug 1981.

Egg (fresh hen's) ....323 ft 2½ in (without breaking it), Johnny Dell Foley to Keith Thomas at Jewett, TX on 12 Nov 1978.

HIGHLAND FLING!

The Scottish haggis is one of the most reviled delicacies in history. The Highland treat has been put to several other uses. Throwing it is perhaps the best known. The record distance for throwing a 1 lb 8 oz haggis is 180 ft 10 in by Alan Pettigrew at Loch Lomond, Scotland on 24 May 1984.

Rolling pin ....175 ft 5 in (2 lb), Lori La Deane Adams, 21, at Iowa State Fair, IA on 21 Aug 1979.

Slingshot ....1,565 ft 4 in (50-in-long sling and a 2½ oz dart), David P. Engvall at Baldwin Lake, CA on 13 Sep 1992.

Spear ....638 ft 8 in (using an atlatl or hand-held device that fits onto a short spear), Wayne Brian at Fairplay, CO on 11 Jul 1992.

Flying disc throwing (formerly Frisbee) The World Flying Disc Federation distance records are: *(men)* 623 ft 7 in, by Sam Ferrans (USA) on 2 Jul 1988 at La Habra, CA; *(women)* 426 ft 10 in, by Amy Bekken (USA) on 25 Jul 1990 at La Habra, CA.

The throw, run and catch records are: *(men)* 303 ft 11 in, by Hiroshi Oshima (Japan) on 20 Jul 1988 at San Francisco, CA; *(women)* 196 ft 11 in, by Judy Horowitz (USA) on 29 Jun 1985 at La Mirada, CA.

The 24-hour distance records for a pair are: *(men)* 362.40 miles, by Leonard Muise and Gabe Ontiveros (USA) on 21–22 Sep 1988 at Carson, CA; *(women)* 115.65 miles, by Jo Cahow and Amy Berard (USA) on 30–31 Dec 1979 at Pasadena, CA.

The records for maximum time aloft are: *(men)* 16.72 sec, by Don Cain (USA) on 26 May 1984 at Philadelphia, PA; *(women)* 11.81 sec, by Amy Bekken (USA) on 1 Aug 1991.

RACQUETBALL

World Championships First held in 1982, the IARF World Championships have been held biennially since 1984. The United States has won all six team titles, in 1981, 1984, 1986 (tie with Canada), 1988, 1990 and 1992.

Egan Inoue (USA) has won the most men's singles titles with two, in 1986 and 1990. Two women have won the world singles championships twice: Cindy Baxter (USA) in 1981 and 1986; Heather Stupp (Canada) in 1988 and 1990.

US titles In 1968, championships were initiated by the AARA (the governing body for the sport in the United States). A record five women's open titles have been won by Michelle Gilman-Gould, 1989–93, and four men's open titles have been won by Ed Andrews of California, 1980–81 and 1985–86.

RAPPELING

Longest descent Wilmer Pérez and Luis Aulestia set a rappeling record of 3,376 ft by descending from above Angel Falls, Venezuela down to its base on 24 Aug 1989. The descent took $1^1/_4$ hr.

The longest descent down the side of a building is one of 1,222 ft by a team of eight men from the Code Four Rescue Unit. They rappeled to the ground from the observation deck of the CN Tower in Toronto, Ontario, Canada on 26 Jun 1985.

Greatest distance The greatest distance rappeled by a team of 10 in an eight-hour period is 45 miles, by Royal Marines from the Commando Training Center in Lympstone, Great Britain. They achieved the record by rappeling 1,382 times down the side of the Civic Center in Plymouth, Great Britain on 22 May 1993.

If the elevator at the top of the CN Tower is out of order, then rappeling down its 1,222-foot facade has been proven a viable alternative for reaching the ground floor. (PO Phot. Ash Amliwala)

REAL/ROYAL TENNIS

Oldest The oldest of the surviving active courts in Great Britain is the one at Falkland Palace, Fife, Scotland built by King James V of Scotland in 1539.

Most titles World The first recorded world tennis champion was Clergé (France), *c.* 1740. Jacques Edmond Barre (France; 1802–73) held the title for a record 33 years from 1829 to 1862. Pierre Etchebaster (1893–1980), a Basque, holds the record for the greatest number of successful defenses of the title, with eight between 1928 and 1952.

The Women's World Championships (instituted in 1985) has been won twice by Judith Clarke (Australia), 1985 and 1987; and Penny Lumley (nee Fellows; Great Britain), 1989 and 1991.

United States Jay Gould, Jr. (1888–1935) won his first US singles title in 1906, and retained the title until he retired from singles play in 1926. During his career he lost only one singles match. He also won 19 US doubles titles between 1909 and 1932.

RODEO

The largest rodeo in the world is the National Finals Rodeo, organized by the Professional Rodeo Cowboys Association (PRCA) and the Women's Professional Rodeo Association (WPRA). The 1991 Finals had a paid attendance of 171,414 for 10 performances. In 1994 a record $2.8 million in prize money was offered for the event.

Most world titles The record number of all-around titles (awarded to the leading money winner in a single season in two or more events) in the PRCA World Championships is six, by Larry Mahan (USA) in 1966–70 and 1973, and, consecutively, 1974–79 by Tom Ferguson.

Jim Shoulders of Henrietta, TX won a record 16 World Championships at four events between 1949 and 1959.

Earnings records Roy Cooper holds the career rodeo earnings mark at $1,489,698 through 29 Jun 1994. The record figure for prize money in a single season is $297,896 by Ty Murray in 1993.

Time records The fastest time recorded for calf-roping under the current PRCA rules is 6.7 sec, by Joe Beaver at West Jordan, UT in 1986, and the fastest time for steer wrestling is 2.4 sec, by James Bynum at Marietta, OK in 1955; Carl Deaton at Tulsa, OK in 1976; and Gene Melton at Pecatonica, IL in 1976.

The fastest team roping time is 3.7 sec, by Bob Harris and Tee Woolman at Spanish Fork, UT in 1986.

YOUNGEST RODEO CHAMPION

"My dad was a cowboy," says Ty Murray in his soft western drawl. "Ever since I could remember I wanted to be like him. I remember trying to ride calves at two-and-a-half or three years. Dad would run beside me and hold my belt so I wouldn't fall off." By the time Murray was five, he rode calves in competition. "I got thrown off," he admits, "but that was not real unusual."

It got unusual soon after that. "I've devoted my whole life to rodeo. I did gymnastics as a kid, rode a unicycle, walked fence lines, practiced every single day, to build up my balance." Nowadays he spends his time in three key events: bareback riding, saddle bronc riding, and bull riding.

(Allsport USA/Ken Levine)

"Asking me if I was scared is like asking a kid who plays football if he was scared of getting tackled. It didn't matter. Unlike some, my dad never told me to do anything. He never said you've got to practice, you've got to get on. He broke colts for a living, and I watched him get thrown. It was just the way he was."

Murray's proudest moment was becoming world champion at age 20. "The previous record was 21, but it was back in the fifties." Apart from a love of animals, which Murray vows all rodeo people have, what makes a good rodeo rider great? "You could take ten champions, all with different personalities, all with determination and heart. What you'd find in common is a lot of *try*. That's it. They've got to put forth a lot of effort. They've got to have *try*."

Women's barrel racing The greatest number of titles won in women's barrel racing is 10, by Charmayne Rodman, 1984–93.

Youngest rodeo champions The youngest winner of a world title in rodeo is Anne Lewis (b. 1 Sep 1958), who won the WPRA barrel racing title in 1968, at 10 years of age. Ty Murray (b. 11 Oct 1969) is the youngest cowboy to win the PRCA All-Around Champion title, at age 20, in 1989.

SCORING RECORDS

Bull riding The highest score in bull riding was 100 points out of a possible 100, by Wade Leslie on Wolfman Skoal at Central Point, OR in 1991.

Top bull The top bucking bull Red Rock dislodged 312 riders, 1980–88, and was finally ridden to the 8-sec bell by Lane Frost (1963–89; world champion bull rider 1987) on 20 May 1988.

Saddle bronc riding The highest scored saddle bronc ride is 95 out of a possible 100, by Doug Vold on Transport at Meadow Lake, Saskatchewan, Canada in 1979. Descent, a saddle bronc owned by Beutler Brothers and Cervi Rodeo Company, received a record six PRCA Saddle Bronc of the Year awards, 1966–69, 1971–72.

Bareback riding Joe Alexander of Cora, WY scored 93 out of a possible 100 on Marlboro at Cheyenne, WY in 1974. Sippin' Velvet, owned by Bernis Johnson, has been awarded a record five PRCA Bareback Horse of the Year titles between 1978 and 1987.

Texas skips Vince Bruce (USA) performed 4,001 Texas Skips (jumps back and forth through a large, vertical spun loop) on 22 Jul 1991 at the Empire State Building, New York City.

Largest loop Using a 100-ft rope, Kalvin Cook spun a loop of 95 feet at the Hacienda Hotel, Las Vegas, NV on 27 Mar 1994.

ROLLER SKATING

Most titles Speed The most world speed titles won is 18, by two women: Alberta Vianello (Italy), eight track and 10 road, 1953–65; and Annie Lambrechts (Belgium), one track and 17 road, 1964–81, at distances from 500 meters to 10,000 meters.

Figure The men's record for most figure titles is five, by Karl Heinz Losch (West Germany) in 1958–59, 1961–62 and 1966, and Sandro Guerra (Italy), 1987–89 and 1991–92.

The women's record is four, by Astrid Bader (West Germany) in 1965–68 and by Rafaella del Vinaccio (Italy), 1988–92. The most world pair titles is six, by Tammy Jeru (USA) in 1983–86 (with John Arishita), and in 1990–91 (with Larry McGrew).

Limbo!

On 10 May 1993, Syamala Gowri shimmied under a limbo bar set at 4.7 in. An achievement in itself, but Gowri was wearing roller skates. This anatomy- and gravity-defying feat was performed at Hyderabad, India.

Speed skating The fastest speed posted in an official world record is 26.85 mph, when Luca Antoniel (Italy) recorded 24.99 sec for 300 meters on a road at Gujan-Mestras, France on 31 Jul 1987. The women's record is 25.04 mph, by Marisa Canofogilia (Italy) for 300 meters on the road at Grenoble, France on 27 Aug 1987.

The world records for 10,000 meters on a road or track are: *(men)* 14 min 55.64 sec, Giuseppe de Persio (Italy) at Gujan-Mestras, France on 1 Aug 1988; *(women)* 15 min 58.022 sec, Marisa Canofogilia (Italy) at Grenoble, France on 30 Aug 1987.

ROLLER HOCKEY

Portugal has won most titles, with 14: 1947–50, 1952, 1956, 1958, 1960, 1962, 1968, 1974, 1982, 1991 and 1993.

SKATEBOARDING

David Frank, 25, covered 270.5 miles in 36 hr 43 min 40 sec in Toronto, Ontario, Canada on 11–12 Aug 1985.

Fastest speed The fastest speed recorded on a skateboard is 78.37 mph in a prone position by Roger Hickey, on a course near Los Angeles, CA on 15 Mar 1990.

The stand-up record is 55.43 mph, achieved by Roger Hickey, at San Demas, CA on 3 Jul 1990.

Jumps The high-jump record is 5 ft 5¾ in, by Trevor Baxter of Burgess Hill, Great Britain at Grenoble, France on 14 Sep 1982.

At the World Professional Championships at Long Beach, CA, on 25 Sep 1977, Tony Alva, 19, jumped 17 barrels (17 ft).

ROWING

Most Olympic medals Seven oarsmen have won three gold medals: John Kelly (USA; 1889–1960), who won at Single Sculls (1920) and Double Sculls (1920 and 1924); his cousin, Paul Vincent Costello (USA; 1894–1986), Double Sculls (1920, 1924 and 1928); Jack Beresford, Jr. (Great

Britain; 1899–1977), Single Sculls (1924), Coxless Fours (1932) and Double Sculls (1936); Vyacheslav Ivanov (USSR), Single Sculls (1956, 1960 and 1964); Siegfried Brietzke (East Germany), Coxless Pairs (1972) and Coxless Fours (1976, 1980); Pertti Karppinen (Finland), Single Sculls (1976, 1980 and 1984); and Steven Redgrave (Great Britain), Coxed Fours (1984) and Coxless Pairs (1988 and 1992).

World Championships World rowing championships distinct from the Olympic Games were first held in 1962, and were held every four years at first, but from 1974 were held annually, except in Olympic years.

The most wins at Single Sculls is five, by Peter-Michael Kolbe (West Germany), 1975, 1978, 1981, 1983 and 1986; Pertti Karppinen, 1979 and 1985, and with his three Olympic wins (above); Thomas Lange (Germany), 1987, 1989 and 1991 and two Olympics 1988 and 1992; and in the women's

Steve Redgrave (foreground) is one of seven oarsmen to win three Olympic titles. (Allsport/Bob Martin)

events by Christine Hahn (nee Scheiblich; East Germany), 1974–75, 1977–78 (and the 1976 Olympic title).

Collegiate Championships The first intercollegiate boat race in the United States was between Harvard and Yale in 1852. The Intercollegiate Rowing Association (IRA) was formed in 1895, and in 1898 inaugurated the Varsity Challenge Cup, which was recognized as the premier event in college racing. In 1979, a women's national championship was inaugurated, followed by an official men's event in 1982.

The University of Washington has won the women's title a record seven times (1981–85, 1987–88). Since 1982 Harvard University has won the most men's titles, with five (1983, 1985, 1987–89).

Longest race The longest annual rowing race is the annual Tour du Lac Leman, Geneva, Switzerland for coxed fours (the five-man crew taking turns as cox) over 99 miles. The record winning time is 12 hr 52 min, by LAGA Delft, Netherlands on 3 Oct 1982.

Fastest speed The fastest recorded speed on non-tidal water for 2,187 yd is by an American eight in 5 min 27.14 sec (13.68 mph) at Lucerne, Switzerland on 17 Jun 1984. A crew from Penn AC was timed in 5 min 18.8 sec (14.03 mph) in the FISA Championships on the River Meuse, Liège, Belgium on 17 Aug 1930.

Twenty-four hours The greatest distance rowed in 24 hours (upstream and downstream) is 135.22 miles, by a coxed quad (Peter Halliday, Paul Turnbull, Mike Skerry, Belinda Goglia and Margaret Munneke) on the Yarra River, Melbourne, Australia on 26–27 Jan 1992.

International Dragon Boat Race In this race, instituted in 1975 and held annually in Hong Kong, the fastest time achieved for the 700-yd course is 2 min 27.45 sec, by the Chinese Shun De team on 30 Jan 1985. Teams have 28 members—26 rowers, one steersman and one drummer.

RUGBY

Records are determined in terms of present-day scoring values, i.e., a try at 4 points; a dropped goal, penalty or goal from a mark at 3 points; and a conversion at 2 points. The actual score, in accordance with whichever of the eight earlier systems was in force at the time, is also given, in parentheses.

Rugby all-arounder Canadian international Barrie Burnham scored all possible ways—try, conversion, penalty goal, drop goal, goal from mark—for Meralomas *v* Georgians (20–11) at Vancouver, Canada on 26 Feb 1966.

Highest rugby posts The world's highest rubgy union goal posts are 110 ft 1/2 in high, at the Roan Antelope Rugby Union Club, Luanshya, Zambia.

Although Emma Murphy looks like she's being restrained from fleeing the field, the opposite is true. She is happily orchestrating England's 1994 Rugby World Cup Victory. (Allsport/Gary Prior)

OLYMPIC GAMES

In competitions held at from 1900 to 1924, the only double gold medalist was the United States, which won in 1920 and 1924, defeating France in the final on both occasions.

WORLD CUP

The World Cup has been held on two occasions, 1987 and 1991, with the winners being New Zealand and Australia respectively. The highest team score was New Zealand's 74–13 victory over Fiji at Christchurch, New Zealand on 27 May 1987. New Zealand scored 10 goals, 2 tries and 2 penalty goals.

The individual match record was 30 (3 tries, 9 conversions), by Didier Camberabero (France) *v* Zimbabwe at Auckland on 2 Jun 1987. The leading scorer in the tournament was the New Zealand goal-kicker, Grant James Fox, with 170 points (including a record 126 in 1987).

HIGHEST SCORES

Teams The highest score in any full international was when Japan beat Singapore by 120–3 in the Asian Championships at Seoul, South Korea on 20 Sep 1992.

Individuals Phil Bennett (Wales) scored 34 points (2 tries, 10 conversions, 2 penalty goals) for Wales *v* Japan at Tokyo on 24 Sep 1975, when Wales won 82–6.

A record eight penalty goals were kicked by Mark Andrew Wyatt when he scored all of Canada's points in their 24–19 defeat of Scotland at St John, New Brunswick, Canada on 25 May 1991.

Career In all internationals, Michael Lynagh scored a record 821 points in 67 matches for Australia, 1984–94. The most tries is 59, by David Campese in 84 internationals for Australia, 1982–94.

SEVEN-A-SIDES

Hong Kong Sevens The record of seven wins is held by Fiji, 1977–78, 1980, 1984, 1990–92.

SHOOTING

Most Olympic medals Carl Townsend Osburn (USA; 1884–1966) won 11 medals, in 1912, 1920 and 1924—five gold, four silver and two bronze. Gudbrand Skatteboe (Norway; 1875–1965) is the only marksman to have won three individual gold medals, in 1906.

The first American to win an Olympic medal in shooting was Margaret L. Murdock, who took the silver at small-bore rifle (3-position) in mixed competition in 1976.

Two American women have won gold medals: Patricia Spurgin at women's air rifle in 1984 and Launi Meili at women's 3-position rifle in 1992.

Highest shooting score in 24 hours The Easingwold Rifle and Pistol Club (Yorkshire, Great Britain) team of John Smith, Edward Kendall, Phillip Kendall and Paul Duffield scored 120,242 points (averaging 95.66 per card) on 6–7 Aug 1983.

Bench rest shooting The smallest group on record at 1,000 yd is 4.076 in, by Robert Frey (USA) with a .308 Baer Magnum in Williamsport, PA on 25 Jul 1993.

The smallest at 500 m (546 yd) is 1.5 in, by Ross Hicks (Australia) using a rifle of his own design at Canberra, Australia on 12 Mar 1994.

Clay pigeon The most world titles have been won by Susan Nattrass (Canada) with six, 1974–75, 1977–79, 1981. The record number of clay birds shot in an hour is 4,557, by John Cloherty (USA) in Seattle, WA on 31 Aug 1992.

The maximum 200/200 was achieved by Ricardo Ruiz Rumoroso at the Spanish Clay Pigeon Championships at Zaragossa on 12 Jun 1983.

Noel D. Townend achieved the maximum 200 consecutive down-the-line targets at Nottingham, Great Britain on 21 Aug 1983.

SHOOTING—INDIVIDUAL WORLD RECORDS

In 1986, the International Shooting Union (UIT) introduced new regulations for determining major championships and world records. Now the leading competitors undertake an additional round with a target subdivided to tenths of a point for rifle and pistol shooting, and an extra 25 shots for trap and skeet. Harder targets have since been introduced, and the table below shows the world records, as recognized by the UIT on 1 Jan 1992, for the 13 Olympic shooting disciplines, giving in parentheses the score for the number of shots specified plus the score in the additional round.

MEN		Score	Name and Country	Venue	Date
FREE RIFLE 50 m 3 × 40 shots	1,287.9	(1,186 + 101.9)	Rajmond Debevec (Slovenia)	Munich, Germany	29 Aug 1992
FREE RIFLE 50 m 60 shots prone	703.5	(599 + 104.5)	Jens Harskov (Denmark)	Zürich, Switzerland	6 Jun 1991
AIR RIFLE 10 m 60 shots	699.4	(596 + 103.4)	Rajmond Debevec (Yugoslavia)	Zürich, Switzerland	8 Jun 1990
FREE PISTOL 50 m 60 shots	672.5	(575 + 97.5)	Sergey Pyzhyanov (Russia)	Milan, Italy	15 Jun 1993
RAPID-FREE PISTOL 25 m 60 shots	698.7	(596 + 102.7)	Ralf Schumann (Germany)	Munich, Germany	29 Aug 1993
AIR PISTOL 10 m 60 shots	695.1	(593 + 102.1)	Sergey Pyzhyanov (USSR)	Munich, Germany	13 Oct 1989
RUNNING TARGET 50 m 30 + 30 shots	679	(582 + 97)	Lubos Racansky (Czechoslovakia)	Munich, Germany	30 May 1991
WOMEN					
STANDARD RIFLE 50 m 3 × 20 shots	689.3	(590 + 99.3)	Vessela Letcheva (Bulgaria)	Munich, Germany	28 Aug 1992
AIR RIFLE 10 m 40 shots	500.8	(399 + 101.8)	Valentina Cherkasova (USSR)	Los Angeles, CA	23 Mar 1991
SPORT PISTOL 25 m 60 shots	693	(593 + 100)	Nino Salukvadse (USSR)	Zagreb, Yugoslavia	13 Jul 1989
AIR PISTOL 10 m 40 shots	492.4	(392 + 100.4)	Lieslotte Breker (West Germany)	Zagreb, Yugoslavia	18 May 1989
OPEN					
TRAP 200 targets	148	(124 + 24)	Giovanni Pellielo (Italy)	Fagnano, Italy	5 Jun 1993
	148	(124 + 24)	Marco Venturini (Netherlands)	Barcelona, Spain	15 Jun 1993
SKEET 200 targets	149	(124 + 25)	Dean Clark (USA)	Barcelona, Spain	20 Jun 1993

SKIING

Most titles *World/Olympic Championships—Alpine* The greatest number of titles won has been by Christel Cranz of Germany, with seven individual—four slalom (1934, 1937–39) and three downhill (1935, 1937, 1939), and five combined (1934–35, 1937–39). She also won the gold medal for the combined in the 1936 Olympics. The most won by a man is seven, by Toni Sailer (Austria), who won all four in 1956 (giant slalom, slalom, downhill and the non-Olympic Alpine combination) and the downhill, giant slalom and combined in 1958.

The only US skier to win two Olympic gold medals has been Andrea Mead-Lawrence, at slalom and giant slalom in 1952.

World/Olympic Championships—Nordic The first World Nordic Championships were those of the 1924 Winter Olympics in Chamonix, France. The greatest number of titles won is 11, by Gunde Svan (Sweden), seven individual—15 km 1989, 30km 1985 and 1991, 50 km 1985 and 1989, and Olympics, 15 km 1984, 50 km 1988; and four relays—4 × 10 km, 1987 and 1989, and Olympics, 1984 and 1988.

The most titles won by a woman is nine, by Galina Kulakova (USSR), in 1970–78. The most medals is 23, by Raisa Smetanina (USSR), including seven gold, 1974–92. Ulrich Wehling (East Germany) has also won four Nordic combined, winning the World Championship in 1974 and the Olympic title, 1972, 1976 and 1980—the only skier to win the same event at three successive Olympics. The record for a jumper is five, by Birger Ruud (Norway), in 1931–32 and 1935–37. Ruud is the only person to win Olympic events in each of the dissimilar Alpine and Nordic disciplines. In 1936 he won the ski-jumping and the Alpine downhill (which was not then a separate event, but a segment of the combined event).

World Cup The World Cup was introduced for Alpine events in 1967 and for Nordic events in 1981. The most individual event wins is 86 (46 giant slalom, 40 slalom from a total of 287 races) by Ingemar Stenmark (Sweden) in 1974–89, including a men's record 13 in one season in 1978/79, of which 10 were part of a record 14 successive giant slalom wins from 18 Mar 1978 to 21 Jan 1980.

Franz Klammer (Austria) won a record 25 downhill races, 1974–84. Annemarie Moser (nee Pröll; Austria) won a women's record 62 individual event wins, 1970–79. She had a record 11 consecutive downhill wins from December 1972 to January 1974. Vreni Schneider (Switzerland) won a record 13 events and a combined including all seven slalom events in 1988/89.

The Nation's Cup, awarded on the combined results of the men and women in the World Cup, has been won a record 15 times by Austria—1969, 1973–80, 1982, 1990–94.

United States The most successful US skier has been Phil Mahre, winner of the overall title three times, 1981–83, with two wins at giant slalom and one at slalom. The most successful US woman has been Tamara McKinney, overall winner 1983, giant slalom 1981 and 1983, and slalom 1984.

The only American to win a Nordic skiing World Cup title has been Bill Koch, at cross-country in 1982.

Ski-jumping The longest ski-jump ever recorded is one of 636 ft, by Piotr Fijas (Poland) at Planica, Yugoslavia on 14 Mar 1987. The women's record is 367 ft, by Eva Ganster (Austria), at Bischofshofen, Austria on 7 Jan 1994. The longest dry ski-jump is 302 ft, by Hubert Schwarz (West Germany) at Berchtesgarten, Germany on 30 Jun 1981.

Fastest speed The official world record, as recognized by the International Ski Federation for a skier, is 145.161 mph by Philippe Goitschel (France) on 21 Apr 1993, and the fastest by a woman is 136.232 mph, by Tarja Mulari (Finland), both at Les Arcs, France on 22 Feb 1992. On 16 Apr 1988 Patrick Knaff (France) set a one-legged record of 115.306 mph.

The fastest average speed in the Olympic downhill race is 64.95 mph, by Bill Johnson (USA), at Sarajevo, Yugoslavia on 16 Feb 1984. The fastest in a World Cup downhill is 69.8 mph, by Armin Assinger (Austria) at Sierra Nevada, Spain on 15 Mar 1993.

Fastest speed—cross-country The record time for a 50 km race is 1 hr 54 min 46 sec by Aleksey Prokurorov (Russia) at Thunder Bay, Canada on 19 Mar 1994, an average speed of 16.24 mph.

United States Bill Koch (USA), on 26 Mar 1981 skied 10 times around a 3.11 mile loop on Marlborough Pond, near Putney, VT. He completed the 50 km (31.07 mile) course in 1 hr 59 min 47 sec, an average speed of 15.57 mph.

MOST OLYMPIC SKIING TITLES

MEN			
Alpine	3	Toni Sailer (Austria)	Downhill, slalom, giant slalom 1956
	3	Jean-Claude Killy (France)	Downhill, slalom, giant slalom 1968
	3	Alberto Tomba (Italy)	Slalom, giant slalom 1988; giant slalom 1992
Nordic	5	Bjorn Daehlie (Norway)	15 km, 50 km, 4 × 10 km 1992; 10 km, 15 km 1994
Jumping	4	Matti Nykänen (Finland)	70 m hill 1988; 90 m hill 1984, 1988; team 1988
WOMEN			
Alpine	3	Vreni Schneider (Switzerland)	Giant slalom, slalom 1988; slalom 1994
Nordic	6	Lyubov Yegorova (Russia)	10 km, 15 km, 4 × 5 km 1992; 5 km, 10 km, 4 × 5 km 1994

La Bomba, Alberto Tomba, won a silver medal at Lillehammer to extend his medal tally to five, matching the all-time mark for alpine skiers. (Allsport/Steve Powell)

Vreni Schneider (above) and Lyubov Yegorova (left) both won gold medals at the Lillehammer Games, extending their career tallies to break the all-time marks. Schneider has a record three alpine titles, and Yegorova six nordic. (Allsport/Chris Cole; Allsport/Shaun Botterill)

Longest run The longest all-downhill ski run in the world is the Weissfluhjoch-Küblis Parsenn course, near Davos, Switzerland, which measures 7.6 miles. The run from the Aiguille du Midi top of the Chamonix lift (vertical lift 9,052 ft) across the Vallée Blanche is 13 miles.

Long-distance (Nordic) In 24 hours Seppo-Juhani Savolainen covered 258.2 miles at Saariselkä, Finland on 8–9 Apr 1988. The women's 24 hr record is 205.05 miles, by Sisko Kainulaisen at Jyväskylä, Finland, on 23–24 Mar 1985.

In 48 hours Bjørn Løkken (Norway) covered 319 miles 205 yd on 11–13 Mar 1982.

Longest races The world's longest Nordic ski race is the Vasaloppet, at 55.3 miles. There were a record 10,934 starters on 6 Mar 1977 and a record 10,650 finishers on 4 Mar 1979. The fastest time is 3 hr 48 min 55 sec, by Bengt Hassis (Sweden) on 2 Mar 1986.

The Finlandia Ski Race, 46.6 miles from Hämeenlinna to Lahti, on 26 Feb 1984, had a record 13,226 starters and 12,909 finishers.

The longest downhill race is the Inferno in Switzerland, 9.8 miles from the top of the Schilthorn to Lauterbrunnen. The record number of entries was 1,401 in 1981, and the record time was 13 min 53.40 sec by Urs von Allmen (Switzerland) in 1991.

Freestyle skiing A record two titles have been won by a number of skiers. Of these, Edgar Grospiron (France), who won moguls, 1989 and 1991, also won an Olympic title, 1992. Donna Weinbrecht (USA) won the women's moguls title in 1991 and at the Olympics in 1992. The most Overall titles in the World Cup (instituted 1980) is 10, by Connie Kissling (Switzerland), 1983–92. The men's record is five, by Eric Laboureix (France), 1986–87, 1989–91.

Longest ski lift The longest gondola ski lift is 3.88 miles long, at Grindelwald-Männlichen, Switzerland (in two sections, but one gondola). The longest chair lift in the world was the Alpine Way-to-Kosciusko Chalet lift above Thredbo, near the Snowy Mountains, New South Wales, Australia. It took from 45 to 74 min to ascend the 3.5 miles, depending on the weather. The chair lift has now collapsed. The highest lift is at Chacaltaya, Bolivia, rising to 16,500 ft.

Snowmobile Fastest speed The fastest speed attained is 103.1 mph, by Erich Brenter (Austria), at Cervinia, Italy in 1964.

World Championships The only snowmobile racers to retain a world championship are: *(men)* Alois Fischbauer (Austria), 1973 and 1975; Robert Mühlberger (West Germany), 1979 and 1981; *(women)* Gerhilde Schiffkorn (Austria), 1967 and 1969; Gertrude Geberth (Austria), 1971 and 1973.

GRASS SKIING

World Championships (now awarded for Super G, giant slalom, slalom and combined) were first held in 1979. The most titles won is 14, by Ingrid Hirschhofer (Austria), 1979–93. The most by a man is seven, by Erwin

Gansner (Switzerland), 1981–87, and Rainer Grossman, 1985–93. The feat of winning all four titles in one year has been achieved by Erwin Gansner, 1987 and Rainer Grossman, 1991, and by (women) Katja Krey (West Germany), 1989 and Ingrid Hirschhofer, 1993.

The speed record is 53.99 mph, by Erwin Gansner at Owen, Germany on 5 Sep 1982.

SLED DOG RACING

Iditarod trail The Iditarod trail is the oldest established trail. It has existed since 1910 and has been raced annually since 1967 by dog teams, 1,049 miles from Anchorage to Nome, AK. The inaugural winner, Dick Wilmarth, took 20 days 49 min 41 sec to complete the course, beating 33 other racers.

The fastest time was set by Martin Buser (Switzerland) in 1994, with 10 days 13 hr 2 min 39 sec. Rick Swenson (USA) has won the race a record five times (1977, 1979, 1981–82 and 1991).

Longest trail The longest race is the 1,243-mile Benergia Trail from Esso to Markovo, Russia. Now established as an annual event, the 1991 race was won by Pavel Lazarev in 10 days 18 hour 17 min 56 sec.

Largest team On 8 Feb 1988 Rev. Donald Ewen McEwen, owner-musher of Nekanesu Kennels, Eldorado, Ontario, Canada drove a 76-dog sled for 2 miles single-handedly on the ice and around the shore of Lingham Lake. The team, consisting of 25 Siberian huskies and 51 Alaskan huskies, was assembled for the filming of a British TV commercial.

SNOOKER

Most world titles The world professional title was won a record 15 times by Joe Davis, on the first 15 occasions it was contested, 1927–40 and 1946. The most wins in the Amateur Championships have been two—by Gary Owen (England) in 1963 and 1966; Ray Edmonds (England) 1972 and 1974; and Paul Mifsud (Malta) 1985–86. Allison Fisher (Great Britain) has won seven Women's World Championships, 1985–86, 1988–89, 1991 and 1993–94.

Maureen Baynton (nee Barrett) won a record eight Women's Amateur Championships between 1954 and 1968, as well as seven at billiards.

Youngest World Champion The youngest man to win a world title is Stephen O'Connor (Ireland; b. 16 Oct 1972), who was 18 yr 40 days when he won the World Amateur Snooker Championship in Colombo, Sri

Lanka on 25 Nov 1990. Stephen Hendry (Scotland; b. 13 Jan 1969) became the youngest World Professional champion, at 21 yr 106 days on 29 Apr 1990.

Stacey Hillyard (Great Britain; b. 15 Sep 1969) won the Women's World Amateur Championship in October 1984 at the age of 15.

Highest breaks Over 200 players have achieved the maximum break of 147. The first to do so was E.J. "Murt" O'Donoghue (New Zealand) at Griffiths, New South Wales, Australia on 26 Sep 1934. The first officially ratified 147 was by Joe Davis against Willie Smith in London, Great Britain on 22 Jan 1955. Cliff Thorburn (Canada) has scored two tournament 147 breaks (the World Professional Championship), on 23 Apr 1983 and 8 Mar 1989. Paul Ebdon (Great Britain) and James Wattana (Thailand) have also achieved this feat.

The highest break by a woman in competition is 137, by Stacey Hilliard (Great Britain) in the General Portfolio Women's Classic at Aylesbury, Great Britain on 23 Feb 1992.

Longest unbroken run From 17 Mar 1990 to his defeat by Jimmy White (Great Britain) on 13 Jan 1991, Stephen Hendry won five successive titles and 36 consecutive matches in ranking tournaments.

SNOWSHOEING

Fastest speed The IASSRF (International Amateur SnowShoe Racing Federation) record for covering one mile is 5 min 56.7 sec, by Nick Akers of Edmonton, Alberta, Canada on 3 Feb 1991. The 100 m record is 14.07 sec, by Jeremy Badeau at Canaseraga, NY on 31 May 1991.

SOARING

Most titles The most World Individual championships (instituted 1937) won is four, by Ingo Renner (Australia) in 1976 (Standard class), 1983, 1985 and 1987 (Open).

The most titles won by a US pilot is two, by George Moffat, in the Open category, in 1970 and 1974.

Women's altitude records The women's single-seater world record for absolute altitude is 41,460 ft, by Sabrina Jackintell (USA) in an Astir GS on 14 Feb 1979.

The height gain record is 33,506 ft, by Yvonne Loader (New Zealand) at Omarama, New Zealand on 12 Jan 1988.

HANG GLIDING

World Championships The World Team Championships (officially instituted in 1976) have been won most often by Great Britain (1981, 1985, 1989 and 1991).

World records The *Fédération Aéronautique Internationale* recognizes world records for rigid-wing, flex-wing and multiplace flex-wing. The following records are for the greatest distance in each category—all by flex-wing gliders.

Men Greatest distance in straight line and declared goal distance: 303.3 miles, Larry Tudor (USA), Hobbs Airpark, NM to Elkhart, KS, 3 Jul 1990.

Height gain: 14,250 ft, Larry Tudor (USA), Owens Valley, CA, 4 Aug 1985.

Out and return distance: 192.8 miles, Larry Tudor (USA) and Geoffrey Loyns (Great Britain), Owens Valley, 26 Jun 1988.

Triangular course distance: 121.79 miles, James Lee (USA), Wild Horse Mesa, CO, 4 Jul 1991.

Women Greatest distance: 208.6 miles, Kari Castle (USA), Owens Valley, 22 Jul 1991.

Height gain: 13,025 ft, Judy Leden (Great Britain), Kuruman, South Africa, 1 Dec 1992.

Out and return distance in a single turn: 181.5 miles, Kari Castle (USA), Hobbs Airpark, 1 Jul 1990.

Declared goal distance: 132.04 miles, Liavan Mallin (Ireland), Owens Valley, 13 Jul 1989.

Triangular course distance: Judy Leden, 70.9 miles, Kössen, Austria, 22 Jun 1991.

SOCCER

Ball control Volkhart Caro (Canada) juggled a regulation soccer ball for 18 hours nonstop with feet, legs and head without the ball ever touching the ground at the St Dominic Catholic Elementary School, Edmonton, Canada on 26–27 Jun 1993. Tomas Lundman (Sweden) "headed" a ball for 7 hr 5 min 5 sec at Nöjeskäallan, Märsta, Sweden on 5 Sep 1992.

Most dismissive referee It was reported on 1 Jun 1993 that in a league soccer match between Sportivo Ameliano and General Caballero in Paraguay, referee William Weiler ejected 20 players. Trouble flared after two Sportivo players were thrown out, a 10-minute fight ensued, and Weiler then dismissed a further 18 players, including the rest of the Sportivo team. Not surprisingly, the game was abandoned.

THE WORLD CUP

Brazil has won the World Cup a record four times, in 1958, 1962, 1970 and 1994. For further details of records set at World Cup '94, see feature on p. 754.

***Team records** Most appearances* Brazil is the only country to qualify for all 15 World Cup tournaments.

Most goals The highest score by one team in a game is 10, by Hungary in a 10–1 defeat of El Salvador at Elche, Spain on 15 Jun 1982. The most goals in tournament history is 148 (in 66 games) by Brazil.

Highest-scoring game The highest-scoring game took place on 26 Jun 1954 when Austria defeated Switzerland 7–5.

***Individual records** Most wins* Pelé (Brazil) is the only player to have played on three winning teams, 1958, 1962 and 1970. He played during the 1962 Finals, but was injured before the final match and was therefore unable to play in it. Franz Beckenbauer is the only man to have both captained and managed a winning side.

Most goals The most goals scored in a final is three, by Geoff Hurst for England *v* West Germany on 30 Jul 1966.

Most games played Four players have appeared in 21 games in the finals tournament: Uwe Seeler (West Germany), 1958–70; Wladyslaw Zmuda (Poland), 1974–86; Diego Maradona (Argentina), 1982–94; and Lothar Matthaus (West Germany/Germany), 1982–94.

Most goals scored The most goals scored in one tournament is 13, by Just Fontaine (France) in 1958, in six games. The most goals scored in a career is 14, by Gerd Muller (West Germany), 10 goals in 1970 and four in 1974.

OLYMPIC GAMES

The leading gold medal winner is Hungary, with three wins (1952, 1964, 1968). The highest Olympic score is 17, by Denmark *v* France in 1908. A record 126 nations took part in qualifying for the 1992 tournament.

NCAA DIVISION I CHAMPIONSHIPS

Men In this competition, first held in 1959, the University of St Louis has won the most Division I titles with 10 victories, including one tie: 1959–60, 1962–63, 1965, 1967, 1969–70, 1972–73.

Women In this competition, first held in 1982, the University of North Carolina has won a record 11 Division I titles. Its victories came in 1982–84, 1986–93.

Largest soccer crowds The top attendance for a soccer match in the USA was 101,799, for France's 2–0 Olympic final win over Brazil at the Rose Bowl, Pasadena, CA on 11 Aug 1984.

SOFTBALL

Most titles The USA has won the men's World Championship (instituted 1966) five times, 1966, 1968, 1976 (shared), 1980 and 1988, and the women's title (instituted 1965) four times, in 1974, 1978 and 1986 and 1990.

US National Championships The most wins in the fast pitch championships (first held in 1933) for men is 10, by the Clearwater (Florida) Bombers between 1950 and 1973, and for women is 23, by the Raybestos Brakettes of Stratford, CT, between 1958 and 1992.

Slow pitch championships have been staged annually since 1953 for men and since 1962 for women. Three wins for men have been achieved by Skip Hogan A.C. of Pittsburgh, 1962, 1964–65, and by Joe Gatliff Auto Sales of Newport, KY, 1956–57, 1963. At super slow pitch, four wins have been achieved by Steele's Silver Bullets, Grafton, OH, 1985–87 and 1990. The Dots of Miami, FL have a record five women's titles, playing as the Converse Dots, 1969; Marks Brothers; North Miami Dots, 1974–75; and Bob Hoffman Dots, 1978–79.

SPEEDWAY

World Championships The World Speedway Championship was inaugurated at Wembley, London, Great Britain on 10 Sep 1936. The most wins have been six, by Ivan Mauger (New Zealand) in 1968–70, 1972, 1977 and 1979. Barry Briggs (New Zealand) made a record 18 appearances in the finals (1954–70, 1972) and won the world title in 1957–58, 1964 and 1966. He also scored a record 201 points in world championship competition in 87 races.

Ivan Mauger also won four World Team Cups (three for Great Britain), two World Pairs (including one unofficial) and three world long track titles. Ove Fundin (Sweden) won 12 world titles: five individual, one pairs, and six World Team Cup medals in 1956–70. In 1985 Erik Gundersen (Denmark) became the first man to hold world titles at individual, pairs, team and long-track events simultaneously.

The World Pairs Championships (instituted unofficially 1968, officially 1970) have been won a record eight times by Denmark, 1979, 1985–91. The most successful individual in the World Pairs has been Hans Nielsen (Denmark) with seven wins. His partners were Ole Olsen, 1979, Erik Gundersen, 1986–89, and Jan O. Pederson, 1990–91. Maximum points (then 30) were scored in the World Pairs Championship by Jerzy Szczakiel and Andrzej Wyglenda (both Poland) at Rybnik, Poland in 1971; and by Arthur Sigalos and Bobby Schwartz (both USA) at Liverpool, New South Wales, Australia on 11 Dec 1982.

The World Team Cup (instituted 1960) has been won a record nine times by England/Great Britain (Great Britain 1968, 1971–73; England

Two riders have won four Long Track Speedway world titles: Karl Maier (Germany), 1980, 1982, 1987–88; and Simon Wigg (Great Britain [left]), 1985, 1989–90, 1993. (Allsport/Mike Powell)

1974–75, 1977, 1980, 1989); and by Denmark 1978, 1981, 1983–88, 1991. Hans Nielsen (Denmark) has ridden in a record eight Team wins.

Maximum points The only speedway rider to have scored maximum points in every test series was Arthur "Bluey" Wilkinson (1911–40), in five matches for Australia *v* England in Sydney in 1937/38.

SQUASH

World Championships Jahangir Khan (Pakistan) won six World Open (instituted 1976) titles, 1981–85 and 1988, and the International Squash Rackets Federation (ISRF) world individual title (formerly World Amateur, instituted 1967) in 1979, 1983 and 1985. Geoff Hunt (Australia) won four World Open titles, 1976–77 and 1979–80, and three World Amateur, 1967, 1969 and 1971. The most women's World Open titles is five, by Susan Devoy (New Zealand), 1985, 1987 and 1990–92.

Australia (1967, 1969, 1971, 1973, 1989 and 1991) and Pakistan (1977, 1981, 1983, 1985, 1987 and 1993) have each won six men's world titles. England won the women's title in 1985, 1987, 1989 and 1990, following Great Britain's win in 1979.

Most titles Open Championship The most wins in the Open Championship held annually in Britain is 10, by Jahangir Khan, in successive years, 1982–91. Hashim Khan (Pakistan) won seven times, 1950–55 and 1957, and also won the Vintage title six times, 1978–83.

The most British Open women's titles is 16, by Heather McKay (nee Blundell; Australia) from 1961 to 1977. She also won the World Open title in 1976 and 1979.

United States The US amateur squash championships were first held for men in 1907 and for women in 1928; the most singles wins is six, by Stanley

Pakistan and Australia have won six world squash titles. Five-time individual champ Jansher Khan led Pakistan to the 1993 championship. (Allsport/Gray Mortimore)

> ## DID YOU KNOW?
>
> The youngest surfing world champion was Frieda Zamba. She was 19 years old when she won the 1984 title. The youngest men's champion was Kelly Slater (USA), who won the 1992 crown at age 20.
>
> The career earnings leader through 1993 is Tom Carroll (Australia) with $488,434. The women's leader is Pam Burridge (Australia), $220,540.

W. Pearson, 1915–17 and 1921–23. G. Diehl Mateer won a record 11 men's doubles titles between 1949 and 1966 with five different partners. Sharif Khan (Pakistan) won a record 13 North American Open Championships (instituted 1953), 1969–74 and 1976–82. Alicia McConnell has won a record seven women's national championships (1982–88).

Unbeaten sequences Heather McKay was unbeaten from 1962 to 1980. Jahangir Khan was unbeaten from his loss to Geoff Hunt at the British Open on 10 Apr 1981 until Ross Norman (New Zealand) ended his sequence in the World Open final on 11 Nov 1986.

Longest and shortest championship matches The longest recorded competitive match was one of 2 hr 45 min when Jahangir Khan beat Gamal Awad (Egypt) 9–10, 9–5, 9–7, 9–2, the first game lasting a record 1 hr 11 min, in the final of the Patrick International Festival at Chichester, Great Britain on 30 Mar 1983. Philip Kenyon (England) beat Salah Nadi (Egypt) in just 6 min 37 sec (9–0, 9–0, 9–0) in the British Open at Lamb's Squash Club, London, Great Britain on 9 Apr 1992.

Most international appearances The men's record is 122 by David Gotto for Ireland. The women's record is 113 by Rebecca O'Callaghan (nee Best) for Ireland.

SURFING

Most titles World Amateur Championships were inaugurated in May 1964 at Sydney, Australia. The most titles is three, by Michael Novakov (Australia), who won the Kneeboard event in 1982, 1984 and 1986. A World Professional series was started in 1976. The men's title has been won four times, by Mark Richards (Australia), from 1979 to 1982, and the women's title (instituted 1979) four times, by Frieda Zamba (USA), 1984–86, 1988; and by Wendy Botha (Australia, formerly South Africa), 1987, 1989, 1991–92.

Longest ride About four to six times each year, ridable surfing waves break in Matanchen Bay near San Blas, Nayarit, Mexico, which makes rides of *c.* 5,700 ft possible.

Highest waves ridden Waimea Bay, HI reputedly provides the most consistently high waves, often reaching the ridable limit of 30–35 ft. The highest wave ever ridden was the tsunami of "perhaps 50 ft" that struck Minole, HI on 3 Apr 1868, and was ridden to save his life by a Hawaiian named Holua.

SWIMMING

Fastest swimmer In a 25-yd pool, Tom Jager (USA) achieved an average speed of 5.37 mph for 50 yards in 19.05 sec at Nashville, TN on 23 Mar 1990. The women's fastest is 4.48 mph, by Yang Wenyi (China) in her 50 m world record (see World Records table).

Most world records *Men:* 32, Arne Borg (Sweden), 1921–29. *Women:* 42, Ragnhild Hveger (Denmark), 1936–42. For currently recognized events (only metric distances in 50 m pools) the most is (*men*) 26, by Mark Spitz (USA), 1967–72, and (*women*) 23, by Kornelia Ender (East Germany), 1973–76. The most by a US woman is 15, by Debbie Meyer, 1967–70.

The most world records set in a single pool is 86, in the North Sydney pool, Australia between 1955 and 1978. This total includes 48 imperial distance records, which ceased to be recognized in 1969.

Most world titles In the World Championships (instituted 1973) the most medals won is 13, by Michael Gross (West Germany)—five gold, five silver and three bronze, 1982–90. The most medals won by a woman is 10, by Kornelia Ender, with eight gold and two silver in 1973 and 1975.

The most gold medals won is six (two individual and four relay) by James Montgomery (USA) in 1973 and 1975. The most medals won at a single championship is seven, by Matt Biondi (USA)—three gold, one silver, three bronze, in 1986.

The most gold medals by an American woman is five, by Tracy Caulkins, all in 1978, as well as a silver. The most medals overall is nine, by Mary T. Meagher—two gold, five silver, two bronze, 1978–82.

US Championships Tracy Caulkins won a record 48 US swimming titles and set 60 US records in her career, 1977–84. The men's record is 36 titles, by Johnny Weissmuller (ne Janos Weiszmuller; 1904–84), between 1921 and 1928.

Largest pools The largest swimming pool in the world is the seawater Orthlieb Pool in Casablanca, Morocco. It is 1,574 ft long and 246 ft wide, and has an area of 8.9 acres.

The largest land-locked pool in current use is Willow Lake in Warren, OH. It measures 600 × 150 ft.

The greatest spectator accommodation is 13,614 at Osaka, Japan.

Only two swimmers have broken the 49-second barrier for the 100 m freestyle: Aleksandr Popov (below), the current world record holder, and Matt Biondi (above). Between them, they have recorded the ten fastest times for the event. (Allsport/Vandystadt/Richard Martin)

Sponsored swim The greatest amount of money collected in a charity swim was £122,983.19 (*c.* $350,000) in "Splash '92," organized by the Royal Bank of Scotland Swimming Club and held at the Royal Commonwealth Pool, Edinburgh, Scotland on 25–26 Jan 1992 with 3,218 participants.

The record for an event staged at several pools was £548,006.14 (*c.* $986,400) by "Penguin Swimathon '88," when 5,482 swimmers participated at 43 pools throughout London, Great Britain, on 26–28 Feb 1988.

OLYMPIC RECORDS

Most medals Men The greatest number of Olympic gold medals won is nine, by Mark Spitz (USA): 100 m and 200 m freestyle, 1972; 100 m and 200 m butterfly, 1972; 4 × 100 m freestyle, 1968 and 1972; 4 × 200 m freestyle, 1968 and 1972; 4 × 100 m medley, 1972. All but one of these performances (the 4 × 200 m freestyle of 1968) were also new world records. He also won a silver (100 m butterfly) and a bronze (100 m freestyle) in 1968, for a record 11 medals. His record seven medals at one Games in 1972 was equaled by Matt Biondi (USA), who took five gold, a silver and a bronze in 1988. Biondi has also won a record 11 medals in total, winning a gold in 1984, and two golds and a silver in 1992.

DID YOU KNOW?

The record for swimming the Golden Gate strait the most times is 61 crossings by Joseph Bruno. He first performed the feat on 17 Sep 1933. His latest crossing was on 11 Sep 1993, two months shy of his 81st birthday.

The youngest male to swim the strait was 10-year-old Andrew Pinetti on 11 Aug 1993.

Women The record number of gold medals won by a woman is six, by Kristin Otto (East Germany) at Seoul in 1988: 100 m freestyle, backstroke and butterfly, 50 m freestyle, 4 × 100 m freestyle and 4 × 100 m medley. Dawn Fraser (Australia) is the only swimmer to win the same event, the 100 m freestyle, on three successive occasions (1956, 1960 and 1964). The most gold medals won by a US woman is three, by 14 swimmers.

The most medals won by a woman is eight, by three swimmers: Dawn Fraser—four golds (100 m freestyle, 1956, 1960 and 1964, 4 × 100 m freestyle, 1956) and four silvers (400 m freestyle, 1956, 4 × 100 m freestyle, 1960 and 1964, 4 × 100 m medley, 1960); Kornelia Ender—four golds (100 m and 200 m freestyle, 100 m butterfly, and 4 × 100 m medley in 1976) and four silvers (200 m individual medley, 1972, 4 × 100 m medley, 1972, 4 × 100 m freestyle, 1972 and 1976); and Shirley Babashoff (USA), who won two golds (4 × 100 m freestyle, 1972 and 1976) and six silvers (100 m freestyle, 1972, 200 m freestyle, 1972 and 1976, 400 m and 800 m freestyle, 1976, 4 × 100 m medley 1976).

Most individual gold medals The record number of individual gold medals won is four, by Charles Daniels (USA [1884–1973), 100 m freestyle, 1906 and 1908, 220 yd freestyle 1904, 440 yd freestyle, 1904); by Roland Matthes (East Germany) with 100 m and 200 m backstroke in 1968 and 1972; by Mark Spitz and Kristin Otto (see Most medals); and by the divers Pat McCormick and Greg Louganis (see Diving).

DIVING

Most Olympic medals The most medals won by a diver is five, by Klaus Dibiasi (Italy), three gold, two silver, 1964–76; and by Greg Louganis (USA), four golds, one silver, 1976, 1984–88. Dibiasi is the only diver to win the same event (highboard) at three successive Games (1968, 1972 and 1976). Two divers have won the highboard and springboard doubles at two Games: Pat McCormick (nee Keller), 1952 and 1956, and Greg Louganis, 1984 and 1988.

Most world titles Greg Louganis (USA) won a record five world titles—highboard in 1978, and both highboard and springboard in 1982 and 1986, as well as four Olympic gold medals, in 1984 and 1988. Three gold medals at one event have also been won by Philip Boggs (USA; 1949–90)—springboard, 1973, 1975 and 1978.

***United States Championships** Most titles* Greg Louganis has won a record 47 national titles: 17 at 1-meter springboard; 17 at 3-meter springboard; 13 at platform. In women's competition Cynthia Potter has won a record 28 titles.

Highest scores Greg Louganis achieved record scores at the 1984 Olympic Games in Los Angeles, CA, with 754.41 points for the 11-dive springboard event and 710.91 for the highboard.

High diving The highest regularly performed head-first dives are those of professional divers from La Quebrada ("The Break in the Rocks") at Acapulco, Mexico, a height of 87½ ft. The base rocks, 21 ft out from the take-off, necessitate a leap of 27 ft out. The water is 12 ft deep.

The world record high dive from a diving board is 176 ft 10 in, by Olivier Favre (Switzerland) at Villers-le-Lac, France on 30 Aug 1987.

The women's record is 120 ft 9 in, by Lucy Wardle (USA) at Ocean Park, Hong Kong on 6 Apr 1985.

LONG-DISTANCE SWIMMING

Longest swims The greatest recorded distance ever swum is 1,826 miles down the Mississippi River between Ford Dam near Minneapolis, MN and Carrollton Ave, New Orleans, LA, by Fred P. Newton of Clinton, OK from 6 Jul to 29 Dec 1930. He was in the water for 742 hr.

Twenty-four hours Anders Forvass (Sweden) swam 63.3 miles at the 25 meter Linköping public swimming pool, Sweden on 28–29 Oct 1989. In a 50-meter pool, Evan Barry (Australia) swam 60.08 miles, at the Valley Pool, Brisbane, Australia on 19–20 Dec 1987.

The women's record is 57.78 miles, by Melissa Cunningham (Australia) at Chandler Aquatic Centre, Brisbane, Australia on 2–3 July 1993.

SWIMMING WORLD RECORDS (set in 50 meter pools)

Event	min : sec	Name & Country	Place	Date
MEN				
Freestyle				
50 meters	21.81	Tom Jager (USA)	Nashville, TN	24 Mar 1990
100 meters	48.21	Aleksandr Popov (Russia)	Monte Carlo, Monaco	18 Jun 1994
200 meters	1:46.69	Giorgio Lamberti (Italy)	Bonn, Germany	15 Aug 1989
400 meters	3:45.00	Evgueni Sadovyi (EUN)[1]	Barcelona, Spain	29 Jul 1992
800 meters	7:46.60	Kieren Perkins (Australia)	Sydney, Australia	14 Feb 1992
1,500 meters	14:43.48	Kieren Perkins (Australia)	Barcelona, Spain	31 Jul 1992
4 × 100 meter relay	3:16.53	United States (Christopher Jacobs, Troy Dalbey, Tom Jager, Matt Biondi)	Seoul, South Korea	25 Sep 1988
4 × 200 meter relay	7:11.95	EUN[1] (Dimitri Lepikov, Vladimir Pychenko, Veniamin Taianovitch, Evgueni Sadovyi)	Barcelona, Spain	27 Jul 1992
Breaststroke				
100 meters	1:00.95	Karoly Guttler (Hungary)	Sheffield, Great Britain	3 Aug 1993
200 meters	2:10.16	Michael Barrowman (USA)	Barcelona, Spain	29 Jul 1992
Butterfly				
100 meters	52.84	Pablo Morales (USA)	Orlando, FL	23 Jun 1986
200 meters	1:55.69	Melvin Stewart (USA)	Perth, Australia	12 Jan 1991
Backstroke				
100 meters	53.86	Jeff Rouse (USA—relay leg)	Barcelona, Spain	31 Jul 1992
200 meters	1:56.57	Martin Lopez-Zubero (Spain)	Tuscaloosa, AL	23 Nov 1991
Medley				
200 meters	1:59.36	Tamás Darnyi (Hungary)	Perth, Australia	13 Jan 1991
400 meters	4:12.36	Tamás Darnyi (Hungary)	Perth, Australia	8 Jan 1991
4 × 100 meter relay	3:36.93	United States (David Berkoff, Richard Schroeder, Matt Biondi, Christopher Jacobs)	Seoul, South Korea	23 Sep 1988

WOMEN

Freestyle

Event	Time	Swimmer	Place	Date
50 meters	24.79	Yang Wenyi (China)	Barcelona, Spain	31 Jul 1992
100 meters	54.48	Jenny Thompson (USA)	Indianapolis, IN	1 Mar 1992
200 meters	1:57.55	Heike Friedrich (East Germany)	Berlin, Germany	18 Jun 1986
400 meters	4:03.85	Janet B. Evans (USA)	Seoul, South Korea	22 Sep 1988
800 meters	8:16.22	Janet B. Evans (USA)	Tokyo, Japan	20 Aug 1989
1,500 meters	15:52.10	Janet B. Evans (USA)	Orlando, FL	26 Mar 1988
4 × 100 meter relay	3:39.46	United States (Nicole Haislett, Dara Torres, Angel Martino, Jenny Thompson)	Barcelona, Spain	28 Jul 1992
4 × 200 meter relay	7:55.47	East Germany (Manuela Stellmach, Astrid Strauss, Anke Möhring, Heike Friedrich)	Strasbourg, France	18 Aug 1987

Breaststroke

Event	Time	Swimmer	Place	Date
100 meters	1:07.91	Silke Hörner (East Germany)	Strasbourg, France	21 Aug 1987
200 meters	2:24.76	Rebecca Brown (Australia)	Brisbane, Australia	16 Mar 1994

Butterfly

Event	Time	Swimmer	Place	Date
100 meters	57.93	Mary Terstegge Meagher (USA)	Milwaukee, WI	16 Aug 1981
200 meters	2:05.96	Mary Terstegge Meagher (USA)	Milwaukee, WI	13 Aug 1981

Backstroke

Event	Time	Swimmer	Place	Date
100 meters	1:00.31	Krizstina Egerszegi (Hungary)	Athens, Greece	22 Aug 1991
200 meters	2:06.62	Krizstina Egerszegi (Hungary)	Athens, Greece	25 Aug 1991

Medley

Event	Time	Swimmer	Place	Date
200 meters	2:11.65	Lin Li (China)	Barcelona, Spain	30 Jul 1992
400 meters	4:36.10	Petra Schneider (East Germany)	Guayaquil, Ecuador	1 Aug 1982
4 × 100 meter relay	4:02.54	United States (Lea Loveless, Anita Nall, Crissy Ahmann-Leighton, Jenny Thompson)	Barcelona, Spain	30 Jul 1992

[1] *EUN=Unified Team*

US NATIONAL SWIMMING RECORDS (set in 50 meter pools)

Event	Time	Name	Place	Date
MEN				
Freestyle				
50 meters	21.81	Tom Jager	Nashville, TN	24 Mar 1990
100 meters	48.42	Matt Biondi	Austin, TX	10 Aug 1988
200 meters	1:47.72	Matt Biondi	Austin, TX	8 Aug 1988
400 meters	3:48.06	Matt Cetlinski	Austin, TX	11 Aug 1988
800 meters	7:52.45	Sean Killion	Clovis, CA	27 Jul 1987
1,500 meters	15:01.51	George DiCarlo	Indianapolis, IN	30 Jun 1984
4 × 100 meter relay	3:16.53	United States (Christopher Jacobs, Troy Dalbey, Tom Jager, Matt Biondi)	Seoul, South Korea	23 Sep 1988
4 × 200 meter relay	7:12.51	United States (Troy Dalbey, Matthew Cetlinski, Douglas Gjertsen, Matt Biondi)	Seoul, South Korea	21 Sep 1988
Breaststroke				
100 meters	1:01.40	Nelson Diebel	Indianapolis, IN	1 Mar 1992
200 meters	2:10.16	Michael Barrowman	Barcelona, Spain	29 Jul 1992
Butterfly				
100 meters	52.84	Pablo Morales	Orlando, FL	23 Jun 1986
200 meters	1:55.69	Melvin Stewart	Perth, Australia	12 Jan 1991
Backstroke				
100 meters	53.93	Jeff Rouse	Edmonton, Canada	25 Aug 1991
200 meters	1:58.66	Royce Sharp	Indianapolis, IN	2 Mar 1992
Medley				
200 meters	2:00.11	David Wharton	Tokyo, Japan	20 Aug 1989
400 meters	4:15.21	Eric Namesnik	Perth, Australia	8 Jan 1991
4 × 100 meter relay	3:36.93	United States (David Berkoff, Richard Schroeder, Matt Biondi, Christopher Jacobs)	Seoul, South Korea	25 Sep 1988

WOMEN

Freestyle

50 meters ....25.20 Jenny Thompson ....Indianapolis, IN ....6 Mar 1992
100 meters ....54.48 Jenny Thompson ....Indianapolis, IN ....1 Mar 1992
200 meters ....1:58.23 Cynthia Woodhead ....Tokyo, Japan ....3 Sep 1979
400 meters ....4:03.85 Janet B. Evans ....Seoul, South Korea ....22 Sep 1988
800 meters ....8:16.22 Janet B. Evans ....Tokyo, Japan ....20 Aug 1989
1,500 meters ....15:52.10 Janet B. Evans ....Orlando, FL ....26 Mar 1988
4 × 100 meter relay ....3:43.26 United States World Championship Team (Nicola Haislett, Julie Cooper, Whitney Hedgepeth, Jenny Thompson) ....Perth, Australia ....9 Jan 1991
4 × 200 meter relay ....8:02.12 United States (Betsy Mitchell, Mary Terstegge Meagher, Kim Brown, Mary Alice Wayte) ....Madrid, Spain ....22 Aug 1986

Breaststroke

100 meters ....1:08.91 Tracey McFarlane ....Austin, TX ....11 Aug 1988
200 meters ....2:25.35 Anita Nall ....Indianapolis, IN ....2 Mar 1992

Butterfly

100 meters ....57.93 Mary T. Meagher ....Brown Deer, WI ....16 Aug 1981
200 meters ....2:05.96 Mary T. Meagher ....Brown Deer, WI ....13 Aug 1981

Backstroke

100 meters ....1:00.84 Janie Wagstaff ....Indianapolis, IN ....3 Mar 1992
200 meters ....2:08.60 Betsy Mitchell ....Orlando, FL ....27 Jun 1986

Medley

200 meters ....2:12.64 Tracy Caulkins ....Los Angeles, CA ....3 Aug 1984
400 meters ....4:37.76 Janet B. Evans ....Seoul, South Korea ....19 Sep 1988
4 × 100 meter relay ....4:05.98 United States (Janie Wagstaff, Keli King, Crissy Ahmann-Leighton, Nicole Haislett) ....Edmonton, Canada ....25 Aug 1991

SHORT-COURSE SWIMMING WORLD BESTS (set in 25 meter pools)

Event	min : sec	Name & Country	Place	Date
MEN				
Freestyle				
50 meters	21.50	Aleksandr Popov (Russia)	Desenzano, Italy	13 Mar 1994
100 meters*	46.74	Aleksandr Popov (Russia)	Gelsenkirchen, Germany	19 Mar 1994
200 meters	1:43.64	Giorgio Lamberti (Italy)	Bonn, Germany	11 Feb 1990
400 meters	3:40.81	Anders Holmertz (Sweden)	Paris, France	4 Feb 1990
800 meters	7:34.90	Kieren Perkins (Australia)	Sydney, Australia	25 Jul 1993
1,500 meters	14:26.52	Kieren Perkins (Australia)	Auckland, New Zealand	15 Jul 1993
4 × 50 meters	1:27.94	Sweden	Espoo, Finland	21 Nov 1992
4 × 100 meters	3:12.11	Brazil	Palma de Mallorca, Spain	5 Dec 1993
4 × 200 meters	7:05.17	West Germany	Bonn, Germany	9 Feb 1986
Backstroke				
50 meters	24.60	Franck Schott (France)	Paris, France	27 Mar 1994
100 meters	51.43	Jeff Rouse (USA)	Sheffield, Great Britain	11 April 1993
200 meters	1:52.51	Martin Zubero (Spain)	Gainesville, FL	10 Apr 1991
Breaststroke				
50 meters	27.15	Dmitriy Volkov (USSR)	Saint-Paul de la Réunion	30 Dec 1989
100 meters	59.07	Philip John Rogers (Australia)	Melbourne, Australia	29 Aug 1993
200 meters	2:07.93	Philip John Rogers (Australia)	Melbourne, Australia	28 Aug 1993
Butterfly				
50 meters	23.68	Mark Foster (Great Britain)	Sheffield, Great Britain	22 Mar 1994
100 meters	52.07	Marcel Gery (Canada)	Leicester, Great Britain	23 Feb 1990
200 meters	1:53.05	Franck Esposito (France)	Paris, France	26 Mar 1994
Medley				
100 meters	53.78	Jani Sievinen (Finland)	Espoo, Finland	21 Nov 1992
200 meters	1:54.65	Jani Sievinen (Finland)	Kuopio, Finland	21 Jan 1994
400 meters	4:07.10	Jani Sievinen (Finland)	Malmo, Sweden	9 Feb 1992
4 × 50 meters	1:38.10	Finland	Espoo, Finland	22 Nov 1992
4 × 100 meters	3:32.57	USA	Palma de Mallorca, Spain	2 Dec 1993

WOMEN

Freestyle

Event	Time	Swimmer	Place	Date
50 meters	24.23	Le Jingyi (China)	Palma de Mallorca, Spain	3 Dec 1993
100 meters	53.01	Le Jingyi (China)	Palma de Mallorca, Spain	2 Dec 1993
200 meters	1:56.35	Birgit Meineke (East Germany)	Indianapolis, IN	7 Jan 1983
400 meters	4:02.05	Astrid Strauss (East Germany)	Bonn, Germany	8 Feb 1987
800 meters	8:15.34	Astrid Strauss (East Germany)	Bonn, Germany	6 Feb 1987
1,500 meters	15:43.31	Petra Schneider (East Germany)	Gainesville, FL	10 Jan 1982
4 × 50 meters	1:40.63	Germany	Espoo, Finland	22 Nov 1992
4 × 100 meters	3:35.97	China	Palma de Mallorca, Spain	4 Dec 1993
4 × 200 meters	7:52.45	China	Palma de Mallorca, Spain	2 Dec 1993

Backstroke

Event	Time	Swimmer	Place	Date
50 meters	27.93	Angel Martino (USA)	Sabadell, Spain	28 Dec 1993
100 meters	58.50	Angel Martino (USA)	Palma de Mallorca, Spain	3 Dec 1993
200 meters	2:06.09	He Cihong (China)	Palma de Mallorca, Spain	5 Dec 1993

Breaststroke

Event	Time	Swimmer	Place	Date
50 meters	31.19	Louise Karlsson (Sweden)	Espoo, Finland	21 Nov 1992
100 meters	1:06.58	Dai Guohong (China)	Palma de Mallorca, Spain	4 Dec 1993
200 meters	2:21.99	Dai Guohong (China)	Palma de Mallorca, Spain	3 Dec 1993

Butterfly

Event	Time	Swimmer	Place	Date
50 meters	26.44	Zhong Weiyue (China)	Beijing, China	6 Jan 1994
100 meters**	58.71	Zhong Weiyue (China)	Beijing, China	5 Jan 1994
200 meters	2:05.65	Mary Meagher (USA)	Gainesville, FL	2 Jan 1981

Medley

Event	Time	Swimmer	Place	Date
100 meters	1:01.03	Louise Karlsson (Sweden)	Espoo, Finland	22 Nov 1992
200 meters	2:07.79	Allison Wagner (USA)	Palma de Mallorca, Spain	5 Dec 1993
400 meters	4:29.00	Dai Guohong (China)	Palma de Mallorca, Spain	2 Dec 1993
4 × 50 meters	1:52.44	Germany	Espoo, Finland	21 Nov 1992
4 × 100 meters	3:57.73	China	Palma de Mallorca, Spain	5 Dec 1993

** Hand timed for first leg.* ****Slower than long-course bests.*

Manhattan swim The fastest swim around Manhattan Island in New York City was in 5 hr 53 min 57 sec, achieved by Kris Rutford (USA) on 29 Aug 1992.

Long-distance relays The New Zealand national relay team of 20 swimmers swam a record 113.59 miles in Lower Hutt, New Zealand in 24 hours, passing 100 miles in 20 hr 47 min 13 sec on 9–10 Dec 1983. The 24-hour club record by a team of five is 100.99 miles, by the Portsmouth Northsea SC at the Victoria Swimming Center, Portsmouth, Great Britain on 4–5 Mar 1993. The women's record is 88.93 miles by the British City of Newcastle ASC on 16–17 Dec 1986.

The most participants in a one-day swim relay is 2,305, each swimming a length, organized by Auburn YMCA-WEIU at Auburn, NY, on 5–6 Mar 1993.

Underwater swimming Paul Cryne (Great Britain) and Samir Sawan al Awami (Qatar) swam 49.04 miles in a 24-hr period from Doha, Qatar to Umm Said and back on 21–22 Feb 1985 using sub-aqua equipment. They were swimming under water for 95.5 percent of the time. A relay team of six swam 94.44 miles in a swimming pool at Olomouc, Czechoslovakia on 17–18 Oct 1987.

CHANNEL SWIMMING

Fastest The official Channel Swim-ming Association (founded 1927) record is 7 hr 40 min by Penny Dean (USA), from Shakespeare Beach, Dover, Great Britain to Cap Gris-Nez, France on 29 Jul 1978.

TABLE TENNIS

Most titles *World (instituted 1926, now held biennially. The following individual records records were set in the era of annual championships.)* G. Viktor Barna (ne Györö Braun; Hungary, 1911–72) won a record five singles, 1930, 1932–35, and eight men's doubles, 1929–35, 1939, in the World Championships (first held in 1926).

Angelica Rozeanu (Romania; b. 15 Oct 1921) won a record six women's singles, 1950–55, and Maria Mednyanszky (Hungary; 1901–79) won seven women's doubles, 1928, 1930–35. With two more at mixed doubles and seven team, Viktor Barna won 22 world titles in all, while 18 were won by Maria Mednyanszky.

The most men's team titles (Swaythling Cup) is 12, by Hungary, 1927–31, 1933–35, 1938, 1949, 1952 and 1979.

The women's record (Marcel Corbillon Cup) is 10, by China, 1965 and eight successive from 1975–89 (biennially) and 1993

United States The US won the Swaythling Cup in 1937 and the Corbillon Cup in 1937 and 1949. Ruth Aarons was the women's world champion in 1936 and 1937, sharing the title in the latter year.

No American has won the men's world singles title, but James McClure won three men's doubles titles, with Robert Blattner in 1936–37 and with Sol Schiff in 1938.

Olympic Games Table tennis was included in the Olympic Games for the first time in 1988.

Most medals Yoo Nam-Kyu (South Korea) has won three medals in Olympic competition: one gold and two bronze, 1988–92. Chin Jing (China) is the only woman to win two medals, one gold and one silver in 1988.

US Championships US national championships were first held in 1931. Leah Neuberger (nee Thall) won a record 21 titles between 1941 and 1961: nine women's singles, 12 women's doubles. Richard Miles won a record 10 men's singles titles between 1945 and 1962.

LONGEST!

The longest span for winning a national championship is 61 years by Keith Gledhill. He won the U.S. National Boys' Doubles Championship (with Sidney Wood) in 1926. In 1987 he won the U.S. National 75 and over Doubles Championship (with Elbert Lewis).

Internationals Joy Foster is the youngest person to represent her country in any international sports contest. She was eight years old when she represented Jamaica in the West Indies Championships at Port of Spain, Trinidad in August 1958.

Counter hitting The record number of hits in 60 sec is 173, by Jackie Bellinger (b. 9 Sep 1964) and Lisa Lomas (nee Bellinger; b. 9 Mar 1967), at the Northgate Sports Center, Ipswich, Great Britain, on 7 Feb 1993.

With a paddle in each hand, Gary D. Fisher of Olympia, WA completed 5,000 consecutive volleys over the net in 44 min 28 sec on 25 Jun 1975.

TAEKWONDO

Taekwondo is a martial art, with all activities based on defensive spirit, developed over 20 centuries in Korea. It was officially recognized as part of Korean tradition and culture on 11 Apr 1955.

World Championships The men's biennial championships were first staged in 1973. Women's events have been officially recognized since 1987.

Most titles The most world titles won is four, by Chung Kook-hyun (South Korea), light-middleweight 1982–83, welterweight 1985, 1987. The women's record is two titles, achieved by three athletes: Kim So-young (South Korea), 1987, 1989; Lee Eun-young (South Korea), 1987, 1989; Lynette Love (USA), 1987, 1991.

Olympic Games Taekwondo was included as a demonstration sport at the 1988 and 1992 Olympic Games.

United States Three American women won gold medals at the 1988 Olympics; one of them, Lynette Love, at heavyweight (over 70 kg), was also world champion in 1987.

Taekwondo is a 20-century-old Korean martial art. The sport has been included as a demonstration sport at the last two Olympics. (Allsport/Simon Bruty)

TEAM HANDBALL

Most championships *Olympic* The USSR won five titles—*(men)* 1976, 1988 and 1992 (by the Unified Team from the republics of the former USSR), *(women)* 1976 and 1980. South Korea has also won two women's titles, in 1988 and 1992.

World Championships (instituted 1938) For indoor handball (now the predominant version of the game), the most men's titles won is three, by Romania, 1961, 1964 and 1970; and by Sweden, 1954, 1958 and 1990. However, Germany/West Germany won the outdoor title five times, 1938–66, and has won the indoor title twice, 1938 and 1978. Three women's titles have been won by three teams: Romania, 1956, 1960 (both outdoor) and 1962 (indoor); the GDR, 1971, 1975 and 1978 (all indoor); and the USSR, 1982, 1986 and 1990 (all indoor).

Highest score The highest score in an international match was recorded when the USSR beat Afghanistan 86–2 in the "Friendly Army Tournament" at Miskolc, Hungary in August 1981.

TENNIS

Longest match The longest match in a grand slam tournament is 5 hr 26 min between Stefan Edberg (Sweden) and Michael Chang (USA) for the semifinal of the US Open on 12–13 Sep 1992. Edberg won 6–7, 7–5, 7–6, 5–7, 6–4.

Fastest service The fastest service timed with modern equipment is 138 mph, by Steve Denton (USA) at Beaver Creek, CO on 29 Jul 1984. The women's best is 115 mph by Brenda Shultz (Netherlands) and Jana Novotna (Czechoslovakia), both at the 1993 Wimbledon Championships, on 25 June and 1 July respectively.

Grand Slam The grand slam for a tennis player is winning all four of the major singles titles—the Australian Open, French Open, Wimbledon and US Open—in the same calendar year. The first man to win the grand slam was Don Budge (USA) in 1938. The first man to achieve the grand slam twice was Rod Laver (Australia), as an amateur in 1962 and again in 1969, when the titles were open to professionals.

Three women have achieved the grand slam: Maureen Connolly (USA; 1934–69), in 1953; Margaret Court (nee Smith; Australia) in 1970; and Steffi Graf (Germany) in 1988, when she also won the women's singles Olympic gold medal.

The most singles championships won in grand slam tournaments is 24, by Margaret Court (11 Australian, 5 US, 5 French, 3 Wimbledon),

Two women have had their serves timed at 115 mph: Jana Novotna (above) and Brenda Schultz. (Allsport/Chris Cole)

1960–73. She also won the US Amateur in 1969 and 1970 when this was held, as well as the US Open. The men's record is 12, by Roy Emerson (Australia), 6 Australian, 2 each French, US, Wimbledon, 1961–67.

The first doubles pair to win the grand slam were the Australians Frank Sedgeman and Ken McGregor in 1951.

Pam Shriver (USA) and Martina Navratilova won a record eight successivc grand slam tournament women's doubles titles, and 109 successive matches in all events from April 1983 to July 1985.

The most grand slam tournament wins by a doubles partnership is 20, by Althea Brough (USA) and Margaret du Pont (nee Osborne; USA)—12 US, 5 Wimbledon, 3 French, 1942–57; and by Martina Navratilova and Pam Shriver—7 Australian, 5 Wimbledon, 4 French, 4 US, 1981–89.

United States The most singles wins in grand slam tournaments by a US player is 19, by Helen Wills Moody—8 Wimbledon, 7 US and 4 French.

Martina Navratilova has won a total of 55 grand slam titles—18 singles, a world record 31 women's doubles and 6 mixed doubles. Billie Jean King (nee Moffit) has the most of US-born players, with 39 titles—12 singles, 16 women's doubles and 11 mixed doubles.

"Golden set" The only known example of a "golden set" (winning a set 6–0 without dropping a single point, i.e., winning 24 consecutive points) in professional tennis was achieved by Bill Scanlon (USA) against Marcos Hocevar (Brazil) in the first round of the WCT Gold Coast Classic at Del Ray, FL on 22 Feb 1983. Scanlon won the match, 6–2, 6–0.

WIMBLEDON

Most wins *Women* Billie Jean King won a record 20 titles between 1961 and 1979—six singles, 10 women's doubles and four mixed doubles. Elizabeth Ryan (USA; 1892–1979) won a record 19 doubles (12 women's, seven mixed) titles from 1914 to 1934.

Men The greatest number of titles by a man has been 13, by Hugh Doherty (Great Britain; 1875–1919) with five singles titles (1902–06) and a record eight men's doubles (1897–1901, 1903–05) partnered by his brother Reginald (1872–1910).

The most titles won by a US man is eight, by John McEnroe—singles 1981, 1983 and 1984; men's doubles 1979, 1981, 1983–84 (all with Peter Fleming), and 1992 (with Michael Stich [Germany]).

Singles Martina Navratilova won a record nine titles, 1978–79, 1982–87 and 1990. The most men's singles wins since the Challenge Round was abolished in 1922 is five consecutively, by Björn Borg (Sweden) in 1976–80. William Renshaw (Great Britain; 1861–1904) won seven singles, in 1881–86 and 1889.

Youngest champions The youngest champion was Lottie Dod (Great Britain; 1871–1960), who was 15 yr 285 days when she won in 1887. The youngest male champion was Boris Becker (West Germany; b. 22 Nov 1967), who won the men's singles title in 1985 at 17 yr 227 days.

US OPEN

Most wins Margaret du Pont won a record 25 titles between 1941 and 1960. She won a record 13 women's doubles, nine mixed doubles and three singles.

The men's record is 16, by Bill Tilden (1893–1953), including seven men's singles, 1920–25, 1929—a record for singles shared with: Richard Dudley Sears (1861–1943), 1881–87; William A. Larned (1872–1926), 1901–02, 1907–11; and at women's singles by Molla Mallory (nee Bjurstedt; 1884–1959), 1915–16, 1918, 1920–22, 1926; and Helen Wills Moody, 1923–25, 1927–29, 1931.

Youngest champions The youngest champion was Vincent Richards (1903–59), who was 15 yr 139 days when he won the men's doubles with

The men's number one ranked player Pete Sampras has set several records in his short career, among them: youngest men's U.S. Open champion and season and tournament earnings records. (Allsport/Chris Cole & Simon Bruty)

Bill Tilden in 1918. The youngest singles champion was Tracy Austin (USA; b. 12 Dec 1962), who was 16 yr 271 days when she won the women's singles in 1979. The youngest men's singles champion was Pete Sampras (USA; b. 12 Aug 1971), who was 19 yr 28 days when he won in 1990.

FRENCH OPEN

Most wins (from international status 1925) Margaret Court won a record 13 titles—five singles, four women's doubles and four mixed doubles, 1962–73. The men's record is nine, by Henri Cochet (France; 1901–1987)—four singles, three men's doubles and two mixed doubles, 1926–30. The singles record is seven, by Chris Evert (USA), 1974–75, 1979–80, 1983, 1985–86. Björn Borg won a record six men's singles, 1974–75, 1978–81.

Youngest champions The youngest doubles champions were the 1981 mixed doubles winners Andrea Jaeger, at 15 yr 339 days, and Jimmy Arias, at 16 yr 296 days. The youngest singles winners have been Monica Seles (Yugoslavia), who won the 1990 women's title at 16 yr 169 days in 1990, and Michael Chang (USA), who won the men's title at 17 yr 109 days in 1989.

AUSTRALIAN OPEN

Most wins Margaret Court won the women's singles 11 times (1960–66, 1969–71 and 1973) as well as eight women's doubles and two mixed doubles, for a record total of 21 titles. A record six men's singles were won by Roy Emerson, 1961 and 1963–67. Thelma Long (nee Coyne) won a record 12 women's doubles and four mixed doubles for a record total of 16 doubles titles. Adrian Quist won 10 consecutive men's doubles from 1936 to 1950 (the last eight with John Bromwich) and three men's singles.

Youngest champions The youngest champions were Rodney W. Heath, age 17 when he won the men's singles in 1905, and Monica Seles (Yugoslavia), who won the women's singles at 17 yr 55 days in 1991.

ATP TOUR CHAMPIONSHIP

The end-of-season tour championship, first know as the Grand Prix Masters Championship, was staged in Tokyo, Japan in 1970. The event was held annually in New York City, 1977–89, with qualification based on season ranking. Since 1990, the event has been known as the ATP Tour Championship and held in Frankfurt, Germany.

Most titles Ivan Lendl has won a record five titles, 1982–83, 1986 (January and December), and 1987. A record seven doubles titles were won by John McEnroe and Peter Fleming, 1978–84.

VIRGINA SLIMS CHAMPIONSHIP

The season end tour championship for women's tennis is the Virginia Slims Championship, first staged in 1971. The championship game is the only women's contest played over the best of five sets (since 1983).

Most titles Martina Navratilova has a record six singles wins, 1978–79, 1981, and 1983–86. She also won nine doubles titles, one with Billie Jean King in 1980 and eight with Pam Shriver, 1981–82, 1984, 1986–89, and 1991.

OLYMPIC GAMES

A record four gold medals, as well as a silver and a bronze, were won by Max Decugis (France; 1882–1978), 1900–20. A women's record five medals (one gold, two silver, two bronze) were won by Kitty McKane (later Mrs Godfree [Great Britain]; 1897–1992) in 1920 and 1924.

INTERNATIONAL TEAM

Davis Cup (instituted 1900) The most wins in the Davis Cup, the men's international team championship, has been 30, by the USA between 1900 and 1992. The most appearances for Cup winners is eight, by Roy Emerson (Australia), 1959–62, 1964–67. Bill Tilden (USA) played in a record 28 matches in the final, winning a record 21—17 out of 22 singles and four out of six doubles. He was on seven winning sides, 1920–26, and then on four losing sides, 1927–30.

Nicola Pietrangeli (Italy) played a record 163 rubbers (66 ties), 1954 to 1972, winning 120. He played 109 singles (winning 78) and 54 doubles (winning 42).

John McEnroe has played for the US team on 31 occasions, 1978 through 1992. He also has the most wins—59 matches in Davis Cup competition (31 singles and 18 doubles).

Federation Cup (instituted 1963) The most wins in the Federation Cup, the women's international team championship, is 14, by the USA between 1963 and 1990. Virginia Wade (Great Britain) played each year from 1967 to 1983, in a record 57 ties, playing 100 rubbers, including 56 singles (winning 36) and 44 doubles (winning 30). Chris Evert won her first 29 singles matches, 1977–86. Her overall record, 1977–89, is 40 wins in 42 singles and 16 wins in 18 doubles matches.

Highest earnings Pete Sampras (USA) won a men's season's record of $3,648,075 and Steffi Graf (Germany) set a women's record of $2,821,337, both in 1993. The career earnings records are (*men's*) $20,453,167 by Ivan Lendl (Czechoslovakia, now USA; b. 7 Mar 1960), and (*women's*) $19,952,177 by Martina Navratilova, both to 27 Jul 1994.

The greatest first-place prize money ever won is $2 million, by Pete Sampras when he won the Grand Slam Cup in Munich, Germany on 16 Dec 1990. In the final he beat Brad Gilbert (USA) 6–3, 6–4, 6–2. Gilbert received $1 million, also well in excess of the previous record figure. The highest total prize money was $9,022,000 for the 1993 US Open Championships.

Largest crowd A record 30,472 people were at the Astrodome, Houston, TX on 20 Sep 1973, when Billie Jean King beat Bobby Riggs (USA). The record for a standard tennis match is 25,578 at Sydney, New South Wales, Australia on 27 Dec 1954, in the Davis Cup Challenge Round (first day), Australia *v* USA.

Most deuces The longest singles game was one of 37 deuces (80 points) between Anthony Fawcett (Rhodesia) and Keith Glass (Great Britain) in the first round of the Surrey Championships at Surbiton, Great Britain on 26 May 1975. It lasted 31 min.

Longest game (elapsed time) Noëlle van Lottum and Sandra Begijn played a game lasting 52 min in the semifinals of the Dutch Indoor Championships at Ede, Gelderland on 12 Feb 1984.

The longest tiebreak was 26–24 for the fourth and decisive set of a first round men's doubles at the Wimbledon Championships on 1 Jul 1985. Jan Gunnarsson (Sweden) and Michael Mortensen (Denmark) defeated John Frawley (Australia) and Victor Pecci (Paraguay) 6–3, 6–4, 3–6, 7–6.

TRACK & FIELD

Fastest speed An analysis of split times at each 10 meters in the 1988 Olympic Games 100 m final in Seoul, South Korea on 24 Sep 1988, won by Ben Johnson (Canada) in 9.79 (average speed 22.85 mph but later disallowed as a world record due to his positive drug test for steroids) from Carl Lewis (USA), 9.92, showed that both Johnson and Lewis reached a peak speed (40 m–50 m and 80 m–90 m respectively) of 0.83 sec for 10 m, i.e., 26.95 mph. In the women's final, Florence Griffith Joyner was timed at 0.91 sec for each 10 m from 60 m–90 m, i.e., 24.58 mph.

Most track records in a day Jesse Owens (USA; 1913–80) set six world records in 45 min at Ann Arbor, MI on 25 May 1935, with a 9.4 sec 100 yd at 3:15 P.M., a 26 ft 8¼ in long jump at 3:25 P.M., a 20.3 sec 220 yd (and 200 m) at 3:45 P.M., and a 22.6 sec 220 yd (and 200 m) low hurdles at 4 P.M.

Highest jump above own head The greatest height cleared above an athlete's own head is 23¼ in, by Franklin Jacobs (USA), 5 ft 8 in tall, who jumped 7 ft 7¼ in at New York City, on 27 Jan 1978. The greatest height cleared by a woman above her own head is 12¾ in, by Yolanda Henry (USA), 5 ft 6 in tall, who jumped 6 ft 6¾ in at Seville, Spain on 30 May 1990.

Most Olympic titles The most Olympic gold medals won is 10 (an absolute Olympic record), by Raymond Ewry (USA; 1873– 1937) in the standing high, long and triple jumps in 1900, 1904, 1906 and 1908.

Women The most gold medals won by a woman is four, shared by Fanny E. Blankers-Koen (Netherlands), with 100 m, 200 m, 80 m hurdles and 4 × 100 m relay, 1948; Betty Cuthbert (Australia), with 100 m, 200 m, 4 × 100 m relay, 1956 and 400 m, 1964; Bärbel Wöckel (nee Eckert; East Germany), with 200 m and 4 × 100 m relay in 1976 and 1980; and Evelyn Ashford (USA), 100 m and 4 × 100 m relay in 1984, 4 × 100 m relay in 1988 and 1992.

Most wins at one Games The most gold medals at one celebration is five,

Wang Junxia (China) set records in the 3,000 and 10,000 meters in 1993. (Allsport/Gary M. Prior)

by Paavo Johannes Nurmi (Finland; 1897–1973) in 1924: 1,500 m, 5,000 m, 10,000 m cross-country, 3,000 m team and cross-country team. The most at individual events is four, by Alvin Kraenzlein (USA; 1876–1928) in 1900: 60 m, 110 m hurdles, 200 m hurdles and long jump.

Most Olympic medals The most medals won is 12 (nine gold and three silver), by Paavo Nurmi (Finland) in the Games of 1920, 1924 and 1928.

Women The most medals won by a woman athlete is seven, by Shirley Barbara de la Hunty (nee Strickland; Australia) with three gold, one silver and three bronze in the 1948, 1952 and 1956 Games. Irena Szewinska (nee Kirszenstein; Poland) won three gold, two silver and two bronze in 1964, 1968, 1972 and 1976, and is the only woman athlete to win a medal in four successive Games.

United States The most Olympic medals won is 10, by Ray Ewry (see Most Olympic titles). The most by a woman is five, by Florence Griffith Joyner: silver at 200 m in 1984, gold at 100 m, 200 m and 4 × 100 m relay, silver at 4 × 400 m relay in 1988. Evelyn Ashford won gold at 100 m and 4 × 100 m relay, silver at 100 m in 1988, and gold at 4 × 100 m relay in 1992. Ashford's four gold medals are the most by an American woman in track and field.

Four gold medals at one Games were won by Alvin Kraenzlein (see above). Jesse Owens (1913–80) in 1936 and Carl Lewis in 1984 both won four gold medals at one Games, both at 100 m, 200 m, long jump and the 4 × 100 m relay.

Olympic champions *Oldest and youngest* The oldest athlete to win an Olympic title was Irish-born Patrick "Babe" McDonald (ne McDonnell; USA, 1878– 1954), who was age 42 yr 26 days when he won the 56 lb weight throw at Antwerp, Belgium on 21 Aug 1920. The oldest female champion was Lia Manoliu (Romania), age 36 yr 176 days when she won the discus at Mexico City on 18 Oct 1968.

The youngest gold medalist was Barbara Pearl Jones (USA), who at 15 yr 123 days was a member of the winning 4 × 100 m relay team, at Helsinki, Finland on 27 Jul 1952. The youngest male champion was Bob Mathias (USA), age 17 yr 263 days when he won the decathlon at the London Games on 5–6 Aug 1948.

The oldest Olympic medalist was Tebbs Lloyd Johnson (Great Britain; 1900–84), age 48 yr 115 days when he was third in the 1948 50,000 m walk. The oldest woman medalist was Dana Zátopková (Czechoslovakia; b. 19 Sep 1922), age 37 yr 348 days when she was second in the javelin in 1960.

World Championships Quadrennial World Championships, distinct from the Olympic Games, were inaugurated in 1983, when they were held in Helsinki, Finland. In 1991 the event became a biennial championship. The most medals won is 10, by Carl Lewis (USA)—eight gold, at 100 m, long jump and 4 × 100 m relay in 1983; 100 m, long jump and 4 × 100 m relay in 1987; 100 m and 4 × 100 m relay, 1991; silver at long jump in 1991; and bronze at 200 m in 1993; and by Merlene Ottey (Jamaica)—two gold, at 200 m in 1993 and 4 × 100 m relay in 1991; two silver, at 100 m in 1993 and 200 m in 1983; and six bronze, at 100 m and 200 m in 1987 and 1991 and at 4 × 100 m relay in 1983 and 1993. The most gold medals won by a woman is

Kenya's William Sigei set a new 10,000 m mark in July 1994. (Allsport)

four, by Jackie Joyner-Kersee (USA)—long jump 1987, 1991; heptathlon 1987, 1993.

Indoor First held as the World Indoor Games in 1985, they are now staged biennially. The most individual titles is four, shared by Stefka Kostadinova (Bulgaria), high jump 1985, 1987, 1989, 1993; and Mikhail Shchennikov (Russia), 5,000 m walk 1987, 1989, 1991, 1993.

World record breakers *Oldest and youngest* For the greatest age at which anyone has broken a world record under IAAF jurisdiction, see General Records. The female record is 36 yr 139 days for Marina Styepanova (nee Makeyeva; USSR) with 52.94 sec for the 400 m hurdles at Tashkent, USSR on 17 Sep 1986.

The youngest individual record breaker is Wang Yan (China; b. 9 Apr 1971), who set a women's 5,000 m walk record at age 14 yr 334 days with 21 min 33.8 sec at Jian, China on 9 Mar 1986. The youngest male is Thomas Ray (Great Britain; 1862–1904) at 17 yrs 198 days when he pole-vaulted 11 ft 2¾ in on 19 Sep 1879 (prior to IAAF ratification).

US Championships The most American national titles won at all events, indoors and out, is 65, by Ronald Owen Laird at various walks events between 1958 and 1976.

Excluding the walks, the record is 41, by Stella Walsh (nee Walasiewicz, 1911–80), who won women's events between 1930 and 1954—33 outdoors and 8 indoors.

The most wins outdoors at one event in AAU/TAC history is 11, by James Mitchel (1864–1921) at 56 lb weight in 1888, 1891–97, 1900, 1903, 1905; Stella Walsh, 220 y/200 m 1930–31, 1939–40, 1942–48, and long jump 1930, 1939–46, 1948 and 1951; Maren Seidler in shot 1967–68, 1972–80; and Dorothy Dodson in javelin 1939–49.

Longest winning sequence Iolanda Balas (Romania) won 150 consecutive competitions at high jump, 1956–67. The record for track is 122, at 400 m hurdles, by Ed Moses (USA) between his losses to Harald Schmid (West Germany) at Berlin, Germany on 26 Aug 1977 and Danny Lee Harris (USA) at Madrid, Spain on 4 Jun 1987.

Longest running races The longest race ever staged was the 1929 transcontinental race from New York City to Los Angeles, CA (3,665 miles). Finnish-born Johnny Salo (1893–1931) was the winner in 1929 in 79 days, from 31 Mar to 18 Jun. His elapsed time was 525 hr 57 min 20 sec (averaging 6.97 mph).

The longest race staged annually is the New York 1,300 Mile race, held since 1987, at Flushing Meadows-Corona Park, Queens, NY. The fastest race time is 16 days 19 hr 31 min 47 sec by Al Howie (Great Britain), from 16 Sep–3 Oct 1991.

Longest runs The longest run by an individual is one of 11,134 miles around the United States, by Sarah Covington-Fulcher (USA), starting and finishing in Los Angeles, CA, 21 Jul 1987– 2 Oct 1988.

Al Howie (Great Britain) ran across Canada, from St Johns, Newfoundland to Victoria, British Columbia, a distance of 4,533.2 miles, in 72 days 10 hr 23 min, 21 Jun–1 Sep 1991. Robert J. Sweetgall (USA) ran 10,608

Overcoming obstacles is important to most champions, but for Colin Jackson (above, far right) and Sally Gunnell (left), hurdle world record-holders, it's a specific requirement. (Allsport/Gray Mortimore; Allsport/Tony Duffy)

Sprinter Merlene Ottey has won a record ten medals at the World Championships since 1983. Her only individual

miles around the perimeter of the United States, starting and finishing in Washington, D.C., 9 Oct 1982–15 Jul 1983. Ron Grant (Australia) ran around Australia, 8,316 miles in 217 days 3 hr 45 min, 28 Mar–31 Oct 1983. Max Telford (New Zealand) ran 5,110 miles from Anchorage, AK to Halifax, Nova Scotia, in 106 days 18 hr 45 min from 25 Jul to 9 Nov 1977.

The fastest time for the cross-America run is 46 days 8 hr 36 min, by Frank Giannino, Jr. (USA) for the 3,100 miles from San Francisco to New York from 1 Sep–17 Oct 1980. The women's trans-America record is 69 days 2 hr 40 min, by Mavis Hutchinson (South Africa) from 12 Mar–21 May 1978.

Mass relay records The record for 100 miles by 100 runners from one club is 7 hr 53 min 52.1 sec, by the Baltimore Road Runners Club, Towson, MD on 17 May 1981. The women's record is 10 hr 47 min 9.3 sec on 3 Apr 1977, by the San Francisco Dolphins Southend Running Club. The record for 100 × 100 m is 19 min 14.19 sec, by a team from Antwerp at Merksem, Belgium on 23 Sep 1989.

The longest relay ever run was 10,806 miles by 23 runners of the Melbourne Fire Brigade, around Australia on Highway No. 1, in 50 days 43 min, 6 Aug–25 Sep 1991. The most participants was 6,500—260 teams of 25—for the Batavierenrace from Nijmegen to Enschede, Netherlands on 25 Apr 1992. The greatest distance covered in 24 hr by a team of 10 is 280.232 miles, by Oxford Striders RC at East London, South Africa on 5–6 Oct 1990.

WORLD RECORDS—*Men*

World records for the men's events scheduled by the International Amateur Athletic Federation. Fully automatic electric timing is mandatory for events up to 400 meters.

Running	min : sec	Name & Country	Place	Date
100 meters	9.85*	Leroy Burrell (USA)	Lausanne, Switzerland	6 Jul 1994
200 meters	19.72†	Pietro Mennea (Italy)	Mexico City, Mexico	12 Sep 1979
400 meters	43.29	Butch Reynolds, Jr. (USA)	Zürich, Switzerland	17 Aug 1988
800 meters	1:41.73	Seb Newbold Coe (Great Britain)	Florence, Italy	10 Jun 1981
1,000 meters	2:12.18	Seb Newbold Coe (Great Britain)	Oslo, Norway	11 Jul 1981
1,500 meters	3:28.86	Noureddine Morceli (Algeria)	Rieti, Italy	6 Sep 1992
1 mile	3:44.39	Noureddine Morceli (Algeria)	Rieti, Italy	5 Sep 1993
2,000 meters	4:50.81	Said Aouita (Morocco)	Paris, France	16 Jul 1987
3,000 meters	7:25.11	Noureddine Morceli (Algeria)	Monte Carlo, Monaco	2 Aug 1994
5,000 meters	12:58.39	Said Aouita (Morocco)	Rome, Italy	22 Jul 1987
10,000 meters	26:52.23	William Sigei (Kenya)	Oslo, Norway	22 Jul 1994
20,000 meters	56:55.6	Arturo Barrios (Mexico)	La Flèche, France	30 Mar 1991
25,000 meters	1 hr 13:55.8	Toshihiko Seko (Japan)	Christchurch, New Zealand	22 Mar 1981
30,000 meters	1 hr 29:18.8	Toshihiko Seko (Japan)	Christchurch, New Zealand	22 Mar 1981
1 hour	13.111 miles	Arturo Barrios (Mexico)	La Flèche, France	30 May 1991

** Ben Johnson (Canada; b. 30 Dec 1961) ran 100 m in 9.79 sec at Seoul, South Korea on 24 Sep 1988, but was subsequently disqualified when he tested positive for steroids. He later admitted to having taken drugs over many years, and this also invalidated his 9.83 sec at Rome, Italy on 30 Aug 1987.*

† This record was set at high altitude—Mexico City 7,349 ft. Best mark at low altitude: 200 m: 19.75 sec, Carl Lewis, Indianapolis, IN, 19 Jun 1983, and Joseph Nathaniel DeLoach (USA; b. 5 Jun 1967) at Seoul, South Korea on 28 Sep 1988.

Hurdling	min : sec	Name & Country	Place	Date
110 meters (3′ 6″)	12.91	Colin Jackson (Great Britain)	Stuttgart, Germany	20 Aug 1993
400 meters (3′ 0″)	46.78	Kevin Young (USA)	Barcelona, Spain	6 Aug 1992
3,000 meter steeplechase	8:02.08	Moses Kiptanui (Kenya)	Zürich, Sweden	20 Aug 1992

Relays

Event	Time	Team	Place	Date
4 × 100 meters	37.40	United States (Mike Marsh, Leroy Burrell, Dennis Mitchell, Carl Lewis)	Barcelona, Spain	8 Aug 1992
	37.40	United States (John A. Drummond Jr, Andre Cason, Dennis A. Mitchell, Leroy Burrell)	Stuttgart, Germany	21 Aug 1993
4 × 200 meters	1:19.11	Santa Monica Track Club (Mike Marsh, Leroy Burrell, Floyd Wayne Heard, Carl Lewis)	Barcelona, Spain	8 Aug 1992
4 × 400 meters	2:55.74	United States (Andrew Valmon, Quincy Watts, Michael Johnson, Steve Lewis)	Barcelona, Spain	8 Aug 1992
4 × 800 meters	7:03.89	Great Britain (Peter Elliott, Garry Peter Cook, Steven Cram, Sebastian Coe)	London, Great Britain	30 Aug 1982
4 × 1,500 meters	14:38.8	West Germany (Thomas Wessinghage, Harald Hudak, Michael Lederer, Karl Fleschen)	Cologne, Germany	17 Aug 1977

Field Events

Field Events	m	ft	in	Athlete	Place	Date
High jump	2.45	8	0½	Javier Sotomayor (Cuba)	Salamanca, Spain	27 Jul 1993
Pole vault	6.14	20	1¾	Sergey Bubka (Ukraine)	Sestriere, Italy	31 Jul 1994
Long jump	8.95	29	4½	Mike Powell (USA)	Tokyo, Japan	30 Aug 1991
Triple jump	17.97	58	11½	Willie Banks (USA)	Indianapolis, IN	16 Jun 1985
Shot 16 lb	23.12	75	10¼	Randy Barnes (USA)	Los Angeles, CA	20 May 1990
Discus 4 lb 8 oz	74.08	243	0	Jürgen Schult (East Germany)	Neubrandenburg, Germany	6 Jun 1986
Hammer 16 lb	86.74	284	7	Yuriy Sedykh (USSR)	Stuttgart, Germany	30 Aug 1986
Javelin	95.54	313	5	Jan Zelezny (TCH)	Pietersburg, South Africa	6 Apr 1993

Decathlon

Points	Athlete	Place	Date
8,891 points	Dan O'Brien (USA; b. 18 Jul 1966) (1st day: 100 m 10.43 sec, Long jump 26 ft ¼ in, Shot put 54 ft 9¼ in, High jump 6 ft 9½ in, 400 m 48.51 sec)	Talence, France (2nd day: 110 m hurdles 13.98 sec, Discus 159 ft 4 in, Pole vault 16 ft 4¾ in Javelin 205 ft 4 in, 1,500 m 4:42.10 sec)	4–5 Sep 1992

WORLD RECORDS—*Women*

World records for the women's events scheduled by the International Amateur Athletic Federation.

Running	min : sec	Name & Country	Place	Date
100 meters	10.49	Delorez Florence Griffith Joyner (USA)	Indianapolis, IN	16 Jul 1988
200 meters	21.34	Delorez Florence Griffith Joyner (USA)	Seoul, South Korea	29 Sep 1988
400 meters	47.60	Marita Koch (East Germany)	Canberra, Australia	6 Oct 1985
800 meters	1:53.28	Jarmila Kratochvílová (Czechoslovakia)	Münich, Germany	26 Jul 1983
1,000 meters	2:30.6	Tatyana Providokhina (USSR)	Podolsk, USSR	20 Aug 1978
1,500 meters	3:50.46	Qu Yunxia (China)	Beijing, China	11 Sep 1993
1 mile	4:15.61	Paula Ivan (Romania)	Nice, France	10 Jul 1989
2,000 meters	5:25.36	Sonia O'Sullivan (Ireland)	Edinburgh, Great Britain	8 Jul 1994
3,000 meters	8:06.11	Wang Junxia (China)	Beijing, China	13 Sep 1993
5,000 meters	14:37.33	Ingrid Kristiansen (nee Christensen; Norway)	Stockholm, Sweden	5 Aug 1986
10,000 meters	29:31.78	Wang Junxia (China)	Beijing, China	8 Sep 1993
Hurdling				
100 meters (2′ 9″)	12.21	Yordanka Donkova (Bulgaria)	Stara Zagora, Bulgaria	20 Aug 1988
400 meters (2′ 6″)	52.74	Sally Jane Janet Gunnell (Great Britain)	Stuttgart, Germany	19 Aug 1993
Relays				
4 × 100 meters	41.37	East Germany (Silke Gladisch [now Möller], Sabine Rieger [now Günther], IngridAuerswald [nee Brestrich], Marlies Göhr [nee Oelsner])	Canberra, Australia	6 Oct 1985
4 × 200 meters	1:28.15	East Germany (Marlies Göhr [nee Oelsner], Romy Müller [nee Schneider], Bärbel Wöckel [nee Eckert], Marita Koch)	Jena, Germany	9 Aug 1980

4 × 400 meters	3:15.17	USSR (Tatyana Ledovskaya, Olga Nazarova [nee Grigoryeva], Maria Pinigina [nee Kulchunova], Olga Bryzgina [nee Vladykina])	Seoul, South Korea	1 Oct 1988
4 × 800 meters	7:50.17	USSR (Nadezhda Olizarenko [nee Mushta], Lyubov Gurina, Lyudmila Borisova, Irina Podyalovskaya)	Moscow, USSR	5 Aug 1984

Field Events

Field Events	m	ft	in			
High jump	2.09	6	10 1/4	Stefka Kostadinova (Bulgaria)	Rome, Italy	30 Aug 1987
Long jump	7.52	24	8 1/4	Galina Chistyakova (USSR)	Leningrad, USSR	11 Jun 1988
Triple jump	15.09	49	6	Anna Biryukova (nee Dereyankina; Russia)	Stuttgart, Germany	21 Aug 1993
Shot 8 lb 13 oz	22.63	74	3	Natalya Lisovskaya (USSR)	Moscow, USSR	7 Jun 1987
Discus 2 lb 3 oz	76.80	25	20	Gabriele Reinsch (East Germany)	Neubrandenburg, Germany	9 Jul 1988
Javelin 24 lb 7 oz	80.00	26	25	Petra Felke (East Germany)	Potsdam, Germany	9 Sep 1988

Heptathlon

7,291 points .... Jacqueline Joyner-Kersee (USA) .... Seoul, South Korea .... 23–24 Sep 1988
(100 m hurdles 12.69 sec; High jump 6 ft 1 1/4 in; Shot 51 ft 10 in; 200 m 22.56 sec; Long jump 23 ft 10 in; Javelin 149 ft 9 in; 800 m 2 min 08.51 sec)

US NATIONAL RECORDS—*Men*

Running	min : sec	Name	Place	Date
100 meters	9.85	Leroy Burrell	Lausanne, Switzerland	6 Jul 1994
200 meters	19.73	Mike Marsh	Barcelona, Spain	6 Aug 1992
400 meters	43.29	Harry "Butch" Reynolds, Jr.	Zürich, Switzerland	17 Aug 1988
800 meters	1:42.60	Johnny Gray	Koblenz, Germany	28 Aug 1985
1,000 meters	2:13.9	Rick Wohlhuter	Oslo, Norway	30 Jul 1974
1,500 meters	3:29.77	Sydney Maree	Cologne, Germany	25 Aug 1985
1 mile	3:47.69	Stevel Scott	Oslo, Norway	7 Jul 1982
2,000 meters	4:52.44	Jim Spivey	Lausanne, Switzerland	15 Sep 1987
3,000 meters	7:33.37	Sydney Maree*	London, Great Britain	17 Jul 1982
	7:35.84	Douglas Floyd Padilla	Oslo, Norway	9 Jul 1983
5,000 meters	13:01.15	Sydney Maree	Oslo, Norway	27 Jul 1985
10,000 meters	27:20.56	Marcus Nenow	Brussels, Belgium	5 Sep 1986
15,000 meters	43:39.8	Bill Rodgers	Boston, MA	9 Aug 1977
20,000 meters	58:25.0	Bill Rodgers	Boston, MA	9 Aug 1977
25,000 meters	1 hr 14:11.8	Bill Rodgers	Saratoga, NY	21 Feb 1979
30,000 meters	1 hr 31:49	Bill Rodgers	Saratoga, NY	21 Feb 1979
1 hour	12 miles 135 yd	Bill Rodgers	Boston, MA	9 Aug 1977
Marathon	2 hr 08:52	Alberto Salazar	Boston, MA	19 Apr 1982

* *Prior to obtaining US citizenship.*

Hurdling				
110 meters	12.92	Roger Kingdom	Zürich, Switzerland	16 Aug 1989
400 meters	47.02	Kevin Young	Barcelona, Spain	6 Aug 1992
3,000 meter steeplechase	8:09.17	Henry Marsh	Koblenz, Germany	28 Aug 1985

Relays

Event	Time	Team	Place	Date
4 × 100 meters	37.40	National Team (Andre Cason, Leroy Burrell, Dennis Mitchell, Carl Lewis)	Tokyo, Japan	1 Sep 1991
	37.40	National Team (Jon Drummond, Andre Cason, Dennis Mitchell, Leroy Burrell)	Barcelona, Spain	8 Aug 1992
4 × 200 meters	1:19.11	Santa Monica Track Club (Daniel Joe Everett, Leroy Burrell, Floyd Heard, Carl Lewis)	Koblenz, Germany	23 Aug 1989
	1:19.11	Santa Monica Track Club (Mike Marsh, Leroy Burrell, Floyd Heard, Carl Lewis)	Philadelphia, PA	25 Apr 1992
4 × 400 meters	2:55.29	National Team (Andrew Valmon, Quincy Watts, Butch Reynolds, Michael Johnson)	Stuttgart, Germany	22 Aug 1993
4 × 800 meters	7:06.5	Santa Monica Track Club (James Robinson, David Mack, Earl Jones, Johnny Gray)	Walnut, CA	26 Apr 1986
4 × 1,000 meters	14:46.3	National Team	Bourges, France	24 Jun 1969

Field Events

Field Events	ft	in	Athlete	Place	Date
High jump	7	10 1/2	Charles Austin	Zürich, Switzerland	7 Aug 1991
Pole vault	19	7	Scott Huffman	Knoxville, TN	18 Jun 1994
Long jump	29	4 1/2	Mike Powell	Tokyo, Japan	30 Aug 1991
Triple jump	58	11 1/2	Willie Banks	Indianapolis, IN	16 Jun 1985
Shot	75	10 1/4	Randy Barnes	Westwood, LA	20 May 1990
Discus*	237	4	Ben Plunknett	Stockholm, Sweden	7 Jul 1981
Hammer	270	8	Lance Deal	Knoxville, TN	17 Jun 1994
Javelin	281	2	Tom Pukstys	Kuortane, Finland	26 Jun 1993

** Ratified despite the fact that it was achieved after a positive drug test.*

Decathlon

Points	Athlete	Place	Date
8,812 points	Dan O'Brien	Talence, France	4–5 Sep 1992

US NATIONAL RECORDS—*Women*

Running	min : sec	Name & Country	Place	Date
100 meters	10.49	Florence Griffith Joyner	Indianapolis, IN	16 Jul 1988
200 meters	21.34	Florence Griffith Joyner	Seoul, South Korea	29 Sep 1988
400 meters	48.83	Valerie Ann Brisco	Los Angeles, CA	6 Aug 1984
800 meters	1:56.90	Mary Slaney (nee Decker)	Berne, Switzerland	16 Aug 1985
1,000 meters	2:34.8	Mary Slaney	Eugene, OR	4 Jul 1985
1,500 meters	3:57.12	Mary Slaney	Stockholm, Sweden	26 Jul 1983
1 mile	4:16.71	Mary Slaney	Zürich, Switzerland	21 Aug 1985
2,000 meters	5:32.7	Mary Slaney	Eugene, OR	3 Aug 1984
3,000 meters	8:25.83	Mary Slaney	Rome, Italy	7 Sep 1985
5,000 meters	14:56.07	Annette Peters	Berlin, Germany	27 Aug 1993
10,000 meters	31:19.89	Lynn Jennings	Barcelona, Spain	7 Aug 1992
Marathon	2 hr 21:21	Joan Samuelson (nee Benoit)	Chicago, IL	20 Oct 1985
Hurdling				
100 meters	12.46	Gail Devers (now Roberts)	Stuttgart, Germany	20 Aug 1993
400 meters	52.79	Sandra Farmer-Patrick	Stuttgart, Germany	19 Aug 1993
Relays				
4 × 100 meters	41.49	National Team (Michelle Finn, Gwen Torrance, Wendy Vereen, Gail Devers)	Stuttgart, Germany	22 Aug 1993
4 × 200 meters	1:32.57	Louisiana State University (Tananjalyn Stanley, Sylvia Brydson, Esther Jones, Dawn Sowell)	Des Moines, IA	28 Apr 1989
4 × 400 meters	3:15.51	National Team (Denean Howard, Diane Lynn Dixon, Valerie Brisco, Florence Griffith Joyner)	Seoul, South Korea	1 Oct 1988
4 × 800 meters	8:17.09	Athletics West (Susan Addison, Lee Arbogast, Mary Decker, Chris Mullen)	Walnut, CA	24 Apr 1983

Field Events	ft	in			
High jump	6	8	Louise Ritter	Austin, TX	8 Jul 1988
	6	8	Louise Ritter	Seoul, South Korea	30 Sep 1988
Long jump	24	7	Jacqueline Joyner-Kersee	New York, NY	22 May 1994
Triple jump	46	8 1/4	Sheila Hudson	New Orleans, LA	21 Jun 1992
	46	8 1/4	Sheila Hudson	Knoxville, TN	16 Jun 1994
Shot	66	2 1/2	Ramona Pagel (nee Ebert)	San Diego, CA	25 Jun 1988
Discus	216	10 1/2	Carol Cady	San Jose, CA	31 May 1986
Javelin	227	5 1/2	Kate Schmidt	Fürth, Germany	11 Sep 1977

Heptathlon

7,291 points	Jacqueline Joyner-Kersee (100 m hurdles 12.69 sec; High jump 6 ft 1 1/4 in; Shot 51 ft 10 in; 200 m 22.56 sec; Long jump 23 ft 10 in; Javelin 149 ft 9 in; 800 m 2 min 08.51 sec)	Seoul, South Korea	23–24 Sep 1988

ULTRA LONG DISTANCE WORLD RECORDS

Track	hr: min: sec	Name & Country	Place	Date
MEN				
50 km	2:48:06	Jeff Norman (Great Britain)	Manchester, Great Britain	7 Jun 1980
50 miles	4:51:49	Don Ritchie (Great Britain)	London, Great Britain	12 Mar 1983
100 km	6:10:20	Don Ritchie (Great Britain)	London, Great Britain	28 Oct 1978
100 miles	11:30:51	Don Ritchie (Great Britain)	London, Great Britain	15 Oct 1977
200 km	15:11:10*	Yiannis Kouros (Greece)	Montauban, France	15–16 Mar 1985
200 miles	27:48:35	Yiannis Kouros (Greece)	Montauban, France	15–16 Mar 1985
500 km	60:23:00	Yiannis Kouros (Greece)	Colac, Australia	26–29 Nov 1984
500 miles	105:42:09	Yiannis Kouros (Greece)	Colac, Australia	26–30 Nov 1984
1,000 km	136:17:00	Yiannis Kouros (Greece)	Colac, Australia	26 Nov–1 Dec 1984
	kilometers			
24 hours	283.600	Yiannis Kouros (Greece)	Montauban, France	15–16 Mar 1985
48 hours	452.270	Yiannis Kouros (Greece)	Montauban, France	15–17 Mar 1985
6 days	1,023.200	Yiannis Kouros (Greece)	Colac, Australia	26 Nov–1 Dec 1984
Road	**hr : min : sec**			
50 km	2:43:38	Thompson Magawana (South Africa)	Claremont–Kirstenbosch, South Africa	12 Apr 1988
50 miles	4:50:21	Bruce Fordyce (South Africa)	London–Brighton, Great Britain	25 Sep 1983
1,000 miles	10d 10hr 30min 35sec	Yiannis Kouros (Greece)	New York City	21–30 May 1988
	kilometers			
24 hours	286.463	Yiannis Kouros (Greece)	New York City	28–29 Sep 1985
6 days	1,028.370	Yiannis Kouros (Greece)	New York City	21–26 May 1988

WOMEN

Track	hr: min: sec			
15 km	49:44.0	Silvana Cruciata (Italy)	Rome, Italy	4 May 1981
20 km	1:06:48.8	Isumi Maki (Japan)	Amagasaki, Japan	20 Sep 1983
25 km	1:29:29.2	Karolina Szabo (Hungary)	Budapest, Hungary	23 Apr 198
30 km	1:47:05.6	Karolina Szabo (Hungary)	Budapest, Hungary	23 Apr 1988
50 km	3:26:45	Carolyn Hunter-Rowe (Great Britain)	Barry, Great Britain	7 Mar 1993
50 miles	6:12:11	Hilary Walker (Great Britain)	London, Great Britain	16 Oct 1993
100 km	7:50:09	Ann Transon (USA)	Hayward, CA	3–4 Aug 1991
100 miles	14:29:44	Ann Transon (USA)	Santa Rosa, CA	18–19 Mar 1989
200 km	19:28:48	Eleanor Adams (Great Britain)	Melbourne, Australia	19–20 Aug 1989
200 miles	39:09:03	Hilary Walker (Great Britain)	Blackpool, Great Britain	5–6 Nov 1988
500 km	77:53:46	Eleanor Adams (Great Britain)	Colac, Australia	13–15 Nov 1989
500 miles	130:59:58	Sandra Barwick (New Zealand)	Campbelltown, Australia	18–23 Nov 1990

	kilometers			
1 hour	18.084	Silvana Cruciata (Italy)	Rome, Italy	4 May 1981
24 hours	240.169	Eleanor Adams (Great Britain)	Melbourne, Australia	19–20 Aug 1989
48 hours	366.512	Hilary Walker (Great Britain)	Blackpool, Great Britain	5–7 Nov 1988
6 days	883.631	Sandra Barwick (New Zealand)	Campbelltown, Australia	18–24 Nov 1990

Road	hr : min : sec			
30 km	1:38:27	Ingrid Kristiansen (Norway)	London, Great Britain	10 May 1987
50 km	3:08:13	Frith van der Merwe (South Africa)	Claremont-Kirstenbosch, South Africa	25 Mar 1989
50 miles	5:40:18	Ann Trason (USA)	Houston, TX	23 Feb 1991
100 km	7:09:44	Ann Trason (USA)	Amiens, France	27 Sep 1993
100 miles	13:47:41	Ann Trason (USA)	Queens, NY	4 May 1991
200 km	19:08:21	Sigrid Lomsky (Germany)	Basel, Switzerland	1–2 May 1993
	(indoors) 19:00:31	Eleanor Adams (Great Britain)	Milton Keynes, Great Britain	3–4 Feb 1990
1,000 km	7d 1hr 11min 00sec	Sandra Barwick (New Zealand)	Queens, NY	16–23 Sep 1991
1,000 miles	12d 14hr 38min 40sec	Sandra Barwick (New Zealand)	Queens, NY	16–29 Sep 1991

** Where superior to track bests and run on properly measured road courses. It should be noted that road times must be assessed with care as course conditions can vary considerably.*

WORLD INDOOR RECORDS

Track performances around a turn must be made on a track of circumference no longer than 200 meters.

Running	min : sec	Name & Country	Place	Date
MEN				
50 meters	5.61*	Manfred Kokot (East Germany)	East Berlin, Germany	4 Feb 1973
	5.61*	James Sanford (USA)	San Diego, CA	20 Feb 1981
60 meters	6.41*	Andre Cason (USA)	Madrid, Spain	14 Feb 1992
200 meters	20.36	Bruno Marie-Rose (France)	Liévin, France	22 Feb 1987
400 meters	45.02	Danny Everett (USA)	Stuttgart, Germany	2 Feb 1992
800 meters	1:44.84	Paul Ereng (Kenya)	Budapest, Hungary	4 Mar 1989
1,000 meters	2:15.26	Noureddine Morceli (Algeria)	Birmingham, Great Britain	22 Feb 1992
1,500 meters	3:34.16	Noureddine Morceli (Algeria)	Seville, Spain	28 Feb 1991
1 mile	3:49.78	Eamonn Coghlan (Ireland)	East Rutherford, NJ	27 Feb 1983
3,000 meters	7:37.31	Moses Kiptanui (Kenya)	Seville, Spain	20 Feb 1992
5,000 meters	13:20.4	Suleiman Nyambui (Tanzania)	New York, NY	6 Feb 1983
50 meter hurdles	6.25	Mark McKoy (Canada)	Kobe, Japan	5 Mar 1986
60 meter hurdles	7.30	Colin Jackson (Great Britain)	Sindelfingen, Germany	6 Mar 1994

** Ben Johnson (Canada) ran 50 m in 5.55 sec at Ottawa, Canada on 31 Jan 1987 and 60 m in 6.41 sec at Indianapolis, IN on 7 Mar 1987, but these were invalidated due to his admission, following his disqualification at the 1988 Olympics, of having taken drugs over many years.*

Relays	min : sec	Name & Country	Place	Date
4 × 200 meters	1:22.11	United Kingdom (Linford Christie, Darren Braithwaite, Ade Mafe, John Regis)	Glasgow, Great Britain	3 Mar 1991
4 x 400 meter	3:03.05	Germany (Rico Lieder, Jens Carlowitz, Karsten Just, Thomas Schönlebe)	Seville, Spain	10 Mar 1991

Walking

Event	Time	Athlete	Place	Date
5,000 meters	18:11.41*	Ronald Weigel (East Germany)	Vienna, Austria	13 Feb 1988
	18:15.25	Grigoriy Kornev (Russia)	Moscow, Russia	7 Feb 1992

** not officially recognized.*

Field Events

Field Events	m	ft	in	Athlete	Place	Date
High jump	2.43	7	11 1/2	Javier Sotomayor (Cuba)	Budapest, Hungary	4 Mar 1989
Pole vault	6.15	20	2 1/4	Sergey Nazarovich Bubka (Ukraine)	Donetsk, Ukraine	21 Feb 1993
Long jump	8.79	28	10 1/4	Carl Lewis (USA)	New York, NY	27 Jan 1984
Triple jump	17.76	58	3 1/4	Mike Conley (USA)	New York, NY	27 Feb 1987
Shot	22.66	74	4 1/4	Randy Barnes (USA)	Los Angeles, CA	20 Jan 1989

Heptathlon

Points	Athlete	Place	Date
6,476 points	Dan O'Brien (USA) (60 m 6.67 sec; Long jump 7.84 m; Shot 16.02 m; High jump 2.13 m; 60 m hurdles 7.85 sec; Pole vault 5.20 m; 1,000 m 2:57.96)	Toronto, Canada	13–14 Mar 1993

WOMEN

Running

Event	Time	Athlete	Place	Date
50 meters	6.00	Merlene Ottey (Jamaica)	Moscow, Russia	4 Feb 1994
60 meters	6.92	Irina Privalova (Russia)	Madrid, Spain	11 Feb 1993
200 meters	21.87	Merlene Ottey (Jamaica)	Liévin, France	13 Feb 1994
400 meters	49.59	Jarmila Kratochvílová (Czechoslovakia)	Milan, Italy	7 Mar 1982
800 meters	1:56.40	Christine Wachtel (East Germany)	Vienna, Austria	13 Feb 1988
1,000 meters	2:33.93	Inna Yevseyeva (Ukraine)	Moscow, Russia	7 Feb 1992
1,500 meters	4:00.27	Doina Melinte (Romania)	East Rutherford, NJ	9 Feb 1990
1 mile	4:17.14	Doina Melinte (Romania)	East Rutherford, NJ	9 Feb 1990
3,000 meters	8:33.82	Elly van Hulst (Netherlands)	Budapest, Hungary	4 Mar 1989
5,000 meters	15:03.17	Elizabeth McColgan (Great Britain)	Birmingham, Great Britain	22 Feb 1992
50 meter hurdles	6.58	Cornelia Oschkenat (East Germany)	Berlin, Germany	20 Feb 1988
60 meter hurdles	7.69	Lyudmila Narozhilenko (USSR)	Chelyabinsk, Russia	4 Feb 1993

(continued)

Relays

Event	Time	Athlete(s)	Place	Date
4 × 200 meters	1:32.55	S. C. Eintracht Hamm (West Germany) (Helga Arendt, Silke-Beate Knoll, Mechthild Kluth, Gisela Kinzel)	Dortmund, Germany	19 Feb 1988
4 × 400 meters	3:27.22	Germany (Sandra Seuser, Katrin Schreiter, Annet Hesselbarth, Grit Breuer)	Seville, Spain	10 Mar 1992

Walking

Event	Time	Athlete	Place	Date
3,000 meters	11:44.00	Alina Ivanova (Ukraine)	Moscow, Russia	7 Feb 1992

Field Events

Field Events	m	ft	in	Athlete	Place	Date
High jump	2.07	6	9½	Heike Henkel (Germany)	Karlsruhe, Germany	9 Feb 1992
Long jump	7.37	24	2¼	Heike Dreschler (East Germany)	Vienna, Austria	13 Feb 1988
Triple jump	14.90	48	10½	Inna Lasovskaya (Russia)	Liévin, France	13 Feb 1994
Shot	22.50	73	10	Helena Fibingerová (Czechoslovakia)	Jablonec, Czechoslovakia	19 Feb 1977

Pentathlon

Points	Athlete	Place	Date
4,991 points	Irina Belova (Russia) (60 m hurdles 8.22 sec; High jump 1.93 m; Shot 13.25 m; Long jump 6.67 m; 800 m 2:10.26)	Berlin, Germany	14–15 Feb 1992

United States The greatest distance covered by an American team of 10 runners in 24 hr is 271.974 miles, by students of Marcus High School in Flower Mound, TX, 17–18 May 1991.

Greatest mileage Gordon Pirie (Great Britain; 1931–91), who set five world records in the 1950s, estimated that he had run a total distance of 216,000 miles in 40 years up to 1981.

Ron Hill (Great Britain), the 1969 European and Commonwealth marathon champion, has not missed a day's training since 20 Dec 1964. His meticulously compiled training log shows a total of 128,030 miles from 3 Sep 1956 to 19 May 1994. He has finished 114 marathons, all in less than 2:52, and has raced in 55 nations.

The greatest competitive distance run in a year is 5,502 miles, by Malcolm Campbell (Great Britain) in 1985.

Joggling *3 objects* Owen Morse (USA), 100 m in 11.68 sec, 1989, and 400 m in 57.32 sec, 1990. Kirk Swenson (USA), 1 mile in 4 min 43 sec, 1986, and 5,000 m (3.1 miles) in 16 min 55 sec, 1986. Ashrita Furman (USA), marathon—26 miles 385 yd—in 3 hr 22 min 32.5 sec, 1988, and 50 miles in 8 hr 52 min 7 sec, 1989. Michael Hout (USA), 110 m hurdles in 20 sec, 1992. Albert Lucas (USA), 400 m hurdles in 1 min 10.37 sec, 1989. Owen Morse, Albert Lucas, Tuey Wilson and John Wee (all USA), 1 mile relay in 3 min 57.38 sec, 1990.

5 objects Owen Morse (USA), 100 m in 13.8 sec, 1988. Bill Gillen (USA), 1 mile in 7 min 41.01 sec, 1989, and 3.1 miles in 28 min 11 sec, 1989.

MARATHON

Fastest There are as yet no official records for the marathon, and it should be noted that courses may vary in severity. The following are the best times recorded on courses whose distances have been verified.

Men 2 hr 6 min 50 sec, by Belayneh Dinsamo (Ethiopia) in Rotterdam, Netherlands, 17 Apr 1988.

Women 2 hr 21 min 6 sec, by Ingrid Kristiansen (nee Christensen; Norway) in London, Great Britain on 21 Apr 1985.

Boston Marathon First run by 15 men on 19 Apr 1897 over a distance of 24 miles 1,232 yards, the Boston Marathon is the world's oldest annual race. The full marathon distance was first run in 1927.

The most wins is seven, by Clarence DeMar (1888–1958), in 1911, 1922–24, 1927–28 and 1930.

Rosa Mota (Portugal) has a record three wins, 1987–88 and 1990, in the women's competition.

The course record for men is 2 hr 7 min 14 sec by Cosmas N'Deti (Kenya) in 1994. The women's record is 2 hr 21 min 45 sec, by Uta Pippig (Germany) in 1994.

John A. Kelley (USA; b. 6 Sep 1907) finished the Boston Marathon 61 times through 1992, winning twice, in 1933 and 1945.

NEW YORK *v* LONDON

Since the first London marathon in 1981, the marathons in New York and London have contested who is the largest in terms of finishers. The New York marathon began with a very small number of entries in 1970, when there were 6,418 finishers, and steadily grew until 1981, when 13,223 runners completed the course. The table at the bottom of page 715 shows how the record progressed from that point.

PROGRESSIVE TIME RECORDS

NEW YORK (since 1976)

	Time	Name	Year
MEN	2:10:10	Bill Rodgers (USA)	1976
	2:09:41	Alberto Salazar (USA)	1980
	2:08:13	Alberto Salazar (USA)	1981*
	2:08:20	Steve Jones (GB)	1988
	2:08:01	Juma Ikangaa (Japan)	1989
WOMEN	2:39:11	Miki Gorman (USA)	1976
	2:32:30	Grete Waitz (Norway)	1978
	2:27:33	Grete Waitz (Norway)	1979
	2:25:42	Grete Waitz (Norway)	1980
	2:25:29	Allison Roe (New Zealand)	1981*
	2:25:30	Ingrid Kristiansen (Norway)	1989
	2:24:40	Lisa Ondieki (Australia)	1992

*Course found to be 170 yd short

LONDON

	Time	Name	Year
MEN	2:11:48	Dick Beardsley (USA) & Inge Simonsen (Norway)	1981
	2:09:24	Hugh Jones (GB)	1982
	2:08:16	Steve Jones (GB)	1985
WOMEN	2:29:57	Joyce Smith (GB)	1981
	2:29:43	Joyce Smith (GB)	1982
	2:25:29	Grete Waitz (Norway)	1983
	2:24:26	Ingrid Kristiansen (Norway)	1984
	2:21:06	Ingrid Kristiansen (Norway)	1985

FINISHERS	CITY	YEAR
13,223	New York	1981
15,758	London	1982
15,776	London	1983
16,580	London	1984
18,175	London	1986
19,710	London	1987
21,141	New York	1987
22,244	New York	1988
22,587	London	1989
24,588	New York	1989
24,871	London	1990
25,797	New York	1991
27,797	New York	1992

GUESS WHAT?

Q. WHAT IS THE FASTEST CREATURE ON LAND?

A. LOOK IN "MAMMALS" (LIVING WORLD)

New York City Marathon In the 1992 competition, there were a record 27,797 finishers.

Grete Waitz (nee Andersen; Norway) was the women's winner nine times, in 1978–80, 1982–86 and 1988. Bill Rodgers (USA) had a record four wins, 1976–79.

The course record for men is 2 hr 8 min 1 sec, by Juma Ikangaa (Tanzania), and for women it is 2 hr 25 min 30 sec, by Ingrid Kristiansen (Norway), both set in 1989. On a course subsequently remeasured as about 170 yd short, Allison Roe (New Zealand) was the 1981 women's winner in 2 hr 25 min 29 sec.

Highest altitude The highest start for a marathon is the biennially held Everest Marathon, first run on 27 Nov 1987. It begins at Gorak Shep at 17,100 ft and ends at Namche Bazar, 11,300 ft. The fastest times to complete this race are *(men)* 3 hr 59 min 4 sec, by Jack Maitland; *(women)* 5 hr 44 min 32 sec, by Dawn Kenwright, both in 1989.

Most competitors The record number of confirmed finishers in a marathon is 27,797 for 28,656 starters in the New York City Marathon on 1 Nov 1992.

A record six men ran under 2 hr 10 min at Fukuoka, Japan on 4 Dec 1983 and at London on 23 Apr 1989. A record nine women ran under 2 hr 30 min in the first Olympic marathon for women at Los Angeles on 5 Aug 1984.

Most run by an individual Norm Frank (USA) had run 525 marathons of 26 miles 385 yd or longer as of 1 May 1994.

Three in three days The fastest combined time for three marathons in three days is 8 hr 22 min 31 sec, by Raymond Hubbard (Belfast, Northern Ireland: 2 hr 45 min 55 sec; London, Great Britain: 2 hr 48 min 45 sec; and Boston: 2 hr 47 min 51 sec) on 16–18 Apr 1988.

Oldest finishers The oldest man to complete a marathon was Dimitrion Yordanidis (Greece), age 98, in Athens, Greece on 10 Oct 1976. He finished in 7 hr 33 min. Thelma Pitt-Turner (New Zealand) set the women's age record in August 1985, completing the Hastings, New Zealand Marathon in 7 hr 58 min at the age of 82.

Pancake race record Dominic M. Cuzzacrea (USA) of Lockport, NY ran the Buffalo, New York Nissan Marathon (26.2 miles) while flipping a pancake in a time of 3 hours 6 min and 22 sec on 6 May 1990.

Half marathon The distance of half the full marathon has become established in recent years as one of the most popular for road races. In 1992 the IAAF held the first official world championships at this distance.

The world best time on a properly measured course is 59 min 47 sec by Moses Tanui (Kenya) at Milan, Italy on 3 Apr 1993.

Ingrid Kristiansen (Norway) ran 66 min 40 sec at Sandes, Norway on 5 Apr 1987, but the measurement of the course has not been confirmed. She holds the recognized best by a woman with 68 min 32 sec at New Bedford, MA on 19 Mar 1989. Liz McColgan (Great Britain) ran 67 min 11 sec at Tokyo, Japan on 26 Jan 1992, but the course was 33 m downhill, a little more than the allowable 1 in 1,000 drop.

Buggy-pushing Priscilla "Tabby" Puzey, 38, pushed a baby buggy while running the Abingdon half marathon in Abingdon, Great Britain, on 13 Apr 1986 in 2 hr 4 min 9 sec.

WALKING

Most titles Four-time Olympian Ronald Owen Laird of the New York AC won a total of 65 US national titles from 1958 to 1976, plus four Canadian Championships.

Most Olympic medals Walking races have been included in the Olympic events since 1906. The only walker to win three gold medals has been Ugo

ROAD WALKING

It should be noted that the severity of the road race courses and the accuracy of their measurement may vary, sometimes making comparisons of times unreliable.

WORLD BESTS

MEN

20 km: 1 hr 17 min 25.5 sec, Bernardo Segura (Mexico) at Fana, Norway on 7 May 1994.

30 km: 2 hr 2 min 41 sec, Andrey Perlov (USSR) at Sochi, USSR on 19 Feb 1989.

50 km: 3 hr 37 min 41 sec, Andrey Perlov (USSR) at Leningrad, USSR on 5 Aug 1989.

WOMEN

10 km: 41 min 30 sec, Kerry Ann Saxby (Australia) at Canberra, Australia on 27 Aug 1988; and Ileana Salvador (Italy) at Livorno, Italy on 10 Jul 1993.

20 km: 1 hr 29 min 40 sec, Kerry Saxby at Varnamo, Sweden on 13 May 1988.

50 km: 4 hr 50 min 28 sec, Kora Sommerfield (Australia) at Neuilly-sur-Marne, France on 13 Sep 1993.

TRACK WALKING WORLD RECORDS

The International Amateur Athletic Federation recognizes men's records at 20 km, 30 km, 50 km and 2 hours, and women's at 5 km and 10 km.

Event	hr : min : sec	Name & Country	Place	Date
MEN				
10 km	38:02.60	Jozef Pribilinec (Czechoslovakia)	Banská Bystrica, Czechoslovakia	30 Aug 1985
20 km	1:18:35.2	Stefan Johansson (Sweden)	Fana, Norway	18 May 1992
30 km	2:01:44.1	Maurizio Damilano (Italy)	Cuneo, Italy	4 Oct 1992
50 km	3:41:38.4	Raul Gonzalez (Mexico)	Fana, Norway	25 May 1979
1 hour	15,447 m	Josef Pribilinec (Czechoslovakia)	Hildesheim, Germany	6 Sep 1986
2 hours	29,572 m	Maurizio Damilano (Italy)	Cuneo, Italy	4 Oct 1992
WOMEN				
3 km	11:48.24	Ileana Salvador (Italy)	Padua, Italy	19 Aug 1993
5 km	20:07.52	Beate Anders (East Germany)	Rostock, Germany	23 Jun 1990
10 km	41:56.23	Nadezhda Ryashkina (USSR)	Seattle, WA	24 Jul 1990

Frigerio (Italy; 1901–68) with the 3,000 m in 1920, and 10,000 m in 1920 and 1924. He also holds the record for most medals, with four (he won the bronze medal at 50,000 m in 1932), a total shared with Vladimir Golubnichiy (USSR), who won gold medals for the 20,000 m in 1960 and 1968, the silver in 1972 and the bronze in 1964.

Longest race The race from Paris to Colmar (until 1980 from Strasbourg to Paris) in France (instituted 1926 in the reverse direction), now about 325 miles, is the world's longest annual race walk.

The fastest performance is by Robert Pietquin (Belgium), who walked 315 miles in the 1980 race in 60 hr 1 min 10 sec (after deducting 4 hr compulsory stops). This represents an average speed of 5.25 mph.

Roger Quémener (France) has won a record seven times, 1979, 1983, 1985–89. The first woman to complete the race was Annie van der Meer (Netherlands; b. 24 Feb 1947), who was tenth in 1983 in 82 hr 10 min.

Twenty-four hours The greatest distance walked in 24 hr is 140 miles 1,229 yd, by Paul Forthomme (Belgium) on a road course at Woluwe, Belgium on 13–14 Oct 1984. The best by a woman is 131.27 miles, by Annie van der Meer-Timmerman (Netherlands) at Rouen, France on 10–11 May 1986.

Mark Kenny, the fastest man on two hands, likes to practice as soon as he gets out of the house—whatever the weather. (David A. Breen)

RUNNING BACKWARDS

He walked at seven months. He started jogging at age eight. But Bud Badyna didn't take up the sport that would make him a champion until he was 23. That's when he got what he calls the "screwball" idea to start running backwards.

These days he's running marathons—and breaking his own record with each one he runs. "I finish in the top 40 or 50 percent every time," Badyna says. "So I'm beating more than half. Sure, I can run faster frontwards—but it's not as much fun. Besides, the gap is narrowing."

(Davida Badyna)

Bud is a paramedic when he's not running backwards. He got his nickname as a kid from his passion for Florida's Busch Gardens and his collection of Budweiser memorabilia. You've heard about the loneliness of the long-distance runner, but it doesn't apply to Bud. He gets attention wherever he goes. When you run backwards, it's not safe to run alone. "My younger brother Troy is my spotter. He rides his bicycle behind me, which means I'm facing him. He has to peek around me to see what's coming." Running backwards has its hazards. "I've only fallen half a dozen times—once over a person, once over a cone. The rest of the time I just tripped over my own feet."

His own feet are the biggest problem. "The balls of my feet under my toes really take a beating. I get tons of blood blisters, and my toenails fall off. They don't grow back for a year."

One thousand hours Ron Grant (Australia) ran 1.86 miles within an hour, every hour, for 1,000 consecutive hours at New Farm Park, Brisbane, Queensland, Australia from 6 Feb–20 Mar 1991.

Roof of the world run Ultra runner Hilary Walker ran the length of the Friendship Highway from Lhasa, Tibet to Kathmandu, Nepal, a distance of 590 miles, in 14 days 9 hrs 36 min from 18 Sep–2 Oct 1991. The run was made at an average altitude of 13,780 ft.

Backwards walking The greatest-ever distance was 8,000 miles, by Plennie L. Wingo, who walked backwards from Santa Monica, CA to Istanbul, Turkey from 15 Apr 1931 to 24 Oct 1932. The longest distance recorded for walking backwards in 24 hr is 95.40 miles, by Anthony Thornton (USA) in Minneapolis, MN on 31 Dec 1988–1 Jan 1989.

Walking on hands The distance record for walking on hands is 870 miles, by Johann Hurlinger (Austria), who in 55 daily 10 hr stints averaged 1.58 mph from Vienna, Austria to Paris, France in 1900.

The four-man relay team of David Lutterman, Brendan Price, Philip Savage and Danny Scannell covered 1 mile in 24 min 48 sec on 15 Mar 1987 at Knoxville, TN.

Mark Kenny (USA) completed a 50-m inverted sprint in 16.93 sec at Norwood, MA on 19 Feb 1994.

TRAMPOLINING

World Championships World Championships were instituted in 1964.

All events The most titles won is nine, by Judy Wills (USA)—a record five individual 1964–68, two pairs 1966–67 and two tumbling 1965–66. The men's record is four, by Yevgeniy Yanes (USSR), two individual 1976 (shared), 1978 and two pairs 1976–78; and Vadim Krasnochapaka (USSR), three pairs 1984–88 and individual 1988. Brett Austine (Australia) won three individual titles at double mini, 1982–86.

Individual event Judy Wills (USA) has won a record five individual world titles, 1964–68. The men's record is two, shared by six trampolinists: Wayne Miller (USA), 1966 and 1970; Dave Jacobs (USA), 1967–68; Richard Tisson (France), 1974–76; Yevgeniy Yanes (USSR), 1976 and 1978; Lionel Pioline (France), 1984 and 1986; and Aleksandr Maskalenko (USSR/Russia), 1990 and 1992.

United States Championships *Most titles* Stuart Ransom has won a record 12 national titles: six, individual (1975–76, 1978–80, 1982); three, synchronized (1975, 1979–80); and three, double mini-tramp (1979–80, 1982).

Leigh Hennessy has won a record 10 women's titles: one, individual (1978); eight, synchronized (1972–73, 1976–78, 1980–82); and one, double mini-tramp (1978).

Somersaults Christopher Gibson performed 3,025 consecutive somersaults at Shipley Park, Derbyshire, Great Britain on 17 Nov 1989.

The most complete somersaults in one minute is 75, by Richard Cobbing of Lightwater, Great Britain, in London, Great Britain on 8 Nov 1989. The most baranis in a minute is 78, by Zoe Finn of Chatham, Great Britain in London, Great Britain on 25 Jan 1988.

TRIATHLON

The triathlon combines long-distance swimming, cycling and running. Distances for each of the phases can vary, but for the best established event—the Hawaii Ironman—competitors first swim 2.4 miles, then cycle 112 miles, and finally run a full marathon of 26 miles 385 yards.

Fastest The fastest time recorded over the Ironman distances is 8 hr 1 min 32 sec, by Dave Scott (USA) at Lake Biwa, Japan on 30 Jul 1989. The fastest time record for a woman is 8 hr 55 min, by Paula Newby-Fraser (Zimbabwe), at Roth, Germany on 12 Jul 1992.

World Championships After earlier abortive efforts, a world governing body, *L'Union Internationale de Triathlon* (UIT), was founded at Avignon, France on 1 Apr 1989, staging the first official World Championships in August 1989.

A World Championship race has been held annually in Nice, France from 1982; the distances are 3,200 m, 120 km and 32 km respectively, with the swim increased to 4,000 m from 1988 on. Mark Allen (USA) has won 10 times, 1982–86, 1989–93. Paula Newby-Fraser has a record four women's wins, 1989–92. The fastest times are: (*men*) 5 hr 46 min 10 sec in 1988, by Mark Allen; (*women*) 6 hr 27 min 6 sec in 1988, by Erin Baker (New Zealand).

IRONMAN!

The oldest triathlete to finish the Ironman Triathlon was 73-year-old Walt Stack in 1981. After swimming 2.4 miles, cycling 112 miles and running 26 miles 385 yd, Stack completed the course in a time of 26 hr 20 min, the longest elapsed time ever.

Hawaii Ironman Dave Scott has won the Ironman a record six times—1980, 1982–84, 1986–87. Mark Allen holds the record for fastest time, at 8 hr 7 min 45 sec in 1993. The women's event has been won a record six times by Paula Newby-Fraser, in 1986, 1988–89, 1991–93. Newby-Fraser holds the course record for women at 8 hr 55 min 28 sec on 10 Oct 1992.

TUG OF WAR

Most titles The most successful team at the World Championships has been England, which has won 16 titles in all categories, 1975–93. Sweden has won the 520 kg twice and the 560 kg three times at the Womens' World Championships (held biennially since 1986).

Longest pulls *Duration* The longest recorded pull (prior to the introduction of AAA rules) is one of 2 hr 41 min when "H" Company beat "E" Company of the 2nd Battalion of the Sherwood Foresters (Derbyshire Regiment) at Jubbulpore, India on 12 Aug 1889.

The longest recorded pull under AAA rules (in which lying on the ground or entrenching the feet is not permitted) is one of 24 min 45 sec for the first pull between the Republic of Ireland and England during the world championships (640 kg class) at Malmö, Sweden on 18 Sep 1988.

The record time for "The Pull" (instituted 1898), across the Black River, between freshman and sophomore teams at Hope College, Holland, MI, is 3 hr 51 min on 23 Sep 1977, but the method of bracing the feet precludes this replacing the preceding records.

Greatest distance The longest tug of war is the 1.616-mile Supertug across Little Traverse Bay, Lake Michigan. It has been contested annually since 1980 between two teams of 20 from Bay View Inn and Harbor Inn.

VOLLEYBALL

Most Olympic titles The sport was introduced to the Olympic Games for both men and women in 1964. The USSR won a record three men's (1964, 1968 and 1980) and four women's (1968, 1972, 1980 and 1988) titles. The only player to win four medals is Inna Ryskal (USSR), who won women's silver medals in 1964 and 1976 and golds in 1968 and 1972. The record for men is held by Yuriy Poyarkov (USSR), who won gold medals in 1964 and 1968 and a bronze in 1972; and by Katsutoshi Nekoda (Japan), who won gold in 1972, silver in 1968 and bronze in 1964.

United States The USA won the men's championship in 1984 and 1988. Three men played on each of the winning teams and on the only US teams to win the World Cup (1985) and World Championships (1986): Craig Buck, Karch Kiraly, and Stephen Timmons. Kiraly is the only player to win an Olympic gold medal and the World Championship of Beach Volleyball.

Most world titles in volleyball World Championships were instituted in 1949 for men and in 1952 for women. The USSR won six men's titles (1949, 1952, 1960, 1962, 1978 and 1982) and five women's (1952, 1956, 1960, 1970 and 1990).

BEACH VOLLEYBALL

US Championships Most wins Three players have won five titles: Sinjin Smith (USA), 1979 and 1981 (with Karch Kiraly), 1982, 1988 and 1990 (with Randy Stoklos); and Mike Dodd (USA) and Tim Hovland (USA), who teamed up to win the 1983, 1985–87, and 1989 titles.

AVP Tour Most wins Sinjin Smith (USA) has won a record 135 AVP tour events, 1977–94.

Highest earnings Karch Kiraly has the highest career earnings, reaching $1,449,349 as of 8 Jul 1994.

WATER POLO

Most Olympic titles Hungary has won the Olympic tournament most often, with six wins, in 1932, 1936, 1952, 1956, 1964 and 1976.

Five players share the record of three gold medals: Britons George Wilkinson (1879–1946), in 1900, 1908, 1912; Paul Radmilovic (1886–1968), and Charles Smith (1879–1951), in 1908, 1912, 1920; and Hungarians Deszö Gyarmati and György Kárpáti, in 1952, 1956, and 1964. Radmilovic also won a gold medal for 4 × 200 m freestyle swimming in 1908.

United States US teams took all the medals in 1904, but there were no foreign contestants. Since then their best result has been silver in 1984 and 1988.

World Championships This competition was first held at the World Swimming Championships in 1973. The most wins is two, by the USSR, 1975 and 1982, and Yugoslavia, 1986 and 1991. A women's competition was introduced in 1986, when it was won by Australia. The Netherlands won the second women's world title in 1991.

Most goals The greatest number of goals scored by an individual in an international match is 13, by Debbie Handley for Australia (16) *v* Canada (10) at the World Championship in Guayaquil, Ecuador in 1982.

Most international appearances The greatest number of international appearances is 412, by Aleksey Barkalov (USSR), 1965–80.

US National Championships In this competition, inaugurated in 1891, the New York Athletic Club has won a record 25 men's championships: 1892–96, 1903–04, 1906–08, 1922, 1929–31, 1933–35, 1937–39, 1954, 1956, 1960–61, 1971. The women's championship was first held in 1926; the Industry Hills Athletic Club (California) has won a record five titles: 1980–81, 1983–85.

WATERSKIING

Most titles World Overall Championships (instituted 1949) have been won four times by Sammy Duvall (USA), in 1981, 1983, 1985 and 1987, and three times by two women, Willa McGuire (nee Worthington; USA), in 1949–50 and 1955, and Liz Allan-Shetter (USA), in 1965, 1969 and 1975. Allan-Shetter has won a record eight individual championship events and is the only person to win all four titles—slalom, jumping, tricks and overall—in one year, at Copenhagen, Denmark in 1969. Patrice Martin (France; b. 24 May 1964) has won a men's record seven titles. The USA has won the team championship on 17 successive occasions, 1957–89.

United States US national championships were first held at Marine Stadium, Jones Beach State Park, Long Island, NY on 22 Jul 1939. The most overall titles is nine, by Carl Roberge, 1980–83, 1985–88, and 1990. The women's record is eight titles, by Willa Worthington McGuire, 1946–51 and 1954–55, and by Liz Allan-Shetter, 1968–75.

Fastest speed The fastest waterskiing speed recorded is 143.08 mph, by Christopher Massey (Australia) on the Hawkesbury River, Windsor, New South Wales, Australia on 6 Mar 1983. Donna Patterson Brice (b. 1953) set a women's record of 111.11 mph at Long Beach, CA on 21 Aug 1977.

Longest run The greatest distance traveled is 1,321.16 miles, by Steve Fontaine (USA) on 24–26 Oct 1988 at Jupiter Hills, FL.

Most skiers towed by one boat A record 100 waterskiers were towed on

WATERSKIING RECORDS

Slalom
MEN: 3.5 buoys on a 10.25 m line, Andrew Mapple (Great Britain) in Miami, FL on 6 Oct 1991.
WOMEN: 2 buoys on a 10.75 m line, Susi Graham (Canada) in Madison, GA on 3 Jul 1993.

Tricks
MEN: 11,150 points, Cory Pickos (USA) in Mulberry, FL on 27 Sep 1992.
WOMEN: 8,580 points, Tawn Larsen (USA) in Groveland, FL on 4 Jul 1992.

Jumping
MEN: 220 ft, Sammy Duvall (USA) in Santa Rosa Beach, FL on 10 Sep 1993.
WOMEN: 156 ft, Deena Mapple (nee Brush; USA) in Charlotte, NC on 9 Jul 1988.

Oh buoy, what a record! 100 waterskiers were towed over a nautical mile by the cruiser *Reef Cat* at Cairns, Australia on 18 Oct 1986. (Yon Ivanovic, Studio One)

double skis over a nautical mile by the cruiser *Reef Cat* at Cairns, Queensland, Australia on 18 Oct 1986. This feat, organized by the Cairns and District Powerboat and Ski Club, was then replicated by 100 skiers on single skis.

Barefoot The first person to waterski barefoot is reported to be Dick Pope, Jr. at Lake Eloise, FL on 6 Mar 1947. The barefoot duration record is 2 hr 42 min 39 sec, by Billy Nichols (USA; b. 1964) on Lake Weir, FL on 19 Nov 1978. The backwards barefoot record is 1 hr 27 min 3.96 sec, by Steve Fontaine at Jupiter, FL, on 31 Aug 1989.

World Championships (instituted 1978) The most overall titles is four, by Kim Lampard (Australia), 1980, 1982, 1985, 1986; and the men's record is three, by Brett Wing (Australia), 1978, 1980, 1982. The team title has been won five times by Australia, 1978, 1980, 1982, 1985 and 1986.

The official barefoot speed record is 135.74 mph, by Scott Michael Pellaton (b. 8 Oct 1956) over a quarter-mile course at Chandler, CA, in November 1989. The fastest by a woman is 73.67 mph, by Karen Toms (Australia) on the Hawkesbury River, Windsor, New South Wales on 31 Mar 1984.

The fastest official speed backwards barefoot is 62 mph, by Robert Wing (Australia; b. 13 Aug 1957) on 3 Apr 1982.

The barefoot jump record is: *(men)* 86 ft 3 in, by John Kretchman (USA); and *(women)* 54 ft 5 in, by Sharon Stekelenberg (Australia), both in 1991.

Walking on water Rémy Bricka of Paris, France "walked" across the At-

Patrice Martin has won a men's record seven water skiing world titles. (Allsport/Vandystadt/Jean Marc Barey)

lantic Ocean on waterskis 13 ft 9 in long in 1988. Leaving Tenerife, Canary Islands on 2 Apr 1988, he covered 3,502 miles, arriving at Trinidad on 31 May 1988.

He also set a speed record of 7 min 7.41 sec for 1,094 yd in the Olympic pool in Montreal, Canada on 2 Aug 1989.

Wearing 11-ft waterski shoes, called Skijaks, and using a twin-bladed paddle, David Kiner walked 155 miles on the Hudson River from Albany, NY to Battery Park, New York City. His walk took him 57 hr, from 22–27 Jun 1987.

WEIGHTLIFTING

Most titles *Olympic* Norbert Schemansky (USA; b. 30 May 1924) won a record four Olympic medals: gold, middle heavyweight 1952; silver, heavyweight 1948; bronze, heavyweight 1960 and 1964.

World The most world title wins, including Olympic Games, is eight, shared by John Henry Davis (USA; 1921–84) in 1938, 1946–52; Tommy Kono (USA; b. 27 Jun 1930) in 1952–59; and Vasiliy Alekseiev (USSR; b. 7 Jan 1942), 1970–77.

Two American women have won world titles: Karyn Marshall, at 82 kg in 1987, and Robin Byrd, at 77.5 kg in 1994.

United States The most US national titles won is 13, by Anthony Terlazzo (1911–66), at 137 lb, 1932 and 1936 and at 148 lb, 1933, 1935, 1937–45.

Youngest world record holder Naim Suleimanov (later Neum Shalamanov [Bulgaria]; (now Naim Suleymanoğlü of Turkey) set 56 kg world records for clean and jerk (160 kg) and total (285 kg), at 16 yr 62 days, at Allentown, NJ on 26 Mar 1983.

Oldest world record holder The oldest is Norbert Schemansky (USA), who snatched 164.2 kg in the then unlimited Heavyweight class, aged 37 yr 333 days, at Detroit, MI on 28 Apr 1962.

Heaviest lift to body weight The first man to clean and jerk more than three times his body weight was Stefan Topurov (Bulgaria), who lifted 396¾ lb at Moscow, USSR on 24 Oct 1983.

Women's World Championships These are held annually; the first was held at Daytona Beach, FL in October 1987. Women's world records have been ratified for the best marks at these championships. Peng Liping (China) won a record 12 gold medals with snatch, jerk and total in the 52-kg class each year, 1988–89 and 1991–92.

POWERLIFTING

Most world titles *World* The winner of the most world titles is Hideaki Inaba (Japan) with 16, at 52 kg, 1974–83, 1985–90. Lamar Gant (USA) holds the record for an American with 15 titles, at 56 kg, 1975–77, 1979, 1982–84; and at 60 kg, 1978, 1980–81 and 1986–90. The most by a woman is six, shared by Beverley Francis (Australia), at 75 kg 1980, 1982; 82.5 kg 1981, 1983–85; and Sisi Dolman (Netherlands) at 52 kg 1985–86, 1988–91.

Timed lifts *24 hours* A deadlifting record of 5,960,631 lb was set by a team of 10 from Her Majesty's Prison, Ayland, Great Britain on 10–11 May 1993. The 24-hr deadlift record by an individual is 818,121 lb, by Anthony Wright at Her Majesty's Prison, Featherstone, Great Britain, on 31 Aug–1 Sep 1990.

A bench press record of 8,873,860 lb was set by a nine-man team from the Forum Health Club, Chelmsleywood, Great Britain on 19–20 Mar 1994. An individual bench press record of 1,231,150 lb was set by Paul Goodall at the Copthorne Hotel, Plymouth, Great Britain on 12–13 Mar 1991. A squat record of 4,780,994 lb was set by a 10-man team from St Albans Weightlifting Club and Ware Boys Club, Hertfordshire, Great Britain on 20–21 Jul 1986. A record 133,380 arm-curling repetitions using three 48¼ lb weightlifting bars and dumbbells was achieved by a team of nine from Intrim Health and Fitness Club at Gosport, Great Britain on 4–5 Aug 1989.

12 hours An individual bench press record of 1,134,828 lb was set by John "Jack" Atherton at Her Majesty's Prison, Featherstone, Great Britain on 27 May 1990.

WRESTLING

Most titles Olympic Three Olympic titles have been won by Carl Westergren (Sweden; 1895–1958), in 1920, 1924 and 1932; Ivar Johansson (Sweden; 1903–79), in 1932 (two) and 1936; and Aleksandr Medved (USSR), in 1964, 1968 and 1972.

Four Olympic medals were won by Eino Leino (Finland; 1891–1986) at freestyle 1920–32; and by Imre Polyák (Hungary) at Greco-Roman in 1952–64.

Three US wrestlers have won two Olympic freestyle titles: George Mehnert (1881–1948), flyweight in 1904 and bantamweight in 1908; John Smith, featherweight in 1988 and 1992; and Bruce Baumgartner, superheavyweight in 1984 and 1992. The only US men to win a Greco-Roman title are Steven Fraser at light-heavyweight and Jeffrey Blatnick at superheavyweight in 1984.

World The freestyler Aleksandr Medved (USSR) won a record 10 World Championships, 1962–64, 1966–72 at three weight categories.

The only wrestler to win the same title in seven successive years has been Valeriy Rezantsev (USSR) in the Greco-Roman 90 kg class in 1970–76, including the Olympic Games of 1972 and 1976.

United States The most world titles won by a US wrestler is six (four world, two Olympic), by John Smith, featherweight 1987–92.

Most wins In international competition, Osamu Watanabe (Japan), the 1964 Olympic freestyle 63 kg champion, was unbeaten and did not concede a score in 189 consecutive matches.

Outside of FILA sanctioned competition, Wade Schalles (USA) won 821 bouts from 1964 to 1984, with 530 of these victories by pin.

WORLD WEIGHTLIFTING RECORDS

From 1 Jan 1993, the International Weightlifting Federation (IWF) introduced modified weight categories, thereby making the then world records redundant. In February, the IWF announced that "the results of major IWF-controlled competitions and championships will be collected until 30 Sep 1993 and the best results be declared as basic performances, with world records to be broken for the first time at the Melbourne World Championships (12–21 November)." This is the current list, with world standards yet to be set and records set as of 1 Jun 1994 for men and 1 Apr 1994 for women.

Bodyweight	Lift	kg	lb	Name and Country	Place	Date
54 kg *119 lb*	Snatch	125	*275 1/2*	Sevdalin Minchev (Bulgaria)	Sokolov, Czech Republic	4 May 1994
	Jerk	157.5	*347 1/2*	*World Standard*		
	Total	277.5	*611 3/4*	Ivan Ivanov (Bulgaria)	Melbourne, Australia	12 Nov 1993
59 kg *130 lb*	Snatch	137.5	*303*	*World Standard*		
	Jerk	167.5	*369 1/4*	Nikolai Pershalov (Bulgaria)	Melbourne, Australia	13 Nov 1993
	Total	305	*672 1/4*	Nikolai Pershalov (Bulgaria)	Melbourne, Australia	13 Nov 1993
64 kg *141 lb*	Snatch	145	*319 3/4*	Naim Suleymanoğlü (Turkey)*	Sokolov, Czech Republic	5 May 1994
	Jerk	180	*396 3/4*	Naim Suleymanoğlü (Turkey)*	Sokolov, Czech Republic	5 May 1994
	Total	325	*716 1/2*	Naim Suleymanoğlü (Turkey)*	Sokolov, Czech Republic	5 May 1994
70 kg *154 1/4 lb*	Snatch	157.5	*347 1/4*	Israil Militosyan (Armenia)	Sokolov, Czech Republic	5 May 1994
	Jerk	192.5	*424 1/4*	Yotov Yoto (Bulgaria)	Sokolov, Czech Republic	5 May 1994
	Total	345	*760 1/2*	Yotov Yoto (Bulgaria)	Sokolov, Czech Republic	5 May 1994
76 kg *167 1/2 lb*	Snatch	170	*374 3/4*	Ruslan Savchenko (Ukraine)	Melbourne, Australia	16 Nov 1993
	Jerk	205	*452*	Pablo Lara (Cuba)	Ponce, Puerto Rico	25 Nov 1993
	Total	370	*815 3/4*	Ruslan Savchenko (Ukraine)	Melbourne, Australia	16 Nov 1993
83 kg *183 lb*	Snatch	175	*385 3/4*	*World Standard*		
	Jerk	210	*463*	Marc Huster (Germany)	Melbourne, Australia	17 Nov 1993
	Total	380	*837 3/4*	*World Standard*		

91 kg *200½ lb*	Snatch	185	*407¾*	Ivan Chakarov (Australia)	Melbourne, Australia	18 Nov 1993
	Jerk	227.5	*501½*	Alexey Petrov (Russia)	Sokolov, Czech Republic	7 May 1994
	Total	412.5	*909¼*	Alexey Petrov (Russia)	Sokolov, Czech Republic	7 May1994
99 kg *218½ lb*	Snatch	190.5	*420*	Sergey Syrtsov (Russia)	Sokolov, Czech Republic	7 May 1994
	Jerk	225	*496*	Sergey Syrtsov (Russia)	Sokolov, Czech Republic	7 May 1994
	Total	415	*915*	Sergey Syrtsov (Russia)	Sokolov, Czech Republic	7 May 1994
108 kg *238lb*	Snatch	197.5	*435¼*	*World Standard*		
	Jerk	235	*518*	Timour Taimazov (Ukraine)	Sokolov, Czech Republic	8 May 1994
	Total	430	*948*	Timour Taimazov (Ukraine)	Sokolov, Czech Republic	8 May 1994
Over 108 kg	Snatch	200.5	*442*	Andrey Chermkin (Russia)	Sokolov, Czech Republic	8 May 1994
	Jerk	250	*551*	Andrey Chermkin (Russia)	Sokolov, Czech Republic	8 May 1994
	Total	450	*992*	Andrey Chermkin (Russia)	Sokolov, Czech Republic	8 May 1994

** Formerly Naim Suleimanov or Neum Shalamanov of Bulgaria*

WOMEN'S WEIGHTLIFTING RECORDS

46 kg *101¼ lb*	Snatch	72.5	*159¾*	Luo Hongwei (China)	Shilong, China	15 Dec 1993
	Jerk	92.5	*204*	Luo Hongwei (China)	Shilong, China	15 Dec 1993
	Total	165	*363¾*	Luo Hongwei (China)	Shilong, China	15 Dec 1993
50 kg *110¼ lb*	Snatch	77.5	*170¾*	Liu Xiuhia (China)	Melbourne, Australia	13 Nov 1993
	Jerk	110	*242½*	Liu Xiuhia (China)	Melbourne, Australia	13 Nov 1993
	Total	187.5	*413¼*	Liu Xiuhia (China)	Melbourne, Australia	13 Nov 1993
54 kg *119 lb*	Snatch	90	*198¼*	Chen Xiaoming (China)	Melbourne, Australia	14 Nov 1993
	Jerk	112.5	*248*	Long Yuiling (China)	Shilong, China	16 Dec 1993
	Total	200	*441*	Chen Xiaoming (China)	Melbourne, Australia	14 Nov 1993

(continued)

59 kg *130 lb*	Snatch	97.5	*215*	Sun Caiyan (China)	Melbourne, Australia	15 Nov 1993
	Jerk	120.5	*265½*	Zuo Feie (China)	Shilong, China	16 Dec 1993
	Total	217.5	*479½*	Sun Caiyan (China)	Melbourne, Australia	15 Nov 1993
64 kg *141 lb*	Snatch	103	*227*	Li Hongyun (China)	Shilong, China	17 Dec 1993
	Jerk	125	*275½*	Lei Li (China)	Shilong, China	17 Dec 1993
	Total	227.5	*501½*	Lei Li (China)	Shilong, China	17 Dec 1993
70 kg *154¼ lb*	Snatch	100	*220½*	Milena Trendafilova (Bulgaria)	Melbourne, Australia	17 Nov 1993
	Jerk	120	*264½*	Milena Trendafilova (Bulgaria)	Melbourne, Australia	17 Nov 1993
	Total	220	*485*	Milena Trendafilova (Bulgaria)	Melbourne, Australia	17 Nov 1993
76 kg *167¼ lb*	Snatch	105	*231½*	Hua Ju (China)	Melbourne, Australia	18 Nov 1993
	Jerk	140	*308½*	Zhang Guimei (China)	Shilong, China	18 Dec 1993
	Total	235	*518*	Zhang Guimei (China)	Shilong, China	18 Dec 1993
83 kg *183 lb*	Snatch	107.5	*237*	Xing Shiwen (China)	Melbourne, Australia	19 Nov 1993
	Jerk	127.5	*281*	Chen Shu-chih (Taipei)	Melbourne, Australia	19 Nov 1993
	Total	230	*507*	Chen Shu-chih (Taipei)	Melbourne, Australia	19 Nov 1993
+83 kg	Snatch	105	*231½*	Li Yajuan (China)	Melbourne, Australia	20 Nov 1993
	Jerk	155	*341½*	Li Yajuan (China)	Melbourne, Australia	20 Nov 1993
	Total	260	*573*	Li Yajuan (China)	Melbourne, Australia	20 Nov 1993

WORLD POWERLIFTING RECORDS (*All weights in kilograms*)

Class	Squat		Bench Press		Deadlift		Total	
MEN								
52 kg	252.5	Andrzej Stanashek (Pol) 1992	172.5	Andrzej Stanashek 1993	256	E S Bhaskaran (Ind) 1993	587.5	Hideaki Inaba (Jap) 1987
56 kg	257.5	Magnus Karlsson (Swe) 1993	175	Magnus Karlsson 1993	289.5	Lamar Gant (USA) 1982	625	Lamar Gant 1982
60 kg	295	Joe Bradley (USA) 1980	180.5	Magnus Karlsson 1993	310	Lamar Gant 1988	707.5	Joe Bradley 1982
67.5 kg	300	Jessie Jackson (USA) 1987	200	Kristoffer Hulecki (Swe) 1985	316	Daniel Austin (USA) 1991	762.5	Daniel Austin 1989
75 kg	328	Ausby Alexander (USA) 1989	217.5	James Rouse (USA) 1980	333	Jarmo Virtanen (Finland) 1988	850	Rick Gaugler (USA) 1982
82.5 kg	379.5	Mike Bridges (USA) 1982	240	Mike Bridges 1981	357.5	Veli Kumpuniemi (Fin) 1980	952.5	Mike Bridges 1982
90 kg	375	Fred Hatfield (USA) 1980	255	Mike MacDonald (USA) 1980	372.5	Walter Thomas (USA) 1982	937.5	Mike Bridges 1980
100 kg	422.5	Ed Coan (USA) 1989	261.5	Mike MacDonald 1977	378	Ed Coan 1989	1032.5	Ed Coan 1989
110 kg	393.5	Dan Wohleber (USA) 1981	270	Jeffrey Magruder (USA) 1982	395	John Kuc (USA) 1980	1000	John Kuc 1980
125 kg	440	Kirk Karwoski (USA) 1993	278.5	Tom Hardman (USA) 1982	387.5	Lars Norén (Swe) 1987	1005	Ernie Hackett (USA) 1982
125+ kg	445	Dwayne Fely (USA) 1982	300	Bill Kazmaier (USA) 1981	406	Lars Norén 1988	1100	Bill Kazmaier 1981
WOMEN								
44 kg	155.5	Raija Koskinen (Fin) 1993	82.5	Irina Krylova (Rus) 1993	165	Nancy Belliveau (USA) 1985	365	Jacquline Janot (Fra) 1993
48 kg	160	Raija Koskinen 1993	92.5	Svetlana Stepanova (Rus) 1993	182.5	Majik Jones (USA) 1984	390	Majik Jones 1984
52 kg	175.5	Mary Jeffrey (USA) (née Ryan) 1991	105	Mary Jeffrey 1991	197.5	Diana Rowell (USA) 1984	452.5	Mary Jeffrey 1991
56 kg	191	Mary Jeffrey 1989	115	Mary Jeffrey 1988	210	Carrie Boudreau (USA) 1993	500	Carrie Boudreau 1993
60 kg	210	Beate Amdahl (Nor) 1993	107.5	Irmgar Wohlhöfler (Ger) 1993	213	Ruthi Shafer 1983	502.5	Vicki Steenrod (USA) 1985
67.5 kg	230	Ruthi Shafer 1984	120	Vicki Steenrod 1990	244	Ruthi Shafer 1984	565	Ruthi Shafer 1984
75 kg	235	Cathy Millen (NZ) 1991	142.5	Liz Odendaal (Neth) 1989	240	Cathy Millen 1991	602.5	Cathy Millen 1991
82.5 kg	240	Cathy Millen 1991	150.5	Cathy Millen 1993	257.5	Cathy Millen 1993	637.5	Cathy Millen 1993
90 kg	255	Cathy Millen 1993	157.5	Cathy Millen 1993	250	Cathy Millen 1992	655	Cathy Millen 1993
90+kg	272.5	Juanita Trujillo (USA) 1993	150	Ulrike Herchenhein (Ger) 1993	238	Ulrike Herchenhein 1993	622.5	Lorraine Constanzo 1987

NCAA Division I Championship Including five unofficial titles, Oklahoma State has won a record 30 NCAA titles, in 1928–31, 1933–35, 1937–1942, 1946, 1948–49, 1954–56, 1958–59, 1961–62, 1964, 1966, 1968, 1971, 1989–90 and 1994. The University of Iowa has won the most consecutive titles, with nine championships from 1978–86.

Heaviest heavyweight The heaviest wrestler in Olympic history was Chris Taylor (USA; 1950–79), bronze medalist in the super-heavyweight class in 1972, who stood 6 ft 5 in tall and weighed over 420 lb.

FILA introduced an upper weight limit of 286 lb for international competition in 1985.

SUMO

The sport's origins in Japan date from *c.* 23 B.C. The heaviest-ever *rikishi* is Samoan-American Salevaa Fuali Atisnoe of Hawaii, alias Konishiki, who weighed in at 580 lb at Tokyo's Ryogaku Kokugikau on 4 Jan 1993. He is also the first foreign *rikishi* to attain the second highest rank of *ozeki*, or champion. Weight is gained by eating large quantities of a high-protein stew called *chankonabe*.

The most successful wrestlers have been *yokozuna* Sadaji Akiyoshi (b. 1912), alias Futabayama, winner of 69 consecutive bouts in the 1930s; *yokozuna* Koki Naya, alias Taiho ("Great Bird"), who won the Emperor's Cup 32 times up to his retirement in 1971; and the *ozeki* Tameemon Torokichi, alias Raiden (1767–1825), who in 21 years (1789–1810) won 254 bouts and lost only 10, for the highest-ever winning percentage of 96.2. Taiho and Futabayama share the record of eight perfect tournaments without a single loss.

The youngest of the 64 men to attain the rank of *yokozuna* (grand champion) was Toshimitsu Ogata, alias Kitanoumi, in July 1974 at the age of 21 years and two months. He set a record in 1978, winning 82 of the 90 bouts that top *rikishi* fight annually.

GUESS WHAT?

Q. WHAT DESSERT WOULD DEFEAT THE HUNGRIEST SUMO WRESTLER?

A. SEE "BIG DEALS" (HUMAN ACHIEVEMENTS)

Yokozuna Mitsugu Akimoto, alias Chiyonofuji, set a record for domination of one of the six annual tournaments by winning the Kyushu Basho for eight successive years, 1981–88. He also holds the record for most career wins, 1,045, and *Makunoiuchi* (top division) wins, 807. He retired in May 1991 but remains in sumo as a training coach.

Hawaiian-born Jesse Kuhaulua, now a Japanese citizen named Daigoro Watanabe, alias Takamiyama, was the first non-Japanese to win an official top-division tournament, in July 1972, and in September 1981 he set a record of 1,231 consecutive top-division bouts.

Kenji Hatano, alias Oshio, contested a record 1,891 bouts in his 26-year career, 1962–88, the longest in modern sumo history. Yukio Shoji, alias Aobajo, contested a record 1,631 consecutive bouts in his 22-year career, 1964–86.

Katsumi Yamanaka, alias Akinoshima, set a new *kinboshi* (gold star) record of 13 upsets over *yokozuna* by a *maegashira*.

Hawaiian-born Chad Rowan (b. 8 May 1969), alias Akebono, scored a majority of wins for a record 18 consecutive tournaments, March 1988–March 1991. He became the first foreign *rikishi* to be promoted to the top rank of *yokuzuna*, in January 1993. He is the tallest (6 ft 8 in) and heaviest ($467^1/_2$ lb) *yokuzuna* in sumo history.

Longest sumo bout The longest recorded wrestling bout was one of 11 hr 40 min, when Martin Klein (Estonia representing Russia; 1885–1947) beat Alfred Asikáinen (Finland; 1888–1942) for the Greco-Roman 75 kg "A" event silver medal in the 1912 Olympic Games in Stockholm, Sweden.

YACHTING

Modern ocean racing (in moderate or small sailing yachts, rather than professionally manned sailing ships) began with a race from Brooklyn, NY to Bermuda, 630 nautical miles, organized by Thomas Day, editor of the magazine *The Rudder*, in June 1906. The race is still held today in every even-numbered year, though the course is now Newport, RI to Bermuda.

The oldest race for any type of craft and either kind of water (fresh or salt) still regularly held is the Chicago-to-Mackinac race on Lakes Michigan and Huron, first sailed in 1898. It was held again in 1904, then annually until the present day, except for 1917–20. The record for the course (333 nautical miles) is 1 day 1 hr 50 min (average speed 12.89 knots), by the sloop *Pied Piper*, owned by Dick Jennings (USA) in 1987.

Olympic titles The first sportsman ever to win individual gold medals in four successive Olympic Games was Paul B. Elvström (Denmark), in the Firefly class in 1948 and the Finn class in 1952, 1956 and 1960. He also won eight other world titles in a total of six classes. The lowest number of penalty points by the winner of any class in an Olympic regatta is three points (five wins, one disqualified and one second in seven starts) by *Superdocious* of the Flying Dutchman class (Lt. Rodney Pattisson and Iain Somerled Macdonald-Smith, both Great Britain), at Acapulco Bay, Mexico in Oct 1968.

United States The only US yachtsman to have won two gold medals is Herman Whiton (1904–67), at six-meter class, in 1948 and 1952.

America's Cup The America's Cup was originally won as an outright prize (with no special name) by the schooner *America* on 22 Aug 1851 at Cowes, Great Britain and was later offered by the New York Yacht Club as a challenge trophy. On 8 Aug 1870 J. Ashbury's *Cambria* (Great Britain) failed

***Enza New Zealand*, skippered by Peter Blake and Robin Knox-Johnston, completed the fastest non-stop circumnavigation at Ushart, France on 1 Apr 1994. (Allsport/Stephen Munday)**

to capture the trophy from *Magic*, owned by F. Osgood (USA). The Cup has been challenged 28 times.

The United States was undefeated, winning 77 races and losing only eight, until 1983, when *Australia II*, skippered by John Bertrand and owned by a Perth syndicate headed by Alan Bond, beat *Liberty* 4–3, the narrowest series victory, at Newport, RI.

Dennis Conner (USA) has been helmsman of American boats four times in succession: in 1980, when he successfully defended; in 1983, when he steered the defender, but lost; in 1987, when the American challenger regained the trophy; and in 1988, when he again successfully defended. He was also starting helmsman in 1974, with Ted Hood as skipper.

The largest yacht to compete in the America's Cup was the 1903 defender, the gaff rigged cutter *Reliance*, with an overall length of 144 ft, a record sail area of 16,160 ft^2 and a rig 175 ft high.

Longest race The world's longest sailing race is the Vendée Globe Challenge, the first of which started from Les Sables d'Olonne, France on 26 Nov 1989. The distance circumnavigated without stopping was 22,500 nautical miles. The race is for boats between 50–60 ft, sailed single-handedly.

The record time on the course is 109 days 8 hr 48 min 50 sec, by Titouan Lamazou (France) in the sloop *Ecureuil d'Aquitaine*, which finished at Les Sables on 19 Mar 1990.

The oldest around-the-world sailing race is the quadrennial Whitbread Round the World race (instituted August 1973), organized by the British Royal Naval Sailing Association. The distance for the 1993–94 race was 32,000 nautical miles from Southampton, Great Britain and return, with stops and restarts at Punta del Este, Uruguay; Fremantle, Australia; Auckland, New Zealand; Punta del Este, Uruguay; and Fort Lauderdale, FL.

The record time for this race is 120 days 5 hr 9 min, by *New Zealand Endeavour*, skippered by Grant Dalton (New Zealand), which finished at Southampton on 3 Jun 1994.

Fastest speeds The fastest speed reached under sail on water by any craft over a 500-meter timed run is 46.25 knots by Simon McKeon and Tim Daddo (Australia) in the tri-foiler *Yellow Pages Endeavour* c. 26 Oct 1993 at Shallow Inlet near Melbourne.

The record for a boardsail is 45.34 knots by Thiery Bielek (France) at Saintes Maries-de-la-Mer Canal, Camargue, France on 24 Apr 1993.

The women's record is held by boardsailer Babethe Coquelle (France), who achieved 39.70 knots at Tarifa, Spain in July 1991.

The fastest speed ever by a true yacht is 36.22 knots (41.68 mph), by Jean Saucet (France) in Charante Maritime on the Bassin de Thau, near Sete, on 5 Oct 1992.

The record for a boat is 43.55 knots (80.65 km/h) by *Longshot*, steered by Russell Long (USA) at Tarifa, Spain in July 1992.

The American with the best time under sail over a 500 meter run is Jimmy Lewis, with 38.68 knots at Saintes Maries-de-la-Mer in February 1988.

Most competitors The most boats ever to start in a single race was 2,072 in the Round Zeeland (Denmark) race on 21 Jun 1984, over a course of 235 nautical miles.

Boardsailing (windsurfing) World Championships were first held in 1973 and the sport was added to the Olympic Games in 1984, when the winner was Stephan van den Berg (Netherlands), who also won five world titles 1979–83.

Longest sailboard The world's longest sailboard, 165 ft, was constructed at Fredrikstad, Norway, and first sailed on 28 Jun 1986.

The longest snake of sailboards was made by 70 windsurfers in a row at the Sailboard Show '89 event at Narrabeen Lakes, Manly, Australia on 21 Oct 1989.

LETTERS TO THE EDITOR

DEAR *GUINNESS BOOK OF RECORDS...*

In 1993 our correspondence editor, Amanda Brooks (above), dealt with about 10,000 claims from potential record-holders. That's more than twice the number that passed through our office three years ago. But while our mailbag expands ceaselessly, one cruel factor remains the same: we simply do not have the space in *The Guinness Book of Records* to mention all the extraordinary talents, stupendous stunts, and fascinating feats we hear about. The result is that we have to disappoint thousands of correspondents each year.

For this edition, by way of a tribute to those whose achievements dwell silently in the cavernous drawers of our filing cabinets, we are putting the spotlight on a handful of would-be's whose charms we could not resist for another year.

Dominique McGarry of Worcester Park, Great Britain, displaying the 14 healthy baby hamsters born to her pet Nibbles in January 1994. Unfortunately, Nibbles' valiant efforts were not enough to beat the world record, although it was the largest claim we had received for some time.

Shri Rajendra K. Tiwari, also known as Dukanji of Allahabad, presents a striking pose while demonstrating mustache dancing—a technique he devised and developed himself. The plastic tubes are there to emphasize the movement of the facial muscles.

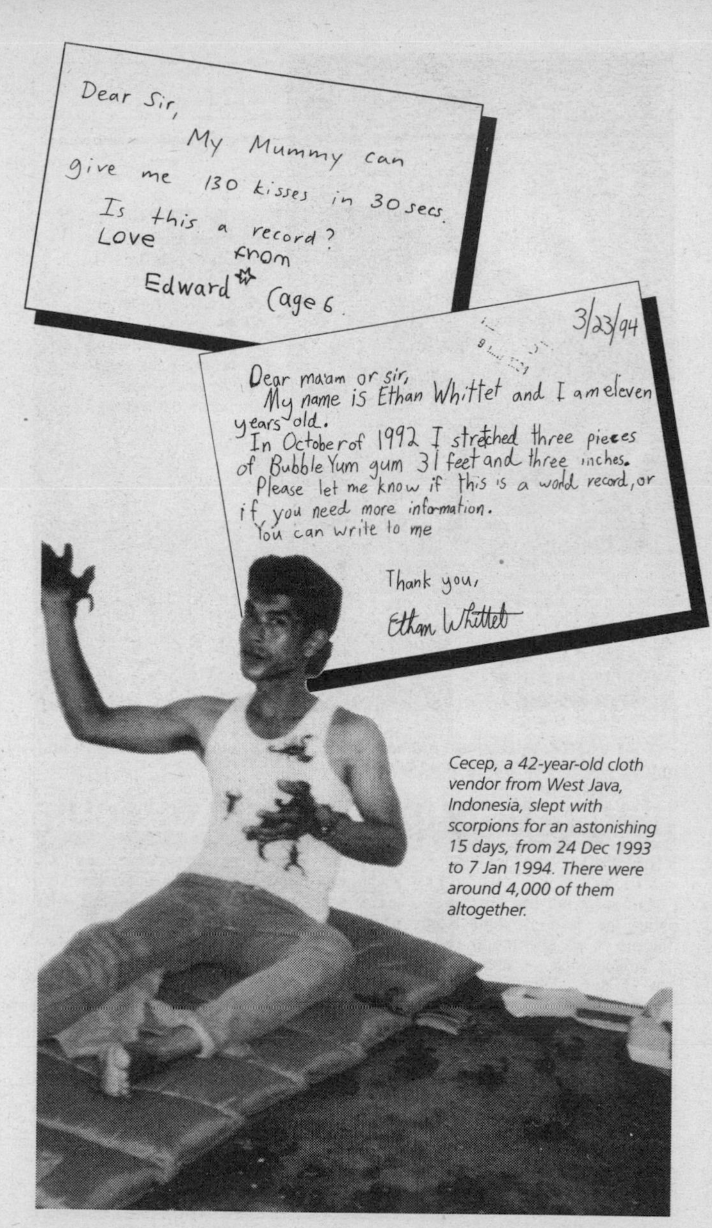

Dear Sir,

My Mummy can give me 130 kisses in 30 secs.
Is this a record?
Love from
Edward (age 6.

3/23/94

Dear ma'am or sir,
My name is Ethan Whittet and I am eleven years old.
In October of 1992 I stretched three pieces of Bubble Yum gum 31 feet and three inches.
Please let me know if this is a world record, or if you need more information.
You can write to me

Thank you,
Ethan Whittet

Cecep, a 42-year-old cloth vendor from West Java, Indonesia, slept with scorpions for an astonishing 15 days, from 24 Dec 1993 to 7 Jan 1994. There were around 4,000 of them altogether.

t human to hold and sculpt a 2000° hot lava f
ld!

ST AT WORK — German Mattias Wendt makes sculptures from lava just
g the molten rock with gloved hands.

man artist uses hands to sculp

I NIELAND
Wall Today

Mattias Wendt has been carefully studying the lava flowing from Volcano in an attempt to get a he molten rock — literally.

out 75 days, Wendt has been the Kamoamoa area of Kilauea, g the moment when he will able to thrust his gloved hands iquid rock pouring into the sea the "ultimate art piece" — rom molten lava.

Wendt, a producer, cameraman and anchorman for German public television, makes sculptures from lava just before it oozes into the ocean.

"It is probably the most dramatic form of art there is," Wendt said of his short-lived sculptures, each of which is returned to the lava flow upon completion.

Wendt said he avoids rangers at Volcanoes National Park in order to film his potentially dangerous work, but said he believes that by educating through enter-

tai

tes
pe
su
pa
He
ga
flo

Self-proclaimed "Lava Man" Matthias Wendt of Paris, France, is surely the first to hold and sculpt molten rock in his hands for 38 seconds. He always makes sure conditions are as favorable as possible before producing what he describes as "probably the most dramatic art form there is."

This 17-ft tea cozy was knitted by the Rainbows, Brownies, Guides and Rangers of Staffordshire, Great Britain—some 11,000 youngsters in all—in 1991. It was used to raise money for the Building Blocks Appeal in Stoke-on-Trent; the cozy was then dismantled to form blankets, which were sent to charities in Romania.

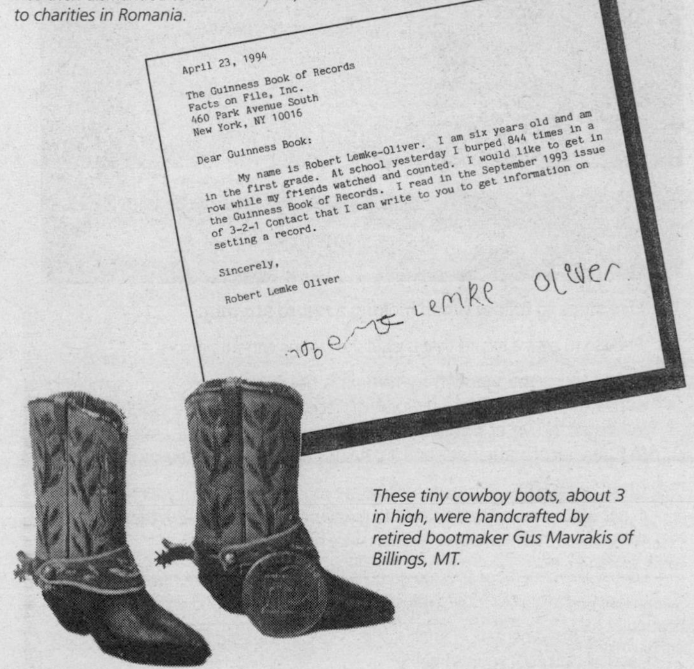

April 23, 1994

The Guinness Book of Records
Facts on File, Inc.
460 Park Avenue South
New York, NY 10016

Dear Guinness Book:

My name is Robert Lemke-Oliver. I am six years old and am in the first grade. At school yesterday I burped 844 times in a row while my friends watched and counted. I would like to get in the Guinness Book of Records. I read in the September 1993 issue of 3-2-1 Contact that I can write to you to get information on setting a record.

Sincerely,

Robert Lemke Oliver

These tiny cowboy boots, about 3 in high, were handcrafted by retired bootmaker Gus Mavrakis of Billings, MT.

This is an 18-ft monument in memory of a rooster called Come On, owned by Guy Valentini of Ontario, Canada. The Valentinis introduced Come On to their household under the erroneous assumption that the little chick would grow up to provide eggs for the family. During his lifetime Come On became somewhat of a local celebrity, and his death in 1993 was much mourned.

Five steps to follow when making a record attempt:

1. Choose to beat a record that is published in the current edition.
2. If the record you want to try to beat is not in the book, your chances of appearing in *The Guinness Book of Records* are slim. We would be most interested, however, if your activity is measurable, if it can be easily compared to future record attempts, and if it has instant popular appeal.
3. Check with us about two months before you proceed. Even if your record is not in the book, we may still be able to give you a target to beat. If the record *is* in the book, it may have been beaten since publication.
4. Follow the general or specific guidelines on rules and authentication that we can provide for your record attempt.
5. Produce documentation at all stages. We cannot send out witnesses, so we need all the proof you can gather.

EXTRA! EXTRA!

HUMAN BEING

Oldest mother (p. 10) Rossanna Dclla Cortc of Canino, Italy gavc birth at age 63 on 18 Jul 1994.

Most-premature twins (p. 12) Joanna and Alexander Bagwell were born 114 days pre-mature on 2 Jun 1993 in Oxford, Great Britain.

Largest biceps (p. 25) Denis Sester of Bloomington, MN has a right bicep measuring $30\frac{5}{8}$ in cold.

Longest surviving heart transplantee (p. 37) Dirk van Zyl of Cape Town, South Africa (1926–1994) survived for 23 yr 57 days, having received an unnamed person's heart in 1971.

Haemodialysis patient (p. 35) Brian Wilson of Edinburgh, Great Britain has suffered from kidney failure since 1964, and began dialysis on 30 May 1964.

LIVING WORLD

Smallest dog (p. 56) The smallest dog in the United States is Chelsi Dijon, a $1\frac{3}{4}$-lb toy poodle belonging to Dollie Childs of Dothan, AL.

Cattle birthweights *Lightest* (p. 113) The lowest live birthweight for a calf is 9 lb, for a Holstein heifer called Christmas, born on 25 Dec 1993 on the farm of Mark and Wendy Theuringer in Hutchinson, MN.

SCIENCE & TECHNOLOGY

Highest temperature (p. 173) The highest temperature produced in a laboratory is 460,000,000 K, during a fusion power experiment at the Princeton University Plasma Physics Laboratory, Princeton, NJ on 27 May 1994.

Fastest chip (p. 184) The world's fastest microprocessor is the DECchip 21064A, developed by Digital Equipment Corporation of Maynard, MA. It can run at speeds of 275 MHz.

Ocean drilling (p. 193) The deepest recorded drilling into the sea bed is 6,926 ft, by the Ocean Drilling Program's vessel *JOIDES Resolution*, in the eastern equatorial Pacific in 1993.

Air-launched records (p. 302) *Columbia STS 65* set the duration record when it touched down on 23 Jul 1994 aftcr 14 days 17 hr 55 min.

BUILDINGS & STRUCTURES

Most durable resident Virginia Hopkins Phillips of Onancock, VA resided in the same house from the time of her birth in 1891 until a few months before her death at age 102 in 1993.

Suspension bridge walking Donald H. Betty of Lancaster, PA has walked over 37 suspension bridges, including the 12 longest in the world.

Snow and ice constructions (p. 245) A snow palace with a volume of 3,658,310.2 ft^3 and 99 ft 5 in high was unveiled on 8 Feb 1994 at Asahikawa, Hokkaido, Japan.

TRANSPORT

Most flying hours *Pilot* (p. 302) Evelyn Bryan Johnson holds the women's record, having logged 53,050 hours in flight as a pilot and flight instructor since 1945.

Submarine *Smallest* William G. Smith of Bognor Regis, Great Britain constructed a fully-functional submarine only 9 ft 8 in long, 3 ft 9 in wide and 4 ft 8 in high. It can reach depths of around 100 ft and remain underwater for four hours.

Longest solo ocean row Peter Bird spent 304 days 14 hours non-stop rowing at sea during a trans-Pacific voyage, which began on 12 May 1993 and was ended prematurely on 12 Mar 1994.

Road cars (p. 271) The highest road-tested acceleration reported (0–60 mph) for a street legal car is 3.07 sec for a Ford RS200 Evolution, driven by Graham Hathaway at the Boreham Proving Ground, Great Britain on 25 May 1994.

Highest mileage (p. 274) Albert Klein's "Beetle" had clocked up 1,531,125 miles as of 7 Jul 1994.

Model trains (p. 290) The greatest distance covered by a model steam locomotive in 24 hours is 167.7 miles, by the 7¼ in gauge "Peggy," at Weston Park Railway, Weston Park, Great Britain on 17–18 Jun 1994.

Peter Bird set the mark for the longest solo Ocean row.

Paper aircraft (p. 312) The level flight duration record for a hand-launched paper aircraft is 18.80 sec by Ken Blackburn in a hangar at John F. Kennedy Airport, New York City on 17 Feb 1994.

The largest flying paper airplane, with a wing span of 140 ft 6 in, was constructed by a team of engineers from BP Chemicals Ltd and flown at Filton, Great Britain on 24 Jun 1994. It was launched indoors and flew 77 ft 4 in.

Coast-to-coast drive *Fastest* Doug Anderson and Jim Addis drove from Atlantic City, NJ to San Diego, CA in 40 hr 43 min. They set off on 13 May 1994 and arrived on 15 May.

Oldest car Raymond H. Carr drove across the United States in a 1902 Northern, the oldest car ever to make the trip. Traveling at 15–20 mph, Carr left San Diego, CA on 8 May 1994 and arrived at Jekyll Island, GA on 31 May 1994.

Parade of cars *United States* A parade of 2,223 Corvettes traveled from the Bloomington Gold Corvette Show in Springfield, IL to Athens, IL and back again on 25 Jun 1994.

ARTS & ENTERTAINMENT

Dancing dragon (p. 364) The longest dancing dragon measured 5,114 ft 10 in from the end of its nose to the tip of its tail. A total of 2,180 people brought it to life on 17 Apr 1994, on a bridge linking Macau with the island of Taipa.

Guitar marathon On 7 May 1994, a gathering of 1,322 guitarists played "Taking Care of Business" in unison for 68 min 40 sec, in an event organized by Music West of Vancouver, Canada.

Largest ground figure (p. 318) The "painted straw" representation of "Will the Great Buffalo" in northeast Wyoming, completed by Robert Berks in September 1993, is 1/2 mile long.

Biggest country line dance A total of 2,578 people danced to the "Boot Scootin' Boogie" in Lebanon, TN on 30 Jul 1994.

Largest and longest dances (p. 363) Rosie Radiator led an ensemble of 12 tap dancers through the streets of San Francisco, CA in a routine covering 9.61 miles on 11 Jul 1994.

Baton twirling (p. 354) The women's record is eight spins, by Danielle Novakowski, in South Bend, IN on 24 Jul 1993.

BUSINESS & PUBLIC AFFAIRS

Rummage sale (p. 397) The greatest amount of money raised at a one-day sale is $214,085.99, at the 62nd sale organized by the Winnetka Congregational Church, IL on 12 May 1994.

Youngest college graduate (p. 455) Michael Kearney became the youngest

graduate in June 1994, at the age of 10 years 4 months, when he obtained his BA in anthropology from the University of South Alabama.

HUMAN ACHIEVEMENTS

Ladder climbing (p. 470) A team of ten firefighters from Frome Fire Station climbed 33.75 miles up a ladder in 24 hours at Frome, Great Britain on 24–25 Jun 1994.

Spitting (p. 473) David O'Dell of Apple Valley, CA spat a tobacco wad 49 ft 5½ in at the 19th World Tobacco Spitting Championships held at Calico Ghost Town, CA on 26 Mar 1994.

Largest cocktail (p. 488) The largest cocktail on record was a Finlandia Sea Breeze of 2,933 gal, made at Maui Entertainment Center, Philadelphia, PA on 5 Aug 1994.

Most marriages (p. 484) Glynn "Scotty" Wolfe married for the 28th time on 27 Jun 1994.

Flags Largest (p. 505) The largest flag in the world is the mile-long, 146,790-ft² "Raise the Rainbow" flag unfurled in New York City on 26 Jun 1994.

Lego tower (p. 234) The world's tallest Lego tower was 70 ft high and built by The East Asiatic Company (Hong Kong) Limited at Time Square, Causeway Bay, Hong Kong on 4 Apr 1994.

The longest dancing dragon (below and opposite), on the bridge linking Macao to Taipa.

The largest flag was unfurled to mark 25 years of the gay rights movement. (Mick Hicks)

Can pyramid (p. 502) Five adults and five children from Dunhurst School in Petersfield, Great Britain built a record-breaking pyramid of 4,900 cans in 25 min 54 sec on 13 May 1994.

Wine glass stacking Alain Fournier of Montreal, Canada put in position and held 45 wine glasses in one hand on "Live! With Regis and Kathie Lee" on 20 Jul 1994.

Parking meters Lotta Sjölin of Solna, Sweden, had a collection of 269 different parking meters as of May 1994.

SPORTS & GAMES

Highest bowling score Couple Brian and Denise Welker of Sugarland, TX bowled 299 and 300 games respectively on 12 Jun 1994 in the Texas State BA Annual Tournament.

Cycling (p. 569) Miguel Induráin (Spain) won the Tour de France for a fourth successive time in 1994, equaling the achievements of Jacques Anquetil and Eddie Merkcx.

Judo (p. 631) Brian Woodward and David Norman complctcd 33,681 judo throws in 10 hr in Rainham, Great Britain on 10 Apr 1994.

Motorcycle racing (p. 636) Rolf Biland (Switzerland) won his 73rd side-car Grand Prix on 23 Jul 1994.

Parachuting Oldest tandem (p. 643) Edward Royds-Jones made a tandem parachute jump at the age of 95 years 170 days at Dunkeswell, Great Britain on 2 Jul 1994

Longest jet-ski journey Richard Chenoweth, Brian Peterson and Dan Walker rode their Yamaha Wave Runners from Pascagoula, MS to Key West, FL, a distance of 922.2 miles, between 31 Mar and 6 Apr 1994.

Weightlifting (p. 728) World records (men): 99 kg class; Snatch 191 kg 421 lb, Jerk 227.5 kg 501½ lb, Total 417.5 kg 920¼ lb by Sergey Syrtsov (Russia) at St Petersburg, Russia on 23 Jul 1994. 108 kg class; Snatch 201 kg 443 lb by Andrey Chemerkin (Russia) at St Petersburg on 23 Jul 1994.

EXTRA! EXTRA! EXTRA! EXTRA!

WORLD CUP USA '94

From 17 Jun to 17 Jul 1994, the world's most watched sporting event, soccer's World Cup, was staged in the United States. World Cup '94 was a colorful event: the flags of the world were waved from the stands and referees handed out yellow and red cards to the players like confetti. Although players were penalized for "diving," everyone was happy to see so many records tumble. Brazil's fourth World Cup win was the most important new record, but there were many others.

(Above) Dunga, Brazil's captain, celebrates his team's record triumph (Allsport USA/B.Stickland)

(Left) Bulgaria snaps Streak v Greece (Allsport USA/J. Daniel)

(Below) Oleg Salenko, the new World Cup marksman (Allsport/S. Dunn)

Most championships

Brazil defeated Italy in a penalty kick shootout to win its fourth title. It was the first time the championship had been decided in that manner.

Most goals in a game

Russian sharpshooter Oleg Salenko scored a record five goals in his team's 6-1 defeat of Cameroon.

(Allsport/S. Botterill)

Most games played in the finals

Diego Maradona of Argentina and Lothar Matthaus of Germany (left) played their 21st World Cup games, tying the previous mark. Both players exited the event in sensational fashion, Maradona to a drug suspension and Matthaus when Bulgaria eliminated Germany.

Longest winless streak

Bulgaria extended its World Cup winless streak to 17 games, but the trend was broken with a 4-0 defeat of Greece, sparking a 4-game winning streak that vaulted Bulgaria to the semi-finals.

Most yellow and red cards

A record 227 yellow cards (an average of 4.36 per game) and 15 red cards were administered.

Oldest player

At 42 years old, Cameroon veteran Roger Mila (right) set two records: the oldest player to play in the finals, and the oldest to score a goal. His efforts were in vain, as he scored his historic goal during a 6-1 loss to Russia.

(Allsport/S. Dunn)

Largest attendance

3,567,994 people attended the 52 games of the tournament, a record for the event. The 68,615 average attendance was also a record.

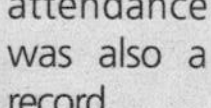

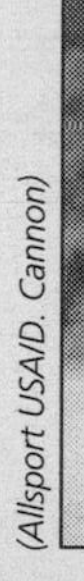

(Allsport USA/D. Cannon)

Most watched television event

A worldwide television audience of 1 billion people watched the World Cup final between Brazil and Italy, staged at the Rose Bowl, Pasadena, CA on 17 July 1994.

Most games played for the United States

Defender Marcello Balboa (left) set the mark for most appearances for the United States team. He played his 94th game in the team's second round loss to Brazil.

INDEX

How To Use:
The typical index entry contains the page number (e.g., **aerobatics** 512). Illustrations appear in *italics.* Tables are indicated by the letter "*t*", features by the letter "*f*" and On the Record by the letter "*r*". The boxes are indicated by "*b.*" Asterisks * denote an updated record in *Extra! Extra!*

A

B

F

H

N

Q

R

S

T

U

V

W